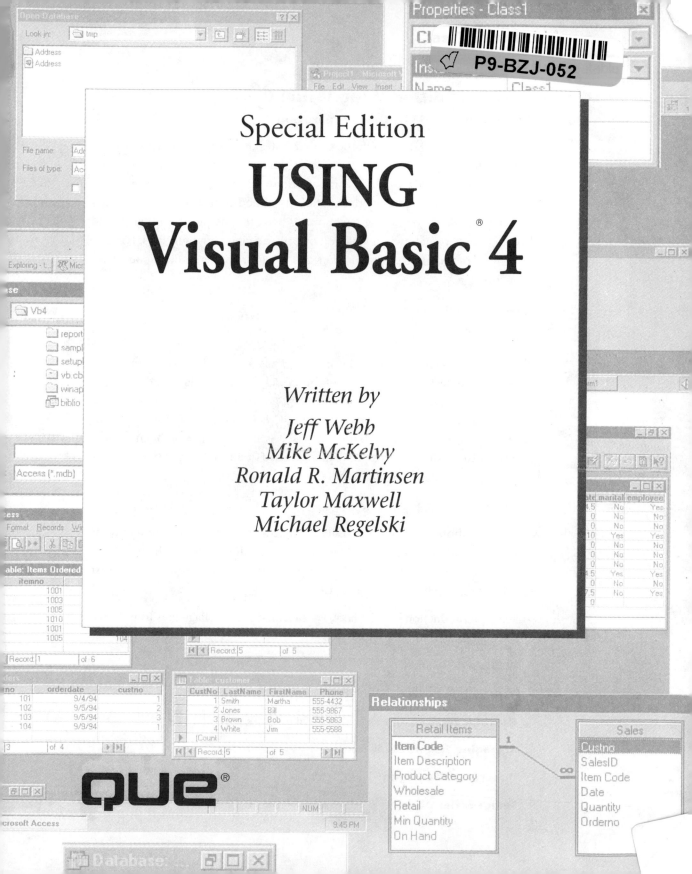

Special Edition

USING
Visual Basic® 4

Written by

Jeff Webb
Mike McKelvy
Ronald R. Martinsen
Taylor Maxwell
Michael Regelski

que®

Special Edition Using Visual Basic 4

Copyright© 1995 by Que® Corporation

Library of Congress Catalog: 95-70635

ISBN: 1-56529-998-1

98 97 96 95   5 4 3 2 1

Interpretation of the printing code: the rightmost double-digit number is the year of the book's printing; the rightmost single-digit number, the number of the book's printing. For example, a printing code of 95-1 shows that the first printing of the book occurred in 1995.

Screen reproductions in this book were created with Collage Plus from Inner Media, Inc., Hollis, NH.

Publisher: Roland Elgey

Associate Publisher: Joseph B. Wikert

Editorial Services Director: Liz Keaffaber

Managing Editor: Sandy Doell

Director of Marketing: Lynn Zingraf

Senior Series Director: Chris Nelson

Dedication

To my daughter, the singer.

—Jeff Webb

To my wife, Wanda, and my children, Laura and Eric, for their support, and for their patience with the long hours.

—Mike McKelvy

To my loving wife Karen for hanging in there during all the nights I missed with her while writing this book.

—Ronald R. Martinsen

To my beloved grandmother Harriet, my loving wife Marcia, and my daughter Robyn Elizabeth.

—Taylor Maxwell

To my son Andrew. He is a very special person to me.

—Michael Regelski

Credits

Publishing Manager
Bryan Gambrel

Acquisitions Editor
Fred Slone

Acquisitions Coordinator
Angela C. Kozlowski

Product Director
Kevin Kloss

Production Editors
Lori Cates
Andy Saff

Copy Editors
Kelli Brooks
Alice Martina Smith

Technical Editors
David Fullerton
Brian Blackman
Jeff Bankston
Ravi-Chandar Ramalingam
Pamela Wilson
Thomas Kiehl

Technical Specialist
Cari Skaggs

Cover Designer
Dan Armstrong

Book Designer
Ruth Harvey

Editorial Assistant
Michelle Newcomb

Production Team
Steve Adams
Angela Bannan
Becky Beheler
Claudia Bell
Maxine Dillingham
Joan Evan
DiMonique Ford
Amy Gornik
Jason Hand
John Hulse
Damon Jordan
Barry Jorden
Clint Lahnen
Bob LaRoche
Beth Lewis
Julie Quinn
Kaylene Riemen
Laura Robbins
Bobbi Satterfield
Craig Small
Mike Thomas
Scott Tullis
Kelly Warner
Todd Wente
Paul Wilson
Jody York

Indexer
Carol Sheehan

Composed in *Stone Serif* and *MCPdigital* by Que Corporation

About the Authors

Jeff Webb was a senior member of the BASIC documentation team at Microsoft. He worked on BASIC PDS, QBASIC, OLE Automation, and all versions of Visual Basic. He contributed to many books and help systems, notably *Visual Basic Reference, OLE 2 Programmer's Reference (Creating Programmable Applications),* and *Programming Integrated Solutions with Microsoft Office.* Currently he runs Wombat Technology in Seattle, Washington.

Mike McKelvy owns McKelvy Software Systems, a software consulting firm in Birmingham, Alabama, specializing in the development of database applications. Mike has been developing software for business and engineering applications for over 15 years. Mike is also the author of *Using Visual Basic 4.* You can contact Mike at the following address:

> McKelvy Software Systems
> P.O. Box 380125
> Birmingham, AL 35238

Ronald R. Martinsen has a bachelors degree in Computer Information Systems Application from Loyola University, and has been programming in Visual Basic since version 1.0. He is also proficent in C and C++, and was the former president and founder of Martinsen's Software. Currently, he is employed by a major software development corporation where he uses Visual Basic daily.

Taylor Hile Maxwell graduated from Alma College in Northern Michigan in 1985. Prior to the release of Visual Basic, Taylor worked creating solutions in dBASE, Foxbase, FoxPro, and Clipper. Taylor has been working in Visual Basic since that language's release. He works extensively with the Visual Basic language solving problems for clients all over the country. Taylor is presently living in Atlanta, Georgia and can be reached via CompuServe at 72371,2435.

Michael Regelski is the Director of Software Development at Lenel Systems International. Lenel is one of the leading developers of Multimedia Development Tools and Multimedia Systems for the Windows, Windows NT, and Windows 95 platforms. Michael has a masters degree in Software Development and Management and a bachelors degree in Computer Engineering, both from Rochester Institute of Technology. Before joining Lenel, Michael was the lead design engineer for Access Control development at Eastman Kodak. When he is not developing software or writing, his interests include golf and basketball.

Acknowledgments

I'd like to acknowledge my indefatigable editor, Fred Slone, who kept me on the ball and made sure this book came together.

—Jeff Webb

My sincere thanks to everyone who helped me with my portion of this book. Thanks especially to Fred Slone, my Acquisitions Editor, for getting me started in this writing adventure. Thanks also to Alice Martina Smith, Lori Cates, and Kevin Kloss for the excellent editing of the manuscript. Finally, thanks to the technical editors for keeping me straight on some of the coding.

—Mike McKelvy

Thanks to my parents for providing me with access to a computer as a child. Also, thanks to Chris Dias and Joe Robison for helping me with some tough issues I faced when writing this book, and to Dan Appleman for being a helpful mentor.

—Ronald R. Martinsen

There are so many people to thank for helping produce this book. My wife Marcia and daughter Robyn gave me the time to write this book when they preferred to have me spending time with them. My chapters are based on experiences solving problems for all of the clients since the publishing of my last book. I want to thank the people at Turner Broadcasting, Bell South, Brown Forman, Dunnings & Frawley, and Cincom for the experiences that inspired the writing of these chapters. I received a great deal of suggestions for my part of this book from people like Sylvester Morgan, Phil Orion, Glenn Engstrand, and Allen Foster.

—Taylor Maxwell

Trademarks

Contents at a Glance

Data Access

Creating OLE Objects

Using OLE

Integrating with Office

Optimization

Contents

3 Implementing the Database Design 59

4 Manipulating Data with a Program 83

13 Controlling OLE Objects   337

14 OLE Container Programming Techniques   361

15 Designing OLE Container Applications   389

16 Distributing OLE Container Applications   419

20 Designing Object Libraries   517

21 Advanced OLE Programming Techniques   545

27 Integration with Other OLE Applications   723

28 Integration with Multiple Office Applications   759

29 Distributing Integrated Applications   821

33 Accessing the Windows API   917

Introduction

The other day I was browsing the software store, kids in tow, poking at the new boxes. I was trying to figure out the feature set described on the various editions of C when another dad informed me that I needed a 32-bit operating system to run the contents of the box that I was reading. I hadn't realized this and thanked him, but told him it was okay, I could do 32-bit. He said it was a *big* problem for him, because he did multimedia work, and much of the DOS work in which he had invested simply didn't work on those platforms.

I'm not sure whether he thought Microsoft should be *entirely* dedicated to building a better DOS, but I choose to think that his comment was somewhat more profound: Programming in a changing environment is really tough. Not tough physically, of course—your typing speed might exceed your ability to bench-press. Change is not even tough intellectually—you're always learning. What's tough about change is leaving behind something on which you have worked hard.

There is perverse frustration in realizing that a general procedure that you spent two days developing has been replaced by a new property on the list box control. This frustration deepens if the new property works better and faster than your original scheme. This type of frustration is a good sign—it means that you've pushed your tools as far as they'll go.

Visual Basic 4.0 contains more new features than any previous update. But simply enumerating new features misses the larger picture: the *nature* of the problems that you are used to solving has changed. Therefore, you might have to leave behind more than just a few procedures. You also might have to shed old ways of thinking about problems to adopt new approaches.

This new version of Visual Basic embodies four fundamental changes in Windows programming:

- *Client/server computing.* An organization can distribute its computing workload among multiple users accessing a single data source by using the new database objects in the Microsoft Jet 2.5 database engine.

- *Object linking and embedding (OLE)*. You can build new applications from the pieces of others, and create new pieces that can fit into other applications.

- *Portability to new operating systems*. You can develop for both 16- and 32-bit platforms to take advantage of the wave of new Windows 95 upgrades without abandoning your installed base.

- *Office development*. You can integrate multiple large applications to create completely new business software solutions.

Each of these topics is big enough to merit its own product version and a book to cover it. As much as we would like to sell you four separate books, Que decided to follow Microsoft's lead and bundle all these features into this single *Special Edition*. By targeting the new areas, this book gives you a leg up understanding both how to use the new features and how to think within this new framework for Windows development.

A New Jet Engine

It's very easy to get started with database programming in Visual Basic—and also very easy to find yourself quickly enmeshed in a tangle of data-oriented programming issues like integrity, multilevel security, efficiency, and normalization. Part I of this book, "Data Access," leads you through the tasks and concepts involved in creating a usable database with Visual Basic's new Jet engine.

Jet 2.5 builds in solutions to many programming problems in earlier versions:

- Jet now enforces referential integrity at the engine level.

- Jet automatically supports cascading updates and deletes.

- Data Definition Language (DDL) queries can create, change, or delete tables or indexes.

- Jet provides user and group permissions on each database object.

Part I explains what each of these features means to you and how you can best take advantage of them when designing and programming with databases.

VB 4.0 Does for OLE What VB 1.0 Did for Windows

You might remember the introduction of Visual Basic. Microsoft had just released Windows 3.0, and the environment was starting to take off. The catch was that you had to program applications for Windows 3.0 in assembly or C, using a huge, obscure application program interface (API). Then Microsoft released Visual Basic 1.0. Suddenly, just about everyone was cranking out good-looking Windows applications. A simple "Hello World" application took only one line to code rather than the 200 lines required in C.

Visual Basic 4.0 is the equivalent epiphany for OLE developers. You can add OLE features to Visual Basic applications with little or no code. In C, you have to deal with hundreds of new functions in the OLE API and write thousands of lines of code to implement similar features. You can't do everything in Visual Basic that you can in C, but you sure can get further faster.

Therefore, you'll soon see thousands more OLE applications. Also, OLE-enabled applications will become the *de facto* industry standard, just as Windows did.

Part II, "Using OLE," tells you how to build applications by using OLE objects from other applications. Part III, "Creating OLE Objects," explains how to create your own "parts" for use in your own applications, other Office applications, or within Visual Basic itself.

Working with 16- and 32-Bit Applications

Visual Basic is code-compatible between 16- and 32-bit operating systems. Therefore, the same code that runs under Windows 3.1 works on Windows NT 3.5 or Windows 95. However, the system services and APIs on 16- and 32-bit systems differ significantly.

Throughout this book, 16- and 32-bit differences are indicated and explained. This enables you to anticipate differences and to create and distribute applications that run naturally on both platforms.

Developing with Office Applications

The Microsoft Office Development Kit (ODK) is a big part of the Visual Basic Professional Edition. Part IV, "Integrating with Office Applications," tells you how to use Microsoft Office applications to create unique applications quickly.

All the Office applications share some form of BASIC. Each dialect and object model differs, however. Part IV compares programming in each product and helps you take advantage of the unique aspects of each Office application.

Advanced Programming Techniques

Part V, "Optimization and Techniques," covers general programming techniques that help you optimize and improve the appearance of your Windows applications.

Special Help for Version 3.0 Users

Appendix A, "Preparing for Visual Basic 4.0," describes how to port your existing Visual Basic applications to the new version. This appendix will help Visual Basic 3.0 users get up and running as soon as possible with the new Visual Basic 4.0 features.

What's Covered in This Book

It's always intriguing how a software product can add huge new regions of features, yet the documentation that accompanies the product stays about the same size. The new features don't *replace* the old ones so... does the print get smaller? What actually gets squeezed is the material—and because the new material is the hardest to create, it usually gets squeezed the hardest.

The advantage of writing a book like this one is that you get to write for a longer period of time than the product documentation team. Therefore, you can include more material without worrying about "busting the box." Because Visual Basic 4.0 introduces so much new material and the Visual Basic *Programmer's Guide* adds so little new documentation, books like this one are becoming essential add-ons for using each new version of Visual Basic.

This book covers in great detail the material that is new to Visual Basic 4.0. Each part introduces its topic carefully before delving into the complete and sometimes gnarly programming details of the topic. The book is broken into these five major parts:

- Part I, "Data Access," includes Chapters 1 to 10.

- Part II, "Using OLE," includes Chapters 11 to 16.

- Part III, "Creating OLE Objects," includes Chapters 17 to 24.

- Part IV, "Integrating with Office Applications," includes Chapters 25 to 29.

- Part V, "Optimization and Techniques," includes Chapters 30 to 34.

Note

Because of the space limitations of this book's pages, a few code lines in this book's listings cannot be printed exactly as you must enter them. In cases where breaking such a line is necessary to fit within the book's margins, you'll find the following graphic:

➡

This character indicates that you must enter the line that you are reading as part of the line that precedes it.

Part I

Data Access

Chapter 1

Designing Your Database Application

When you build a house, you need a blueprint to tell you what the finished product will look like and to define the steps of construction. Without the blueprint, the results of the construction effort will not yield the desired results. Building a computer program is the same way: you need a good design if you are to obtain a good final product. This is especially important in building database applications.

In designing a *database application*, not only must you set up the program's routines for maximum performance, you must also pay attention to the physical and logical layout of the data storage as well. A good database design provides minimum search times when locating specific records. It also stores the data in the most efficient manner possible to keep the database from growing too large. It makes data updates as easy as possible. A good design should also be flexible enough to allow inclusion of new functions required of the program.

This chapter covers the basics of good database design and points out the key areas for making your database application work as well as possible. This chapter is not an exhaustive discussion—several entire books have been written on the subject of database design. However, the information presented here provides you with what you need to know to begin writing database applications.

This chapter uses several examples of "databases." It also presents a sample case that is used in other chapters of this section as you work through designing and developing a database application.

In this chapter, you learn the following:

- What a database is

- What objects make up a relational database

- How to design a database

- What data normalization is and how to use it

- How to use key fields to relate data tables

- The difference between physical order and logical order of a database

- How and when to use an index

Defining the Term "Database"

In the broadest definition, a *database* is a collection of information, usually organized in a particular order. A familiar example of a database is a phone book. It is a collection of names, addresses, and phone numbers organized in alphabetical order. As many people know, some phone books list phone numbers by street address. This presentation contains the same data as the original phone book, but presents it in a different order.

> **Note**
>
> A phone book is an example of a "flat file" database, where a single record stores all the information for each entry, and a single table contains the records. This is in contrast to relational databases, where the information is stored in multiple tables that are related by key fields.

A *relational database management system* (RDBMS) is used to store information in a manner that allows people to look at it in different ways. An RDBMS consists of a database, tables, records, fields, indexes, queries, and views. Table 1.1 defines the key elements of a database.

Table 1.1   Elements of a Relational Database Management System

Element	Description
Database	A group of data tables that contain related information. Note that a database may consist of only a single table.
Table	A group of data records, each containing the same type of information. In the example of the phone book, the book itself is a data table.
Record	A single entry in a table; the entry consists of a number of data fields. In a phone book, a record is one of the single-line entries.
Field	A specific item of data contained in a record. In a phone book, at least four fields can be identified: last name, first name, address, and phone number.
Index	A special type of table that contains the values of a key field or fields (defined by the user) and pointers to the location of the actual record. These values and pointers are stored in a specific order (again defined by the user) and may be used to present the data in the database in that order. For the phone book example, one index may be used to sort the information by last name and first name; another index may be used to sort the information by street address. If you want, you can also create an index to sort the information by phone number.
Query	A SQL command designed to retrieve a certain group of records from one or more tables or to perform an operation on a table. Although SQL commands can be executed directly from a program, a query allows you to name the command and store it in the database itself—useful if the SQL commands are used often, as are commands that retrieve records for a specific monthly report. When a query is stored in the database, it is usually *compiled*. Compiling queries gives your program a performance improvement over just issuing the SQL statement because the database engine does not have to interpret (or *parse*) the SQL command.
Filter	A filter is not actually a part of the database but it is used in conjunction with indexes and sort orders to determine what data is displayed or processed. A filter is a condition imposed on the data, such as "Last name starts with *M*."
View	A view of the data consists of the number of records seen (or processed) and the order in which they are displayed (or processed). A view is typically controlled by filters and indexes. Two examples of views of phone book data are an alphabetical listing of all people who live on Main Street and the first ten people whose last names start with *S*.

Tip

Structured Query Language (SQL, pronounced "SEE-kwel") is a set of commands that manipulate information in a database. A single SQL command can replace many lines of traditional program code.

Types of Applications

Database applications can be used to handle a wide variety of data processing needs. Most programs require a mix of user interface functions and calculational functions. How each of these functions uses the data in the database impacts the design in areas of table relations, index expressions, and data validation.

User-Intensive Functions

Functions in which the user directly manipulates the data in the database are defined as *user-intensive* functions. An example is an order entry function, in which the user enters a customer's name, address, purchase information, and payment information. The design objective for this type of function is to make the data entry as quick and error free as possible.

Process-Intensive Functions

Process-intensive functions are those in which data from a table or tables is used to perform a series of calculations, with the results stored in an output table or printed to a report. Process-intensive functions usually require little or no user interaction, other than possibly to start the processes. The design objective for this type of function is to make calculations as quick as possible and to store output data as efficiently as possible for later retrieval and further processing. An example of this is a bank transaction. When you make a withdrawal, the teller enters your account number and the amount. The computer then looks up your account number, verifies that you have sufficient funds, and debits your account for the amount requested. These functions take place without any further interaction from the teller.

Database Design Decisions

Creating a good database design involves seven key activities:

- Modeling the application

- Determining the data required for the application

- Organizing the data into tables

- Establishing the relationships between tables

- Setting index and validation requirements for the data

- Creating and storing any necessary queries for the application

- Reviewing the design

Considering a Sample Application

To help explain the concepts involved in database design, this chapter uses a sample application. The task is to develop a database system for an aquarium supply store called Triton's Treasures. The owner of Triton's Treasures, Mr. Herman Crabb, wants to handle sales, inventory tracking, special order processing, and a customer mailing list. Mr. Crabb has also decided to expand his business beyond the walk-in retail outlet. He is setting up a mail order and local delivery portion of the business for people who are outside his local area, or are in the area but too busy to come to his shop. The database design must take into account this business expansion.

Modeling the Application

Modeling the application involves determining the functions to be performed, the inputs and outputs of the application, and the performance requirements of the application. A well-defined application model leads to a good database design.

Defining the Application's Functions

The first step in designing the application is to determine what the user wants the application to do. This is often called determining the *functional specifications*. Functional specifications can usually be expressed in terms of an action, such as "produce a report of all items sold during the last week" or "calculate the amortization schedule of a loan given the loan amount, interest rate, and length of the loan." From this type of information, the developer can determine the data necessary to achieve the desired functions.

In designing an application, the information for the functional specifications is gathered by talking to the users of the application. This usually involves not only talking to the key person on the project (the department manager or store owner), but also to others who will work with the application, such as the department employees or store clerks. In some cases, it may also be useful to talk to other people with similar business needs. For example, to learn about data handling for local deliveries, you or Mr. Crabb may want to talk to the person who owns May's Flowers, a floral delivery service.

Knowing Where to Start Gathering Information

The easiest place to start determining the functional specifications is frequently with the desired output of the application. Once the outputs are known, you can start constructing the data and processes required to achieve that output.

Often, clients have examples of reports that they currently use, such as the one shown in figure 1.1. Using these reports as a starting point, clients can show you what information must be added to the reports, or request different ways of displaying the information so that they can do their work more efficiently. This kind of investigation provides valuable insight into the needs of the clients and the information they currently have and will need in the future. It also provides the developer with a first look at how the database may have to be organized.

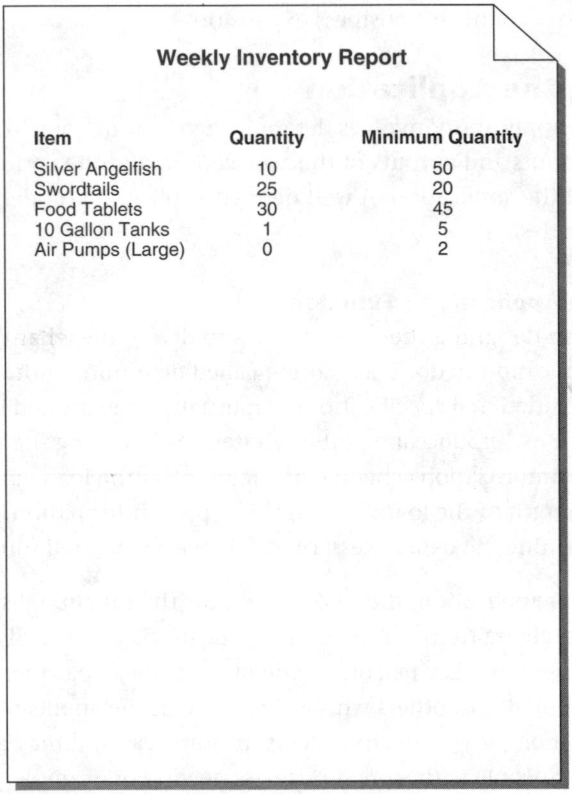

Fig. 1.1
Information for functional specifications can often be obtained from sample reports.

Weekly Inventory Report

Item	Quantity	Minimum Quantity
Silver Angelfish	10	50
Swordtails	25	20
Food Tablets	30	45
10 Gallon Tanks	1	5
Air Pumps (Large)	0	2

As you may guess, the process of determining the functional specifications for an application is mainly about observation and listening. It is also necessary to see possibilities for providing additional functions that the database can perform and presenting these to the client.

Planning Process Flow
After you determine what functions the application must perform, it is useful to work through each function to determine the processes involved

in performing the function. This involves determining where the user input is required, any table lookups that may be needed, calculations to be performed, and outputs to be generated.

Many people use a process flow diagram (also called a flow chart) to show where all of the pieces of the process fit in. Once the processes are defined, this diagram can be used to add the types of data required for each step to produce a data flow diagram. The data flow diagram can help the developer determine the organization of data tables and what indexes (if any) are required for the tables. Figure 1.2 shows a generic process flow diagram.

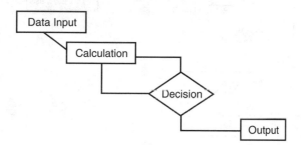

Fig. 1.2
A process flow diagram aids in the design of the database.

Determining the Functional Specifications for the Sample Case

For the sample case, suppose that you have determined that Mr. Crabb must get the following outputs from the system:

- Sales receipts for each sale in the retail store at the time of sale.

- A listing of the inventory level for each stock item on a weekly basis and necessary supplier orders.

- Invoice for each mail order to be sent out.

- A listing of the deliveries to be made for the day.

- A mailing list and labels for all customers and, if possible, their buying preferences (so that mailings can be appropriately targeted).

To find out more about handling deliveries, Mr Crabb talked to the owner of May's Flowers and found that it would be beneficial to have the delivery list grouped into geographic regions. This arrangement allows the delivery drivers to reduce travel time by making all the deliveries in a specific region before moving on to the next region. Grouping the delivery list can make the drivers' work more efficient—and Mr. Crabb can perceive some real value from the application. To achieve the desired results, you may decide to group the local deliveries by ZIP code (an already defined set of geographic regions) or break down the ZIP-code groups further if a number of businesses are in one particular location, such as a mall or office tower. Figure 1.3 shows the process flow diagram for this task. You must also provide some sort of regional grouping for the mail order portion of the business to help determine shipping charges, because many charges are based on the distance between shipper and receiver.

Fig. 1.3
The process flow diagram for the delivery scheduling task helps isolate the data required to achieve the task.

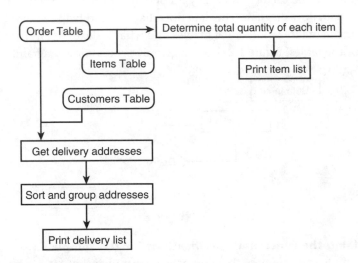

Determining Data Required for the Application

Part of the design process is defining the data that must be in the database. Of equal importance is determining what data does *not* have to be kept. Superfluous data can bloat the database and diminish performance.

Selecting the Required Information

Using the functional specifications for the application, the developer can begin to define the data that goes into the database. This is done by examining each task to be performed by the application and finding the pieces of data required for that task.

Begin by looking at one of the tasks of the sample case, the scheduling of local deliveries. Each day, the delivery driver needs a report of the locations of each delivery and a list of the items to be delivered to each customer. Obtaining the list of items involves not only printing the order for each customer, but also printing the list by item number to make retrieval from inventory more efficient.

To group the deliveries by geographic region, you need to know what region the customer is in. You also need the customer's phone number and address so that you can notify the customer of the timing of the delivery and get directions to the location if necessary.

As you can see, a lot of different data may be required just to fulfill one task of the application. Fortunately, as you see later, the data required for many tasks can be placed in similar formats and in the same data tables.

Determining the Format of the Information

Formatting data basically consists of determining whether the item of data is a character, a number, a date, or a logical (yes/no) value. Beyond the basic description of the data, certain other criteria must be determined, such as whether a number is an integer or a decimal number and whether a character string is of a fixed or variable length. Further definition of the formats may be required depending on the database engine being used. The native database engine for Visual Basic (the Jet engine) is capable of supporting all these data types. A detailed description of the Jet database engine formats is presented in Chapter 2, "Looking at the Capabilities of the Jet Engine."

Typical Information Formatting. Table 1.2 shows the types of data formats used for various types of information.

Table 1.2 Various Data Formats Used to Handle Information in the Database	
Data Format	**Used to Contain**
Text	Variable-length character strings up to 255 characters long. Examples of this are names, addresses, and alphanumeric item codes. Although it is true that not every name has the same number of characters, a length can be set that can accommodate most names. Character strings are often used for index and filter expressions. When text fields are created, they are assigned a maximum length. The data stored in the field can contain any number of characters up to that maximum.
Memo	Large variable-length character strings. Examples of memo fields are product descriptions or doctor's notes. They are used instead of the character data format either because of limitations on the size of the character format in some database engines or because the information is stored more efficiently.
Integer	Numerical data that has no decimal component. Examples are quantities of items and populations.
Decimal	Numerical quantities such as fractional amounts and money.

(continues)

Table 1.2 Continued	
Data Format	**Used to Contain**
Date	Month, day, and year information. Although this is usually in the mm/dd/yyyy (06/28/1995) format, most database engines support date formats for countries other than the United States. Most also allow you to input only the last two digits of the year and assume that the first two digits are *19*.
Logical/Boolean	Items with a true/false or yes/no value or any items that have only two possible choices. For example, is a person married or is the phone number a business phone?
Binary	Pictures, sound clips, or OLE objects. In the sample case, you can use the binary format to store pictures of the fish available for sale.

Other Formatting Considerations. Although the necessary format for most data items is quite obvious, some items require additional consideration. A good example is a person's social security number. The social security number is made up of nine numeric digits but is often stored in databases in a character format. ZIP codes are also typically stored in a character format instead of a numeric format. The reason you may want to store numbers in a character format is typically because you want to sort and index the numbers, usually when the field is used in conjunction with other fields. Consider these two items when you choose formatting:

■ For *compound expressions* (those using two or more fields), all fields must be of the same format.

■ Numeric fields can be combined and this may determine the sort order. Numeric fields can be combined either as an arithmetic sum or as the combination of character strings representing the numbers.

Organizing Data into Tables

After determining what data you need for the application, you need to organize the data in a manner that allows for easy maintenance and retrieval of the data. Within a database, data is stored in one or more tables. For most database applications, efficient data management is accomplished by storing data in multiple tables and establishing relationships between these tables. The following sections will describe how you can determine what data belongs in each table of your database.

Tables as Topics

A *table* is a collection of information related to a particular topic. By thinking of a key topic for the table, you can determine whether a particular piece of data fits into the table. For example, if a store owner wants to track information about both customers and employees, the owner may be tempted to put both in the same table (because both groups refer to people). However, look at the data required for each group. Although both groups require information about a person's name, address, and possibly phone number, the employee group also requires information about the person's social security number, job category, payroll, and tax status. If you were to create just one table, many of the entries would be blank for the customers. You would also have to add a field to distinguish between a customer and an employee. Clearly, this technique would result in a lot of wasted space. It could also result in slower processing of employee transactions or customer transactions because the program would have to skip a number of records in the table. Figure 1.4 shows a database table with the two groups combined. Figure 1.5 shows the reduction in the number of fields in a customer-only database table.

Note the blank fields in the customer records

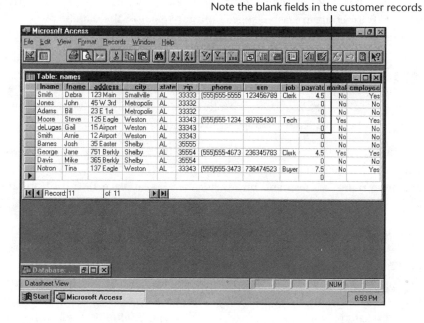

Fig. 1.4
Combining the employee and customer tables creates wasted space.

Fig. 1.5
A separate
database table for
customers has
only the required
fields and is more
efficient.

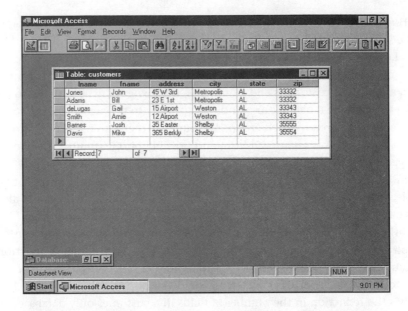

By thinking of the topic to which a table relates, it is easier to determine whether a particular piece of information belongs in the table or not. If the information results in wasted space for many records, the data belongs in a different table.

Data Normalization

Data normalization is the process of eliminating redundant data within the database. Taking data normalization to its fullest extent results in each piece of information in a database appearing only once.

Consider the example of the customer order function. For each item ordered, you need the item number, description, price, order number, order date, and customer name, address, and phone number. If you place all this information in one table, the result looks like the table shown in figure 1.6.

As you can see, much of the data in the table is repeated over and over. This introduces two problems. The first problem is wasted space because you repeat information such as the customer name, address, and phone number. The second problem is one of data *accuracy* or *currency*. If, for example, one of the customers changes her phone number, you have to change it for all the records that apply to that customer—with the possibility that you will miss one of the entries. In the table in figure 1.7, notice that Martha Smith's phone number was changed in the latest entry, but not in the two earlier entries. If an employee looked up Martha Smith and used an earlier entry, that employee would not find Martha's updated phone number.

Repeated information

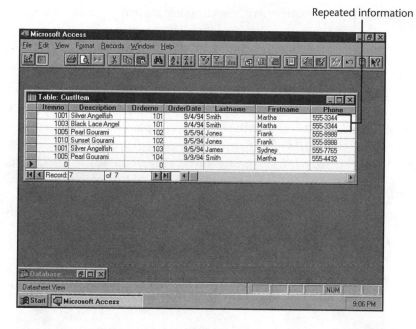

Fig. 1.6
Nonnormalized
data produces a
large, inefficient
data table.

A better solution for handling the data is to put the customer information in
one table and the sales order information in another table. You assign each
customer a unique ID and include that ID in the sales order table to identify
the customer. This arrangement yields two tables with the data structure
shown in figure 1.7.

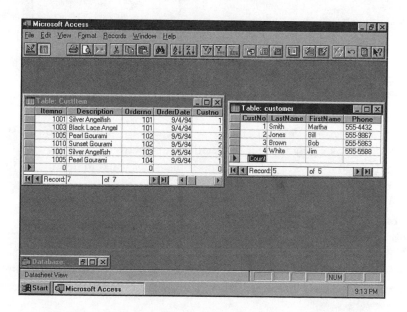

Fig. 1.7
Normalized
customer and
order tables
eliminate data
redundancy.

With this type of arrangement, the customer information only appears in one place. Now, if a customer changes his or her phone number, you have to change only one record.

You can do the same thing to the items sold and order information. This thinking leads to the development of four tables, but the organization of the tables is much more efficient and you can be sure that when information must be changed, it has to change in only one place. This arrangement is shown in figure 1.8. With the four-table arrangement, the Orders table and the Items Ordered table provide the links between the customers and the retail items they purchased. The Items Ordered table contains one record for each item of a given order. The Orders table relates the items to the date of purchase and the customer making the purchase.

Fig. 1.8
Complete normalization of the tables provides the greatest efficiency.

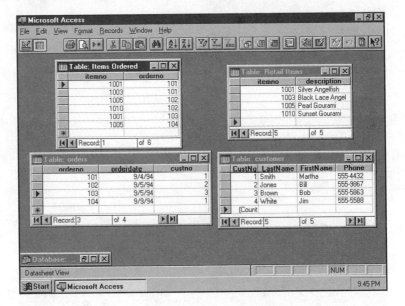

When information is moved out of one table and into another, you must have a way of keeping track of the relationships between the tables. This is done through the use of *data keys*. This topic is discussed in depth later in this chapter.

Data Volume Estimates

Another part of the design process is estimating the maximum desirable size of your database and the rate at which the size of the database will increase. This is important for getting an idea of the performance and space requirements of a database. The more data in the database, the more disk space required for it, and the slower database operations will be. The maximum desirable size will be determined by a number of factors such as the size of the user's disk and the data transfer rates of their network, if they use one. For example, if the user has only a 70 megabyte hard drive and the application is expected to be creating two megabytes of data per week, the user will quickly run out of available space. This fact may indicate the need to redesign the database.

By analyzing the data volume, you may see areas where the database can grow much larger than desired, indicating the need for a change to the design. Remember that it is much easier to implement design changes in the early phases of the project than it is later. Often, you may have to discuss a change with the client and may even have to make a change to the functional specifications of the application.

One of the things the sample application has to do is produce a sales receipt for each sale. Originally, it was determined that a record should be entered into the database for each item sold. This record contains the customer number, item number, price, and date sold. Mr. Crabb wants this so that he can look at each customer's buying habits and notify them of appropriate sales or special events that may interest them. After you talk to Mr. Crabb about his sales volume (which is directly related to the number of records that go into the database), you determine that the item sales table would grow at a rate of 1.5M per month. This growth rate will rapidly chew up space on the disk and has the potential to slow down many database transactions.

Because this information isn't needed for anything else (you use the sales information for inventory processing but don't have to retain it), you suggest to Mr. Crabb that a better approach may be to add a preference field to the customer database and simply ask the customer what particular areas of the aquarium hobby he or she is interested in. You may even suggest that a customer information response card be produced with predefined interest categories on it. This card, shown in figure 1.9, can be filled out by the customer and the information entered into the system. If properly designed, the card can be directly translated into a data entry form in the application to make it easy for employees to enter the data.

If Mr. Crabb insists that the information is necessary for some other needs of his store, you might consider archiving the sales history on a monthly basis. This can be done using a query to transfer the data to another database, which can then be stored either on tape or on floppies.

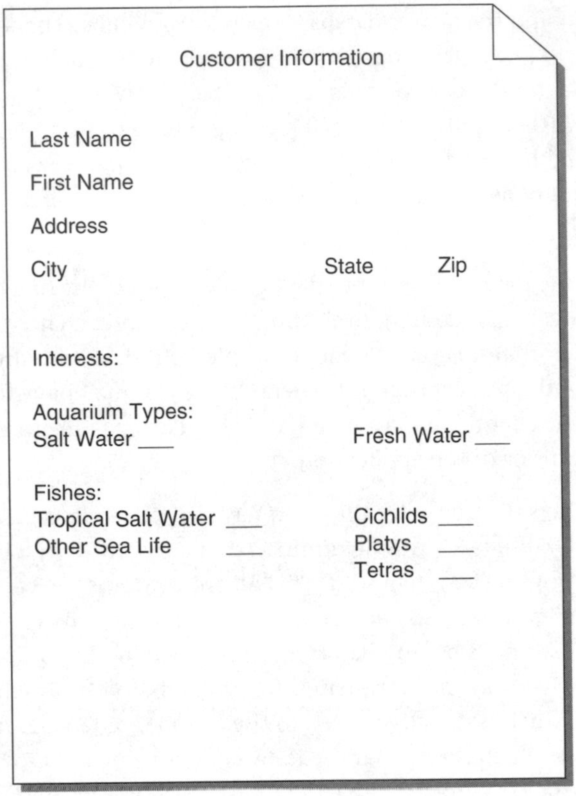

Fig. 1.9
A customer
information card
can eliminate the
tracking of some
data.

```
                        Customer Information


        Last Name

        First Name

        Address

        City                                State        Zip



        Interests:

        Aquarium Types:
        Salt Water ____                     Fresh Water ____


        Fishes:
        Tropical Salt Water ____            Cichlids ____
        Other Sea Life      ____            Platys   ____
                                            Tetras   ____
```

If you had not analyzed the data volume, a problem may have occurred
within a few months when Mr. Crabb started complaining that his system
was running slowly or that he got an Out of disk space error message. Once
the problem arises, consolidating the data and changing the database structure is much more difficult. This example also shows that database design
requires an understanding of the user's intended application as well as the
principles of programming.

Child Tables

A *child table* is a table in which all the entries share some common information, and the common information is stored in another table. A simple example of this is a membership directory: the family shares a common last
name, address, and phone number but each family member has a different
first name. The table containing the common information is called the *parent
table*, and the table containing the member's first names is the child table.
Figure 1.10 shows a parent table and its related child table. The use of child
tables is a form of data normalization.

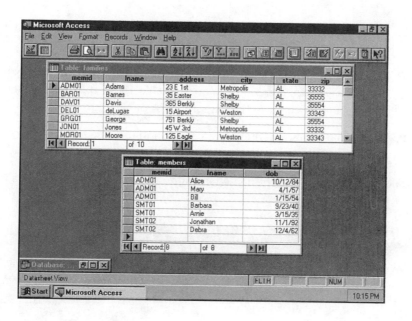

Fig. 1.10
Parent and child
tables are a form
of data normal-
ization.

Lookup Tables

A *lookup table* is typically a table used to store valid data entries (for example,
a state abbreviations table). When a person enters the state code in an application, the program looks in the abbreviations table to make sure that the
code exists.

A lookup table can also be used in data normalization. If you have a large
mailing list, many of the entries use the same city and state information. In
this case, you can use a ZIP code table as a related table to store the city and
state by ZIP code (remember that each ZIP code corresponds to a single city
and state combination). Using the ZIP code table requires that the mailing list
use only the ZIP code of the address and not the city and state. During data
entry, you can have the program check an entered ZIP code against the valid
entries.

Rules for Defining Tables

Although there are no absolute rules for defining what data goes into which
tables, here are some general guidelines to follow for efficient database
design:

- Determine a topic for each table and make sure that all data in the table
  relates to the topic.

- If a number of the records in a table have fields intentionally left blank,
  split the table into two similar tables. (Remember the example of the
  employee and customer tables.)

- If information is repeated in a number of records, move that information to another table and set up a relationship between the tables.

- Repeated fields indicate the need for a child table. For example, if you have Item1, Item2, Item3, and so on in a table, move the items to a child table that relates back to the parent table.

- Use lookup tables to reduce data volume and increase the accuracy of data entry.

- Do not store information in a table if it can be calculated from data in other tables.

Note

As stated above, the guidelines for defining tables are not hard and fast rules. There are times when it makes sense for the developer to deviate from the guidelines.

Performance Considerations

One of the most frequent reasons for deviating from the guidelines just given is to improve performance. For example, if obtaining a total sales figure for a given salesperson requires summing several thousand records, it may be worthwhile to include a Total Sales field in the salesperson table that is updated each time a sale is made. This way, when reports are generated, the application doesn't have to do large numbers of calculations and the report process is dramatically faster.

Another reason to deviate from the guidelines is to avoid opening a large number of tables at the same time. Because each open table uses a file handle and takes up memory, having too many open tables can slow down your application.

There are two major consequences of deviating from the guidelines. The first is increasing the size of the database because of redundant data. The second is the possibility of having incorrect data in some of the records because a piece of data was changed and not all the affected records were updated.

There are trade-offs between application performance and data storage efficiency. For each design, the developer must look at the trade-offs and decide what the optimum design is.

Establishing Relationships between Tables

When data is normalized and information is moved from one table to another, a method must exist to relate the two tables. The method of relating tables is the use of data keys. This section discusses the two types of table relationships and how data keys are established.

Data keys are usually referred to as either *primary keys* or *foreign keys*. A primary key is the one that uniquely identifies a record in a table. For example, in the Customers table, each record contains information about a specific customer. The primary key then provides a unique identifier for each customer record. In the case of the sales order tables shown earlier in figure 1.9, the Custno field in the Customers table is the primary key. A foreign key is one used to relate a record in one table to a specific record in another table. There may be multiple records in the second table relating to a single record in the primary table. In the order system, the customer key in the Orders table is a foreign key, linking the order records back to the Customers table.

One-to-Many Relationships

A *one-to-many relationship* occurs when a record in one table is related to one or more records in a second table, but each record in the second table is related to only one record in the first table. One-to-many relationships comprise the majority of the table relations in a database system.

In the sales order application example, a customer may make many purchases, but each purchase is made by only one customer (see fig. 1.11). In the membership directory example, each family record is related to one or more member name records, but each member name record is tied to only one family record.

Many-to-Many Relationships

Many-to-many relationships occur when each record from the first table relates to each record in the second table, and vice versa. When this occurs, an intermediate table is usually introduced that provides a one-to-many relationship with each of the other two tables.

An example of a many-to-many relationship is the items purchased by customers. Each customer may purchase many items, and each item can be purchased by many customers. Figure 1.12 shows how the data is structured with all the information in a single table. Figure 1.13 shows how the data is structured as separate item and customer tables with intermediate tables.

The "many" side of a relationship is indicated by the infinity symbol (∞)

Fig. 1.11

A one-to-many relationship between tables shows the use of key fields.

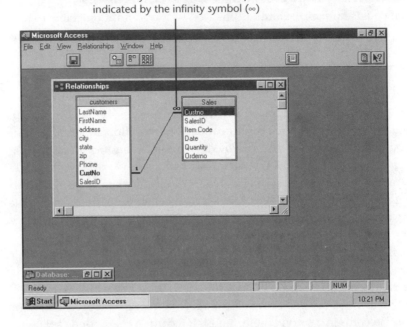

Fig. 1.12

Item and customer information in a single table is an inefficient means of handling the data.

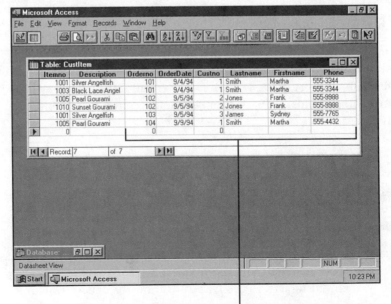

Repeated information in these fields

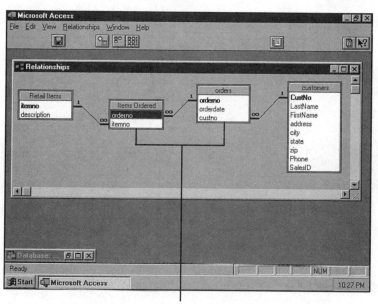

Fig. 1.13
Separate item and
customer tables
with intermediate
tables show the
resolution of the
many-to-many
relationship.

Data Access

Intermediate tables

Key Fields

Tables are related to each other through key fields. A *key field* is one that
uniquely identifies a record. A key field may be one that has meaningful data
in it or it may be a created field that serves the sole purpose of providing a
unique identifier for the record. The main criteria for the key field is that it
must be unique. Figure 1.14 shows a table with a key field added to provide a
unique ID for each record.

The key field is present in both databases of the relationship. For the membership directory, you can assign a unique identifier to each family record.
You then include the same identifier in each of the name records to indicate
the family to which the name belongs. If the key-field value is not unique,
there is confusion about the family information for a member.

If you are developing an employee database, it is possible that several people
have the same name. One possible unique identifier is the social security
number. However, because this nine-digit number must be stored in every
related record, it may be better to create a smaller, unique employee ID. If
you know that there will never be more than 9,999 employees, for example, a
four-digit ID can be used, saving five digits in every related record. Depending on the number of related records, the space savings can be significant.

Fig. 1.14

A table showing an added key field to ensure unique record IDs.

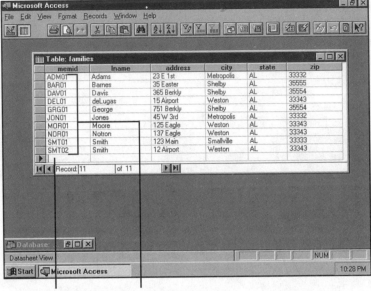

Key field added — Unique IDs for each record

> **Note**
>
> One way to ensure unique IDs is to use a counter field for the primary key. A counter field is an integer number field the database engine automatically increments when a new record is added. The counter field takes the responsibility of creating unique keys away from the user and places it on the database engine. One drawback in using a counter field is that the ID has no intrinsic meaning to the user.

Using Indexes, Filters, and Sorts

Indexes, filters, and sorts are used to control the appearance and processing of tables in a database. An index or sort controls the order of the database; a filter controls the range of records accessed.

Why Use an Index?

When information is entered into a table, records are stored in the order in which they are entered. This is the *physical order* of the data. However, you usually want to view or process data in an order different from the order of entry. You also frequently have to find a specific record in a table. Doing this by scanning the table in its physical order is quite time consuming.

An *index* provides a method of showing a table in a specific order. An index is a special table that contains a key value (usually derived from the values of one or more fields) for each record in the data table stored in an order requested by the user. The index also contains pointers that tell the database engine where the actual record is located.

The structure of an index allows for rapid searches of the data. If you have a table of names indexed alphabetically, you can rapidly retrieve the record for John Smith by searching the index. To get an idea of the value of such an index, imagine a phone book that lists the customer names in the order in which they signed up for phone service. If you live in a large city, it could take forever to find a person's number because you have to look at each line until you find the one you want.

A table can have a number of different indexes associated with it to give you several different organizations of the data. An employee table may have indexes on last name, date of birth, date of hire, and pay scale. Each index shows the same data in a different order, for a different purpose.

> **Caution**
>
> Although it may be desirable to have many different views of the data, keeping multiple indexes can take a toll on performance. Once again, there are trade-offs in the database design.

> **Note**
>
> You can also create different views of the information in a table by sorting the records or by specifying an order using a SQL statement.

Single-Key Expressions

The most common type of index is the *single-key index*, an index based on the value of a single field in a table. Examples of this type of index are social security number, ZIP code, employee ID, and last name. If multiple records exist with the same index key, those records are shown in physical order within the sort order imposed by the single-key index. Figure 1.15 shows the physical order of a names table and how the table appears after being indexed on the last name field.

Fig. 1.15
The physical and
logical order of
a table may be
different. Logical
order depends on
indexes.

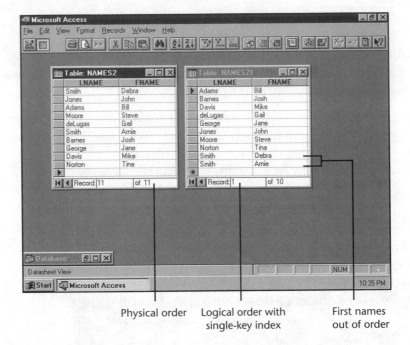

Physical order   Logical order with   First names
single-key index   out of order

Multiple-Key Expressions

Although single-key expressions are valuable in presenting data in a specific order, it is often necessary to impose an even more detailed order on the table. This can be done through the use of *multiple-key indexes*. As you can infer from the name, a multiple-key index is based on the values of two or more fields in a table. A prime example is to use last name *and* first name when indexing a membership list. Figure 1.16 updates the view of the table shown in figure 1.15 to show how using the first name field to help sort the records changes the order of the table. As with single-key indexes, if the key values of several records are the same, the records are presented in physical order within the index order.

Caution

The order of the fields in the index expression has a dramatic impact on the order of the records in the table. Although this may be obvious, the point should be stressed. Indexing on first name and then last name produces different results than indexing on last name and then first name. Figure 1.17 shows the undesirable results of using a first name/last name index on the table used in figure 1.16.

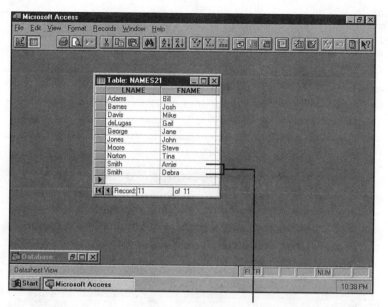

Fig. 1.16
Multiple-key indexes further refine the logical order of a table.

First names now in order

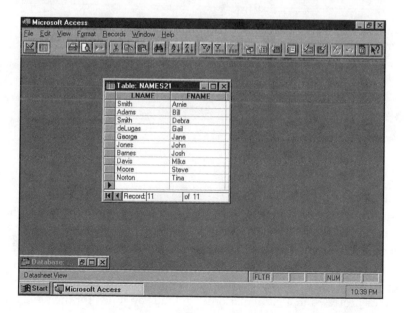

Fig. 1.17
Improper index field order yields undesirable results.

> ### Caution
>
> Use care when using multiple numeric fields as an index expression. Because the key value is a combination of the individual keys, a key value obtained *adding* two numbers may yield a different order than a key value obtained by *concatenating* the character representation of the two numeric fields. Figure 1.18 shows a simple example of this phenomenon.

Fig. 1.18
Different ways of combining numeric fields in an index expression can result in different arrangements of information.

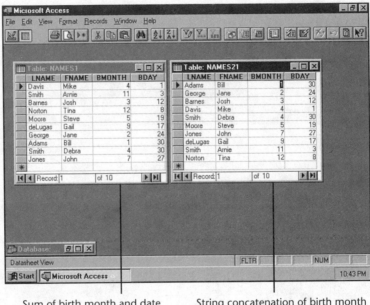

Sum of birth month and date numbers—bad results

String concatenation of birth month and date numbers—good results

Which Keys to Include in Indexes

The functional specifications for the application helps determine which fields should be used as key fields for an index in a table. For lookup tables, an index is often included on the field being searched. Using an index speeds up the search for a specific value; as a table gets larger, the speed advantage of using an index increases. If a function calls for data from a table to be displayed or processed in a particular order, include an index for the table that results in that order.

In the sample case, you determine that you need two indexes on the table containing customer information. The first index is on the customer name (so that you can quickly locate a particular customer in the table, and so that you can prepare a list of all customers presented in alphabetical order).

The second index is on ZIP code (so that you can sort deliveries by geographic area, and so that you can prepare mailing lists sorted by ZIP code to use discounted mailing rates).

Another of the tables is the inventory items table, which includes item numbers, inventory levels, prices, and item descriptions. You decide to use an index on the item number for this table (so that you can find the item quickly to update the inventory quantity, and so that you can look up the price of the item for the point-of-sale portion of the application).

How to Use Filters

Another way to control the information an application displays or processes is with the use of filters. A *filter* limits the number of records to those that meet a certain condition (for example, people with last names beginning with S or people who live in Florida). A filter is expressed as a logical condition in which the value of a field is compared to the filter value. Operators typically used for filters are equal to, not equal to, greater than, less than, and so on. For filter conditions, the comparison value must be of the same data type as the fields being compared. The most common error of mismatched data types occurs when a number is compared to the character representation of another number.

As with indexes, filter conditions can use comparisons of multiple fields (for example, "people named *Smith* who live in Florida). When you use multiple filter conditions, the individual conditions are joined by logical operators such as AND and OR. Obviously, the joined condition has a big impact on the records that meet the filter condition. For example, the condition `Birthdate<01/01/65 AND Birthdate>12/31/54` yields a list of people aged 30 to 39; the condition `Birthdate>01/01/65 OR Birthdate<12/31/54` yields a list of people that *excludes* those in the 30 to 39 age bracket.

When multiple conditions are used, each condition can use a different data type. Therefore, a filter condition of `Lastname='Smith' AND Age>30` is perfectly valid.

How to Use Sorts

A *sort* is used to create a recordset presented in a specific order from one or more base recordsets. In Visual Basic, a sort is used when you have a `dynaset` and want to change the presentation order of the records. Because an index cannot be assigned to a `dynaset`, you must set a sort condition and create a second `dynaset` from the first one. A sort is also implied when you use the `ORDER BY` clause of a SQL statement.

> **Note**
>
> The term *recordset* is used to refer to any collection of records from one or more tables. A *dynaset* refers to a specific type of recordset used in Visual Basic. These terms are further defined in Chapter 4, "Manipulating Data with a Program."

How to Use Functions and Calculated Values in Indexes and Filters

When setting up index and filter expressions, it is not always possible to achieve the desired results with direct comparisons to field values. Therefore, most database engines allow the use of calculated values or functions in the expression. For example, if you want to find the people whose names start with *S*, you actually create a condition such as `Firstletter(Lastname)='S'`, where `Firstletter` is a function that returns the first letter of the string (the `Lastname`) passed to it.

In the sample case, you must look for service calls that should be performed when the period of time since the last service exceeds the recommended service frequency. The data you have available is the date of the last service call and the current date. Therefore, you can generate a filter condition similar to this one: `CurrentDate-ServiceDate>ServiceFrequency`.

Another common use of functions in filter and index expressions is to put character data in uppercase (or lowercase). This change ensures that the index or filter is independent of the case of the information in the field. Some people have last names that begin with lowercase letters. If you do not use a function to convert the last name to uppercase letters in the index, these names are sorted out of order with other names that start with the same letter (see fig. 1.19).

Understanding Data Validation and Integrity

Two other issues in database design are *data validation* and *data integrity*. The first is concerned with making sure that data entered into the database is correct. The second refers to maintaining proper relationships between tables.

Validating Data

Data validation is the process of ensuring that the data stored in a field meets certain criteria. Common validation checks are dates (to make sure that someone hasn't entered February 31, for example), numbers (someone's age can't be less than 0), or lookup table values (to ensure that a ZIP code does exist). Validation checks can also be used to make sure that the data entered meets the design criteria of a database or table (not allowing a blank social security number in a personnel table).

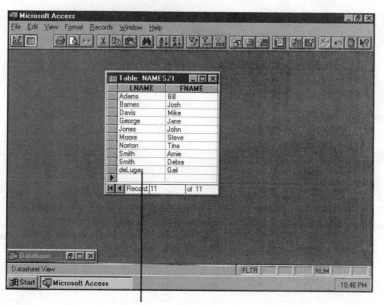

Fig. 1.19
An example of
not using a func-
tion in an index
expression.

Name starting with lowercase letter is out of desired order

Depending on the database engine in use, the validation of data can be
handled by the rules embedded in the table, or it may have to be handled by
rules set in the program that is processing the data. In either case, the deter-
mination of the validation rules is part of the design process, and the rules
are developed from the functional specifications.

The Jet database engine supports the use of validation rules embedded in the
tables. This is known as *engine-level validation*. These rules are stored in the
database itself. Validation rules can also be defined within the program commands used to access the database.

Maintaining Database Integrity

Data integrity refers to making sure that references between tables remain
valid (also known as *referential integrity*). A common problem arises when a
record in one table is deleted, and that record is related to other records in a
dependent table. Consider the case of the membership directory: if a family
name is deleted from the family table, information contained in that record
is no longer available to the records in the member name table. The member
names left without a family record are referred to as *orphan records*.

Determining whether or not to allow orphan records is one of the decisions
to be made during database design. As with data validation, some database
engines can automatically handle the maintenance of referential integrity.

For other database engines, referential integrity is the responsibility of the programmer.

The Jet database engine supports referential integrity. This support is optional and must be turned on when relationships between tables are defined.

Making Queries

If you perform operations on a repetitive basis, you may want to create a query to perform the operation and store the query in the database. For example, in the sales order function, you want to be able to produce a billing report for each customer every month. This report is shown in the following table:

Order Number	Date	Total Cost	Customer Name
10001	9/1/94	4.25	Martha Smith
10002	9/2/94	2.15	Bill Jones
10003	9/2/94	5.50	Bob Brown
10004	9/5/94	1.35	Jim White

To generate the report, you need the orders for the specific time period, total them by customer number, and add the customer information to the report. This can easily be done with the following SQL statement:

```
SELECT Or.OrderDate, Or.Totcost, Cs.Lastname, Cs.Firstname FROM _
    Orders AS Or, Customers As Cs WHERE Or.OrderData>#09/01/94#
```

This SQL statement asks the database engine to return a recordset containing specific data fields (the names between the SELECT and FROM keywords). The statement also defines in which tables the records are found (the names after the FROM keyword), and a condition that the returned records should meet (the text following the WHERE keyword). A complete description of SQL statements is in Chapter 6, "Understanding Structured Query Language (SQL)."

Because this query is run on a regular basis, you can store the query in the database. Creating a query and storing it is covered in Chapter 3, "Implementing the Database Design."

Reviewing the Design

After you complete the initial design of the database, review the design to look for any omissions or any inefficiencies that should be resolved. The best way to review the design is to input sample data for the application. This data is preferably a subset of the real data that will be used once the application is completed.

Does the Design Meet Objectives?

The first question to be addressed is, "Does the design meet the objectives?" In other words, can it perform all the functions asked for by the client? Common causes of missing an objective are omission of a piece of data, not creating a specific index, or not linking a table correctly to other tables. To determine this, the developer should walk through the processes involved in each function using the data in the sample database. If a process reaches a dead end or takes a wrong turn, some redesign is in order.

Questions Raised by the Design

Here is a list of several other things you can look for in the design that may show up when you use the sample data:

- Are there duplicate records—and should duplicates be allowed? If duplicates should not be allowed, you may want to set a primary key or unique index on the table.

- Are there blank fields in a number of records in a table? If so, you may want to break the information up into two or more related tables to eliminate wasted space.

- Do the key fields for relating tables yield unique values? If not, you may have to define another key field.

Data Tables Developed for the Sample Case

Tables 1.4 through 1.9 list the structures of the data tables developed for the sample case. The Length column in these tables has different meanings for the different data types. For character fields, the length indicates the maximum number of characters contained in the string. For numbers, the length column indicates the specific type of number, which in turn defines the number of bytes used to represent the number. For other field types, the number of bytes for the field is predefined, and no further information is needed. This is summarized in table 1.3.

Table 1.3 Use of Length Column for Data Types

Data Type	Meaning
Character	The number of characters in the text string.
Numeric	Indicates whether a number is an integer (2 bytes), long integer (4 bytes), or a single or double precision real number (4 or 8 bytes, respectively).
Memo	Length predefined.
Binary	Length predefined.
Long Binary	Length predefined.
Date	Length predefined.
Yes/No	Length predefined.

Table 1.4 Data Structure of the Customer Data Table

Field Name	Type	Length	Description
Custno	Numeric	Long Integer	Unique customer ID
Lastname	Character	30	Last name
Firstname	Character	30	First name
Address	Character	40	Street address
City	Character	30	City
State	Character	2	State abbreviation code
ZIP	Character	5	Postal ZIP code
Phone	Character	13	Phone number
Interests	Memo		Customer interests
SalesID	Character	6	ID of salesperson assigned to customer

Table 1.5 Data Structure of the Salesperson Data Table

Field Name	Type	Length	Description
SalesID	Character	6	ID of salesperson
SalesLast	Character	30	Last name of salesperson
SalesFirst	Character	30	First name of salesperson

Table 1.6 Data Structure of the Retail Items Data Table

Field Name	Type	Length	Description
Item Code	Numeric	Integer	Unique item ID
Item Description	Character	50	Item description
Product Category	Character	10	Product category
Wholesale	Numeric	Single	Wholesale price
Retail	Numeric	Single	Retail price
Min Quantity	Numeric	Integer	Desired minimum inventory
On Hand	Numeric	Integer	Current inventory level
SupplierID	Numeric	Long Integer	Supplier ID for item
Photo	Picture	Long Binary	Picture of product

Table 1.7 Data Structure for Orders Data Table

Field Name	Type	Length	Description
Orderno	Numeric	Long Integer	Unique order ID
Custno	Numeric	Long Integer	Unique customer ID
SalesID	Character	6	ID of salesperson
OrderDate	Date		Date order was placed
Totcost	Numeric	Single	Total cost of order

Table 1.8 Data Structure for Sales Data Table

Field Name	Type	Length	Description
Orderno	Numeric	Long Integer	Unique order ID
Item Code	Numeric	Integer	Unique item ID

Table 1.9 Data Structure for Suppliers Data Table

Field Name	Type	Length	Description
SupplierID	Numeric	Long Integer	Supplier ID
Name	Character	50	Name of supplier
Contact	Character	50	Name of contact person
Address	Character	50	Supplier's address
City	Character	30	City
State	Character	2	State abbreviation
ZIP	Character	5	ZIP code
Phone	Character	13	Phone number

From Here...

This chapter introduced the concepts used in designing a database. You learned about data modeling, the organization of data into tables, and the use of relations and data normalization to prevent redundant data. The chapter also explained the workings of indexes, sorts, and filters.

To learn more, refer to these chapters:

- Chapter 2, "Looking at the Capabilities of the Jet Engine," describes in detail how Visual Basic's native database engine stores data and handles data validation, data integrity, and security.

- Chapter 7, "Creating Multiuser Programs," reviews additional design considerations involved for programs on a network.

Looking at the Capabilities of the Jet Engine

The Microsoft Jet (Joint Engine Technology) database engine that comes with Visual Basic (and is shared with Microsoft Access) provides the developer with a feature-rich database environment for creating any type of data access application. This chapter covers the following topics regarding the Jet database engine:

- How a database management system works
- Database management features supported by the Jet engine
- How the database management features are accessed from Visual Basic

What's New in This Release?

Bundled with Visual Basic 4 is the latest version of the Microsoft Jet engine. If you worked with data access applications in Visual Basic 3, you worked with version 1.1 of the Jet engine (or possibly version 2 with the compatibility layer). The following list provides a quick summary of the enhancements made to version 1.1 to result in the latest version of the Jet engine:

- Engine-level enforcement of referential integrity
- Support for cascading updates and deletes
- Engine-level field and table validation

- ■ Data definition language queries for creating and modifying database objects

- ■ Enhanced security model that allows permission assignments by database object and user

These features are discussed in greater detail later in this chapter. The implementation of many of the features is covered in other chapters in this book.

How a Database Management System Works

Most programs created by developers must be able to retrieve, analyze, and store information. Before the advent of *database management systems* (DBMS), the developer not only had to handle the user interface (input and output) and analytical portions of the program, but also had to develop the methods of storing and retrieving the data in either sequential or random access files. The developer also had to handle any forms of searches or indexing that the program required. This type of data handling is shown in figure 2.1.

Fig. 2.1
Data retrieval and storage without a DBMS was a major effort.

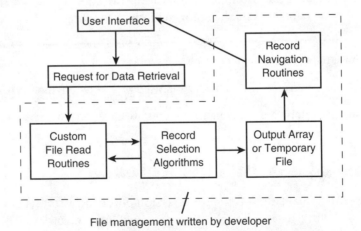

File management written by developer

With a DBMS, the developer initially defines the type of data to be stored. When data must be retrieved or stored, the program issues a request to the DBMS, and all the gory details of data management are handled automatically. The DBMS also handles searches and creates indexes as instructed by the developer. Data handling using a DBMS is shown schematically in figure 2.2.

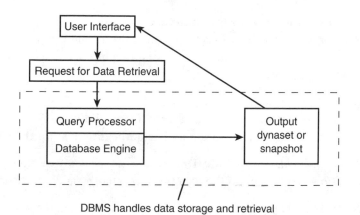

Fig. 2.2
Data handling is
much easier with a
database manage-
ment system.

Data Access

Advantages of a DBMS

As indicated in the preceding section, a DBMS frees developers from the tasks of defining the data storage and retrieval mechanisms. This provides several advantages.

First, the initial design of the program is easier because you don't have to program search algorithms or read-and-write statements to work with the current record. This can speed the initial development of a program.

Second, a DBMS makes it much easier to change the format of some of the data if it becomes necessary to do so (as it often does). With a DBMS, you change only the data definition stored in the database. The DBMS takes care of the rest. The routines in the programs that access an individual piece of data remain unchanged. Without a DBMS, you have to write a routine to port data files to the new format and then change the input and output statements in each affected program to reflect the change to the data format.

Finally, it is easier for users and other developers to create additional programs to access the data in the database. This is because they don't have to know the format in which the data was stored, only the names of the data fields and the types of data they contain. This information is easily found because most DBMSes contain methods to report the *structure* (field names and types) of the database.

Parts of a DBMS

A DBMS consists of two major parts, the programming interface (which consists of the user interface and the data retrieval requests) and the database engine. These two parts are shown in the DBMS block of figure 2.2.

Functions of the Programming Interface

The *programming interface* provides the commands that allow a program to tell the database engine what to do. The programming interface usually includes the following elements:

- A *data definition language* (DDL) that tells the database engine the format of the data objects (tables, records, fields, and indexes). The DDL also defines the data validation and data integrity rules for the database.

- A *data manipulation language* (DML) that tells the database engine the functions to perform on the data (retrieve, change, add, delete, store).

- A *data control language* (DCL) that tells the database engine what type of access is allowed to the data by various users.

Functions of the Database Engine

The simplest form of database engine provides mechanisms for the physical storage of the data, retrieval and updating of data, and data search and index capabilities. A database engine may also provide methods for ensuring data validity, data integrity, and data security.

The design of the database engine also determines what data manipulation features are supported. For example, if you need to increase the price of every item in a retail sales table, one database engine may support the use of "action queries" that allow a single program line to perform the function. With a different database engine, you may have to use a program loop to retrieve each record, change the price, and store the changes.

The Jet Database Engine

The Microsoft Jet database engine supports most of the functions described in the preceding section. The data definition features of Jet support the creation, modification, and deletion of tables, indexes, and queries. Jet also supports field level and record level data validation. Data integrity is supported in the form of primary keys and referential integrity between tables.

For data manipulation, Jet supports the use of Structured Query Language (SQL). SQL provides the means for a single statement to retrieve, add, delete, or update groups of records based on user-defined criteria. (The SQL supported by the Jet engine is close to but not fully compliant with ANSI SQL-89.) In addition, the Visual Basic-Jet engine combination supports the use of *data access objects.* These objects allow the developer to manipulate information in the database by setting the properties of the objects and executing the methods attached to the objects. Table 2.1 lists these objects and gives a brief description of their functions. How these data access objects are used to manipulate data is covered in Chapters 4 and 5.

Table 2.1	Visual Basic Data Access Objects
Object	**Description**
DBEngine	The object referring the Jet database engine.
Workspace	An area in which the user can work with one or more databases.
Database	A collection of information organized into tables, along with index and relation information about the tables.
TableDef	A definition of the physical structure of a data table.
QueryDef	A stored SQL query of information in the database.
Recordset	A collection of information records about a single topic.
Field	A single unit of information in a database.
Index	An ordered list of records in a recordset based on a defined key field.
Relation	Stored information about the relationship between two tables.

The data access objects and SQL statements are also used to provide data definition language support. The *data definition language* is used to create or modify the actual structure of the database. The use of some of the forms of data definition language is covered in Chapter 3, "Implementing the Database Design."

Jet also provides support for security features. These features allow the developer to assign a user ID and password that must be given before the user can access the database. Jet also supports the use of permissions, or access levels (for example, read-only or read/write accessibility), for individual tables and queries. This allows the database administrator to assign each user or group of users specific access to different parts of the database. For example, you can set up security so that everyone can look at the address and phone number information in an employee database but so that only the department manager can view salary and performance information.

Data Types Supported by the Jet Engine

The Jet engine supports a wide variety of data types, including several types of text and numeric fields. These different data types allow the developer a great deal of flexibility in designing a database application. Table 2.2 shows all the different data types available.

Table 2.2 The Data Types Available with the Jet Engine		
Name	**Information Stored**	**Size or Range**
Text	Character strings	255 characters maximum
Memo	Long character strings	Up to 1.2G
Byte	Integer (numeric data)	0 to 255
Integer	Integer (numeric data)	−32,768 to 32,767
Long	Integer (numeric data)	−2,147,483,648 to 2,147,483,647
Counter	Long integer, automatically incremented	
Single	Real (numeric data)	-3.4×10^{38} to 3.4×10^{38}
Double	Real (numeric data)	-1.8×10^{308} to 1.8×10^{308}
Yes/No	Logical/Boolean	
Date	Date and time values	
Binary	Binary data	Up to 1.2G
OLE	OLE objects	Up to 1.2G

Data Integrity and Validation

One of the key functions of a database application is ensuring, as much as possible, the accuracy of the data in the tables. Data accuracy refers not only to making sure that the individual data items are correct, but also to making sure that relationships between data tables are properly maintained. These two functions are referred to, respectively, as *data validation* and *data integrity*.

The Jet engine supports two main types of data integrity monitoring—*primary-key integrity* and *referential integrity*. It also supports two key forms of data validation—*field-level validation* and *record-level validation*. These items are discussed later in this section.

In Visual Basic 4, the developer can invoke all these integrity and validation features using the data access objects. The features are determined by setting the properties of the various objects at design time when the database and tables are created. (See Chapter 3 for more information on creating data tables and fields and setting the object properties.) In Visual Basic 3, these features (with the exception of primary-key integrity) could only be set using Microsoft Access.

Primary-Key Integrity

Primary-key integrity ensures that each record in a table is uniquely identified by a field or combination of fields. Unique keys are essential for properly relating tables. For example, if you make a sale to a customer named John Smith, but have no identifier other than his name, how do you determine which John Smith to send the bill to?

You can implement a primary key in either of two ways. You can define a unique field or combination of fields that is meaningful to you, or you can create a counter field. If you create a counter field, Jet automatically creates a new value for the field for each record you add, ensuring the uniqueness of the key. If you define your own field (for example, the first three letters of a person's first and last names, such as JOHSMI), you are responsible for making sure that the values are unique and for resolving any conflicts if a new value is not unique. That is, you must provide a program function that generates the key value (or gets an input value from the user) and verifies that the value is unique. If the value is not unique, you must provide a way to change the value and reverify its uniqueness.

With either method, Jet enforces primary integrity by verifying that the value of the primary key is unique before it allows the addition or updating of a record. If the value is not unique, a trappable error is returned. Your program must be able to handle this error.

Referential Integrity

To relate one table to another, the same value must appear in both tables. In a one-to-many relationship, the table on the one side of the relationship contains the primary key for the table (as described in the preceding section). The table on the many side of the relationship contains a reference to this primary key in a field. This field is known as the *foreign key*. Figure 2.3 shows the relationship between the Retail Items and Sales tables of the sample case, with the primary and foreign keys labeled.

Fig. 2.3
The foreign key in one table is related to the primary key in another table.

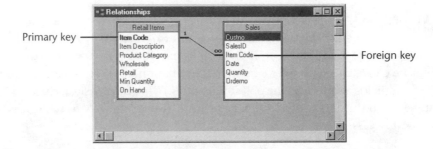

In this relationship, each record in the Retail Items table can be linked to many items in the Sales table. However, each item in the Sales table can be linked to only one item in the Retail Items table. A one-to-many relationship is often referred to as a *parent-child relationship*, with the primary-key table being the parent table and the foreign-key table being the child table.

Referential integrity is responsible for making sure that the relationship between two tables is maintained. Jet supports the following functions of referential integrity:

- When a foreign key is added or changed in a child table, the existence of the key value is verified in the parent table.

- When a new record is added to a child table, a foreign key must be specified.

- When a parent record is deleted, or the primary key is changed, Jet can either cascade the update or deletion through the child tables or reject the operation if there are child records. The choice of behavior is made by the developer.

With Visual Basic 4, you can define the relationships between tables using the data access objects available for relations. With previous versions of Visual Basic and versions of the Jet engine before 2.0, referential integrity was either not available or could be set only using Microsoft Access. If you have a copy of Access, however, it provides a nice graphical method of setting table relationships (see fig. 2.4).

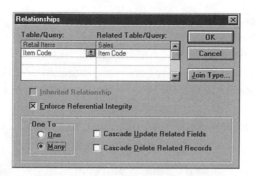

Cascading Updates and Deletions

Allowing the cascading of updates and deletions from the parent table to
the child tables is a new feature of the Jet engine, initially implemented in
Jet 2.0. Cascading is an optional property of a relationship. You may choose
to use cascading updates, cascading deletes, or both. If you choose these
options, changes to the parent table are automatically propagated through
the child table. For updates, if you change the primary key of the parent
table, the related foreign keys in the child table are changed to reflect the
new value. For deletions, if you delete a record in the parent table, all related
child records are also deleted.

Without cascading, the programmer is responsible for handling conflicts that
arise from making changes to a parent record when there are dependent
records in a child table. The programmer must either verify that no child
records exist before making the change or deletion, or let the program make
the change when a record is found or an error occurs. If you do not have the
cascading options turned on, you get an error when you try to change or
delete a record with dependent records in a child table.

Cascading options are set when a relation is created. The options are properties of the Relation object. The tasks of creating a relation and setting its
properties are covered in Chapter 3, "Implementing the Database Design."

Caution

Although cascading is a very useful and powerful method for preserving referential
integrity, it should be used with caution—especially cascading deletions. Accidentally
deleting a parent record can wipe out quite a bit of data.

Data Access

Handling Rejected Changes

For any type of data integrity rule defined in the database, the Jet engine issues an error message if the rule is violated. When this happens, the program must have routines to *trap* the error and either handle the problem or inform the user of decisions to be made about the erroneous data. If you do not include an error-handling routine, the user sees the error message box, the attempted operation is aborted, and, in extreme cases, the program locks up.

You handle database errors the same as other errors in your code: by using the `On Error GoTo` statement and an error-handling routine. Visual Basic's manuals and online Help cover basic error handling fairly well. Chapter 7, "Creating Multiuser Programs," covers some of the specific database errors that you might encounter.

Data Validation

Data validation is the process of ensuring that the data input or changed by a user meets certain criteria. Data validation can take several forms, all of which are described in the following sections:

- Field level validation

- Record level validation

- Required field validation

Field Level Validation

Field level validation ensures that the information in the field is within a certain range of values. Jet supports the use of simple expressions in field level validation. A simple expression can compare the value of the field to a constant. Additional types of field level validation include the use of user-defined functions or checking for valid entries in another table. Although Jet does not support these types of validation at the engine level, they can be programmed into your Visual Basic code. Alternatively, if you are accessing an external database server, check to see whether these types of validation are supported by your host system.

How to Validate Data in a Database Application

Database applications created with Visual Basic can provide data validation functions using either engine-level validation or program validation. Engine-level validation uses rules about data fields and tables that are stored in the database itself. When data is changed, the Jet engine checks the data against the rule prior to writing the update to the database. If the new data does not conform to the rules, an error message is returned. Program validation is made up of data rules embedded in the actual program code. These rules check the value of the data against the defined criteria when particular program events occur. A program validation rule might be placed in the data-changed event of an object or the click event code of a command button.

In addition to setting a validation rule, you can also specify a custom message that displays if the validation rule is violated. This message is displayed in the standard message box when needed. In version 4, field level validation can be set by setting the optional `ValidationRule` and `ValidationText` properties of the data access objects. You can also use Microsoft Access or the Data Manager application that comes with Visual Basic. Figure 2.5 shows how the validation rule and text are set using the Data Manager. In Visual Basic, field level validation expressions are checked when an update method is called.

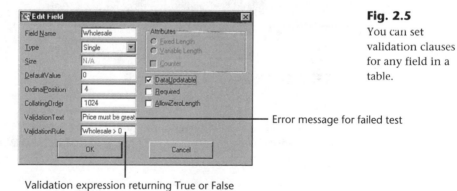

Fig. 2.5
You can set validation clauses for any field in a table.

Error message for failed test

Validation expression returning True or False

Record Level Validation
Record level validation checks the information in a field against data in other fields of the record, or checks the results of a combination of fields against a criterion. For example, you can verify that the ratio of the retail price to the wholesale price is greater than 25 percent or that the length of the combined first and last name fields is less than 40 characters (for mailing labels). As with field level validation, Jet only supports the use of simple expressions for

record level validation. In addition, only one validation criterion can be set for each table. As with field level validation, you can enter validation text that provides a custom error message if the validation rule is violated.

Record level validation can also be set using the data access objects or Microsoft Access. When your program violates the record level validation, a message is shown indicating the error. Any text you entered as validation text is included in the message that appears.

Required Field Validation

The Jet engine also allows you to specify any field as a required field. If you specify a field as required, a value *must* exist for it when a record is added or changed. Jet checks each required field for a null value whenever a record is updated. If you attempt to update a record without a value in a required field, an error is generated.

As with field validation, required field validation can be set using the data access objects, the Data Manager, or Microsoft Access.

Caution

If you specify required fields, make sure that you include the field on any data-entry form that adds new records to the table. Otherwise, you provide no means to input a value for the required field, and no new records can be created.

Support for Queries

The Jet engine supports the use of Structured Query Language (SQL) statements for defining and manipulating data. There are two main groupings of SQL statements, Data Manipulation Language statements and Data Definition Language statements.

Data Manipulation Language (DML)

The Data Manipulation Language statements provide the means to insert, delete, update, and retrieve groups of records in a database. Two basic types of queries are defined: action queries and retrieval queries.

Action Queries

Action queries operate on groups of records. These types of queries let you delete records, insert new records, update fields in records, or create new tables from existing records. Jet supports all of these types of action queries.

The queries are based on SQL syntax. You can run action queries with either a database execute method or a query execute method. The syntax of these queries and how to execute them are discussed in detail in Chapter 6, "Understanding Structured Query Language (SQL)." Table 2.3 summarizes the action queries supported by the Jet engine.

> **Note**
>
> The Execute method is one of the methods associated with the Database and QueryDef objects. By using this method, you can run a SQL query in your code.

Table 2.3   Action Queries Supported by the Jet Engine

Keywords	Function
DELETE...FROM	Removes records from a table based on the selection criteria.
INSERT INTO	Appends records to a table from another data source.
UPDATE...SET	Changes the values of selected fields.
SELECT INTO	Creates a new table from information in other tables.

> **Note**
>
> The selection criteria for deleting records is defined by a logical expression such as Price > 1.00. Any record that meets this criteria is deleted; all other records are left alone. The syntax of this statement is explained further in Chapter 6, "Understanding Structured Query Language (SQL)."

Retrieval Queries

Retrieval queries tell the database engine to return a group of records in a dynaset or snapshot for viewing or processing. These queries are SQL SELECT statements that define the fields to be retrieved; the tables in which the fields are located; and the filter criteria for the fields. Jet supports standard SQL clauses such as WHERE, ORDER BY, GROUP BY, and JOIN. In addition, Jet supports the new clauses UNION, TOP *n*, and TOP *n*%. Jet also supports the use of subqueries, in which the results of one SELECT statement can be used as part of the WHERE clause of another statement. These capabilities of the SELECT statement provide the developer with a lot of flexibility in grouping and manipulating data. Table 2.4 summarizes the clauses of the SELECT statement supported by the Jet engine.

Table 2.4   Types of Retrieval Queries and Conditional Clauses Supported by the Jet Engine

Keywords	Function
UNION	Creates a recordset containing all records from the defined tables.
SELECT...FROM	Retrieves a group of fields from one or more tables subject to the conditional clauses.
WHERE *comparison*	A conditional clause that compares an expression to a single value.
WHERE...LIKE	A conditional clause that compares an expression to a pattern of values.
WHERE...IN	A conditional clause that compares an expression to a group of values.
INNER¦LEFT¦RIGHT JOIN	A conditional clause that combines information from two tables based on identical values in a key field in each table.
ORDER BY	A conditional clause that determines the sort sequence of the output recordset.
GROUP BY	A conditional clause that combines summary information on records into groups based on the value of one or more listed fields.

Data Definition Language (DDL)

Data definition language (DDL) queries are a new feature of the Jet engine (versions 2.0 and later). In previous versions of the Jet engine, you created tables in a database by defining field and index objects and then adding them to the table definition. With the new DDL queries, you can issue a single command to create, change, or delete a table, and create or delete an index. Table 2.5 summarizes the various DDL queries.

Table 2.5   DDL Queries Used to Modify a Database Structure

Keywords	Function
CREATE TABLE	Creates a new table from a list of field definitions.
ALTER TABLE	Adds new fields to a table.
DROP TABLE	Deletes a table from the database.

Keywords	Function
CREATE INDEX	Creates a new index for a table.
DROP INDEX	Deletes an index from a table.

Security

The security features of the Jet engine include the assignment of user IDs, passwords, and permissions for objects in the database. In Visual Basic 4, you control these features through data access objects. In earlier versions, security features could be set only using Microsoft Access.

The security features allow you to assign different permissions to each user or group of users for each object in the database. Table 2.6 summarizes the permission levels available for database objects.

Table 2.6 Security Features Available with the Jet Engine	
Permission Type	**Allows User to...**
Open	Open a database in shared mode, so that more than one user can access it at a time.
Open Exclusive	Open a database for exclusive use.
Read Design	Read database definition objects.
Modify Design	Add or change database definition objects.
Administer	Modify any database component—including security information.
Read Data	Read information in the object.
Update Data	Change information but not add or delete records.
Insert Data	Insert records but not change data or delete records.
Delete Data	Delete records but not change data or insert records.

From the application developer's standpoint, the only links to the security system are to include the user ID and password when opening a database that has the security features enabled.

Access to Other Databases

The Jet engine provides direct access to several external database formats: FoxPro, dBASE, Paradox, and Btrieve. In addition, the Jet engine can link to any Open Database Connectivity (ODBC) database through the ODBC drivers.

From Here...

The capabilities of the Jet engine are explained in more detail in other chapters of this book:

- Chapter 3, "Implementing the Database Design," explains more about creating and maintaining a database.

- Chapter 6, "Understanding Structured Query Language (SQL)," explains how to build SQL statements.

- Chapter 8, "Accessing Other Databases with the Jet Engine," explains how to access external databases.

- Chapter 9, "Using ODBC to Access Databases," explains how to access ODBC databases.

Chapter 3

Implementing the Database Design

When you use Visual Basic to develop database applications, you have a number of data access options. The option designed to be most easily integrated into Visual Basic applications, and the one that is the subject of Chapters 3 through 5, is the Microsoft Jet database engine. However, if a situation warrants, you should be aware that data can be stored in sequential or random-access files and accessed using Visual Basic's file read and write commands (alternatively, a third-party data access engine can be used). This chapter looks only at using the Jet engine and, in particular, using Microsoft Access databases (the native database for Visual Basic). (Accessing other databases through the Jet engine is covered in Chapters 8 and 9.)

There are three main methods of creating an Access database for use with Visual Basic:

- Using the data access objects with a program to create the database

- Using the Data Manager application provided with Visual Basic

- Using Microsoft Access

This chapter demonstrates how to do the following:

- Create a database with program commands

- Create a database with the Data Manager

- Modify existing databases

- Add and delete relationships in a database

- Add and delete queries in a database

What's New in Visual Basic 4

If you have used Visual Basic Version 3 to create a database, you will note several changes in the methods used to create databases in Version 4. Any of your existing programs should still run (Version 4 supports the older methods of creating databases for backward compatibility). The major changes you should be aware of are as follows:

- New `CreateTableDef` and `CreateField` methods are used to define tables and fields.

- You can define field and table level validation for your database by setting the appropriate properties.

- You can create relationships between tables to establish and enforce referential integrity.

- Data definition SQL statements are available to create or modify tables.

- You can delete a field from a table under certain conditions. In earlier versions, you could not delete fields from tables at all.

Creating a Database

This chapter focuses on using data access objects to create portions of the sample database defined in Chapter 1. There are several ways to implement the data access objects. Although each method is not described in detail, the sample case on the companion CD contains examples of the various methods. Each group of commands is tied to a command button on the form. By examining the code, you can see the different methods. The project file for this sample case is CHAPTER3.MAK. The sample case also uses the SQL DDL statements that are covered in Chapter 6, "Understanding Structured Query Language (SQL)." In addition to discussions about using data access objects, this chapter presents a section on using Data Manager to create a database.

Writing a Program to Create a Database

You can use Visual Basic's database commands to write a program that creates a database for use in your design work, or to write a program that creates a new database while the program is running. The database creation commands are the only way to make a new database at program run time. Using the program to create the database is particularly useful in creating and distributing commercial applications because you don't have to worry about

Data Access

including and installing the database files with the application. The database is created the first time the user runs your application.

Creating files at run time is also useful if the user is expected to create different database files with the same structure but different user-defined names. Each time the user wants to create a new file, the program asks for the file name and then creates the database accordingly.

Creating a new database involves the following eight steps:

1. Creating a new database object with the `Dim` statement.

2. Using the `CreateDatabase` method to create the new database.

3. Creating `TableDef` objects with the `Dim` statement and `CreateTableDef` method.

4. Setting the properties for the new tables.

5. Creating `Field` and `Index` objects with the `Dim` statement and `CreateField` and `CreateIndex` methods.

6. Setting the properties for the fields and indexes.

7. Using the `Append` method to add fields and indexes to the tables.

8. Using the `Append` method to add the table to the database.

To explain the process of creating a new database, this chapter steps you through the process of creating the database and Retail Items table from the sample application described in Chapter 1. The designed structure of the Retail Items table is repeated in table 3.1 for your convenience.

Table 3.1   Data Structure of the Retail Items Data Table

Data Element	Type	Length	Description
Item Code	Numeric	Integer	Unique item ID
Item Description	Character	50	Item description
Product Category	Character	10	Product category
Wholesale	Numeric	Single	Wholesale price
Retail	Numeric	Single	Retail price

(continues)

Table 3.1	Continued		
Data Element	**Type**	**Length**	**Description**
Min Quantity	Numeric	Integer	Desired minimum inventory
On Hand	Numeric	Integer	Current inventory level
SupplierID	Numeric	Long Integer	Supplier ID for item
Photo	Picture	Long Binary	Picture of product

Creating the Database

Previous versions of Visual Basic used the CreateDatabase statement to create a new database. Visual Basic 4 contains the DBEngine and Workspace objects as data access objects. In Visual Basic 4, the CreateDatabase statement was changed to a method of the Workspace object. A default workspace is always created for you whenever you access the Jet database engine. You can create other workspaces if necessary. If you do not include the ID of a workspace when using the functions, the default workspace is assumed.

Listing 3.1 shows the statements used to define a database object and create the database (steps 1 and 2 defined in the preceding section). The first part of the listing shows the full syntax of using the CreateDatabase method of the workspace. This is the method used for Visual Basic 4. The second part of the listing shows the use of the CreateDatabase statement used in Visual Basic 3. Either listing creates a new database. The CreateDatabase statement is supported in Visual Basic 4 for backward-compatibility. However, it is recommended that you use the workspace's CreateDatabase method for any new work, since the old methods may not be supported in future versions.

Listing 3.1   Defining a Database Object and Creating a Database

```
'***********************************
'Full syntax of CreateDatabase method
'***********************************
Dim NewDb As Database, NewWs As Workspace
Set NewWs = DBEngine.Workspaces(0)
Set NewDb = NewWs.CreateDatabase("A:\TRITON.MDB",dbLangGeneral)
'*************************************************
'Syntax of CreateDatabase function (Old method)
'*************************************************
Dim NewDb As Database
Set NewDb = CreateDatabase("A:\TRITON.MDB",dbLangGeneral)
```

Any valid variable name can be defined as a database object using the `Dim` statement. Although a database (`"A:\TRITON.MDB"`) was specified in the argument of the `CreateDatabase` function, a string variable could have been used to hold the name of the database to be created. This arrangement gives the user the flexibility of specifying a database name meaningful to him or her or allows the programmer to create multiple databases with the same structure.

The constant `dbLangGeneral` is a required argument of the `CreateDatabase` method. It specifies the language and code page information for the database.

Another optional argument is available for the `CreateDatabase` method: the options argument allows you to create an Access 1.0, 1.1, 2.0, or 3.0 database (the default is Access 2.0 for Windows 3.1 and 3.0 for Windows 95) and to encrypt your database. To invoke these options, the constants for each option are summed to a long integer and specified as the last argument of the function. The code below shows how you can change the code in listing 3.1 to create an Access 1.1 database and encrypt it.

```
Dim NewDb As Database, NewWs As Workspace
Set NewWs = DBEngine.Workspaces(0)
Dim DbOpts As Long
DbOpts = dbVersion11 + dbEncrypt
Set NewDb = NewWs.CreateDatabase("A:\TRITON.MDB", _
    dbLangGeneral,DbOpts)
```

Caution

When you use the `CreateDatabase` method, a trappable error occurs if the file to be created already exists. You should include a trap for this error in your error-handling routine or, better yet, check for the existence of the file name before invoking the function.

Creating the Tables

Creating a database creates a file on a disk. You can't do anything with that file until the tables have been created and added to the database (refer to steps 3 through 8 in "Writing a Program to Create a Database," earlier in this chapter).

Note

Although this book typically refers to "tables" in a database, keep in mind that a database may contain only a single table.

Defining the *TableDef* Object. The first step in creating a new table is to create a new TableDef object. This object allows you to set the properties for the new table. The following lines of code show how to create a TableDef object and give your table a name. In earlier versions of Visual Basic, the use of the New keyword in the Dim statement was required. Visual Basic 4 no longer uses this keyword.

```
Dim NewTbl As TableDef
Set NewTbl = NewDb.CreateTableDef("Retail Items")
```

The Name property of the table is only one of several properties for the TableDef object, but it is typically the only one required for the creation of an Access database. Some of the other properties (Attributes, Connect, and SourceTableName) may be used when attaching an external table to the database. You can set the Attributes, SourceTableName, and Connect properties in successive arguments of the CreateTableDef method. You can also specify other properties by setting them equal to a value, as you do if you want to set the validation rule and validation error message for a table (as shown below). These statements follow the CreateTableDef method.

```
NewTbl.ValidationRule = "Retail > Wholesale"
NewTbl.ValidationText = _
      "Retail price must exceed wholesale price."
```

Defining the Fields. After defining the TableDef object for the new table, the field objects must be defined. A table can contain one field or a number of fields. For each field, you must define its name and type. Depending on the type of field, you may be required to define other properties, or you may want to set some optional properties.

For text fields, you must set the size property to specify how long a string the field can contain. The valid entries for the size property of the text field are 1 to 255. If you want to allow longer strings, set the field type to memo.

You should be aware of two optional settings for the Attribute property. The first is the auto-increment setting, which tells the database to increment the value of the field each time a new record is added. This setting can provide a record counter and can be used to ensure a unique value in that field for each record. The auto-increment field can then be used as a primary key field. The auto-increment setting is only valid for fields with the long data type. The other optional setting is the updatable setting, which allows you to specify whether a field can be changed. This setting is not typically used when initially creating a table but can be very useful in limiting access to information, particularly in a multiuser environment.

Listing 3.2 shows how the field objects are created and the field properties set for the Retail Items table of the sample application. The field name, type, and size can be specified as optional arguments of the `CreateField` method. You can also use the `CreateField` method without any arguments and then set all the field properties with assignment statements. Both of these methods are shown in listing 3.2. Any other properties must be set using an assignment statement. As an example of an assignment statement, the listing sets a validation rule for the wholesale price field.

Listing 3.2   Creating Field Objects and Setting Properties

```
Dim F1 As Field, F2 As Field, F3 As Field, F4 As Field
Dim F5 As Field, F6 As Field, F7 As Field
'*************************************************************
'Specify field name, type, and size as CreateField arguments
'*************************************************************
Set F1 = NewTbl.CreateField("Item Code", dbText, 10)
Set F2 = NewTbl.CreateField("Item Description", dbText, 50)
Set F3 = NewTbl.CreateField()
'******************************
'Explicitly set field properties
'******************************
F3.Name = "Product Category"
F3.Type = dbText
F3.Size = 10
Set F4 = NewTbl.CreateField("Wholesale", dbSingle)
'************************************
'Set validation properties for a field
'************************************
F4.ValidationRule = "Wholesale > 0"
F4.ValidationText = "Wholesale price must be greater than 0."
Set F5 = NewTbl.CreateField("Retail", dbSingle)
Set F6 = NewTbl.CreateField("Min Quantity", dbInteger)
Set F7 = NewTbl.CreateField()
F7.Name = "On Hand"
F7.Type = dbInteger
```

Once you define each of the fields to be included in the table, the `Append` method is used to add the fields to the table definition, as shown in listing 3.3.

Listing 3.3   Adding Fields to the Table Definition

```
NewTbl.Fields.Append F1
NewTbl.Fields.Append F2
NewTbl.Fields.Append F3
```

(continues)

Tip
If you have many
fields, or want to
create a generic
routine for adding
fields to a table,
consider using an
array to define
your fields. Arrays
allow you to write
a simple FOR loop
to add all the fields
to the table. De-
pending on the
table's structure,
you may be able to
use a loop to set
the type properties
of several fields,
although you must
still define each
field you intend to
add to the table.

Listing 3.3   Continued

```
NewTbl.Fields.Append F4
NewTbl.Fields.Append F5
NewTbl.Fields.Append F6
NewTbl.Fields.Append F7
ReDim Fld(1 To 7) As Field
'************************************************
'Field definition statements go here for each
'array element.
'************************************************
FOR I = 1 To 7
  NewTbl.Fields.Append Fld(I)
NEXT I
```

Defining the Indexes. Defining indexes for a table is another key aspect of developing your database. If you have created an index with Visual Basic 3, forget everything you know about the process. Remember, however, *why* you want to create an index and how indexes are used. Visual Basic 4 introduces a new method for creating indexes. This method is more closely related to the creation of the table itself than to the creation of a field (as was the case in Visual Basic 3). For each index, you must still assign a name, define the fields to be included in the index, and determine whether the index is a primary index and whether duplicate values are allowed in the fields that comprise the index key.

To create an index, follow these six steps:

1. Use the CreateIndex method of the TableDef object to create the Index object.

2. Set any optional properties of the index (such as primary or unique).

3. Use the CreateField method of the Index object to create the field objects.

4. Set any optional properties of the field objects.

5. Append the fields to the Index object.

6. Append the index to the TableDef object.

Two of the most commonly used optional properties of the Index object are the Primary property and the Unique property. A *primary index* is one that is typically used for finding a specific record in a table. To make an index primary, set the Primary property to True. Making an index primary ensures that the value of the index key for each record is unique and that there are no null values.

Use the Unique property on a nonprimary index to make sure that the values of fields other than the primary field are unique (for example, to make sure that you enter a unique social security number for each employee in a table).

> **Note**
>
> You can specify only one primary index per table.

For the field objects, the only property of concern for creating indexes is the Attributes property. This property is used to determine whether the sort order of the field is ascending (from A to Z) or descending (from Z to A). The default value is ascending. If you want to sort the field in descending order, set the Attributes property to the value of the constant dbDescending.

You can create a multiple-field index (for example, an index on the first and last names of a customer). To create such an index, simply create multiple fields using the CreateField method. Remember that the order of the fields can have a dramatic impact on the order of your records. The order of the fields in an index is determined by the order in which the fields are appended to the index.

As described in the preceding section, after you create the fields and set the properties of the fields and index, use the Append method to add the fields to the index and the index to the table definition.

> **Note**
>
> You can create a maximum of 32 indexes per table.

For the sample case, create a primary index on the Item Code field and an index on the Wholesale price in descending order. Listing 3.4 shows how this is accomplished.

Listing 3.4   Creating Index Objects, Assigning Properties, and Adding Indexes to the Table

```
Dim Idx1 As Index, Idx2 As Index, Fld1 As Field, Fld2 As Field
Set Idx1 = NewTbl.CreateIndex("Item Code")
Idx1.Primary = True
Set Fld1 = Idx1.CreateField("Item Code")
Idx1.Fields.Append Fld1
```

(continues)

Data Access

Listing 3.4   Continued

```
Set Idx2 = NewTbl.CreateIndex("Price_Paid")
Idx2.Unique = False
Set Fld2 = Idx2.CreateField("Wholesale")
Fld2.Attributes = dbDescending
Idx2.Fields.Append Fld2
NewTbl.Indexes.Append Idx1
NewTbl.Indexes.Append Idx2
```

Note

Although spaces are acceptable in field names, they are not allowed in index names. If you want a multiple word index name, separate the words with an underscore.

Adding the Table to the Database

The final step in creating a database is adding the table or tables to the database. Use the Append method of the Database object to accomplish this as shown in the following code. The code also shows the Close method, which closes the database file and releases the system resources associated with the database object.

```
NewDb.TableDefs.Append NewTbl
NewDb.Close
```

Using a Query to Add a Table and Index

As an alternative to using the data access objects, you can also create tables and indexes using a DDL query. The details of DDL queries are presented in Chapter 6, "Understanding Structured Query Language (SQL)," but the following code shows an example of how DDL queries can be used to create tables and indexes.

```
'*****************************************
'Create a table in the current database
'*****************************************
CREATE TABLE Orders (Orderno COUNTER, Custno LONG, SalesID
➥TEXT(6),
  OrderDate DATETIME, Totcost SINGLE)
'*****************************************************************
'Create a primary index in the Orders table on the Orderno field
'*****************************************************************
CREATE INDEX Ordernum ON Orders (Orderno) WITH PRIMARY
```

Creating Tables for the Sample Case

To further demonstrate the various commands used to create tables, the CHAPTER3.MAK file on the companion CD contains the source code to create all the tables used in the sample case. Each table is created using a different set of commands as follows:

- Salesperson table created by Visual Basic 3 methods for comparison.

- Customer table created by Visual Basic 4 methods with the CreateField arguments used.

- Retail Items table created by Visual Basic 4 methods without the CreateField arguments. All field properties are explicitly assigned.

- Orders table created using the DDL query.

The creation of each table is assigned to a command button on the form. Before you run the table commands, make sure that you run the Create Database section of the form.

Creating a Relationship

Chapter 1, "Designing Your Database Application," discussed normalizing data and the need to relate normalized tables. The way tables are related with the Jet engine is through the use of a Relation object stored in the database. The relation tells the database which two tables are related, which table is the parent and which is the child, and the key fields used to specify the relationship.

To create a relationship between two tables, follow these seven steps:

1. Use the Dim statement to define a Relation variable.

2. Create the Relation object using the CreateRelation method of the Database object.

3. Set the primary table and the foreign table properties of the relationship.

4. Create the relation field for the primary table using the CreateField method of the Relation object.

5. Set the foreign field property of the Field object.

6. Append the field to the Relation object.

7. Append the Relation object to the database.

Listing 3.5 demonstrates the creation of a relationship, showing how to create a relation between the Customer (primary) table and the Orders (foreign) table of the sample database.

Listing 3.5 Specifying a Relationship between Two Tables Using the Relation Object

```
Dim NewRel As Relation
Dim Fld1 As Field
'***************************
'Create the Relation object
'***************************
Set NewRel = NewDb.CreateRelation("Customers_Orders")
'***********************************
'Set the properties of the relation
'***********************************
NewRel.Table = "Customers"
NewRel.ForeignTable = "Orders"
'*****************************************************
'Create the relating field and set the properties
'*****************************************************
Set Fld1 = NewRel.CreateField("Custno")
Fld1.ForeignName = "Custno"
'*************************************************************************
'Append the field to the relation and the relation to the database
'*************************************************************************
NewRel.Fields.Append Fld1
NewDb.Relations.Append NewRel
```

A War Story

If you're like me, you sometimes get ahead of yourself in a program. I did the first time I tried to create a relationship. I had set up the commands just like the manual said, but kept getting the error message, `Customer_Orders is not an index in this table`.

The problem was that I had forgotten to create a primary index on the `Custno` field in the Customers table. Although the documentation does not point this out, you *must* have a primary key field in your primary table. This is the field that identifies the records to the relationship.

Using the Data Manager Application to Create a Database

The Data Manager application that comes with Visual Basic provides the user with an interactive way of creating and modifying Access databases. The application is invoked by selecting the Data Manager bar under the Add-Ins pad on the Visual Basic main menu.

Once the Data Manager application is active, choose File, New Database to create a new Access database. The New Database dialog box appears (see fig. 3.1) so that you can name the database and select the location for it. Enter a valid file name and click OK; you enter the design mode shown in figure 3.2.

> ### Note
>
> If you are working in Windows 3.1, the Data Manager will create an Access 2.0 database. If you are working in Windows 95, the Data Manager will create an Access database for the Jet 3.0 engine. This database format is not compatible with earlier versions.

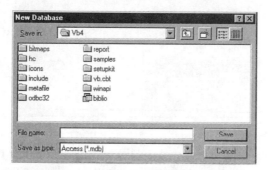

Fig. 3.1
The New Database dialog box allows you to specify the name of your new database.

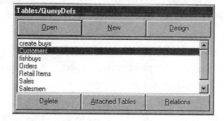

Fig. 3.2
The Data Manager design window provides access to the design functions for tables, fields, indexes, and relations.

Adding a New Table

The database design window gives you the choice of creating a new table, opening an existing table to "browse" the data, changing the design of a table, deleting a table, attaching an external table, or creating table relations. To create a new table, click the New button; the Add Table design area opens (see fig. 3.3). This design window allows you to specify the table name and enter the names, types, and sizes of each field in the table. To add a field to the table, follow these steps:

1. Enter the name of the field.

2. Select the field type from the Data Type drop-down list.

3. Enter the size of the field (if necessary).

4. Click the > button to add the field to the table list on the right side of the dialog box.

Fig. 3.3
The Add Table dialog box allows you to specify a name for and add fields to a new table.

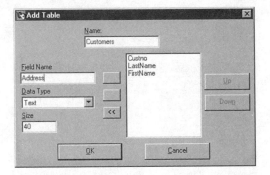

If you want to remove a field from the list, highlight the field in the list at the right of the dialog box and click the < button. Clicking the << button removes all fields from the list. When you are satisfied with the fields in the table, click the OK button to create the table.

Making Changes to the Fields in Your Table

After you create a new table, you are returned to the main Data Manager design window. If you want to set any optional properties for the fields in the table, highlight the table name and click the Design button to enter the Table Editor window (fig. 3.4 shows the table design window). This window allows you to add new fields, edit existing fields, delete fields (edit and delete functions are new for Visual Basic 4), add and delete indexes, and process key fields.

To add a new field, click the Add button. The Add Field data screen appears (see fig. 3.5). This screen allows you to enter the field name, type, and size (if necessary), and set optional properties such as validation rules, default values, and required entry flag. When you finish entering the data for the field, click OK to add the field to the table.

To edit a field, open the Table Editor dialog box, highlight the field you want to change, and click the Edit button. The same dialog box you used to add a field (see fig. 3.5) appears. Make your changes and click OK to save the changes.

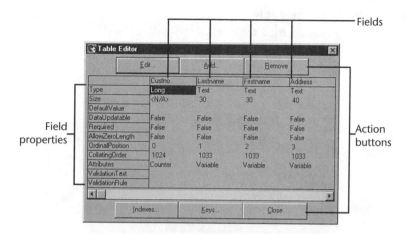

Fig. 3.4
You can add, edit, and delete fields, or add indexes from the Table Editor dialog box.

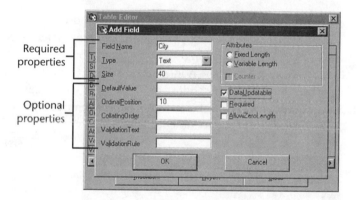

Fig. 3.5
You can specify the name and properties of a field with the Add Field dialog box.

Caution

If you change the properties of a field that contains data, the data in that field is lost. The Data Manager cannot preserve the data.

To delete a field from a table, highlight the field in the Table Editor dialog box and click the Remove button. This action deletes the field *and all its associated data.*

Note

Visual Basic does not allow you to edit or delete any field that is part of an index expression or a relation. If it is necessary to delete such a field, you must delete the index or relation containing the field and then make the changes to the field.

Adding an Index to the Table

To work with the indexes for a table, click the Indexes button in the Table Editor dialog box; the Indexes dialog box is presented (see fig. 3.6).

Fig. 3.6
You can add, edit, or delete indexes for a table from the Indexes dialog box.

To add a new index, click the Add button; the Add Index window is presented (see fig. 3.7). In this dialog box, first enter an index name. Then select the fields to be included in the index by highlighting your choice in the Fields in Table list and clicking either the Add(ASC) or Add(DEC) button (depending on whether you want an ascending or descending sequence). The fields you select are added to the Fields in Index list. To remove a field from the Fields in Index list, highlight it and click Remove.

Fig. 3.7
The Add Index dialog box provides a visual means of creating the indexes for a table.

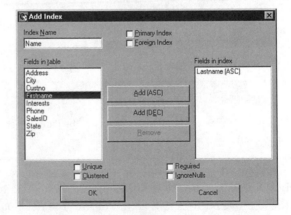

Once you define the fields for the index, you may choose to require the index to be unique or to be a primary index by choosing the appropriate check box in the window. When the index is completed to your liking, save it by clicking OK. The index you have just created is added to the index list on the

Indexes dialog box. To delete an index, simply highlight it in the list box and click Remove.

When you finish all your indexes, click the Close button in the Indexes dialog box to return to the table design window.

Creating Relationships

You can also establish the relationship between two tables with Data Manager. To set a relationship, click the Relations button from the main design window. The Relationships dialog box opens (see fig. 3.8). To start setting up the relation, you choose your primary table from the Primary Table drop-down list and the related table (also known as child table) from the Related Table drop-down list. After you have chosen the primary table, you see a list of available primary key fields in the area of the dialog box under the label Primary Key Fields. For most primary tables, there will be only one primary key field listed. If there is more than one, you will need to choose one of the fields in this block as the primary relation key for this relation.

Relations list

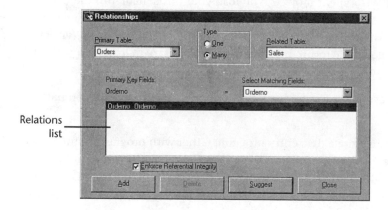

Fig. 3.8
You can create or delete relations between tables with the Relationships dialog box.

Once the primary key field is defined, you need to choose the matching field for the related table from the Select Matching Fields drop-down list. You may also define the type of relation (one-to-one or one-to-many) by selecting the appropriate option button under the "Type" label at the top of the dialog box. The default type is one-to-many. If you want to have the relation enforce referential integrity, you will need to mark the check box at the bottom of the dialog box. When you have entered all the information for the relation, add it to the database by clicking the Add button. Clicking the Close button returns you to the database design window.

Returning to the Visual Basic Design Screen

Closing the Data Manager window or opening the File menu and choosing Exit takes you back to the Visual Basic main design screen. To manipulate databases without having to start Visual Basic every time, you may find it convenient to make the Data Manager application a program item in your Visual Basic group.

Using Microsoft Access to Create a Database

The other option for creating an Access database for use with a Visual Basic application is to use Microsoft Access. Access has a good visual design interface for setting up tables, indexes, queries, and table relationships. Obviously, this option is only available if you have a copy of Access.

If you have Access and want more information on using it to create and modify databases, Que's *Special Edition Using Microsoft Access 2* is recommended.

Loading the Initial Data for a Database

For many development projects, you load your initial data into the database after you create the database. This is typically the case in custom development work when your client already has some data for the system (either in written or electronic form). It is also usually necessary to load data into a test database in order to check out the functions of your system.

You have several choices for loading this data into the database you have created:

- You can write a data entry program, either with program commands or using the data control and bound controls. Chapter 4, "Manipulating Data with a Program," and Chapter 5, "Using Visual Basic's Data and Bound Controls," show examples of data-entry programs for these two methods.

- If you have the initial data in electronic form, you can write a short program in Visual Basic to import the data. An example of this method is included as part of the Chapter 3 application on the companion CD.

- You can use Microsoft Access to input the data.

- You can use the Data Manager application to input the data.

To use Data Manager, start the Data Manager application and open the database as just explained (assuming that the Data Manager is not already open).

From the Data Manager design window, select a table from the table list and click the Open button. The Table Editing dialog box appears (see fig. 3.9). This window is similar to the data-entry panel you will create in Chapter 5, "Using Visual Basic's Data and Bound Controls." From this panel, you can add new records, update the data in existing records, and delete records. When finished, close the Data Entry window and exit Data Manager.

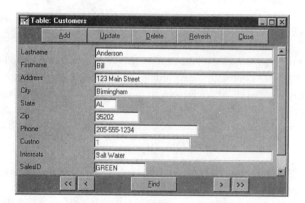

Fig. 3.9
You can edit your database from the Data Manager.

Modifying the Database Structure

Even if you create the perfect database for an application, sooner or later someone will come along and say, "Well, I really need this program to handle other data, too." At this point, you must modify the structure of your database and tables. Modifications can take the form of new tables, new fields or indexes in tables, or changes in the properties of tables, fields, or indexes. On occasion, you may also have to delete a table, field, or index.

The following sections cover the modification of a database through the use of Visual Basic 4 program commands. As with the creation of a database, you can also use the Data Manager application or Microsoft Access to perform the modifications.

Adding and Deleting Tables

To add a table, follow the same steps that you took to create tables in a new database:

1. Define the table, field, and index objects using the Dim statement and appropriate create methods.

2. Define the properties of the table, fields, and indexes.

3. Append the fields and indexes to the table.

4. Append the table to the database.

To delete a table from a database, you can use the `Delete` method of a database object as shown in this statement:

```
OldDb.TableDefs.Delete "Customers"
```

> **Caution**
>
> Use the `Delete` method with extreme caution. When you delete a table, all fields, indexes, and—most importantly—data is deleted with it. And when it's gone, it's gone. The only way to get it back is to create the table again from scratch and reload all your data.

Adding, Deleting, and Editing Indexes

Adding a new index involves the same steps as creating an index for a new table. You must define an index object, set the properties of the index, and append the new index to the table. An example of these steps was shown earlier in listing 3.4.

To delete an index, simply use the `Delete` method shown in this statement. This code deletes the `Price_Paid` index from the Retail Items table.

```
OldDb.TableDefs("Retail Items").Indexes.Delete "Price_Paid"
```

It is not possible to edit the properties of an index in a table. Therefore, if a change to an index is required, the old index must be deleted from the table and a new index with the new desired properties created. This is accomplished using the methods shown in the section "Defining the Indexes" earlier in this chapter.

> **Note**
>
> You cannot delete an index that is required by a relation. To delete such an index, you must first delete the relation.

Adding, Deleting, and Editing Fields

As you learned when creating a new database, you add a field to a table by defining the field object, setting its properties, and appending it to the table. These commands were presented in listings 3.2 and 3.3.

Unlike Visual Basic 3, Version 4 provides you with a method to delete a field from a table. To delete a field, use the `Delete` method shown here. This example deletes the Address field from the Customers table:

```
NewDb.TableDefs("Customer").Fields.Delete "Address"
```

Unfortunately, there is no direct way of changing a field's properties. There are, however, two indirect ways to accomplish this task. If you have a new table that contains no data, or if you don't care about losing the data in the field, you can delete the field from the table and then recreate it with the new properties. If you have a table that contains data and want to preserve the data, you must create a whole new table (making the appropriate changes), move the data to the new table, and then delete the old table. The difficulty of this process of making changes to fields dramatically underscores the importance of a good initial design.

To move data from one table to another existing table, you must follow these steps:

1. Open both tables.

2. Set up a loop to process each record in the table currently containing the data.

   Then for each record in the old table, follow these steps:

3. Retrieve the value of each field to be transferred from the old table.

4. Add a record to the new table.

5. Set the values of the field in the new table.

6. Update the new table.

> **Note**
>
> If you have Microsoft Access, you can change the properties of a table's fields while preserving the fields' contents.

Remember that you cannot delete a field that is part of an index or relation.

Deleting a Relation

If it is necessary to delete a relation, you can do this with the `Delete` method of the database object. The following statement shows how to delete the relation created in listing 3.5:

```
NewDb.Relations.Delete "Customers_Orders"
```

Why Use a Program Instead of Data Manager?

In this chapter, you have learned that the Data Manager application and Microsoft Access can create, modify, and load data into a database. So the question you may be asking is: "Why do I ever need to bother with the Visual Basic 4 program commands for these functions?" The answer is that, in many cases, you don't. If you have direct control over the database (that is, you are the only user or you can access the database at any time), you may never need to use program commands to create or change a database.

However, if you have an application with many customers—either throughout your company or across the country—there are several benefits to using a program. One benefit is in initial installation. If the database creation routines are in the program itself, you don't have to include empty database files on your installation disks. This may reduce the number of disks required and certainly reduces the possibility that a key file is left out. Another benefit occurs when you distribute updates to the program. With changes embedded in a program, your user merely runs the update program to change the file structure. There is no need to reload data into a new, blank file. Also, by modifying the file in place, you can preserve most structure changes in the database made by the end user.

Another reason for putting database creation and maintenance commands in a program is for performance considerations. There are times when it is desirable from a performance standpoint to create a temporary table to speed up a program or to store intermediate results and then delete the table at the completion of the program. It may also be desirable to create a temporary index that creates a specific order or speeds up a search and then delete the index later.

Introducing Queries

Queries are a powerful method of gathering information from more than one table or of selecting information from a table that matches a specific criteria (for example, customer records for people who live in Alabama). As you will learn in Chapter 4, "Manipulating Data with a Program," an object called a dynaset can store this type of information for use in your programs. In fact, using a query is one method of creating a dynaset. The advantage of creating a query is that the information about it is saved in the database itself, making it convenient to test and store information needed to create recordsets that are used often.

Creating a Query

To create a query, you define a QueryDef object and then use the CreateQueryDef method of the database. When calling the function, you must specify the name of the query. You can specify the Structured Query Language (SQL) syntax of the query, or you can define the SQL statement in a separate program line. The following code shows the two different methods of creating a query.

```
Dim OldDb As Database, NewQry As QueryDef
Set OldDb = OldWs.OpenDatabase("A:\TRITON.MDB")
Set NewQry = OldDb.CreateQueryDef("Fish")
NewQry.SQL = "SELECT * FROM [Retail Items];"
'****************************************************
'Alternative form of query creation statement.
'****************************************************
Set NewQry = OldDb.CreateQueryDef("Fish", "SELECT * FROM [Retail _
Items];")
```

The heart of defining queries is the SQL statement. This statement defines the fields to be included, the source of the fields, record filters, and the sort order of the resulting recordset. SQL statements are covered in Chapter 6, "Understanding Structured Query Language (SQL)."

Note

Queries can be created and stored in the database only for Access databases.

Deleting a Query

As with most other objects in the database, if you create it, you may, at some time, need to delete it. Queries are no exception. If you have a query that you no longer need in your database, you can remove it using the following command:

```
OldDb.DeleteQueryDef "Fish"
```

From Here...

To learn more about some of the subjects mentioned in this chapter, please refer to the following chapters:

- Chapter 4, "Manipulating Data with a Program," explains how to manipulate data in a database with a program.

- Chapter 6, "Understanding Structured Query Language (SQL)," explains how to create SQL statements.

Tip

When you use a query in your program, you open the query by creating a data access object for it. Therefore, when you need to delete the query, you should specifically close a query variable before you try to delete it. Closing the variable ensures that the query is not in use, and that no error occurs during the deletion. The syntax for closing a query is NewQry.Close.

Chapter 4

Manipulating Data with a Program

A data access application can be written with only program commands, with only the data control and bound controls, or with a combination of these two methods. The data control and bound controls provide the user with easy access to a database. You connect them to the database by setting specific properties of the controls. This chapter discusses only the program commands. Chapter 5, "Using Visual Basic's Data and Bound Controls," discusses using the data control and bound controls.

When you use just the program commands, you work with the data access objects of Visual Basic. Using the data access objects and their associated program commands is a little more complex than using the data control and bound controls, but does offer greater programming flexibility for some applications. The data access objects and programming commands also provide the basis for the actions of the data control and the bound controls. Therefore, they will help you understand the concepts behind the controls. And even if you use the data control, you also need some of the programming commands to augment the capabilities of the data control.

To demonstrate the similarities and differences between data access objects and the data control, this chapter and Chapter 5 instruct you to build a data entry screen that allows you to see how the programming commands work and how the data control implements the commands. Figure 4.1 shows the data entry screen that you build in this chapter.

The key reason you use program commands is the flexibility they give in addition to the data control. Because program commands do not directly access the database, you can perform more detailed input validation than is possible with just the data engine rules. You also can cancel changes to your edited data without using transactions. Program commands also provide a more efficient way to handle data input and searches that do not require user interaction. Examples of this are receiving data from lab equipment or across a modem, or looking up the price of an item in a table. Program commands also allow you to do transaction processing.

Fig. 4.1
This data entry screen is used as an example in this chapter.

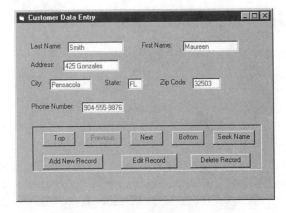

In this chapter, you learn about the following:

- How and when to use different recordset types

- How to move from one record to another in a recordset

- How to find a specific record

- How to add, edit, and delete records in a database

The Recordset Object—A New Addition for Version 4

The main new feature of version 4, with regard to data access objects, is the new recordset object. This object takes the place of the table, dynaset, and snapshot objects in earlier versions of Visual Basic. Instead of opening a table or creating a dynaset, you now open a recordset. Because you can still open a recordset with table, dynaset, or snapshot properties, it still makes sense to refer to these recordset types. Later in this chapter, the advantages and disadvantages of each type is discussed.

In addition, Visual Basic 4 provides three new methods of positioning the record pointer:

- **Move *n* method:** Moves the record pointer *n* records from the current record or from a bookmark.

- **Absolute position property:** Moves the record pointer to a specific location in the recordset.

- **Percent position property:** Moves the record pointer to a record with the approximate percent position.

Opening an Existing Database

The first step in writing most data access programs is setting up a link to the database with which you want to work. When you create a new database (as described in Chapter 3), that database is available for you to work with in your program until you exit the program or explicitly close the database. If you have an existing database, you must open it before your program can work with it. Opening a database is done using the OpenDatabase method of the Workspace object. To use the OpenDatabase method, you create a database object and call the method as shown in this bit of code:

```
Dim OldDb As Database, OldWs As Workspace
Set OldWs = DBEngine.Workspaces(0)
Set OldDb = OldWs.OpenDatabase("A:\TRITON.MDB")
```

These commands open an Access database with the default options of read/write data access and shared access. The full syntax of the OpenDatabase method allows you to specify that the database should be opened exclusively (no other users or programs may access it at the same time), that it be opened in read-only mode (no updates are allowed), or, if you are connecting to a non-Access database, you can specify the database type. The use of exclusive access and read-only access is usually required for multiuser applications (as discussed in Chapter 7, "Creating Multiuser Programs"). The use of non-Access databases is covered in Chapter 8, "Accessing Other Databases with the Jet Engine."

However, you may want to use the read-only mode even in a single-user application for a lookup database (for example, a ZIP code database or a state abbreviations database you include with your application but do not want the user to be able to modify). To open the database as read-only, change the Set statement to the form shown in the following listing. The first parameter after the database name indicates whether the database is opened for exclusive access; the second parameter indicates whether read-only mode is to be used.

```
Set OldDb = OldWs.OpenDatabase("A:\ZIPCODE.MDB",False,True)
```

After the database is opened, you must still define a recordset to access the data in the database. Think of opening the database as telling the program where to go to find the data and defining the recordset as telling the program what data to use.

There are three types of recordsets available in Visual Basic:

- Tables—The physical structures in a database that contain the actual data.

- dynaset—A set of pointers that provide access to fields and records in one or more tables of a database.

- snapshot—a read-only copy of data from one or more tables. It is stored in memory.

The following sections describe each type of recordset, point out some of the advantages and disadvantages of each, and demonstrate the commands used to access the recordset.

Using Tables

A *table* is the physical representation of the database design. Because all data in a database is stored in tables, accessing tables provides the most direct link to the data. Tables are also the only form of recordset that supports indexes; therefore, searching a table for a specific record is quicker than searching a dynaset or snapshot.

When using tables, data is addressed or modified one table at a time, one record at a time. This arrangement provides very fine control over the manipulation of data but does not allow the convenience of changing records in multiple tables with a single command such as an action query.

Advantages of Using Tables

There are several advantages in using tables in your programs:

- You can use or create indexes to change the presentation order of the data in the table during program execution.

- You can perform rapid searches for an individual record using an appropriate index and a Seek command.

- Changes made to the table by other users or programs are immediately available. It is not necessary to "refresh" the table to gain access to these records.

Disadvantages of Using Tables

Of course, there are also disadvantages in using tables in your programs:

- You cannot set filters on a table to limit the records being processed to those that meet a certain criteria.

- You cannot use find commands on a table; the Seek command finds only the first record that meets its criteria. This implies that, to process a series of records in a range, the programmer must provide the methods to find the additional records.

These disadvantages can usually be overcome with programming, but the solutions are often less than elegant. Some of the workarounds are discussed later in this chapter when you look at the various methods for moving through a recordset and finding specific records.

Opening a Table for Use

To open a table for use by the program, you define a Recordset object and then use the OpenRecordset method to access the table. You also specify the dbOpenTable constant in the parameters of the method to identify the type of recordset to create, as shown in the following segment of code. This listing assumes that you have already opened the database using the OldDb object and that the database contains a table called Customers.

```
Dim OldTbl As Recordset
Set OldTbl = OldDb.OpenRecordset("Customers",dbOpenTable)
```

These commands open an Access table with the default parameters of shared use and read/write mode. Optional parameters may be included in the OpenRecordset method to open the table for exclusive use or to open the table in read-only mode. These options are summarized in table 4.1.

Table 4.1 Options Used to Modify the Access Mode of Tables	
Option	**Action**
dbDenyWrite	Prevents others in a multiuser environment from writing to the table while you have it open.
dbDenyRead	Prevents others in a multiuser environment from reading the table while you have it open.
dbReadOnly	Prevents you from making changes to the table.

> **Note**
>
> If you have existing code that uses table objects and the OpenTable function, Visual Basic 4 still supports this code. However, you should use the new methods for any future work you do.

Using *dynasets*

A dynaset is a grouping of information from one or more tables in a database. This information is comprised of selected fields from the tables, often presented in a specific order and filtered by a specific condition. dynasets address the records present in the base tables at the time the dynaset was created. dynasets are an updatable recordset, so any changes made by the user are stored in the database. However, dynasets do not reflect additions or deletions of records made by other users. This makes dynasets less useful for some types of multiuser applications.

A dynaset is actually a set of record pointers that point to the specified data that existed when the dynaset was created. Changes made to information in the dynaset are reflected in the base tables from which the information was derived as well as in the dynaset itself. These changes include additions, edits, and deletions of records.

Advantages of Using *dynasets*

Some of the advantages provided by dynasets are as follows:

- dynasets give you the ability to join information from multiple tables.

- You can use Find methods to locate or process every record meeting specified criteria.

- dynasets make use of filters and sort order properties to change the view of data.

Disadvantages of Using *dynasets*

dynasets do have some limitations:

- You cannot create an index for a dynaset. This prevents you from changing the presentation order of a dynaset by changing the index or creating a new one.

■ A dynaset does not reflect additions or deletions made to the data by other users or other programs. A dynaset must be explicitly refreshed or re-created to show the changes.

Setting Up a *dynaset*

To set up a dynaset for use within a program, you must define the recordset object with the Dim statement and then generate the dynaset using the OpenRecordset method. The key part of the OpenRecordset method is the SQL statement that defines the records to be included, the filter condition, the sort condition, and any join conditions for linking data from multiple tables. The code shown in listing 4.1 shows the simplest form of creating a dynaset, in which all records and fields are selected from a single table with no sort or filter conditions specified. This is the type of dynaset created by default when using a data control.

Listing 4.1   How to Create a Simple dynaset

```
Dim OldDb As Database, NewDyn As Recordset,OldWs As Workspace
Set OldWs = DBEngine.Workspaces(0)
Set OldDb = OldWs.OpenDatabase("A:\TRITON.MDB")
Set NewDyn = OldDb.OpenRecordset("SELECT * FROM Customers", _
    dbOpenDynaset)
```

In the creation of a dynaset, any valid SQL statement can be used. (The details of using SQL statements are covered in Chapter 6, "Understanding Structured Query Language (SQL).") In creating a dynaset, you may also specify options that affect its behavior. These options are listed in table 4.2.

Table 4.2   Options Used to Modify the Access Mode of a dynaset

Option	Action
dbDenyWrite	Prevents others in a multiuser environment from writing to the dynaset while you have it open.
dbReadOnly	Prevents you from making changes to the dynaset.
dbAppendOnly	Allows you to add new records but prevents you from reading or modifying existing records.
dbSQLPassThrough	Passes the SQL statement used to create the dynaset to an ODBC database server to be processed.

> **Note**
>
> An ODBC server is a database engine such as Microsoft SQL Server or Oracle that conforms to the Open Database Connectivity (ODBC) standards. The purpose of a server is to handle query processing at the server level and return to the client machine only the results of the query. ODBC drivers, which are usually written by the vendor of the database engine, handle the connection between Visual Basic and the database server. The advantage of using ODBC is that the Visual Basic programmer can connect to the information on the database servers without having to know the inner workings of the engine.

A dynaset can also be created from another dynaset or from a QueryDef (listing 4.2 shows the creation from another dynaset). The reason for creating a second dynaset from an initial dynaset is that you can use the filter and sort properties of the first dynaset to specify the scope of records and the presentation order of the second dynaset. Creating a second dynaset allows you to create a subset of your initial data. The second dynaset is usually much smaller than the first, which allows faster processing of the desired records. In listing 4.2, a dynaset was created from the customer table to result in a national mailing list. A second dynaset was then created, which includes only the customers living in Alabama and sorts them by city name for further processing. The results of these two dynasets are shown in figures 4.2 and 4.3.

Listing 4.2 How to Set the Filter and Sort Properties of a dynaset and Create a Second dynaset from the First

```
Dim OldDb As Database, NewDyn As Recordset, ScnDyn As Dynaset
Dim OldWs As Workspace
Set OldWs = DBEngine.Workspaces(0)
Set OldDb = OldWs.OpenDatabase("A:\TRITON.MDB")
Set NewDyn = OldDb.OpenRecordset("SELECT * FROM Customers", _
    dbOpenDynaset)
NewDyn.Filter = "State = 'AL'"
NewDyn.Sort = "City"
Set ScnDyn = NewDyn.OpenRecordset(dbOpenDynaset)
```

You may well ask, "If I need the results in the second dynaset, can't I just create it from the base tables in the first place?" The answer is that you can do it if your application needs *only* the second table. However, consider an order entry system in which you want access to all your customers (the creation of the first dynaset), and one of the functions of the system is to generate a mailing list for a sales region (the creation of the second dynaset). Because the pointers to all the required information are already present in the first dynaset, the creation of the second dynaset is faster than if it were created from scratch.

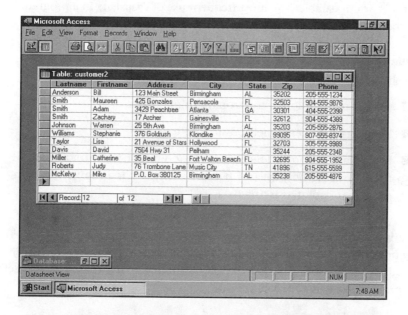

Fig. 4.2
The results of the creation of a dynaset from base tables.

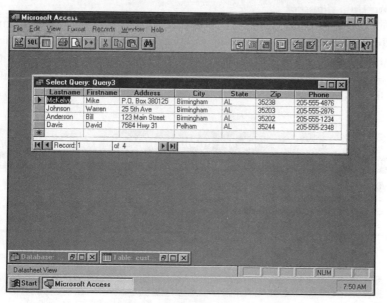

Fig. 4.3
The results of creating one dynaset from another dynaset after filter and sort conditions have been set.

Using *snapshots*

A snapshot, as the name implies, is a "picture," or copy, of the data in a recordset at a particular point in time. A snapshot is very similar to a dynaset in that it is created from base tables using a SQL statement, or created from a QueryDef, dynaset, or another snapshot. A snapshot differs from a dynaset in that it is not updatable. The most frequent use of snapshots in a program is to generate reports or informational screens in which the data is static.

Advantages of Using *snapshots*

snapshots provide the programmer with the following advantages:

- They can join information from multiple tables.

- You can use the Find methods to locate records.

- Record navigation and recordset creation can be faster for a snapshot than for a read-only dynaset because a snapshot is a copy of the data, not a set of pointers to the data.

Disadvantages of Using *snapshots*

The primary disadvantage of using a snapshot is that it is not an updatable recordset. In addition, you cannot create an index on a snapshot to help set the order of the data or locate specific records.

Setting Up a *snapshot*

A snapshot is created by defining a recordset object with the Dim statement and then using the OpenRecordset method to assign the records to the object (as shown in listing 4.3). As with a dynaset, there are optional parameters that can be specified in the OpenRecordset method. These parameters are summarized in table 4.3.

Listing 4.3   Create a snapshot in Much the Same Way You Create a dynaset

```
Dim OldDb As Database, NewSnap As Recordset, OldWs As Workspace
Set OldWs = DBEngine.Workspaces(0)
Set OldDb = OldWs.OpenDatabase("A:\TRITON.MDB")
Set NewSnap = OldDb.OpenRecordset("Customers",dbOpenSnapshot)
```

Table 4.3   Options Used to Modify the Access Mode of a snapshot

Option	Action
dbDenyWrite	Prevents others in a multiuser environment from writing to the snapshot while you have it open.
dbForwardOnly	Allows only forward scrolling through the snapshot.

Option	Action
dbSQLPassThrough	Passes the SQL statement used to create the snapshot to an ODBC database to be processed.

Placing Information on the Screen

Suppose that you have written a data entry screen using the data and bound controls. To get information on the screen, you simply draw the bound control and then set the appropriate data field for the control. The display of the information is automatic. Using the data access objects, the process is only slightly more involved. You still use control objects (text boxes, labels, check boxes, and so on) to display the information, but you have to assign the data fields to the correct control properties with each record displayed. When used in this manner, the control objects are typically referred to as *unbound controls*. One advantage of using unbound controls is that you can use any control in the toolbox to display data, not just the controls specifically designated for use with the data control.

For the sample case in this chapter, you create a customer data entry screen based on the Customers table of the sample database. To begin building this screen, start a new project in Visual Basic. Then on the default form, you add the data labels and text boxes to hold the data from the table. The form with these controls added is shown in figure 4.4.

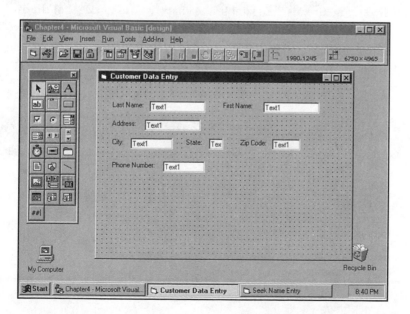

Fig. 4.4
Use unbound controls to display data from the data access objects.

To set up the table for use, you must open the table using the OpenRecordset method. For this case, place the Dim statement that defines the data access objects in the Declarations section of the form so that the objects are available throughout all the code in the form. You then open the database and table in the Form_Load event (see listing 4.4). At this point, the table is open and you are positioned at the first record in the table.

Listing 4.4   Placing the OpenDatabase and OpenRecordset in the Form Load Event

```
Set OldWs = DBEngine.Workspaces(0)
'********************************
'Open database and Customer table
'********************************
Set OldDb = OldWs.OpenDatabase("A:\TRITON.MDB")
Set RcSet = OldDb.OpenRecordset("Customers",dbOpenTable)
'**********************************************
'Move to first record and display information
'**********************************************
RcSet.MoveFirst
Call ShowFields
```

To display the data, assign the value of the desired data fields to the display properties of the controls (captions for labels, text for text boxes, and so on) that contain the data. This process is shown in listing 4.5. Notice that the listing defines the text boxes as a control array so that a loop can be used to quickly modify certain properties of the controls such as foreground color or visibility. This method is used later in the chapter. Also notice that the assignments are placed in a subroutine so that the same routine can be called from a number of command button events instead of repeating the code in each event. This arrangement makes the code more efficient and easier to maintain.

Listing 4.5   Assigning Data Fields to the Display Properties of the Form's Controls

```
Private Sub ShowFields()
Text1(0).Text = RcSet("Lastname")
Text1(1).Text = RcSet("Firstname")
Text1(2).Text = RcSet("Address")
Text1(3).Text = RcSet("City")
Text1(4).Text = RcSet("State")
Text1(5).Text = RcSet("Zip")
Text1(6).Text = RcSet("Phone")
End Sub
```

> **Note**
>
> You can find the commands from these listings, and the other listings used to build the data entry screen, in the CHAPTER4.MAK file on the companion disk.

Positioning the Record Pointer

Because a database with only one record is fairly useless, a database engine must provide methods for moving from one record to another within recordsets. Visual Basic provides four classes of such methods:

- Move methods—Change the position of the record pointer from the current record to another record.

- Find methods—Locate the next record that meets the find condition. Find methods work on dynasets and snapshots.

- Seek method—Finds the first record in a table that meets the requested condition.

- Bookmark property—Identifies the location of a specific record.

Each of these methods has benefits and limitations, as described in the following sections.

Using the Move Methods

You can use the move methods on any recordsets available in Visual Basic. The move methods are as follows:

- MoveFirst. Moves the record pointer from the current record to the first record in the opened recordset.

- MoveNext. Moves the record pointer from the current record to the next record (the record following the current record) in the opened recordset. If there is no "next record" (that is, if you are already at the last record), the end-of-file (EOF) flag will be set.

- MovePrevious. Moves the record pointer from the current record to the preceding record in the opened recordset. If there is no "previous record" (that is, if you are at the first record), the beginning-of-file (BOF) flag will be set.

- MoveLast. Moves the record pointer from the current record to the last record in the opened recordset.

■ Move *n*. Moves the record pointer from the current record *n* records down (if *n* is positive) or up (if *n* is negative) in the opened recordset. If the move would place the record pointer beyond the end of the recordset (either BOF or EOF), an error will occur.

These commands move the record pointer to the record indicated based on the current order of the recordset. The current order of the recordset is the physical order—unless an index was set for a table or a dynaset or snapshot was created with the order specified. To show the use of the MoveFirst, MovePrevious, MoveNext, and MoveLast methods, add command buttons to the data entry screen so that the user can move through the recordset (see fig. 4.5). To activate these buttons, add the code shown in listing 4.6. The code for each button is preceded by an identifying comment line.

Fig. 4.5
Add command buttons to allow the user to navigate through the recordset.

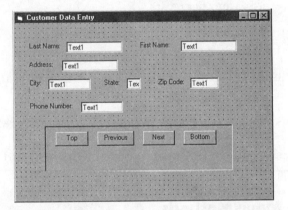

Listing 4.6   Assigning Move Methods to Navigation Command Buttons to Make Them Work

```
'*************************************************
'The MoveFirst method activates the "Top" button.
'*************************************************

RcSet.MoveFirst
Call ShowFields
'*****************************************************
'The MovePrevious method activates the "Previous" button.
'*****************************************************

RcSet.MovePrevious
Call ShowFields
'*************************************************
'The MoveNext method activates the "Next" button.
'*************************************************
```

```
RcSet.MoveNext
Call ShowFields
'*****************************************************
'The MoveLast method activates the "Bottom" button.
'*****************************************************
RcSet.MoveLast
Call ShowFields
```

The Move *n* method allows you to move more than one record from the current position. The value of *n* is the number of records to move in the recordset. This value can be either positive or negative to indicate movement either forward or backward in the recordset. The following piece of code shows the use of this method to move two records forward from the current record.

```
RcSet.Move 2
```

Using the Find Methods

The find methods are available for use only on dynasets and snapshots. You cannot use find methods on table objects. (Because the data entry screen was created with a table, you cannot use the find methods in the sample.) The find methods are used to locate records that meet specified criteria. The criteria is expressed in the same way that the Where clause of a SQL command is specified—except without the Where keyword. The four find methods are as follows:

- FindFirst. Starting at the top of the database, finds the first record in the recordset with the specified criteria.

- FindNext. Starting at the current location in the recordset, finds the next record down with the specified criteria.

- FindPrevious. Starting at the current location in the recordset, finds the next record up with the specified criteria.

- FindLast. Starting at the bottom of the recordset, finds the last record in the database with the specified criteria.

After the find method is run, you should check the status of the NoMatch property. If NoMatch is true, the method failed to find a record that matched the requested criteria. If NoMatch is false, the record pointer is positioned at the found record.

Listing 4.7 shows the use of the find methods to move through a dynaset.

Listing 4.7   How to Move through Selected Records in a dynaset **Using Find Methods**

```
'*************************************
'Set up the database and Dynaset objects
'*************************************
Dim OldDb As Database, NewDyn As Recordset, FindCrit As String
Dim OldWS As Workspace
Set OldWs = DBEngine.Workspaces(0)
Set OldDb = OldWs.OpenDatabase("E:\VB4BOOK\SAMPLES\TRITON.MDB")
Set NewDyn = OldDb.OpenRecordset("SELECT * FROM Customers", _
    dbOpenDynaset)
'*************************************************
'Set the search criteria for the find methods
'*************************************************
FindCrit = "State = 'AL'"
'*************************************************
'Find the first record matching the criteria
'*************************************************
NewDyn.FindFirst FindCrit
Do While Not NewDyn.NoMatch
'*************************************************************
'Loop forward through all records matching the criteria
'*************************************************************
    NewDyn.FindNext FindCrit
Loop
'*********************************************
'Find the last record matching the criteria
'*********************************************
NewDyn.FindLast FindCrit
Do While Not NewDyn.NoMatch
'*************************************************************
'Loop backward through all records matching the criteria
'*************************************************************
    NewDyn.FindPrevious FindCrit
Loop
```

Tip

In many cases, it is faster to re-create the dynaset using the search criteria than to use the find methods to process all matching records. You can also create a second filtered dynaset from the first dynaset by using the search criteria as the filter condition. Listing 4.8 shows the comparison of these two methods.

The find methods work by scanning each record, starting with the current record, to locate the appropriate record that matches the specified criteria. Depending on the size of the recordset and the criteria specified, this search operation can be somewhat lengthy. Searches can by optimized by the Jet engine if an index is available for the search field. If you will be doing many searches, you should consider creating an index for the field in its base table.

Listing 4.8   Creating a dynaset **with a Filter Condition in the SQL Statement or Creating a Second after Setting the Filter Property of the First** dynaset

```
'**********************
'Create Initial Dynaset
'**********************
```

```
Dim OldDb As Database, NewDyn As Recordset, ScnDyn As Recordset
Dim OldWs As WorkSpace
Set OldWs = DBEngine.Workspaces(0)
Set OldDb = OpenDatabase("E:\VB4BOOK\SAMPLES\TRITON.MDB")
Set NewDyn = OldDb.OpenRecordset("SELECT * FROM Customers", _
    dbOpenDynaset)
'********************************
'Use Find method to search records
'********************************
NewDyn.FindFirst "State = 'FL'"
Do Until NewDyn.NoMatch
    NewDyn.FindNext "State = 'FL'"
Loop
'*****************************************************************
'Create second dynaset and use Move methods to process records
'*****************************************************************
NewDyn.Filter = "State = 'FL'"
Set ScnDyn = NewDyn.OpenRecordset()
ScnDyn.MoveFirst
Do Until ScnDyn.EOF
    ScnDyn.MoveNext
Loop
'************************************************************
'Create initial dynaset with "Where" clause and use Move
'************************************************************
Set NewDyn = OldDb.OpenRecordset _
    ("SELECT * FROM Customers WHERE State = 'FL'", dbOpenDynaset)
NewDyn.MoveFirst
Do Until NewDyn.EOF
    NewDyn.MoveNext
Loop
```

Comparing Variables with the Find Method

When you use variables as the value to be compared to, you may encounter the error
Cannot bind name *item* when you run the program.

When the field and the variable you are comparing are string (or text) variables,
surround the variable name by single quotes (') as shown in the following sample
code. For the sake of readability, you can also assign the single quote to a constant
and use that constant in your code.

```
Dim FindCrit As String, FindStr As String
FindStr = "Smith"
FindCrit = "Lastname = '" & FindStr & "'"
NewDyn.FindFirst FindCrit
```

In the same manner, you would surround a date variable with the pound symbol to
compare it to a date field. You do not need to include any additional symbols when
comparing numbers.

When a find method is successful, the record pointer moves to the new record. If the find method is not successful, the recordset's `NoMatch` property is set to `True` and the record pointer does not move. One way to use the `NoMatch` property is to write an `If` condition that checks the value as shown in the following code:

```
If NewDyn.NoMatch Then
    'Notify user of event
    MsgBox "Record not found"
Else
    'Process found record.
    command
End If
```

Using the *Seek* Method

The `Seek` method is the fastest way to locate an individual record in a table—however, it is also the most limiting of the record-positioning methods. The limitations of the `Seek` method are as follows:

- A `Seek` can only be performed on a table; it cannot be used with a dynaset or snapshot.

- A `Seek` can be used only with an active index. The parameters of the `Seek` method must match the fields of the index in use.

- A `Seek` finds only the first record that matches the specified index values. Subsequent uses do not find additional matching records.

A `Seek` method, as shown in listing 4.9, consists of the method call, the comparison operator, and the values of the key fields. The comparison operator can be <, <=, =, >=, >, or <>. The key values being compared must be of the same data type as the fields in the controlling index. Although you are not required to include the same number of key values as there are fields in the index, you *do* have to include a key value for each field you want to search. These values must appear in the same order as the fields in the index and be separated by commas, as shown in the second part of listing 4.9.

Listing 4.9 Using the Seek Method to Find a Specific Record in a Table

```
Dim OldDb As Database, OldTbl As Recordset
Dim OldWs As WorkSpace
Set OldWs = DBEngine.Workspaces(0)
Set OldDb = OldWs.OpenDatabase("A:\TRITON.MDB")
Set OldTbl = OldDb.OpenRecordset("Customers",dbOpenTable)
'***********************************
'Set the index property for the table
'***********************************
```

```
OldTbl.Index = "Name"
'*********************************************
'Execute the seek for the desired condition
'*********************************************
OldTbl.Seek ">", "Smith"
'***************************************************************
'Display information or "Not Found" message as appropriate
'***************************************************************
If OldTbl.NoMatch Then
   MsgBox "Not Found"
Else
   MsgBox OldTbl("Lastname") & ", " & OldTbl("Firstname")
End If
'***************************************************************
'Seek method with first and last name information supplied
'***************************************************************
OldTbl.Seek ">=", "Smith", "M"
```

You must carefully plan for one behavior of the Seek method. When the Seek method uses the comparison operators =, >=, >, or < >, Seek starts with the first record for the current index and scans forward through the index to find the first matching occurrence. If the comparison operator is < or <=, Seek starts with the last record in the table and scans backward through the table. If the index has unique values for each record, this presents no problem. However, if there are duplicate index values for the key fields being specified, the record found depends on the comparison operator and the sort order of the index. Figure 4.6 shows a table of first and last names indexed on last name and then first name. The table on the top is indexed in ascending order; the table on the bottom is indexed in descending order. Listing 4.10 shows four possible combinations of controlling index and comparison operator for finding a record for the last name of *Smith*. Each of these combinations is labeled in the comments of the code. The results of each of these Seek operations are shown in table 4.4.

Listing 4.10 Varying Results Are Obtained Using Different Seek Operators and Index Orders on a Table

```
Dim OldDb As Database, OldTbl As Recordset
Dim OldWs As WorkSpace
Set OldWs = DBEngine.Workspaces(0)
Set OldDb = OldWs.OpenDatabase("A:\TRITON.MDB")
Set OldTbl = OldDb.OpenTable("Customers", dbOpenTable)
'************************
'Set ascending order index
'************************
OldTbl.Index = "Name"
OldTbl.Seek ">=", "Smith", "A"
```

(continues)

Listing 4.10 Continued

```
printer.Print OldTbl("Lastname") & ", " & OldTbl("Firstname")
OldTbl.Seek "<=", "Smith", "Z"
printer.Print OldTbl("Lastname") & ", " & OldTbl("Firstname")
'************************
'Set descending order index
'************************
OldTbl.Index = "Name2"
OldTbl.Seek ">=", "Smith", "A"
printer.Print OldTbl("Lastname") & ", " & OldTbl("Firstname")
OldTbl.Seek "<=", "Smith", "Z"
printer.Print OldTbl("Lastname") & ", " & OldTbl("Firstname")
```

Fig. 4.6

These tables show the difference between using ascending and descending order in an index.

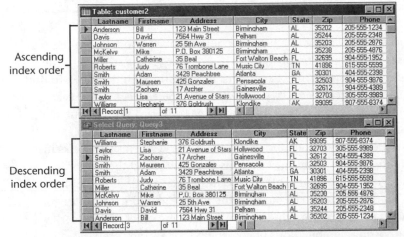

Table 4.4 Different Seek **Comparison Operators and Index Sort Orders Yield Different Results**

Comparison Operator	Index Order	Resulting Record
>= Smith,A	Ascending	Smith, Adam
<= Smith,Z	Ascending	Smith, Maureen
>= Smith,A	Descending	Roberts, Judy
<= Smith,Z	Descending	Smith, Zachary

Notice that you must also be careful when using the > or < operator on a descending index. The > operator is interpreted as finding the record that occurs later in the index than the specified key value. That is why the >= "Smith" search on a descending index returns the record Roberts, Judy. Similar behavior is exhibited by the < operator. As can be seen from the preceding example, use care when choosing both the index sort order and the comparison operator with the Seek method to ensure that the desired results are achieved.

As with the find methods, if a Seek is successful, the record pointer moves. Otherwise, the recordset's NoMatch property is set to True and the record pointer does not change. Figure 4.7 shows the Seek Name button and dialog box added to the sample case.

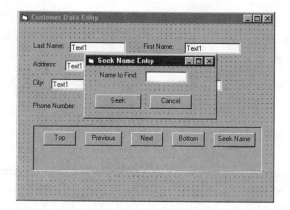

Fig. 4.7
Using a dialog box to obtain the Seek condition desired by the user.

Using the Bookmark Property

It is often desirable to find a specific record, even after the record pointer moves or new records are added. You can do so by using the Bookmark property of the recordset. The Bookmark is a system-assigned variable that is correlated to the record and is unique for each record in a recordset. Listing 4.11 shows how to obtain the value of the Bookmark for the current record, move to another record, and then return to the original record using the Bookmark previously obtained.

Listing 4.11 Using a Bookmark to Return to a Specific Record in a Recordset

```
Dim OldDb As Database, NewDyn As Recordset
Dim OldWs As WorkSpace
Set OldWs = DBEngine.Workspaces(0)
Set OldDb = OldWs.OpenDatabase("A:\TRITON.MDB")
Set NewDyn = OldDb.OpenRecordset _
```

(continues)

Listing 4.11   Continued

```
        ("SELECT * FROM Customers", dbOpenDynaset)
'******************************************************
'Set a variable to the bookmark of the current record
'******************************************************
CrntRec = NewDyn.Bookmark
'**********************
'Move to another record
'**********************
NewDyn.MoveNext
'*************************************************************************
'Return to the desired record by setting the Bookmark property
'  to the previously defined value.
'*************************************************************************
NewDyn.Bookmark = CrntRec
```

Caution

If you are working with a database other than an Access database, check the bookmarkable property of the recordset you are using to see whether bookmarks are supported before you execute any methods that depend on the bookmarks.

Listing 4.12   Storing Multiple Bookmarks in an Array

Tip

If you must store multiple Bookmark values, consider storing them in an array for faster processing. Listing 4.12 shows code that, while processing a mailing list, uses a bookmark array to identify customers whose birthdays are coming up.

```
ReDim BkMrk(1)
nmbkmk = 0
NewDyn.MoveFirst
Do Until NewDyn.EOF
'***************************
'Check for birthday in month
'***************************
    If birthday Then
'*********************
'Add bookmark to array
'*********************
        nmbkmk = nmbkmk + 1
        If nmbkmk > 1 Then
            ReDim BkMrk(1 To nmbkmk)
        End If
        BkMrk(nmbkmk) = NewDyn.Bookmark
    End If
    NewDyn.MoveNext
Loop
'*****************
'Process bookmarks
'*****************
For I = 1 To nmbkmk
    NewDyn.Bookmark = BkMrk(I)
    Debug.Print Lastname, Birthday
Next I
```

Using Filters, Indexes, and Sorts

Filters, sorts, and indexes are properties of the recordset object. These properties are set using an assignment statement such as

```
NewDyn.Filter = "Lastname = 'Smith'"
```

Filters, indexes, and sorts allow the programmer to control the scope of records being processed and the order in which records are processed. *Filters* (which are available only for dynasets and snapshots) limit the scope of records by specifying that they meet certain criteria, such as "last name starts with *M*." *Indexes* (available only for tables) and *sorts* (available only for dynasets and snapshots) specify the order of a recordset based on the value of one or more fields in the recordset. For sorts and indexes, ascending or descending sort order can also be specified.

Setting the Filter Property

The filter property is available only for dynasets and snapshots. Although the following discussion refers only to dynasets, the same statements hold true for snapshots. When set, the filter property does not affect the current dynaset, but filters records that are copied to a second dynaset or snapshot created from the first.

The filter property of a dynaset is specified in the same manner as the Where clause of a SQL statement—but without the Where keyword. The filter can be a simple statement such as State = 'AL' or one that uses multiple conditions such as State = 'FL' AND Lastname = 'Smith'. You can also use an expression such as Lastname LIKE 'M*' to find people whose last names begin with *M*. The following sample code shows how these filter properties are set for a dynaset created from the customer information tables.

```
Dim NewDyn As Recordset, ScnDyn As Recordset
Set NewDyn = OldDb.OpenRecordset("Customers",dbOpenDynaset)
NewDyn.Filter = "State = 'FL' AND Lastname = 'Smith'"
'Second recordset contains only "filtered" records.
Set ScnDyn = OldDb.OpenRecordset(dbOpenDynaset)
```

You can include added flexibility in your filter conditions by using functions in the condition. For example, if you want to filter a dynaset of all states with the second letter of the state code equal to *L*, use the Mid function as shown here:

```
NewDyn.Filter = "Mid(State,2,1) = 'L'"
```

Using functions does work, but it is an inefficient way to filter a dynaset. The better approach would be to include the condition in the query used to create the dynaset.

Data Access

More about Filters

The filter condition of the dynaset has no effect on the current dynaset—only on secondary dynasets created from the current one. The only way to "filter" the existing recordset is to move through the recordset with the find methods. By setting the find condition to your filter condition, you will only process the desired records.

If you work with only the filtered dynaset, it is more efficient to create the required dynaset using the appropriate SQL clause in the OpenRecordset method. This method is shown here:

```
Fltr = "State = 'FL' AND Lastname = 'Smith'"
Set NewDyn = OldDb.OpenRecordset _
        ("SELECT * FROM Customers WHERE Fltr")
```

Setting the Sort Property

As with the filter property, the sort property is available only for dynasets and snapshots. Although the following discussion refers only to dynasets, the same statements apply to snapshots. The sort property is specified by providing the field names and order (ascending or descending) for the fields on which the dynaset is to be sorted. You can specify any field or combination of fields in the current dynaset. The syntax for setting the sort property is shown in listing 4.13.

Listing 4.13 Two Methods for Creating a Filtered dynaset

```
Dim OldDb As Database, NewDyn As Recordset, ScnDyn As Recordset
Dim OldWs As WorkSpace
Set OldWs = DBEngine.Workspaces(0)
Set OldDb = OldWs.OpenDatabase("A:\TRITON.MDB")
'*******************************************************************
'The first method sets the sort property of one dynaset then
'    creates a second dynaset from the first.
'*******************************************************************
Set NewDyn = OldDb.OpenRecordset("SELECT * FROM Customers")
NewDyn.Sort = "Lastname,Firstname"
Set ScnDyn = NewDyn.OpenRecordset()
'**********************************************************
'The second method creates the sorted dynaset directly
'**********************************************************
Set ScnDyn = OldDb.OpenRecordset _
        ("SELECT * FROM Customers ORDER BY Lastname,Firstname")
```

> **Caution**
>
> When specifying a multiple field sort, the order of the fields is important. A sort on
> first name and then last name yields different results than a sort on last name and
> then first name.

As was the case for the filter property, the sort property has no effect on the current dynaset; it specifies the order of any dynaset created from the current one. You can also achieve the same results of a sorted dynaset by specifying the Order By clause of the SQL statement used to create the dynaset. This alternate technique is also shown in listing 4.13.

Setting the Current Index in a Table

An index is used with a table to establish a specific order for the records or to work with the Seek method to find specific records quickly. For an index to be in effect, the index property of the table must be set to the name of an existing index for the table. If you want to use an index that does not already exist, you must create it using the methods described in Chapter 3, then set the index property of the recordset to the new index name. Following is an example of how to use a program command to set the current index.

```
OldTbl.Index = "Name"
```

The index specified for the table must be one that has already been created and is part of the indexes collection for the given table. If the index does not exist, an error occurs. The index is not created for you!

Creating an Index for a New Situation

If the index you want does not exist, create it as described in Chapter 3, "Implementing the Database Design," and then set the index property of the table to the newly created index. The example shown in listing 4.14 creates a Zip Code index for the Customers table.

Listing 4.14 Creating a New Index and Setting the Index Property

```
Dim Idx1 As New Index
Idx1.Name = "Zip_Code"
Idx1.Fields = "Zip"
NewTbl.Indexes.Append Idx1
NewTbl.Index = "Zip"
```

If your program needs an index, why not just create it at design time and not worry about having to create it at run time? There are several reasons for not doing this:

- It takes time for the data engine to update indexes after records are added, deleted, or changed. If there are a large number of indexes, this process can be quite time consuming. It may be better to create the index only when it is needed. Also, indexes take up additional disk resources, so many indexes on a large table may cause your application to exceed available resources.

- You are limited to 32 indexes for a table. Although this is a fairly large number, if you need more than 32, you must create some indexes as they are needed and then delete them.

- You may not be able to anticipate all the ways a user of your application may want to view data. By providing a method for creating indexes specified by the user at run time, you add flexibility to your application.

Of these reasons, the performance issue of updating multiple indexes is the one most often considered. To determine whether it is better to add the index at design time or create it only when you need it, set up the application both ways and test the performance both ways.

> **Note**
>
> Although it is desirable to limit the number of indexes your table has to keep current, it is advisable to have an index for each field that is commonly used in SQL queries. This is because the Jet engine (starting with version 2.0) employs query optimization that uses any available indexes to speed up queries.

Considering Programs That Modify Multiple Records

There are some programs, or program functions, concerned with finding one specific piece of information in a database. However, the vast majority of programs and functions work with multiple records from the database. There are two basic methods of working with multiple records:

- Program loops—Groups of commands contained inside a DO...WHILE or DO...UNTIL programming structure. The commands are repeated until the exit condition of the loop is met.

■ SQL statements—Commands written in the Structured Query Language that tell the database engine to process records. SQL is covered in detail in Chapter 6.

Using Loops

Most programmers are familiar with the use of DO...WHILE and FOR...NEXT loops. In working with recordsets, all the programming principles for loops still apply. That is, you can perform a loop *while* a specific condition exists or *for* a specific number of records. Loops of this type were shown earlier in this chapter (refer to listings 4.4 and 4.5).

Another way of working with multiple records forms an *implied loop*. Most data entry or data viewing programs include command buttons on the form to move to the next record or previous record. When a user repeatedly presses these buttons, he or she executes a type of program loop by repeating the move events. A special consideration for this type of loop is what to do when you are at the first record, the last record, or if you have an empty recordset. The problem is that if you move backward from the first record, forward from the last record, or try to move anywhere in an empty recordset, an error occurs. Fortunately, the Jet database engine provides some help in this area. There are properties of the recordset that can tell you when these conditions exist, as described in the following section.

Using the *BOF, EOF, RecordCount,* and *NoMatch* Properties

There are four main recordset properties that can be used to control the processing of multiple records in a recordset. The definitions of these properties are given in table 4.5.

Table 4.5   Properties Used to Control Loop Processing

Property	Indicates
BOF	Beginning of File flag, indicates whether the record pointer is at the first record (BOF = True) or not (BOF = False).
EOF	End of File flag, indicates whether the record pointer is at the last record (EOF = True) or not (EOF = False).
RecordCount	Indicates the number of records in the recordset which have been accessed. This will give a count of the total records in the recordset only after the last record has been accessed (for example, by using a MoveLast method.)
NoMatch	Indicates that the last find method or Seek method was unsuccessful in locating a record that matched the desired criteria.

These properties can be used to terminate loops or prevent errors. Consider the data entry form in figure 4.5. To prevent an error from occurring when the user presses the Next button, you may want to use code that allows the move only if the recordset is not at the end of the file (the following code takes this possibility into account). Alternatively, you may want to disable the Next button when you reach the end of file. The same principal can be applied to the Previous button and the BOF condition. You may also want to check the RecordCount property of a recordset and enable only the Add Record button if the count is zero.

```
If NOT OldDyn.EOF Then
    OldDyn.MoveNext
End If
```

Using SQL Statements

In addition to processing records with a program loop, you can use SQL statements to handle a number of functions that apply to multiple records. The following sections discuss two main types of functions:

- Calculation queries—Provide cumulative information about the requested group of records.

- Action queries—Insert, delete, or modify groups of records in a recordset.

Calculation Queries

Calculation queries allow you to determine cumulative information about a group of records such as the total; average, minimum, and maximum values; and the number of records. Calculation queries also let you specify the filter criteria for the records. For example, you can extract total sales for all salesmen in the Southeast region or the maximum price of a stock on a given day (assuming, of course, that the base data is in your tables). Figure 4.8 shows a table of purchasing data for the fish inventory of the sample case. The code in listing 4.15 shows how to determine the total purchase costs for one type of fish and the minimum, maximum, and average unit cost of all the fish. Figure 4.9 shows the results table from the SQL query.

Listing 4.15 Using Calculation Queries to Determine Information about Data in the Recordset

```
Dim OldDb As Database, NewDyn As Recordset, _
    NewDyn2 As Recordset, SQL As String
Dim OldWs As WorkSpace
```

```
Set OldWs = dbEngine.Workspaces(0)
Set OldDb = OldWs.OpenDatabase("E:\VB4BOOK\SAMPLES\TRITON.MDB")
'************************************************
'Use the SUM function to get the total cost.
'************************************************
SQL = "SELECT SUM([Total Cost]) As Grand FROM Fishbuys
      ➥WHERE Fishcode = 1001"
Set NewDyn = OldDb.OpenRecordset(SQL)
Print NewDyn("Grand")
NewDyn.Close
'*********************************************************************
'Use the MIN, AVG, and MAX functions to get unit price statistics.
'*********************************************************************
SQL = "SELECT MIN([Unit Price]) As Mincst,
      ➥AVG([Unit Price]) As Avgcst, "
SQL = SQL + _
    " MAX([Unit Price]) As Maxcst FROM Fishbuys WHERE Fishcode > 0"
Set NewDyn2 = OldDb.OpenRecordset(SQL)
Print NewDyn2("Mincst"), NewDyn2("Avgcst"), NewDyn2("Maxcst")
NewDyn2.Close
OldDb.Close
```

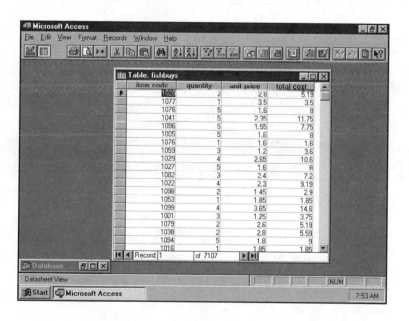

Fig. 4.8
Purchasing data
shown here can be
processed with
calculation queries
or action queries.

Using a calculation query can replace many lines of program code that would
be required to produce the same results. In addition, a query is usually faster
than the equivalent program code. The query and the equivalent program
code are contained in the project SQLCALC.MAK on the companion disk.

Fig. 4.9
The calculation
query produces a
dynaset with a
single record
containing the
results.

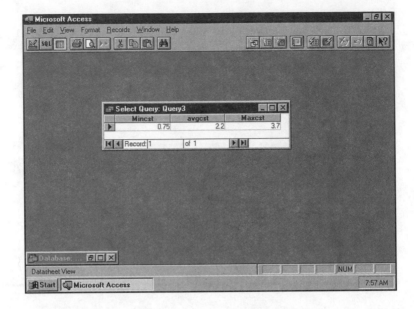

Action Queries

Action queries operate directly on a recordset to insert, delete, or modify
groups of records based on specific criteria. As with calculation queries, action
queries perform the same work that would require many lines of program
code. Listing 4.16 shows examples of several action queries.

Listing 4.16 Using Action Queries to Perform Operations on Multiple Records

```
Dim OldDb As Database, NewDyn As Recordset, NewQry As QueryDef
Dim OldWs As WorkSpace
Set OldWs = DBEngine.Workspaces(0)
Set OldDb = OldWs.OpenDatabase("E:\VB4BOOK\SAMPLES\TRITON.MDB")
'********************************************
'Calculate the total cost of each purchase.
'********************************************
SQL = _
    "Update Fishbuys Set [Total Cost] = [Quantity] * [Unit Price]"
Set NewQry = OldDb.CreateQueryDef("Calc Total", SQL)
NewQry.Execute
NewQry.Close
'**************************************
'Delete all records for Fishcode = 1003
'**************************************
SQL = "Delete From Fishbuys WHERE Fishcode = 1003"
Set NewQry = OldDb.CreateQueryDef("Del Fish", SQL)
NewQry.Execute
NewQry.Close
OldDb.DeleteQueryDef ("Calc Total")
```

```
OldDb.DeleteQueryDef ("Del Fish")
OldDb.Close
```

> **Caution**
>
> When using action queries to modify groups of records, be very careful in specifying the Where clause of the query that defines the records to be modified. Improperly setting this clause can produce disastrous results, such as the deletion of all records in a recordset.

Understanding Other Programming Commands

In this chapter, you have learned how to find specific records and how to move through a group of records. However, in most programs, you also must add, modify, and delete records. The commands covered in the following sections apply only to tables and dynasets (remember that snapshots are not updatable).

Adding Records

To add a new record to a recordset, use the AddNew method. AddNew does not actually add the record to the recordset; it clears the copy buffer to allow information for the new record to be input. To physically add the record, use the Update method. Listing 4.17 shows how to add a new record to the recordset.

Listing 4.17 Using AddNew and Update to Add a Record to the Recordset

```
'*******************************
'Use AddNew to set up a new record
'*******************************
NewDyn.AddNew
'*********************************************************
'Place the necessary information in the recordset fields
'*********************************************************
NewDyn("Lastname") = "McKelvy"
NewDyn("Firstname") = "Mike"
NewDyn("Address") = "6995 Bay Road"
NewDyn("City") = "Pensacola"
NewDyn("State") = "FL"
NewDyn("Zip") = "32561"
```

(continues)

Data Access

Listing 4.17 Continued

```
'**************************************************************
'Use the update method to add the new record to the recordset
'**************************************************************
NewDyn.Update
```

> **Caution**
>
> Because AddNew places information only in the copy buffer, reusing the AddNew method or moving the record pointer with any move or find method clears the copy buffer. Any information entered in the record is therefore lost.

Editing Records

In a manner similar to adding a record, you use the Edit method to make changes to a record. The Edit method places a copy of the current record's contents into the copy buffer so that information can be changed. As with AddNew, the changes take effect only when the Update method is executed. Listing 4.18 shows the use of the Edit method.

Listing 4.18 Using Edit and Update to Change the Data in a Record

```
'*********************************************************
'Use the find method to locate the record to be changed.
'*********************************************************
NewDyn.FindFirst "Lastname = 'McKelvy'"
'*********************************************
'Check the NoMatch Property to avoid an error
'*********************************************
If NewDyn.NoMatch Then
    MsgBox "Not Found"
Else
'********************************************************
'Use the edit method to set up the record for changes
'********************************************************
    NewDyn.Edit
'*****************************************************
'Change the necessary information in the copy buffer
'*****************************************************
    NewDyn("Address") = "P. O. Box 380125"
    NewDyn("City") = "Birmingham"
    NewDyn("State") = "AL"
    NewDyn("Zip") = "35238"
'**********************************************************
'Use the update method to write the changes to the recordset
'**********************************************************
    NewDyn.Update
End If
```

> **Caution**
>
> Because Edit only places information in the copy buffer, reusing the Edit method or moving the record pointer with any move or find method clears the copy buffer. Any information entered in the record is therefore lost.

Updating Records

The Update method is used in conjunction with the AddNew and Edit methods to make changes to the recordsets. The Update method writes the information from the copy buffer to the recordset. In the case of AddNew, Update also creates a blank record in the recordset to which the information is written. In a multiuser environment, the Update method also clears the record locks associated with the pending add or edit method. (The use of the Update method is shown in listings 4.17 and 4.18.)

> **Note**
>
> If you use data controls to work with recordsets, the use of the Update method is not required. An update is automatically performed when a move is executed by the data control.

Deleting Records

Deleting a record requires the use of the Delete method, as shown in listing 4.19. This method removes the record from the recordset and sets the record pointer to a null value.

Listing 4.19   Using Edit to Remove a Record from the Recordset

```
'*********************************************************
'Use the find method to locate the record to be deleted
'*********************************************************
NewDyn.FindFirst "Lastname = 'McKelvy'"
'**********************************************
'Check the NoMatch property to avoid an error
'**********************************************
If NewDyn.NoMatch Then
    MsgBox "Not Found"
Else
    '********************************************
    'Use the delete method to remove the record
    '********************************************
    NewDyn.Delete
End If
```

Caution

Once you delete a record, it is gone. You can recover the record only if you issued a BeginTrans command before you deleted the record, in which case you can RollBack the transaction. Otherwise, the only way to get the information back into the database is to re-create the record with the AddNew method.

Incorporating Add, Edit, and Delete Functions in the Sample Case

Figure 4.10 shows some command buttons added to the data entry screen for the sample case. These buttons make use of the add, edit, and delete capabilities described in the preceding sections. The Delete Record button deletes the current record. The Add New Record button blanks out the text boxes to prepare them for new input. The Edit Record button prepares the recordset for editing. As a visual indication of editing, the foreground color of the text boxes also changes. Both the Edit Record and Add New Record buttons cause the normal command buttons (the Top, Previous, Next, Bottom, and Seek Name buttons) to be hidden and two new buttons to be displayed. The new buttons are Save and Cancel. The Save button stores the values displayed in the text boxes to the appropriate fields in the recordset and issues the Update method. The Cancel button terminates the edit or add process and restores the original information for the current record. After either Save or Cancel is selected, both buttons disappear and the eight main buttons are again shown.

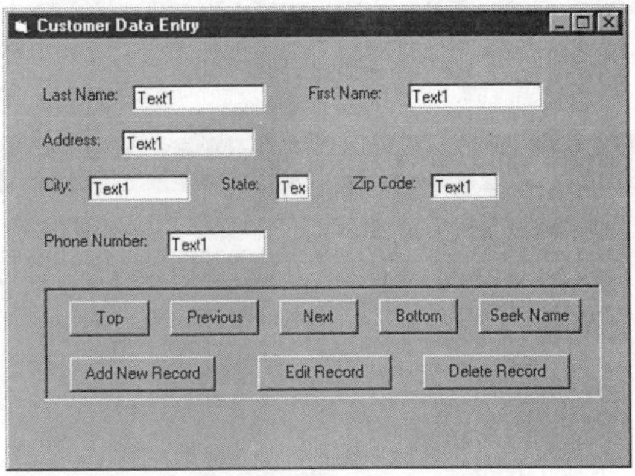

Fig. 4.10

Add, edit, and delete functions are added to the data entry screen with new command buttons.

Introducing Transaction Processing

Transaction processing allows you to treat a group of changes, additions, or deletions to a database as a single entity. This is useful when one change to a database depends on another change, and you want to make sure that all changes are made before any of the changes become permanent. For example, you have a point-of-sale application that updates inventory levels as sales are made. As each item is entered for the sales transaction, a change is made to the inventory database. However, you only want to keep the inventory changes if the sale is completed. If the sale is aborted, you want to return the inventory database to its initial state before the sale was started. Transaction processing is a function of the Workspace object and, therefore, affects all databases open in a particular workspace.

Visual Basic provides three statements for transaction processing. These statements perform the following functions:

- BeginTrans: Starts a transaction and sets the initial state of the database.

- RollBack: Returns the database to its initial state before the BeginTrans statement was issued. When RollBack is executed, all changes made after the last BeginTrans statement are discarded.

- CommitTrans: Permanently saves all changes to the database made since the last BeginTrans statement. Once the CommitTrans statement has been issued, the transactions cannot be undone.

Listing 4.20 shows the BeginTrans, RollBack, and CommitTrans statements in use in the sales example mentioned earlier in this section.

Listing 4.20   Using Transaction Processing to Handle Multiple Changes to a Database as One Group

```
BeginTrans
'************************************************
'Perform loop until user ends sales transaction
'************************************************
Do While Sales
'************************************************
'Get item number and sales quantity from form
' Input Itemno,SalesQty
' Find item number in inventory
'************************************************
   Inv.FindFirst "ItemNum = " & Itemno
'************************
```

(continues)

Listing 4.20 Continued

```
'Update inventory quantity
'*************************
   Inv.Edit
   Inv("Quantity") = Inv("Quantity") - SalesQty
   Inv.Update
Loop
'*****************************************
'User either completes or cancels the sale
'*****************************************
If SaleComp Then
   CommitTrans
Else
   Rollback
End If
```

From Here...

Some of the topics mentioned in this chapter are covered in greater detail in other portions of the book. Please refer to these chapters:

■ Chapter 5, "Using Visual Basic's Data and Bound Controls," explains how to write programs that use the data control.

■ Chapter 6, "Understanding Structured Query Language (SQL)," explains more about the SQL statements used in creating dynasets, snapshots, and queries.

Chapter 5

Using Visual Basic's Data and Bound Controls

Chapter 4, "Manipulating Data with a Program," introduced you to the data access objects and the way program commands are used to manipulate these objects. You learned that you can write powerful database applications using these methods. The discussions in Chapter 4 also provided a good basis for the discussion of the data and bound controls; these objects automate and simplify many of the data access tasks. With the improvements in the data control and the addition of more bound controls (these topics are discussed in this chapter), these controls provide an excellent means of developing data entry and data viewing programs for almost any need.

As good as the data control is, there are still occasions when the data control is not the right tool to use for your application. For example, you would not want to use it for an application that reads data directly from a COM port into the database. You will find, however, that the data control is a powerful tool for many applications, both by itself and in combination with the methods of the data access objects.

This chapter discusses how the data and bound controls are used. Also in this chapter, you build a data entry screen using many of the bound controls discussed. The data entry screen allows the user two views of the data: a single record view and a browse view, which allows editing of multiple records. The two views of the data entry screen are shown in figures 5.1 and 5.2.

Fig. 5.1

The sample data entry screen in single record mode.

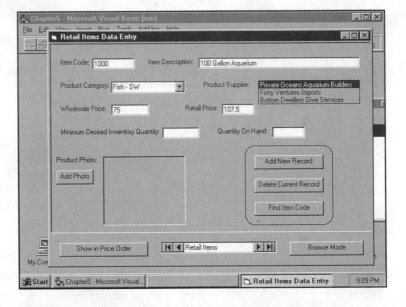

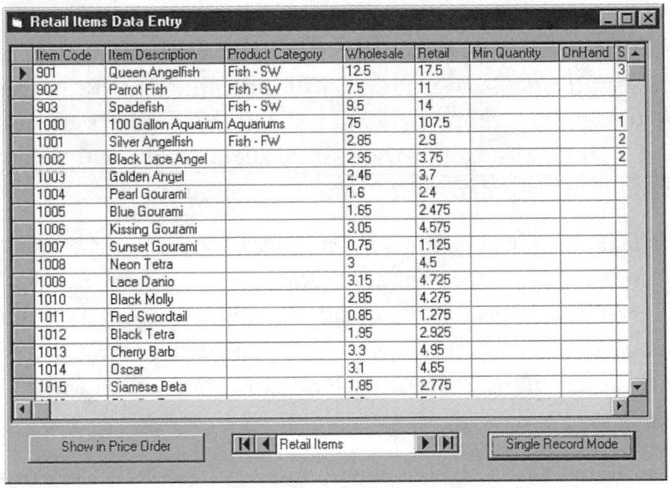

Fig. 5.2

The sample data entry screen in browse mode for modifying data.

In this chapter, you learn about the following:

■ How to use the data control to access your databases

■ How to use the bound properties of controls to display data from your databases

■ The limitations of the data control and how to get around them

What's New in Version 4?

Visual Basic Version 4 offers some great improvements over Version 3 in the area of the data control and bound controls. These improvements dramatically extend their capabilities and overcome most of the deficiencies of the earlier version. For the data control itself, the key improvements are as follows:

- The ability to create any of the three recordset types (table, dynaset, or snapshot).

- The ability to assign a recordset created with the data access objects to a control, or vice versa.

- The addition of BOF and EOF action properties, which allow the developer to automatically invoke a specific action when the file boundaries are reached.

The ability to create any of the recordset types is the most important of these three improvements. This ability allows you to set an index for a data control that uses a table-type recordset, thus allowing the use of the Seek method to quickly find records. Being able to set indexes means that you can change the presentation order of the recordset more easily. Another advantage of being able to use tables is that any updates made by others in a multiuser environment are immediately available to the current user. This was not the case when the data control was limited to using dynasets only.

In addition to the improvements in the data control, Version 4 adds five new data-bound controls. These controls are listed here:

- List box

- Combo box

- DBList box

- DBCombo box

- DBGrid

The differences between the two types of list and combo boxes are covered later in this chapter. The addition of these new controls greatly expands the flexibility of programs that can be developed with the bound controls.

Understanding the Data Control

The *data control* is designed to provide an easy means of access to a database. To use the data control, you follow these five steps:

1. Select the control from the toolbox.

2. Draw the control on your form.

3. Set the DatabaseName property.

4. Set the RecordSource property.

5. Set the RecordsetType property.

At this point, you have created the links to the database and recordset with which you want to work. This method requires far less work than having to specify all the functions to do this with program code.

The data control also provides record-movement functions for your applications. The buttons on the data control take the place of command buttons that you would have to program and they perform the equivalent functions of the MoveFirst, MovePrevious, MoveNext, and MoveLast methods.

When setting up the data control, you typically set the DatabaseName and RecordSource properties at design time. However, you can also set properties at run time. It is also possible to create a recordset with the data access objects (see Chapter 4) and assign that recordset to a data control.

Looking at How the Data Control Works

The data control provides access to your data by creating a recordset based on the information in the database Name and RecordSource properties. The default recordset type is a dynaset, but you can also use a table or snapshot.

> **Note**
>
> You cannot create a new table with the data control. You can only access an existing table in the database. However, if you specify the recordset type as table, you get all the advantages of using a table (as described in Chapter 4).

With the data control, you can create a dynaset (or snapshot) from a table, a query, or a SQL statement. You are not limited to using an Access database. You can use the data control and bound controls with any database files accessible through the Jet engine.

If you specify the properties of the data control at design time, the recordset is created when your form is loaded and the data control is displayed. If you specify (or subsequently change) the data control properties at run time, the new recordset is created when the properties are set.

Adding a Data Control to a Form

The first step in using a data control is to add the control to your application's form. To do this, first select the data control object from the Visual Basic Toolbox (see fig. 5.3). Then, place and size the data control just as you do any other design object. After you set the desired size and placement of the data control on your form, you can set the Name and Caption properties of the data control.

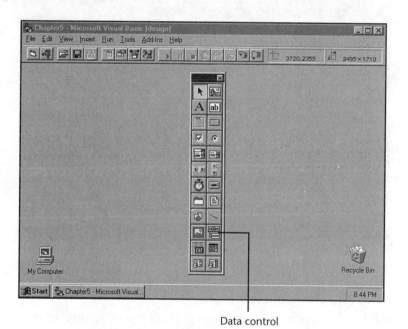

Data control

Fig. 5.3
The data control is one of the tools in the Visual Basic Toolbox.

The Name property sets the control name, which identifies the control and its associated data to the bound controls. The Name property is also the name of the recordset object that you use with any program commands that your application needs. The default name for the first data control added to a form is Data1. Additional data controls added to a form are sequentially numbered as Data2, Data3, and so on. You can change the name of the data control by selecting the Name property from the Properties window and typing the desired name.

Tip
You can quickly access the Properties window by pressing F4 or clicking the Properties icon on the toolbar.

The Caption property specifies the text that appears on the data control. You usually want the caption to be descriptive of the data the control accesses. The default for the Caption property is the initial setting of the Name property (for example, Data1 for the first data control). You can change the Caption property the same way you change the Name property.

For the examples in this chapter, add a data control with the name Items and the caption Retail Items. The form with this control added is shown in figure 5.4.

Fig. 5.4

Draw the data control on your form and set its caption to an expression meaningful to your application.

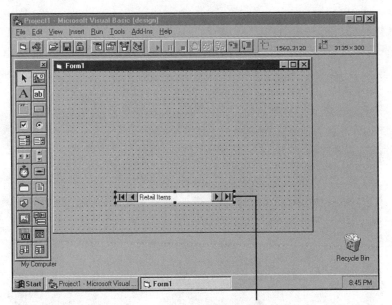

Data control, sized, with caption set

Setting the Properties

You attach a database and recordset to a data control by setting the properties of the control. The only two properties required are DatabaseName and RecordSource. These are the minimum specifications for using an Access database with the data control. Specifying these two properties defines the information you want in the data control and creates a dynaset with the default of nonexclusive, read/write access to the data. If you want to create a recordset other than a dynaset, you also must set the RecordsetType property.

> **Note**
>
> The DatabaseName property is not the same as the Name property mentioned earlier. The Name property specifies the name of the data control object. This is used to reference the object in code. The DatabaseName property specifies the name of the database file that the data control is accessing.

The *DatabaseName* Property

For Access databases, the DatabaseName property is the name of the database file, including the full path name. You can enter the name by selecting the DatabaseName property from the Properties dialog box and either typing the database name or selecting the database from a list. Figure 5.5 shows the Properties dialog box with the DatabaseName property selected.

Fig. 5.5
Use the Properties dialog box to set the database name for the control.

To select the database name from the dialog box, click the ellipsis button (...) at the right of the property input line. This action displays a DatabaseName dialog box (see fig. 5.6). Select the file name you want and click OK. The selected file name then appears next to the DatabaseName property of the data control.

If you use the data control with databases other than Access, the DatabaseName property requires different values such as the path name for the data subdirectory. The required values for some common databases are summarized in table 5.1.

Fig. 5.6
You can enter a
database name or
choose it from the
DatabaseName
dialog box.

Table 5.1	Property Requirements for Various Database Types
Database Type	**Database Name Value**
Access	Name of database including path (d:\sub\name.MDB)
FoxPro	Subdirectory path (d:\sub\) for database files
dBASE	Subdirectory path (d:\sub\) for database files
Paradox	Subdirectory path (d:\sub\) for database files
Btrieve	Data definition file including path (d:\sub\name.DDF)

The *RecordSource* Property

After you designate the database to use with the DatabaseName property,
specify the information you want from the database with the RecordSource
property. If you are working with a single table as your recordset, you can
enter the table name or select it from the list of tables (see fig. 5.7).

Fig. 5.7
You can select the
RecordSource from
a list of tables
available in the
database.

Table list

You can access only selected information from a table or use information from multiple tables by using a SQL statement. To use a SQL statement to define the recordset, you set the RecordSource property to the name of a QueryDef (which contains the SQL statement) in the database or enter a valid SQL statement in the property definition. You can use any SQL statement that creates a dynaset (you can also include functions in your SQL statement). If you are using a QueryDef, it must be a QueryDef that has already been defined and stored in the database.

If you are using the data control to work with a non-Access database, you must set the RecordSource property to the proper table name or SQL statement for that database. Again, if you are using only a table, you can select it from the drop-down list for the RecordSource property.

The *RecordsetType* Property

The default recordset type for a data control is a dynaset. If you need to create a snapshot or access a table directly, you must change the setting of the RecordsetType property. Do this by selecting the desired type from a drop-down list in the Properties dialog (see fig. 5.8).

Fig. 5.8
Use the RecordsetType property to determine whether the data control uses a table, dynaset, or snapshot.

Type options

The *BOF* and *EOF* Action Properties

The action properties tell the data control what to do when either the beginning-of-file (BOF) or end-of-file (EOF) is reached. For the BOF property, you have two choices:

■ Execute the MoveFirst method to set the record pointer at the first record and the BOF flag to False (property value of 0).

■ Set the BOF flag to True (property value of 1).

For the EOF property, you have three choices:

- Execute the MoveLast method to set the record pointer at the last record and the EOF flag to False (property value of 0).

- Set the EOF flag to True (property value of 1).

- Execute the AddNew method to set up the recordset for the addition of a new record (property value of 2).

The values of each of these properties can be chosen from a drop-down list in the Properties dialog box. The AddNew setting of the EOFAction property can be useful if you have an application that adds a number of new records. As with most other properties of the data control, these properties can be reset to other values at run time.

> **Note**
>
> These BOF and EOF actions are triggered only when the beginning or end of the file is reached using the data control (in other words, pressing the next button). They have no effect if the beginning or end of file is reached using the data access methods in code (as in MoveNext).

Other Optional Properties

Four other properties can be set for the data control:

- Connect. Necessary only if you are using a database other than Access. The Connect property tells the Jet engine what kind of database you are using. Table 5.2 summarizes the values of the Connect property for several common database types.

- Exclusive. Determines whether or not others can access the database while it is in use by your application. The property is set to either True (your application is the only one that can access the database) or False (others may access the database). The default value is False.

- Readonly. Determines whether or not your application can modify the data in your defined recordset. The property may be set to True (your application cannot modify data) or False (your application can modify data). The default value is False.

- Options. Allows you to specify other properties for the dynaset created by the data control. These properties were summarized in Chapter 4, "Manipulating Data with a Program" (refer to table 4.2).

Table 5.2 Property Settings for Various Database Types	
Database Type	**Value of Connect Property**
Access	Access
FoxPro 2.0	FoxPro 2.0
FoxPro 2.5	FoxPro 2.5
FoxPro 2.6	FoxPro 2.6
dBASE III	dBASE III
dBASE IV	dBASE IV
Excel	Excell
Paradox 3.x	paradox 3.x;pwd=password
Paradox 4.x	paradox 4.x;pwd=password
Btrieve	btrieve
ASCII Text	Text

Troubleshooting

I tried to set an index for my recordset using the Index *property of the data control, but was unable to do so.*

The Index property does not refer to a database index but to the index position in an array. A data control, like any other Visual Basic control object, can be part of a control array. If you have such an array, the Index property specifies the position of the current control in that array. Remember that a data control by default creates a dynaset—and you cannot apply an index to a dynaset. You can use an index if you specify that the data control should use a table, but the index can be set only with a program command such as this one:

```
Data1.Recordset.Index = "Price"
```

Setting Properties at Run Time

You can choose to set (or reset) the DataBaseName, RecordSource, and RecordsetType properties of the data control at run time. Following are three cases in which it is desirable to set the properties at run time.

You want to allow the user to select a specific database file from a group of related files. For example, a central office application keeps a separate database for each store of a chain; your application must allow the user to select the store with which he or she wants to work.

You want to allow users to set specific conditions on the data they want to see. These conditions may take the form of filters or sort orders (for example, show only salespeople with over $10,000 in sales in order of total sales). Alternatively, your application may have to set the filters as part of an access control scheme, such as allowing a department manager to see data about only the people in his or her department. In the case of the application setting the filters, the information is set at design time, but is incorporated in code instead of in the initial setting of the data control properties.

You want the user to specify the directory in a configuration file (or have your setup program do it for them) and then use the information from the configuration file to set your data control properties. If you are developing a commercial application, there is no guarantee that the user has the same directory structure you have. In fact, many users are annoyed if you impose a specific directory structure or drive designation as a requirement for your program.

If you need to set the parameters at run time, simply set the properties with code statements shown in listing 5.1. As shown in the listing, you must specify the name of your data control, the property name, and the desired property value.

After the properties have been set, use the Requery method of the data control to implement the changes. This method is shown in the last line of listing 5.1. The changes to the data control (that is, the creation of the new recordset) take effect *after* the Requery method is run.

Listing 5.1 Setting or Changing the DatabaseName and RecordSource Properties of a Data Control at Run Time

```
'*******************************************
'Set the value of the DatabaseName property
'*******************************************
Items.DatabaseName = "A:\TRITON.MDB"
'*******************************************
'Set the value of the RecordSource property
'*******************************************
Items.RecordSource = "Retail Items"
'***********************************************************
'Set the value of the RecordsetType property to table (0)
'***********************************************************
```

```
Items.RecordsetType = 0
'*************************************************
'Use the Requery method to implement the changes
'*************************************************
Items.ReFresh
```

Looking at Advantages of the Data Control

The key advantage to using the data control is that less programming is required to develop a data access application. You do not have to provide program code to open or create a database or recordset, to move through the records, or to edit the existing records in the recordset. The data control makes the initial application development much quicker and makes maintenance of your code much easier.

When using the data control, you also have the advantage of specifying your data objects (database and recordset) at design time, and you can select these options from dialog boxes and lists. Selecting options from lists cuts down on errors that can be introduced into the application by eliminating the typographic errors to which many developers (especially this author!) are prone.

The other advantage of the data control is that it provides a direct link to the data. You do not have to specifically invoke the Edit and Update methods to modify the data in the database. The advantage to you is that your changes show up in the database as soon as you enter them.

In addition to these advantages of using the data control, several of the bound controls that are new for Version 4 provide an easy way to accomplish tasks that are quite difficult using just the data access objects and program commands. These controls are the data bound list box, data bound combo box, and data bound grid. These controls are discussed in detail later in this chapter.

Looking at Limitations of the Data Control

As useful as the data control is, it also has a few limitations. (Doesn't everything?) These limitations are listed here:

- There are no add or delete functions built in to the data control.

- Because the Edit and Update functions are automatic, it is more difficult to implement transaction processing in the data control.

Later in this chapter, you see how to overcome some of these limitations when you look at combining the data control with program code.

Understanding the Bound Controls

Bound controls are simply Visual Basic control objects that can be linked to fields in one or two data controls. In addition, the bound controls have a data-changed property that triggers a data-changed event in the data control. Visual Basic provides 13 bound controls:

- Picture box

- Label

- Text box

- Check box

- Image

- List box

- Combo box

- Data bound list box

- Data bound combo box

- Data bound grid

- Masked edit

- 3-D check box

- 3-D panel

These controls are called out on the Visual Basic Toolbox shown in figure 5.9.

Fig. 5.9
There are 13 bound controls available in Visual Basic.

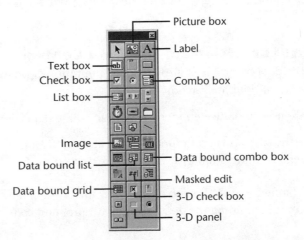

In addition, many vendors of third-party controls are making their controls data aware so that they can be used with the data control.

Looking at What the Bound Controls Do

The *bound controls* display the data from the field and data source specified in the control's properties. The data source for a bound control is *always* a data control. As the user moves from record to record using the data control, the bound controls are updated to reflect the contents of the current record. Table 5.3 lists the bound controls, the type of data they can handle, and the control property that displays the data.

Table 5.3   The Relationship between Bound Controls and Types of Data in the Underlying Recordset

Control Name	Data Type(s)	Control Property
Picture box	Long Binary	Picture
Label	Text, Numeric, Date	Caption
Text box	Text, Numeric, Date	Text
Check box	True/False, Yes/No	Value
Image	Binary	Picture
List box	Text, Numeric, Date	Text
Combo box	Text, Numeric, Date	Text
Data bound list box	Text, Numeric, Date	Text
Data bound combo box	Text, Numeric, Date	Text
Data bound grid	Text, Numeric, Date	Text, Value
Masked edit	Text, Numeric, Date	Text
3-D check box	True/False, Yes/No	Value
3-D panel	Text, Numeric, Date	Caption

The bound controls also provide a direct link to the data in the recordset. Any changes made in the control are reflected in the recordset. There are no intermediate steps of setting the field value equal to the value of the control and updating the record.

Adding Bound Controls to a Form

To add one of the bound controls to your form, select the control from the Toolbox and position and size the control on the form. Figure 5.10 shows a text box added to the form with the data control on it.

Bound text box

Fig. 5.10
You draw bound controls on your form just like any other control.

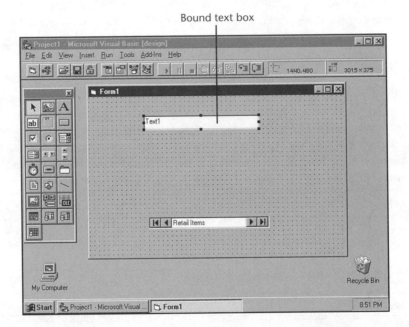

Tip
If you hold down the Ctrl key when you click on a control in the toolbar, you can add multiple controls of that type to your form. This eliminates the hassle of having to click on the control icon for each occurrence of the control that you add.

The Name property of the bound control defines the object by which the control is referenced in any program statements. If you are using only the data control, you may want to leave the Name property with its default value. If you are going to use program statements, you may want to change the name to one that has some meaning to you. The Name property does not affect how the bound control performs.

Setting the Properties of the Bound Controls

For a bound control to work with the data from a recordset, you must tie the bound control to the data control representing the recordset. Do this by setting the DataSource property of the bound control. Depending on the specific control used, you may have to set other properties. By working on the sample Retail Items data entry screen throughout the remainder of this chapter, you learn many of the bound controls, which properties must be set, and how to set them.

Setting the *DataSource* Property

To set the DataSource property, select the property from the Properties dialog box for your control. Click the arrow to the right of the input area to see a list of all the data controls on the current form. Select one of the controls from the list and the DataSource property is set. This procedure is shown in figure 5.11.

— Data control list

Fig. 5.11
Select the
DataSource for the
bound control
from the list of
data controls on
the form.

Using the Label and Text Box Controls

The label and text box controls are used for the display of any type of alphanumeric data. Use the text box control to edit any type of alphanumeric data; use the label control if you want to keep the displayed data from being updated. For both of these types of controls, you set the DataField property after you set the DataSource property. In the sample case, you want to allow editing of all the fields, so you do not use labels as bound controls. Figure 5.12 shows the data entry screen with the text boxes and unbound labels displayed.

To set the DataField property of the control, select the DataField property from the Properties dialog box, click the arrow to the right of the input area, and choose one of the fields from the displayed list. The list includes all available fields from the recordset defined in the specified DataSource (see fig. 5.13).

Tip
Double-clicking on
the DataSource
property will scroll
through the list of
available data
controls.

Fig. 5.12
You can use the
label and text box
controls to display
alphanumeric
data.

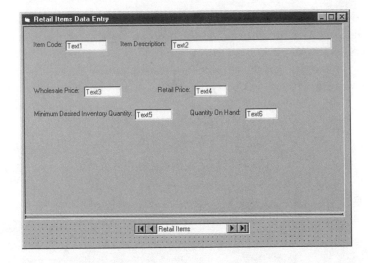

Fig. 5.13
Select the
`DataField` for the
bound control
from the list of
fields in the
selected data
control.

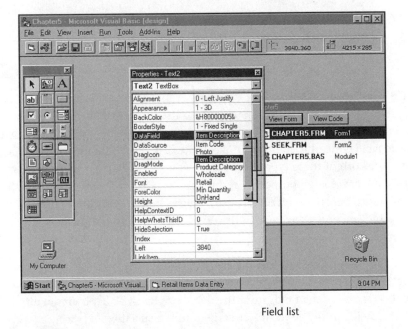

Field list

Tip
Double-clicking
on the `DataField`
property will scroll
through a list of
available fields.

Using the Picture Box and Image Controls

The picture box and image controls are used to display Windows graphics
files (.BMP, .WMF, .ICO, and .DIB formats). When tied to a long binary field
in a recordset, these controls can display and store photos, graph images,
drawings, and so on in a database. To bind either of these control types to a
recordset, set the `DataSource` and `DataField` properties as described in the
preceding sections.

The main difference between the picture box and image controls is the way in which they display pictures. By default (Stretch property set to False), the image control changes size to fit the picture it contains. If you set the Stretch property to True, the image control changes the size of the picture to fit the control. This may change the aspect ratio (height to width ratio) of the picture and change its appearance. By default (Autosize property set to False), the picture box control displays as much of the picture as fits in the control without changing the aspect ratio. If you want to see the whole picture, set the Autosize property of the picture box to True, which causes the control to change size to fit the picture.

For the sample case, you want to display a picture of the fish in the inventory. Figure 5.14 shows a picture box added to the form and tied to the Photo field in the recordset.

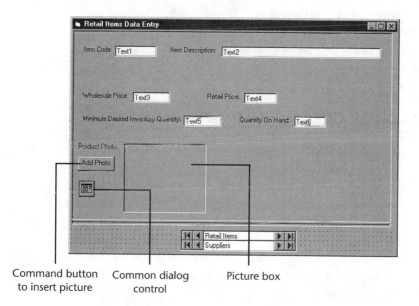

Command button   Common dialog   Picture box
to insert picture   control

Fig. 5.14
You can add pictures to your form and database with the picture or image control.

Unlike most other bound controls, the picture and image controls do not allow you to edit their contents directly. The best way to get a picture into the recordset is to use the LoadPicture function to retrieve a picture from a file and place it in the control (see listing 5.2). This capability is added to the sample case with the Add Photo button shown in figure 5.14. The common dialog control was added to the form to allow the user to select the file to import. The use of the common dialog button is also shown in listing 5.2.

Listing 5.2 Using the Common Dialog Control and the LoadPicture Function to Add a Picture to the Picture or Image Control and the Recordset

```
'*****************************************************
'Use the Common Dialog to get the file name to load
'*****************************************************
Getfile.Filter = "Bitmap Files (*.BMP)¦*.bmp¦ All Files¦*.*"
Getfile.DefaultExt = "BMP"
Getfile.ShowOpen
DataName = Getfile.FileName
'*******************************************************
'Use the LoadPicture function to add the picture to the control
'*******************************************************
Picture2.Picture = LoadPicture(DataName)
```

Using the Check Box Control

The check box control displays True and False information. The box is checked if the bound field has a True value; it is unchecked if the bound field has a False value. The check box is bound to the recordset by setting the DataSource and DataField properties.

Using the List Box and Combo Box Controls

The list box and combo box controls allow the user to choose one item from a list of items; in addition, the combo box allows the user to enter a different item. These controls in Visual Basic 4 are enhancements of the controls available in the previous versions of Visual Basic. The enhancement allows you to bind the control to a data field to store the user's choices in a field. You do this by setting the DataSource and DataField properties of the control. To give your user a list of items from which to select, you use the AddItem method of the control. For the sample case, use a combo box to allow users to select the product category for the item they are editing (see fig. 5.15). Listing 5.3 shows the population of the list.

Listing 5.3 Populating the List with the AddItem Method

```
Combo1.AddItem "Aquariums"
Combo1.AddItem "Fish - FW"
Combo1.AddItem "Fish - SW"
Combo1.AddItem "Plants"
Combo1.AddItem "Supplies"
```

Combo box

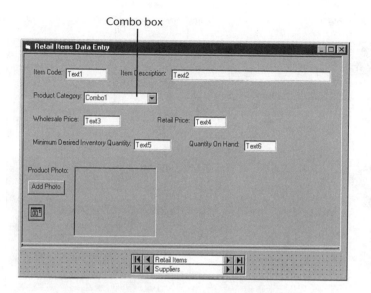

Fig. 5.15
Use a list or combo
box to present
your user with a
list of choices.

Using the Data Bound List Box and Data Bound Combo Box

The data bound list box and combo box are similar in function to their standard counterparts. They are designed to present the user with a list of choices. The key difference is that the data bound list and combo box controls get their list information from a recordset instead of from a series of AddItem statements.

Consider an example from the sample case. As your users enter data about a product, you want them to also tie the product to a supplier. One of the tables in the database contains supplier information. You can use the data bound list box to allow your users to select a supplier from those contained in the supplier table. The data bound list takes the supplier ID selected from the Supplier table and stores it in the appropriate field of the Retail Items table. You may think it would be hard to select the appropriate supplier if all you can see is the ID. However, the data bound list and combo boxes allow you to select a second field from the source table to serve as the display in the list. This means that you can display the name of the supplier in the list box but store only the supplier ID in the Retail Items table. This concept is shown graphically in figure 5.16.

Fig. 5.16
The data bound
list and combo
boxes let you pick
an item from one
table for inclusion
in another table.

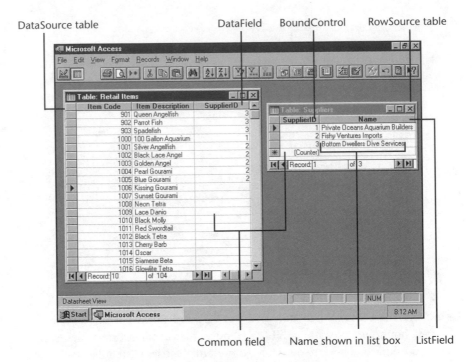

DataSource table   DataField   BoundControl   RowSource table

Common field   Name shown in list box   ListField

You set up the data bound list or combo box by specifying five properties.
These properties are described in table 5.4.

Property	Sample Case Setting	Description
Table 5.4 Properties for Data Bound List Box or Combo Box		
RowSource	Suppliers	The name of the data control containing the information used to populate the list.
BoundColumn	SupplierID	The name of the field containing the value to be copied to the other table.
ListField	Name	The name of the field to be displayed in the list.
DataSource	Items	The name of the data control containing the recordset that is the destination of the information.
DataField	SupplierID	The name of the destination field.

You can set each of these properties by selecting the property from the Properties dialog box and choosing the setting from a drop-down list. Several notes must be considered when setting the properties of the data bound list and combo boxes:

- The data controls specified for the RowSource and DataSource properties can be the same control or different controls.

- The fields for the BoundColumn and DataField properties must be of the same type.

- The ListField property can be set to the same field as the BoundColumn property.

- All five properties must be set, or a run-time error occurs.

Figure 5.17 shows the data bound list box added to the sample data entry form.

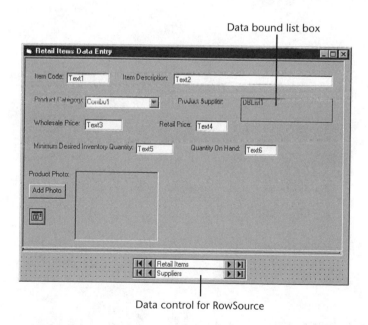

Data bound list box

Data control for RowSource

Fig. 5.17
A data bound list box added to the screen to allow the user to select from a list of suppliers.

Using the Data Bound Grid

The data bound grid provides a means to view the fields of multiple records at the same time. The data bound grid is similar to the table view used in Access or the Browse command used in FoxPro. The data bound grid displays information in a spreadsheet style of rows and columns. It can be used to display any alphanumeric information or pictures.

Tip

To conserve re-
sources used by
your application,
use a QueryDef or
SQL statement in
the RecordSource
property of the data
control that the
grid will use. This
allows you to keep
to a minimum the
number of records
and fields handled
by the grid.

To set up the data bound grid, you only need to specify the DataSource property to identify the data control containing the data. Once this is set, the grid
displays all fields of all records in the recordset. If the information is larger
than the area of the grid you defined, scroll bars are presented to allow you to
view the remaining data.

Your user can select a grid cell to edit by clicking on the cell with the mouse.
To add a new record, the user positions the pointer in the last row of the grid
indicated by an asterisk (*) and enters the desired data. You must specifically
allow editing and record addition in the grid by setting the AllowAddNew and
AllowUpdate properties of the grid to True.

For the sample case, use the data bound grid to display the Retail Items information in a browse mode. To save screen real estate, allow the user to switch
between the browse mode and single-record mode by using the command
button at the bottom-right corner of the screen. The data bound grid for the
sample case is shown in figure 5.18.

Data bound grid

Fig. 5.18

You can use the
data bound grid to
display informa-
tion from several
records at once.

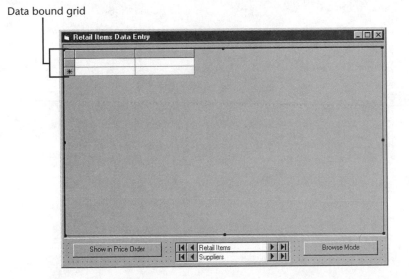

Knowing When to Use the Data Control and When to Use Code

As part of your application design, you must determine whether to use only
the data control, only code statements, or a combination of both. The following sections examine types of programs that lend themselves to each type of

programming. These are not hard-and-fast rules for development but merely examples of the uses of the various programming techniques.

Using the Data Control Alone

You may want to use the data control by itself for applications in which the user access is read only or when there is no need to add or delete records. In these cases, you don't need anything beyond the capabilities of the data control—and the ease of programming makes it an excellent choice.

The data control is also great for prototyping an application. With it, you can rapidly develop data forms and see how your data will appear. Prototype applications can be shown to a client, and adjustments or improvements can be made very quickly. (Clients are usually really impressed by prototypes.) Once the prototype is developed, you can keep the data control as the basis of your application and enhance its functionality using some additional program code. You may, however, decide to write the entire application in program code. In this case, the prototype you developed provides a detailed model from which you can work.

A more unusual application is to provide global information about a database. Suppose that you have an engineer who wants to see the statistical variation of a set of experimental data. You could write the SQL statement of your data control's RecordSource to return the minimum, maximum, and average values of the data as well as the standard deviation. These returned fields could then be bound to a set of controls for display on the form. Because only one record is returned, you may choose to hide the data control to keep the form cleaner. In this case, the bound controls make the display of the data easier than if you were working with a program.

Using a Program Alone

It is better to use a program alone when much of the data entry is done by other programs or equipment. Also, for a heavily used multiuser system, the data control may not be the best choice of techniques.

For unattended data entry from another program or from an instrument, the data control is inappropriate because it is designed only to respond to user input events. The data control performs updates only when the record movement buttons are pushed or when the data control is closed. A program, on the other hand, can be set up to read files for input on a timed basis or to read data directly from a serial port and add it to the database.

For heavily used multiuser applications, a data control may increase the possibility of record-locking conflicts because the control of the locking is not as fine as in a "program command only" application. Also, transaction processing is not as easily implemented with the data control.

Using the Data Control in Combination with a Program

Probably the best solution for many applications is to use the data control in combination with program commands. You can use the program commands to enhance the basic functionality of the data control by including such features as these:

- Adding and deleting records.

- Finding a specific record in a recordset. (The data control itself only executes Move commands; it does not use the Find or Seek commands.)

- Responding to other events of the controls (for example, click, double-click, got focus, and change).

- Transaction processing.

The next section looks at examples of some of these functions.

Enhancing the Data Control

As flexible as the data control is, it lacks a few functions that are necessary for most data entry applications. These functions were listed in the preceding section. To overcome these shortcomings, you can add the functions to the data entry screen using program commands assigned to either a command button or to events of the data control and bound controls.

Adding Record Addition and Deletion Capabilities

The next step in developing the sample application is to add the ability to add and delete records. To do this, add two command buttons to the form named Add and Delete. To make the buttons functional, add the code segments shown in listing 5.4 to the click event of the appropriate button.

Listing 5.4   Program Statements Placed in the `Click` Event of Command Buttons to Add Capabilities to the Data Entry Screen

```
'*********************************************************************
'Command to add a new record,
'place in click event of Add button
'*********************************************************************
Items.Recordset.AddNew
'*********************************************************************
'Commands to delete a record,
'placed in click event of Delete button
'*********************************************************************
Items.Recordset.Delete
Items.Recordset.MoveLast
```

As you can see, this listing did not enter a command to invoke the `Update` method (updates are done automatically by the data control whenever you move to a new record or close the form).

Note

The move command was added to the Delete button to force a move to a new record. After a record is deleted, it is no longer accessible but still shows on the screen until a move is executed. If you did not force a move and tried to access the deleted record, an error would occur.

The data entry form now looks like the one shown in figure 5.19.

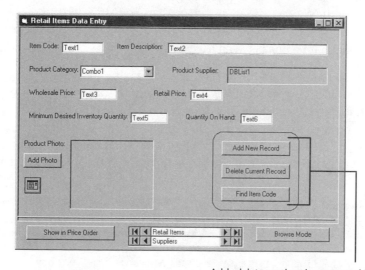

Fig. 5.19
New capabilities added to the data entry screen by adding command buttons and using program commands.

Add, delete, and seek command buttons

Data Access

Finding a Specific Record

Another enhancement to the capabilities provided by the data control is the ability to search for a specific record. To add this feature, you must use either the Find method or the Seek method of the data control recordset, depending on the recordset type. For a table, use the Seek method; for a dynaset or snapshot, use the Find method. To implement the search, add a command button to the form. This command button invokes a dialog box that requests the ID to be found and then uses the appropriate method to perform the search (see listing 5.5).

Listing 5.5 Use the Seek or Find Method to Search for a Specific Record

```
'***********************************************************************
'The variable SrchCond contains the value of the search criteria
'***********************************************************************
If Items.RecordsetType = 0 Then
  Items.Recordset.Seek ">=", SrchCond
Else
    Items.Recordset.FindFirst "Items.Recordset([Item Code]) >= " _
        & SrchCond
End If
```

Linking In Other Data

Earlier in this chapter, when you used the data bound list box, you made a link between the data in two tables. Suppose that you also want to display the name of the contact person at the supplier. You already have a data control that provides access to the supplier table, so you only have to display the data and maintain a link between the two tables.

To make the link work on the form, add a text box to the form that shows the supplier ID from the Retail Items table. Then, in the change event of the text box, add the search code shown in listing 5.6. This code takes the supplier ID from the text box and uses the FindFirst (or Seek) method on the supplier data control to find the correct record. When the pointer moves in the supplier table, the name of the contact person on the screen is updated.

Listing 5.6 Maintaining the Link between the Retail Items and Supplier Tables in the Change Event of the Supplier ID Text Box

```
'**********************************************************
'Set the find criteria to the text value of the text box.
'This value is the SupplierID from the Retail Items table.
```

```
'**********************************************************
FndCrit = "SupplierID = '" + Text8.Text + "'"
'**********************************************************
'Execute the Find method to locate the proper supplier.
'**********************************************************
Supplier.Recordset.FindFirst FndCrit
```

Using Multiple Data Controls

The last addition to the data entry screen (in the preceding section) raises some interesting programming points. First, you added another data control to the form. One obvious question is, "Why didn't you just include the additional fields in a SQL statement to generate the recordset for the original data control?" This could have been done using the following statement:

```
SELECT [Retail Items].*, Supplier.Contact FROM [Retail Items], _
    Supplier
    WHERE [Retail Items].SupplierID = Supplier.SupplierID
```

The advantage of doing this is that you wouldn't have to go through the trouble of establishing the Retail Items and Supplier link using the supplier ID text box and the change event. The downside of using the SQL statement is that the supplier information could have changed. Because you cannot set read-only properties for individual fields in the data controls recordset, you cannot prevent the update of the text boxes.

By using two data controls, you were able to protect the data in the Supplier table from unwanted changes. Another reason for using the two controls is that you can add controls to the form to switch between the Retail Items view and a Supplier view. Then you need the supplier data control to navigate through the recordset.

The other point illustrated by adding the supplier contact information is that other events can be used to change or affect the data control.

> **Note**
>
> The validate event is triggered any time the record pointer is moved to a new record, an update is issued, or the database or form is closed. The validate event passes variables that tell what action triggered the event and whether any data in the current bound controls has been changed. By placing program code in the validate event, you can perform data checking in addition to engine-level data validation. You can also perform transaction processing with code in the event. It is not required that any code be put in the validate event; it is an optional feature. For the sample case, you do not include any code in the validate event.

(continued)

The data entry screen you built in this chapter is contained on the companion disk as CHAPTER5.MAK. Running this application allows you to see the data control and the bound controls in action.

From Here...

Some of the topics mentioned in this chapter are covered in greater detail in other portions of the book. Please refer to these chapters for more information:

■ Chapter 4, "Manipulating Data with a Program," explains more about program commands and data access objects.

■ Chapter 6, "Understanding Structured Query Language (SQL)," explains more about the SQL statements necessary to create the dynasets used by the data control.

Chapter 6

Understanding Structured Query Language (SQL)

This chapter explains the basics of SQL statements as they apply to Visual Basic programming. All the examples in this chapter use an Access database. This chapter discusses both data manipulation language (DML) SQL statements and data definition language (DDL) SQL statements. Unless otherwise identified, SQL statements are of the DML type.

In this chapter, you learn how to do the following:

- Retrieve information from your database by using SQL statements

- Limit the records and field returned by a query

- Retrieve information from multiple related tables

- Modify the structure of the database by using SQL

What Is SQL?

Structured Query Language (SQL) is a specialized set of programming commands that enable the developer (or end user) to do the following kinds of tasks:

- Retrieve data from one or more tables in one or more databases.

- Manipulate data in tables by inserting, deleting, or updating records.

- Obtain summary information about the data in tables, such as totals; record counts; and minimum, maximum, and average values.

- Create, modify, or delete tables in a database (Access databases only).

- Create or delete indexes for a table (Access databases only).

SQL statements enable the developer to perform functions in one line or a few lines of code that would take 50 or 100 lines of standard BASIC code to perform.

As the name implies, Structured Query Language statements create a query that is processed by the database engine. The query defines the fields to be processed, the tables containing the fields, the range of records to be included, and, for record retrieval, the order in which the returned records are to be presented.

When retrieving records, a SQL statement usually returns the requested records in a dynaset. Recall that a dynaset is an updatable recordset that actually contains a collection of pointers to the base data. dynasets are temporary and are no longer accessible once they are closed. SQL does have a provision for the times when permanent storage of retrieved records is required.

> **Note**
>
> The Microsoft SQL syntax used in this chapter is designed to work with the Jet database engine and is compatible with ANSI SQL (there are, however, some minor differences between Microsoft and ANSI SQL). In addition, if you use SQL commands to query an external database server such as SQL Server or Oracle, read the documentation that comes with the server to verify that the SQL features you want to use are supported and that the syntax of the statements is the same.

Understanding the Parts of the SQL Statement

A SQL statement consists of three parts:

- The parameter declarations—These are optional parameters that are passed to the SQL statement by the program.

- The manipulative statement—This part of the statement tells the Query engine what kind of action to take, such as SELECT or DELETE.

- The options declarations—Tells the Query engine about any filter conditions, data groupings, or sorts that apply to the data being processed. This includes the WHERE, GROUP BY, and ORDER BY clauses.

These parts are arranged as follows:

```
[Parameters declarations] Manipulative statement [options]
```

Most of this chapter uses only the manipulative statement and the options declarations. Using these two parts of the SQL statement, you can create queries to perform a wide variety of tasks. Table 6.1 lists the five manipulative clauses and their purposes.

Table 6.1   Parts of the Manipulative Statement

Manipulative Statement	Function
DELETE FROM	Removes records from a table
INSERT INTO	Adds a group of records to a table
SELECT	Retrieves a group of records and places the records in a dynaset or table
TRANSFORM	Creates a summary table using the contents of a field as the column headers
UPDATE	Sets the values of fields in a table

Although manipulative statements tell the database engine what to do, the options declarations tell it what fields and records to process. The discussion of the optional parameters makes up the bulk of this chapter. In this chapter, you first look at how the parameters are used with the SELECT statement and then apply them to the other manipulative statements. Many of the examples in this chapter are based on the sales transaction table of the sample Triton's Treasures database originally defined in Chapter 1.

The following discussions of the different SQL statements show just the SQL statement syntax. Be aware that these statements cannot be used alone in Visual Basic. The SQL statement is always used to create a QueryDef, to create a dynaset or snapshot, or as the RecordSource property of a data control. Following the explanation of the parts of the SQL statement is an explanation of how you can actually implement these statements in your programs. In addition, look back through Chapters 4 and 5 for other examples of using SQL statements.

Using *SELECT* Statements

The SELECT statement retrieves records (or specified fields from records) and places the information in a dynaset or table for further processing by a program. The SELECT statement follows this general form:

```
SELECT [predicate] fieldlist FROM tablelist [table relations]
       [range options] [sort options] [group options]
```

> **Note**
>
> In demonstrating code statements, words in all caps are SQL keywords, and italicized words or phrases are used to indicate terms that a programmer would replace in an actual statement. For example, *fieldlist* would be replaced with Lastname, Firstname. Phrases or words inside the square brackets are optional terms.

The various components of this statement are explained in this chapter. Although a SQL statement can be greatly complex, it can also be fairly simple. The simplest form of the SELECT statement is shown here:

```
SELECT * FROM Sales
```

Defining the Desired Fields

The *fieldlist* part of the SELECT statement is used to define the fields to be included in the output recordset. You can include all fields in a table, selected fields from the table, or even calculated fields based on other fields in the table. You can also choose the fields to be included from a single table or from multiple tables.

The *fieldlist* portion of the SELECT statement takes the following form:

```
[tablename.]field1 [AS alt1][,[tablename.]field2 [AS alt2]]
```

Selecting All Fields from a Table. The *, or wild-card, parameter is used to indicate that you want to select all the fields in the specified table. The wild card is used in the *fieldlist* portion of the statement. The statement SELECT * FROM Sales, when used with the sample database you are developing, produces the output recordset shown in figure 6.1.

Selecting Individual Fields from a Table. Frequently, you need only a few fields from a table. You can specify the desired fields by including a *fieldlist* in the SELECT statement. Within the *fieldlist*, the individual fields are separated by commas. In addition, if the desired field has a space in the name, such as *Order Quantity*, the field name must be enclosed within square brackets, []. The recordset that results from the following SELECT statement is shown in figure 6.2. A recordset created with fields specified is more efficient than one created with the wild card (*), both in terms of the size of the recordset and speed of creation. As a general rule, you should limit your queries to the smallest number of fields that can accomplish your purpose.

```
SELECT [Item Code], Quantity FROM Sales
```

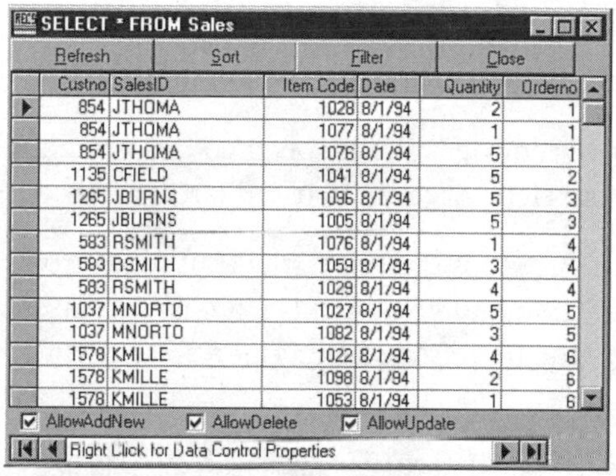

SELECT * FROM Sales

Custno	SalesID	Item Code	Date	Quantity	Orderno
854	JTHOMA	1028	8/1/94	2	1
854	JTHOMA	1077	8/1/94	1	1
854	JTHOMA	1076	8/1/94	5	1
1135	CFIELD	1041	8/1/94	5	2
1265	JBURNS	1096	8/1/94	5	3
1265	JBURNS	1005	8/1/94	5	3
583	RSMITH	1076	8/1/94	1	4
583	RSMITH	1059	8/1/94	3	4
583	RSMITH	1029	8/1/94	4	4
1037	MNORTO	1027	8/1/94	5	5
1037	MNORTO	1082	8/1/94	3	5
1578	KMILLE	1022	8/1/94	4	6
1578	KMILLE	1098	8/1/94	2	6
1578	KMILLE	1053	8/1/94	1	6

Fig. 6.1
Using * in the *`fieldlist`* parameter selects all fields from the source table.

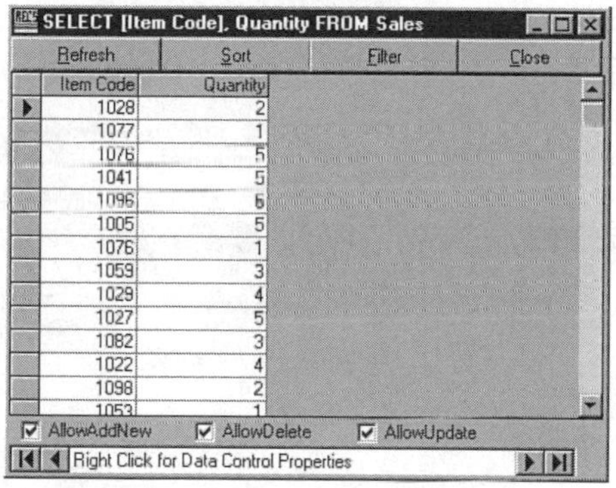

SELECT [Item Code], Quantity FROM Sales

Item Code	Quantity
1028	2
1077	1
1076	5
1041	5
1096	5
1005	5
1076	1
1059	3
1029	4
1027	5
1082	3
1022	4
1098	2
1053	1

Fig. 6.2
This recordset results from specifying individual fields in the `SELECT` statement.

Selecting Fields from Multiple Tables. As you remember from the discussions on database design in Chapter 1, you normalize data by placing it in different tables to eliminate data redundancy. When you retrieve this data for viewing or modification, you want to see all the information from the related tables. SQL allows you to combine information from various tables into a single recordset.

To select data from multiple tables, you specify three things:

- The table from which each field is selected.
- The fields from which you are selecting the data.
- The relationship between the tables.

Specify the table for each field by placing the table name and a period in front of the field name (for example, Sales.[Item Code] or Sales.Quantity). (Remember, square brackets must enclose a field name that has a space in it.) You also can use the wild-card identifier (*) after the table name to indicate that you want all the fields from that table.

To specify the tables you are using, place multiple table names (separated by commas) in the FROM clause of the SELECT statement.

The relationship between the tables is specified by either a WHERE clause or a JOIN condition. These elements are discussed later in this chapter.

The statement in listing 6.1 is used to retrieve all fields from the Sales table and the Item Description and Retail fields from the Retail Items table. These tables are related by the Item Code field. The results of the statement are shown in figure 6.3.

> **Note**
>
> The listing shows an underscore character at the end of each of the first two lines. This is a line continuation character. It is used to tell Visual Basic that the next line is still part of the same statement.

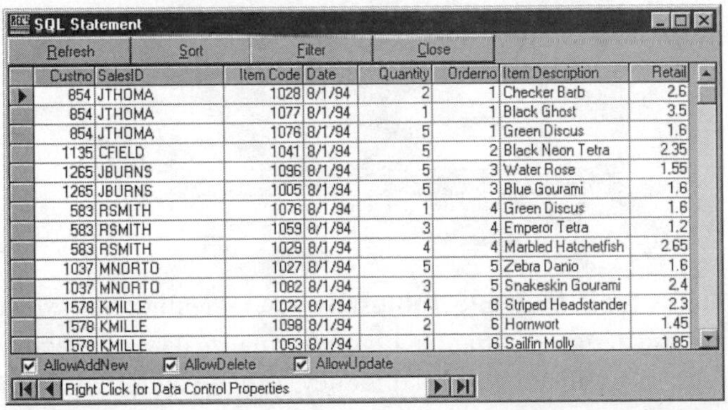

Fig. 6.3
Selecting fields from multiple tables produces a combined recordset.

Custno	SalesID	Item Code	Date	Quantity	Orderno	Item Description	Retail
854	JTHOMA	1028	8/1/94	2	1	Checker Barb	2.6
854	JTHOMA	1077	8/1/94	1	1	Black Ghost	3.5
854	JTHOMA	1076	8/1/94	5	1	Green Discus	1.6
1135	CFIELD	1041	8/1/94	5	2	Black Neon Tetra	2.35
1265	JBURNS	1096	8/1/94	5	3	Water Rose	1.55
1265	JBURNS	1005	8/1/94	5	3	Blue Gourami	1.6
583	RSMITH	1076	8/1/94	1	4	Green Discus	1.6
583	RSMITH	1059	8/1/94	3	4	Emperor Tetra	1.2
583	RSMITH	1029	8/1/94	4	4	Marbled Hatchetfish	2.65
1037	MNORTO	1027	8/1/94	5	5	Zebra Danio	1.6
1037	MNORTO	1082	8/1/94	3	5	Snakeskin Gourami	2.4
1578	KMILLE	1022	8/1/94	4	6	Striped Headstander	2.3
1578	KMILLE	1098	8/1/94	2	6	Hornwort	1.45
1578	KMILLE	1053	8/1/94	1	6	Sailfin Molly	1.85

Listing 6.1 Selecting Fields from Multiple Tables in a SQL Statement

```
SELECT Sales.*, [Retail Items].[Item Description], _
    [Retail Items].Retail
    FROM Sales, [Retail Items] _
    WHERE Sales.[Item Code]=[Retail Items].[Item Code]   _
```

> **Note**
>
> You can leave out the table name when specifying fields as long as the requested field is present only in one table in the list. However, it is very good programming practice to include the table name, both for reducing the potential for errors and for readability of your code.

Creating Calculated Fields. The example in listing 6.1 has customer order information consisting of the item ordered, quantity of the item, and the retail price. Suppose that you also want to access the total cost of the items. You can achieve this by using a calculated field in the SELECT statement. A *calculated field* can be the result of an arithmetic operation on numeric fields (for example, Price * Quantity) or the result of string operations on text fields (for example, Lastname & Firstname). For numeric fields, you can use any standard arithmetic operation (+, −, *, /, ^). For strings, you can use the concatenation operator (&). In addition, you can use Visual Basic functions to perform operations on the data in the fields (for example, you can use the MID$ function to extract a substring from a text field, the UCASE$ function to place text in uppercase letters, or the SQR function to calculate the square root of a number). Listing 6.2 shows how some of these functions can be used in the SELECT statement.

In the listing, no field name is specified for the calculated field. The Query engine will automatically assign a name such as Expr1001 for the first calculated field. The next section describes how you can specify a name for the field.

Listing 6.2   Creating a Variety of Calculated Fields with the SELECT Statement

```
'****************************************
'Calculate the total price for the items
'****************************************
SELECT [Retail Items].Retail * Sales.Quantity FROM _
      [Retail Items],Sales  _
      WHERE Sales.[Item Code]=[Retail Items].[Item Code]
'********************************************************************
'Create a name field by concatenating the Lastname and
'Firstname fields
'********************************************************************
SELECT Lastname & ', ' & Firstname FROM Customers
'********************************************************************
'Create a customer ID using the first 3 letters of the Lastname
' and Firstname fields and make all letters uppercase.
```

(continues)

Listing 6.2 Continued

```
'************************************************************
SELECT UCASE$(MID$(Lastname,1,3)) & UCASE$(MID$(Firstname,1,3)  _
    FROM Customers
'************************************************************
'Determine the square root of a number for use in a data report.
'************************************************************
SELECT Datapoint, SQR(Datapoint) FROM Labdata
```

Calculated fields are placed in the recordset as read-only fields: they cannot be updated. In addition, if you update the base data used to create the field, the changes are not reflected in the calculated field.

Note

If you use a calculated field with a data control, it is best to use a label control to show the contents of the field. This prevents the user from attempting to update the field and causing an error. You could also use a text box with the locked property set to True. (You can learn more about the data control and bound controls in Chapter 5.)

Specifying Alternative Field Names. Listing 6.2 created calculated fields to include in a recordset. For many applications, you will want to use a name for the field other than the one automatically created by the Query engine.

You can change the syntax of the SELECT statement to give the calculated field a name. You assign a name by including the AS clause and the desired name after the definition of the field (refer to the second part of listing 6.3). You can also use this technique to assign a different name to a standard field if you want.

Listing 6.3 How to Access the Value of a Calculated Field and How to Name the Field

```
'*********************************************
'Set up the SELECT statement without the name
'*********************************************
Dim NewDyn As RecordSet
SQL = "SELECT Lastname & ', ' & Firstname FROM Customers"
'*********************************************
'Create a dynaset from the SQL statement
'*********************************************
NewDyn = OldDb.OpenRecordset(SQL)
```

```
'*********************************
'Get the value of the created field
'*********************************
Person = NewDyn.Recordset(0)
'*************************************************************
'Set up the SELECT statement and assign a name to the field
'*************************************************************
SQL = "SELECT Lastname & ', ' & Firstname As Name FROM Customers"
'*********************************************
'Create a dynaset from the SQL statement
'*********************************************
NewDyn = OldDb.OpenRecordset(SQL)
'*********************************
'Get the value of the created field
'*********************************
Person = NewDyn.Recordset("Name")
```

Specifying the Data Sources

In addition to telling the database engine what information you want, you must tell it in which table to find the information. This is done with the FROM clause of the SELECT statement. Here is the general form of the FROM clause:

```
FROM table1 [IN data1] [AS alias1][,table2 [IN data2] [AS alias2]]
```

Various options of the FROM clause are discussed in the following sections.

Specifying the Table Names. The simplest form of the FROM clause is used to specify a single table. This is the form of the clause used in this statement:

```
SELECT * FROM Sales
```

The FROM clause can also be used to specify multiple tables (refer to listing 6.1). When specifying multiple tables, separate the table names with commas. Also, if a table name has an embedded space, the table name must be enclosed in square brackets [ ] (refer again to listing 6.1).

Using Tables in Other Databases. As you develop more applications, you may have to pull data together from tables in different databases. For example, you may have a ZIP code database that contains the city, state, and ZIP code for every postal code in the United States. You do not want to duplicate this information in a table for each of your database applications that requires it. The SELECT statement allows you to store that information once in its own database and pull it in as needed. To retrieve the information from a database other than the current one, you use the IN portion of the FROM clause. The SELECT statement for retrieving the ZIP code information along with the customer data is shown in listing 6.4.

Listing 6.4   Retrieving Information from More Than One Database

```
'****************************************************************
'We are working from the TRITON database which is already open.
'****************************************************************
SELECT Customers.Lastname, Customers.Firstname, Zipcode.City, _
    Zipcode.State  FROM Customers, Zipcode IN USZIPS  _
    WHERE Customers.Zip = Zipcode.Zip
```

Assigning an Alias Name to a Table. Notice the way the table name for each of the desired fields was listed in listing 6.4. Because these table names are long and there are a number of fields, the SELECT statement is fairly long. The statement gets much more complex with each field and table you add. In addition, typing long names each time increases the chances of making a typo. To alleviate this problem, you can assign the table an alias by using the AS portion of the FROM clause. Using AS, you can assign a unique shorter name to each table. This alias can be used in all the other clauses in which the table name is needed. Listing 6.5 is a rewrite of the code from listing 6.4 using the alias CS for the Customers table and ZP for the ZIP code table.

Listing 6.5   Using a Table Alias to Cut Down on Typing

```
'*********************************************************
'We use aliases to make the statement easier to enter.
'*********************************************************
SELECT CS.Lastname, CS.Firstname, ZP.City, ZP.State  _
    FROM Customers AS CS, Zipcode IN USZIPS AS ZP  _
    WHERE CS.Zip = ZP.Zip
```

Using *ALL, DISTINCT,* or *DISTINCTROW* Predicates

In most applications, you select all records that meet specified criteria. You can do this by specifying the ALL predicate in front of your field names or by leaving out any predicate specification (ALL is the default behavior). Therefore, the following two statements are equivalent:

```
SELECT * FROM Customers
SELECT ALL * FROM Customers
```

However, there may be times when you want to determine the unique values of fields. For these times, use the DISTINCT or DISTINCTROW predicate. The DISTINCT predicate causes the database engine to retrieve only one record with a specific set of field values—no matter how many duplicates exist. For a record to be rejected by the DISTINCT predicate, its values for all the selected fields must match those of another record. For example, if you were selecting first and last names, you can retrieve several people with the last name *Smith*, but you cannot retrieve multiple occurrences of *Adam Smith*.

If you want to eliminate records that are completely duplicated, use the DISTINCTROW predicate. DISTINCTROW compares the values of all fields in the table, whether or not they are among the selected fields. For the pet store example, you can use DISTINCTROW to determine which products have been ordered at least once. DISTINCTROW has no effect if the query is only on a single table.

Listing 6.6 shows the uses of DISTINCT and DISTINCTROW.

Listing 6.6   Obtaining Unique Records with the DISTINCT or DISTINCTROW Predicates

```
'*****************************
'Use of the DISTINCT predicate
'*****************************
SELECT DISTINCT [Item Code] FROM Sales
'********************************
'Use of the DISTINCTROW predicate
'********************************
SELECT DISTINCTROW [Item Code] FROM [Retail Items], Sales _
    [Retail Items] INNER JOIN Sales _
        ON [Retail Items].[Item Code]=Sales.[Item Code]
```

Setting Table Relationships

When you design a database structure, you use key fields so that you can relate the tables in the database. For example, you use a salesperson ID in the Customers table to relate to the salesperson in the Salesperson table. You do this so that you don't have to include all the salesperson data with every customer record. You use these same key fields in the SELECT statement to set the table relationships so that you can display and manipulate the related data. That is, when you view customer information, you want to see the salesperson's name, not his or her ID.

There are two ways to specify the relationships between tables:

- Use a JOIN clause—This combines two tables based on the contents of specified fields in each table and the type of JOIN.

- Use a WHERE clause—This usually is used to filter the records returned by a query, but can be used to emulate an INNER JOIN.

> **Note**
>
> Using the WHERE clause to join tables creates a read-only recordset. To create a modifiable recordset, you must use the JOIN clause.

Using a *JOIN* Clause. The basic format of the JOIN clause is as follows:

```
table1 {INNER¦LEFT¦RIGHT} JOIN table2 ON table1.key1 = table2.key2
```

The Query engine used by Visual Basic (also used by Access, Excel, and other Microsoft products) supports three types of JOIN clauses: INNER, LEFT, and RIGHT. Each of these clauses returns records that meet the JOIN condition, but each behaves differently in returning records that do not meet that condition. Table 6.2 shows the records returned from each table for the three JOIN conditions. For this discussion, *table1* is the "left" table and *table2* is the "right" table. In general, the left table is the first one specified (left side of the JOIN keyword) and the right table is the second table specified (right side of the JOIN keyword).

> **Note**
>
> You can use any comparison operator (<, <=, =, >=, >, or <>) in the JOIN clause to relate the two tables.

Table 6.2   Records Returned Based on the Type of JOIN Used

JOIN Type Table	Records from Left Table	Records from Right Table
INNER	Only records with corresponding record in right table	Only records with corresponding record in left table
LEFT	All records	Only records with corresponding record in left table
RIGHT	Only records with corresponding record in right table	All records

To further explain these concepts, consider the sample database with its Customers and Salesmen tables. In that database, you created a small information set in the tables consisting of ten customers and four salespeople. Two of the customers have no salesperson listed, and one of the salespeople has no customers (he's a new guy!). You select the same fields with each JOIN but specify an INNER JOIN, LEFT JOIN, and RIGHT JOIN (refer to listing 6.7). Figure 6.4 shows the two base data tables from which this listing is working. Figure 6.5 shows the resulting recordsets for each of the JOIN operations.

Listing 6.7   Examples of the Three Different JOIN Types

```
'***************************
'Select using an INNER JOIN
'***************************
SELECT CS.Lastname, CS.Firstname, SL.Saleslast, SL.Salesfirst _
    FROM Customers AS CS, Salesmen AS SL, _
    CS INNER JOIN SL ON CS.SalesID=SL.SalesID
'***************************
'Select using an LEFT JOIN
'***************************
SELECT CS.Lastname, CS.Firstname, SL.Saleslast, SL.Salesfirst _
    FROM Customers AS CS, Salesmen AS SL, _
    CS LEFT JOIN SL ON CS.SalesID=SL.SalesID
'***************************
'Select using an RIGHT JOIN
'***************************
SELECT CS.Lastname, CS.Firstname, SL.Saleslast, SL.Salesfirst _
    FROM Customers AS CS, Salesmen AS SL, _
    CS RIGHT JOIN SL ON CS.SalesID=SL.SalesID
```

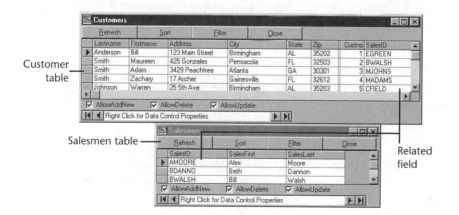

Customer table

Salesmen table

Related field

Fig. 6.4
The base tables used for the JOIN example.

Data Access

Fig. 6.5
Different records
are returned with
the different JOIN
types.

INNER JOIN

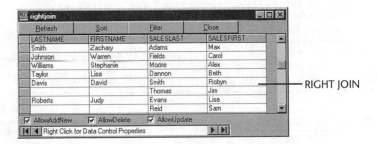

LEFT JOIN

RIGHT JOIN

Note that in addition to returning the salesperson with no customers, the RIGHT JOIN returned all customer records for each of the other salespeople, not just a single record. This is because a RIGHT JOIN is designed to return all the records from the RIGHT table even if they have no corresponding record in the LEFT table.

Using the *WHERE* Clause. You can use the WHERE clause to relate two tables. The WHERE clause has the same effect as an INNER JOIN. Listing 6.8 shows the same INNER JOIN as listing 6.7 but using the WHERE clause instead of the INNER JOIN.

Listing 6.8   A WHERE Clause Performing the Same Function as an INNER JOIN

```
'*****************************************
'Select using WHERE to relate two tables
'*****************************************
SELECT CS.Lastname, CS.Firstname, SL.Saleslast, SL.Salesfirst  _
    FROM Customers AS CS, Salesmen AS SL,  _
    WHERE CS.SalesID=SL.SalesID
```

Setting the Filter Criteria

One of the most powerful features of tablesSQL commands is that you can control the range of records to be processed by specifying a filter condition. You can use many types of filters such as Lastname = "Smith", Price < 1, or birthday between 5/1/94 and 5/31/94. Although the current discussion is specific to the use of filters in the SELECT command, the principles shown here also work with other SQL commands such as DELETE and UPDATE.

Filter conditions in a SQL command are specified using the WHERE clause. The general format of the WHERE clause is as follows:

```
WHERE logical-expression
```

There are four types of predicates (logical statements that define the condition) that you can use with the WHERE clause:

- Comparison predicate—Compares a field to a given value.

- LIKE predicate—Compares a field to a pattern (for example, A*)

- IN predicate—Compares a field to a list of acceptable values.

- BETWEEN predicate—Compares a field to a range of values.

Using the Comparison Predicate. As its name suggests, the *comparison predicate* is used to compare the values of two expressions. There are six comparison operators (the symbols that describe the comparison type) you can use; the operators and their definitions are summarized in table 6.3.

Table 6.3 Comparison Operators Used in the WHERE Clause	
Operator	**Definition**
<	Less than
<=	Less than or equal to
=	Equal to
>=	Greater than or equal to
>	Greater than
<>	Not equal to

Here is the generic format of the comparison predicate:

```
expression1 comparison-operator expression2
```

For all comparisons, both expressions must be of the same type (for example, both must be numbers or both must be text strings). Several comparisons of different types are shown in listing 6.9. The comparison values for strings and dates require special formatting. Any strings used in a comparison must be enclosed in single quotes (for example, 'Smith', 'AL'). Likewise, dates must be enclosed between pound signs (for example, #5/15/94#). The quotes and the pound signs tell the Query engine the type of data that is being passed. Note that numbers do not need to be enclosed within special characters.

Listing 6.9 Comparison Operators Used with Many Types of Data

```
'********************************************************
'Comparison of text data using customer table as source
'********************************************************
SELECT * FROM Customers WHERE Lastname='Smith'
'********************************************************
'Comparison of numeric data using Retail Items table
'********************************************************
SELECT * FROM [Retail Items] WHERE Retail<2
'*********************************************
'Comparison of date data using Sales table
'*********************************************
SELECT * FROM Sales WHERE Date>#8/15/94#
```

Using the *LIKE* Predicate. With the LIKE predicate, you can compare an expression (that is, a field value) to a pattern. The LIKE predicate allows you to make comparisons such as last names starting with *S*, titles containing

SQL, or five-letter words starting with *M* and ending with *H*. You use the wild cards * and ? to create the patterns. The actual predicates for these comparisons would be `Lastname LIKE 'S*'`, `Titles LIKE '*SQL*'`, and `Word LIKE 'M???H'`, respectively.

The `LIKE` predicate is used exclusively for string comparisons. The format of the `LIKE` predicate is as follows:

```
expression LIKE pattern
```

The *pattern*s defined for the `LIKE` predicate make use of wild-card matching and character-range lists. When you create a pattern, you can combine some of the wild cards and character lists to allow greater flexibility in the pattern definition. When used, character lists must meet three criteria:

■ The list must be enclosed within square brackets.

■ The first and last characters must be separated by a hyphen.

■ The range of the characters must be defined in ascending order (for example, a-z, and not z-a).

In addition to using a character list to match a character in the list, you can precede the list with an exclamation point to indicate that you want to exclude the characters in the list. Table 6.4 shows the type of pattern matching you can perform with the `LIKE` predicate. Listing 6.10 shows the use of the `LIKE` predicate in several `SELECT` statements.

Table 6.4   The `LIKE` Predicate Using a Variety of Pattern Matching

Wild Card	Used to Match	Example Pattern	Example Results
*	Multiple characters	S*	Smith, Sims, sheep
?	Single character	an?	and, ant, any
#	Single digit	3524#	35242, 35243
[list]	Single character in list	[c-f]	d, e, f
[!list]	Single character not in list	[!c-f]	a, b, g, h
combination	Specific to pattern	a?t*	art, antique, artist

Listing 6.10 The LIKE Predicate Provides Powerful Pattern Matching Capabilities

```
'***************************
'Multiple character wild card
'***************************
SELECT * FROM Customers WHERE Lastname LIKE 'S*'
'***************************
'Single character wild card
'***************************
SELECT * FROM Customers WHERE State LIKE '?L'
'***********************
'Character list matching
'***********************
SELECT * FROM Customers WHERE MID$(Lastname,1,1) LIKE '[a-f]'
```

Using the *IN* Predicate. The IN predicate allows you to determine whether the expression is one of several values. Using the IN predicate, you can check state codes for customers to determine whether the customer's state matches a sales region. This example is shown in the following sample code:

```
SELECT * FROM Customers WHERE State IN ('AL', 'FL', 'GA')
```

Using the *BETWEEN* Predicate. The BETWEEN predicate lets you search for expressions with values within a range of values. You can use the BETWEEN predicate for string, numeric, or date expressions. The BETWEEN predicate performs an *inclusive search*, meaning that if the value is equal to one of the endpoints of the range, the record is included. You can also use the NOT operator to return records outside the range. The form of the BETWEEN predicate is as follows:

```
expression [NOT] BETWEEN value1 AND value2
```

Listing 6.11 shows the use of the BETWEEN predicate in several scenarios.

Listing 6.11 Using the BETWEEN Predicate to Check an Expression against a Range of Values

```
'******************
'String comparison
'******************
SELECT * FROM Customers WHERE Lastname BETWEEN 'M' AND 'W'
'******************
'Numeric comparison
'******************
SELECT * FROM [Retail Items] WHERE Retail BETWEEN 1 AND 2.5
```

```
'***************
'Date comparison
'***************
SELECT * FROM Sales WHERE Date BETWEEN #8/01/94# AND #8/10/94#
'***********************
'Use of the NOT operator
'***********************
SELECT * FROM Customers WHERE Lastname NOT BETWEEN 'M' AND 'W'
```

Combining Multiple Conditions. The WHERE clause can also accept multiple conditions so that you can specify filtering criteria on more than one field. Each individual condition of the multiple conditions is in the form of the conditions described in the preceding sections. These individual conditions are then combined using the logical operators AND and OR. By using multiple condition statements, you can find all the *Smith*s in the Southeast, or find anyone whose first or last name is *Scott*. Listing 6.12 shows the statements for these examples. Figure 6.6 shows the recordset resulting from a query search for *Scott*.

Listing 6.12   Combining Multiple WHERE Conditions with AND or OR

```
'*********************************
'Find all Smiths in the Southeast
'*********************************
SELECT * FROM Customers WHERE Lastname = 'Smith' AND _
    State IN ('AL', 'FL', 'GA')
'*********************************************************
'Find all occurrences of Scott in first or last name
'*********************************************************
SELECT * FROM Customers WHERE Lastname = 'Scott' _
    OR Firstname = 'Scott'
```

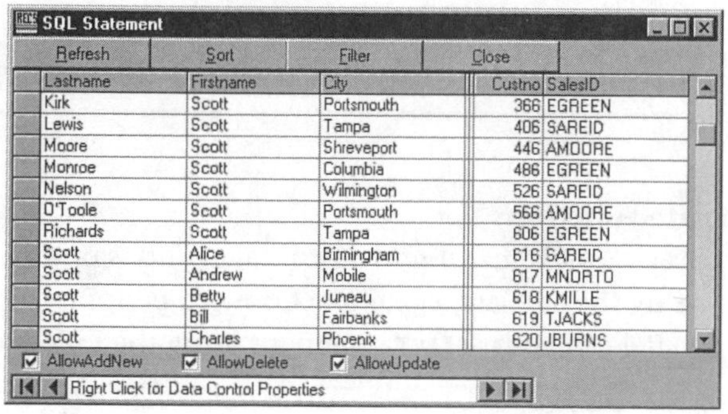

Lastname	Firstname	City	Custno	SalesID
Kirk	Scott	Portsmouth	366	EGREEN
Lewis	Scott	Tampa	406	SAREID
Moore	Scott	Shreveport	446	AMOORE
Monroe	Scott	Columbia	486	EGREEN
Nelson	Scott	Wilmington	526	SAREID
O'Toole	Scott	Portsmouth	566	AMOORE
Richards	Scott	Tampa	606	EGREEN
Scott	Alice	Birmingham	616	SAREID
Scott	Andrew	Mobile	617	MNORTO
Scott	Betty	Juneau	618	KMILLE
Scott	Bill	Fairbanks	619	TJACKS
Scott	Charles	Phoenix	620	JBURNS

☑ AllowAddNew   ☑ AllowDelete   ☑ AllowUpdate

Right Click for Data Control Properties

Fig. 6.6
You can use multiple conditions to enhance a WHERE clause.

Setting the Sort Conditions

In addition to specifying the range of records to process, you can also use the SELECT statement to specify the order in which you want the records to appear in the output dynaset. The SELECT statement controls the order in which the records are processed or viewed. Sorting the records is done by using the ORDER BY clause of the SELECT statement.

You can specify the sort order with a single field or with multiple fields. If you use multiple fields, the individual fields must be separated by commas.

The default sort order for all fields is ascending (that is, A–Z, 0–9). You can change the sort order for any individual field by specifying the DESC keyword after the field name (the DESC keyword affects only the one field, not any other fields in the ORDER BY clause). Listing 6.13 shows several uses of the ORDER BY clause. Figure 6.7 shows the results of these SELECT statements.

Note

When you are sorting records, the presence of an index for the sort field can significantly speed up the SQL query.

Listing 6.13 Specifying the Sort Order of the Output

```
'*****************
'Single field sort
'*****************
SELECT * FROM Customers ORDER BY Lastname
'*******************
'Multiple field sort
'*******************
SELECT * FROM Customers ORDER BY Lastname, Firstname
'*********************
'Descending order sort
'*********************
SELECT * FROM Customers ORDER BY Lastname DESC, Firstname
```

Using Aggregate Functions

You can use the SELECT statement to perform calculations on the information in your tables using the SQL aggregate functions. To perform the calculations, define them as a field in your SELECT statement using the following syntax:

function(expression)

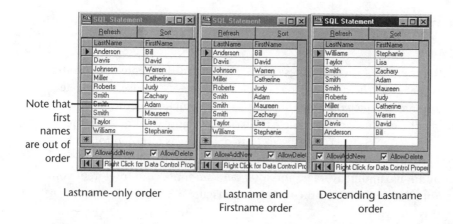

Fig. 6.7
The ORDER BY clause specifies the sort order of the dynaset.

Note that first names are out of order

Lastname-only order

Lastname and Firstname order

Descending Lastname order

The *expression* can be a single field or a calculation based on one or more fields such as Quantity * Price, or SQR(Datapoint). The Count function can also use the wild card * as the expression, because it only returns the number of records. There are 11 aggregate functions available in Microsoft SQL:

- Avg—Returns the arithmetic average of the field for the records that meet the WHERE clause.

- Count—Returns the number of records that meet the WHERE clause.

- Min—Returns the minimum value of the field for the records that meet the WHERE clause.

- Max—Returns the maximum value of the field for the records that meet the WHERE clause.

- Sum—Returns the total value of the field for the records that meet the WHERE clause.

- First—Returns the value of the field for the first record in the recordset.

- Last—Returns the value of the field for the last record in the recordset.

- StDev—Returns the standard deviation of the values of the field for the records that meet the WHERE clause.

- StDevP—Returns the standard deviation of the values of the field for the records that meet the WHERE clause.

- Var—Returns the variance of the values of the field for the records that meet the WHERE clause.

Data Access

■ VarP—Returns the variance of the values of the field for the records that meet the WHERE clause.

As with other SQL functions, these aggregate functions operate only on the records that meet the filter criteria specified in the WHERE clause. Aggregate functions are unaffected by sort order. Aggregate functions return a single value for the entire recordset unless the GROUP BY clause (described in the following section) is used. If GROUP BY is used, a value is returned for each record group. Listing 6.14 shows the SELECT statement used to calculate the minimum, maximum, average, and total sales amounts, and total item volume from the Sales table in the sample case. Figure 6.8 shows the output from this query.

Listing 6.14   Using Aggregate Functions to Provide Summary Information

```
SELECT Min(SL.Quantity * RT.Retail) AS Minsls,  _
       Max(SL.Quantity * RT.Retail) AS Maxsls,  _
       Avg(SL.Quantity * RT.Retail) AS Avgsls,  _
       Sum(SL.Quantity * RT.Retail) AS Totsls,  _
       Sum(SL.Quantity) AS Totvol _
       FROM Sales AS SL, [Retail Items] AS RT  _
       WHERE SL.[Item Code]=RT.[Item Code]
```

Fig. 6.8
A table showing the summary information from aggregate functions.

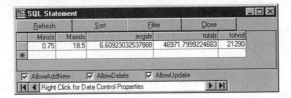

Creating Record Groups
Creating record groups allows you to create a recordset that has only one record for each occurrence of the specified field. For example, if you group the Customers table by state, you have one output record for each state. This arrangement is very useful when combined with the calculation functions described in the preceding sections. When groups are used in conjunction with aggregate functions, you can easily obtain summary data by state, salesperson, item code, or any other desired field.

Most of the time, you want to create groups based on a single field. You can, however, specify multiple fields in the GROUP BY clause. If you do, a record is returned for each unique combination of field values. You can use this technique to get sales data by salesperson and item code. Separate multiple fields in a GROUP BY clause with commas. Listing 6.15 shows an update of listing 6.14 to add groups based on the salesperson ID. Figure 6.9 shows the results of the query.

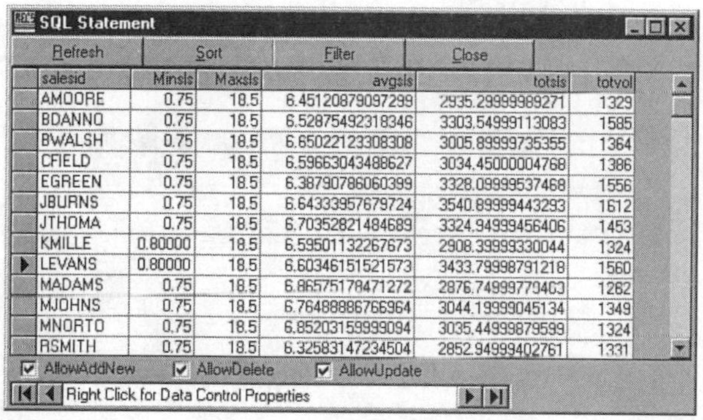

Fig. 6.9
Using GROUP BY creates a summary record for each defined group.

Listing 6.15 Using the GROUP BY Clause to Obtain Summary Information for Record Groups

```
SELECT SL.SalesID, Min(SL.Quantity * RT.Retail) AS Minsls, _
    Max(SL.Quantity * RT.Retail) AS Maxsls, _
    Avg(SL.Quantity * RT.Retail) AS Avgsls, _
    Sum(SL.Quantity * RT.Retail) AS Totsls, _
    Sum(SL.Quantity) AS Totvol _
    FROM Sales AS SL, [Retail Items] AS RT _
    WHERE SL.[Item Code]=RT.[Item Code] _
    GROUP BY SL.SalesID
```

The GROUP BY clause can also include an optional HAVING clause. The HAVING clause works similarly to a WHERE clause but examines only the field values of the returned records. The HAVING clause determines which of the selected records to display; the WHERE clause determines which records to select from the base tables. You can use the HAVING clause to display only those salespeople with total sales exceeding $3,000 for the month. This example is shown in listing 6.16; the output from this listing is shown in figure 6.10.

Listing 6.16 The HAVING Clause Filters the Display of the Selected Group Records

```
SELECT SL.SalesID, Min(SL.Quantity * RT.Retail) AS Minsls, _
       Max(SL.Quantity * RT.Retail) AS Maxsls, _
       Avg(SL.Quantity * RT.Retail) AS Avgsls, _
       Sum(SL.Quantity * RT.Retail) AS Totsls, _
       Sum(SL.Quantity) AS Totvol _
       FROM Sales AS SL, [Retail Items] AS RT _
       SL INNER JOIN RT ON SL.[Item Code]=RT.[Item Code] _
       GROUP BY SL.SalesID _
       HAVING Sum(SL.Quantity * RT.Retail) > 3000
```

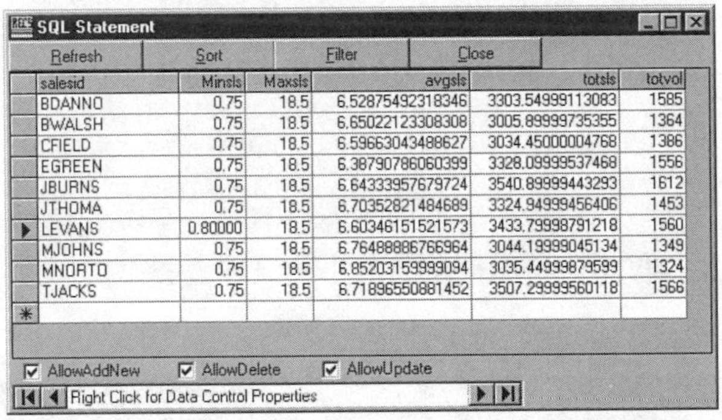

Fig. 6.10
The HAVING clause limits the display of group records.

salesid	Minsls	Maxsls	avgsls	totsls	totvol
BDANNO	0.75	18.5	6.52875492318346	3303.54999113083	1585
BWALSH	0.75	18.5	6.65022123308308	3005.89999735355	1364
CFIELD	0.75	18.5	6.59663043488627	3034.45000004768	1386
EGREEN	0.75	18.5	6.38790786060399	3328.09999537468	1556
JBURNS	0.75	18.5	6.64333957679724	3540.89999443293	1612
JTHOMA	0.75	18.5	6.70352821484689	3324.94999456406	1453
LEVANS	0.80000	18.5	6.60346151521573	3433.79998791218	1560
MJOHNS	0.75	18.5	6.76488886766964	3044.19999045134	1349
MNORTO	0.75	18.5	6.85203159999094	3035.44999879599	1324
TJACKS	0.75	18.5	6.71896550881452	3507.29999560118	1566

Creating a Table

In all the examples of the SELECT statement used earlier in this chapter, the results of the query are output to a dynaset or a snapshot. Because these recordsets are only temporary, their contents exist only as long as the recordset is open. Once a close method is used or the application is terminated, the recordset disappears (although any changes made to the underlying tables are permanent).

Sometimes, however, you may want to store the information in the recordset permanently for later use. Do so with the INTO clause of the SELECT statement. With the INTO clause, you specify the name of an output table (and optionally the database for the table) in which to store the results. You may want to do this to generate a mailing list table from your customer list. This mailing list table can then be accessed by your word processor to perform a mail merge function or to print mailing labels. Listing 6.4, earlier in this chapter, generated such a list in a dynaset. Listing 6.17 shows the same basic SELECT statement as was used in listing 6.4, but uses the INTO clause to store the information in a table.

Listing 6.17   Using the INTO Clause to Save Information to a New Table

```
SELECT CS.Firstname & ' ' & CS.Lastname, CS.Address, ZP.City, _
    ZP.State, CS.ZIP INTO Mailings FROM Customers AS CS, _
    Zipcode IN USZIPS AS ZP WHERE CS.Zip = ZP.Zip
```

Caution

The table name you specify should be a new table. If you specify the name of a table that already exists, that table is overwritten with the output of the SELECT statement.

Using the *DELETE* Statement

The DELETE statement is used to create an action query. Its purpose is to delete specific records from a table. An action query does not return a group of records into a dynaset like SELECT queries do. Instead, action queries work like program subroutines. That is, an action query performs its functions and returns to the next statement in the calling program.

The syntax of the DELETE statement is as follows:

```
DELETE FROM tablename [WHERE clause]
```

The WHERE clause is an optional parameter. If it is omitted, all the records in the target table are deleted. You can use the WHERE clause to limit the deletions to only those records that meet specified criteria. In the WHERE clause, you can use any of the comparison predicates defined in the section, "Using the Comparison Predicate," earlier in this chapter. Following is an example of the DELETE statement used to eliminate all customers who live in Florida:

```
DELETE FROM Customers WHERE State='FL'
```

Caution

Once the DELETE statement has been executed, the records are gone and cannot be recovered. The only exception is if transaction processing is used. If you are using transaction processing, you can use a ROLLBACK statement to recover any deletions made since the last BEGINTRANS statement was issued.

Using the *INSERT* Statement

The INSERT statement is another action query, like the DELETE statement. The INSERT statement is used in conjunction with the SELECT statement to add a group of records to a table. The syntax of the statement is as follows:

```
INSERT INTO tablename SELECT rest-of-select-statement
```

You build the SELECT portion of the statement exactly as explained in the first part of this chapter. The purpose of the SELECT portion of the statement is to define the records to be added to the table. The INSERT statement defines the action of adding the records and specifies the table that is to receive the records.

One use of the INSERT statement is to update tables created with the SELECT INTO statement. Suppose that you are keeping a church directory. When you first create the directory, you create a mailing list for the current member list. Each month, as new members are added, you can either rerun the SELECT INTO query and re-create the table, or you can run the INSERT INTO query and add only the new members to the existing mailing list. Listing 6.18 shows the creation of the original mailing list and the use of the INSERT INTO query to update the list.

Listing 6.18   Using the INSERT INTO Statement to Add a Group of Records to a Table

```
'*******************************
'Create a new mailing list table
'*******************************
SELECT CS.Firstname & ' ' & CS.Lastname, CS.Address, ZP.City, _
    ZP.State, CS.ZIP INTO Mailings FROM Members AS CS, _
    Zipcode IN USZIPS AS ZP WHERE CS.Zip = ZP.Zip
'*******************************
'Update the mailing list each month
'*******************************
INSERT INTO Mailings SELECT CS.Firstname & ' ' & CS.Lastname, _
    CS.Address, ZP.City, ZP.State, CS.ZIP _
    FROM Customers AS CS, Zipcode IN USZIPS AS ZP _
    WHERE CS.Zip = ZP.Zip AND CS.Memdate>Lastmonth
```

Using the *UPDATE* Statement

The UPDATE statement is another action query. It is used to change the values of specific fields in a table. The syntax of the UPDATE statement is as follows:

```
UPDATE tablename SET field = newvalue [WHERE clause]
```

You can update multiple fields in a table at one time by listing multiple *field = newvalue* clauses, separated by commas. The inclusion of the WHERE *clause* is optional. If it is excluded, all records in the table are changed.

Listing 6.19 shows two examples of the UPDATE statement. The first example changes the salesperson ID for a group of customers, as happens when a salesperson leaves the company and his or her accounts are transferred to someone else. The second example changes the retail price of all retail sales items, as can be necessary to cover increased operating costs.

Listing 6.19   Using the UPDATE Statement to Change Field Values for Many Records at Once

```
'**********************************************
'Change the SalesID for a group of customers
'**********************************************
UPDATE Customers SET SalesID = 'EGREEN' WHERE SalesID='JBURNS'
'*************************************************************
'Increase the retail price of all items by five percent
'*************************************************************
UPDATE [Retail Items] SET Retail = Retail * 1.05
```

Using Data Definition Language Statements

Data definition language (DDL) statements allow you to create, modify, and delete tables and indexes in a database with a single statement. For many situations, these statements take the place of the data access object methods described in Chapter 3, "Implementing the Database Design." However, there are some limitations to using the DDL statements. The main limitation is that these statements are supported only for Jet databases; remember that data access objects can be used for any database accessed with the Jet engine. The other limitation of DDL statements is that they support only a small subset of the properties of the table, field, and index objects. If you need to specify properties outside of this subset, you must use the methods described in Chapter 3.

Defining Tables with DDL Statements

Three DDL statements are used to define tables in a database:

- CREATE TABLE—Defines a new table in a database.

- ALTER TABLE—Changes the structure of the table.

- DROP TABLE—Deletes a table from the database.

Creating a Table

To create a table with the DDL statements, you create a SQL statement containing the name of the table and the names, types, and sizes of each field in the table. The following code shows how to create the Orders table of the sample case.

```
CREATE TABLE Orders (Orderno LONG, Custno LONG, SalesID TEXT (6), _
        OrderDate DATE, Totcost SINGLE)
```

Notice that when you specify the table name and field names, you do not have to enclose the names in quotation marks. However, if you want to specify a name with a space in it, you must enclose the name in square brackets (for example, [Last name]).

When you create a table, you can specify only the field names, types, and sizes. You cannot specify optional parameters such as default values, validation rules, or validation error messages. Even with this limitation, the DDL CREATE TABLE statement is a powerful tool you can use to create many of the tables in a database.

Modifying a Table

By using the ALTER TABLE statement, you can add a field to an existing table or delete a field from the table. When adding a field, you must specify the name, type, and (if necessary) the size of the field. You add a field using the ADD COLUMN clause of the ALTER TABLE statement. To delete a field, you only need to specify the field name and use the DROP COLUMN clause of the statement. As with other database modification methods, you cannot delete a field used in an index or a relation. Listing 6.20 shows how to add and then delete a field from the Orders table created in the preceding section.

Listing 6.20   Using the ALTER TABLE Statement to Add or Delete a Field from a Table

```
'***************************************************
'Add a shipping charges field to the "Orders" table
'***************************************************
ALTER TABLE Orders ADD COLUMN Shipping SINGLE
'*********************************
'Delete the shipping charges field
'*********************************
ALTER TABLE Orders DROP COLUMN Shipping
```

Deleting a Table

You can delete a table from a database using the DROP TABLE statement. The following simple piece of code shows how to get rid of the Orders table. Use caution when deleting a table; the table and all its data are gone forever once the command has been executed.

```
DROP TABLE Orders
```

Defining Indexes with DDL Statements

You can use two DDL statements with indexes:

- CREATE INDEX—Defines a new index for a table.

- DROP INDEX—Deletes an index from a table.

Creating an Index

You can create a single-field or multifield index with the CREATE INDEX statement. To create the index, you must give the name of the index, the name of the table for the index, and at least one field to be included in the index. You can specify ascending or descending order for each field. You can also specify that the index is a primary index for the table. Listing 6.21 shows how to create a primary index on customer number, and a two-field index with the sort orders specified. These indexes are set up for the Customers table of the sample case.

Listing 6.21   Create Several Types of Indexes with the CREATE INDEX Statement

```
'*******************************************
'Create a primary index on customer number
'*******************************************
CREATE INDEX Custno ON Customers (Custno) WITH PRIMARY
'*****************************************************************
'Create a two field index with ascending order on Lastname and
'    descending order on Firstname.
'*****************************************************************
CREATE INDEX Name2 ON Customers (Lastname ASC, Firstname DESC)
```

Deleting an Index

Getting rid of an index is just as easy as creating one. To delete an index from a table, use the DROP INDEX statement as shown in the following example. These statements delete the two indexes created in listing 6.21. Notice that you must specify the table name for the index you want to delete.

```
DROP INDEX Custno ON Customers
DROP INDEX Name2 ON Customers
```

Using SQL

As stated at the beginning of the chapter, you cannot place a SQL statement by itself in a program. It must be part of another function. This part of the chapter describes the various methods used to implement the SQL statements you can create.

Executing an Action Query

The Jet engine provides an execute method as part of the database object. The execute method tells the engine to process the SQL query against the database. An action query can be executed by specifying the SQL statement as part of the execute method for a database. An action query can also be used to create a QueryDef. Then the query can be executed on its own. Listing 6.22 shows how both of these methods are used to execute the same SQL statement.

Listing 6.22   Execute a SQL Statement Using the Database Execute or Query Execute Method

```
Dim OldDb AS Database, NewQry AS QueryDef
'*********************************************************
'Define the SQL statement and assign it to a variable
'*********************************************************
SQLstate = "UPDATE Customers SET SalesID = 'EGREEN'"
SQLstate = SQLstate + " WHERE SalesID='JBURNS'"
'*******************************************
'Use the database execute to run the query
'*******************************************
OldDb.Execute SQLstate
'*****************************************
'Create a QueryDef from the SQL statement
'*****************************************
Set NewQry = OldDb.CreateQueryDef("Change Sales", SQLstate)
'**************************************
'Use the query execute to run the query
'**************************************
NewQry.Execute
'*********************************************************
'Run the named query with the database execute method
'*********************************************************
OldDb.Execute "Change Sales"
```

Creating a *QueryDef*

Creating a QueryDef allows you to name your query and store it in the database with your tables. You can create either an action query or a retrieval query (one that uses the SELECT statement). Once the query is created, you can call it by name for execution (shown in the previous section, "Executing an Action Query") or for creation of a dynaset (as described in the following section). Listing 6.22 shows how to create a QueryDef called Change Sales that is used to update the salesperson ID for a group of customers.

Creating *dynasets* and *snapshots*

To use the SELECT statement to retrieve records and store them in a dynaset or snapshot, it must be used in conjunction with the OpenRecordset method. Using the OpenRecordset method, you specify the type of recordset with the options parameter. With this method, you can either use the SELECT statement directly or use the name of a retrieval query that you have previously defined. Listing 6.23 shows these two methods of retrieving records.

Listing 6.23   Using the Create Methods to Retrieve the Records Defined by a SELECT Statement

```
Dim OldDb As Database, NewQry As QueryDef, NewDyn As Recordset
Dim NewSnap As Recordset
'**********************************************************
'Define the SELECT statement and store it to a variable
'**********************************************************
SQLstate = "SELECT RI.[Item Description], SL.Quantity,"
SQLstate = SQLstate & " RI.Retail, _
     SL.Quantity * RI.Retail AS Subtot"
SQLstate = SQLstate & "FROM [Retail Items] AS RI, Sales AS SL"
SQLstate = SQLstate & "WHERE SL.[Item Code]=RI.[Item Code]"
'***********************
'Create dynaset directly
'***********************
Set NewDyn = OldDb.OpenRecordset(SQLstate, dbOpenDynaset)
'***************
'Create QueryDef
'***************
Set NewQry = OldDb.CreateQueryDef("Get Subtotals", SQLstate)
NewQry.Close
'*****************************
'Create snapshot from querydef
'*****************************
Set NewSnap = OldDb.OpenRecordset("Get Subtotals", dbOpenSnapshot)
```

In addition to the use of SELECT statements to create dynasets and snapshots, the comparison WHERE and ORDER BY clauses are used in setting dynaset properties. The filter property of a dynaset is a WHERE statement without the WHERE keyword. When setting the filter property, you can use all the predicates described in the section, "Using the WHERE Clause," earlier in this chapter. In a like manner, the sort property of a dynaset is an ORDER BY clause without the ORDER BY keywords.

Using SQL Statements with the Data Control

The data control uses the RecordSource property to create a recordset when the control is loaded. The RecordSource may be a table, a SELECT statement, or a predefined query. Therefore, the entire discussion on the SELECT statement (in the first part of this chapter) applies to the creation of the recordset used with a data control.

> **Note**
>
> When you specify a table name for the RecordSource property, Visual Basic uses the name to create a SELECT statement such as this:
>
> ```
> SELECT * FROM table
> ```

Creating SQL Statements

When you create and test your SQL statements, you can program them directly into your code and run the code to see whether they work. This process can be very time-consuming and frustrating, especially for complex statements. There are, however, three easier ways of developing SQL statements that may be available to you:

- The VISDATA application that ships with Visual Basic.
- The Data Manager Add-in that comes with Visual Basic.
- Microsoft Access (if you have a copy).

> **Note**
>
> Users of Microsoft Excel or Office also have access to Microsoft Query, the tool in Access.

The VISDATA application, the Data Manager, and Access all have Query Builders that can help you create SQL queries. They provide dialog boxes for selecting the fields to include, and help you with the various clauses. When you have finished testing a query with either application, you can store the query as a QueryDef in the database. This query can then be executed by name from your program. As an alternative, you can copy the code from the Query Builder into your program using standard cut and paste operations.

> **Note**
>
> The VISDATA application is more flexible in the types of SQL statements it can handle than the Data Manager. However, for simply creating recordsets, the Data Manager works quite well. Also, the Query Builder in the VISDATA application helps you create complex queries.

Using the VISDATA Application

The VISDATA application allows you to open a database, construct and test SQL queries, and, if desired, create a QueryDef from the debugged SQL statement. To use the VISDATA application, you must run Visual Basic and load the .VBP file. This file is the VISDATA.VBP file found in the sample applications subdirectory of Visual Basic. You can also compile the VISDATA application and add it to one of your Windows program groups. (The authors prefer the latter method.) Using the method you prefer, start the VISDATA application. Then choose File, Open Database; when the dialog box appears, choose a database from the list of available databases. Once the database is opened, a list of tables and queries in the database appears in the left panel. The VISDATA application with the Triton database open is shown in figure 6.11.

To develop and test SQL statements, first enter the statement in the text box of the SQL dialog box (the one on the right of fig. 6.11). When you are ready to test the statement, click the Execute SQL button. If you are developing a retrieval query, a dynaset is created and the results are displayed in a data control (or a grid) if the statement has no errors. If you are developing an action query, a message box appears, telling you that the execution of the query is complete (again, assuming that the statement is correct). If you have an error in your statement, a message box appears informing you of the error.

Fig. 6.11
You can use the
VISDATA applica-
tion to develop
SQL queries.

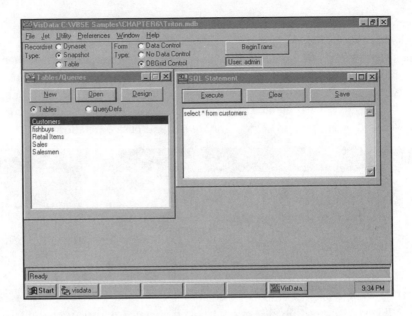

The VISDATA application also includes a Query Builder that allows you to
create a query by following these steps:

1. Select the tables to include from the select tables list.

2. Select the fields to include from the select fields list.

3. Set the WHERE clause (if any) using the Field Name, Operator, and Value
   drop-down lists at the top of the dialog box.

4. Set the table JOIN conditions (if any) by clicking the Set Table Joins
   command button.

5. Set a single-field ORDER BY clause (if any) by selecting the field from the
   Order By drop-down box and selecting either the Asc or Desc option.

6. Set a single GROUP BY field (if any) by selecting the field from the Group
   By drop-down box.

Once you have set the Query Builder parameters, you can run the query,
display the SQL statement, or copy the query to the SQL statement window.
The Query Builder provides an easy way to become familiar with constructing
SELECT queries. Figure 6.12 shows the Query Builder screen.

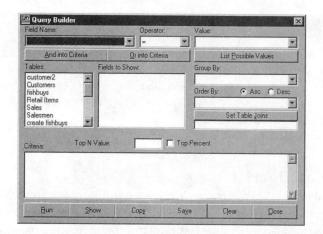

Fig. 6.12
You can use VISDATA's Query Builder to create SQL statements.

When you have developed the query to your satisfaction (either with the Query Builder or by typing the statement directly), you can save the query as a QueryDef in your database. In your Visual Basic code, you can then reference the name of the query you created. Alternatively, you can copy the query from VISDATA and paste it into your application code.

Using Microsoft Access

If you have a copy of Microsoft Access, you can use its Query Builder to graphically construct queries. You can then save the query as a QueryDef in the database and reference the query name in your Visual Basic code.

Optimizing SQL Performance

Developers always want to get the best possible performance from every aspect of their application. Wanting high performance out of SQL queries is no exception. Fortunately, there are several methods you can use to optimize the performance of your SQL queries.

Using Indexes

The Microsoft Jet database engine uses an optimization technology called Rushmore. Under certain conditions, Rushmore uses available indexes to try to speed up queries. To take maximum advantage of this arrangement, you can create an index on each of the fields you typically use in a WHERE clause or a JOIN condition. This is particularly true of key fields used to relate tables (for example, the Custno and SalesID fields in the sample database). An index also works better with comparison operators than with the other types of WHERE conditions such as LIKE or IN.

> **Note**
>
> Only certain types of queries are optimizable by Rushmore. For a query to use Rushmore optimization, the WHERE condition must use an indexed field. In addition, if you use the LIKE operator, the expression should begin with a character, not a wild card. Rushmore works with Jet databases and FoxPro and dBASE tables. Rushmore does not work with ODBC databases.

Compiling Queries

Compiling a query refers to creating a QueryDef and storing it in the database. If the query already exists in the database, the command parser does not have to generate the query each time it is run, and this increases execution speed. If you have a query that is frequently used, create a QueryDef for it.

Keeping Queries Simple

When you are working with a lot of data from a large number of tables, the SQL statements can become quite complex. Complex statements are much slower to execute than simple ones. Also, if you have a number of conditions in WHERE clauses, this increases complexity and slows execution time. Keep statements as simple as possible. If you have a complex statement, consider breaking it into multiple smaller operations. For example, if you have a complex JOIN of three tables, you may be able to use the SELECT INTO statement to create a temporary table from two of the three, then use a second SELECT statement to perform the final JOIN. There are no hard-and-fast rules for how many tables is too many or how many conditions make a statement too complex. If you are having performance problems, try some different ideas and find the one that works best.

Another way to keep things simple is to try to avoid pattern matching in a WHERE clause. Because pattern matching does not deal with discrete values, pattern matching is much harder to optimize. In addition, patterns that use wild cards for the first character are much slower than those that specifically define that character. For example, if you are looking for books about SQL, finding ones with *SQL* anywhere in the title (pattern = "*SQL*") requires looking at every title in the table. On the other hand, looking for titles that start with *SQL* (pattern = "SQL*") allows you to skip over most records. If you had a Title index, the search would go directly to the first book on SQL.

Passing SQL Statements to Other Database Engines

Visual Basic has the capability of passing a SQL statement through to an ODBC database server such as SQL Server. When you pass a statement through, the Jet engine does not try to do any processing of the query, but sends the query to the server to be processed. Remember, however, that the SQL statement must conform to the SQL syntax of the host database.

To use the pass-through capability, set the option parameter in the `OpenRecordset` or `Execute` methods to the value of the constant `dbSQLPassThrough`.

> **Note**
>
> The project file, CHAPTER6.VBP, on the companion disk contains many of the listings used in this chapter. Each listing is assigned to a command button. Choosing the command button creates a dynaset using the SQL statement in the listing and displays the results in a data bound grid. The form containing the grid also has a text box that shows the SQL statement.

From Here...

To see how SQL statements are used in programs and with the data control, refer to the following chapters:

- Chapter 4, "Manipulating Data with a Program," explains how to write data access programs.

- Chapter 5, "Using Visual Basic's Data and Bound Controls," explains how to use the data control.

Chapter 7

Creating Multiuser Programs

Previous chapters discussed several aspects of database programming, focusing mainly on developing an application that would be used by a single user on a stand-alone PC. However, many of today's database applications must be written for a network environment, where multiple users will be reading, modifying, deleting, and adding to the data in the database. This presents an additional set of challenges for the database developer.

The main considerations that are involved in multiuser program development are the following:

- Database access

- Database security

- Data currency

- Record-locking to prevent simultaneous update attempts

- Application performance

Even if you don't develop applications for a network environment, you still need to be aware of some of the multiuser considerations. In Windows or any other multitasking environment, it is possible for two programs on the same machine to try to access the same data. As an example, consider a PC monitoring a manufacturing process. You might have one program receiving the process data from instruments and storing the data in a database. You would then have another program for generating reports on the data, or modifying erroneous or abnormal data points. Although both programs may be run by the same user on the same machine, they appear to the database to be multiple users of the data.

Determining the multiuser needs of the application is part of the design process. And, as with other aspects of programming, a good design will help tremendously in producing a good and efficient application.

In this chapter, you learn about the following:

- Controlling the access of users to the database

- Using locking to keep one user from changing a record while another user is using it

- Using Jet engine security features

- Dealing with some common database errors

Data Access

Controlling data access involves placing restrictions on part or all of a database. Data access restrictions may be put in place as either user restrictions or function restrictions.

You need user restrictions when you want to prevent certain people (or, as a corollary, allow only certain people) from looking at sensitive information. An example would be a payroll system, where most people would be allowed to view the names of employees, but only a select few would be able to see or modify the actual pay information. These restrictions are usually handled through user IDs and passwords, and are the basis of data security.

Function restrictions, on the other hand, place limits on specific parts of a program, regardless of who the user is. An example of this would be opening a price table in read-only mode in an order-entry system. This would be done so that a user could not inadvertently change the price of an item while processing an order.

There are two ways of handling the restrictions in an application: programmatic controls and database engine controls. A *programmatic control* is one that the developer puts into the application itself. *Engine-level controls* restrict any program trying to access the information in the database.

Using a Database Exclusively

The most restrictive limit that can be placed on a database is to open it exclusively. This prevents any other user or program from gaining access to any information in the database while it is in use. Because this method is so restrictive, it should be used only for operations that affect the entire database. These operations include

- Compacting a database.

- Updating entire tables (for example, using the UPDATE query).

- Changing the structure of the database by adding or deleting tables, fields, or indexes.

Within a program, you can open a database exclusively using the options portion of the OpenDatabase functions, as shown in the following code.

```
Dim OldDb As Database, OldWs As Workspace
Set OldDb = OldWs.OpenDatabase("A:\TRITON.MDB,True,False")
```

If the database is not in use, the database will be opened and no one else will be able to access it until it is closed. If the database is in use, an error will be returned. (Handling errors is discussed later in this chapter in the section "Handling Errors and Conflicts.")

Denying Table Access to Others

A less restrictive form of locking part of a database is to deny other users or programs access to the table in use by your program function. You can do this using the options of the OpenRecordset method to deny read and/or write access to the information with which you will be working. Similarly, you can deny write access to the information in a dynaset using the options of the OpenRecordset method.

Caution

When you use the deny options on a recordset, it locks out other users from the base tables used to create the dynaset.

As with exclusive access, these options should be used only for administrative functions, when you don't want others viewing or updating information during the process.

Using the Deny Read Option (*dbDenyRead*)

The dbDenyRead option for the OpenRecordset method prevents other users from looking at the data in the affected table until you close the table. You would use this option if you needed to update information in the entire table, such as a global price increase. The following code shows the use of this option:

```
Dim OldTbl As Recordset
lopt = dbDenyRead
Set OldTbl = OldDb.OpenRecordset("Retail Items", _
dbOpenTable, lopt)
```

> **Note**
>
> The dbDenyRead option is available only for table type recordsets. It cannot be used with dynasets or snapshots.

Using the Deny Write Option (*dbDenyWrite*)

The dbDenyWrite option used in the OpenRecordset methods also restricts other users' access to information. In this case, however, the user may view but not update information in the affected table(s). Again, other users' access is restricted only until you close the table or dynaset. You might use the dbDenyWrite option if you are inserting new records into a table, but not making changes to existing records. The dbDenyWrite option is available for both table and dynaset type recordsets. Listing 7.1 shows the use of the dbDenyWrite option for the two functions.

Listing 7.1   Use dbDenyWrite to Prevent Others from Updating Tables While You Are Working with Them

```
Dim OldTbl As Recordset, NewDyn As Recordset
lopt = dbDenyWrite
'*****************************************
' Open a table with the dbDenyWrite option.
'*****************************************
Set OldTbl = OldDb.OpenRecordset("Retail Items",dbOpenTable,lopt)
'*******************************************
' Create a dynaset with the dbDenyWrite option.
'*******************************************
lopt = dbDenyWrite
SQLSel = "Select * From Sales"
Set NewDyn = OldDb.OpenRecordset(SQLSel, dbOpenDynaset, lopt)
```

Using Read-Only Tables

Using the deny options does restrict other users' access to information in the database, but only if they open a table while you are using it with one of the options in effect. There will often be functions in your applications that have data you do not want the user to be able to modify. There will also be some tables that you do not want modified except by certain people. In these cases, you can open a table or dynaset as a read-only recordset, or you can use a snapshot.

Using Lookup Tables

One example of read-only tables is a *lookup table*. A lookup table contains reference information that is necessary for the user to see, but that the user does not need to change. For instance, your application might use a ZIP code table for a mailing list application or a price table for an order-entry system. In either of these cases, you would open the table in read-only mode using the options as shown in listing 7.2. Unlike the deny options, the read-only option does not restrict other users' access to the information.

Listing 7.2   Use the Read-Only Option to Prevent a User from Modifying Data

```
Dim OldTbl As Recordset
lopt = dbReadOnly
Set OldTbl = OldDb.OpenRecordset("Zip Code", dbOpenTable, lopt)
```

Using *snapshots*

Another way to restrict a program function to read-only is to use a snapshot for the recordset. snapshots are always read-only. A snapshot can be used when data in the base tables is not being frequently changed by others, or when a point-in-time look at the data is sufficient. snapshots are usually used for reporting functions. An advantage to using snapshots is that they are stored in memory. Therefore, some operations using snapshots are faster than the same operations using tables or dynasets. However, because of the memory requirements for a snapshot and the time that it takes to load the data into memory, snapshots are best used for queries that return fewer than 200 records.

Restricting Specific Users

Finally, you may have occasion to want to restrict certain users to read-only access, no matter what program functions they are performing. This can be done only through the Jet security system. These security features are described later in this chapter in the section "Jet Security Features."

Record-Locking Schemes

The features described in the preceding section place restrictions on an entire table or even the entire database. These features are useful in multiuser programming but are often too restrictive for some aspects of an application. One of the biggest considerations in multiuser programming is assuring that a record is not in use by another user at the same time that you are trying to update it. This is done through the use of *record locks*. A record lock temporarily limits the access of other users to a specific record or group of records.

In a typical application, a record lock is set while a user updates the data in the record, and then is released after the update is completed. The developer must take into account several considerations in the use of record locks. These are the following:

- What to do if the record cannot be locked (for example, if another user is accessing the record).

- How to prevent a user from keeping a record locked for too long.

- Whether to lock the record when the user first accesses it or only when the changes are being written to the database.

How you handle these considerations will have an impact on many aspects of the application development. Therefore, you should address these as much as possible in the design phase of the application.

Page-Locking versus Record-Locking

The Jet engine does not support true record-locking. In record-locking, only the individual record currently being accessed by the user is locked. Instead, Jet uses a page-locking scheme. Jet reads data in pages of 2K (2048 bytes). When it places a lock on a record, it locks the entire page containing the record.

What this means to the developer and users is that multiple records are locked each time a lock is issued. The number of records locked depends on the size of each record. For example, each record in the customer table of the sample database is 230 bytes long. This would mean that nine records would be locked each time. On the other hand, the sales table has records that are only 30 bytes long, so each record lock would affect 68 records.

When a page is locked by one user, another user cannot modify any records on that page (although the other user can read the records), although the first user is working with only one of the records. This aspect of page-locking requires you to be even more careful in the application of record locks because it increases the chances of a conflict between users.

Visual Basic has no commands to specifically request a record lock. Instead, the record locks are automatically created and released when the Edit and

Update methods are used. Visual Basic supports two locking methods: pessimistic and optimistic.

Pessimistic Locking

Pessimistic locking locks the page containing a record as soon as the Edit method is used on that record. The lock on the page is released when the Update method is used and the data is written to the file. The advantage of this method is that it prevents other users from changing the data in a record while you are editing it. The disadvantage is that it keeps the record locked for a longer period of time. In the worst case, a user could open a record for editing, place a lock on it, then head out to lunch. This could keep other users from editing that record, or any others on the same page, for a long time.

Optimistic Locking

Optimistic locking locks the page containing a record only when the Update method is invoked. The lock on the page is immediately released when the update operation is completed. The advantage of optimistic locking is that the lock is on the page for only a short period of time, reducing the chance that another user may try to access the same data page while the lock is in place. The disadvantage is that it is possible for another user to change the data in the record between the time the Edit and Update methods are used. If the data has changed in that time period, VB will issue an error message.

Which Locking Method to Use and When

For most database applications, optimistic locking is the better choice of the two methods. The probability that someone else will change or delete the record you are working on is less than the probability that someone will try to access a record on the page that you have locked. If, however, you have an application where many users are accessing and editing records simultaneously, you may want to use pessimistic locking to ensure that the record is not changed while you are performing your edits. In this case, you will want to put some method in place to limit the time that the record is locked.

Pessimistic locking is the default method used by Visual Basic. To set the method of record-locking, you must set the Lockedits property of the table or dynaset with which you are working. Setting the property to True gives you pessimistic locking. Setting the property to False yields optimistic locking. Listing 7.3 shows how to set the Lockedits property for pessimistic and optimistic locking, respectively.

Data Access

Listing 7.3   Set the Recordset's Lockedits Property to Choose the Record-Locking Method

```
Dim OldTbl As Recordset
'****************************************
'Set the locking method to pessimistic
'****************************************
OldTbl.LockEdits = True
'****************************************
'Set the locking method to optimistic
'****************************************
OldTbl.LockEdits = False
```

Releasing Locks

As stated previously, the record locks are released automatically when the Update method has completed. However, releasing record locks is a background process, and there are times when other activities are occurring so rapidly that the database does not have time to catch up. If you are developing a data-entry-intensive program, you may need to pause the processing in the application momentarily. You can do this with the Idle method of the database engine.

The Idle method pauses the application and allows the database engine to catch up on its housekeeping work. The following line shows the syntax of the Idle method:

```
DBEngine.Idle dbFreeLocks
```

Using the Data Control

Since the data control uses tables and/or dynasets (the default) as its record source, the same locking schemes mentioned previously are used with the data control. Pessimistic locking is the default; therefore, as each record is accessed, the data control automatically performs the Edit method, which in turn automatically locks the record's page. When you move from one record to another, the lock on the current record is released by the Update method, and a lock is placed on the next record by the Edit method. In a multiuser system where you want to use optimistic locking, you will need to change the locking scheme of the data control. You do this by adding a LockEdits statement (see listing 7.3) to the Activate event of the form containing the data control.

Note

You must be careful when using transactions in a multiuser environment. This is because any record locks that are set by the Edit or Update method are not released until the transaction is committed or rolled back. Therefore, it is best to keep transactions as short as possible to avoid a large number of records being locked for a long period of time. In addition, you should be careful when using cascaded updates or deletes, because these create more transactions and therefore more locks.

Jet Security Features

Another consideration of multiuser database programming is database security. Since a network environment may allow other people access to your database file, you may want to use methods to prevent them from viewing specific information in your database, or possibly prevent them from viewing any of the information.

The Jet engine provides a database security model based on user IDs and passwords. In this model, you may assign to individual users or groups of users permissions to the entire database, or any parts of the database. As each user is added to the security file, you must assign him to one or more user groups. He then inherits the permissions of that group. In addition, you may assign other permissions to the user.

If you are working with a secured database, you must do three things to gain access to the database from your VB program. These are the following:

- Create an .INI file for your program that tells the program the name of the system database.

- Run the IniPath method of the database engine to tell the program where the .INI file is located.

- Use the CreateWorkspace method with the workspace name, user ID, and user password specified to create a workspace to contain the database.

Listing 7.4 shows the syntax for these statements.

Listing 7.4   To Gain Access to a Secured Database, You Must Specify the Location of the System Database, and Include the User ID and Password in Your `CreateWorkspace` Method

```
'********************************************
'Statements to be included in the INI file.
'********************************************
[Options]
SystemDB=C:\VB4\test1.mda
'**********************************************
'Set the location of the application INI file
'**********************************************
DBEngine.IniPath = "C:\VB4\TEST1.INI"
'****************************
'Set the user ID and password
'****************************
DBEngine.CreateWorkspace ("WORKNAME", "MIKEMCKE", "BESTGUESS")
```

Database Permissions

Within the Jet security system, there are two database-level permissions that may be set. These are Run/Open and Open Exclusive. The Run/Open permission is required for anyone who needs access to the database. Without it, a user cannot open a database for any function. The Open Exclusive permission lets a user open the database exclusively. This permission should be given only to administrative users. Otherwise, another user of an application may inadvertently lock the entire database.

Table Permissions

Although database permissions affect the entire database (and every table in it), you will often need finer control over the access of users to individual tables. The Jet engine allows you to set table-level permissions for any table in a database. As with the database permissions, the table permissions can be assigned to individual users or groups of users. There are seven table-level permissions available with the Jet engine. These are the following:

- Read design—Allows the user to view the structure of the table.

- Modify design—Allows the user to change the structure of the table.

- Administer—Allows the user full control over the table.

- Read data—Allows the user to read information from the table, but not to make any changes.

- Modify data—Allows the user to modify existing data, but not to add or delete data.

- Insert data—Allows the user to add new data to the table.

- Delete data—Allows the user to remove data from the table.

The read and modify design permissions allow the user to work with the structure of the table. The administer permission gives a user full access to a table, including table-deletion capabilities. The four data permissions control the type of access a user has to the actual data in the table. These permissions may be assigned by table, and different users may be granted different access rights to each table.

Setting Up the Security System

Visual Basic has no means of creating the system database file (usually SYSTEM.MDA) that is needed for the security system. This file can only be created using Microsoft Access. Access also provides the easiest means of establishing and modifying user IDs and setting database and table permissions. However, from Visual Basic, you can create new user IDs, assign users to existing groups, and delete users as described in the following list:

- To add a new user, you create the user object by specifying the user name, user ID, and password. You then append the new user to the workspace. This will add the new user to the system database that was in use when the workspace was created.

- To add a user to an existing user group, you create the user object, then add the user to the Groups collection.

- To delete a user, you use the delete method for the Users collection of the workspace.

Each of these activities is shown in listing 7.5.

Listing 7.5   You Can Perform Some Security System Maintenance Using Commands from Visual Basic

```
'****************************************
'Add a new user to the system database
'****************************************
Dim OldWs As Workspace, NewUser As User, NewGrp As Group
DBEngine.IniPath = "C:\VB4\TEST1.INI"
Set OldWs = DBEngine.Workspaces(0)
Set NewUser = OldWs.CreateUser("BJONES", "44587", "HOOPS")
OldWs.Users.Append NewUser
'**************************
```

(continues)

Listing 7.5   Continued

```
'Add a user to a user group
'***************************
Dim OldWs As Workspace, NewUser As User, NewGrp As Group
DBEngine.IniPath = "C:\VB4\TEST1.INI"
Set OldWs = DBEngine.Workspaces(0)
Set NewUser = OldWs.CreateUser("BJONES", "44587", "HOOPS")
OldWs.Groups("Users").Users.Append NewUser
'************************************
'Delete a user from the system database
'****************************************
Dim OldWs As Workspace, NewUser As User, NewGrp As Group
DBEngine.IniPath = "C:\VB4\TEST1.INI"
Set OldWs = DBEngine.Workspaces(0)
OldWs.Users.Delete "BJONES"
```

Encryption

In addition to the security system, the Jet engine provides a means of encrypting a database that you create. *Encryption* is a method of disguising the data in a database so that someone using a disk-editing program cannot view the contents of the database. Encryption may be specified when the database is first created using the options portion of the CreateDatabase function. After a database has been created, encryption may be added or removed using the CompactDatabase function. The use of these functions for encrypting data is shown in listing 7.6.

Listing 7.6 You Can Add Encryption to Your Database Using the CreateDatabase or CompactDatabase Statement

```
Dim NewDb As Database, OldDb As Database, OldWs As Workspace
'*****************************
'Create an encrypted database
'*****************************
Set NewDb = OldWs.CreateDatabase("A:\TRITON2.MDB", _
    dbLangGeneral,dbEncrypt)
'*****************************
'Encrypt an existing database
'*****************************
DBEngine.CompactDatabase "A:\TRITON.MDB", _
    "A:\TRITON3.MDB",,dbEncrypt
'*********************************
'Remove encryption from a database
'*********************************
DBEngine.CompactDatabase "A:\TRITON.MDB", _
    "A:\TRITON3.MDB",,dbDecrypt
```

The encryption method used by the Jet engine encrypts the entire database, including table definitions and queries. Also, the encryption results in a performance degradation of about 10 to 15 percent.

For some applications, it may be desirable to encrypt only a portion of the data. For instance, in a payroll system, you may need to encrypt only the actual pay rates, not the entire database. Although there is no built-in way to do this, you can create your own encryption schemes for these situations.

As an example, a simple encryption scheme for numeric data would be to convert each digit (including leading and trailing zeros) to a character, inverting the character string, then storing the data as text. In this way, the number 2534.75 could be stored as EGDCEB. Although this type of encryption is by no means foolproof, it does provide some data security from casual lookers.

Application Passwords

In addition to, or in place of, the security built in to the database, you may also choose to put a user ID and password system into your application. With an application-level system, you control the type of access people have to the functions of your application. The drawback to this approach is that someone could access your database using another program.

Using Network Security

Finally, most network operating systems have their own security system built in. Many of these systems are quite good and can prevent unauthorized users from even knowing that the database exists. To determine the capabilities of your network's security system, refer to your network program manuals or contact your network administrator.

Maintaining Data Currency

Currency of the data is a big issue in multiuser applications, especially those that handle a high volume of data entry and modification. *Maintaining currency* refers to making sure that the data at which you are looking is the most up-to-date information available. The data you are working with becomes noncurrent if another user changes or deletes the records since you retrieved them. Additionally, your recordset may be noncurrent if other users have added records since you retrieved data.

Using Only Tables

The only way to be sure that your data is always the most current is to work exclusively with tables. Only a table will immediately reflect changes, additions, or deletions made by other users. If your application or function works with only one table, using the table instead of a dynaset is probably the best way to go. If your application must work with multiple tables, the drawback to using just the tables is that you have to maintain the table relationships instead of using a dynaset to do it. To decide whether to use tables or dynasets, you must determine the probability that your data will not be current, the consequences of having noncurrent data, and the effort involved in maintaining the table relationships. Weighing these three factors will let you decide which access method is best.

Requerying a *dynaset*

If you need to work with a dynaset in a multiuser application, you can use the Requery method to make the dynaset current with the database. The Requery method basically re-executes the SQL query used to create the dynaset. Here is the Requery method:

```
NewDyn.Requery
```

There is a limit to the number of times that you can requery a dynaset. Therefore, it is a good idea after several requeries to close the dynaset and recreate it completely.

Performance Considerations

The performance of your multiuser application is dependent on, among other things, the type of network, the number of users, and the size of the databases with which you are working. At best, with you as the only user attached to a server, the data-transfer rates across a network are five to ten times slower than from your local hard drive. This means that you have to work harder in a network environment to keep the performance of your application crisp. The following sections list some ideas for helping the performance of your application.

Keep *dynasets* Small

The trick to keeping your dynasets small is to make your queries as specific as possible. This allows you to avoid repeatedly reading data across the network as you move through the dynaset.

Copy a Database or Table to a Local Drive

If you have a database that does not change, such as a ZIP code database, you could make a copy of the database on your local drive. This improves the speed of access during searches and queries. For other databases that might change only occasionally (such as a price database), you could consider making the changes at a time when no one else is using the database. That way, the data would always be static to the users of the system. In other words, do your data maintenance at night.

Use *snapshot*s Where Possible

Because snapshots are a read-only copy of the data stored in memory, they access the network only when the snapshot is created. Therefore, if you don't need to make changes to the data, use a snapshot, but only if the recordset is small.

Use Transactions for Processing Updates

Each time an update is issued, data is written to the database, requiring a disk write—that is, unless transaction processing is used. All the updates between a BeginTrans and a CommitTrans are stored in memory until the transaction is committed. At that time, all the updates are processed at once. This cuts down on the amount of writes being performed across the network. However, you should be careful not to allow too many updates to stack up at one time because of the record-locking concerns described earlier.

Handling Errors and Conflicts

In a multiuser application, errors are triggered when you attempt to open a table or update a record that is locked by another user. These errors can be trapped by your code and appropriate steps can be taken to either retry the operation or exit the application gracefully. You will look at these errors in three major groups:

- Database/Table locking errors

- Record-locking errors

- Permission errors

The way to handle most errors that occur when trying to lock a table, database, or record is to wait for a few seconds, then try the operation again. Unless the other user that has the record locked maintains the lock for a long time, this method will work. In an interactive environment, I usually give the user the choice of retrying or aborting the operation.

Database/Table Locking Errors

Database or table locking errors occur when you try to access information that is currently locked or in use by another user. These errors occur either when you try to open the database or table, or when you try to lock them. When the errors occur, it is necessary to wait until the other user has released the lock or quit using the recordset. Table 7.1 lists the error numbers and when they occur.

Table 7.1   Locking Errors That Apply to Tables and Databases

Error Number	Error Occurs When
3008	You attempt to open a table that is exclusively opened by another.
3009	You attempt to lock a table that is in use by another.
3211	Same as 3009
3212	Same as 3009

Each of these errors may be handled as described previously, with a choice by the user to abort or retry the operation.

Record-Locking Errors

Record-locking errors occur when you try to add, update, or delete records on a page locked by another user. Depending on the type of locking you use, the error may occur either when you use the Edit method (pessimistic locking) or when you use the Update method (optimistic locking). To determine which locking method is in effect when the error occurs, you can check the LockEdits property of the recordset you are attempting to lock. Then, if you choose to retry the operation, you can re-execute the correct method. This routine is shown in listing 7.7.

Listing 7.7   Determine Which Locking Method Is in Effect When an Error Occurs

```
'*******************************************
'Determine the type of locking being used
'*******************************************
```

```
If NewDyn.LockEdits Then
'**********************************
'If pessimistic locking, retry Edit
'**********************************
    NewDyn.Edit
Else
'**********************************
'If optimistic locking, retry Update
'**********************************
    NewDyn.Update
End If
```

Most of the record errors pertain to problems encountered while locking the record. However, one error requires special handling. This error (3197) occurs when a user attempts to update a record that has already been changed by another user. This error will occur only when optimistic locking is in effect. When it occurs, you need to present your user with the choices of "Make the new changes anyway" or "Keep the changes made by the other user." It would also be beneficial to show what the other user's changes were. If the user decides to make the changes anyway, the Update method may be executed a second time to make the changes.

Several other errors might occur when you attempt to lock a record. Table 7.2 lists the error numbers for these errors and when they occur.

Table 7.2   Other Record-Locking Errors

Error Number	Cause
3046	You attempt to save a record locked by another user.
3158	You attempt to save a record locked by another user.
3186	You attempt to save a record locked by another user, but give the name of the user who placed the lock.
3187	You attempt to read a record locked by another user.
3188	You attempt to update a record that another program on your machine already has locked.
3189	You attempt to access a table that another user has exclusively locked.
3218	You attempt to update a locked record.
3260	You attempt to save a record locked by another user, but give the name of the user who placed the lock.

Data Access

Permission Errors

The other major group of errors is permission errors. These errors occur when the Jet security is in operation and the current user does not have the appropriate permission to perform the operation. The only way to handle these errors is to inform the user of the error and abort the operation. Table 7.3 summarizes the permission errors.

Table 7.3 Permission Errors Occur When a User Does Not Have the Appropriate Rights for an Operation

Error Number	Permission Required
3107	Insert
3108	Replace
3109	Delete
3110	Read definitions
3111	Create
3112	Read

From Here...

As you can see, there are many more design considerations involved in creating a multiuser application than in a single-user application. This is made even more difficult by the fact that each multiuser situation is different, in terms of hardware and network software used, the number of users of the system, and the functional requirements of the individual application. The intent of this section was not to provide specific solutions, but to make you aware of the challenges involved in multiuser programming and some of the tools available in Visual Basic to help you meet the challenges. Refer to the following chapters for more information:

- See Chapter 1, "Designing Your Database Application," to learn about general database design considerations.

- See Chapter 3, "Implementing the Database Design," to learn how to create and modify a database.

Chapter 8

Accessing Other Databases with the Jet Engine

Very often, database systems do not present data to application developers in their "home" or "native" format. Often, your application uses one DBMS (database management system) and the information your application needs resides in another DBMS. When designing database systems, there are two likely scenarios that can occur:

- You develop an application that needs to access data in a database used or shared by other applications.

- You need to import data from an external database to populate your database.

Each of these situations demands different techniques that fortunately can be addressed with Visual Basic—without losing a lot of sleep in the process.

In this chapter, you learn the following:

- What is the Jet engine architecture

- When to import external data and when to attach to external tables

- How to manage attached tables

- More about database-specific issues

Examining Jet Engine Architecture

The Jet engine was developed by Microsoft to provide all of the database connectivity features for Visual Basic. It originally previewed in Access 1.0. In Visual Basic 4, the Jet engine is comprised of six main Dynamic Link Libraries (*.DLL): MSAJT200.DLL, MSJETERR.DLL, MSJETINT.DLL, VBAJET.DLL, VBDB16.DLL, and DOA2516.DLL. A variety of other DLLs are shipped with Visual Basic; these DLLs are libraries used for external database support and ODBC support. There is a separate DLL for each database type. Table 8.1 shows the DLLs used for each database type.

Table 8.1   DLLs Used for Each Database Type

Database Type	DLL
FoxPro, dBASE III, dBASE IV	XBS200.DLL
Paradox	PDX200.DLL
Btrieve	BTRV200.DLL
Excel spreadsheet	MSXL2016.DLL
Delimited and fixed-length text	MSTX2016.DLL
ODBC Database Drivers	ODBC.DLL, ODBCCURS.DLL, ODBCINST.DLL

Visual Basic is a Windows executable which, like many Windows applications, is comprised of a core executable (*.EXE) and a set of DLLs (*.DLL). A DLL is a code library that contains a set of API (Application Programming Interface) functions. Visual Basic 4 uses Visual Basic for Applications (VBA) as the language interpreter. VBA is the programming language used across all Microsoft products including Microsoft Excel and Microsoft Word. VBA allows for multienvironment usage of Visual Basic programming modules.

The main Visual Basic DLL is VBA2.DLL, the Visual Basic for Applications DLL. When a Visual Basic program issues a Database API call, it is through a new object-oriented interface. This interface is called the *data access object* (DAO) and is a set of OLE Automation objects that Visual Basic uses for data access. The data access object is contained in DAO2516.DLL.

When the data access object is called from a Visual Basic program, many DLLs are used in the process. Figure 8.1 shows the succession of events that occur when your application calls one of these APIs.

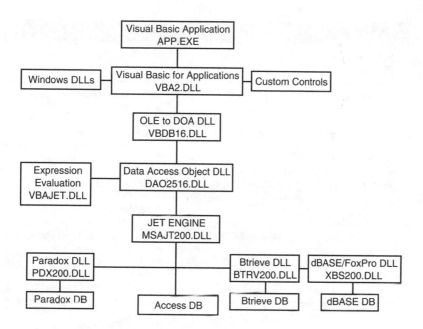

Fig. 8.1
DLLs used when accessing the data access object.

The following code fragment is used to illustrate the succession of DLLs that are called when using Visual Basic's data access object. The first line of code declares an object variable of type Database. The second line calls the OpenDatabase method of the DBEngine object.

```
DIM db as Database
Set db = DbEngine.Workspaces(0).OpenDatabase( "C:\path\mydb.dbf" ,
  False , False , "dBase IV" )
```

The following list explains what happens when the OpenDatabase call is issued from a Visual Basic application.

■ The OpenDatabase call is interpreted by VBA2.DLL.

■ The call is interpreted as a database access call and is passed to DAO2516.DLL.

■ The call is then passed to the Jet engine DLL, MSAJT200.DLL. The Jet engine DLL then determines what type of database is to be opened. A LoadLibrary call is then issued to load the appropriate DLL (because you are looking at a dBASE IV file in this case, XBS200.DLL is loaded) and the database file MYDB.DBF is opened.

Visual Basic 4 has a 16-bit version and a 32-bit version of the development environment. Visual Basic allows for the same code base to be used by each version, but the underlying DLLs that are used are different. Table 8.2 is a comparison of the Visual Basic 16-bit and 32-bit DLLs.

Table 8.2 Jet 2.0 16-Bit DLLs versus Jet 2.0 32-Bit DLLs

Jet Engine 2.0 16-Bit	Jet Engine 2.0 32-Bit	Description
VBAJET.DLL	VBAJET32.DLL	Expression evaluation services for Jet engine
MSAJT200.DLL	MSJT3032.DLL	Jet database engine
XBS200.DLL	MSXB3032.DLL	FoxPro/dBASE ISAM driver
PDX200.DLL	MSPX3032.DLL	Paradox ISAM driver library
BTRV200.DLL		Btrieve ISAM driver library
DAO2516.DLL	DAO3032.DLL	MS data access object library
MSJETERR.DLL	MSJTER32.DLL	MS Jet error library
VBDB16.DLL	VBDB32.DLL	OLE to DOA implementation DLL

The Jet 2.0 engine provides a host of new functionality to Visual Basic developers. Here are some of the highlights of the Jet 2.0 engine:

- A fully object-oriented Data Definition Language (DDL) that provides complete support for creating and modifying database, table, query, index, field, security, and referential integrity objects.

- Cascading updates and deletes that allow users to delete or update a record and have all dependent records reflect the change.

- A new recordset object for increased database performance and data manipulation.

- Enhanced data integrity and security through table-level validation. Relation objects can be used to define and enforce referential integrity.

- Rushmore query optimization that greatly increases search speed (this technology is currently used in Microsoft FoxPro).

- Support for Paradox 4.x database files.

- Support for Btrieve 6.x database files.

- Improved SQL support and support for UNION and subqueries as well as SQL passthrough for nonstandard SQL statements that must be executed in the server.

Importing External Data

Leveraging external data is very important not only to application developers but to your customers. If you are developing a custom or vertical-market application, leveraging external data is essential because most applications of this type start with a populated database with which you must preload your system or that you must access. Even shrink-wrapped products offer their users a tremendous benefit by leveraging external data. Users do not like to reenter information; your users will be very appreciative if they can import or attach to the information they need.

This section covers "importing" external data and "attaching" to external data. A sample application is developed to provide examples of both attaching to and importing external data.

> **Note**
>
> When importing external data, there are some issues that must be addressed to maintain the integrity of the data. Data verification is essential. Does the database being imported contain field types that are not supported by my database? Is importing the data the correct choice for my application, or should I attach to the table instead?

Imported Data Verification and Manipulation

Depending on the version of the Jet engine you are using, data verification used to be a difficult task. Earlier versions of the Jet engine recognized only default relationships and referential integrity rules for Access databases. These rules could not be established through the Data Definition Language (DDL). These rules could be set only when creating the Access database with Access. Additionally, Version 1.1 of the Jet engine had no support for table-level validation.

Visual Basic 4 greatly enhances the programmer's data validation and manipulation capabilities. The Data Definition Language (DDL) provides Visual Basic with the ability to create databases, tables, fields, queries, and indexes. The Data Definition Language has added creating and editing of referential integrity and security objects also.

Jet 2.0 adds some additional enhancements for Visual Basic programmers: Table-level validation is supported as are cascading updates and deletes. These enhancements are available to the Visual Basic programmer during database construction with Access 2.0 or the Data Manager add-on tool. The enhancements can also be achieved programmatically.

When you are importing data or attaching to external databases, it is extremely important that you know the relationships that exist among the tables and the fields. Not knowing this information increases the chances of data corruption when manipulating the database.

When to Import and When to Attach

When should you import data and when should you attach to external tables? This answer to this question is often complex. The responses you make to the next few questions can help you arrive at the correct answer for your application:

- Is your application going to be the only application to access and manipulate the data?

- Will any of the important data be lost by importing the data? By attaching to the data?

- If other applications update the database, is your application dependent on the updated information?

If your application is going to be the only application to access and manipulate the data, importing the data is probably the correct choice. The Jet engine is optimized to work with native database formats as opposed to foreign formats. However, if the data resides in a database on the network, and the data is shared by many applications, attaching to the database is probably the better choice.

Importing data from external databases is not always a trivial task. Not all database formats support the same field types as others (an example of this is the Binary Large Object—BLOB). Importing data can result in the loss of information contained in the original database. If you attach to the database, your application still cannot access these fields, but it won't lose the data either.

When importing data, it is important to know what field types are in both the source and destination tables. This is necessary because the source and destination databases may not support all of the same field types. You need to know these two pieces of information when you're designing your application. If the same field types are not supported, importing the data may not be the correct solution.

If your application does not need to contain all the fields contained in a source database, you can populate your application's database by importing the relevant information from the source database.

Relevant Functions and Commands

Visual Basic provides two sets of objects in the Jet engine: the DDL group (Data Definition Language, which deals with defining and creating a database) and the DML group (Data Manipulation Language). Visual Basic offers methods of programmatically adding table-level validation rules and enforcement. This chapter does not use the DDL to create a database for import; it assumes that you have already defined the database definition of the destination (import) database and that any table-level validation rules were added at table creation.

The following data manipulation objects listed in table 8.3 are used when importing data.

Table 8.3 Database Objects Used to Import External Data		
Object	**Definition**	**Creation Functions**
workspace	A container that holds a collection of databases.	CreateWorkspace
database	A container or structure that holds all the information of a database.	CreateDatabase Open Database
recordset (type table)	A structure that holds data in a database. This object organizes the data into rows and columns. A *table* is a type of recordset, which in turn is a group of records.	OpenRecordset
recordset (type dynaset)	A group of records that is a result of a query. This object can have updatable records. This is a dynamic image of a set of records.	OpenRecordset
recordset (type snapshot)	This is similar to a dynaset object. It is a group of records created through the result of a query. Unlike a dynaset, this object contains a static image of the records and is not updatable.	OpenRecordset

(continues)

Data Access

Table 8.3 Continued		
Object	**Definition**	**Creation Functions**
QueryDef	This object stores a SQL-like statement in the database. It is used to indicate the table values used for searching database tables.	CreateQueryDef OpenQueryDef

To demonstrate the use of the database objects indicated in table 8.2, this chapter uses a simple address-book database application. The database layout is listed in table 8.4 (the database layout was created in Microsoft Access).

Table 8.4 Database Layout for Address Book Application			
Field Name	**Data Type**	**Length**	**Indexed**
Name	Text	64	Yes
Street	Test	100	No
Street2	Text	100	No
City	Text	32	No
State	Text	2	No
Zip	Text	10	No
Phone	Text	20	No
WorkPhone	Text	20	No
Fax	Text	20	No

The address book application was designed to keep track of names, addresses, and phone information about people and companies. This application demonstrates the following concepts:

- How to open a database using the Jet engine.

- How to import information from an external database. An external dBASE IV database is used for this application.

- How to attach to an external database.

■ How to update both the native database and the attached database with imported data.

■ How to search for information from both the native and attached database.

Figure 8.2 shows the main screen of the address book application.

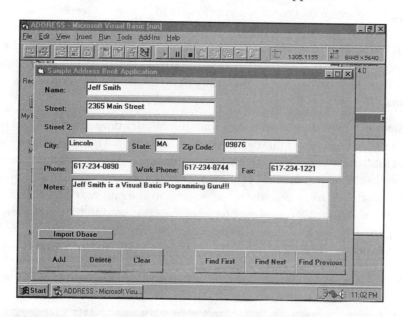

Fig. 8.2
The main screen of the address book application.

The application's database contains one table, the Address table. This table has one primary key, Name. The application also attaches a dBASE IV table, AddInfo, to the Address database. The AddInfo table contains a Memo field for additional information about the name of the entry. The AddInfo table also has a Name field, which is identical to the Name field of the Address table.

The FormLoad function performs two services. The first is to open the Address database for the application and create a recordset object of type table for adding records. The second service is to attach the AddInfo dBASE table to the open database and create a recordset object of type dynaset for adding information to the AddInfo table. Notice that on FormUnload, the AddInfo table is detached from the Address database. If the table wasn't detached, a run-time error would occur in Visual Basic the next time the application ran because the table would already be attached.

When adding a record (Add_Click), the AddressCtl control array copies values from the screen to the Address table. A new record is then added. The screen value in the Additional Information field of the AddressCtl control array is copied to the attached recordset object in the AddInfo table and a new record is added.

To search a record, a SQL statement is generated to create a greater-than-or-equal-to search on the value in the Name field. A global recordset object (SearchSet) is created from this query. The subroutine FillFormfromRecord is then called. This subroutine fills the screen with the recordset record information. This subroutine also creates an additional recordset object on the attached table, based on an equal-to search on the Name field. If a value is found, the Notes field on the screen is updated.

When the application imports data from dBASE IV, information is added to both the Address table and the attached AddInfo table. The import table contains the same fields as the Address table as well as the Notes field contained in the AddInfo table. The Import_Click subroutine opens the external database and creates a recordset of all records in the Address table. Notice that the same global recordset object (SearchSet) is used so that the application can call the subroutines already provided for adding records and searching.

The code for the address book application is given in listing 8.1.

Listing 8.1   The Address Book Application

```
' Since all fields are in a control array
' I will set up defines for accessing them
Const NAME_FLD = 1
Const STREET_FLD = 2
Const STREET2_FLD = 3
Const CITY_FLD = 4
Const STATE_FLD = 5
Const ZIP_FLD = 6
Const PHONE_FLD = 7
Const WORK_FLD = 8
Const FAX_FLD = 9
Const NOTES_FLD = 10
Const FIRST_FLD = NAME_FLD
Const LAST_FLD = NOTES_FLD

' Objects and variables used in this module
Dim Ws As Workspace
Dim Db As Database
Dim Tbl As Recordset
Dim SearchSet As Recordset
```

```
Dim MemoSet As Recordset
Dim AddInfoAdd As Recordset
Dim SrchValue As String

Sub Add_Click ()
    If Not (AddressCtl(NAME_FLD) = "") Then
Tbl.AddNew
    Tbl.Fields("Name").Value = AddressCtl(NAME_FLD)
    Tbl.Fields("Street").Value = AddressCtl(STREET_FLD)
    Tbl.Fields("Street2").Value = AddressCtl(STREET2_FLD)
    Tbl.Fields("City").Value = AddressCtl(CITY_FLD)
    Tbl.Fields("State").Value = AddressCtl(STATE_FLD)
    Tbl.Fields("ZipCode").Value = AddressCtl(ZIP_FLD)
    Tbl.Fields("Phone").Value = AddressCtl(PHONE_FLD)
    Tbl.Fields("WorkPhone").Value = AddressCtl(WORK_FLD)
    Tbl.Fields("Fax").Value = AddressCtl(FAX_FLD)
    Tbl.Update
    'Tbl.Fields("Notes").Value = AddressCtl(NOTES_FLD)
    'Tbl.Update

    AddInfoAdd.AddNew
    AddInfoAdd.Fields("Name").Value = AddressCtl(NAME_FLD)
    AddInfoAdd.Fields("Notes").Value = AddressCtl(NOTES_FLD)
    AddInfoAdd.Update
    End If
End Sub

Sub Command1_Click ()
    Dim i As Integer
    For i = FIRST_FLD To LAST_FLD Step 1
    AddressCtl(i) = ""
    Next i
End Sub

Sub Delete_Click ()
    If Not SearchSet.NoMatch Then
        SearchSet.Delete
        If Not MemoSet.NoMatch Then
    MemoSet.Delete
        End If
        Command1_Click
        FindFirst_Click
    End If
End Sub

Sub FillFormfromImport ()
    If Not SearchSet.NoMatch Then
    AddressCtl(NAME_FLD) = ValidateRecordField("Name")
    AddressCtl(STREET_FLD) = ValidateRecordField("Street")
    AddressCtl(STREET2_FLD) = ValidateRecordField("Street2")
    AddressCtl(CITY_FLD) = ValidateRecordField("City")
    AddressCtl(STATE_FLD) = ValidateRecordField("State")
    AddressCtl(ZIP_FLD) = ValidateRecordField("ZipCode")
    AddressCtl(PHONE_FLD) = ValidateRecordField("Phone")
    AddressCtl(WORK_FLD) = ValidateRecordField("WorkPhone")
```

Data Access

(continues)

Listing 8.1   Continued

```
        AddressCtl(FAX_FLD) = ValidateRecordField("Fax")
        AddressCtl(NOTES_FLD) = ValidateRecordField("Notes")
    End If

End Sub

Sub FillFormfromRecord ()
    If Not SearchSet.NoMatch Then
        AddressCtl(NAME_FLD) = ValidateRecordField("Name")
        AddressCtl(STREET_FLD) = ValidateRecordField("Street")
        AddressCtl(STREET2_FLD) = ValidateRecordField("Street2")
        AddressCtl(CITY_FLD) = ValidateRecordField("City")
        AddressCtl(STATE_FLD) = ValidateRecordField("State")
        AddressCtl(ZIP_FLD) = ValidateRecordField("ZipCode")
        AddressCtl(PHONE_FLD) = ValidateRecordField("Phone")
        AddressCtl(WORK_FLD) = ValidateRecordField("WorkPhone")
        AddressCtl(FAX_FLD) = ValidateRecordField("Fax")

        Dim AttachStatement As String
        AttachStatement = "SELECT * FROM Addinfo WHERE Name = '" +
        AddressCtl(NAME_FLD) + "'"
      Set MemoSet = Db.OpenRecordset(AttachStatement, dbOpenDynaset)
        If MemoSet.BOF = False Then
            If MemoSet.Fields("Notes").Value > "" Then
              AddressCtl(NOTES_FLD) = MemoSet.Fields("Notes").Value
            Else
              AddressCtl(NOTES_FLD) = ""
            End If
        End If
      End If
    End Sub

Sub FindFirst_Click ()
    Dim Statement As String
    Statement = "SELECT * FROM Address WHERE Name >= '" +
    AddressCtl(NAME_FLD) + "'"
    Set SearchSet = Db.OpenRecordset(Statement, dbOpenDynaset)
    FillFormfromRecord
End Sub

Sub FindNext_Click ()
    SearchSet.FindNext "Name > ' '"
    FillFormfromRecord
End Sub

Sub FindPrevious_Click ()
    SearchSet.FindPrevious "Name > ' '"
    FillFormfromRecord
End Sub

Sub Form_Load ()
    Dim TblDef As New TableDef
    ' first create the default workspace
```

```
        Set Ws = DBEngine.Workspaces(0)
        ' second open the access database
        Set Db = Ws.OpenDatabase("c:\vb\address.mdb")

        ' now attach the dbase IV table to the open db
        TblDef.Connect = "dBASE IV;DATABASE=C:\VB\ADDINFO"
        TblDef.SourceTableName = "ADDINFO"    ' The name of the file.
        TblDef.Name = "Addinfo"      ' The name in your database.
        Db.TableDefs.Append TblDef  ' Create the link.

        ' now open a table info the main database
        Set Tbl = Db.OpenRecordset("Address", dbOpenTable)

        ' now we need to create a dynaset from the attached table
        Statement = "SELECT * FROM Address WHERE Name >= '" +
        AddressCtl(NAME_FLD) + "'"
        Set AddInfoAdd = Db.OpenRecordset("SELECT * FROM Addinfo",
        dbOpenDynaset)
End Sub

Sub Form_Unload (Cancel As Integer)
    Tbl.Close
    AddInfoAdd.Close
    Db.TableDefs.Delete "Addinfo"
End Sub

Sub ImportDbase_Click ()
    Dim dbdb As Database
    Dim DTable As RecordSet
    Dim Statement As String

    Set dbdb = Ws.OpenDatabase("c:\vb", False, False, "dBase IV")
    Set DTable = dbdb.OpenRecordSet("Address", dbOpenTable)

    Statement = "SELECT * FROM Address"
    Set SearchSet = dbdb.OpenRecordset(Statement, dbOpenRecordset)
    While Not SearchSet.EOF
     FillFormfromImport
     Add_Click
     Command1_Click
     SearchSet.MoveNext
    Wend
End Sub

Function ValidateRecordField (Field As String) As String
    If SearchSet.BOF = False Then
    If SearchSet.Fields(Field).Value > "" Then
        ValidateRecordField = SearchSet.Fields(Field).Value
    Else
        ValidateRecordField = ""
    End If
    End If
End Function
```

Database and File Issues

If all databases were created equal, there would only be one database vendor and only one method of entering, searching, changing, and deleting information. There would be no reason to worry about attaching to or importing external data because the world could be viewed as one giant database with many tables.

However, this is not the case. Many database vendors and competing products give the user a variety of choices. Each database provides unique features that other databases may or may not support.

This section deals with the issues involved when importing data from different databases and file formats. This chapter assumes that you are importing data *from* a specified database or file format *into* a Jet 3.0 database file.

One element that applies to using foreign databases with the Jet engine is that either the system registration database or your APP.INI must contain a section called [Installable ISAMs]. (Note: You can view the system registration database by running the application REGEDIT. You can find the Installable_ISAM section in the following path: HKEY_LOCAL_MACHINE\software\microsoft\jet20\Installable_ISAM.) In this section, you *must* indicate the database engine type you want to access followed by the path. The section shown in listing 8.2 contains all the installable ISAMs for the Jet engine.

Listing 8.2 The Required [Installable ISAMs] Section in System Registration Database or the APP.INI File

```
[Installable ISAMs]
dBase III=c:\windows\system\xbs200.dll
dBase IV=c:\windows\system\xbs200.dll
Paradox 4.x = c:\windows\system\pdx200.dll
Paradox 3.x = c:\windows\system\pdx200.dll
Foxpro 2.0 = c:\windows\system\xbs200.dll
Foxpro 2.5 = c:\windows\system\xbs200.dll
Btreive=c:\windows\system\btrv200.dll
Excel 5.0=c:\windows\system\msxl2016.dll
Excel 4.0=c:\windows\system\msxl2016.dll
Excel 3.0=c:\windows\system\msxl2016.dll
Text = c:\windows\system\mstx2016.dll
```

Note that the each entry label matches the string that is passed into the OpenDatabase function as the database type parameter.

Databases That Use Jet 3.0

The Jet 3.0 file format—or, more appropriately, the Access 95 database file format—is the native database format for Visual Basic 4. Users of Jet 3.0 will have no problem importing data from other Jet 3.0 database files. All the data in the database can be transferred completely.

Databases That Use Jet 2.x and Jet 1.1

Jet 3.0 can access Jet 2.x and 1.1 database file formats. All the field types supported in Jet 3.0 are supported in Jet 2.x and 1.1. This makes the job of importing data from a Jet 1.1 format easy. Just as with a Jet 3.0 format, all the data in a Jet 2.x and 1.1 database can be transferred completely.

Delimited and Fixed-Width Text Files

The Jet engine in Visual Basic 4 can open a text file as though it were a foreign database. This capability makes importing data from a text file into an existing database a simple task. Text files are accessed through the Jet engine by using MSTX2016.DLL (16-bit) or MSTX3032.DLL (32-bit).

In previous versions of Visual Basic, importing text data required writing custom code to open the text file and parse through its contents—a tedious and inflexible task. Fortunately, the Jet engine now relieves programmers of this burden.

A *delimited text file* contains text in which each line represents a row in a database table. Each column in the row is delimited, or separated, by a known character (such as a tab or a comma). Visual Basic recognizes tabs, commas, and custom deliminators in text files. The only limitation is that the same deliminator *must* be used throughout the file. Missing field values or null data is represented by two consecutive delimiters.

A *fixed-width text file* contains text in which each line represents a row in a database table. In contrast to a delimited text file, each column in the fixed-width text file is a fixed width. The width of each column in a row is defined in SCHEMA.INI. Null data is represented by the space character " "entered for the width of the field.

For both types of text files, the first row can contain the names of the fields that each column represents.

The following statements open a text file as a database:

```
Dim Db As Database
Set Db = DBEngine.Workspaces(0).OpenDatabase ("c:\path\text.txt" ,
 False, False, "Text" )
```

When accessing text files with the Jet engine, settings in VB.INI or your APP.INI file control how the file's data is interpreted. These values are found in the [Text I-ISAM] section and are listed in table 8.5.

Table 8.5 Values in the [Text I-ISAM] Section of VB.INI or APP.INI		
Section Entry	**Description**	**Default Value**
Extensions	Indicates the files to be browsed when looking for text-based data.	N/A
ColNameHeader	Indicates whether the first record (row) in the file contains column names. Set to True or False.	True
Format	Set to one of the following: TabDelimited, CVSDelimited, Delimited(<singlecharacter>) or Fixed Length. If single-character delimited, any character except for the quotation mark (") can be used.	N/A
MaxScanRows	The number of rows to scan when guessing the column type. If 0, the entire file is scanned.	N/A
CharacterSet	Set to OEM or ANSI, depending on the code page of the text file.	N/A

SCHEMA.INI Settings. To import or export text data with the Jet engine, you must create and specify settings in SCHEMA.INI in addition to the [Text I-ISAM] section in VB.INI or APP.INI. SCHEMA.INI instructs the Jet engine how the text file is formatted and how it is to be read at import time.

SCHEMA.INI can contain multiple sections. Each section in SCHEMA.INI represents a file name or a saved export format.

Table 8.6 shows the settings that Visual Basic uses in SCHEMA.INI.

Table 8.6 Values in SCHEMA.INI for Text Data	
Section Entry	**Description**
ColNameHeader	Indicates whether the first record (row) in the file contains column names. Set to True or False.

Section Entry	Description
Format	Set to one of the following: `TabDelimited`, `CVSDelimited`, `Delimited(<singlecharacter>)` or `Fixed Length`. If single-character delimited, any character except for the quotation mark (") can be used.
MaxScanRows	The number of rows to scan when guessing the column type. If 0, the entire file is scanned.
CharacterSet	Set to `OEM` or `ANSI`, depending on the code page of the text file.
DateTimeFormat	A format string used for dates and times. This entry should be specified if all date and time fields in the import or export file use the same format. If no format string is specified, the control panel short date and time options are used. Format strings are specified by indicating the number of entries for each date or time entry— for example *mm-dd-yy hh:mm:ss*.
CurrencySymbol	Indicates the currency symbol to be used for any currency values in the text file. If no value is specified, the control panel setting is used.
CurrencyDigits	Specifies the number of digits used for the fractional (change) part of currency values. If no value is specified, the control panel setting is used.
CurrencyNegativeFormat	Set to one of the following values:

Value	Example
0	($1)
1	-$1
2	$-1
3	$1-
4	(1 $)
5	-1 $
6	1-$
7	1$-
8	-1 $
9	-$ 1
10	1 $-
11	$ 1-
12	$ -1
13	1- $
14	($ 1)
15	(1 $)

(continues)

Table 8.6 Continued	
Section Entry	**Description**
	When specifying the entry in SCHEMA.INI, only the numeric number is used. For example: `CurrencyNegativeFormat=13`.
	If this entry is not present, the control panel setting is used.
	Note: The dollar sign ($) is used here only as an example. The actual symbol used is specified with CurrencyFormat.
DecimalSymbol	Indicates the single character separating the whole and fractional parts of the currency value. If not specified, the control panel setting is used.
NumberDigits	Indicates the number of decimal digits in the fractional portion of the currency value. If not specified, the control panel setting is used.
NumberLeadingZeros	Specifies whether decimal values less than 1 and greater than -1 should contain leading zeros. Valid values are 0 (no leading zeros) or 1.

Listing 8.3 shows the SCHEMA.INI values for the address book application.

Listing 8.3   SCHEMA.INI Values for the Address Book Application

```
[address.txt]
ColNameHeader=True
Format=TabDelimited
MaxScanRows=0
CharacterSet=ANSI
```

Limitations on Text Data Files. Some limitations exist when you open a text data file: Data in a text file cannot be updated or deleted. You cannot build indexes on the text file either. Text files can be opened only in exclusive mode (that is, the text file cannot be shared by simultaneous users). Tables are limited to a maximum of 256 columns. The maximum length of a row is 65,536 bytes. Column widths are limited to 65,500 characters and column names are limited to 64 characters.

Microsoft Excel (2.x, 3.0, 4.0, and 5.0) Files

A spreadsheet is set up much like a database table. Spreadsheets are comprised of rows and columns. The Visual Basic Jet engine allows you to import Microsoft Excel 2.x, 3.0, 4.0, and 5.0 spreadsheets.

Microsoft Excel spreadsheets can be opened in the same manner as a foreign database. The Jet engine uses MSXL2016.DLL (16-bit) or MSXL2032.DLL (32-bit) to access the Excel spreadsheet.

The following sample of code opens an Excel spreadsheet as a database.

```
Dim Db As Database
Set Db = DBEngine.Workspaces(0).OpenDatabase _
    ("C:\path\address.XLS", False, False, "Excel 5.0")
```

When accessing Excel files through the Jet engine, settings in VB.INI or your APP.INI file control how the file's data is interpreted. These values are found in the [Microsoft Excel ISAM] section and are listed in table 8.7.

Table 8.7   Values in VB.INI or APP.INI for Excel Spreadsheets

Section Entry	Description	Default Value
TypeGuessRows	The number of rows to be checked for a data type. The data type is determined by the maximum number of kinds of data found. If more than one data type is found in a column, the data is determined in the following order: Number, Currency, Date, Text, Boolean. If a data type is encountered that is not the type guessed for the column, NULL is returned.	N/A
AppendBlankRows	Number of blank rows to be appended to the end of an Excel 3.0 or 4.0 worksheet before new data is appended.	0
FirstRowHasNames	Set to Yes or No. Yes indicates that the first row contains column names. No indicates that no column names are present.	N/A

The following limitations are imposed on using Excel worksheets as a database: Rows cannot be deleted from the worksheet. Data can be cleared from individual cells but formulas cannot be cleared. Indexes cannot be created on the worksheet. Excel spreadsheets are opened in exclusive mode (that is, simultaneous users of a spreadsheet are not allowed). If the Jet engine encounters encrypted data, the open or attachment operation fails.

Data Access

Paradox (3.x or 4.x DB) Files

Foreign databases such as Paradox are accessed in the same manner as Access databases. The OpenDatabase function takes additional arguments so that you can specify the type of database to open. The following code opens a Paradox database:

```
Dim ParadoxDB As Database
Set ParadoxDB = OpenDatabase ( "C:\paradox" , False , False , _
    "Paradox" )
```

After the database is opened, the Jet engine provides the same capabilities to Paradox as it does to an Access database.

> **Note**
>
> The Jet engine still cannot open password-protected files.

Notice that you do not specify a Paradox file name in the OpenDatabase call as you do for Access. This is because Paradox maintains each table in a separate file with the file name matching the table name. Paradox maintains a primary key for each table in the database in a file with the extension .PX. Remember the Address database example; in Paradox, the database for the Address table has a file called ADDRESS.DB, in which the data is stored, and an associated index file called ADDRESS.PX. The Jet engine needs the index file to open the table. If the Paradox table doesn't have a primary key for the table, the Jet engine cannot update the table. This means that only snapshot objects can be created, not dynaset objects. For the purposes of importing data, this isn't a big concern.

Data Types from Paradox to Access

When importing data, one of the greatest concerns is when different database engines use different data types. The following table indicates the field compatibility types when you import from Paradox to Access:

Paradox Data Type	Paradox DB Version	Jet Data Type
Alphanumeric	3.x, 4.x	Text
Currency	3.x, 4.x	Numeric (Double)
Date	3.x, 4.x	Date/Time

Paradox Data Type	Paradox DB Version	Jet Data Type
Short Number	3.x, 4.x	Numeric (Integer)
Number	3.x, 4.x	Numeric (Double)
Memo	3.x, 4.x	Memo
OLE	3.x, 4.x	OLE object
Graphic	4.x	Not supported
Binary	4.x	Not supported
Formatted Memo	4.x	Not supported

When accessing a database engine like Paradox, the Jet engine uses settings contained in VB.INI (when your application is running under the control of Visual Basic) or in APP.INI (when running a compiled version of your application). (*APP* is replaced with the compiled name of your executable.) Jet uses a section called [Paradox ISAM] to retrieve values the Paradox database needs. Table 8.8 lists the Paradox entries you can include in this section.

Table 8.8 Values in VB.INI or APP.INI for Paradox Databases

Section Entry	Description	Default Value
ParadoxNetPath	Specifies the path to PARADOX.NET, a file used for locking tables or records in a multiuser system.	C:\
ParadoxNetStyle	Specifies the locking type to use. When using Paradox 4.x files, set this entry to 4.x.	3.x
ParadoxUserName	Specifies the name of the user placing a lock on a Paradox table or record.	None
CollatingSequence	Determines the sort sequence of text fields.	ASCII
PageTimeout	Specifies the length of time in tenths of a second that your application waits to move data from a table to a virtual table.	600

Data Access

FoxPro (2.0, 2.5, and 2.6 DBF) and dBASE III and dBASE IV (DBF) Files

FoxPro, dBASE III, and dBASE IV are accessed by the Jet engine through the Installable ISAM driver XBS200.DLL. This driver must be listed in the `[Installable ISAM]` section of either VB.INI or APP.INI.

The following sample code shows how to open a FoxPro 2.5 database:

```
Dim Db As Database
Set Db = OpenDatabase ( "C:\foxpro" , False , False , "Foxpro 2.5")
```

As with Paradox, once a FoxPro or dBASE database is opened, all Visual Basic's data access objects can be used to retrieve and access data.

Even though the FoxPro and dBASE databases share the same file extension for data tables (.DBF), their index extensions are different: FoxPro uses .IDX and .CDX; dBASE uses .NDX or .MDX. Like Paradox, the file name in FoxPro or dBASE is the table name with the .DBF extension. If an index is present, it carries the same file name with the index extension.

If the index file is not located in the current directory, the Jet engine accesses the index's through an information file (.INF). The location of this information file is obtained through the INFPath entry in the `[dBase ISAM]` section in VB.INI or APP.INI.

Data Types from FoxPro or dBASE to Access

To import a FoxPro or dBASE table, your application must follow these conversion rules:

FoxPro/dBASE Data Type	Version	Jet Data Type
Character	FoxPro 2.x, dBASE III, dBASE IV	Text
Numeric (Double)	FoxPro 2.x, dBASE III, dBASE IV	Numeric
Logical	FoxPro 2.x, dBASE III, dBASE IV	Yes/No
Float (Double)	dBASE III, dBASE IV	Numeric
Date	FoxPro 2.x, dBASE III, dBASE IV	Date/Time
Memo	FoxPro 2.x, dBASE III, dBASE IV	Memo
General	FoxPro 2.x	OLE object

One additional note about memo fields. dBASE and FoxPro store memo fields in a separate file from the rest of the information. Memo fields are stored in the associated file *TABLENAME*.DBT. The .DBT file must be in the same location as the related .DBF file.

The Jet engine uses a section in VB.INI or APP.INI to control the dBASE or FoxPro database. This section is called [dBase ISAM]; table 8.9 lists the entries this section contains. Note that the section name is the same whether the database is dBASE or FoxPro.

Table 8.9   Values in VB.INI or APP.INI for dBASE and FoxPro Databases

Section Entry	Description	Default Value
INFPath	Location of the information file that maintains the locations for database index files.	None
PageTimeout	Specifies the length of time in tenths of a second that your application waits to move data from a table to a virtual table.	600
CollatingSequence	Determines the sort sequence of text fields.	ASCII
Deleted	Causes the Jet engine to not operate on deleted files. Equivalent to the dBASE instruction SET DELETED.	ON
Mark	The ASCII value of the mark character. Equivalent to the dBASE instruction SET MARK.	47
Date	The country used for setting and retrieving date information. Equivalent to the dBASE instruction SET DATE.	AMERICAN
Century	The country used for setting and retrieving date information. Equivalent to the dBASE instruction SET CENTURY.	OFF

Btrieve (FILE.DDF and FIELD.DDF) Files

Btrieve was the database from Novell. Although opening a Btrieve database with the Jet engine is similar to opening other databases, you use a much more complicated setup procedure with Btrieve than with other database systems.

Data Access

You must have the following items in place if the Jet engine is to import or attach to a Btrieve database:

- Obtain the WBTRDLL.DLL file. This file must be present for the Jet engine to use a Btrieve database. This DLL is *not* distributed with Visual Basic or the Jet 2.0/Visual Basic compatibility layer. You must get this file from Novell or from another application that uses the DLL. Beware that problems can occur from applications overwriting the [Btrieve] section of the WIN.INI file.

- The Jet engine must locate Btrieve files in the same directory as the .DDF file you specify when opening the database, or must use the locations for the Btrieve files specified in the FILE.DDF file. Optionally, the Btrieve file locations can be specified by the environment variable XTRPATH. This environment variable takes the same format as the PATH environment variable.

- The XTRPATH variable can be set in the environment or in VB.INI or APP.INI in the section [Btrieve ISAM].

- If your Btrieve database uses Xtrieve security options, the Jet engine may not be able to access the database. If the only option is the owner name, Jet can use the database if the DDFPAssword option is set in the VB.INI or APP.INI file. Otherwise, the security options must be removed.

- When you use Btrieve files in a multiuser environment, a transaction file called BTRIEVE.TRN must be present. This file must be located so that all users of the database access the same .TRN file. The location of this file is specified by an entry in the [Btrieve] section of WIN.INI.

- The Jet engine cannot use Btrieve files that have indices with the attributes Manual or Null. Indexes that have alternate collating sequences specified or that have segmented keys cannot be used.

Once you are sure that the preceding Btrieve requirements are taken care of, set the [Btrieve] section of WIN.INI. Following is the default entry for this section:

```
[Btrieve]
options=/m:64 /p:4096 /b:16 /f:20 /l:40 /n:12 /t:c:\Btrieve.trn
```

All the Btrieve options that can be specified in this section are listed in table 8.10.

Table 8.10	Values in the [Btrieve] Section of WIN.INI	
Option	**Description**	**Required Value**
/m	Memory size	>= 38
/p	Page size	4096
/b	Preimage buffer size	16
/f	Open files	>= 4
/l	Multiple locks	Open files (/f) value * 2
/n	Files in a transaction	>= 4
/t	Transaction file	Path and file name of transaction file (.TRN). In a multiuser environment, this file must be shared by all users.
/u	Compression buffer size	If Btrieve files are compressed, this value must be >= length of longest record in the database.
/I	Preimage file drive	N/A
/c	Image compaction	N/A
/a	Activate logging	N/A
/s	Discard unneeded segments	N/A

The following commands open a Btrieve database:

```
Dim Db As Database
Set Db = OpenDatabase( "c:\btrieve\file.ddf", False, False, _
    "Btrieve");
```

In a Btrieve database, each table is contained in a file with the extension .DAT. Btrieve uses FILE.DDF to specify the location of the .DAT files in the database. Btrieve also uses FIELD.DDF and INDEX.DDF to complete the data dictionary definition of the database.

It is important to note that once the database is defined and created, if either the data dictionary files or the data files themselves are moved, the database cannot be opened.

The Jet engine uses a section in VB.INI or APP.INI to control the Btrieve database. This section is called [Btrieve ISAM]; table 8.11 lists the entries this section contains.

Data Types from Btrieve to Access

To import a Btrieve database, your application must follow these conversion rules:

Btrieve Data Type	Btrieve Version	Jet Data Type
Integer, 1 byte	5.1x, 6.x	Numeric (Byte)
Integer or autoinc, 2 bytes	5.1x, 6.x	Numeric (Integer)
Integer or autoinc, 4 bytes	5.1x, 6.x	Numeric (Long)
Decimal	5.1x, 6.x	Numeric (Double)
Float or bfloat, 4 bytes	5.1x, 6.x	Numeric (Single)
Float or bfloat, 8 bytes	5.1x, 6.x	Numeric (Double)
Logical or bit	5.1x, 6.x	Yes/No
Lvar	5.1x, 6.x	OLE object
Money	5.1x, 6.x	Currency
String or lstring or zstring	5.1x, 6.x	Text
Date or Time	5.1x, 6.x	Date/Time

As it does for other foreign databases, the Jet engine uses the [Btrieve ISAM] section in VB.INI or APP.INI for Btrieve options. Table 8.11 lists these options.

Table 8.11 Values in VB.INI or APP.INI for Btrieve Databases

Section Entry	Description	Default Value
DataCodePage	Determines the code page to use for reading and writing data.	OEM
OpenAccelerated	Uses the Btrieve option to accelerate access. If used, it must be used by all users.	OFF
NetworkAccess	Determines whether file locking is to be used. If OFF, files are opened as exclusive.	ON

Section Entry	Description	Default Value
PageTimeout	Specifies the length of time in tenths of a second that your application waits to move data from a table to a virtual table.	600
DDFPassword	Owner name for opening FILE.DDF if Xtrieve security is used.	None
IndexDDF	Determines whether Jet maintains the INDEX.DDF file. Require and Maintain are the values that maintain the file.	Ignore
XTRPATH	List of file paths for locating Btrieve data files.	None
XTRENV	The location of the Xtrieve environment file.	None
XTRPINDX	Indicates which path in the XTRPATH variable to use for creating Btrieve files.	None

When using the server version of Btrieve, BTRIEVE.NLM (a NetWare Loadable Module), you must follow these rules:

- The following section must exist in WIN.INI:

```
[BREQUESTDPMI]
datalength=4096
tasks=10
local=no
chkparms=no
```

- Your NLM server must have transactions enabled.

- The NLM server files (BREQUEST.EXE, WBTRCALL.DLL, and WBTRVRES.DLL) must be Version 6.x.

Attaching to External Tables

Importing data is frequently not the preferred method of accessing data. Your application may need only temporary access to information that resides in another database and is maintained by other applications. Such a situation calls for *attaching* to the tables in the external database rather than importing the external database.

Data Access

When attaching to external tables, your application temporarily adds the table definition to your database. This has the same effect as defining the table in your database definition and importing the data. The attached table remains in the database until explicitly deleted. This means that if you try to attach the table every time you run the program without first detaching the table, a Visual Basic run-time error is generated.

> **Note**
>
> When you try to attach to a table that is already attached, you generate a trappable Visual Basic run-time error. You should trap this error before your application goes into production.

If you want to temporarily use a table in another database, open the database temporarily with OpenDatabase. Then open the specific table with the OpenRecordset command. Although this procedure does not place the table definition into your database, the table can still be accessed. The following code sample shows how to open a new database table without attaching the table:

```
Dim NewDatabase As Database
Dim NewRecordset As Recordset
Set NewDatabase = DBEngine.Workspaces(0).OpenDatabase _
    ("C:\path\dbase" , False , False , "dBASE IV")
Set NewRecordset = NewDatabase.OpenRecordset("Address")
```

Minimizing Overhead

Attaching a foreign database to your application adds additional overhead. To minimize the overhead, follow these guidelines to achieve the best results:

- View only the data you need. Avoid jumping to the last record in the table or loading unneeded records into memory. One method of doing this is to design queries that limit the number of records searched (for example, the query SELECT * is not optimized).

- Avoid locking records for longer than necessary; remember that other people may also be accessing the foreign tables.

Attaching Tables with Data Manager

Visual Basic 4 provides a convenient method for setting up database attachments during application design mode rather than in run mode. This is made possible with the add-in tool Data Manager. Data Manager allows application developers to design and view the database layout and schema; and view, add, change, and delete the table contents. To access Data Manager, choose Add-Ins, Data Manager in Visual Basic.

To attach a table using Data Manager, choose File on the Data Manager menu bar and then Open Database. The dialog box shown in figure 8.3 appears.

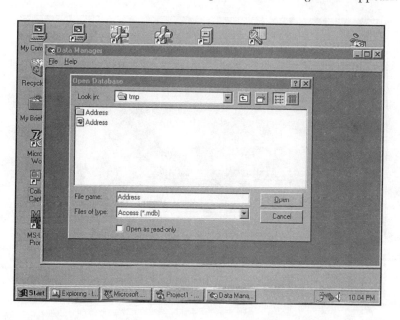

Fig. 8.3
Opening a database using Visual Basic's Data Manager.

Select the name of Access database and click Open. The Access database is opened and the tables contained in the database are listed in a modeless dialog box (see fig. 8.4). The database that was just opened is the database that is used by the application. This is not the database that the application is using to import data from.

To attach a table, choose the Attached Tables button. The Attach Tables dialog box appears as shown in figure 8.5.

Choose the New button to attach a table to the opened database. The New Attached Table dialog box (fig. 8.6) appears. The dialog box has four fields that you must fill in to attach a table. The first field is Attachment Name. The Attachment Name is the name of the table after you attach it to your Jet database. The second field, Database Name, lists the directory that contains the database tables to attach. The third field, Connect String, is a combo box that contains the name of all databases that the Jet engine supports. The last field, Table to Attach, is a combo box that dynamically fills in values based on the three preceding fields. Figure 8.6 shows values used for the Address Book application.

After you finish filling in all the fields in the New Attached Table dialog box, choose the Attach button to attach the table to your Jet database. The Attached Tables dialog box is then updated with the new information, as shown in figure 8.7.

Fig. 8.4

The Table/ QueryDefs dialog box showing information about opened database.

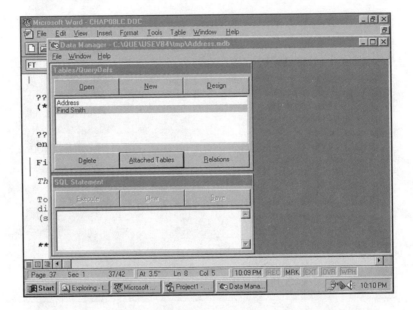

Fig. 8.5

Showing all attached databases with the Attached Tables dialog box.

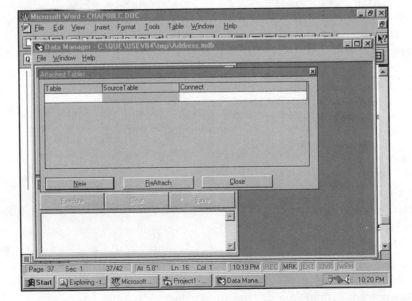

Relevant Functions and Commands

As you know, Visual Basic provides two sets of objects in the Jet engine: the DDL group (Data Definition Language), which deals with defining and creating a database, and the DML group (Data Manipulation Language).

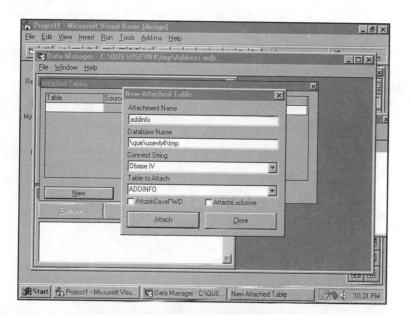

Fig. 8.6
Filling out the New Attached Table dialog box.

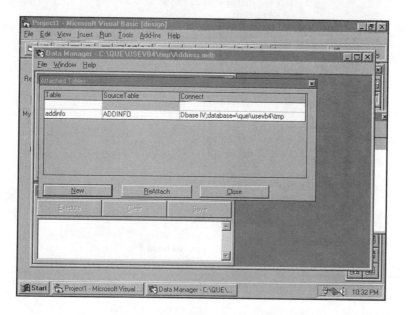

Fig. 8.7
An updated list of tables in the Jet database.

One key difference between importing and attaching database files is that attaching uses the `TableDef` object. The `TableDef` object adds the definition of the attached table to the open database so that you can create `dynaset` and `snapshot` objects as though the table were native to the database.

Table 8.12 lists the objects you can use when you attach to database tables.

Table 8.12 Database Objects Used to Attach to External Data		
Object	**Definition**	**Creation Functions**
workspace	A container that holds a collection of databases.	CreateWorkspace
database	A container or structure that holds all the information in a database.	CreateDatabase OpenDatabase
recordset (type table)	A structure that holds data in a database. This object organizes the data into rows and columns. A *table* is a type of recordset, which in turn is a group of records.	OpenRecordset
recordset (type dynaset)	A group of records that is a result of a query. This object can have updatable records. This is a dynamic image of a set of records.	OpenRecordset
recordset (type snapshot)	This is similar to a dynaset object. It is a group of records created through the result of a query. Unlike a dynaset, this object contains a static image of the records and is not updatable.	OpenRecordset
QueryDef	This object stores a SQL-like statement in the database. It is used to indicate the table values used for searching database tables.	CreateQueryDef OpenQueryDef
TableDef	This object represents a stored table definition. `TableDef` objects corresponding to attached tables cannot have their definitions changed.	CreateTableDef

Database-Specific Issues

Whether you are attaching or importing data from foreign databases, the setup requirements for the Jet engine are identical. Refer to "Database and File Issues," earlier in this chapter in the "Importing External Data" section, for more information.

From Here...

This chapter demonstrates the techniques and requirements for accessing other databases with the Jet engine. The Jet engine is extremely versatile in its capability to use foreign database systems even though it is highly optimized for working with the native Access database.

Attaching is a more attractive option when you need to access but not manage small amounts of data in another database. You must pay a performance penalty, but with careful planning you can minimize this penalty.

Importing data is necessary when an external database contains information that your database needs to access and manage. The Jet engine provides the same data access objects for external databases as for the Access database. This makes selecting the data necessary for import relatively easy.

In other chapters of this book, you can find more details about some of the topics mentioned in this chapter. Please refer to these chapters for more information:

- Chapter 4, "Manipulating Data with a Program," explains more about program commands and data access objects.

- Chapter 6, "Understanding Structured Query Language (SQL)," explains more about the SQL statements necessary to create the dynasets used by the data control.

Chapter 9

Using ODBC to Access Databases

Visual Basic, with its powerful drawing tools and easy programming method-ologies, is an excellent tool for creating front-end data-access programs. The Jet engine enables Visual Basic users to create powerful database applications. In the world of corporate computing with large networks and multiple users, client/server database applications are the required solution.

When creating database applications with the Jet engine, the Database engine is a part of the application. The database files can reside on a shared file server, but each application that uses the database contains the Database engine code. Such an application is called *remote* database application. Many users can share the database, but the methodology is actually that of sharing files. To enable users to share a database, all the applications that use the database *must* have access to the database files. Also, none of the applications can open the database in "exclusive" mode. When you open a database in exclusive mode, you prevent other applications from using the database.

In this chapter, you learn about the following:

- Considering performance issues when developing client/server applications

- Using ODBC to access database servers

- Using the data access object to retrieve data

- Considering performance issues when using ODBC

- Using the ODBC API directly

- How to perform SQL (Structured Query Language) pass-through to access servers directly

Exploring Visual Basic and Client/Server Computing

In client/server applications, the Database engine and the database files reside on a machine separate from the applications that access the database files. Therefore, the Database engine can run on a powerful server platform while the client applications run on less powerful machines. The server can even be running a non-Windows operating system. Figure 9.1 depicts the differences between remote and client/server database applications.

Fig. 9.1
An architectural diagram of the client/server application environment.

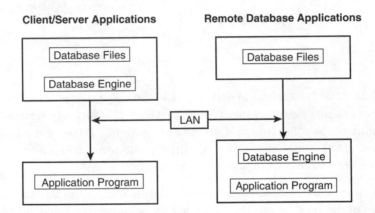

A client/server application accesses data by having the client application send a query to the server. The client application usually sends the query through a networking (interprocess communications, or IPC) protocol. The protocol that the application uses is determined by the protocol stacks in the computing environment. Some common protocol stacks include NetBEUI, NetBIOS, TCP/IP, and IPX/SPX. Even though the query is being made across the computer network, the database server blocks the application calling it until the server retrieves the data and sends the data back to the client application.

Open Database Connectivity (ODBC) is a method of communication to client/server databases in Visual Basic. ODBC is part of Microsoft's Windows Open Systems Architecture (WOSA), which provides a series of application program interfaces (APIs) to simplify and provide standards for various programming activities. The goal is to have all applications communicating through the same set of APIs. ODBC is just one piece of the WOSA picture. Other components include telephone services (TAPI), messaging services (MAPI), and open data services (ODS).

This chapter covers the basics and the advanced issues in developing client/server applications.

> **Note**
>
> Although ODBC is intended for client/server applications, ODBC drivers are available for remote databases like Access and dBASE. In this chapter, these drivers are used to develop the sample application and code samples.

Understanding ODBC Operation

Before you can access ODBC databases, you must configure the ODBC data source names, the ODBC drivers, and the configuration values used in ODBC.INI. You also should understand the structure of an ODBC driver and the ODBC API as well as some ODBC-related terminology.

Defining ODBC Terminology

ODBC drivers are classified as either single-tier or multiple-tier:

- A *single-tier* driver is designed for use with remote desktop database management systems (DBMSs). Such drivers include Access, FoxPro, dBASE, spreadsheets, and text files. The SQL statement issued to the ODBC driver is converted into low-level instructions that operate on the database files directly.

- A *multiple-tier* driver uses a client/server database to process the SQL statement that the application sends. The remote database server processes the statement and returns the statement's result.

Each ODBC driver conforms to one of three levels of capabilities: Core Level, Level 1, and Level 2.

The Core Level is the base set of capabilities that an ODBC driver must contain. All ODBC drivers *must* meet the requirements of this level. The Core Level capabilities for an ODBC driver are the following:

- Providing applications with database connections

- Preparing and executing SQL statements

- Returning results from queries

- Processing transactions, including rollbacks and commits

- Providing error information

Level 1 includes the capabilities of Core Level ODC drivers plus data-source connectivity through driver-specific dialogs. All ODBC drivers that the Jet engine uses must meet or exceed this level.

Level 2 includes the capabilities of a Level 1 ODBC driver plus the following capabilities:

- Browsing available connections to data sources

- Retrieving query results in array format

- Providing scrollable cursors

- Obtaining additional information such as stored procedures

Adding ODBC Drivers

Before accessing an ODBC database, you must install on your system the appropriate ODBC driver for that database. You install this driver by using the ODBC Manager applet in the Windows Control Panel. You can also use the ODBCADM.EXE program supplied with Visual Basic.

To install an ODBC driver, just perform the following steps:

1. Click on the ODBC Manager applet in the Control Panel as shown in figure 9.2.

Fig. 9.2
Opening the ODBC Manager application to maintain ODBC drivers and data sources.

2. The Data Sources dialog box, shown in figure 9.3, appears. This dialog box contains all the data sources listed in ODBC.INI.

3. Select the Drivers button. The Drivers dialog box appears (see fig. 9.4), displaying all ODBC drivers installed on the system.

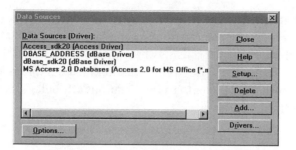

Fig. 9.3
Browsing the available data sources with the ODBC Manager.

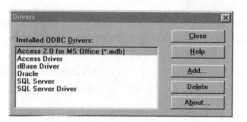

Fig. 9.4
Using the ODBC Manager to add a new ODBC driver to the system.

4. To add an ODBC driver, choose the <u>A</u>dd button. The Add Driver dialog box appears (see fig. 9.5), prompting you to enter the ODBC driver disk to install.

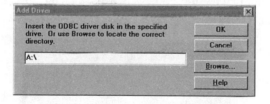

Fig. 9.5
Completing the ODBC driver installation.

5. Insert the disk and follow the installation instructions. The installation process adds the ODBC driver to the system and updates the ODBCINST.INI file with the installed driver information.

Caution

The ODBC driver that you install *must* be at least Level 1 compliant. Most ODBC drivers meet this requirement. The driver's manufacturer can tell you whether its product has all the Level 1 capabilities.

Creating and Naming ODBC Data Sources

An *ODBC data source* is a named connection to a database. ODBC.INI stores the data-source entry, which consists of the information necessary for connecting to the database server. This information includes the database name and location, the ODBC driver to use, and various attributes specific to the ODBC driver that you are using.

To create an ODBC data source, two methods are available:

■ Through the ODBC Data Manager

■ Through the data access object using the Database engine's RegisterDatabase method.

Adding an ODBC data source is easy. To add a data source through the ODBC Data Manager control applet, perform the following steps:

1. Open the Windows Control Panel and click on the ODBC Data Manager applet or start the ODBCADM.EXE program included with Visual Basic. The Data Sources dialog box appears, containing all the data sources listed in ODBC.INI.

2. Select the Add button. The Add Data Source dialog box appears as shown in figure 9.6. This dialog box lists all ODBC drivers installed on the system.

Fig. 9.6
Choosing an
ODBC driver to
use when adding a
data source.

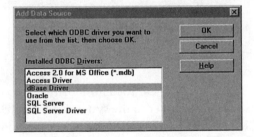

3. Select the appropriate driver from the list. A driver-specific dialog box appears for ODBC setup. For example, figure 9.7 shows the dialog box that you see if you select the dBASE driver in the Add Data Source dialog box.

4. Enter the appropriate information, including the data source name and description along with the driver-specific information, and choose OK. The ODBC Data Manager then adds the data source to the data-source list and ODBC.INI.

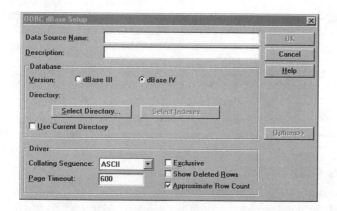

Fig. 9.7
Setting the ODBC driver-specific options for a data source.

To add a data-source name using the RegisterDatabase method in DBEngine, you first must examine the method to understand the information that it requires:

```
DBEngine.RegisterDatabase dbName, driver, silent, attributes
```

The parameters in this syntax are the following:

Parameter	Definition
dbName	A user-definable string expression that specifies the data source's name (for example, MyDatabase).
driver	A string expression that indicates the installed driver's name (for example, ORACLE) as listed in ODBCINST.INI. Note that this expression is the name of the driver section in ODBCINST.INI, not the driver's DLL name.
silent	True specifies that the next parameter (attributes) indicates all connection information. False specifies to display the Driver Setup dialog box and ignore the contents of the attributes parameter.
attributes	All connection information for using the ODBC driver. This parameter is ignored if silent is set to False.

Listing 9.1 is a code example that demonstrates how to add a data source programmatically for the Address Book example in Chapter 8.

Listing 9.1   Adding a Data Source Programmatically for the Address Book Example

```
Dim Attrib As String
    Attrib = "Description=Address dBase" & Chr$(13)
```

(continues)

```
Listing 9.1  Continued
    Attrib = Attrib & "Driver=C:\WINDOWS\SYSTEM\simba.dll" & _
            Chr$(13)
    Attrib = Attrib & "FileType = dBase4" & Chr$(13)
    Attrib = Attrib & "DataDirectory=C:\VB4\Address" & Chr$(13)
    Attrib = Attrib & "SingleUser = False" & Chr$(13)
    DBEngine.RegisterDatabase "DBASE ADDRESS", "dBase Driver", _
            True, Attrib
```

Setting ODBC Time-Out Values

Because you use ODBC primarily for accessing client/server databases, delays are possible in database logins and queries, particularly when the database server resides on a mainframe or host computer connected by a modem or bridge. The delay is primarily due to the time necessary to issue calls to the database server through the local area network (LAN) or dial-up communication lines.

Visual Basic maintains a default database-login time of 20 seconds. This value is used when the user issues an OpenDatabase command. If Visual Basic cannot establish the connection within this timeframe, the OpenDatabase call fails. You can alter this value through DBEngine's LoginTimeout property, as in the following statement:

```
DBEngine.LoginTimeout = 120 'set time-out for 2 minutes
```

The default time-out value for database queries is 60 seconds. You can alter this value by changing the database QueryTimeout property or a QueryDef's ODBCTimeout property. Be careful when performing queries on tables that contain BLOB (Binary Large Objects) information. Queries on such tables are typically very slow, so you might want to increase the time-out value according to the BLOB data's size and the database server's speed. If you specify 0, no time-out occurs. The following examples demonstrate alterations to the default time-out:

```
MyDatabase.QueryTimeout = 120 ' 2 minutes
MyQueryDef.ODBCTimeout = 180 ' 3 minutes
```

The ODBC section of VB.INI or APP.INI also maintains these time-out values, as you will see in the upcoming sections.

Examining ODBC.INI and ODBCINST.INI

As mentioned earlier, ODBC operation depends on two files that the ODBC Data Manager creates: ODBC.INI and ODBCINST.INI.

ODBCINST.INI is located in the Windows directory and contains information about the ODBC drivers installed on the system. Listing 9.2 shows a sample ODBCINST.INI file.

Listing 9.2   A Sample ODBCINST.INI File

```
[ODBC Drivers]
SQL Server=Installed
Access 2.0 for MS Office (*.mdb)=Installed
Oracle=Installed
SQL Server Driver=Installed
Access Driver=Installed
dBase Driver=Installed

[SQL Server]
Driver=C:\WINDOWS\SYSTEM\SQLSRVR.DLL
Setup=C:\WINDOWS\SYSTEM\SQLSRVR.DLL

[Access 2.0 for MS Office (*.mdb)]
Driver=C:\WINDOWS\SYSTEM\ODBCJT16.DLL
Setup=C:\WINDOWS\SYSTEM\ODBCJT16.DLL

[Oracle]
Driver=C:\WINDOWS\SYSTEM\sqora.dll
Setup=C:\WINDOWS\SYSTEM\orasetup.dll

[MS Code Page Translator]
Translator=C:\WINDOWS\SYSTEM\mscpxlt.dll
Setup=C:\WINDOWS\SYSTEM\mscpxlt.dll

[ODBC Translators]
MS Code Page Translator=Installed

[SQL Server Driver]
Driver-C:\WINDOWS\SYSTEM\sqlsrvr.dll
Setup=C:\WINDOWS\SYSTEM\sqlsrvr.dll

[Access Driver]
Driver=C:\WINDOWS\SYSTEM\simba.dll
Setup=C:\WINDOWS\SYSTEM\simadmin.dll
SQLLevel=0
APILevel=1
FileUsage=2
FileExtns=*.mdb
DriverODBCVer=01.00
ConnectFunctions=YYN

[dBase Driver]
Driver=C:\WINDOWS\SYSTEM\simba.dll
Setup=C:\WINDOWS\SYSTEM\simadmin.dll
SQLLevel=0
APILevel=1
FileUsage=1
FileExtns=*.dbf
DriverODBCVer=01.00
ConnectFunctions=YYN
```

At the top of the ODBCINST.INI file is the [ODBC Drivers] section. This section lists all installed ODBC drivers. The Installed Drivers dialog box of the

ODBC Data Manager lists all installed ODBC drivers. Note that for client/server databases or multiple-tier drivers, the entries are simple. Each section contains a "Driver" and "Setup" entry. Single-tier drivers have additional parameters, such as the SQLLevel and APILevel that the driver supports.

The ODBC.INI file maintains a list of all defined ODBC data sources. The file contains all the information about the data source as specified through the Add Data Source dialog box (see fig. 9.6) or by the *attributes* parameter of the RegisterDatabase method. Listing 9.3 shows a sample ODBC.INI file.

Listing 9.3   A Sample ODBC.INI File

```
[ODBC Data Sources]
MS Access 2.0 Databases=Access 2.0 for MS Office (*.mdb)
Access_sdk20=Access Driver
dBase_sdk20=dBase Driver
DBASE ADDRESS=dBase Driver

[MS Access 2.0 Databases]
Driver=C:\WINDOWS\SYSTEM\ODBCJT16.DLL
DBQ=ADDRESS.MDB
DefaultDir=C:\VB4\ADDRESS
Description=Address
FIL=Microsoft Access
JetIniPath=MSACC20.INI
UID=Admin

[ODBC]
TraceAutoStop=1
Trace=0
TraceFile=\SQL.LOG

[Access_sdk20]
Driver=C:\WINDOWS\SYSTEM\simba.dll
Description=Sample Access Data
FileType=RedISAM
DataDirectory=C:\ODBCSDK\SMPLDATA\ACCESS\SAMPLE.MDB
SingleUser=False
UseSystemDB=False

[dBase_sdk20]
Driver=C:\WINDOWS\SYSTEM\simba.dll
Description=Sample dBase Data
FileType=dBase4
DataDirectory=C:\ODBCSDK\SMPLDATA\DBASE
SingleUser=False

[DBASE ADDRESS]
Driver=C:\WINDOWS\SYSTEM\simba.dll
Description=Address DBase
DataDirectory=C:\VB4\Address
FileType=dBase4
SingleUser=False
```

Using the ODBC Section in VB.INI or APP.INI

The last set of parameters that affect ODBC operation is contained in an ODBC section of VB.INI or your application's initialization file, APP.INI. Table 9.1 indicates the valid entries, their purpose, and any default values.

Table 9.1 Application-Specific Parameters That Affect ODBC Operation

Entry	Purpose	Valid Values
TraceSQLMode	Trace the ODBC API calls that the Jet engine sends	0 = Don't Trace (default) 1 = Trace
QueryTimeout	Abort queries that don't finish within the specified number of seconds	60 seconds (default)
LoginTimeout	Abort login attempts that don't finish within the specified number of seconds	20 seconds (default)
ConnectionTimeout	Close active connections that are idle for the specified number of seconds	600 seconds (default)
AsyncRetryInterval	Set the interval for asking the server whether the query is finished; specified in milliseconds	500 milliseconds (default)
AttachCaseSensitive	Use case-sensitivity when attaching to tables	0 = No case sensitivity (default) 1 = Use case sensitivity
SnapshotOnly	Create both dynaset and snapshot recordset objects or only snapshots	0 = Create both (default) 1 = Create only snapshots
AttachableObjects	List (in a string) the database server object types to which you can connect	"TABLE,VIEW,SYSTEM TABLE,ALIAS,SYNONYM" (default)

Converting ODBC Data Types

When applications read in external data types, a one-to-one correspondence between types does not always occur. Such is the case when reading external ODBC data sources. You need to understand how ODBC data types relate to Jet engine data types. Such an understanding is important when you attach an ODBC table to a database. The Jet engine maps ODBC data types to Jet data types. Table 9.2 describes these relationships.

Table 9.2   Comparing ODBC and Jet Data Types

ODBC Data Type	Description	Visual Basic Data Type
SQL_BIT	Single-bit binary data	YES/NO
SQL_TINYINT	A whole number between 0 and 255 inclusive	Integer
SQL_SMALLINT	A whole number between 32,767 and −32,768, inclusive	Integer
SQL_INTEGER	A whole number between 2,147,483,647 and −2,147,483,648, inclusive	Long
SQL_REAL	A floating point number with seven-digit precision	Single
SQL_FLOAT, SQL_DOUBLE	A floating-point number with 15-digit precision	Double
SQL_TIMESTAMP, SQL_DATE, SQL_TIME	Date and time data	DateTime
SQL_CHAR	Character string	If 255 characters or more, Text; if less than 255 characters, Memo
SQL_VARCHAR	A variable-length character string with a maximum length of 255	Text
SQL_BINARY	Fixed-length binary data	If 255 characters or more, Binary, where the precision is Field Size; if less than 255 characters, OLE Field
SQL_VARBINARY	Variable-length binary data with a maximum length of 255 characters	Binary

ODBC Data Type	Description	Visual Basic Data Type
SQL_LONGVARBINARY	Variable-length binary data with a source-dependent maximum length	OLE Field
SQL_LONGVARCHAR	A variable-length character string with a source-dependent maximum length	Memo
SQL_DECIMAL, SQL_NUMERIC	Signed, exact, numeric value with precision and scale	If the scale is 0, then ?; if the precision is 4 or greater, Integer; if the precision is 9 or greater, Long; if the precision is 15 or greater, Double; if the scale is less than 0 and the precision is greater than 15, Double

Comparing the ODBC API and Jet's Data Access Objects

When accessing ODBC databases, you can use two methods: directly through the ODBC API or with the Jet data access object. Note that for Jet to access the ODBC databases, the data access object calls the ODBC API internally.

The ODBC API

The ODBC API consists of approximately 30 functions. It supports field-by-field data retrieval and uses the SQL syntax for manipulating and defining data. The various ODBC drivers conform to one of the three levels of capabilities (Core Level, Level 1, and Level 2). To use the ODBC API directly, you must know the level of ODBC that the driver supports.

The Jet data access object can use ODBC drivers that provide Level 1 support. Therefore, Jet does *not* support the complete set of ODBC functions. Table 9.3 lists all the ODBC functions that the Jet engine supports.

Table 9.3   ODBC API Functions Supported by the Jet Engine

Function	Purpose
SQLAllocConnect	Obtains a connection handle.

(continues)

Table 9.3 Continued

Function	Purpose
SQLAllocEnv	Obtains an environment handle. You use one environment handle for one or more connections.
SQLAllocStmt	Allocates a statement handle.
SQLCancel	Cancels a SQL statement.
SQLColumns	Returns the list of column names in specified tables.
SQLDescribeCol	Describes a column in the result set.
SQLDisconnect	Closes the connection.
SQLDriverConnect	Connects to a specific driver by a connection string or requests that the Driver Manager and the driver display connection dialog boxes for the user.
SQLError	Returns additional error or status information.
SQLExecDirect	Executes a statement.
SQLExecute	Executes a prepared statement.
SQLFetch	Returns a result row.
SQLFreeConnect	Releases the connection handle.
SQLFreeEnv	Releases the environment handle.
SQLFreeStmt	Ends statement processing, closes the associated cursor, discards pending results, and, optionally, frees all resources associated with the statement handle.
SQLGetData	Returns part or all of one column of one row of a result set.
SQLGetInfo	Returns information about a specific driver and data source.
SQLGetTypeInfo	Returns information about supported data types.
SQLNumResultCols	Returns the number of columns in the result set.
SQLParamData	Used with SQLPutData, supplies parameter data at execution time.
SQLPrepare	Prepares a SQL statement for later execution.
SQLPutData	Sends part or all of a data value for a parameter.
SQLRowCount	Returns the number of rows affected by an insert, update, or delete request.

Function	Purpose
SQLSetConnectOption	Sets a connection option.
SQLSetParam	Binds a buffer to a parameter in a SQL statement. Replaced with SQLBindParam.
SQLSetStmtOption	Sets a statement option.
SQLSpecialColumns	Returns information about the optimal set of columns that uniquely identifies a row in a specified table, or the columns that are automatically updated when a transaction updates any value in the row.
SQLStatistics	Returns statistics about a single table and the list of indexes associated with the table.
SQLTables	Returns the list of table names stored in a specific data source.
SQLTransact	Commits or rolls back a transaction.

Visual Basic does not include the ODBC constants and functions that Visual Basic developers need. However, this exclusion does not prohibit you from using the ODBC API. All the ODBC functions are in the file ODBC.DLL, which Visual Basic includes. The documentation for these functions, as well as the Visual Basic prototypes, are available in the ODBC Developer's SDK.

Using the ODBC API directly has some advantages. The API is quite flexible because it is a very low-level API. In other words, the ODBC API is used for directly issuing commands to a database server. The developer must build all data structures for retrieving data. This gives the programmer maximum power in designing applications. Also, the API is fast, goes directly to the database server, and imposes no additional overhead. Finally, ODBC is designed to provide connectivity to all databases and thus is portable across languages and databases.

On the other hand, the ODBC also presents some disadvantages. First, you need an external development kit, the ODBC SDK, to get the prototypes and documentation required for using the API functions. Because the ODBC is a very low-level API, you find yourself building many "wrapper" or helper functions to provide a higher level of interface for your application. The API provides no object model on which you can build and use. Additionally, the ODBC API is subject to change, leaving the developer with the possibility of developing to a moving target. And finally, only rarely will an application be likely to need to access the ODBC API directly.

The Jet Data Access Object

Visual Basic's data access object is the preferred method for accessing ODBC databases because it uses the ODBC API internally, provides a higher-level interface, and is based on an object model.

The data access object consists of two sets of functions: the Data Definition Language (DDL) and the Data Manipulation Language (DML). Table 9.4 lists the interfaces that comprise the data access object and their purpose.

Table 9.4   Data Access Object Interfaces

Data Access Object Interface	Purpose	Type
DBEngine	A top-level object that corresponds to the Jet engine	DML, DDL
Workspace	A container for open databases that supports simultaneous transactions	DML, DDL
Database	Represents the database layout; corresponds to a native Jet database, an external database, or an ODBC connection	DML, DDL
TableDef	Represents a physical database table definition	DDL
QueryDef	Defines a stored query or precompiled SQL statement; stored in the database rather than the code	DDL
Recordset	Returns the results of a query into a database	DML
Field	Represents a column of data in a table	DDL
Index	Represents a stored index for a table	DDL
Parameter	Represents a stored query parameter associated with a parameterized query	DDL
User	Defines and enforces database security	DDL
Group	A collection of users with similar privileges	DDL
Relation	Defines relationships among fields in two or more tables	DDL
Property	Represents a stored property associated with an object	DDL

Data Access Object Interface	Purpose	Type
Container	Enumerates all objects stored in a database	DDL
Document	Objects of a common type that share a container	DDL

When using the data access object, your Visual Basic program can access ODBC databases in the same manner as desktop databases. The preferred method for accessing ODBC databases is to attach the tables in an ODBC data source to your application's database. Listing 9.4 shows how you attach tables to an ODBC database.

Listing 9.4   Attaching Tables to an ODBC Database

```
Dim Db As Database
Dim Table As TableDef
' first open your application's database
Set Db = DBEngine.Workspaces(0).OpenDatabase(c:\path\app.mdb)
' now create the table definition object
Set Table = Db.CreateTableDef("Attached ODBC Database")
' create the connection information
Table.Connect =
"ODBC;DATABASE=ADDRESS;UID=Guest;PWD=Password;DSN=DataSource"
Table.SourceTableName="ADDRESS"
' now append the table definition to the open db
Db.TableDefs.Append Table
```

In listing 9.4, the string passed into the CreateTableDef method is the TableDef name. The Connect string consists of the following items:

- The database type, which in this case is ODBC.

- A string of parameters specific to the ODBC driver that you are using. The string contains the database name or path, the user login ID, the user password, the Data Source Name as identified by ODBC.INI, and an optional Logintimeout.

Direct Access to the Database Server

Attaching a table as just described is one method for accessing an ODBC database with the data access object. You also can use the data access object by directly opening and using DBEngine's OpenDatabase method and specifying an ODBC connection string. You shouldn't use this access method, however, because it slows your application's performance.

When attaching to an ODBC database, the Jet engine stores a great deal of information about the table locally, including table and field information as well as server capabilities. When an application opens an ODBC database directly, Jet asks the server for this information every time that the application performs a query.

Performance Concerns: *dynasets* versus *snapshots*

To access ODBC data from Visual Basic, you can use one of two methods: by writing directly to the ODBC API or by using the data access object.

When developing client/server applications with ODBC, you must consider a different set of performance concerns than when working with remote databases.

Visual Basic 4.0 replaces Visual Basic 3.0's dynaset, snapshot, and Table objects with one generic object, Recordset.

> **Note**
>
> Visual Basic 4.0 still preserves the dynaset, snapshot, and Table objects and syntax to provide backward compatibility.

When creating a Recordset object, you specify the type of recordset that you are creating. The type can be dynaset, snapshot, or Table. When accessing remote data through an ODBC connection, you can create two types of Recordset objects: dynaset or snapshot.

A Recordset object of type dynaset or snapshot returns as the result of a data query. The dynaset type contains a "live," updatable view of the data in the underlying tables. When the dynaset changes, the underlying tables are immediately updated; conversely, when the tables change, the dynaset is updated. A snapshot is a static or nonupdatable view of the data in the underlying tables.

To understand more clearly when to choose one type rather than another, you need to know how each type of recordset is populated. When you create a snapshot, Visual Basic retrieves all the data in the selected columns of the matching rows and places the retrieved data in the recordset. Conversely, when you create a dynaset object, Visual Basic retrieves only the primary key (or *bookmark*) of the query. For both recordsets, Visual Basic stores in memory the results of the query.

The Jet engine is optimized to return only as many records as it needs to fill the resulting display screen. The rest of the data is retrieved either in idle time or through user scrolling (scrolling indicates an on-demand situation where the records are retrieved only when the user moves to records not visible on the screen). Again, the snapshot recordset retrieves all the selected columns in the matching rows, but dynaset retrieves the matching primary keys.

When you need rows of information, the snapshot recordset has all the information in memory and readily accessible for use. Because a dynaset recordset contains only the primary keys in memory, the Jet engine sends a separate query to the server to request all the selected columns. Jet optimizes this process by requesting clusters of information rather than one row at a time. The dynaset retrieves about 100 records surrounding the current record to create the impression that data is being retrieved rapidly.

Because they use different methods to retrieve and cache data, the performance of snapshot and dynaset recordsets differs greatly. The following are performance considerations for each type:

- If your result set is small and you don't need to update data or to see changes that other users have made, use a snapshot recordset. It is faster to open and scroll through. Also, if you need to make only one pass through the results, use the dbForwardOnly option when creating the recordset. This option prohibits copying the data to a scrollable buffer.

- When working with very large result sets, use a dynaset recordset. Unlike snapshots, dynasets retrieve only the primary key, so jumping from beginning to end to retrieve data from both the first and last groups of data, for example, is much faster.

- When using a dynaset recordset, limit the number of tables and columns that the query selects. Select only the columns that you need. (For example, don't use the * indicator for all columns.)

- If your result set contains memo or OLE fields, using a dynaset is much more efficient. dynasets retrieve memo and OLE fields *only* if your application is to display them on-screen. A snapshot retrieves all columns selected for the matching rows, and thus retrieves results in the memo fields during the query.

Understanding SQL Pass-through

When accessing data, your application can use two methods: queries based on the Jet engine and pass-through queries. In a Jet engine query, the engine compiles the statement and then sends it to the server. In a pass-through query, your application sends directly to the database server the SQL statement that you enter.

Pass-through queries offer a few advantages over compiled queries:

- Instead of the client machine processing and sending the query in chunks, the server processes the query, thus reducing network bandwidth.

- You can log the informational messages and statistics that the server returns.

- You can access server-specific functionality. Often, no equivalent Jet function or statement corresponds to the server's function.

- You can provide access to nonstandard SQL extensions that the server supports. You can also directly access data-definition, administration, and security commands.

- You can support joins of multiple tables in multiple databases.

- Action queries such as update, delete, and add are faster than compiled queries that are based on attached tables.

Using SQL pass-through statements also has some disadvantages:

- Such queries return snapshots only.

- The client must know the server's exact SQL syntax. Therefore, the code is not portable.

- You cannot parameterize pass-through queries.

Using Stored Procedures

A stored procedure is analogous to a Jet engine QueryDef. Such a procedure consists of a set of SQL statements that the server stores. The application program accesses a stored procedure to retrieve and update data. In some environments, stored procedures perform all data requests and updates because the application programs have no direct access to the remote tables.

If your application must update data in an environment in which you have no direct access to remote tables, you must execute a SQL pass-through that calls a stored procedure.

From Here...

Client/server computing offers network users great power and flexibility. A powerful database server can reside on a fast CPU to provide information to a host of clients. As this chapter has shown, Visual Basic offers a variety of methods for accessing ODBC database servers. You can use the ODBC APIs for directly accessing the database, and use the Jet engine's data access objects to provide a higher-level object interface. You can combine this interface with SQL pass-through statements to access a server's functionality directly. Visual Basic showcases these capabilities in providing a quality database-development environment.

To learn more about the Jet engine, see Chapter 8, "Accessing Other Databases with the Jet Engine." This chapter provides more information about the Jet engine and demonstrates how to use it to bring external data into database applications.

Chapter 10

Linking Databases to Other Programs

A database is a repository of systematically organized information. Applications that use database systems hide the database structure from users and instead present logically ordered information. Often, external (nondatabase) applications that do not have database access, such as a word processor or spreadsheet, must retrieve database information. How can you provide data to such applications while hiding database-access techniques from the application integrator? The answer lies in creating distributed applications that you can easily integrate into external applications.

In this chapter, you learn about the following:

- Using DDE to share data among applications

- Creating programmable applications with OLE Automation

- Choosing between DDE or OLE

- Understanding architectural concerns related to data sharing

- Database-enabling other applications

Creating Distributed Applications and Systems Integration

Distributed applications enable you to divide complex computing tasks into separate processes that can run on the same or different machines. Creating distributed applications requires a different set of design and coding skills than creating stand-alone applications. Knowledge of distributed architectures, interprocess communications, and systems integration is essential.

To create distributed applications, you need a thorough understanding of the operating environment. The Windows operating systems provide several interprocess communications (IPC) facilities that applications can use, including Dynamic Data Exchange (DDE) and Object Linking and Embedding (OLE). Some of the operating systems (Windows for Workgroups, Windows NT, and Windows 95) enable you to use DDE across the network with NetDDE. Soon, you will also be able to distribute OLE across the network.

The Distributed Operating Environment

In today's operating environments, no application stands alone. In typical operating environments, users often work with many applications simultaneously, frequently with data common to some or all applications. Microsoft has introduced many technologies into its operating systems to facilitate the integration of data sharing and application interoperability.

These technologies have moved the desktop from an application-centered to a data-centered mode of operation. No longer do you use monolithic applications for all tasks. Now, more dedicated applications share and move information seamlessly among one another. These applications form a distributed operating environment. In layman's terms, a *distributed environment* is one in which you use many applications to accomplish a task. A simple example of a distributed environment is one in which you fax a word processing document. You use the word processor to create your fax, and the word processor's print menu sends the document to a background fax spooler, which sends the document to its final destination.

Database applications fit naturally into the distributed operating environment. You can employ many methods to share such applications' data. Many users can open and use the same data in a file server environment, in which the database tables reside on a common server and many instances of an application access them. The client/server environment is inherently distributed, as a client application accesses a database server for information.

Windows incorporates many technologies that enable interprocess communication among applications. The interprocess capabilities enable your applications to share data with other applications. The interprocess communication capabilities also enable you to build business solutions by integrating many applications, thus letting your application become part of the distributed environment. These technologies include OLE, DDE, OLE Automation, and Remote Procedure Calls (RPC).

Database-Enabling Other Applications

For a database application to share information with an external application, the two applications must communicate. A typical database application resides on a local computer or on a local area network (LAN). To database-enable an external application, you must establish an interprocess communication protocol between the two applications. The Windows family of operating systems provides several methods of interprocess communication (IPC) to data-enable other applications. These methods include Dynamic Data Exchange (DDE) and Object Linking and Embedding (OLE).

Each of these protocols makes your application programmable from external applications. Because the Windows operating systems are multitasking (capable of running many programs simultaneously), program interoperability is crucial to a user-friendly operating environment. In the days of MS-DOS, you could run only one program at a time, so interprocess communications were not very important. Today, your applications must employ an IPC mechanism to provide users with a powerful programming tool that they can use to solve their computing problems.

Systems Integration: A New Type of Computing Problem

The distributed operating environment creates a new problem that didn't exist in the application-centered environment: systems integration. *Systems integration* involves creating an environment in which, ideally, all applications run together and share information among each other. Unfortunately, this environment is easier to create on paper than in a real computing environment.

In the real world, claims that an application is "OLE-enabled" or "supports DDE" don't carry the same meaning from vendor to vendor. The meaning of such claims changes even from application to application. Although this chapter doesn't solve the problem of application coexistence, it does describe some techniques that you can employ in your applications to make them "well-behaved" Windows applications.

Architectural Concerns in Exposing the Database to Other Applications

When exposing your database to other applications, be particularly careful that you do not compromise your database's integrity. After all, a database is only as good as the information that it contains.

Determining which features of your database application to expose to other applications is often your toughest choice. Keep in mind that your application should contain all the error checking and data dictionary rules to follow for performing database operations. External applications do not contain all of your application's error-checking and referential-integrity features. With this in mind, you should design your application to be an object, or a "black box," to external applications. The black box approach provides an interface for external applications while sheltering the internal implementation details from external applications.

The object or black box concept provides meaningful functionality to other applications without providing direct access to your application's data. By denying such access, you prevent rogue applications from corrupting your data or causing your application to behave incorrectly. Also, by denying direct access to your application's data members, you can change the internal implementation of your application's interfaces. By doing so, you ensure that as you release new versions of your application, it remains compatible with other programs.

Figure 10.1 contrasts the black box concept with direct access to data members.

Fig. 10.1
Implementation differences between black box and direct-access interfaces.

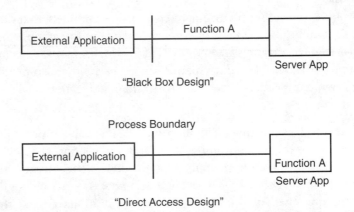

"Black Box Design"

"Direct Access Design"

Planning for a Distributed Architecture

When planning for a distributed architecture, one of the foremost decisions that you must make is whether to use DDE or OLE Automation. DDE is an existing protocol that Microsoft is phasing out, and OLE Automation is the new standard that many existing applications do not support.

Implementing a DDE server is a simple and quick task that you can accomplish during the design phase of building your applications. You probably should implement such a server to provide backward compatibility with existing programs.

> **Note**
>
> OLE Automation is one of the most important technologies that Microsoft has released. You should provide this support in your applications. Windows 95, Windows NT, and future versions of the Windows operating systems will support OLE and OLE Automation. Implementing these technologies is critical to running on future operating system platforms.

When implementing OLE Automation in your application, it is easier to place your upfront thought in the design and creation of your programmable objects. After designing your objects, incorporate these objects into your application. If you define the interfaces that you are providing to external applications, many of the helper functions that you need for the user interface will reside in your object and can then be used by the user interface forms.

For distributed applications, take special precautions for code maintenance. Your solution depends on many different components, so you must carefully design the interfaces among applications. In a distributed environment, you can easily add functionality to one application and simultaneously break the interface to another.

Using DDE and OLE to Pass Data

The most common form of IPC is to pass data among applications. DDE and OLE both are capable of sharing and passing data, but the mechanics that you use are quite different.

DDE uses shared memory to exchange data among processes. To obtain shared memory, you use the function GlobalAlloc. This function returns a handle to memory of the size specified by the user. When creating shared memory, you must pass the flag GMEM_DDESHARE in a parameter to the function call. This flag informs Windows that many programs besides the one allocating the memory can access the memory block. The GlobalAlloc function then fills the memory block with the data and sends the block to the destination program. Fortunately, the Visual Basic environment handles all the memory management details, so you only see the data passing between programs.

OLE also uses shared memory, but the memory is allocated within the OLE libraries instead of being specified by the sending application. As data passes from the sending program, the OLE libraries perform boundary marshaling across process or DLL boundaries. OLE allocates shared memory for the receiving program and copies the data it is sending into this memory space. The receiving program then gets a copy of the data. Figure 10.2 illustrates OLE data passing.

Fig. 10.2
How OLE passes data between applications.

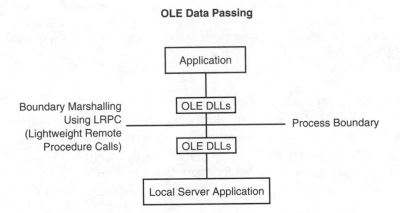

OLE Data Passing

Boundary Marshalling Using LRPC (Lightweight Remote Procedure Calls)

Process Boundary

Dynamic Data Exchange (DDE)

Dynamic Data Exchange (DDE), which Microsoft introduced with Windows 1.0, defines a standard protocol for exchanging data among active applications. DDE was the first IPC protocol implemented in the Windows environment, so most existing programs provide support for DDE. This is in contrast to OLE technologies, which are much harder to implement. Today, most application vendors add OLE support into their applications.

DDE enables your program to be a client, server, or both. Therefore, your application can both provide data to and receive data from other applications. Later you learn how to create DDE clients and servers, but the next section first provides an overview of DDE.

DDE Overview

All DDE connections or conversations require a few basic items: the application, topic, and item. These items establish the protocol used in forming the conversation. In this context, the term *application* refers to the application name. In Visual Basic, this name is that of the makefile, without the .MAK extension, when running from the Visual Basic development environment, or the name of a compiled executable program without the .EXE extension.

The *topic* refers to nature of the conversation. Some default conversations are system-wide and usually supported by most programs. The most widely available topic is the system topic. Each application creates its own unique conversations. You should document your applications' conversions so that other programs can take advantage of them. The application and topic uniquely identify a conversation.

The *item* is a reference to data that is meaningful to both applications. Each application should create and document its own items. When an application's control (such as an edit field) is the client (or *destination*) in a conversation, the control's LinkItem property defines the item. When the control is to be a server (or *source*), the control's name is used as the item name.

DDE's capability to establish connections automatically is limited. Before you can establish a DDE connection, both the client and server application must be running. Unlike OLE, DDE does not automatically start the server application. If the DDE server isn't already running, the Visual Basic function Shell can start it.

DDE terminology and documentation refer to the server application as the *source* and the client application as the *destination*. A conversation starts when a source application receives a request for a topic that it recognizes. After establishing a conversation, neither the source nor destination applications can switch topics. If either the application or topic changes, the conversation terminates.

During a conversation, the applications can exchange information about one or more items. Either the source or the destination can change without affecting the state of the conversation. Combined, the application, topic, and item uniquely identify the data that applications pass between each other.

DDE conversations are often referred to as *links*, because the source and destination applications are linked by the data that they are exchanging. As table 10.1 indicates, applications can establish three kinds of links. The difference among the links is the manner by which the source updates the destination.

Data Access

Table 10.1   The DDE Links Available with Windows

Connection/Link Type	Description
None	No DDE connection is specified.
Manual	The source supplies data to the destination only when requested.
Automatic	The source supplies data to the destination each time that the data defined by the LinkItem property changes.
Notify	The source notifies the destination when the data changes but supplies the data only when requested.

Note

Using the DDE Execute command is similar to issuing a function call (or calling a function in a DLL) to the server applications. After establishing a connection, an application can use the Execute command to send command strings.

Table 10.2 lists Visual Basic methods that you can use to manipulate other applications after establishing a conversation. These methods are part of the Visual Basic controls.

Table 10.2   Visual Basic Methods Available for DDE Conversations

Method	Description
LinkPoke	Transfers a control's contents to the source application.
LinkRequest	Asks the source application to update a control's contents.
LinkExecute	Sends a command string to an application.
LinkSend	Transfers a picture control's contents to the destination application.
Shell	Starts an external application. You can use this function to start the DDE server application.

Your application must provide handlers for two DDE events: LinkNotify and LinkExecute. The LinkExecute event attaches to a form and defines the set of commands to which your application responds. The LinkNotify event attaches to controls and performs the action required to notify destination applications when data changes within the control.

Today, DDE offers one significant advantage over other IPC technologies: remote or network access to other applications. Starting with Windows for Workgroups, the Windows operating systems include NetDDE, which enables you to establish links to applications running on remote computers. Visual Basic 4.0 offers an implementation of distributed OLE, although distributed OLE will not become a standard part of the Windows operating systems until the Cairo version of Windows NT is available.

Creating a DDE Server

Creating a DDE server application is relatively easy. In the Visual Basic development environment, the project name determines the application name, and if you are running a stand-alone application, the executable name determines the application name. The form that performs the DDE conversation specifies the topic name, which you set in the form's LinkTopic property. You set the form's LinkMode property to 1 (Source), indicating that the application will supply information.

Individual controls that you place on the form (such as text boxes and edit boxes) comprise the topic's items. The control names, which you specify in the name property, identify these items. After you specify these settings, Visual Basic handles all the conversation negotiations.

Most applications that support DDE also provide support for the System topic. You can use this topic to request from the application such information as which topics and data formats the application supports. To support the System topic, create a form and set the LinkTopic property to System. Then create controls on that form that correspond to the various system topics. One of the more typical system items is the topic item, which specifies all the topics to which the application can respond. Table 10.3 describes the common items supported by applications responding to the System topic.

Table 10.3   Available Items Used for System Conversations

Item	Description
Topics	Generates a tab-separated list of all topics that the application supports, including System
Status	Returns Busy or Ready
Format	Generates a tab-separated list of formats that the source application can copy to the Clipboard
SysItems	Generates a tab-separated list of all items supported by the System topic.

Data Access

In summary, the following steps are necessary to create a DDE server:

1. Set the LinkTopic property in the form that will respond to the conversation topic. This property corresponds to the topic name.

2. Set the form's LinkMode property to 1 (Source). If you do not set this property, no destination application can initiate a conversation with that form as a topic. All the form's controls are topic items.

> **Note**
>
> At design time, you *must* set the LinkMode property to 1 (SOURCE). You cannot switch the form from None at design time to SOURCE at run time. If you set the property to SOURCE at design time, you can set it to None and then back to SOURCE.

Creating a DDE Client

Creating a DDE client is also fairly simple in Visual Basic. You can do so either at run time or at application design time. In either case, the rules that you follow are the same.

To establish a DDE conversation, both the client and the server must know the application name, topics, and items. You might be able to query the names of the topics and items that an application supports through the System topic, but when you establish a DDE conversation, you usually do so for a specific purpose. Typically, the names of the topics and items available are queried as a method of error checking to ensure that the server supports the requested conversation.

You specify the application name and topic in a control that you place on a form. To do so, you use a control's LinkTopic property. In Visual Basic, the application name and topic both reside on this code line, which you specify with the pipe symbol, |. For example, to connect to the Address Book application, you set the LinkTopic property as follows:

```
Control.LinkTopic = "Address | Address"
```

A control's LinkItem property specifies the item for the conversation defined in the LinkTopic property. The LinkItem property contains the name of the control in the source application from which you want to receive data.

The last item that you must set is the control's LinkMode property. This property specifies how the control is to establish the DDE link. The possible values are None, Automatic, Manual, or Notify. If you set these values at design time, the source application *must* be running if you want to assign a value other than None. Usually, you set this property at run time rather than design time.

If you use the `Notify` link mode, you must fill in the control's `LinkNotify` event to perform an action when the source data changes.

Listing 10.1 establishes an automatic connection to the Address Book application for a Text1 text box. The text box needs to receive information about an employee name.

Listing 10.1   Establishing an Automatic Connection

```
Text1.LinkMode = vbLinkNone ' terminate any connection
Text1.LinkTopic = "Address¦Address"
Text1.LinkItem = "AddressCtl(1)"
Text1.LinkMode = vbLinkAutomatic
       ' Automatic connection to Address Name field
```

Responding to DDE Execute Commands

After establishing a DDE conversation, you can send commands to the source application to instruct it to perform an action. For example, the Address Book application supports the command string `"Find Name,"` where `"Name"` is the search criteria for the Address Book application. This support can be useful for updating automatic links in an application based on the results of a database query.

To process DDE Execute, the source form processes the `LinkExecute` command. This command processes the string that the source application sends. The `LinkExecute` event acts like a filter because it is responsible for processing all execute commands for the form topic.

Listing 10.2 is the code for the Address Book `LinkEvent`. This subroutine handles only one event, a database search. `LinkEvent` parses the string that the event receives and places the string's "Name" portion in the database Name field. The event then searches the database, using the name as the search criteria.

Listing 10.2   The Address Book

```
Private Sub Form_LinkExecute(CmdStr As String, Cancel As Integer)
    Dim LWord, Msg, RWord, SpcPos   ' Declare variables.
    SpcPos = InStr(1, CmdStr, " ")  ' Find space.
    If SpcPos > 0 Then
        LWord = Left(CmdStr, SpcPos - 1)    ' Get left word.
        RWord = Right(CmdStr, Len(CmdStr) - SpcPos) ' Get right word.
    End If
    If 0 = StrComp(LWord, "Name", 1) Then
      AddressCtl(NAME_FLD) = RWord
      FindFirst_Click
    End If
End Sub
```

Object Linking and Embedding (OLE)

OLE (Object Linking and Embedding) provides a new method, OLE Automation, that you can use to share data with other applications. OLE Automation creates programmable objects and applications that other applications can call. Visual Basic 4.0 provides the capability both to create a programmable application (OLE Automation server) and to access programmable applications (OLE Automation client).

Using OLE Automation to Provide Database Access

OLE Automation is one of the greatest technological advances that Microsoft has ever provided for the Windows operating systems. The method is part of OLE 2.0, which Microsoft introduced in 1993.

The "holy grail" for the software development industry is a way to create application-independent software—code that developers can use repeatedly without modification. To create such reuseable code, you must hide from the user the internal implementation details, and call the code with an interface that is independent of the development environment. The internal implementation doesn't matter, only the interface and the expected results.

Windows started a smaller subset of this capability with the *DLL* (Dynamic Link Library). A DLL enables developers to bind code to one of many executables at run time rather than link time. This creates an environment in which many applications can use the same code base. Windows is based on the DLL concept.

The DLL is very function-oriented. Newer software techniques like object-oriented design don't follow the DLL function call paradigm. Even though languages like C++ can expose objects in a DLL, the object is not transportable among development environments. Even in the C++ environment, compilers such as Borland's and Microsoft's follow different naming conventions for their objects so that you cannot link them together.

OLE Automation is the first step toward producing truly reusable software components. These object-oriented components are independent of the development environment. In OLE, you work with containers and servers. A *container* is the program that uses a server's services. An example of a container application is Visual Basic. A *server* is an entity that provides services for a container. OLE Automation servers can be either in-process (.DLL) or local (.EXE). Soon, distributed OLE will provide access to OLE Automation servers residing on a LAN.

OLE Automation provides access to an application's *objects* to the programmer. The objects contain properties and methods. A *property* represents data variables that the container manipulates to shape the server object's appearance and behavior. A *method* is an action that the object performs.

You have already seen an example of OLE Automation in action by using the data access objects (DAO) in Visual Basic 4. The DBEngine is an OLE Automation object that provides all the database-access services to Visual Basic. This DBEngine is the primary object, and contains a few properties and methods. DBEngine's true power derives from the aggregate objects (such as workspaces, databases, and fields) that DBEngine provides to the programmer. All the data access objects are OLE Automation objects that you can use in your program.

The Windows registration database registers OLE Automation objects. You can view this database by invoking the program REGEDIT.EXE (Windows 3.x and Windows 95) or REGEDT32.EXE in the Windows NT environment. The registration database contains the IDs and the OLE Automation objects that are available for system use. Figure 10.3 shows a sample registration database.

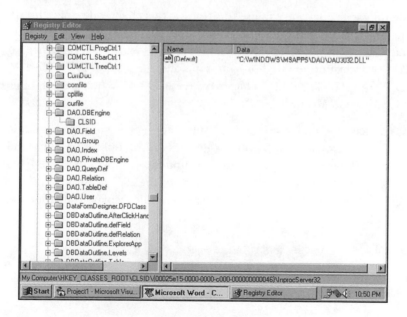

Fig. 10.3
Viewing the Windows registration database.

Windows registers an OLE Automation object in two parts: by the object's name and by the GUID (globally unique identifier), a 32-bit ID generated from the time/date stamp and a network interface card ID.

In figure 10.3, you can see that the DBEngine object is registered as DAO.DBEngine. By searching under the CLSID (Class ID) key in the registration and using the DAO.DBEngine GUID, you can see that DAO.DBEngine resides in an in-process server, DAO3032.DLL.

Using an OLE Automation object is quite simple, and much like using any other form of control (such as a DAO, .VBX , or .OCX). The Visual Basic function CreateObject loads the OLE Automation server and creates an instance of the object. The following lines of code can create an OLE Automation object for DBEngine, then get the workspace for the object:

```
Dim DB As Object
Dim Ws As Workspace
Set DB = CreateObject("DAO.DBEngine")
Set Ws = DB.Workspaces(0)
```

Creating OLE Automation Objects

Visual Basic 3.0 enabled you to use OLE Automation servers to obtain additional functionality for your programs. Visual Basic 4.0 provides the additional capability of enabling you to create your own OLE Automation objects for use in other programs—a very powerful feature.

To demonstrate how you can use this feature, this chapter describes how to create an OLE Automation interface to the Address Book application, which you developed in Chapter 8, "Accessing Databases with the Jet Engine," to provide information to other programs. Before you create this interface, however, you must understand the basics of creating an OLE Automation object in Visual Basic.

In Visual Basic, you represent an OLE Automation object as a class module. You create a *class module* by choosing Insert, Class Module. This command creates a code-entry window for the class module, as shown in figure 10.4. Press F4 to invoke the Properties dialog box for the class, as shown in figure 10.5. The Properties dialog box for the class module displays the properties listed in table 10.4.

Fig. 10.4
Adding code to the OLE Automation object.

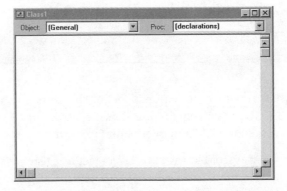

Fig. 10.5
Viewing the
properties of the
OLE Automation
object.

Data Access

Table 10.4 Class Module Properties	
Property	**Description**
Createable	If the value is True, you can create the object from an external application. In Visual Basic, you accomplish this by using the CreateObject function. If the value is False, only objects within the application can create the object.
Name	Visual Basic supplies this user-callable name of the object as the argument to the CreateObject function call. Visual Basic uses this name as an extension to the project name. For example, if the name of the object is test, the user-callable name will be projectname.test.
Instancing	The setting of this property determines instancing capabilities of a class:
	0 - Not Creatable. This default setting enables you to create instances of the class inside the project only.
	1 - Creatable SingleUse. You can create instances of the class both inside and outside the project. Each request for an instance of the class by an OLE client outside the project starts a separate copy of the OLE server.
	2 - Creatable MultiUse. You can create instances of the class both inside and outside the project. An already running copy of the OLE server supplies any requests for an instance of the class by an OLE client outside the project. If no copies of the OLE server are running, Visual Basic starts a copy to supply the class.

To add properties and methods to the object, choose Insert, Procedure.
The Insert Procedure dialog box then appears as shown in figure 10.6.

Fig. 10.6
Adding properties
and methods to a
class module.

In the Insert Procedure dialog box, you type the property or method name in the Name edit box. In the Type group, choose the appropriate option (Sub, Function, or Property) for the property or method. Sub (subroutine) specifies a method that returns no value, Function specifies a method that returns a value, and Property specifies a property or data member.

In the Scope group, you indicate whether external applications can access the property or method. Public specifies access for external applications, and Private limits use to within the program.

In the check box All Local Variables as Statics, you indicate whether to make all local variables or properties static. If you select this check box, the data members can retain memory between calls to the object. Usually you should select this check box.

The Insert Procedure dialog box adds only template code to the class programming module. You still have some work to do to make the object functional. For methods, this work is fairly simple: you must add the return types and parameters to the function or subroutine declaration. For properties, slightly more work is involved.

Listing 10.3 shows the code that you add to the code module for the Address Book application's Name property. The implementation of the Name property appears later in this section.

Listing 10.3 Additional Code for the Address Book Application's Name Property

```
Public Static Property Get Name()
End Property

Public Static Property Let Name()
End Property

Public Static Property Get Name() As String
    FirstName = Address.AddressCtl(NAME_FLD)
End Property
```

```
Public Static Property Let Name(Value As String)
    Address.Command1_Click
    Adress.AddressCtl(NAME_FLD) = Value
End Property
```

For properties, Visual Basic has `Property Get` and `Property Let` operations.
The `Get` function retrieves the property's value. The example application
shown in listing 10.4 implements the `Get` property by retrieving the value of
an edit control in the application's form. The `Let` function sets the property's
value. To implement the `Let` property, you first clear your application's form
and then set the edit control to the value passed into the function.

Listing 10.4   The Implementation of the `Name` Property

```
Const NAME_FLD = 1
Const STREET_FLD = 2
Const STREET2_FLD = 3
Const CITY_FLD = 4
Const STATE_FLD = 5
Const ZIP_FLD = 6
Const PHONE_FLD = 7
Const WORK_FLD = 8
Const FAX_FLD = 9
Const NOTES_FLD = 10
Const FIRST_FLD = NAME_FLD
Const LAST_FLD = NOTES_FLD

Private Sub Class_Initialize()
    Address.Visible = False
    Load Address
    Address.Command1_Click
End Sub

Private Sub Class_Terminate()
    If Address.Visible = False Then
        Unload Address
    End If
End Sub
Public Sub FindTelephoneNumbers()
    Address.FindFirst_Click
End Sub

Public Static Property Get Name() As String
    FirstName = Address.AddressCtl(NAME_FLD)
End Property

Public Static Property Let Name(Value As String)
    Address.Command1_Click
    Adress.AddressCtl(NAME_FLD) = Value
End Property
```

(continues)

Listing 10.4 Continued

```
Public Static Property Get Phone() As String
    Phone = Address.AddressCtl(PHONE_FLD)
End Property

Public Static Property Let Phone(Value As String)
    Address.Command1_Click
    Adress.AddressCtl(PHONE_FLD) = Value
End Property

Public Static Property Get Workphone() As String
    Workphone = Address.AddressCtl(WORK_FLD)
End Property

Public Static Property Let Workphone(Value As String)
    Address.Command1_Click
    Adress.AddressCtl(WORK_FLD) = Value
End Property

Public Static Property Get Fax() As String
    Fax = Address.AddressCtl(FAX_FLD)
End Property
Public Static Property Let Fax(Value As String)
    Address.Command1_Click
    Adress.AddressCtl(FAX_FLD) = Value
End Property
```

Listing 10.4 shows the code for the class module that you add to the Address Book application. The AddressObject uses the application's form extensively for storing, searching, and retrieving values. You could move the functions located in the address form into the class module, but this example simply reuses the existing application code.

Each class module contains a Class_Initialize and a Class_Terminate function. The Class_Initialize function is where all object-instance initialization code resides. The Class_Terminate function is where you put any object-instance exit code. Visual Basic executes the initialization and termination code for each instance of the class module, *not* once each time that you load or unload the application.

When you first load the object, you also load into memory the application that contains the object. This scheme is exactly the same as starting the program from Program Manager. You load the startup form, call the Class_Initialize code, and create the object.

After removing all references to the object, you unload the program, unless the user starts it (for example, through Program Manager).

From Here...

As this chapter has shown, Visual Basic provides easy access to Windows interprocess communications facilities. This enables your application to use other applications as part of a system solution, and also enables other applications to use your application as part of a solution.

OLE Automation is one technology that you should implement for compatibility with future versions of the Windows operating systems. You should use DDE to provide network access and to maintain compatibility with older applications. Also, any of the Visual Basic OLE applications that you create can be used from Microsoft Office or any other OLE 2.0 enabled applications.

For further information on using the Jet database engine for creating database applications, see the following chapters:

- Chapter 8, "Accessing Other Databases with the Jet Engine," covers all the fundamental database-access techniques.

- Chapter 9, "Using OBDC to Access Databases," provides insight into using client/server databases and ODBC for implementing database front-ends.

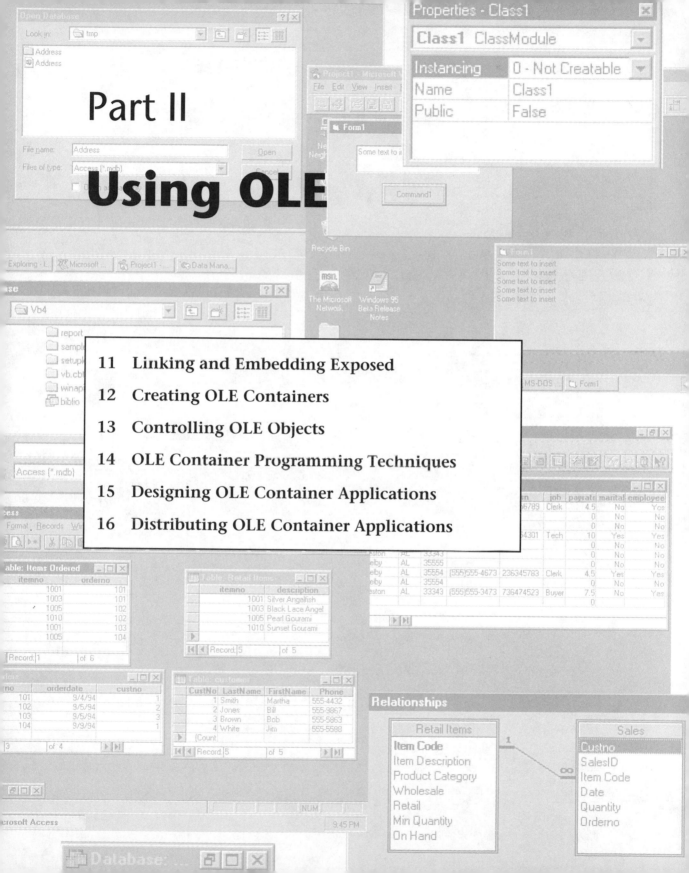

Part II

Using OLE

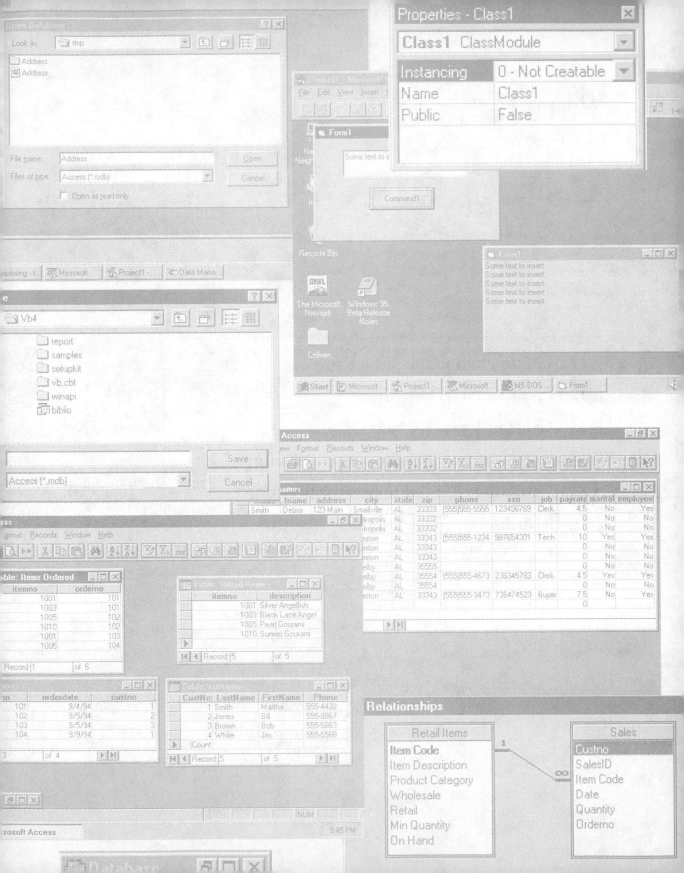

Chapter 11

Linking and Embedding Exposed

Object Linking and Embedding (OLE) is at the center of most of the changes in the new version of Visual Basic. In version 4.0, Visual Basic itself is an OLE container, and Microsoft provides the core language as an OLE object. This chapter describes these changes and how they affect you.

In this chapter, you learn about the following:

- The OLE features that are new to version 4.0

- How to use OLE to create a new application from the parts of others

- How OLE evolved from attempts to share data across applications

- How applications provide OLE objects and how containers use those objects

- How to use OLE Automation to share tasks between applications

- The difference between OLE Automation objects, custom controls, and DLLs

- How OLE manages the interactions between applications and the OLE DLLs

OLE Features New to Version 4.0

If you're already familiar with Visual Basic 3.0's OLE features, this section helps you take advantage of the new features and changes in Visual Basic 4.0. This section is just a summary, however. These new features are explained in greater depth throughout the rest of Parts II and III of this book.

- The OLE 2 custom control is now built in to Visual Basic as the OLE container control in the Visual Basic Toolbox.

- Visual Basic forms now support *menu negotiation* for OLE objects. Embedded OLE objects can add their application's menu items and toolbars to Visual Basic menu bars.

- You can add OLE objects to the Visual Basic Toolbox, just like custom controls.

- OLE now offers a new type of custom control: the OLE control (.OCX).

- An Object Browser enables you to view the objects, properties, methods, and procedures contained in Visual Basic modules, OLE controls, and OLE applications.

- Visual Basic incorporates language improvements from Visual Basic's Applications Edition to help you work with objects.

- A new type of module, the *class module*, enables you to define objects, properties, and methods for your application. You can also add properties and methods to forms, and call event procedures externally.

- You can build applications as stand-alone applications or as OLE object applications, which expose their objects, properties, and methods to other applications through OLE Automation.

- You can run multiple instances of the Visual Basic programming system simultaneously to test and debug applications that interact with each other.

- An Add-In Manager enables you to add third-party tools to extend the Visual Basic development environment.

- The Visual Basic development environment provides objects that you can use to build your own add-ins with Visual Basic.

OLE 2 Container Control

The OLE control is now built in to Visual Basic. The control appears in the Toolbox, just as it did in Visual Basic 3.0 (see fig. 11.1). The new control contains code improvements and bug fixes, plus changes to accommodate updates to the OLE 2.0 DLLs.

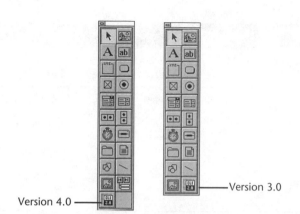

Version 4.0 ──────

────── Version 3.0

Fig. 11.1
The built-in OLE
control on the
Visual Basic 4.0
Toolbox looks
the same as the
version 3.0 custom
control.

Unlike custom controls, built-in controls can have their own methods.
Therefore, Visual Basic now provides the Action property setting as methods.
Although Visual Basic still provides the Action property for compatibility
with existing programs, the new OLE control methods make the code much
easier to read and understand. Table 11.1 compares the old Action property
settings to their new method equivalents.

**Table 11.1   Visual Basic 3.0's OLE Control Action Property
Settings Compared to Version 4.0's Methods**

Action **Property Setting**	**Equivalent Method Name**	**Task**
OLE_CREATE_EMBED (0)	CreateEmbed	Creates an embedded object
OLE_CREATE_LINK (1)	CreateLink	Creates a linked object from a file's contents
OLE_COPY (4)	Copy	Copies the object to the system Clipboard
OLE_PASTE (5)	Paste	Copies data from the system Clipboard to an OLE container control
OLE_UPDATE (6)	Update	Retrieves the current data from the application that supplied the object and displays that data as a picture in the OLE container control

(continues)

Table 11.1 Continued

Action Property Setting	Equivalent Method Name	Task
OLE_ACTIVATE (7)	DoVerb	Opens an object for an operation, such as editing
OLE_CLOSE (9)	Close	Closes an object and terminates the connection to the application that provided the object
OLE_DELETE (10)	Delete	Deletes the specified object and frees the memory associated with it
OLE_SAVE_TO_FILE (11)	SaveToFile	Saves an object to a data file
OLE_READ_FROM_FILE (12)	ReadFromFile	Loads an object that the user saved to a data file
OLE_INSERT_OBJ_DLG (14)	InsertObjDlg	Displays the Insert Object dialog box
OLE_PASTE_SPECIAL_DLG (15)	PasteSpecialDlg	Displays the Paste Special dialog box
OLE_FETCH_VERBS (17)	FetchVerbs	Updates the list of verbs that an object supports
OLE_SAVE_TO_OLE1FILE (18)	SaveToOle1File	Saves an object to the OLE 1 file format

Menu Negotiation for In-Place Editing

When you edit an OLE object in-place, the object's application can supply menu items and toolbars for editing the object. Visual Basic 3.0 ignored these OLE features, but version 4.0 enables you to include them on your form, as shown in figure 11.2.

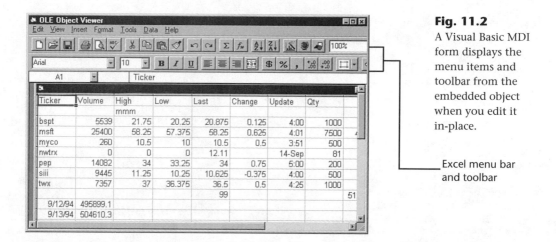

Fig. 11.2
A Visual Basic MDI
form displays the
menu items and
toolbar from the
embedded object
when you edit it
in-place.

Excel menu bar
and toolbar

To get menu negotiation to work on your forms, set the Negotiate Position
option for the form's menu in the Menu Editor (fig. 11.3).

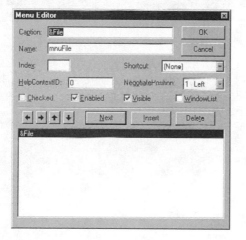

Fig. 11.3
The Negotiate
Position list box in
the Menu Editor
determines how
OLE in-place
menus appear
on a form.

Insertable OLE Objects

You can add embedded objects directly to the Toolbox and then draw them
on the form, just as you would any other control (fig. 11.4).

To add insertable OLE objects to the Toolbox, use the new Custom Controls
dialog box (fig. 11.5).

II

Using OLE

Fig. 11.4
Add insertable
OLE objects to the
Toolbox.

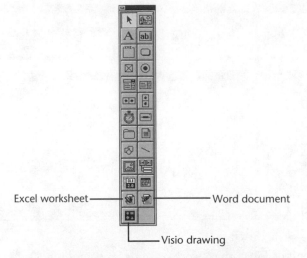

Excel worksheet———————————————— Word document

———— Visio drawing

Fig. 11.5
Choose Tools,
Custom Controls
to display the
Custom Controls
dialog box.

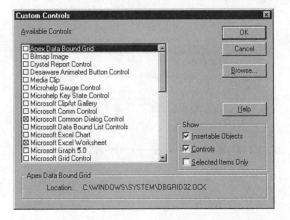

OLE Custom Controls

OLE custom controls (.OCX) look and work the same as old-style custom
controls (.VBX). However, .OCX controls provide the following advantages
over .VBX controls:

- They can provide 32-bit versions to take advantage of performance
  improvements available in the new versions of Windows. .VBXs run
  only in 16-bit mode on the new operating systems.

- They can have methods.

- They enable you to view their properties and methods with the new
  Object Browser.

Visual Basic 4.0 ships OLE custom controls that replace all the .VBX controls included in Visual Basic 3.0 Professional Edition. Visual Basic can automatically upgrade projects that contain .VBX controls so that they can use their .OCX control equivalents.

Browse Procedures, Objects, Properties, and Methods

You use the new Object Browser, shown in figure 11.6, for viewing the objects, properties, methods, constants, modules, and Visual Basic procedures. Visual Basic itself is an OLE application, so you can use the Browser to view Visual Basic's objects and language.

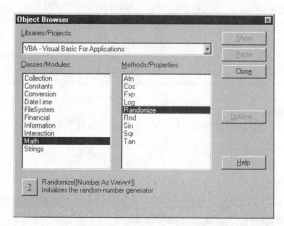

Fig. 11.6
Choose View, Object Browser or press F2 to display the Object Browser dialog box.

II

Using OLE

The Object Browser displays the syntax of the item selected in the Methods/ Properties list box. You can find help on the item by clicking on the question mark (?).

Language Improvements from the Applications Edition

The Visual Basic language gains some new keywords from Visual Basic Applications Edition (VBA). If you have programmed in Excel with VBA, you are already familiar with most of the new items listed in table 11.2.

Table 11.2   Visual Basic 4.0's New Language Features

Item	Use
For Each...Next	Iterate over the items in an array or a collection of objects, such as the Controls or Forms collection.
With...End With	Apply a set of methods or properties to a specific object.

(continues)

Table 11.2 Continued	
Item	**Use**
Line continuation (_)	Break a long line of code over two or more lines.
Optional parameters	Define parameters that the code might omit when calling the procedure.
IsMissing function	Determine whether the code omits an optional argument.
Property procedures	Create object properties in a class module or form.
Public/Private	Control the scope and visibility of variables, procedures, and constants. You can make event procedures Public to call them from modules outside of the form that contains them.
TypeName function	Determine a variable's object type or data type.

Create Objects, Properties, and Methods

By using several of these new language features together, you can create your own objects in Visual Basic. Table 11.3 describes how you use these features to create an object.

Table 11.3 Features for Creating Visual Basic Objects	
Feature	**Use**
Class modules	Create an invisible object that provides general services. Through OLE Automation, other applications can use objects in class modules.
Form modules	Create a visible object. Other modules in an application can use objects in form modules. Also, you can make such modules available to other applications by using methods defined in a class module.
Property procedures	Add properties to an object defined in a class or form module.
Sub or Function	Add methods to an object defined in a procedures class or form module.
Public and Private scope declarations	Make a property or method available to all other modules or local to the containing module.

Feature	Use
Class module `Instancing` property	Make an object available to other applications through the `CreateObject` and `GetObject` functions.
Class module `Public` property	Make an object visible to other applications in the Object Browser.

Figure 11.7 shows a class module in a Visual Basic project.

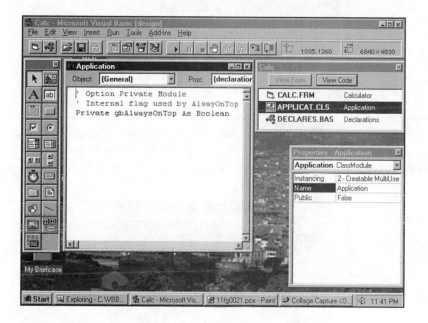

Fig. 11.7
Use a class module to contain code that you want to package as an object.

Expose OLE Automation Objects

The Options properties pages enable you to set two startup modes for the applications that you create: stand-alone application and OLE server (fig. 11.8). OLE servers expose their class modules as objects that can be used from other applications.

Run Multiple Instances of Visual Basic

Visual Basic applications can use each other's objects, so you need a way to debug multiple Visual Basic applications at the same time. Visual Basic now enables you to run several copies of itself simultaneously. By doing so, you can trace code execution from one application to another.

Fig. 11.8
Choose Tools,
Options to display
the Options
properties pages.

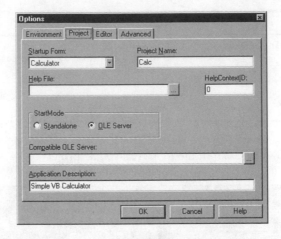

Load Add-Ins

The new Add-In Manager dialog box (fig. 11.9) enables you to load extensions to the Visual Basic programming system. Add-on tools from third-party vendors, such as Sheridan's VB Assist, can add items to the Visual Basic menus and respond to events in the Visual Basic programming environment.

Fig. 11.9
Choose Add-Ins,
Add-In Manager to
display the Add-In
Manager dialog
box.

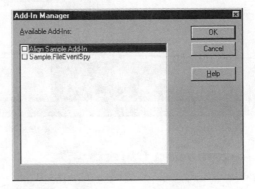

Create Your Own Add-Ins

Visual Basic Professional Edition includes tools and documentation for creating your own Visual Basic add-ins. Visual Basic accesses these add-ins through OLE Automation, using the objects, methods, and properties defined in the add-in's class module. Figure 11.10 shows the Regadd add-in that is used as a sample in Chapter 24, "Creating Add-Ins."

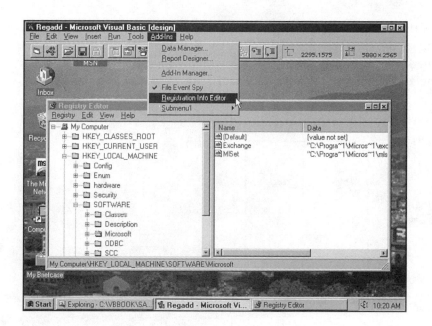

Fig. 11.10
The Regadd sample
add-in enables you
to run the Registry
Editor from within
Visual Basic.

The Evolution of OLE

OLE makes it much easier for applications to share data effectively with one
another. Because they can so easily share data, individual applications can
focus on the tasks that they perform best instead of trying to be all things to
all users. Figure 11.11 illustrates how desktop applications have evolved to
share data with each other.

As shown in figure 11.11, early desktop applications written for MS-DOS had
a very hard time sharing data among applications. Only one application
could run at a time, so you had to save your data to disk, exit, and load the
data in the next application. Some applications, like SideKick, worked around
this laborious process by using a technique called *terminate-and-stay-resident*
(TSR). A TSR application could "pop up" as you worked in another application, perform a task, and then return you to your previous application. TSRs
were tricky to write, however, and took up blocks of the limited memory
(640K) available to your main application.

Another DOS programming approach to sharing data was to build all your
needed applications into a single .EXE file. Lotus 1-2-3 1.0 is the most successful example of this approach. By combining spreadsheet, word processing, and data management tasks, Lotus 1-2-3 could meet most users' needs

within a single application. Users could share the data among the pieces of the application without exiting. In later versions, however, Lotus 1-2-3 ran into problems related to its size. Because the application tried to fit three specialized tasks into a limited space, it had to sacrifice features or speed.

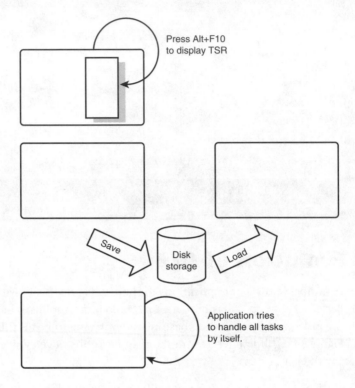

Fig. 11.11
Under DOS, applications struggled to share data with each other.

By the time Lotus 1-2-3's size became a serious problem, Lotus had several approaches that it could employ to address it. Most of these approaches involved "end-runs" around the operating system to gain access to additional memory. Those were turbulent times full of expanded memory managers, complicated strings of drivers in CONFIG.SYS, and many hardware and software incompatibilities.

Windows 3.0 and the Intel 80386 CPU finally laid all these divergent approaches to rest. Windows used the new CPU's protected-memory features to enable multiple applications to run at the same time. In addition, Windows added a system service, the Clipboard, to enable applications to share data.

The Clipboard was very limited, however. It could hold only one item at a time, and any application could overwrite its contents with new data at any time. To share data between two applications reliably, the two applications needed a dedicated channel. OLE 1.0 introduced this channel as *Dynamic Data Exchange* (DDE).

Using DDE, a source application could transmit data to a target application, and the target would send back an acknowledgment after receiving the data. Although more reliable than the Clipboard, DDE was still prone to problems. If the connection failed, it was difficult to determine why. Did the other application terminate? Was the system busy? Another limitation of DDE was that it supported only the transfer of textual data. Bitmaps, formatted text, and other binary data could not cross a DDE channel.

What's the Object?

OLE breaks everything into small, usable parts called *objects*. On a technical level, OLE defines the way that these objects fit together. Think of OLE objects as Lego blocks, with OLE as the little, stubby pegs and corresponding orifices on the tops and bottoms of the blocks that enable the blocks (objects) to fit together snugly, as shown in figure 11.12.

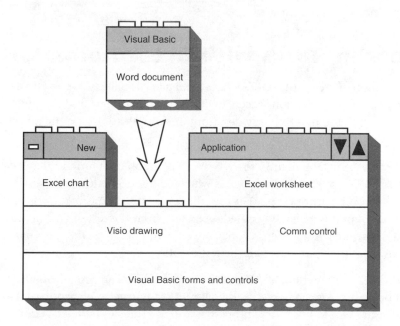

Fig. 11.12
OLE defines how objects fit together. You can use OLE objects to assemble whatever you want.

With Legos, you don't have to worry about which parts fit together—they all interconnect the same way. You don't think about the little doohickies on each block that make these connections possible, until you step on a block with your bare feet one cold morning.

The same principle applies to OLE objects: You don't have to worry about why the pieces snap together as long as you remember to put your toys away when you finish playing with them. Visual Basic keeps OLE objects in the Toolbox (fig. 11.13).

Fig. 11.13
In Visual Basic 4.0, you can add OLE objects directly to the Visual Basic Toolbox and then add the objects directly on a form by drawing them.

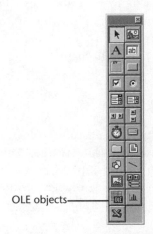

OLE objects

Sharing Tasks with OLE Automation

As mentioned previously, OLE objects are data plus behavior. The OLE DLLs give container applications access to both the object's data and the functions (behavior) that the object provides. Container applications use the object's application code to display, activate, and edit the object.

You can extend OLE slightly to make more of an object's functions available to a container application—which is where OLE Automation comes in. OLE Automation is part of OLE 2.0; it uses the same DLLs and is part of the same standard, but it is generally treated separately from the rest of OLE because a separate group within Microsoft developed it and because OLE Automation serves a different purpose than the rest of OLE.

Under OLE Automation, an OLE object's application can provide methods and properties for each object. Programming languages such as Visual Basic and Visual C++ can use these properties and methods to perform actions within the OLE object's application (fig. 11.14).

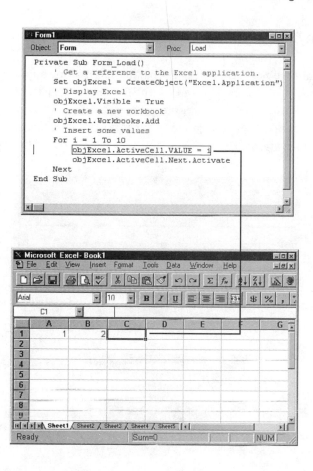

Fig. 11.14
OLE Automation
enables Visual
Basic to use an
OLE object's
properties and
methods.

Although the code resides in your Visual Basic project, it executes within the object's application. You can use OLE Automation to control other applications remotely, or to control OLE objects that you embed on your forms.

Why Use OLE Automation?

OLE Automation enables you to build an application from precompiled parts (OLE objects) instead of having to create your own components for everything. If you have used custom controls extensively, you already understand the utility of component architecture. Building an application with components rather than with line-by-line code saves time and simplifies maintenance.

For example, inserting a Word document on a form is easier than programming all your own word processing tasks into a text box. When you insert a Word document on a form, you also provide your form with thousands of features, including formatting, printing, and spell checking. Using a text box, you would have to write code for each of those features.

II

Using OLE

Differentiating OLE Automation from Custom Controls

OLE Automation objects are part of a separate, stand-alone application, such as Microsoft Excel or Word. Custom controls exist only as part of another application. Although you can access custom control methods and properties from within your current application, you cannot access custom controls from other applications. Figures 11.15 and 16 illustrate this difference.

Fig. 11.15
OLE Automation objects' cross-application boundaries.

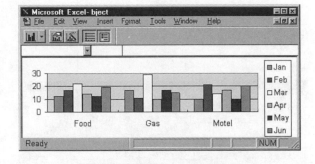

Fig. 11.16
Custom controls are available only within an application.

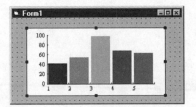

Differentiating OLE Automation from DLLs

With OLE Automation, you can use the methods and properties that are in another application. DLLs enable you to do something similar: call functions from the DLL in your Visual Basic code. OLE Automation provides the following important differences, however:

- OLE Automation methods and properties are self-describing. They provide documentation and access to online Help (.HLP) files through the Visual Basic Object Browser.

- OLE Automation objects are *type-safe*. That is, if you pass them the wrong sort of variable, an error occurs. DLLs often cause general protection faults (GPFs) if you pass in a variable of the wrong size.

- OLE Automation objects use `object.property` and `object.method` syntax, just like other Visual Basic objects. DLLs use only function syntax.

- OLE Automation objects use Visual Basic data types, such as length-deliniated strings, objects, and arrays. DLLs require special care when dealing with these types.

Because of these differences, OLE Automation is much easier to use than DLLs in Visual Basic code. Chapter 18, "Creating Objects," shows you how to repackage DLLs, such as the Windows API, in the form of OLE Automation objects.

Understanding How OLE Works

Container applications don't call OLE objects directly; instead, they send their requests to the OLE DLLs, which pass the requests to the OLE object's application. Figure 11.17 illustrates this interaction and table 11.4 describes the OLE DLLs.

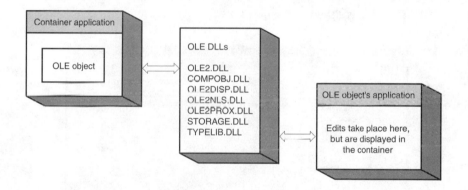

Fig. 11.17
The OLE DLLs intercede between OLE containers and OLE objects.

Table 11.4   OLE DLLs and the Services That They Provide

DLL File	Function
COMPOBJ.DLL	Create and access OLE objects
OLE2.DLL	Perform standard OLE actions on objects
OLE2CONV.DLL	Convert data in an OLE object from one type to another
OLE2DISP.DLL	Access OLE Automation objects by invoking methods and properties
OLE2NLS.DLL	Perform string comparisons based on the user's national language

(continues)

Table 11.4 Continued	
DLL File	**Function**
OLE2PROX.DLL	Coordinate access to objects across processes
STORAGE.DLL	Save OLE objects to files and read OLE objects from files
TYPELIB.DLL	Access object libraries that describe OLE Automation objects

The OLE DLLs are interdependent; they must all be present for OLE to work.

How OLE Finds Objects

OLE uses the system registration database to find the .EXE and .DLL files that provide OLE objects and to determine what services the OLE objects provide. You can view the system registration database by using the Registry Editor (REGEDIT.EXE), as shown in figure 11.18.

Fig. 11.18
Enter the command **REGEDIT /V** to see a full listing of the system registration database.

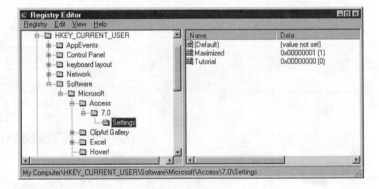

The system registry is the Windows equivalent of the MS-DOS PATH environment variable, although the system registry includes much more information. Applications that support OLE write to the system registry their location on disk and the services that they support. The OLE DLLs check this information whenever a request is made for an OLE object (fig. 11.19).

How OLE Describes Objects, Properties, and Methods

OLE objects that support OLE Automation have another file, an *object library*, that contains much more information than the system registry. The object library contains a complete description of an object's properties, methods, and constants. You can view an object's object library by using the Visual Basic Object Browser, as shown in figure 11.20.

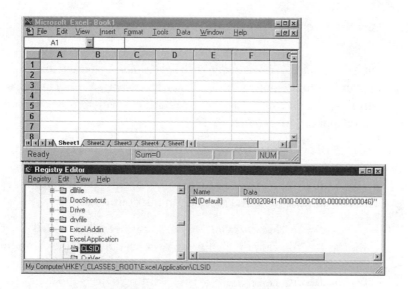

Fig. 11.19
Applications
register their
information, and
then OLE uses the
information to fill
requests.

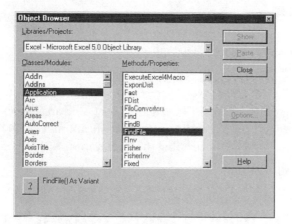

Fig. 11.20
The Object
Browser lists
the properties,
methods, and
constants that an
OLE Automation
object defines.

Visual Basic uses the information in the object library to bind to the code in
an OLE object's application. When you compile your application, Visual
Basic writes these bindings into your application so that your application
calls the code directly.

Exploring the Limitations in OLE 2.0

OLE 2.0 is certainly a great improvement over OLE 1.0. It extends applications beyond their traditional boundaries to let them share data and tasks
smoothly. However, many important areas could still use improvement.
Some of the areas are within OLE itself, others are within the applications

that provide OLE objects. The following are some of the current limitations of OLE 2.0:

- *Objects are interdependent within each application.* You must load an entire application to use one of the application's objects. A more modular design approach could reduce the amount of memory that OLE container applications require.

- *The OLE DLLs are interdependent.* As one Microsoft program manager has said, "OLE is modular, you just need to include all the modules." You must distribute and install all the OLE DLLs with your application. This consumes a good deal of space on distribution disks.

- *You cannot easily customize OLE objects.* Currently, all compiled objects come "as-is." You cannot redefine an existing object slightly and then pass it to other parts of your application. This capability, sometimes called *subclassing*, could make reusing existing objects much easier.

- *OLE objects don't provide events.* In Visual Basic, you can only detect OLE container control events. When you activate the OLE object, it suspends these events; the OLE object doesn't pass user events back to Visual Basic.

- *Applications that provide OLE objects are sometimes unreliable or bug-ridden.* Nothing can be more frustrating than spending an afternoon trying to work around a bug in someone else's application. If an OLE object's application crashes, recovering that application within your application is difficult.

OLE 2.0 Objects and Containers

Microsoft developed OLE 2.0 specifically to solve the problems with OLE 1.0. OLE 2.0 needed to provide the following:

- More reliable communication, including better notification when problems occur sharing data

- A broader range of the types of data that you can transmit among applications

A little word like *data* can hide a lot of complexity. You might tend to think of data as neat little 80-column rows of ASCII characters, but in fact, data is more like any sort of gooey stuff that an application might decide is useful.

Because there's no accounting for some applications' taste, you have no way to anticipate the type of data that one application might want to share with another.

Instead of trying to enumerate all the types of data that an application can share, OLE defines a set of services that each application must provide for each type of data to share. These services enable other applications to do the following:

- Retrieve and store data from the source application

- Display data from the source application

- Activate and perform actions on data shared from the source application

Data that defines all these services is called an *OLE object* (data + behavior = object).

OLE also defines how applications request and use services from an OLE object. Applications that follow these rules are called *OLE containers*. Figure 11.21 shows how an OLE container and an OLE object interact.

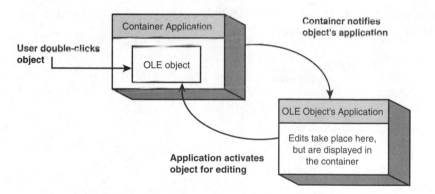

II

Using OLE

Fig. 11.21
An OLE container with an OLE object.

Where OLE Stores Data

Because OLE is all about sharing data, the document in which an OLE object appears may or may not store that object. OLE objects stored in the currently open document are called *embedded objects*. Objects displayed in one document but actually stored in a separate file are called *linked objects*. Figure 11.22 illustrates the difference between linked and embedded objects.

Fig. 11.22
Linked objects
versus embedded
objects; the
difference is where
the data resides.

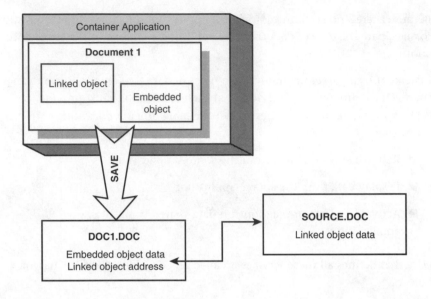

Figure 11.22 glosses over a sticky issue: Under OLE, the word *file* is no longer synonymous with the word *document*. A *document* can contain several different OLE objects, some of which may be stored in other files. OLE calls such documents *compound documents*. Figure 11.23 shows what actually is stored in an OLE compound document file.

Fig. 11.23
A compound
document
includes the data
for embedded
objects and the
location of linked
objects.

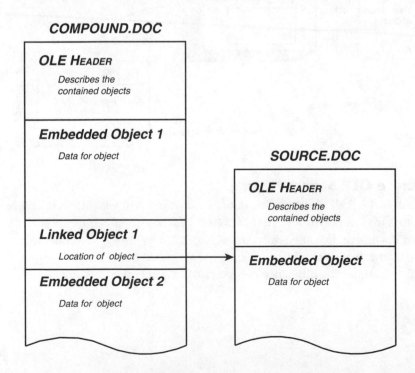

How OLE Displays Objects

When a user opens a compound document, the container application displays a picture of each of the OLE objects that the document contains. You can edit directly objects that the container application created (called *native data*). If the objects are from other applications, you must *activate* them before you can edit them.

When you activate an object, the OLE DLLs start the application that created the object. You activate embedded objects *in place*—that is, you can edit them without leaving the compound document. You open linked objects in a separate window that contains the application that created the linked object. Figures 11.24 and 11.25 show the difference between editing embedded and linked objects.

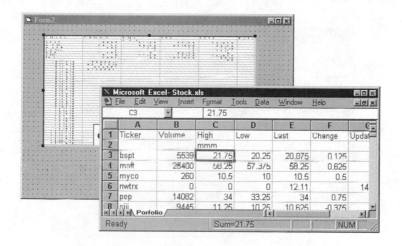

Fig. 11.24
Double-click a linked object to edit it in a separate window.

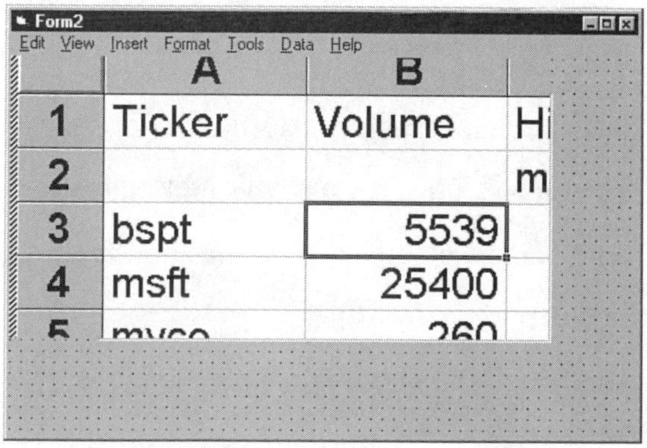

Fig. 11.25
Double-click an embedded object to edit it in place.

When an embedded object is active for editing, the menu bars and toolbars from the object's application replace the menu bars and toolbars that the container application normally displays. Only the container application's File menu remains unchanged, because the container application is still responsible for saving the compound document or opening new documents. This feature is called *menu negotiation*.

How OLE Performs Actions on Objects

Not every object provides the same actions. For example, you may not be able to "edit" an embedded video clip. Similarly, you cannot "play" a word processing document. The user actions that an object supports are the object's *verbs*. A pop-up menu displays an object's verbs when the user right-clicks on the object (see fig. 11.26).

Fig. 11.26
To display an object's verbs, right-click on the object.

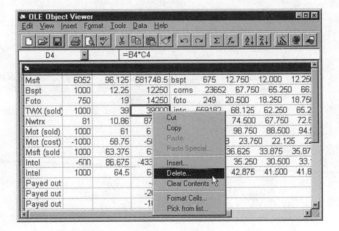

When a user chooses one of the object's verbs, the OLE DLLs do the following tasks:

1. Check whether the application is loaded

2. If the application is not loaded, start the application

3. Increment the number of references to the application

4. Activate the object

5. Pass the user's action to the object's application

The user can deactivate the object by closing the object from the File menu or by activating another object. After the user deactivates the object, the OLE DLLs do the following:

1. Deincrement the number of references to the object's application

2. If the number of references equals zero, close the object's application

Keeping track of the number of references to an application is one of the central tasks that the OLE DLLs perform.

How to Drag and Drop Objects

OLE 2.0's goal is to enable the user to move data between applications as directly as possible. The most direct way to manipulate things in Windows is by dragging and dropping objects with the mouse. Naturally, OLE provides this capability between applications (see fig. 11.27).

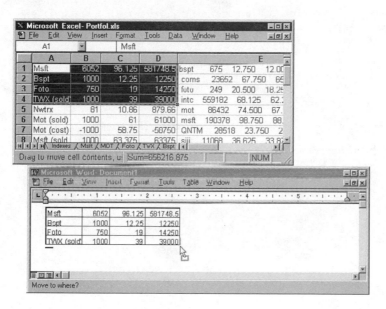

Fig. 11.27
Dragging an object from one application and dropping it into another.

From Here...

For more information on the following topics, see the indicated chapters:

- Chapter 12, "Creating OLE Containers," explains how to create applications that use linked and embedded objects.

- Chapter 13, "Controlling OLE Objects," explains how to control linked and embedded objects in code.

- Chapter 17, "OLE Objects Exposed," discusses the OLE Automation features.

Chapter 12

Creating OLE Containers

You create OLE container applications by using OLE custom controls, linked and embedded objects, and object applications. This chapter tells you how to use Visual Basic's tools to assemble these OLE building blocks.

In this chapter, you learn how to do the following:

- Add OLE custom controls to the Visual Basic Toolbox and draw those controls on forms

- Upgrade existing projects that use .VBX controls to OLE custom controls

- Add embedded objects to the Toolbox and draw those objects on forms

- Link and embed objects on forms using the OLE 2.0 control

- Run OLE Automation object applications from code

- Use the properties and methods of object applications

- Close OLE Automation object applications

- Explore the system registration database that OLE uses

A New Type of Custom Control

Visual Basic 4.0 introduces a whole new type of control: the OLE custom control. OLE custom controls (.OCX) look and work the same as old-style custom controls (.VBX). In fact, Microsoft provides tools to third-party developers to help them convert their .VBXs to .OCXs.

Why the Change?

The standards on which .VBXs were built were written specifically and (at the time) exclusively for Visual Basic. Since then, other development tools, such as Microsoft Visual C++ and Borland C++, have added support for .VBXs. The differences between these development environments and Visual Basic are significant, so the .VBX standard no longer suffices for all custom controls.

Additionally, Visual Basic is now available on several different operating systems—Windows 3.1, Windows NT, and Windows 95 (Chicago). Soon, Visual Basic might also be available on the Macintosh and other platforms. The .VBX standard was written for Windows 3.x and took advantage of features that change under the new versions of Windows. Rather than invest a lot of effort in maintaining the .VBX standard on all platforms, Microsoft (wisely) decided to leverage the work that was already being done by its OLE developers.

The OLE standard is much broader than the original .VBX standard. This broader scope enables such applications as Microsoft Access and Excel to incorporate custom controls. In all, the .VBX to .OCX evolution is an inevitable step in the onward march of computer technology.

.OCX versus .VBX

The advantages of OLE custom controls over .VBXs might not be immediately obvious. For example, OLE custom controls are not faster than .VBXs, nor do they require less memory. Instead, OLE custom controls promise these future advantages:

■ As more applications support OLE custom controls, control developers will flourish and there will be more competition among them. Hopefully, this competition will result in more controls, wider choices, and lower prices.

■ Using OLE custom controls enables you to build applications for operating systems on many different hardware platforms. These configurations include 386 machines running Windows 3.1, 486 or Pentium computers running Windows 95, and PowerPC, DEC Alpha, or MIPS machines running Windows NT.

■ OLE custom controls provide a standard way to get information about the control. Using the Object Browser, you can view OLE custom control properties and methods and get help on the control.

- The system locates OLE custom controls by using the standard system registry instead of requiring that you install the files in the Windows system directory. This should make it easier to manage and maintain custom control files.

- OLE custom controls can provide methods. .VBX controls had to use awkward "Action" properties because they couldn't provide methods.

Although none of these advantages provides an immediate, tangible benefit today, they are almost certain to provide a return on your investment in the near future.

For instance, it is easy to imagine tools that might run in the background maintaining the associations between the system registry and the custom controls that you've installed. If you move a file to a new directory, the tool might update REG.DAT automatically. Such a tool might be included with Windows 95 or be developed by some enterprising reader looking to make it big.

Using OLE Custom Controls

OLE custom controls appear and behave nearly identically to old-style .VBX controls. However, Visual Basic 4.0 incorporates several new features that change the way that you work with custom controls:

- You now add custom controls from the Tools menu instead of using the File menu's Load command.

- OLE custom controls list their methods and properties in the Object Browser, making it easier to get syntax and Help information.

- You can upgrade existing projects that use .VBX controls to use OLE custom controls.

The following sections describe these tasks in greater detail.

Drawing a Custom Control on a Form

To draw a custom control on a form, follow these steps:

1. Click on the toolbar button for the control to draw.

2. Click on the form and drag the control until it is the size that you want, then release the mouse button (see fig. 12.1).

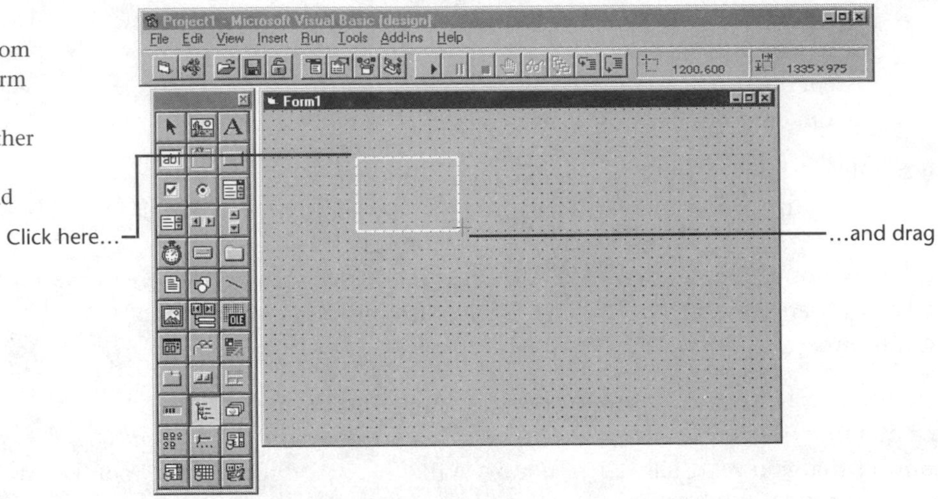

Fig. 12.1

Drawing a custom control on a form is the same as drawing any other control—you simply click and drag.

Click here...

...and drag

Adding an OLE Custom Control to the Toolbox

To add an OLE custom control (.OCX) to the Toolbox, follow these steps:

1. Choose Tools, Custom Controls. Visual Basic displays the Custom Controls dialog box (see fig. 12.2).

Fig. 12.2

The Custom Controls dialog box.

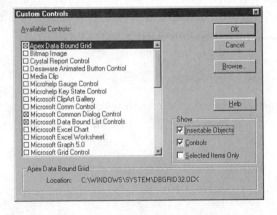

2. Select the check box next to the name of the control that you want to add to the Toolbox. Visual Basic adds the control to the toolbar (see fig. 12.3).

Fig. 12.3
Visual Basic adds
custom controls to
the Toolbox.

If You're Having Trouble

If a custom control appears on the Available Controls list of the Add Custom Control dialog box but does not appear on the Toolbox when you select the control, check whether the file that contains the control (.OCX) is still available in your Windows system directory (usually \WINDOWS\SYSTEM). The file might have been moved or deleted. The locations of custom controls are maintained in the system registry and if files have been moved or deleted, the path recorded in the system registry might not agree with the actual path on your hard disk.

To fix this problem, copy the custom control file to the Windows system directory.

The Insertable Objects and Controls check boxes on the Custom Controls dialog box (see fig. 12.2) enable you to show or hide either type of OLE object in the Available Controls list box. If you have many applications installed on your system but don't often use objects from those applications, you might want to select only Custom Controls. This choice makes it a little easier to find the custom control that you want.

Adding a Custom Control to the List of Available Controls

Normally, Visual Basic adds a custom control to its list of available controls when you install the control. If you do not properly install a control, it might not appear in the Available Controls list on the Add Custom Control dialog box.

To add a control to Visual Basic's list of available controls, follow these steps:

1. Choose Tools, Custom Controls. Visual Basic displays the Custom Controls dialog box (see fig. 12.2).

2. Choose Browse. Visual Basic displays the Add Custom Control dialog box (see fig. 12.4).

Fig. 12.4

Choose Browse in the Custom Controls dialog box to display the Add Custom Control dialog box, in which you can add a custom control to the list of available custom controls.

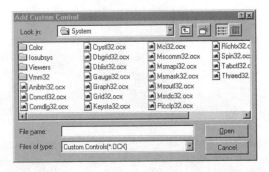

3. Select a custom control file to add, then choose OK. Visual Basic adds the control to the Toolbox and to the list of available controls.

Viewing OLE Custom Control Methods and Properties

One of the advantages that OLE custom controls have over .VBX controls is that you can view control methods and procedures by using the new OLE Object Browser.

To view the methods and properties for an OLE custom control, follow these steps:

1. Add the custom control to your form. The Object Browser lists only those custom controls that you have already used somewhere in the current project.

2. Choose View, Object Browser. Visual Basic displays the Object Browser dialog box (see fig. 12.5). You can also display the Object Browser by pressing F2 or by clicking the Object Browser toolbar button.

3. From the Libraries/Projects drop-down list, select the custom control to view. The Object Browser displays the classes and modules for that control. Most controls have one class for the control itself, but others might have more than one.

4. Select the class and the method or property to view. The Object Browser displays the syntax for the method or property and a brief description, as shown in figure 12.6.

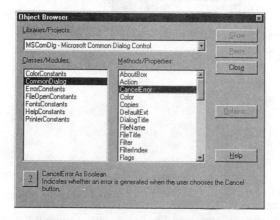

Fig. 12.5
The Object Browser displays the methods and properties of any OLE custom control, object, or library of objects.

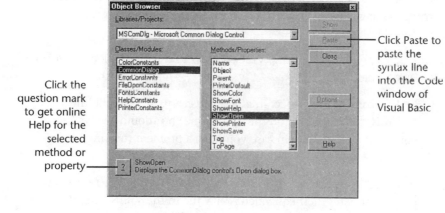

Click Paste to paste the syntax line into the Code window of Visual Basic

Click the question mark to get online Help for the selected method or property

Fig. 12.6
The Object Browser lists the syntax and a brief description of the properties and methods of all OLE objects.

The Object Browser does not list the events an object supports. To add event procedures for a custom control, use the Object and Proc list boxes on the Visual Basic Code window (see fig. 12.7).

Upgrading .VBXs to .OCXs

Visual Basic 4.0 ships OLE custom controls that replace all the .VBX controls included in Visual Basic 3.0 Professional Edition. The version 3.0 controls still work with Visual Basic 4.0, but if you want to run your applications on 32-bit operating systems, such as Windows NT or Windows 95, you should upgrade those projects to use the new OLE custom controls.

Fig. 12.7
Use the Code
window to view
the events that an
OLE custom
control supports.

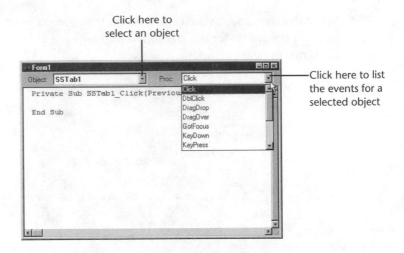

Click here to
select an object

Click here to list
the events for a
selected object

Many other custom control vendors also provide OLE custom controls to replace their older .VBX controls. You might want to contact your custom control provider before you begin upgrading your projects—it is easier to perform the upgrade for all controls once instead of upgrading a project in a piecemeal fashion.

To upgrade a project containing .VBX controls to use new OLE custom controls, follow these steps:

1. Make a copy of the project in a new directory. After upgrading your controls, you cannot undo the operation. You should always keep a copy of the old project in case you have a problem running the upgraded version.

2. Install all the new OLE custom controls on your system. These new controls register their equivalent .VBX file in the VB.INI file. Visual Basic automatically uses this information for the upgrade.

3. Open the project to upgrade by using Visual Basic 4.0. Visual Basic displays the Custom Control Upgrade dialog box (see fig. 12.8). Choose Yes to proceed with the upgrade.

4. If you are upgrading the project from Visual Basic 3.0, Visual Basic displays a warning that it will save the files in a new format for Visual Basic 4.0 (see fig. 12.9). Click OK For All to proceed with the upgrade.

    If you are upgrading your project from Visual Basic 3.0, Visual Basic displays another warning (see fig. 12.10). Data access objects are OLE objects in Visual Basic 4.0, not objects built in to the language.

Therefore, projects that use data access objects must reference the Microsoft Data Object Library. Click Add if your project uses data access; otherwise, click Don't Add.

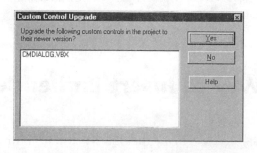

Fig. 12.8
The Custom Control Upgrade dialog box appears before Visual Basic converts .VBX controls to .OCX controls in a project.

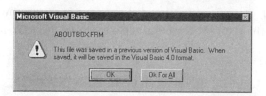

Fig. 12.9
Visual Basic 4.0 files are not backwardly compatible with earlier versions.

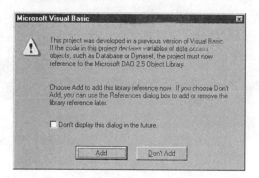

Fig. 12.10
If you ask it to, Visual Basic will add a reference to the Microsoft Data Object Library.

5. Visual Basic replaces your .VBX custom controls with the equivalent OLE custom controls installed on your system. This process can take a little while, depending on the complexity and size of your project.

Visual Basic doesn't upgrade .VBX controls that lack equivalent OLE custom controls installed on your system. The setup program written by the custom control provider handles the installing and registering of the mapping between .VBX controls and OLE custom controls. If you have problems upgrading a control, you might want to contact the custom control provider to see whether it knows of the problem and offers special procedures to use when upgrading its custom controls.

II

Using OLE

> **Note**
>
> Not all .VBX controls have .OCX equivalents. Before planning any migration to Windows 95 or Windows NT 3.51, check with your custom control vendor to make sure updated controls are available.

A New Way to Insert Embedded Objects

In Visual Basic 3.0, you had to use the OLE 2.0 custom control (MSOLE2.VBX) to add linked or embedded objects to a form. In Visual Basic 4.0, you can add embedded objects directly to the Toolbox and then draw them on the form, just as you would any other control (see fig. 12.11).

Fig. 12.11
Add insertable OLE objects to the Toolbox, then draw them directly on a form.

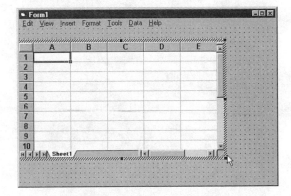

Visual Basic refers to these embedded OLE objects as *insertable objects* throughout its documentation.

Adding an Embedded Object to the Toolbox

The Setup program doesn't install embedded objects in the Toolbox because they are provided by OLE applications, such as Microsoft Word and Excel, that don't ship with Visual Basic.

To add an embedded object to the Toolbox, follow these steps:

1. Choose Tools, Custom Controls. Visual Basic displays the Custom Controls dialog box (see fig. 12.12).

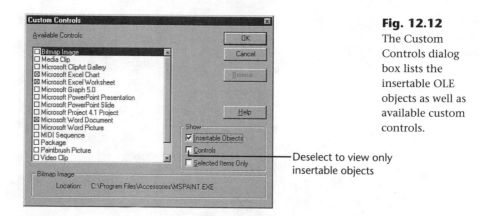

Fig. 12.12
The Custom
Controls dialog
box lists the
insertable OLE
objects as well as
available custom
controls.

—Deselect to view only
insertable objects

2. Select the check box next to the name of the embedded object that you
want to add to the Toolbox. Visual Basic adds the control to the toolbar
(see fig. 12.13).

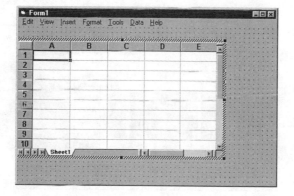

Fig. 12.13
An Excel
worksheet
embedded on
a form.

The Insertable Objects and Controls check boxes on the Custom Controls
dialog box (see fig. 12.12) enable you to show or hide either type of OLE
object in the Available Controls list box. You might want to select only
Insertable Objects if you are not adding custom controls to your Toolbox.
This makes it a little easier to find the object that you want.

Drawing Embedded Objects on a Form

To draw an embedded object on a form, follow these steps:

1. Click on the Toolbox button for the object to draw.

2. Click on the form and drag the control until it is the size that you want,
then release the mouse button (see fig. 12.14).

Fig. 12.14
Drawing an
embedded object
on a form is the
same as drawing a
control—simply
click and drag.

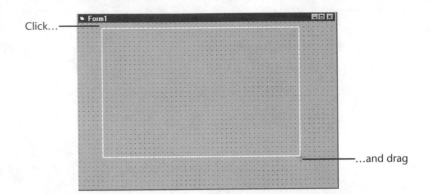

Click...

...and drag

Embedded Objects and In-Place Editing

Embedded objects need not support in-place editing. If an object supports in-place editing, Visual Basic starts the application that provides the object and displays the object's toolbar or menu on the form, as shown in figure 12.15.

Fig. 12.15
The Microsoft
Excel Chart object
supports in-place
editing, so it
displays the
charting menu
right on the form.

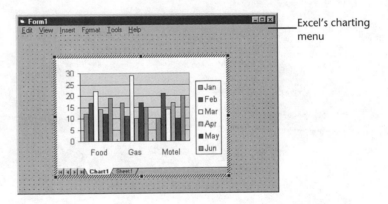

Excel's charting
menu

If an object does not support in-place editing, the application that provides the object starts up when you release the mouse button.

Table 12.1 lists widely installed applications, their embedded objects, and whether they support in-place editing.

Table 12.1 Many Applications Now Provide Embedded Objects, but Only Some Support In-Place Editing			
Application	**Version**	**Object**	**Supports In-Place Editing (Y/N)**
Microsoft Access	7.0	Database	Y

Application	Version	Object	Supports In-Place Editing (Y/N)
Microsoft Excel	7.0	Worksheet	Y
		Chart	Y
		Graph	Y
Microsoft Excel	5.0	Worksheet	Y
		Chart	Y
		Graph	Y
Microsoft Equation	2.0	Equation	Y
Microsoft Graph	3.0	Graph	N
Microsoft PowerPoint	7.0	Presentation	Y
		Slide	Y
Microsoft Windows	3.1	Package	N
		Paintbrush Picture	N
		Sound	N
Microsoft Windows	95	Package	N
		Sound	Y
		Paintbrush Picture	Y
		Video clip	Y
		WordPad Document	Y
Shapeware Visio	3.0	Drawing	Y
Shapeware Visio	2.0	Drawing	N
Microsoft Word	2.0	Document	N
Microsoft Word	6.0	Document	Y
		Picture	Y
Microsoft Word	7.0	Document	Y
		Picture	Y
Microsoft WordArt	2.0	WordArt	Y

II

Using OLE

Adding Data to Embedded Objects

When you draw an embedded object on a form, the object appears without data. You can enter new data directly in the object at that time. If you select another control on the form, the embedded object is closed. To reopen an embedded object for editing, follow these steps:

1. Right-click on the embedded object. The object displays its pop-up menu (see fig. 12.16).

Fig. 12.16

An embedded Excel worksheet object displaying its pop-up menu.

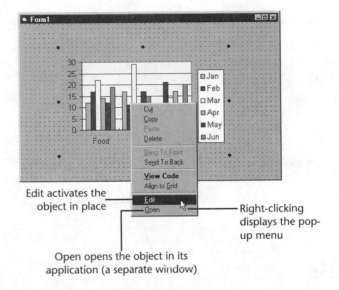

Edit activates the object in place

Right-clicking displays the pop-up menu

Open opens the object in its application (a separate window)

2. Choose Edit to edit the object in place. Choose Open to open the object in its application (not in place).

3. If you finish editing the object in place, simply click another control on the form to close the object. If you are editing the object in its application, choose File, Close from the application's menus to close the object.

Creating Embedded Objects from Files

Drawing embedded objects on forms using the Toolbox button for the object works great for new objects that don't yet contain data. However, moving the contents of an existing file into one of these embedded objects is awkward; you must open the object in its application, then cut and paste the data into the file.

It is easier to create an embedded object from a file by using the OLE 2.0 control. To create an embedded object from a file, follow these steps:

1. Click the OLE 2.0 control button in the Visual Basic Toolbox.

2. Click on the form and drag the control until it is the size that you want, then release the mouse button. Visual Basic displays the Insert Object dialog box (see fig. 12.17).

Fig. 12.17
Use the Insert Object dialog box to create an embedded object from a file.

3. On the Insert Object dialog box, click Create from File. Visual Basic changes the Insert Object dialog box to enable you to select a file (see fig. 12.18).

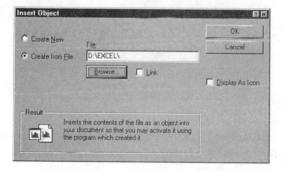

Fig. 12.18
Type the file name or choose Browse to specify a file to use.

4. On the Insert Object dialog box, type the name and path of the file to link or choose Browse to select a file in the Browse dialog box.

5. Click OK. Visual Basic makes a copy of the data in the file and inserts the object on the form.

An embedded object created in this way is a copy of the data in the file—it is stored and updated separately from the original file. To ensure that an object is updated and kept in sync with its source file, use a linked object rather than an embedded one.

Inserting Linked Objects with the OLE 2.0 Control

In Visual Basic 3.0, linking and embedding was provided through the OLE 2.0 custom control (MSOLE2.VBX). In Visual Basic 4.0, the OLE 2.0 control is built in. The OLE 2.0 control works the same way that it did in Visual Basic 3.0—you can still use it to add linked or embedded objects to forms.

Drawing Linked Objects on a Form

To draw a linked object on a form, follow these steps:

1. Click the OLE 2.0 control button in the Visual Basic Toolbox.

2. Click on the form and drag the control until it is the size that you want, then release the mouse button. Visual Basic displays the Insert Object dialog box (see fig. 12.19).

Tip

When adding embedded objects, it is easier to use the Toolbox. For more information, see "A New Way to Insert Embedded Objects," earlier in this chapter.

Fig. 12.19

Use the Insert Object dialog box to add linked objects to a form.

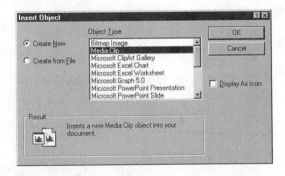

3. On the Insert Object dialog box, click Create from File. Visual Basic changes the Insert Object dialog box to enable you to select a file (see fig. 12.20).

Fig. 12.20

Type the file name or click Browse to specify a file to use.

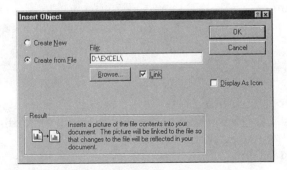

4. On the Insert Object dialog box, type the name and path of the file to link, or choose Browse to select a file in the Browse dialog box.

5. Select Link to link the object on the form to the file, then click OK. Visual Basic inserts the object on the form and displays the data from the file in the object.

Editing Linked Objects

Unlike embedded objects, linked objects never support in-place editing. When you edit a linked object, the object's application always starts up in another window and loads the linked file.

To edit a linked object on a form, follow these steps:

1. Right-click on the object. The object displays its pop-up menu (see fig. 12.21).

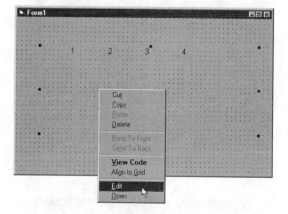

Fig. 12.21
An Excel worksheet object displaying its pop-up menu.

2. From the pop-up menu, choose Open or Edit. The object's application starts and loads the linked file (see fig. 12.22).

3. Edit the file for the linked object, then save the file and exit. Visual Basic updates the linked object.

An OLE object might look different in design mode or run mode, as shown in figure 12.23.

Fig. 12.22
Editing a linked
worksheet file
with Excel.

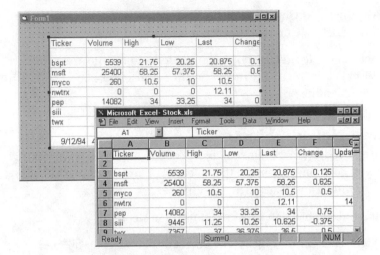

Fig. 12.23
In design mode,
Visual Basic
updates the linked
object as the file
changes. In run
mode, the object
is grayed until the
file is closed.

Design mode ——

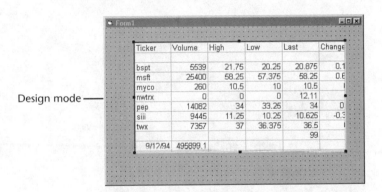

Run mode ——

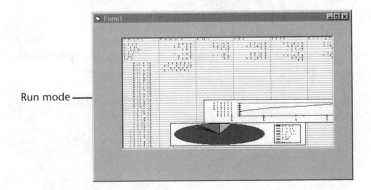

A New Type of OLE Object: Object Applications

Linked and embedded objects are no longer the only type of OLE objects that you can use in Visual Basic. Object applications differ from linked and embedded objects in that you can't place them on a form. Instead, object applications can display their own dialog boxes and forms to perform services, such as access to databases or retrieving a password from a user. Figure 12.24 shows the differences between linked and embedded objects and object applications.

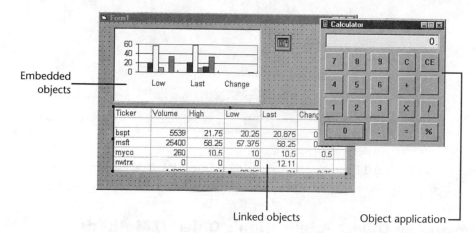

Embedded objects

Linked objects

Object application

Fig. 12.24
Linked and embedded objects appear on a form. Object applications might display their own forms or run invisibly in the background.

Building the Sample Object Application

You can create object applications in Visual Basic or Visual C++. Part III, "Creating OLE Objects," teaches you how to create your own object applications using Visual Basic. This chapter is concerned only with using those applications after they exist.

However, to see how to use an object application, you must have one installed on your system. The easiest way around this catch-22 is to go ahead and build one of the sample applications that ship with Visual Basic: GRAVITY.VBP.

To build GRAVITY.VBP, follow these steps:

1. Load the project GRAVITY.VBP in Visual Basic. You can find the GRAVITY.VBP project in the Visual Basic \SAMPLES\OLESERV directory.

2. Choose File, Make EXE File. Visual Basic displays the Make EXE File dialog box (see fig. 12.25).

Fig. 12.25
Compile the
GRAVITY.VBP
sample file to see
how to use an
object application.

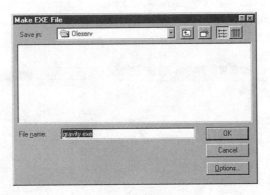

3. Click OK. Visual Basic compiles the project into GRAVITY.EXE and adds an entry in your system's registry for the application.

Viewing an Object Application's Objects, Methods, and Properties

You use the Object Browser to view the objects, properties, and methods that an object application contains. However, before you can browse an application object, you must first establish a reference to that application. It's not absolutely necessary to establish a reference before using an object application, but doing so does enable the Object Browser and provides syntax checking for properties and methods.

To view GRAVITY.EXE's objects, methods, and properties, follow these steps:

1. Create a new project or open an existing one (other than GRAVITY.VBP). References to object applications are saved with each project.

2. Choose Tools, References. Visual Basic displays the References dialog box (see fig. 12.26). A reference enables your project to use objects, methods, and properties included in other applications or libraries.

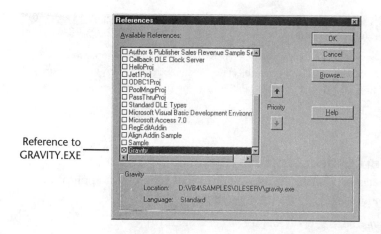

Reference to
GRAVITY.EXE

Fig. 12.26
The References
dialog box
establishes a
reference between
the open project
and object
applications or
object libraries.

3. In the Available References list box, select the check box next to the
words "What goes up..." This is the reference for GRAVITY.EXE.

4. Click OK. Visual Basic closes the References dialog box.

5. Choose View, Object Browser or press F2. Visual Basic displays the
Object Browser dialog box (see fig. 12.27).

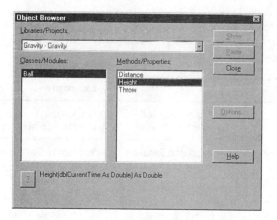

Fig. 12.27
GRAVITY.EXE
contains one
object and three
methods or
properties.

6. From the Libraries/Projects drop-down list, select Gravity. The Object
Browser displays the objects, methods, and properties contained in
GRAVITY.EXE.

You can use the objects, methods, and properties listed for GRAVITY anywhere in code. Unlike other types of objects, however, object applications do
not provide events that you can use in Visual Basic.

II

Using OLE

If You're Having Trouble...

If you are having trouble establishing a reference to an object application, run the object application and then try again. Object applications check their system registry entries every time that they start up. Often this fixes the problems in the system registry.

Running an Object Application

Use the CreateObject and GetObject functions to run an object application. CreateObject and GetObject use this syntax:

```
Set objVariable = CreateObject(programmaticID)

Set objVariable = GetObject([objectname], programmaticID)
```

The placeholder *objVariable* is an object variable that contains the object that CreateObject and GetObject return. This is the variable used throughout your code to refer to the object application.

The placeholder *programmaticID* is the name of the object application as it is entered in the system registry. This name has the form *ApplicationName.ObjectName*. For example, excel.application or gravity.ball.

CreateObject and GetObject both return an object from the application, as shown in the following table:

Use	To	Example
CreateObject	Start a new copy of the object application	Set objBall = CreateObject ("gravity.ball")
GetObject (first argument null)	Get a running instance of the object application	Set objBall=GetObject ("","gravity.ball")
GetObject (first argument provided)	Get a specific object from the object application	Set xlsExcel = _GetObject ("c:\excel\stock.xls", "excel.sheet")

To run the GRAVITY object application, follow these steps:

1. Create a new project.

2. Open the Code window for Form1 in the project and add the following lines of code:

   ```
   Option Explicit
   ' Declare an object variable for the object application.
   Dim mobjBall As Object
   ```

The variable `mobjBall` is declared at the form level, so other procedures in the form can use it. This ensures that the object variable is still available after the `Form_Load` event creates the object in the next step.

3. Add the following lines to the `Form_Load` event:

```
Private Sub Form_Load()
    ' Run the object application
    ' by calling CreateObject.
    ' CreateObject returns the object
    ' from the application.
    Set mobjBall = CreateObject("gravity.ball")
End Sub
```

The `CreateObject` line starts GRAVITY.EXE, returns the `Ball` object, and assigns it to the object variable `mobjBall`. You must use `Set` when assigning object variables.

4. Run the new project. When Form1 loads, Visual Basic starts GRAVITY.EXE. GRAVITY.EXE doesn't display any forms or dialog boxes, but you can see it if you view the Windows Task List.

Finding Programmatic IDs

One of the hardest parts about using `CreateObject` and `GetObject` is finding the right programmatic ID for the object application that you want to start. Table 12.2 lists some commonly installed applications and the programmatic IDs for their objects.

Table 12.2 Many Applications Provide Objects, but Their Programmatic IDs Are Often Hard to Find

Application	Object	Programmatic ID
Microsoft Excel	Application Worksheet Chart	excel.application excel.sheet excel.chart
Shapeware Visio	Application	visio.application
Microsoft Word	Basic	word.basic

The programmatic ID of an object application created in Visual Basic consists of the application name and the object name, as in gravity.ball or calc.application.

The application name is the name entered in the Project Name text box of the Project tab of the Options properties pages. The object name is the name of the class (see fig. 12.28).

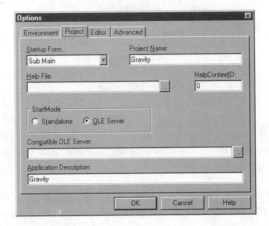

Using Object Application Methods and Properties

After starting an object application as described in the previous section, you can use the object's methods and properties just as you would with any other Visual Basic object or control.

To see how this works with the GRAVITY.EXE object application, follow these steps:

1. Create a module-level variable to contain the reference to the Ball object and write code in the Form Load event to initialize the Ball object:

```
Dim mobjBall

Private Sub Form_Load()
    Set mobjBall = CreateObject("Gravity.Ball")
End Sub
```

2. Draw an option button on Form1 of the project that you created in the previous section. Add the following lines to the option button's click event:

```
Private Sub Option1_Click()
    ' Call the Throw method for the Ball object.
    mobjBall.Throw dblHorizontalVelocity:=1000, _
    dblVerticalVelocity:=1000
    Timer1.Enabled = Option1.Value
    Timer1.Interval = 1000
End Sub
```

The Ball object's Throw method starts GRAVITY.EXE tracking the trajectory of a hypothetical ball influenced by the earth's gravity.

3. Draw a timer control on Form1 and add the following lines to the timer event:

```
Private Sub Timer1_Timer()
    ' Call the Distance and Height properties
    ' for the Ball object.
    Form1.Print "Distance: " _
    & mobjBall.Distance(dblCurrentTime:=Now) _
        & "      Height: " _
    & mobjBall.Height(dblCurrentTime:=Now)
End Sub
```

The `Ball` object's `Distance` and `Height` properties return the coordinates of the hypothetical ball that was thrown in step 1.

4. Run the project. When you click the option button, Form1 displays the coordinates of the ball's trajectory (see fig. 12.29).

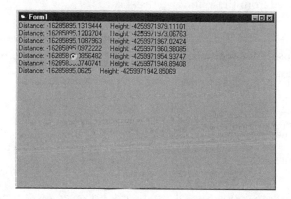

Fig. 12.29
The application that you create in these steps demonstrates how to use the Throw method and Height and Distance properties of the Ball object provided by GRAVITY.EXE.

The application shown in this section isn't terribly exciting. You can improve on the application by moving the option button to follow the ball's trajectory on the form. See the sample GRAVTEST.VBP in the \SAMPLES\OLESERV directory for more ideas.

Closing an Object Application

After you start an application by using `CreateObject` or `GetObject`, it continues running as long as one or more object variables refer to an object in the application. This principle is fundamental to OLE.

OLE keeps track of the number of references to an application. If the application is not visible and the count goes to zero, OLE closes the application. If the application is visible and the count goes to zero, OLE leaves the application running.

To see how this works with the GRAVITY.EXE object application, follow these steps:

1. In the project created in the previous two sections, add this code to the form's unload event:

```
Private Sub Form_UnLoad(Cancel As Integer)
        ' Set the object variable to Nothing
        ' to close the object application.
        Set mobjBall = Nothing
End Sub
```

    Setting the object variable `mobjBall` to `Nothing` changes the reference count of GRAVITY.EXE to zero. Because GRAVITY does not have a visual interface, OLE closes the application.

2. Run the project. When you close Form1, GRAVITY.EXE shuts down and is removed from the Windows Task List.

Applications that have a visual interface usually provide a `Quit` or `Exit` method to close. For example, these lines start Microsoft Excel, then close that application:

```
Sub Main()
    Dim appExcel As Object
    Set appExcel = CreateObject("excel.application")
    appExcel.Visible = True
                    ' Excel starts invisibly, so make it visible.
    appExcel.Quit              ' Close Excel
End Sub
```

Not all applications follow the OLE standard, however. Most notably, Microsoft Word closes when no longer referenced, even if it is visible. These lines start Microsoft Word 6.0, then close the application:

```
Sub Main()
  Dim appWord As Object
  Set appWord = CreateObject("word.basic")
                        ' Start Microsoft Word.
  appWord.Insert "Add some text" ' Insert some text in a document.
  Set appWord = Nothing              ' Closes Word without saving!
End Sub
```

In this regard, Word is not a "well-behaved" OLE application. In all cases, it is important to experiment with object applications to determine how well they follow the OLE standards.

Exploring the System Registry

Each OLE object installed on your system has one or more entries in the system registry. One of the best tools for exploring the OLE objects on your system is the Registry Editor (REGEDIT.EXE). This tool ships with Windows and comes installed in the Windows directory.

To explore your system's registry, follow these steps:

1. Run the command line `regedit /v`. (You might want to add an item with this command line to your Visual Basic program group.) The Registry Editor appears as shown in figure 12.30.

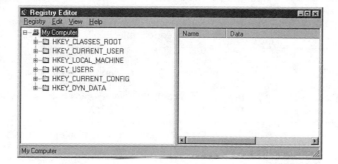

Fig. 12.30
The Registry Editor lets you view the entries in your system's registry.

2. Choose <u>E</u>dit, <u>F</u>ind. The Registry Editor displays the Find dialog box (see fig. 12.31).

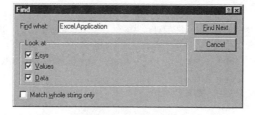

Fig. 12.31
Use the Find dialog box to search for insertable objects, programmatic IDs, or applications by name.

3. Enter the name of a key for which to search and click <u>F</u>ind Next. For example, you might want to search on `progid` to see programmatic IDs or `word` to locate the entries for Microsoft Word.

4. Press F3 to find the next entry that matches the entered key.

II

Using OLE

The listing that appears in the Registry Editor is confusing at best. Table 12.3 describes what some of the items mean.

Table 12.3 The Meanings of Some of the Keys in the System Registry	
Key Item	**Meaning**
CLSID	The item's *class ID*, a number that identifies the object to OLE, and that is used by the OLE .DLLs when referring to the object.
insertable	An indicator that this object supports in-place editing for embedded objects.
notinsertable	An indicator that this object does not support in-place editing for embedded objects.
progid	The *programmatic identifier* used to start the application as an application object. You cannot use all objects with programmatic identifiers CreateObject or GetObject, however. You can't readily tell which objects are creatable by looking at the system registry.
server	A list of the path and file specification of the application that provides the object.
verb	The menu items that this object adds to the pop-up menu when right-clicked. Typical actions are Edit and Open, but some objects may support additional verbs, such as Play.

From Here...

For more information on the following topics, see the indicated chapters:

- Chapter 13, "Controlling OLE Objects," explains how to control linked and embedded objects in code.

- Chapter 15, "Designing OLE Container Applications," explains the different types of applications that you can create using OLE objects.

- Chapter 17, "OLE Objects Exposed," discusses the OLE Automation features.

Chapter 13

Controlling OLE Objects

You control OLE objects by using the OLE control's properties and methods. All OLE objects share these properties and methods, whether they were created with the OLE control or with an insertable object. This chapter tells you how to control OLE objects in code.

In this chapter, you learn how to do the following:

- Create linked and embedded objects at run time
- Control the display of OLE objects by resizing, scrolling, and scaling
- Enable the user to move or resize embedded objects in place
- Capture the image of an OLE object and display it in a picture box or image control
- Update linked objects
- Activate and deactivate linked and embedded objects
- Save OLE objects in special files that Visual Basic can read directly
- Get the OLE Automation object from linked or embedded objects

Creating OLE Objects at Run Time

To create OLE objects at run time, you use the OLE control. It provides the methods listed in table 13.1 to create objects.

Table 13.1 OLE Control Methods for Creating Objects

OLE Control Method	Use
oleobject.InsertObjDlg	Displays the standard OLE Insert Object dialog box to enable the user to select an OLE object to create
oleobject.CreateEmbed *file*[, *type*]	Creates an embedded object in code without displaying the OLE Insert Object dialog box
oleobject.CreateLink *file*	Creates a linked object from a file without displaying the OLE Insert Object dialog box

Follow these steps to create an OLE object at run time:

1. Draw an OLE control on a form. Visual Basic displays the standard Insert Object dialog box (fig. 13.1).

Fig. 13.1
To create a linked or embedded object at run time, click the Insert Object dialog box's Cancel button.

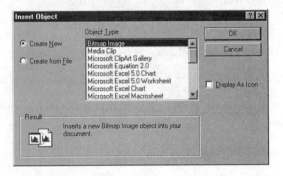

2. Click Cancel to close the Insert Object dialog box without selecting an OLE object to create.

3. In an event procedure, use the InsertObjDlg, CreateEmbed, or CreateLink methods to create an object for the control, as in the following example:

```
Private Sub OLE1_DblClick()
    OLE1.InsertObjDlg
            ' Let the user choose an object to create.
End Sub
```

These lines display the Insert Object dialog box (fig. 13.1) when the user double-clicks the OLE object control.

Creating an Embedded Object

To create an embedded object without displaying the Insert Object dialog box, follow the procedure in the preceding section, but substitute this code in step 3:

```
Private Sub OLE1_DblClick()
    OLE1.CreateEmbed "", "excel.sheet"
        ' Create a new embedded Excel worksheet.
End Sub
```

The preceding lines of code embed a new, empty worksheet in the OLE control OLE1. To base the embedded object on a file, specify the file name in the first argument, as in the following example:

```
Private Sub OLE1_DblClick()
    OLE1.CreateEmbed "c:\excel\stock.xls" ' Embed STOCK.XLS.
End Sub
```

If you specify a file name for CreateEmbed, Visual Basic ignores the second argument. If a file contains more than one type of object, Visual Basic simply uses the first object in the file. You cannot specify an object within a file by using CreateEmbed.

Class Types of Embedded Objects

The CreateEmbed method uses the class type of the OLE object to create new embedded objects (the *type* argument). Table 13.2 lists the class types for some commonly available OLE objects.

Table 13.2 Class Types for Common OLE Objects

Application	Class Type
Microsoft Equation Editor	Equation
Microsoft Equation Draw	MSDraw
Microsoft Word document (any version)	WordDocument
Microsoft Word document (any version)	Word.Document
Microsoft Word document (version 6.0)	Word.Document.6
Microsoft Word picture (version 6.0)	Word.Picture.6
Microsoft Note-It	Note-It
Microsoft WordArt	WordArt
A package (a file of any format)	Package

(continues)

Table 13.2 Continued	
Application	**Class Type**
Microsoft Paintbrush	PBrush
Microsoft Quick Recorder	SoundRec
Microsoft Excel chart	Excel.Chart
Microsoft Excel worksheet	Excel.Sheet
Microsoft Excel worksheet (version 5.0)	Excel.Sheet.5
Microsoft Excel worksheet (version 5.0)	Excel.Chart.5
ShapeWare Visio Drawing (version 2.0)	ShapewareVISIO20

The OLE class type differs from the OLE programmatic ID that CreateObject
and GetObject methods use. See Chapter 12, "Creating OLE Containers," for
more information on CreateObject and GetObject.

Creating a Linked Object

To create a linked object without displaying the Insert Object dialog box,
follow the procedure in the section "Creating OLE Objects at Run Time," but
substitute this code in step 3:

```
Private Sub OLE1_DblClick()
    OLE1.CreateEmbed "c:\excel\stock.xls"
        ' Create a new link to an Excel worksheet.
End Sub
```

Obviously, this procedure causes an error if C:\EXCEL\STOCK.XLS does not
exist. To prompt a file name from the user, add a Common Dialog control to
the form and use the code in listing 13.1.

Listing 13.1 Getting a File Name to Create a Linked Object

```
Private Sub OLE1_DblClick()
    ' Show FileOpen dialog to get a file to open.
    CommonDialog1.FileName = "*.*"
    CommonDialog1.ShowOpen
    ' Check if file exists before creating link
    ' (see Function below).
    If FileExists(CommonDialog1.FileName) Then
        ' Attempt to create an embedded object.
        OLE1.CreateLink CommonDialog1.FileName
    End If
End Sub
```

```
' Checks if a file exists (uses full path and file name).
Function FileExists(strFileName) As Boolean
    ' Turn on error checking.
    On Error Resume Next
    ' FileLen causes error if file doesn't exist.
    FileLen (strFileName)
    If Err Then
        FileExists = False
        Err = 0
    Else
        FileExists = True
    End If
    ' Turn off error checking.
    On Error GoTo 0
End Function
```

The function `FileExists` verifies that the user entered a valid file name in the Open File dialog box. Using `FileLen` and error checking is one of the faster ways of checking for a file, although it certainly is not the only way.

Controlling the Display of OLE Objects

One of biggest problems with creating OLE objects at run time is getting them to display correctly on screen. When you create objects at design time, you draw the object and can adjust its appearance manually. When you create OLE objects at run time, you must write code to handle the object's display. To handle the display of OLE objects at run time, you can use several techniques:

- Resize the control to fit the object

- Scroll the object on the form

- Scale the object to fit in the control

- Scale the object *and* size the control to create the best fit for both the object and the control

The following sections describe how to use the OLE control's `SizeMode` property and `Resize` event to perform these programming tasks.

How the *SizeMode* Property and *Resize* Event Interact

The OLE control's `SizeMode` controls how the OLE control displays an OLE object. Table 13.3 lists the possible settings for the `SizeMode` property.

II

Using OLE

Table 13.3 `SizeMode` **Property Settings**

`SizeMode` **Constant**	**Value**	**Use**
`vbOLESizeClip` (default)	0	Clip the object to fit in the control
`vbOLESizeStretch`	1	Stretch or shrink the object's height and width to match the control without retaining the object's original proportions
`vbOLESizeAutoSize`	2	Resize the control to match the object's height and width
`vbOLESizeZoom`	3	Stretch or shrink the object's height and width to match the control while retaining the object's original proportions

If the OLE control does not match the size of the OLE object that it contains, Visual Basic triggers a `Resize` event for the object. The `Resize` event has the following form for the OLE control:

```
Private Sub OLE1_Resize(HeightNew As Single, WidthNew As Single)
    ' ... your code here.
End Sub
```

The `HeightNew` and `WidthNew` arguments indicate a recommended size for the object. This size is that of the OLE object in its original form. You can use these arguments with the `SizeMode` property to control the scaling of an OLE object. To learn more about this technique, see the section "Scaling the Object to Fit the Control," later in this chapter.

The `Resize` event occurs when the displayed size of an OLE object changes, as in the situations described in table 13.4.

Table 13.4 Situations That Result in a `Resize` **Event**

A `Resize` **Event Occurs When**	**If the Current** `SizeMode` **Setting Is**
A new object is inserted in the control	Any setting
The size of an object changes because it was updated	Any setting but `vbOLESizeClip`
The OLE control's `Height` and `Width` properties are used to change the object's size	Any setting but `vbOLESizeClip`

A Resize Event Occurs When	If the Current SizeMode Setting Is
The SizeMode property changes to a new setting	vbOLESizeClip
The SizeMode property changes to vbOLESizeAutosize	vbOLESizeStretch or vbOLESizeZoom

The Resize event does *not* occur when SizeMode changes from any setting to vbOLESizeClip or vbOLESizeAutoSize to any setting. In the latter situation, the control size matches the object size, so no visual change occurs either.

Displaying Objects in a Sizable Window (Form)

A simple way to size an OLE object is to display it on a separate form that matches the size of the OLE control, and then enable the user to resize the form. Use the ScaleMode settings vbOLESizeClip or vbOLESizeAutoSize when creating OLE objects to display in a sizable window.

To see how this scheme works, follow these steps:

1. Create a new project.

2. Add an OLE control to Form1 and move the control so that its upper-left corner is in the form's upper-left corner.

3. Add the following lines of code to the Form1_Load event procedure:

```
Private Sub Form_Load()
    ' Automatically adjust the control to fit the object.
    OLE1.SizeMode = vbOLESizeAutosize
    ' Display the Insert Object dialog
    ' to get an object to display.
    OLE1.InsertObjDlg
End Sub
```

4. Add these lines of code to the Form1_Resize event procedure:

```
Private Sub Form_Resize()
    ' Prevent the form from exceeding
    ' the size of the OLE object.
    If OLE1.Width < Form1.Width Then Form1.Width = OLE1.Width
    If OLE1.Height < Form1.Height Then Form1.Height = OLE1.Height
End Sub
```

5. Run the project and select an OLE object to display. The object appears on the form as shown in figure 13.2.

Fig. 13.2
When you resize a form, you can see more of the object. This "object in a window" approach is good for multiple-document interface (MDI) applications.

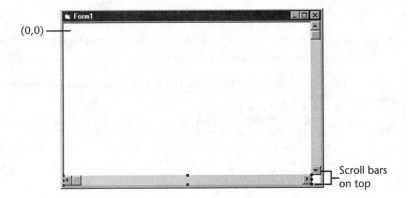

Scrolling the Control for Large Objects

Another way to size objects is to enable the user to scroll large objects up, down, right, or left. To create scrollable OLE objects, you use the ScaleMode setting vbOLESizeAutoSize, as described in these steps:

1. Create a new project.

2. Draw horizontal and vertical scroll bars on the form and an OLE control (see fig. 13.3).

Fig. 13.3
The OLE control starts at the form's origin (0,0) and covers the entire form. The scroll bars appear on top of the OLE control, so they are obscured when you activate the object for editing.

3. Add the following lines of code to the form's Load event procedure:

```
Private Sub Form_Load()
    ' Use the default SizeMode, OLE control
    ' automatically resize to match the object's size.
        OLE1.SizeMode = vbOLESizeAutoSize
    ' Display the InsertObject dialog box to
    ' let the user choose an object to embed or link.
        OLE1.InsertObjDlg
End Sub
```

4. Add the following lines of code to the scroll bars' Scroll event procedures. These lines scroll the OLE object on the form when the user moves either scroll bar.

```
Private Sub HScroll1_Change()
    OLE1.Left = 0 - HScroll1.Value
End Sub

Private Sub VScroll1_Change()
    OLE1.Top = 0 - VScroll1.Value
End Sub
```

5. Add the following lines of code to the OLE control's `Resize` event procedure. These lines control the scroll bars' display and determine the
scroll bars' scale and maximium values based on the OLE object's size.

```
Private Sub OLE1_Resize(HeightNew As Single,
    WidthNew As Single)
    If HeightNew > Form1.Height Then
        VScroll1.Visible = True
        VScroll1.Max = HeightNew
        VScroll1.LargeChange = _
            HeightNew / (HeightNew / OLE1.Height)
        VScroll1.SmallChange = VScroll1.LargeChange / 10
    Else
        VScroll1.Visible = False
    End If
    If WidthNew > Form1.Width Then
        HScroll1.Visible = True
        HScroll1.Max = WidthNew
        HScroll1.LargeChange = WidthNew / _
            (WidthNew / OLE1.Width)
        HScroll1.SmallChange = HScroll1.LargeChange / 10
    Else
        HScroll1.Visible = False
    End If
End Sub
```

6. Add the following lines of code to the form's `Resize` event procedure.
These lines trigger the OLE control's `Resize` event to elicit the correct
behavior when the user resizes the form.

```
Private Sub Form_Resize()
    ' Skip first Resize on Load.
    Static bFlag As Boolean
    If bFlag Then
        ' If form resizes, trigger OLE control
        '   resize behavior.
        OLE1_Resize OLE1.Height, OLE1.Width
    Else
        bFlag = True
    End If
    ' Call support procedure to adjust the placement
    ' and size of scroll bars on the form.
    AdjustScrollBars Me
End Sub
```

7. Run the project. When displaying on the form, the OLE object
appears with scroll bars if it is larger than the current form, as shown
in figure 13.4.

Fig. 13.4
After creating the
sample in this
section, you can
resize the form or
scroll it to see
more of the object.

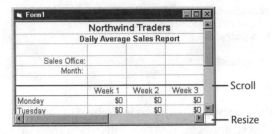

In step 6, you use the support procedure in listing 13.2 to adjust the scroll
bar's positions on the form. This procedure is useful in a variety of contexts,
so the companion CD presents it as a separate procedure instead of building
it in to the form's Resize event.

Listing 13.2   A Procedure for Adjusting Scroll Bars When a Form Is Resized

```
' AdjustScrollBars procedure
'
' Keeps scroll bars on the outer edges of a form
' after resizing. Assumes that the horizontal
' and scroll bars in the form's controls
' collect apply to the form.
Sub AdjustScrollBars(frmTarget As Form)
    ' Declare size and object variables.
    Dim sHeight As Single, sWidth As Single
    Dim objCount As Object
    Dim scrHScroll As Control, scrVScroll As Control
    ' Search through the form's controls collection...
    For Each objCount In frmTarget.Controls
        ' Find the horizontal scroll bar.
        If TypeName(objCount) = "HScrollBar" Then
            ' Initialize object variable.
            Set scrHScroll = objCount
            ' If visible, then record height to help position
            ' vertical scroll bar later.
            If scrHScroll.Visible = True Then
                sHeight = scrHScroll.Height
            End If
        ' Find the vertical scroll bar.
        ElseIf TypeName(objCount) = "VScrollBar" Then
            ' Initialize object variable.
            Set scrVScroll = objCount
            ' If visible, then record width to help position
            ' horizontal scroll bar later.
            If scrVScroll.Visible = True Then
                sWidth = scrVScroll.Width
            End If
        End If
```

```
    Next objCount
    ' Set position of horizontal scroll bar (if one exists).
    If Not IsEmpty(scrHScroll) Then
        scrHScroll.Top = frmTarget.ScaleHeight - sHeight
        scrHScroll.Width = frmTarget.ScaleWidth - sWidth
    End If
    ' Set position of vertical scroll bar (if one exists).
    If Not IsEmpty(scrVScroll) Then
        scrVScroll.Left = frmTarget.ScaleWidth - sWidth
        scrVScroll.Height = frmTarget.ScaleHeight - sHeight
    End If
End Sub
```

Scaling the Object to Fit the Control

OLE objects are often (but not always) much larger than the OLE control drawn on a form. Therefore, scaling the object to fit in the control often results in an object that's hard to read on screen.

This type of display is useful when legibility is not an issue or when you are displaying small objects, such as small graphics. Use the `ScaleMode` settings `vbOLESizeZoom` or `vbOLESizeStretch` when scaling objects to fit the OLE control.

Zooming an Object for the Best Fit

Scaling enables you to fit more on screen than other display methods. However, to create legible objects, you must combine scaling with sizing the OLE control. To create a best fit, use the `SizeMode` setting `vbOLESizeZoom`, the `Resize` event, and the `Height` and `Width` properties together.

To see how to create the best fit for OLE objects inserted at run time, follow these steps:

1. Create a new project.

2. Add an OLE control to the form and move the control so that its upper-left corner is in the form's upper-left corner. Then add to the form a vertical scroll bar to control zooming. Figure 13.5 shows the desired form.

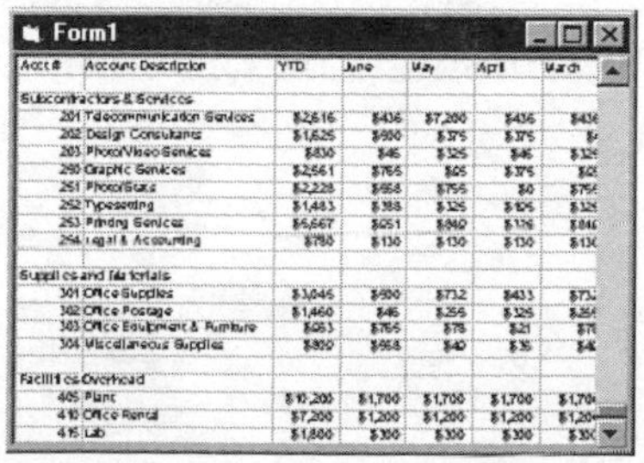

Tip
Usually `vbOLESizeZoom` is more useful than `vbOLESizeStretch`, because it maintains the object's original proportions.

Fig. 13.5
The scroll bar controls the zoom ratio of the OLE control.

3. Add the following lines of code to the form's Load event procedure. When run, these lines display the Insert Object dialog box that enables the user to select an OLE object to insert in the control.

```
' Declare module-level variables used.
Dim msHeightRatio As Single, msWidthRatio As Single

Private Sub Form_Load()
    ' Scale the object to fit the control.
    OLE1.SizeMode = vbOLESizeZoom
    ' Display the Insert Object dialog to get
    ' an object to display.
    OLE1.InsertObjDlg
End Sub
```

4. Add the following lines of code to the OLE object's Resize event procedure. This event procedure calculates the ratio of the object's actual size (HeightNew and WidthNew) to the size of the control. It also determines the display and Max value of the scroll bar used to control zooming.

```
Private Sub OLE1_Resize(HeightNew As Single, _
  WidthNew As Single)
' Choose which ratio is greater.
msHeightRatio = HeightNew / OLE1.Height
msWidthRatio = WidthNew / OLE1.Width
' If control is big enough to contain object, don't
' display scroll bar.
If msWidthRatio <= 1 And msHeightRatio <= 1 Then
   VScroll1.Visible = False
   ' Exit now.
   Exit Sub
End If
' Use the greater ratio for the scroll bar zoom.
If msHeightRatio >= msWidthRatio Then
    ' Set the maximum value (100%)
    VScroll1.Max = HeightNew
    ' Set the initial scroll bar position.
    VScroll1.Value = OLE1.Height
Else
    ' Set the maximum value (100%)
    VScroll1.Max = WidthNew
    ' Set the initial scroll bar position.
    VScroll1.Value = OLE1.Width
End If
End Sub
```

5. Add the following lines of code to the scroll bar's Change event procedure. This code scales the size of the OLE control up or down, and also automatically scales the object displayed in the control to match the control's size.

```
' Zoom OLE control.
Private Sub VScroll1_Change()
    ' Increase Height or Width, depending on which
    ' ratio is greater.
```

```
      If msHeightRatio >= msWidthRatio Then
          OLE1.Height = VScroll1.Value
      Else
          OLE1.Width = VScroll1.Value
      End If
End Sub
```

6. Run the project. When the OLE object displays on the form, drag the scroll bar slider to scale the object up or down (fig. 13.6).

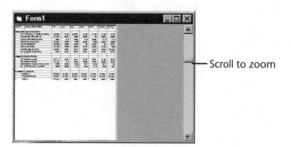

Scroll to zoom

Fig. 13.6
After creating the sample in this section, you can zoom the size of the object by using the scroll bar.

II

Using OLE

Unfortunately, relying on the `ScaleMode` property settings `vbOLESizeZoom` and `vbOLESizeStretch` does not work well for all applications. In particular, Microsoft Word updates scaled objects in a peculiar way. You can work around these display problems by capturing the image of the OLE control with its `Picture` property. To learn how to do so, see the section "Capturing the Object's Picture," later in this chapter.

Moving and Sizing Embedded Objects during In-Place Editing

By default, Visual Basic prevents you from moving embedded objects while they are being edited in place (see fig. 13.7).

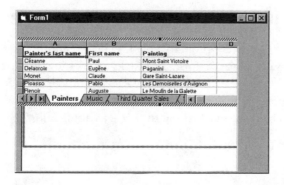

Fig. 13.7
When you try to move or resize an embedded object, it "snaps back" to its original position.

To enable users to move or size OLE objects at run time, use the `ObjectMove` event procedure. `ObjectMove` has the following form:

```
Private Sub OLE1_ObjectMove(Left As Single, Top As Single, _
    Width As Single, Height As Single)

    '...your code here
End Sub
```

The arguments to the `ObjectMove` event procedure are the position and dimensions to which the user dragged the object. To make the object respond to the user's action, simply assign the `ObjectMove` arguments to the OLE control's `Left`, `Top`, `Width`, and `Height` properties, as follows:

```
Private Sub OLE1_ObjectMove(Left As Single, Top As Single, _
    Width As Single, Height As Single)
    OLE1.Left = Left
    OLE1.Top = Top
    OLE1.Width = Width
    OLE1.Height = Height
End Sub
```

Now when the user moves or resizes the OLE object, the OLE control adjusts to the new size and location as shown in figure 13.8.

Fig. 13.8
The `ObjectMove` event procedure enables the OLE control to respond when the user moves or resizes an embedded object.

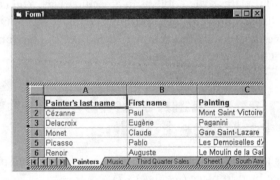

Capturing the Object's Picture

The OLE control's `Picture` property enables you to capture the image on the control. This is useful for performance tricks and for low-level control of the object's appearance. You need to use the `Picture` property when the object's application doesn't update the display correctly or when you want to display the object quickly, without loading the object's application.

To see how to capture the OLE object's picture, follow these steps:

1. Create a project.

2. Add an OLE control and picture box to Form1.

3. Add the following lines of code to the form's Load event procedure. When run, these lines display the Insert Object dialog box to enable the user to select an OLE object to insert in the control. Then the code captures the OLE control's image and displays it in the picture box. The code automatically scales the image to fit in the picture box.

```
Private Sub Form_Load()
    ' Use the automatic size mode to get a picture
    ' of the whole object.
    OLE1.SizeMode = vbOLESizeAutoSize
        OLE1.InsertObjDlg
    ' Capture the image of the control.
    Picture1.Picture = OLE1.Picture
End Sub
```

4. Add the following lines of code to the form's Resize event procedure. These lines resize the picture control to match the size of the form.

```
Private Sub Form_Resize()
    Picture1.Height = Form1.Height
    Picture1.Width = Form1.Width
End Sub
```

5. Run the project. The OLE object's image displays in a picture box (fig. 13.9). Notice that when you resize the form, the image in the picture box scales up or down.

Fig. 13.9
Displaying the image of an OLE object in a picture box or image control can fix display problems with scaling. It can also speed up applications and save memory.

II

Using OLE

You can also save an OLE object's image as a Windows metafile by using the SavePicture statement, as in the following example:

```
SavePicture OLE1.Picture "OLE1.WMF"
```

By saving the images of objects to disk before exiting, you can make your OLE container applications appear to start up instantaneously—without waiting for other applications to load. For more information on this, see Chapter 14, "OLE Container Programming Techniques."

Updating Linked Data

By default, Visual Basic updates linked objects whenever the user saves the source data while editing the linked object. However, Visual Basic currently does not automatically handle changes that other users make to the source file (such as storing a file on a network), nor do such changes currently trigger events in Visual Basic.

To control updating in code, use the OLE control's UpdateOptions property, the Updated event, and the Update method.

Table 13.5 describes the UpdateOptions property's three settings.

Table 13.5 The UpdateOptions Property Settings		
UpdateOptions Setting	**Value**	**Description**
vbOLEAutomatic (default)	0	Updates the OLE control when the user changes or saves the data in the linked object. Not all applications update the OLE control on every edit, however.
vbOLEFrozen	1	The user can edit the object, but the displayed object does not reflect the edits. Calling the Update method does *not* update the object from its source.
vbOLEManual	2	The user can edit the object, but the displayed object doesn't reflect the edits. You can use the Update method to update the object from its source.

The Updated event occurs when the user edits, closes, or renames the source file while editing the object from within the OLE control. The Updated event can also occur when the OLE control first loads (as at startup) if the source file for the link has changed since the last time that the control loaded.

These events occur regardless of the UpdateOptions property setting. However, not all applications notify the OLE control as they are updated. For instance, Microsoft Word does not trigger the Updated event until the user saves or closes the file. Microsoft Excel, however, triggers the Updated event each time that a cell of data on a worksheet changes.

The Updated event procedure has this form:

```
Private Sub OLE1_Updated(Code As Integer)
      '... your code here.
End Sub
```

The Code argument corresponds to the type of update that occurred. Table 13.6 describes the possible values.

Table 13.6   Possible Values of the Code Argument

Code Constant	Value	Meaning
vbOLEChanged	0	The object's data has changed
vbOLESaved	1	The application that created the object has saved the object's data
vbOLEClosed	2	The application that created the linked object has closed the file that contains the object's data
vbOLERenamed	3	The application that created the linked object has renamed the file that contains the linked object's data

Some actions might cause more than one event to occur. For example, if the user closes a file and saves changes, the OLE control receives three Updated successive events: vbOLEChanged, vbOLESaved, and vbOLEClosed.

Use the Update method to update linked objects from their source files. In Visual Basic 4.0, Microsoft has changed this method, which in Visual Basic 3.0 used the Action property setting OLE_UPDATE to update links. In Visual Basic 4.0, the Action property still works, but using the Update method makes code clearer and easier to understand.

II

Using OLE

Controlling Object Activation

By default, the OLE control activates its linked or embedded object as specified by the application that provides the object (usually by double-clicking) or when the user chooses Edit or Open from the object's pop-up menu. To control activation in code, use the AutoActivate property and the DoVerb method.

Table 13.7 describes the AutoActivate property's settings.

Table 13.7 The AutoActivate Property Settings		
AutoActivate Constant	Value	Description
vbOLEActivateManual	0	Activates the object when you call the DoVerb method
vbOLEActivateGetFocus	1	Activates the object when the OLE control receives focus
vbOLEActivateDoubleClick (default)	2	Activates the object when the user double-clicks the OLE control
vbOLEActivateAuto	3	Activates the object when the application-specified event occurs; usually this is the same as vbOLEActivateDoubleClick

The DoVerb method has this form:

```
olecontrol.DoVerb [verbnumber]
```

The *verbnumber* argument corresponds to the index of the verb on the object's pop-up menu. If you omit this argument, the method performs the default verb (usually Edit).

Activating an Object for Editing

To activate an object for editing, use the DoVerb method with no arguments. This triggers the default response from the object's application, which is usually to edit the object.

To ensure that the action taken is Edit, check the OLE control's ObjectVerbs property. The following code checks the OLE object's list of verbs. If it finds an Edit verb, it performs it.

```
Private Sub Command1_Click()
    Dim iVerbCount As Integer
    ' Check each verb in the object's verb list.
    For iVerbCount = 0 To oleObject.ObjectVerbsCount - 1
        ' If the object contains an Edit verb, perform that verb.
        If oleObject.ObjectVerbs(iVerbCount) = "&Edit" Then
            oleObject.DoVerb iVerbCount
            Exit Sub
        End If
    Next iVerbCount
End Sub
```

Opening an Object within Its Application

When you activate a linked object, it opens in its application. Embedded objects can activate in place. To ensure that an object opens in its application, use the object's Open verb.

The following code checks the OLE object's list of verbs. If the code finds an Open verb, it performs that verb.

```
Private Sub Command1_Click()
    Dim iVerbCount As Integer
    ' Check each verb in the object's verb list.
    For iVerbCount = 0 To oleObject.ObjectVerbsCount - 1
        ' If the object contains an Edit verb, perform that verb.
        If oleObject.ObjectVerbs(iVerbCount) = "&Open" Then
            oleObject.DoVerb iVerbCount
            Exit Sub
        End If
    Next iVerbCount
End Sub
```

Deactivating an Object

To deactivate an object, switch focus to another object on the form. Switching focus does not close any objects open in another application window.

When you open objects in another application window, you also must close those objects from within that application. If the application supports OLE Automation, you can close the objects programmatically through the OLE control's Object property.

The following lines of code activate an Excel object for editing. These lines open the object in the Excel application. Then the code uses the Excel Close method to close the workbook in Excel.

```
Private Sub cmdOpenClose_Click ()
    ' Open an Excel worksheet in the application window.
    shtExcel.DoVerb 2
    ' Close the sheet's workbook in Excel.
    oleExcel.Object.Parent.Close SaveChanges:=True
End Sub
```

To use the `Object` property, you need special knowledge of the objects, properties, and methods that the application exposes. For instance, the following code shows how to close a Microsoft Word document. Note that this example differs significantly from the previous Excel example.

```
Private Sub cmdOpenClose_Click ()
    ' Open a Word document in the application window.
    docWord.DoVerb 2
    ' Close the document in Word.
    docWord.Object.Application.WordBasic.DocClose Save:=1
End Sub
```

For more information on using OLE Automation methods and properties with an OLE object, see the section "Getting the OLE Automation Object from Linked or Embedded Objects" later in this chapter.

Storing and Retrieving OLE Objects

As previously mentioned, you store linked objects in separate files on disk and store embedded objects with their container. When you embed an object on a form, you store the embedded object's data with the form in your Visual Basic application.

The application that provides an OLE object supplies ways to save linked or embedded objects through the application's user interface. If your application saves its objects, you can load them into an OLE control by using the `CreateEmbed` or `CreateLink` methods. For information on using `CreateEmbed` and `CreateLink`, see the section "Creating OLE Objects at Run Time" earlier in this chapter.

To save a linked or embedded object from within code, use the OLE control's `SaveToFile` method. If you save OLE objects this way, their original application cannot open them directly; instead, you must open them by using the OLE control's `ReadFromFile` method. `SaveToFile` and `ReadFromFile` enable you to store and retrieve individual OLE objects in code.

Saving OLE Objects to Files

Use the OLE object's `SaveToFile` method to save a linked or embedded object directly to a file, by following these steps:

1. Open a file for binary access. The following code opens the file FOO.OLE:

```
Open "foo.ole" For Binary As #1
```

2. Call the `SaveToFile` method on the OLE control that contains the object that you want to save. The following code saves the object in the oleObject control:

```
oleObject.SaveToFile 1
```

3. Close the file. The following code line closes the file opened in step 1:

```
Close 1
```

When you use `SaveToFile`, you cannot save more than one object to a particular file. The method always overwrites the entire file.

Reading OLE Objects from Files

Use the OLE object's `ReadFromFile` method to load a linked or embedded object directly from a file. To read an OLE object from a file, follow these steps:

1. Open the file to read for binary access. The following code opens the file FOO.OLE:

```
Open "foo.ole" For Binary As #1
```

2. Call the `ReadFromFile` method on the OLE control that should display the object. The following code loads the object into the control oleObject:

```
oleObject.ReadFromFile 1
```

3. Close the file. The following code line closes the file opened in step 1:

```
Close 1
```

Tip

Reading a linked object that `SaveToFile` saved restores the link to the original file.

Getting the OLE Automation Object from Linked or Embedded Objects

Use the OLE control's `Object` property to get the OLE Automation object from a linked or embedded object on a form. Not all applications provide OLE Automation objects. If an object does not support OLE Automation, the `Object` property returns `Nothing`.

When working with OLE Automation objects, you should create an object variable to contain the OLE Automation object. For example, the following lines of code declare an object variable and establish a reference to an embedded worksheet when the form loads:

II

Using OLE

```
Option Explicit
Dim mobjExcelSheet

Private Sub Form_Load()
    ' Embed a worksheet in the OLE control named oleExcel.
    oleExcel.CreateEmbed "c:\excel\stock.xls"
    ' Establish a reference to the OLE Automation object for the
    ' embedded worksheet.
    Set mobjExcelSheet = oleExcel.Object
End Sub
```

In the preceding example, the variable mobjExcelSheet has *module-level scope*; that is, other procedures in the module have access to the variable. For instance, the following Click event procedure uses the OLE Automation object mobjExcelSheet to print the embedded worksheet:

```
Private Sub cmdPrintSheet()
    mobjExcelSheet.PrintOut
End Sub
```

Unlike other applications that support OLE Automation, Microsoft Word requires the following special syntax to get its OLE Automation object:

```
Set objVar = olecontrol.Object.Application.WordBasic
```

You must use this special syntax because Word exposes only the WordBasic language for OLE Automation. When working with the Word OLE Automation object, remember that methods and properties apply to the current document, which might not be the one that the OLE control is currently displaying.

The following lines of code establish a reference to the WordBasic OLE Automation object:

```
Option Explicit
Dim mobjWordBasic

Private Sub Form_Load()
    ' Embed a Word document in the OLE control named oleWord.
    oleWord.CreateEmbed "c:\docs\products.doc"
    ' Establish a reference to the OLE Automation object for the
    ' embedded worksheet.
    Set mobjWordBasic = oleWord.Object.Application.Word
End Sub
```

The following two event procedures demonstrate how the WordBasic methods apply to the current document. If cmdOpenNew runs before cmdPrintDocument, Word prints the newly opened document rather than the one that the OLE control is currently displaying.

```
' Open a new file in Word (changes the current document).
Private Sub cmdOpenNew()
    mobjWordBasic.FileOpen
End Sub

' Print the current document in Word.
Private Sub cmdPrintDocument()
    mobjWordBasic.Print
End Sub
```

Troubleshooting

My OLE controls do not always update the display correctly.

If the control appears grayed after you edit an object, try closing the object's application. If that does not help, reload the object on the form. In extreme cases, you might have to capture the OLE object's image and display it within a picture box or image control. For information on how to do so, see the section "Capturing the Object's Picture" earlier in this chapter.

When I edit linked or embedded objects, my application crashes.

Be careful when opening linked or embedded objects for editing. Having more than one object open in the same application might cause that application to crash.

When using an OLE object's OLE Automation object, I frequently encounter "Method or property does not exist" errors.

Usually this error indicates that you are using the wrong syntax. Check the application's documentation for the method. Often the problem involves the number of arguments or their data types.

My application doesn't recognize an object that it created.

Even if your application creates an object, it doesn't recognize that object after the SaveToFile method saves it. You can load such objects only by using the ReadFromFile method.

From Here...

For more information on the following topics, see the indicated chapters:

- Chapter 14, "OLE Container Programming Techniques," describes how to save OLE objects to files.

- Chapter 15, "Designing OLE Container Applications," explains how to build efficient OLE container applications.

II

Using OLE

Chapter 14

OLE Container Programming Techniques

Visual Basic provides some powerful OLE features, but those features alone aren't enough to create applications that fulfill the entire vision of OLE. This chapter tells you how to extend Visual Basic so that you can create OLE applications that are document-centric. In this chapter, you learn how to do the following:

- Create applications that start when the user double-clicks on a document file in the Windows Desktop or Explorer.

- Balance memory and performance when developing OLE container applications.

- Test a user's hardware configuration at run time.

- Locate lost OLE references that consume memory.

- Create an OLE object storage system.

- Maintain the system registry.

- Register your application in the system registry.

- Check and maintain your application's system registry entries at run time.

Creating Document-Centric Applications

Most OLE container applications are *document-centric*. That is, the user uses the document to load the application. This approach becomes increasingly important in Windows 95, where documents are often displayed in the Program Manager. Figure 14.1 shows an example of how a user activates and uses a document-centric application.

1) User clicks on the document icon   2) Container application displays the document

Fig. 14.1
Document-centric applications let the user think about content rather than the process of using a computer.

3) User clicks on an object in the document to activate it for editing

Although document-centric applications make life easier for computer users, they complicate things for us programmers. In order to create an application that is document-centric, you must consider the following programming tasks:

- Manage memory/performance tradeoffs when initializing OLE objects. By default, OLE objects start their applications when they are activated; however, loading an OLE application such as Word or Excel can take a while.

- Create a system for saving and loading the OLE objects used in your documents.

- Create a file to register the file type for your application's documents. File types are registered in the system registry.

- Register your application when it starts. This ensures that the Registry doesn't become outdated if your application's executable file is moved to another directory.

The rest of this chapter explains each of these tasks in greater detail. Remember, you can use any of these techniques to create applications that aren't document-centric. But when you combine these techniques, you're probably working on the type of OLE application that Bill Gates envisions as the future of computing.

The Big Tradeoff: Memory versus Performance

An OLE container application can use some very big chunks of code. For instance, editing a single Excel worksheet requires the entire Excel application to be loaded in memory. If Excel isn't in memory already, the user must wait while it is loaded (see fig. 14.2).

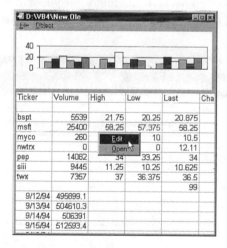

Fig. 14.2
Small user actions can have big effects! Activating an Excel worksheet loads the entire Excel application in memory.

You can reduce the delay by loading the Excel application when your application loads. However, your target system must be able to keep all the components you need in *physical* memory at once. Otherwise, performance will degrade as Windows uses *virtual* memory by swapping to disk (see fig. 14.3).

Fig. 14.3
When physical memory fills up, Windows starts using virtual memory on disk. Physical memory is much faster, since it doesn't require disk access.

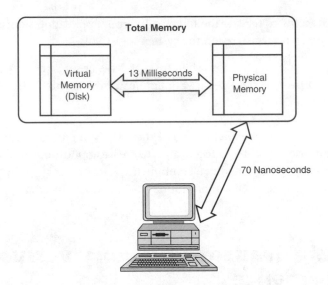

Determining Hardware Requirements

To balance performance against memory requirements, you need to know the hardware configuration on which your application will be run. In a corporate environment, it's a good idea to set up a couple of test machines to help you tune your application. Table 14.1 provides some guidelines for hardware requirements based on the type of OLE applications you are using.

Table 14.1   Estimated Minimum Hardware Guidelines for OLE Container Applications Written in Visual Basic

Item	Minimum Processor	Minimum Physical Memory (M)
.OCX	486	8
Jet data objects	486	8
Small OLE object (Paint, MS Graph)	486	8
One large OLE object (Excel worksheet)	486	12
Two large OLE objects (Excel worksheet, Word document)	486	16
The kitchen sink	Pentium	16

Table 14.1 shows *minimum* requirements based on very subjective criteria—performance as perceived by someone who's just downed his third cup of coffee. OLE applications will run in leaner configurations than those shown in table 14.1, but they won't run very fast.

> **Note**
>
> Table 14.1 assumes that you are running your application under Windows 95. Windows 3.x has similar requirements, although you might be able to squeak by with less memory in a minimum configuration. If you are running under Windows NT, add 4–8M to each minimum physical memory guideline in table 14.1.

Checking Hardware Configurations at Run Time

Ideally, you should test your application on an average configuration and on a "worst-case" hardware configuration. Don't make all your decisions based on the worst-case scenario, however. Instead, create a fall-back strategy for machines that don't have adequate processors or memory. The following code sets a global flag if the user's hardware doesn't meet some minimum requirements:

```
' Global flags section.
Public gDisableAdvanced As Boolean

Private Sub Form_Load()
    Dim System As Object
    Set System = CreateObject("WinAPI.Information")
    If System.MeetsCriteria(486, 8) = False Then
        ' Set flag to disable some features.
        gbDisableAdvanced = True
        ' Notify user.
        MsgBox ("Your computer does not meet the minimum " & _
            "requirements of 8 megabytes memory and 486 or " & _
            "later processor. Some features have been disabled.")
    Else
        gbDisableAdvanced = False
    End If
End Sub
```

The preceding code uses the method MeetsCriteria to test a hardware configuration at run time. The MeetsCriteria method in listing 14.1 uses Windows API functions to get system information. The MeetsCriteria method is part of the SYSTEM.VBP OLE server found on the companion CD. Chapter 21, "Advanced OLE Programming Techniques," describes SYSTEM.VBP more completely.

Listing 14.1   Testing Hardware Configuration (SYSTEM.VBP)

```
#If Win16 Then
Private Declare Function GlobalCompact Lib "Kernel" _
    (ByVal dwMinFree As Long) As Long
Private Declare Function GetWinFlags Lib "Kernel" () As Long
Const WF_CPU286 = &H2
Const WF_CPU386 = &H4
Const WF_CPU486 = &H8
#Else
Private Declare Sub GetSystemInfo Lib "kernel32" _
    (lpSystemInfo As SYSTEM_INFO)
Private Declare Sub GlobalMemoryStatus Lib "kernel32" _
    (lpBuffer As MEMORYSTATUS)
' Type declaration for system information.
Private Type SYSTEM_INFO
    dwOemId As Long
    dwPageSize As Long
    lpMinimumApplicationAddress As Long
    lpMaximumApplicationAddress As Long
    dwActiveProcessorMask As Long
    dwNumberOfProcessors As Long
    dwProcessorType As Long
    dwAllocationGranularity As Long
    dwReserved As Long
End Type
' Type declaration for system information.
Private Type MEMORYSTATUS
    dwLength As Long          ' sizeof(MEMORYSTATUS)
    dwMemoryLoad As Long      ' percent of memory in use
    dwTotalPhys As Long       ' bytes of physical memory
    dwAvailPhys As Long       ' free physical memory bytes
    dwTotalPageFile As Long   ' bytes of paging file
    dwAvailPageFile As Long   ' free bytes of paging file
    dwTotalVirtual As Long    ' user bytes of address space
    dwAvailVirtual As Long    ' free user bytes
End Type
#End If


' Checks if a system meets processor and memory
' hardware requirements.
' iProcessor is a three-digit number: 286, 386, or 486
' iMemory is the number of megabytes of physical memory required.
Public Function MeetsCriteria(iProcessor As Integer, _
    iMemory As Integer) As Boolean
    Dim iAvailableMemory  As Integer, lWinFlags As Long
    Dim bProcessor As Boolean
    #If Win16 Then
        lWinFlags = GetWinFlags()
    #Else
        Dim SysInfo As SYSTEM_INFO
        GetSystemInfo SysInfo
        lWinFlags = SysInfo.dwProcessorType
    #End If
    Select Case iProcessor
```

```
           Case 286
               ' Windows 3.1 won't run on earlier machines, so True.
               bProcessor = True
           Case 386
               ' If meets criteria, set to True.
               #If Win16 Then
                   If lWinFlags >= WF_CPU386 Then bProcessor = True
               #Else
                   If lWinFlags >= 386 Then bProcessor = True
               #End If
           Case 486
               #If Win16 Then
                   If lWinFlags And WF_CPU486 Then bProcessor = True
               #Else
                   If lWinFlags >= 486 Then bProcessor = True
               #End If
           Case 586
               #If Win16 Then
                   ' There is no test for 586 under Win16,
                   ' so test for 486 -- probably
                   ' better than returning an error.
                   If lWinFlags And WF_CPU486 Then bProcessor = True
               #Else
                   If lWinFlags >= 586 Then bProcessor = True
               #End If
       End Select
       ' Win16 and Win32 have different ways of getting
       ' available physical memory.
       #If Win16 Then
           ' Get available physical memory.
           iAvailableMemory = GlobalCompact(0) _
               / (1024000)
       #Else
           Dim MemStatus As MEMORYSTATUS
           GlobalMemoryStatus MemStatus
           iAvailableMemory = MemStatus.dwTotalPhys / (1024000)
       #End If
       ' Combine results of two tests: True And True = True.
       MeetsCriteria = bProcessor And iAvailableMemory >= iMemory
   End Function
```

Loading Object Applications at Startup

To reduce the amount of time it takes to activate an OLE object for editing,
load the object's application at startup. For example, the following code loads
the Excel application if it is not already running:

```
Private Sub Form_Load()
    Dim System As Object
    Set System = CreateObject("WinAPI.Information")
    If System.IsRunning("Microsoft Excel") = False Then
        ' Start Excel minimized.
        Shell "c:\excel\excel.exe", 6
    End If
End Sub
```

The preceding code uses the IsRunning method to determine whether Microsoft Excel is running. The IsRunning method in listing 14.2 uses Windows API functions to check whether the application is loaded.

Listing 14.2 Checking Whether an Application Is Running (SYSTEM.VBP)

```
#If Win16 Then
Private Declare Function GetNextWindow Lib "User" _
    (ByVal hWnd As Integer, ByVal wFlag As Integer) As Integer
Private Declare Function GetActiveWindow Lib "User" () As Integer
Private Declare Function GetWindowText Lib "User" _
    (ByVal hWnd As Integer, ByVal lpString As String, _
     ByVal aint As Integer) As Integer
Private Declare Function APIFindWindow Lib "User" _
    Alias "FindWindow" _
    (ByVal lpClassName As Any, ByVal lpWindowName _
     As Any) As Integer
#Else
Private Declare Function GetNextWindow Lib "user32" _
    Alias "GetNextQueueWindow" _
    (ByVal hWnd As Long, ByVal wFlag As Integer) _
    As Long
Private Declare Function GetActiveWindow Lib "user32" _
    () As Long
Private Declare Function GetWindowText Lib "user32" _
    Alias "GetWindowTextA" (ByVal hWnd As Long, _
    ByVal lpString As String, ByVal cch As Long) _
    As Long
Private Declare Function APIFindWindow Lib "user32" _
    Alias "FindWindowA" (ByVal lpClassName As String, _
    ByVal lpWindowName As String) As Long
#End If

Const GW_HWNDNEXT = 2

Const SW_SHOW = 5

Public Function IsRunning(strAppName) As Boolean
    #If Win16 Then
    Dim hWnd As Integer, hWndStop As Long, hWndNext _
        As Integer, iLen As Integer
    #Else
    Dim hWnd As Long, hWndStop As Long, hWndNext _
        As Long, iLen As Long
    #End If
    Dim strTitle As String * 80
    ' Get a handle to the active window (first in task list).
```

```
hWnd = GetActiveWindow()
hWndStop = hWnd
' Loop until you reach the end of the list.
Do
    ' Get the next window handle.
    hWndNext = GetNextWindow(hWnd, GW_HWNDNEXT)
    ' Get the text from the window's caption.
    iLen = GetWindowText(hWndNext, strTitle, Len(strTitle))
    If iLen Then
        ' If found, return True.
        If InStr(strTitle, strAppName) Then
            IsRunning = True
            Exit Function
        End If
    End If
    hWnd = hWndNext
Loop Until hWnd = hWndStop
' Not found, so return False.
IsRunning = False
End Function
```

Loading Object Applications on Demand

By default, Visual Basic loads an OLE object's application when the object is activated for editing. The OLE control's `AutoActivate` property controls how the user activates the object. For information on the `AutoActivate` property, see "Controlling Object Activation" in Chapter 13.

If the object's application is already running, Visual Basic simply increments the Windows reference count to the running application. Visual Basic deincrements the Windows reference count for an object's application when the form containing the object is closed. The object's application continues running until the user closes the application manually, or until the reference count goes to zero. Figure 14.4 shows how OLE loads and unloads an OLE object's application used on a Visual Basic form.

Fig. 14.4
OLE controls when an object's application starts and quits.

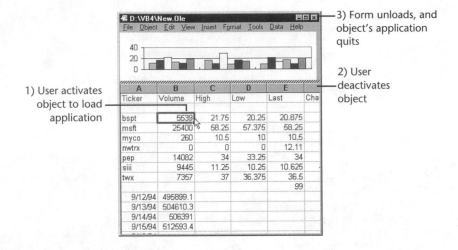

1) User activates object to load application

3) Form unloads, and object's application quits

2) User deactivates object

Table 14.2 describes the steps shown in figure 14.4.

	Table 14.2 How OLE Loads, Activates, and Deactivates OLE Object Applications		
Step	**User Action**	**OLE Action**	**Object's Application Reference Count**
1.	Activates object on form.	OLE loads object's application if it is not already running.	References + 1
2.	None.	OLE object's application loads.	References + 1 (if application is visible)
3.	User deactivates object.	Updates object, closes object.	No change.
4.	Form unloads.	Decrement reference count.	References − 1
5.	None.	Close object's application.	References = 0

Whether or not an object's application quits when a form unloads is determined by the reference count of that application. The application will not quit if the reference count is not zero. There are three main reasons an object's application won't close after a form unloads:

■ The application is visible. Under OLE, the application's reference count is incremented by 1 just for being visible. Visible applications are assumed to be under user control. This prevents OLE from closing an application that a user may be using.

■ Another object has a reference to the application. A single application may be shared by many objects. The application won't close until all the objects are done using it.

■ The application is not following the OLE standard. It is possible for invisible applications to remain loaded after all objects have released their references to the application. The application may remain loaded until the user exits Windows.

Raiders of the Lost OLE Reference

In the movie *Raiders of the Lost Ark*, they never explained how the Ark got lost in the first place—the point of the movie was that they wanted it back. The same thing is true of OLE references. Applications may or may not track their references correctly. When they don't, you need to find them. Lost references to objects keep the object's application loaded in memory. This consumes precious Windows resources and can affect performance or require the user to reboot his or her system.

Excel is a good example of an application that doesn't always track its references. For example, the following steps cause a "lost reference" to the Excel application, leaving it loaded in memory with no easy way to shut it down:

1. Start Excel using the `CreateObject` function. The following procedure starts the Excel application invisibly and returns a reference to the OLE object for the Excel application:

   ```
   Sub CreateReference()
       Dim objExcel As Object
       Set objExcel = CreateObject("excel.application")
   End Sub
   ```

2. Run the `CreateReference` procedure. The `CreateObject` function starts Excel and returns a reference to the object. But when the object variable `objExcel` loses scope at the end of the procedure, Excel remains loaded in memory.

3. Notice that Excel does not appear on the taskbar—there is no obvious way for you to activate the Excel application so that you can shut it down!

Since you know that you just started Excel, this situation is easy to fix. To find Excel after you've lost its reference, follow these steps:

1. Use the `GetObject` function to obtain a reference to the running instance of Excel.

2. Set the returned object's Visible property to True. The following procedure finds a lost reference to the Excel application object and makes the application visible:

```
Sub FindLostReference()
    Dim objExcel As Object
    Set objExcel = GetObject(, "excel.application")
    objExcel.Visible = True
End Sub
```

You can avoid this specific situation by using object variables that are global in scope and by being fastidious about closing instances of Excel that you've started in your application.

However, you can't always account for the behavior of other applications or unanticipated interruptions of your own application. For these cases, you need to be able to find all hidden instances of applications running on a system; and to do that, you need to make some Windows API calls. The `MakeVisible` method in listing 14.3 makes all of the applications on your system visible using common window-manipulation functions from the Windows API. Listing 14.3 shows the declarations for the API functions used in the `MakeVisible` method.

Listing 14.3   Making Hidden Application Instances Visible (SYSTEM.VBP)

```
' Makes all applications visible.
Public Sub MakeVisible()
    #If Win16 Then
    Dim hWnd As Integer, hWndFirst As Integer, iTemp _
        As Integer, iLen As Integer
    #Else
    Dim hWnd As Long, hWndFirst As Long, iTemp As Long, _
        iLen As Long
    #End If
    Dim strTitle As String * 80
    ' Get a handle to the active window (first in task list).
    hWnd = GetActiveWindow()
    hWndFirst = hWnd
    ' Loop until you reach the end of the list.
```

```
        Do
            iLen = GetWindowText(hWnd, strTitle, Len(strTitle))
            If iLen Then
                iTemp = ShowWindow(hWnd, SW_SHOW)
            End If
            ' Get the next window handle.
            hWnd = GetNextWindow(hWnd, GW_HWNDNEXT)
        Loop Until hWnd = hWndFirst
    End Sub
```

Caution

Don't close an OLE object's application in code unless you are *absolutely sure* no other objects on the system have references to that application. Doing so can lose data and disrupt file integrity. It is much safer to allow the user to close an application.

Creating an OLE Storage System

By default, Visual Basic stores OLE objects in the form that contains them. For linked objects, Visual Basic stores the image of the object and the source of the object. For embedded objects, Visual Basic stores the image of the object and the object's data.

When you compile a Visual Basic form, the object's image, source, or data is written into your application's executable file. This has the affect of "freezing" the initial state of the object. Changes you make to embedded objects at run time are lost when the application closes. Changes to linked objects are preserved, but the startup image of the object doesn't reflect those changes.

As mentioned in Chapter 13, you save OLE objects to files using the SaveToFile method and read OLE files using the ReadFromFile method. The following code shows using a form's Load event procedure to update an OLE object when the form is displayed:

```
    Option Explicit
    Const OLE_FILE = "c:\foo.ole"
    Dim miOLE_File As Integer

    Private Sub Form_Load()
        miOLE_File = FreeFile()
        Open OLE_FILE For Binary As miOLE_File
        oleObject.ReadFromFile miOLE_File
    End Sub
```

This code shows using the Unload event to save changes to the OLE object in a file:

```
Private Sub Form_Unload(Cancel As Integer)
        oleObject.SaveToFile miOLE_File
        Close miOLE_File
End Sub
```

Since the file you use with ReadFromFile and SaveToFile is open for Binary access, you don't have to close the file between loading and saving the OLE object. Binary access files support read/write access.

Storing Multiple Objects in a Single File

The Load and Unload event procedures in the preceding section support access to only one OLE object per file. To store more than one object in a single file, repeat the SaveToFile method for each OLE object in your application. The following cmdSave event procedure shows how to save multiple OLE objects in a control array to a single file:

```
Private Sub cmdSave_Click()
    ' Get a file number.
    iFileNum = FreeFile()
    ' Open the file for Binary access.
    Open "NEW.OLE" For Binary As iFileNum
    ' For each object in the oleObjects control array
    For Each oleControl In oleObjects
        ' Save the object to the open file.
        oleControl.SaveToFile iFileNum
    Next oleControl
    ' Close the file when done.
    Close iFileNum
End Sub
```

> **Caution**
>
> The ReadFromFile and SaveToFile methods don't correctly reposition the file pointer, so the Loc function is useless when saving or loading OLE objects.

Loading Multiple Objects from a Single File

The process of loading OLE objects from an existing file is similar to that of saving them as described in the preceding section. Use the OLE object's ReadFromFile method, as shown in the following cmdLoad_Click event procedure:

```
Private Sub cmdLoad_Click()
    ' Get a file number.
    iFileNum = FreeFile()
    ' Open the file for Binary access.
```

```
        Open "NEW.OLE" For Binary As iFileNum
        ' For each object in the oleObjects control array
        For Each oleControl In oleObjects
            ' Save the object to the open file.
            oleControl.ReadFromFile iFileNum
        Next oleControl
        ' Close the file when done.
        Close iFileNum
    End Sub
```

The preceding code is simple enough, but it makes one major assumption: that the number of OLE objects contained in the file matches the number of controls in the oleObjects control array. To load an unknown number objects from a file, you must add a loop that contains the ReadFromFile method and poll for error number 31037. Listing 14.4 shows how to load all the objects from a file.

Listing 14.4 Loading All the Objects from a File (STORE.VBP)

```
Private Sub mnuOpen_Click()
    ' Get a file name.
    dlgFile.ShowOpen
    ' If the file name if valid, open it.
    If Len(Dir(dlgFile.filename)) Then
        mstrFileName = dlgFile.filename
        ' Get a file number.
        iFileNum = FreeFile()
        ' Open a file to read.
        Open mstrFileName For Binary As iFileNum
        ' Update the form caption.
        Me.Caption = mstrFileName
        ' Enable the Save menu.
        mnuSave.Enabled = True
    Else
        ' Do nothing.
        Exit Sub
    End If
    ' Clear the existing OLE control array.
    For Each oleControl In oleObjects
        ' Keep the control with Index = 0.
        If oleControl.Index Then
            Unload oleControl
        End If
    Next oleControl
    ' Turn on error handling.
    On Error GoTo cmdLoad_Err
    ' Repeat until an error indicating you've reached
    ' the last object in the file, which causes an error.
    Do
        ' Load an object into the control.
        oleObjects(Index).ReadFromFile iFileNum
        ' Increment the count.
```

(continues)

Listing 14.4   Continued

```
            Index = Index + 1
            ' Create another control in the control array.
            Load oleObjects(Index)
            ' Make the object visible
            oleObjects(Index).Visible = True
            ' Reposition each object.
            oleObjects(Index).TOP = oleObjects(Index - 1).TOP _
                + oleObjects(Index - 1).Height
        Loop
cmdLoad_Err:
    If Err = 31037 Then
            ' Unload the last control since it's empty.
            Unload oleObjects(Index)
            ' Update the display.
            Me.Refresh
            ' Close the file
            Close iFileNum
            ' Update the number of objects.
            mIndex = Index
            Exit Sub
    Else
            MsgBox "An unhandled error occurred: " & _
            Err & Error
    End If
End Sub
```

Note

Listing 14.4 uses a rather simple system for positioning OLE objects on a form—it simply lays them out end to end. Ideally, users should be able to drag objects to new positions and have the program record those positions in the file. This gets tricky, because you must store dissimilar data in the same file. It's even further complicated by the fact that ReadFromFile and SaveToFile don't reposition the file pointer. There is no easy way to tell where in a file OLE objects begin and end. The easiest solution to this problem is to store position information in a separate, random-access file.

Maintaining the System Registry

Applications use the Registry to store the following information:

- The name of the executable file that is associated with a given file name extension.

- The command line to execute or Dynamic Data Exchange (DDE) messages to send when the user opens a file from Windows.

- The command line to execute or DDE messages to send when the user prints a file from Windows.

- Initialization data for the application (formerly stored in an .INI file under Windows 3.x).

- Details about the implementation of OLE if the application is an OLE server.

You can edit the system registry directly using the Registry Editor (see fig. 14.5). To run the Registry Editor, use this command line:

```
regedit
```

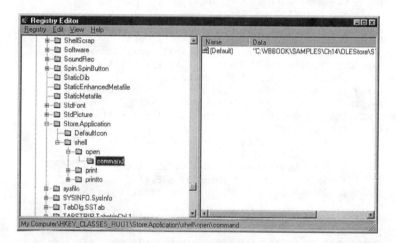

Fig. 14.5
The Windows 95 Registry Editor displays a hierarchical list of the system registry.

Note

When running the Registration Info Editor under Windows 3.x, you must use the /v switch if you want to see all levels of detail.

The Structure of the System Registry

The data in the system registry is hierarchical. Below HKEY_CLASSES_ROOT are all the entries for registered applications and file types. Below them are sub-entries for the types of actions each application supports. These entries and sub-entries are referred to as registration *keys*. Most keys have a setting, as shown by the system registry entries for the Paint accessory included with Windows 95 (see listing 14.5).

Listing 14.5   Registry Entries for Paint (PAINT.REG)

```
REGEDIT4
*********************************************************************
Register file types for the Paint application.
[HKEY_CLASSES_ROOT\.bmp]
@="Paint.Picture"
[HKEY_CLASSES_ROOT\.bmp\ShellNew]
"NullFile"=""
[HKEY_CLASSES_ROOT\.pcx]
@="Paint.Picture"


*********************************************************************
Register the command lines that Windows uses for opening and
printing Paint documents.
[HKEY_CLASSES_ROOT\Paint.Picture]
@="Bitmap Image"
[HKEY_CLASSES_ROOT\Paint.Picture\shell]
[HKEY_CLASSES_ROOT\Paint.Picture\shell\open]
[HKEY_CLASSES_ROOT\Paint.Picture\shell\open\command]
@="\"C:\\PROGRA~1\\ACCESS~1\\MSPAINT.EXE\" \"%1\""
[HKEY_CLASSES_ROOT\Paint.Picture\shell\print]
[HKEY_CLASSES_ROOT\Paint.Picture\shell\print\command]
@="\"C:\\PROGRA~1\\ACCESS~1\\MSPAINT.EXE\" /p \"%1\""
[HKEY_CLASSES_ROOT\Paint.Picture\shell\printto]
[HKEY_CLASSES_ROOT\Paint.Picture\shell\printto\command]
@="\"C:\\PROGRA~1\\ACCESS~1\\MSPAINT.EXE\" /pt \"%1\" \
      %2\" \"%3\" \"%4\""
[HKEY_CLASSES_ROOT\Paint.Picture\DefaultIcon]
@="C:\\Progra~1\\Access~1\\MSPAINT.EXE,1"
[HKEY_CLASSES_ROOT\Paint.Picture\Insertable]
@=""
[HKEY_CLASSES_ROOT\Paint.Picture\protocol]
[HKEY_CLASSES_ROOT\Paint.Picture\protocol\StdFileEditing]
[HKEY_CLASSES_ROOT\Paint.Picture\protocol\StdFileEditing\verb]
[HKEY_CLASSES_ROOT\Paint.Picture\protocol\StdFileEditing\verb\0]
@="&Edit"
[HKEY_CLASSES_ROOT\Paint.Picture\protocol\StdFileEditing\server]
@="C:\\PROGRA~1\\ACCESS~1\\MSPAINT.EXE"
[HKEY_CLASSES_ROOT\Paint.Picture\CLSID]
@="{D3E34B21-9D75-101A-8C3D-00AA001A1652}"


*********************************************************************
Register the class ID for the application.
[HKEY_CLASSES_ROOT\CLSID\{0003000A-0000-0000-C000-000000000046}]
@="Paintbrush Picture"
[HKEY_CLASSES_ROOT\CLSID\{0003000A-0000-0000-C000-000000000046}\
TreatAs]@="{D3E34B21-9D75-101A-8C3D-00AA001A1652}"
[HKEY_CLASSES_ROOT\CLSID\{0003000A-0000-0000-C000-000000000046}
\Ole1Class]@="PBrush"
[HKEY_CLASSES_ROOT\CLSID\{0003000A-0000-0000-C000-000000000046}
\ProgID]@="PBrush"
(other registration entries omitted here)
```

Because you can't create all types of OLE applications using Visual Basic, you don't need to worry about all the different keys that can appear for each application. In fact, listing 14.5 omits many lines that register features that are either handled automatically or are unavailable through Visual Basic. The keys that are of interest to Visual Basic programmers are shown in table 14.3.

Table 14.3   Registry Keys

Key	Example and Description

ProgID	`[HKEY_CLASSES_ROOT\.bmp]`
	`@="Paint.Picture"`
	
	Identifies the application within the system registry. The programmatic ID Paint.Picture is used in all the subsequent keys. The setting for *ProgID* is the text that appears in the standard OLE Insert Object dialog box.

FileType	`[HKEY_CLASSES_ROOT\.bmp]`
	`@="Paint.Picture"`
	
	Associates a file type with the ProgID. For instance, double-clicking on a .BMP file in Windows loads the file in Paint.

CLSID	`[HKEY_CLASSES_ROOT\Paint.Picture\CLSID]`
	`@="{D3E34B21-9D75-101A-8C3D-00AA001A1652}"`
	
	Identifies the application to OLE. OLE uses the class ID (the very long number in braces) internally when starting an OLE object's application.

protocol	Identifies the OLE services that the application supports.
StdFileEditing	Identifies the OLE file editing services that the application supports.

server	`[HKEY_CLASSES_ROOT\Paint.Picture\protocol\`
	`StdFileEditing\server]`
	`@="C:\\PROGRA~1\\ACCESS~1\\MSPAINT.EXE"`
	
	Identifies the application's .EXE file to use as the server for OLE editing services.

verb	`[HKEY_CLASSES_ROOT\Paint.Picture\protocol\`
	`StdFileEditing\verb\0]`
	`@="&Edit"`
	
	Identifies the OLE verbs the application supports. These are the verbs listed in the object's pop-up menu when the OLE object is right-clicked.

II

Using OLE

(continues)

Table 14.3	Continued
shell	Lists the Windows shell services that the application supports. Shell services include the Windows Explorer and Desktop.
open\command	[HKEY_CLASSES_ROOT\Paint.Picture\shell\ open\command] @="\"C:\\PROGRA~1\\ACCESS~1\\MSPAINT.EXE\" \"%1\""
print\command	[HKEY_CLASSES_ROOT\Paint.Picture\shell\ print\command] @="\"C:\\PROGRA~1\\ACCESS~1\\MSPAINT.EXE\" /p \"%1\"" Provides the command line Windows uses when the Explorer prints a file with a file type associated with this application's programmatic identifier (see the *FileType* key in this table).

Changing Registry Entries and Seeing the Effects

You can edit system registry entries directly using the Registry Editor, then save those entries to a separate .REG file. This is useful when creating .REG files for your own applications.

To use the Registry Editor to change the value of an entry, follow these steps:

1. Select an item to edit by clicking on it in the list box.

2. Type the new key value in the Value text box.

To use the Registry Editor to save an entry to an .REG file, follow these steps:

1. Select an item to save by clicking on it in the list box. The Registry Editor saves all the entries subordinate to the entry that you select. To save the entire database to an .REG file, select the root entry, \, as shown in figure 14.6.

Fig. 14.6
Select the root entry to save the entire Registry to a file.

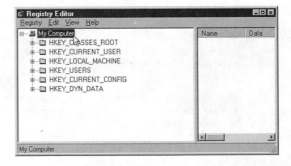

2. Choose Registry, Export Registration File. The Registry Editor displays the Export Registry File dialog box (see fig. 14.7).

Fig. 14.7
Registration files use the .REG file type by convention.

3. Type the name of the file to create and click OK. The Registry Editor saves the entry and all its subordinate entries in a text format file.

Deleting Registry Entries

You might want to delete entries manually from your Registry after you delete an OLE application from your system. The old entries don't do any direct harm, but they can clutter up OLE dialog boxes with invalid entries. To use the Registry Editor to delete a key, follow these steps:

1. Select the item to delete from the Registration Info Editor list box.

2. Choose Edit, Delete.

Registering Your Application

Under Windows 3.x, you ran most Visual Basic applications by double-clicking on the application's icon in the Windows Program Manager. You can run document-centric applications by double-clicking on an icon on the Windows 95 desktop or on the file name in the Windows Explorer (see fig. 14.8).

II

Using OLE

Fig. 14.8
Document-centric
applications can
start directly from
the documents
that they create.

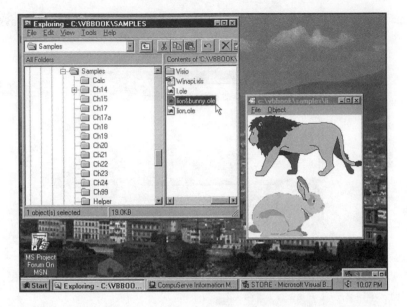

You should register your application in the system registry if you want your users to be able to open application documents directly through the Windows Desktop or Explorer.

There are currently two system registration tasks that are of interest to Visual Basic programmers:

■ Associating a file type with your application.

■ Identifying the icon to display for application-specific documents.

The following sections describe these tasks in greater detail.

Registering a File Type for Your Application

The Registry contains *FileType* keys that identify specific file extensions as belonging to specific applications. These keys enable the Windows shell functions to start to load the file when the user double-clicks on the file name in the Explorer or a shortcut for the file on the Windows Desktop.

To associate a file type with your application, follow these steps:

1. Create a registration file for your application. The following file registers STORE.EXE and creates associations for loading and printing the file:

```
REGEDIT4
**********************************************************************
Register file types for the STORE application.
```

```
[HKEY_CLASSES_ROOT\.ole]
@="Store.Application"

[HKEY_CLASSES_ROOT\.cdoc\ShellNew]
"NullFile"=""

*********************************************************************
Register the command lines that Windows uses for opening and
printing  STORE documents.

[HKEY_CLASSES_ROOT\Store.Application]
@="OLE Storage Demo"

[HKEY_CLASSES_ROOT\Store.Application\shell]

[HKEY_CLASSES_ROOT\Store.Application\shell\open]

[HKEY_CLASSES_ROOT\Store.Application\shell\open\command]
@="\"C:\\VBBOOK\\SAMPLES\\CH14\\STORE.EXE\" \"%1\""

[HKEY_CLASSES_ROOT\Store.Application\shell\print]

[HKEY_CLASSES_ROOT\Store.Application\shell\print\command]
@="\"C:\\VBBOOK\\SAMPLES\\CH14\\STORE.EXF\" /p \"%1\""

[HKEY_CLASSES_ROOT\Store.Application\shell\printto]

[HKEY_CLASSES_ROOT\Store.Application\shell\printto\command]
@="\"C:\\VBBOOK\\SAMPLES\\CH14\\STORE.EXE\" /pt
        \"%1\" \"%2\" \"%3\" \"%4\""

[HKEY_CLASSES_ROOT\Store.Application\DefaultIcon]
@="C:\\VBBOOK\\SAMPLES\\CH14\\STORE.EXE,1"
```

2. Merge the registration file. The following command line merges the file
STORE.REG with the system registry. The -s switch merges the changes
silently—no confirmation dialog box is shown.

```
regedit -s store.reg
```

3. After merging the file, you can view the changes using the Registry
Editor (see fig. 14.9).

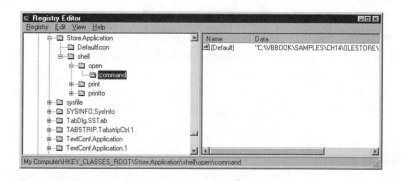

Fig. 14.9
The Registry
entries for
STORE.REG.

Registering Document Icons

Registering a file type for your application causes Windows to use your application's default icon for program items created from files with the specified type (see fig. 14.10).

Fig. 14.10
When you add a program item with the file type .OLE, Windows 95 displays it with the icon from STORE.EXE.

Shortcut for .OLE file

Visual Basic applications have always used the first icon stored in the executable file as their document icon. You can't use other icons stored in the executable as document icons.

Check Registry Entries at Startup

If your application has an entry in the system registry, it should check its registered entries at startup to verify that the executable's file path has not changed since the application was last run. If the executable's current file path does not match the registered file path, the application should update its registration.

Visual Basic does not provide built-in support for checking system registry entries at startup, so you must use Windows API functions. Table 14.4 lists the functions Windows provides to help you maintain the system registry.

Table 14.4   Windows System Registry Functions

Function	Use
RegCloseKey	Closes a key after opening it with RegOpenKey.
RegCreateKeyA	Creates a new key.
RegDeleteKey	Deletes an existing key.
RegEnumKey	Gets the next subkey of a specified key.
RegOpenKey	Opens a key.
RegQueryValueA	Retrieves the value setting of a key as a text string.
RegSetValueA	Sets the value of a key.

Note

There are many more registration API functions than are shown in table 14.4. The ones listed in the table are compatible with Windows 3.x and provide the capability to check and update Registry entries as discussed in this chapter.

To check a registered key in the system registry, follow these steps:

1. Use RegOpenKeyA to open the registration key that contains path and file name information, such as store.application\shell\open.

2. Use RegQueryValueA to return the value of the subentry containing path and file name information.

3. Compare the returned value to the application's current path and file name. If the two values don't match, use RegSetValueA to change the registered value of the subentry.

4. Use RegCloseKey to close the registration key opened in step 1.

The CheckRegistrationEntry procedure in listing 14.6 shows the declarations for the system registry Windows API functions, and demonstrates how to check the registry entry for the STORE.VBP application found on the companion CD.

Listing 14.6   Checking Registry Entries at Startup (STORE.VBP)

```
Option Explicit

' Registry APIs used to check entry.
#If Win16 Then
Declare Function RegOpenKey Lib "Shell" _
    (ByVal HKeyIn As Long, _
    ByVal LPCSTR As String, _
    HKeyOut As Long) _
    As Long
Declare Function RegCloseKey Lib "Shell" _
    (ByVal HKeyIn As Long) _
    As Long
Declare Function RegQueryValue Lib "Shell" _
    (ByVal HKeyIn As Long, _
    ByVal SubKey As String, _
    ByVal KeyValue As String, _
    KeyValueLen As Long) _
    As Long
Declare Function RegSetValue Lib "Shell" _
    (ByVal HKeyIn As Long, _
    ByVal SubKey As String, _
    ByVal lType As Long, _
    ByVal strNewValue As String, _
    ByVal lIngnored As Long) _
    As Long
Declare Sub RegDeleteKey Lib "Shell" _
    (ByVal HKeyIn As Long, _
    ByVal SubKeyName As String)
#Else
Declare Function RegOpenKey Lib "advapi32" _
    Alias "RegOpenKeyA" _
    (ByVal HKeyIn As Long, _
    ByVal LPCSTR As String, _
    HKeyOut As Long) _
    As Long
Declare Function RegOpenKeyEx Lib "advapi32" _
    Alias "RegOpenKeyExA" _
    (ByVal HKeyIn As Long, ByVal LPCSTR _
    As String, ByVal dwRes _
    As Long, ByVal dwAccess _
    As Long, HKeyOut As _
    Long) As Long _


Declare Function RegCloseKey Lib "advapi32" _
    (ByVal HKeyIn As Long) _
    As Long
Declare Function RegQueryValue Lib "advapi32" _
    Alias "RegQueryValueA" _
    (ByVal HKeyIn As Long, _
    ByVal SubKey As String, _
    ByVal KeyValue As String, _
    KeyValueLen As Long) _
    As Long
```

```
Declare Function RegSetValue Lib "advapi32" _
    Alias "RegSetValueA" _
    (ByVal HKeyIn As Long, _
    ByVal SubKey As String, _
    ByVal lType As Long, _
    ByVal strNewValue As String, _
    ByVal lIngnored As Long) _
    As Long
Declare Function RegDeleteKey Lib "advapi32" _
    Alias "RegDeleteKeyA" _
    (ByVal HKeyIn As Long, _
    ByVal SubKeyName As String) _
    As Long
#End If

#If Win16 Then
    Const HKEY_CLASSES_ROOT = &H1
#Else
    Const HKEY_CLASSES_ROOT = &H80000000
    Const HKEY_CURRENT_USER = &H80000001
    Const HKEY_LOCAL_MACHINE = &H80000002
    Const HKEY_USERS = &H80000003
    Const HKEY_PERFORMANCE_DATA = &H80000004
#End If

Public Const ERROR_SUCCESS = 0

Sub CheckRegistrationEntry(strSearchKey As String)
    Dim hkroot As Long, lError As Long, lLen As Long
    Dim strKeyID As String, strKeyDesc As String
    Dim strAppName As String
    ' Get current application path and file name.
    strAppName = Chr(34) & App.Path & "\" & App.EXEName & _
        ".EXE" & _
        Chr(34) & Chr(32) & Chr(34) & "%1" & Chr(34)
    lLen = 255
    ' Specify subentry value to check.
    strKeyID = "command"
    ' Initialize key description (value returned by RegQueryValue).
    strKeyDesc = String(lLen, 0)
    ' Get the registry entry for the Open key.
    lError = RegOpenKey(HKEY_CLASSES_ROOT, strSearchKey & _
        "\shell\open", hkroot)
    ' Get the value of the entry.
    lError = RegQueryValue(hkroot, strKeyID, strKeyDesc, lLen)
    ' If RegOpenKey or RegQueryValue return an error,
    ' display a message and end.
    If lError Then
        MsgBox "Couldn't find registry entry. Please reinstall" & _
            "the application."
        End
    End If
    ' Check the value against the current installation.
    If Left(strKeyDesc, lLen - 1) <> strAppName Then
            ' If it doesn't match, change the registered value.
            lError = RegSetValue(hkroot, strKeyID, 1, strAppName, 0)
```

(continues)

Listing 14.6 Continued

```
        End If
        ' If RegOpenKey or RegQueryValue return an error,
        ' display a message and end.
        If lError Then
            MsgBox "Couldn't update registry entry."
            End
        End If
        ' Close the registration key.
        lError = RegCloseKey(hkroot)
End Sub
```

From Here...

For more information on OLE container applications, see the following chapters:

- Chapter 15, "Designing OLE Container Applications," discusses creating efficient OLE container applications.

- Chapter 16, "Distributing OLE Container Applications," discusses installing OLE container applications.

Chapter 15

Designing OLE Container Applications

This chapter describes the types of applications you can create using Visual Basic's OLE container features. It tells you how to go about creating each of these types of applications and provides guidelines on dealing with general programming problems such as control flow and error handling in OLE container applications.

In this chapter, you learn how to do the following:

- Create applications that simplify the interface of large OLE applications.

- Add user-interface features to an existing OLE application.

- Make an ordinary OLE application programmable.

- Manage the flow of an application as control passes from the OLE container to OLE objects and back.

- Decide whether code should reside in your Visual Basic 4.0 (VB4) project or in procedures stored in application documents.

- Call procedures stored in application documents from VB4 code.

- Track down OLE trappable errors.

Types of Applications You Can Create

You can create Visual Basic OLE container applications that accomplish any of the following tasks:

- Provide a simplified shell for an application that limits user actions to specific tasks.

- Add features, such as e-mail or data access, by superclassing an OLE application.

- Make an ordinary OLE application programmable through Visual Basic's OLE Automation features.

- Integrate a suite of OLE applications, such as Microsoft Office or Lotus SmartSuite, to create complete business software systems.

The following sections discuss each of these types of applications in turn.

Creating a Simplified Shell

Most OLE applications are highly customizable, but even so they never match the level of control you have in Visual Basic. This makes Visual Basic a very good tool for creating simplified interfaces for more complicated underlying applications.

Figure 15.1 shows how easy it is to create limited access to a variety of OLE objects. The Object Viewer is simply an OLE control on a single form with a common dialog control to allow the user to select a file to view.

Fig. 15.1
The OLE Object Viewer (VIEW.VPJ) displays any object the user selects.

Click here to select a file

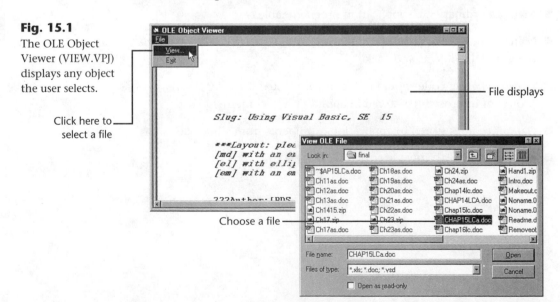

File displays

Choose a file

The code for the Object Viewer is extremely short. The View menu item's Click event procedure, shown in listing 15.1, displays the File Open common dialog box and then loads the selected file into the OLE control using the CreateEmbed method.

Listing 15.1 Use CreateEmbed to Load OLE Objects from Files Quickly

```
Option Explicit

Private Sub mnuView_Click()
    ' Show all file names.
    cmnDlg.FileName = "*.*"
    ' Display the Open common dialog.
    cmnDlg.ShowOpen
    ' Make sure a file name was entered and that the file exists.
    If (cmnDlg.FileName <> "") And Len(Dir(cmnDlg.FileName)) Then
        ' Display the file in the OLE object.
        oleObject.CreateEmbed cmnDlg.FileName
    End If
End Sub
```

The Exit menu item's Click event procedure merely gives the user a way to close the application:

```
Private Sub mnuitExit_Click()
    End
End Sub
```

And finally, the OLE control's Resize event procedure sizes the form to match the object. This assumes that the OLE control's SizeMode property is set to vbOLESizeAutoSize—otherwise, the object is clipped to fit in the control.

```
' Resize the form to fit the object.
Private Sub oleObject_Resize(HeightNew As Single, _
    WidthNew As Single)
    Me.Height = HeightNew
    Me.Width = WidthNew
End Sub
```

The Object Viewer is about as simple as an OLE container application can get, yet it is still extremely useful for viewing files without worrying about what application they came from. Of course, the Viewer doesn't handle non-OLE files very elegantly—to do this, you need to add some error handling, such as the modifications to the View_Click event procedure shown in listing 15.2.

II

Using OLE

Listing 15.2   Modify `mnuView_Click` to Handle Non-OLE Objects

```
Private Sub mnuView_Click()
    ' New: Set up error handling.
    On Error Resume Next
    ' Show all file names.
    cmnDlg.FileName = "*.*"
    ' Display the Open common dialog.
    cmnDlg.ShowOpen
    ' Make sure a file name was entered and that the file exists.
    Len(Dir(cmnDlg.FileName)) Then
        ' Display the file in the OLE object.
        oleObject.CreateEmbed cmnDlg.FileName
        ' New: If the file was not an OLE object,
        ' load the file as a non-OLE object.
        If Err Then DisplayNonOLEObject (cmnDlg.FileName)
        ' New: Hide other objects
        imgObj.Visible = False
        txtObj.Visible = False
        oleObject.Visible = True
    End If
End Sub
```

It is safer to try `CreateEmbed` and catch the error than to try to determine whether the file is a valid OLE file by looking at the extension in the file name (.XLS, .DOC, and so on). Any file may have these extensions—not just OLE files. The `DisplayNonOLEObject` procedure, shown in listing 15.3, handles the other file types. Graphic files are displayed in an image control and other file types (.TXT, .INI, and so on) are displayed in a text box control.

Listing 15.3   `DisplayNonOLEObjects` Uses Text Box and Image Controls to Display Other Types of Objects

```
' Handles displaying other types of files.
Sub DisplayNonOLEObject(strFile As String)
    ' Check for errors.
    On Error Resume Next
    Dim strBuffer As String, iFile As Integer
    ' If the file is a graphic, display it in
    ' an Image control.
    imgObj.Picture = LoadPicture(strFile)
    ' If the file was a valid picture, then
    ' display the image control and hide others.
    If Err = 0 Then
        ' Hide other objects
        imgObj.Visible = True
        txtObj.Visible = False
        oleObject.Visible = False
        ' Reset form's Height and Width to match
        ' Image control.
        Me.Height = imgObj.Height
        Me.Width = imgObj.Width
```

```
            ' If the file wasn't a valid picture, then
            ' load the data into a text box and hide other
            ' controls.
            Else
                iFile = FreeFile
                Open strFile For Binary As iFile
                strBuffer = Space(LOF(iFile))
                Get iFile, 1, strBuffer
                Close iFile
                txtObj.Text = strBuffer
                ' Hide other objects
                imgObj.Visible = False
                txtObj.Visible = False
                oleObject.Visible = False
                ' Reset form's Height and Width to match
                ' Text Box control.
                Me.Height = txtObj.Height
                Me.Width = txtObj.Width
            End If
        End Sub
```

Listings 15.2 and 15.3 use a style of error checking called *polling*. The On Error Resume Next statement tells Visual Basic to temporarily ignore trappable run-time errors and continue executing code—you check the value of Err after each line that you expect might return an error (If Err...Then...). This style of error handling is very useful when working with OLE objects. For more information on error handling with OLE objects, see the section "Trapping and Skinning OLE Errors" later in this chapter.

It's a Bird, It's a Plane, It's a Superclass!

Relative to the processing and memory requirements of a full-blown drawing, spreadsheet, or word processing application, the overhead you incur by adding Visual Basic is minimal. You may choose to operate an OLE application—with all of its user interface intact—from within an OLE control on a form. This provides a way to add menu items and features to an application that is not otherwise programmable.

Figure 15.2 shows a Visual Basic application that adds two menu items to the Visio file menu. Visio automatically adds its own menu bar and toolbar to the Visual Basic MDI form. You only have to program the items on the File menu. Creating a new object that modifies a contained object is called *superclassing* the object. In this case, you are using Visual Basic to superclass an entire application.

Fig. 15.2
You use Visual
Basic to "super-
class" OLE
applications such
as Visio to add
menu items and
other features.

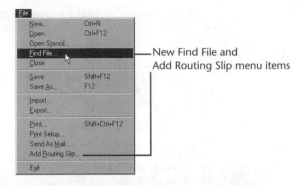

New Find File and
Add Routing Slip menu items

To superclass an OLE application using Visual Basic, follow these steps:

1. Create a new project.

2. Add an MDI parent form to the project (see fig. 15.3). The MDI parent
form will display the OLE object's application menu and toolbar when
the application runs. If the application you are superclassing doesn't
display multiple windows, you can skip this step.

Fig. 15.3
Create an MDI
parent form to
contain OLE
applications that
display multiple
windows.

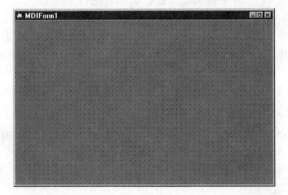

3. Add an MDI child form with an OLE control to contain an embedded
object from the application you want to superclass (see fig. 15.4). You
must use an embedded object (not linked) in order to get in-place
editing.

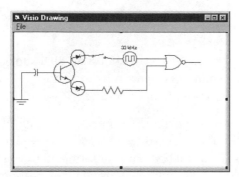

Fig. 15.4
The MDI child form contains the OLE object from the application you want to modify—in this case, Shapeware's Visio drawing application.

4. Add a File menu to the MDI child form. Be sure to set the Negotiate Position option to Left in the Menu Editor (see fig. 15.5).

Fig. 15.5
Setting Negotiate Position in the Menu Editor allows OLE objects to insert their application's menu and toolbar on the MDI parent form.

II

Using OLE

5. Write code to perform the actions on the File menu on the MDI child form. Embedded objects do not provide File menu items, so you'll have to write code for these as well as for the new features you add to the File menu. Usually, you can delegate most of these tasks to the OLE application.

Note

The form's `NegotiateMenus` property also determines whether OLE objects can display their menus on the form's menu bar. This property is `True` by default.

When superclassing an OLE application, you need to write code for two important tasks:

1. Initialize the OLE object at start-up. For an MDI application, this means displaying the child forms containing the embedded objects and activating those objects for in-place editing.

2. Handle menu events from the File menu. Since embedded objects don't provide a File menu when edited in-place, you need to replicate the application's File menu both on your form and in your code. This is easy to do if the application supports OLE Automation, since you can delegate most tasks using methods provided by the application.

The following Load event procedure for an MDI parent form displays an MDI child form and activates the OLE object it contains for editing:

```
Private Sub MDIForm_Load()
    ' Show Visio drawing child form.
    frmDrawing.Show
    ' Activate the object on the form for
    ' in-place editing.
    frmDrawing.oleVisio.DoVerb
End Sub
```

The MDI child form frmDrawing contains the File menu for Visio, plus two new menu items (Find File and Add Routing Slip). Since Visio supports OLE Automation, you can use Visio methods to reproduce the standard File menu actions. For example, the Click event for the Print menu item simply calls the Visio Print method on the OLE object, as shown here:

```
' Delegate Printing to the Visio application.
Private Sub mnuitPrint_Click()
  ' The Object property returns a Visio Page object,
  ' but Print applies to the Document object, so use
  ' Document.Print to print the object as shown here.
  oleVisio.Object.Document.Print
End Sub
```

Using the object's application methods in this way is called *delegating*—your application delegates the task to the OLE application. Of course you can't delegate tasks that Visio doesn't ordinarily provide, such as Find File. To perform this task, you need your own code, as shown here:

```
' Event procedure for Find File command
' (new feature).
Private Sub mnuitFindFile_Click()
    ' Display the Find File dialog box.
    frmFindVisoFiles.Show vbModal
End Sub
```

Adding OLE Automation to an Existing Application

You can use Visual Basic's OLE Automation features to add objects, properties, and methods to an existing OLE application. Part III of this book, "Creating OLE Objects," covers Visual Basic's OLE Automation features in great detail, but this task is worth mentioning here since it deals with developing OLE container applications. To make an existing OLE application programmable as a Visual Basic OLE server, follow these steps:

1. Create a new project.

2. Add an OLE control to Form1 that contains an object from the application that you want to make programmable. Figure 15.6 shows a WordArt object inserted on a form.

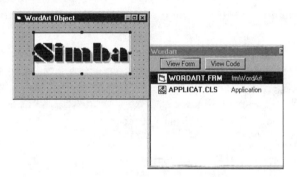

Fig. 15.6
The WordArt application is not programmable, although it does support other OLE features.

3. Choose <u>T</u>ools, <u>O</u>ptions. Visual Basic displays the Options property pages (see fig. 15.7).

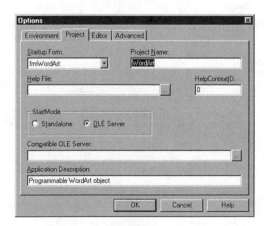

Fig. 15.7
The project name appears in the system registry after you compile and run the application from the resulting executable.

II

Using OLE

4. In the Project Name text box, type the name of the OLE application to which you are adding OLE Automation features. Then select the StartMode OLE Server option button and click OK.

5. Choose Insert, Class Module to add a class module to the project.

6. In the Properties box for the class module, set both properties to True and name the module Application.

7. Add code to the class module for the objects, properties, and methods to expose the OLE object you inserted in step 2.

8. Compile and run the project.

Listing 15.4 demonstrates how to create a method in a class module. The InsertText method inserts a string into the WordArt object on the form frmWordArt.

Listing 15.4   Adding a Method to Insert Text in the WordArt OLE Application (WORDART.VBP)

```
' Inserts WordArt text in an OLE control.
Public Sub InsertText(strText As String)
    ' Using the WordArt object on frmWordArt
    With frmWordArt.oleWordArt
        ' Embed a WordArt object in the passed-in OLE control.
        .CreateEmbed "", "MSWordArt.2"
        ' Activate the object.
        .Verb = -3
        ' Set the data format to text.
        .Format = "CF_TEXT"
        .DataText = strText
        .UPDATE
        .Close
        ' Pause to let the OLE application load.
        ' On Error Resume Next
        'Do
            ' Err = 0
            ' DoEvents
            ' Activate the OLE application.
            ' AppActivate "Microsoft WordArt", False
        ' Loop While Err = 5
        ' On Error GoTo 0
        ' Set the text in the object.
        ' SendKeys strText, True
        ' Update the object
        ' SendKeys "%A", True
        ' Close the object
        ' SendKeys "{Esc}", True
        ' .UPDATE
```

```
                ' Close the object.
                ' .Close
          End With
     End Sub
```

Listing 15.5 demonstrates how to create an object property in a class module. The `Object` method copies the object contained in the `oleWordArt` object to the object on the left side of a Visual Basic `Set` statement (for example, `Set objTarget = objWordArt.Object`).

Listing 15.5   Adding an Object Property to the WordArt OLE Application (WORDART.VBP)

```
     ' APPLICAT.CLS
     ' Application class module for WordArt object.
     '
     ' Pastes the WordArt object into the target control when
     ' the user performs and object Set.
     Public Property Set Object(objTarget)
          ' Using the WordArt object on frmWordArt
          With frmWordArt.oleWordArt
               ' Activate the object, hiding the running application.
               .DoVerb -3
               ' Copy the object to the Clipboard.
               .Copy
               ' Paste the object into the OLE target.
               objTarget.Paste
               ' Close the object.
               .Close
          End With
     End Property
```

Figure 15.8 shows using the new OLE Automation application from another Visual Basic application.

Listing 15.6 demonstrates how to call the OLE Automation application you just created from another Visual Basic application. The `CreateObject` function starts the application and returns a reference to an instance of the `WordArt.Application` class shown in listing 15.5. Then the method `InsertText` draws a text string using WordArt, and the `Set` statement displays the object in an OLE object on the current form.

II

Using OLE

Fig. 15.8

The Test application calls the new WordArt application to insert text in a WordArt object and display it.

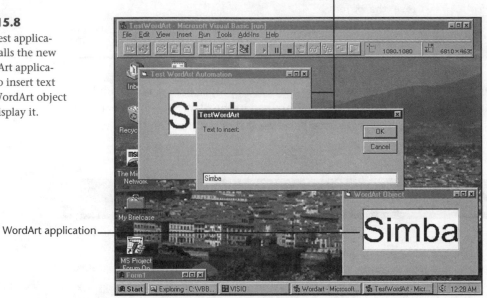

Listing 15.6   Using the New WordArt Methods and Properties from Another Application (TESTWORDART.VBP)

```
Private Sub cmdInsertText_Click()
    ' Create a new object variable.
    Dim oleWordArt As Object
    ' Set the object variable to the VB
    ' WordArt.Application class created to
    ' make WordArt programmable.
    Dim strText As String
    strText = InputBox("Text to insert:")
    Set oleWordArt = GetObject("", "wordart.application")
    ' Use the InsertText method from WordArt.Application.
    oleWordArt.InsertText strText
    ' Insert the WordArt object into an OLE
    ' control on the current form.
    oleWordArt.CopyObject
    OLE1.Paste
End Sub
```

Integrating OLE Applications

Of course, the biggest single advantage of OLE is that it lets you integrate applications so that they can work together. You can create sophisticated software applications by borrowing features from a suite of OLE applications, such as Microsoft Office or Lotus SmartSuite.

From the standpoint of creating OLE container applications using suites of applications, you need to consider a few major points:

- How much memory and disk space is the application going to require?

- Do all of the applications work well together? OLE is terrific glue, but different application developers implement things slightly differently. You should test all the applications in your suite to make sure they are consistent and to note the exceptions.

- Do all applications support the same color palettes? Embedding a million-color object into an application that supports only 256 colors can cause some weird color shifts.

- Are the applications programmable in Visual Basic? Being able to get at each application's object through OLE Automation is much easier and more reliable than using dynamic data exchange (DDE) or SendKeys.

Part IV of this book, "Integrating with Office Applications," is dedicated to doing this type of system integration using the Microsoft Office Development Kit.

Who's in Control?

OLE containers pass control back and forth between the applications that provide the OLE objects and the application that contains them. Since OLE objects may themselves contain embedded objects, it can be difficult to determine who's currently in control, as shown in figure 15.9.

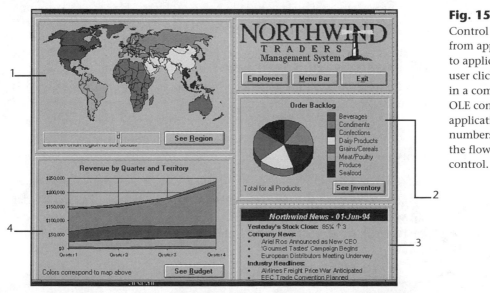

Fig. 15.9
Control passes from application to application as a user clicks around in a complicated OLE container application; the numbers indicate the flow of control.

Knowing who is in control is critical to tracking down errors and anticipating the behavior of an application. For instance, if the user opens another document in an application while editing an embedded object, does the container application know *not* to close the object's application—and thereby avoid losing the user's edits? Alternatively, how does your OLE container application recover if an OLE object's application crashes?

Here are some guidelines that help contain these problems when programming with OLE objects:

- Don't close an OLE object's application in code if it is visible to the user. If the application is visible, the user may have created a new document or made changes to an existing document. You can't always rely on the object's application to prompt the user to save changes if you close the application using Visual Basic statements.

- Don't make a visible application invisible. This is related to the preceding point—the user may lose edits.

- Test whether the OLE object's application is running before performing operations on the object. You can't detect whether the user closes the application or the application crashes, so it is best to check that the application is running at the beginning of every task that requires the object's application to be loaded.

- Limit retries. If an OLE object's application closes unexpectedly, it's dangerous to try restarting it. You've probably lost a chunk of memory somewhere that will eventually cause problems. It's better to attempt a graceful exit, saving changes along the way.

Where Does the Code Live?

OLE doesn't just distribute control between applications, it also lets you distribute code. For example, you can use Visual Basic 4.0 (VB4) to call Visual Basic for Applications (VBA) procedures that reside in an Excel worksheet. The VBA procedures can function just like VB4 procedures, receiving arguments and returning values.

When designing your container application, you must decide where code should live. Keeping all your code in the VB4 project makes it easier to maintain your code, since all files are stored in the same format in a single location. Using VBA procedures has performance advantages for some tasks, however.

VB4 versus VBA

The Visual Basic Programming System, version 4.0 (VB4) includes the same "engine" that drives Visual Basic for Applications (VBA). VBA is the programming language shipped with Microsoft Excel, Project, and (eventually) other Microsoft Office applications. Programming in VBA is very much like programming in VB4—there is a code window and a similar debugger, and all the "core" language is the same. Many of the OLE features that are available in VB4 are also available to VBA from within the application.

So why program in VB4? VB4 has these advantages over VBA:

- Includes built-in forms and controls.

- Allows custom controls.

- Creates compiled executable files.

- Reads resource files (.RES).

- Provides its own storage mechanism for OLE objects (the `SaveToFile` and `ReadFromFile` methods).

- Provides direct access to database objects through Jet 2.5 or 3.0.

The disadvantage of VB4 is that it takes longer to access an OLE object's properties and methods from VB4 than it does to access that object's properties and methods from within its application using VBA. The reason for this is that VB4 must cross-process boundaries to get at an OLE object's properties and methods, whereas VBA has *in-process* access to all of the application's objects. Figure 15.10 shows the difference between in-process and cross-process access.

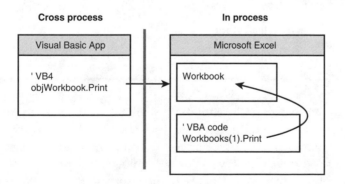

Fig. 15.10

Cross-process versus in-process access to objects.

Cross-process access to an object's properties is 2 to 20 times slower than in-process access. Access to methods is 15 to 30 times slower cross-process than in-process. To see the performance difference between cross-process and in-process access, try listing 15.7's lines of code in VB4 using an embedded worksheet from Microsoft Excel named oleObject.

Listing 15.7   Timing In-Process Access (ACCESS.VBP)

```
Sub VB4AccessTime()
    Dim Sheet1 As Object, x As Object
    Set Sheet1 = OLEOBJECT.object
    time1 = Timer
    For i = 1 To 1000
        temp = Sheet1.UsedRange
    Next i
    MsgBox "Property access time: " & CSng(Timer - time1) / 1000
    time1 = Timer
    For i = 1 To 1000
        Sheet1.Unprotect
    Next i
    MsgBox "Method access time: " & CSng(Timer - time1) / 1000
End Sub
```

Next, try listing 15.8's lines of code in VBA within a Microsoft Excel workbook.

Listing 15.8   Timing Cross-Process Access (ACCESS.VBP)

```
Sub VBAAccessTime()
    Dim Sheet1 As Object, Temp As Object
    Set Sheet1 = Sheets("Sheet1")
    time1 = Timer
    For i = 1 To 1000
        temp = Sheet1.UsedRange
    Next i
    MsgBox "Property access time: " & CSng(Timer - time1) / 1000
    time1 = Timer
    For i = 1 To 1000
        Sheet1.Unprotect
    Next i
    MsgBox "Method access time: " & CSng(Timer - time1) / 1000
End Sub
```

The access time between VB4 and VBA is significantly different for the UsedRange property and Unprotect method: UsedRange takes twice the amount of time cross-process; Unprotect takes 19 times more time cross-process. These differences vary greatly depending on the property or method used. Operations that cause a change in the display of the object can mask performance differences since the screen update takes a fixed amount of time, regardless of the source of the request.

Calling VBA Procedures from VB4 for Better Performance

If an OLE application includes VBA, you can write performance-critical procedures in VBA, then call them from VB4. Access to properties and methods stays in-process, so these actions take place much more quickly.

To use VBA procedures from VB4, follow these steps:

1. Add the VBA procedure to the OLE object.

2. Activate the OLE object.

3. Call the VBA procedure.

4. Deactivate the OLE object when you are finished calling VBA procedures.

Adding VBA Procedures to Embedded Objects

You can add VBA procedures to linked or embedded objects on a VB4 form. With linked objects, the procedures are stored in the separate, linked source file. With embedded objects, the procedures are stored in the VB4 form as part of the OLE object.

To add a VBA procedure to an OLE object, follow these steps:

1. Open the OLE object in its application, as shown in figure 15.11. You must use the Open command rather than the Edit command in order to be able to edit VBA code in an embedded object.

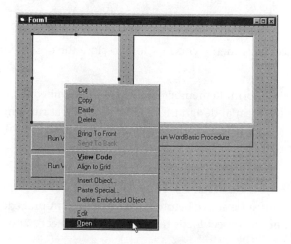

Fig. 15.11
You must open the worksheet object in Excel to be able to add a module sheet for VBA code.

2. From Excel's Insert menu, choose Macro, then choose the subitem Module to create a new module for your VBA code (see fig. 15.12).

Fig. 15.12
Inserting a new VBA module into an embedded object.

3. Add your VBA procedure(s) to the new module. While in the object's application, you have access to VBA's Help and debugging features (see fig. 15.13).

Fig. 15.13
You can run, debug, and get Help on VBA statements as you write procedures for an OLE object.

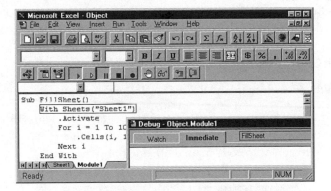

4. From Excel's File menu, choose Close to close the object and return to VB4.

5. Save the VB4 form. Remember that changes to embedded objects are saved in the form at design time. Changes made at run time are lost unless you are using a linked object or have written special code to store changes to the embedded object before exiting.

Calling VBA Procedures from VB4

The OLE object must be active before you can call a VBA procedure in the object. Activating the object loads the object in the object's application and makes the VBA procedures available to run. Each OLE application provides different methods for running VBA procedures, as shown in the following table:

Application	Method	Example
Microsoft Excel	Run	`oleObject.Object.Application.Run "FillSheet"`
Microsoft Project	MacroRun	`oleObject.Object.Application .MacroRun "AssignTask"`
Microsoft Word*	ToolsMacro	`oleObject.Object.Application. WordBasic.ToolsMacro _ "CreateLetter", 1`

Microsoft Word includes WordBasic, which also can be called from VB4.

To run a VBA procedure from VB4, follow these steps:

1. Activate the OLE object using the DoVerb method. For example, this line of code activates an object using its default OLE verb—usually this is Edit or Open:

   ```
   oleObject.DoVerb
   ```

2. Call the object's Run method. The actual name of the method varies from application to application. This line runs the procedure FillSheet in Excel:

   ```
   oleObject.Object.Application.Run "FillSheet"
   ```

3. Use the OLE object's Close method to deactivate the object when you are done calling VBA procedures. This line of code deactivates the OLE object used previously in this procedure:

   ```
   oleObject.Close
   ```

Calling Excel VBA Procedures

Use the Excel Application object's Run method to call VBA procedures from VB4. You can get a reference to the Excel Application object two ways:

■ Directly using the CreateObject or GetObject functions. For example, the following code starts Excel and returns a reference to the Excel application:

   ```
   Set objExcel = CreateObject("excel.application")
   ```

■ From a linked or embedded Excel object using the OLE control's `Object` property and the Excel `Application` property. For example, the following code returns a reference to the Excel application for an OLE control containing a worksheet:

```
Set objExcel = oleWorksheet.Object.Application
```

Once you've obtained a reference to the Excel `Application` object, use the `Run` method to run the VBA procedure. `Run` has the following form for VBA `Sub` procedures:

```
appobject.Run [workbook!]procedurename[, arguments...]
```

The `Run` method has the following form for VBA `Function` procedures:

```
appobject.Run([workbook!]procedurename[, arguments...])
```

The following table describes the parts of Excel's `Run` method:

Item	Description
appobject	A reference to the Excel `Application` object. In VBA this item is optional, but it's required when calling from VB4.
Run [*workbook!*]	The `Run` method. The file name of the open workbook that contains the procedure. If omitted, Excel uses the current workbook. Excel does not automatically open *workbook* if it is not already loaded.
procedurename [, arguments...]	The name of the procedure to run. A list of the arguments to pass to the VBA procedure.

If the VBA procedure is a function, `Run` returns the result of the function. For example, the code in listing 15.9 runs the `SumColumn` function in Excel and returns the total of all the cells in a column on a worksheet.

Listing 15.9 Using VBA Procedures Stored in an Embedded Object (OLECHART.VBP)

```
Private Sub cmdSum_Click()
    Dim objExcel As Object, lTotal As Long
    ' Activate the embedded worksheet before running the VBA
    ' procedure.
    oleSheet.DoVerb
    ' Get a reference to the Excel Application object.
    Set objExcel = oleSheet.Object.Application
    ' Run the VBA procedure SumColumn on the first column
    lTotal = objExcel.Run("SumColumn", 1)
    ' Close the OLE object.
    oleSheet.Close
```

```
        ' Display result
        Msgbox lTotal
End Sub
```

The `SumColumn` VBA function is shown in the following code. This function can be inserted in a module in the workbook of the `oleSheet` object, or it can be in any workbook currently loaded in Excel.

```
Function SumColumn(iCol As Integer) As Long
    Dim i As Integer
    For i = 1 To ActiveSheet.UsedRange.Rows.Count
        lTotal = lTotal + Cells(i, iCol)
    Next i
    SumColumn = lTotal
End Function
```

You can't pass objects to VBA procedures, since VB4 evaluates all items in the argument list before passing them on to the procedure. In other words, VB4 attempts to pass the `Value` property of an object, rather than the object itself, when you use the `Run` method. Similarly, you can't receive objects as return values from the `Run` method—Excel simply returns an error. Even if you could receive an object back from `Run`, you couldn't use it to set the OLE control's `Object` property, since it is read-only.

Calling WordBasic Macros

Use the WordBasic object's `ToolsMacro` method to call WordBasic macros from VB4. You can get a reference to the Word `WordBasic` object two ways:

- Directly using the `CreateObject` or `GetObject` functions. For example, the following code starts Excel and returns a reference to the Excel application:

```
Set wrdBasic = GetObject("", "Word.Basic")
```

- From a linked or embedded Word object using the OLE control's `Object` property and the Word `Application` and `WordBasic` properties. For example, the following code returns a reference to the Word application for an OLE control containing a Microsoft Word document:

```
Set wrdBasic = oleWordDocument.Object.Application.WordBasic
```

Once you've obtained a reference to the `WordBasic` object, use the `ToolsMacro` method to run the WordBasic macro. `ToolsMacro` has the following form for running WordBasic macros:

```
wordbasic.ToolsMacro macroname, Run:=1
```

The following table describes the parts of Word's `ToolsMacro` method:

Item	Description
wordbasic	A reference to the `WordBasic` object.
ToolsMacro	The `ToolsMacro` method.
macroname	The name of the macro to run. WordBasic macros are stored in Word template files (.DOT). Only macros in currently active templates are available from VB4.
Run:=1	Tells Word to run the macro. `ToolsMacro` has other arguments for displaying and editing macros. See the WordBasic documentation for more information on these arguments.

WordBasic macros are available only if the Word application is open for editing. You can't use WordBasic macros on embedded objects that are activated for in-place editing. The VB4 code in listing 15.10 opens an embedded Word document in Word and runs the `CreateLetter` procedure.

Listing 15.10   Running a WordBasic Macro from VB4 (ACCESS.VBP)

```
Private Sub cmdWord_Click()
    Dim wrdBasic As Object
    ' Open the embedded object. Note, you must open
    ' Word objects -- WordBasic procedures are not
    ' available in Word's OLE Edit mode.
    oleWordDocument.DoVerb 2
    ' Set wrdBasic = GetObject("", "Word.Basic")
    ' Get a reference to the WordBasic object from the
    ' embedded OLE object.
    Set wrdBasic = oleWordDocument.Object.Application.WordBasic
    ' Call the ToolsMacro method on the WordBasic object.
    wrdBasic.toolsmacro Name:="CreateLetter", run:=1
    ' Close the embedded object.
    oleWordDocument.Close
End Sub
```

The `CreateLetter` WordBasic macro, shown in listing 15.11, must exist in the global template (NORMAL.DOT) or the document's current template file in order to be run from VB4.

Listing 15.11   The WordBasic Macro to Run

```
' NORMAL.DOT.This is a new letter
' CreateLetter WordBasic macro.
Sub MAIN
```

```
' Insert some text -- not very interesting,
'  but you get the idea...
Insert "This is a new letter"
InsertPara
Insert "Dear Jane:"
InsertPara
Insert "I'm sorry I won't make it to your party."
Insert "I'm too busy programming VBA."
End Sub
```

WordBasic macros can't receive arguments or return values. However, you can use Word's document variables to achieve the same effect. In Word, a *document variable* is a static, global variable that all macros can read from or write to within the document. Use the WordBasic SetDocumentVar and GetDocumentVar$ methods to set and return values from document variables. The two methods have this form when used from VB4:

```
wordbasic.SetDocumentVar varname, value
```

```
wordbasic.[GetDocumentVar$] varname
```

Be sure to enclose GetDocumentVar$ in square brackets in your VB4 code, since it includes a dollar sign ($), which has special meaning to Visual Basic. The VB4 code in listing 15.12 uses a document variable to return the number of styles contained in the style sheet for a document.

Listing 15.12   Getting Values Back from WordBasic Macros (WORD.VBP)

```
Private Sub cmdGetStyles_Click()
    Dim wrdBasic As Object, strStyles As String
    ' Open the embedded object.
    oleWordDocument.DoVerb 2
    ' Get a reference to the WordBasic object from the
    ' embedded OLE object.
    Set wrdBasic = oleWordDocument.Object.Application.WordBasic
    ' Call the ToolsMacro method on the WordBasic object.
    wrdBasic.toolsmacro Name:="ListStyles", run:=1
    ' Get the result from the StyleCount document variable.
    strStyles = wrdBasic.[GetDocumentVar$]("gStyleName")
    ' Close the embedded object.
    oleWordDocument.Close
    ' Display the result
    MsgBox strStyles
End Sub
```

The ListStyles WordBasic macro, shown in listing 15.13, must exist in the global template (NORMAL.DOT) or the document's current template file in order to be run from VB4.

Listing 15.13 Sending Values to VB4 from a WordBasic Macro

```
' ListStyles Macro in NORMAL.DOT
Sub MAIN
    ' Build a list of all the styles in a document.
    For i = 1 To CountStyles()
        sNames$ = sNames$ + Chr$(13) + StyleName$(i)
    Next i
    ' Set the document variable -- notice that the variable name
    ' is in quotes.
    SetDocumentVar "gStyleName", sNames$
End Sub
```

Trapping and Skinning OLE Errors

When programming with OLE objects, you may receive trappable errors from three sources:

- Visual Basic. The Visual Basic OLE trappable error codes range from 430 to 450. Most of these errors deal with OLE Automation objects.

- The OLE DLLs. These errors come across as user-defined error codes in the range 31000 to 32000. These are the error codes you'll usually see when dealing with linked and embedded objects.

- The OLE object's application. Each application has its own defined range of error codes it returns. Word error messages range from 1000 to 1600. Excel's error codes range from 1000 to 1006. These errors occur only when you're working with each application's objects through OLE Automation.

There are two programming strategies for trapping these errors:

- Polling using `On Error Resume Next`.

- Error handlers using `On Error Goto`.

Polling is essential when you're programming with OLE objects. Errors from OLE object applications tend to be vague—Excel defines seven errors to cover about 1400 methods and properties—you usually need to know exactly what line of code failed in order to handle the situation effectively.

Polling for Errors

This method is called *polling* because you check for errors after each statement that might cause an error. The advantage of this is that you know exactly what line of code caused the error. Listing 15.14 shows how to poll for errors.

Listing 15.14   When Polling for Errors, Don't Abandon the Punt in Favor of the Pole

```
Sub PollingDemo()
    ' (1) Start polling for errors.
    On Error Resume Next
    ' (2) This line returns error 1004 if an outline can't be
    ' created.
    oleSheet.Object.Selection.AutoOutline
    ' (3) If there was an error...
    If Err Then
        ' (4) Alert user of the error.
        MsgBox "Can't create outline on this selection."
        Beep
        ' (5) Important! Reset error back to 0.
        Err = 0
    End If
    '(6) Turn off error trapping.
    On Error GoTo 0
End Sub
```

Listing 15.14 uses the following steps to poll for errors:

1. The first step is to turn on polling. On Error Resume Next prevents errors from halting the program—instead, Visual Basic simply assigns the error value to Err and continues to the next line of code.

2. The Excel Worksheet object's AutoOutline method does not work on all selections, and it is impossible to test the selection to see if it will work *before* you call AutoOutline. Your only choice is to test *after*—possibly causing an error.

3. If there was an error, Err is set to a nonzero value (in this case 1004). This tells you that the method failed, but unless you parse the string returned by Error, you can't tell *what* method failed. Parsing error strings is a bad idea, since they may change from version to version of Visual Basic. Your only real solution is to poll for errors after each method you think might fail.

4. Alerting the user is a good idea. Here it is done through the status bar. Using the status bar rather than a message box is less intrusive and doesn't interrupt the user's work. Be sure to clear the status bar on the next user action so that the message doesn't stay up forever.

5. Reset Err to 0. Otherwise, subsequent polling will reflect the current error value (1004) even if no error occurs.

6. Turn off polling before exiting the procedure.

II

Using OLE

Using Error Handlers

Error handlers are blocks of code that handle a general set of errors. One of the nice things about handlers is that they move all the error-handling code to the end of the procedure—out of the main logic of the procedure.

Unlike polling, execution doesn't continue in a straight line from the top to the bottom of a procedure. Instead, execution jumps to the error handler when an error occurs. Listing 15.15 shows how you might use error trapping by setting up an error handler.

Listing 15.15 Using Error Handlers (ERROR.VBJ)

```
' Opens a file for Input. Returns file number if successful,
' 0 if failure.
Function iOpenFile(sFilename As String) As Integer
    Dim iFilenumber As Integer, iTries As Integer
    ' (1) Turn on error handling.
    On Error GoTo iOpenFileErr
    ' Get a free file number.
    iFilenumber = FreeFile()
    ' (2) Open file. We don't know if the file exists yet,
    ' so might cause an error.
    Open sFilename For Input As iFilenumber
    ' (7) Return file number so user can manipulate file.
    iOpenFile = iFilenumber
    ' Important! Turn off error handling.
    On Error GoTo 0
    ' Clear status bar.
    Application.StatusBar = ""
    ' (8) Important! Exit procedure before the error handler.
    Exit Function
' (3) Label identifies error handler. This label must be unique
' to the workbook.
iOpenFileErr:
    ' Classic way to do this: Select Case on the error code,
    ' with a Case statement for each possibility.
    Select Case Err
        Case 52, 53, 75, 76 ' Bad file name or number,
                            ' file not found, or path error.
            ' (4) Display a status message
            ' indicating the error.
            Application.StatusBar = "File not found."
            ' Prompt the user for the file to open.
            sFilename = Application.GetOpenFilename _
                (, , "Choose file to open")
            ' If the user chose Cancel...
            If sFilename = "False" Then
                ' Return 0 to indicate that function didn't
                ' open a file.
                iOpenFile = 0
                ' Turn off error handling and exit.
                On Error GoTo 0
                Exit Function
            End If
```

```
        Case 55 ' File already open by VB for an incompatible
                    ' read/write access.
            ' This shouldn't happen, but if it does, return 0
            ' and exit.
            iOpenFile = 0
            On Error GoTo 0
            Exit Function
        Case 67 ' (5) Too many files are open
            Application.StatusBar = "Too many files or " & _
                applications open."
            MsgBox "Close one or more files or " & _
                "applications and try again."
            iOpenFile = 0
            On Error GoTo 0
            Exit Function
        Case 70 ' Permission denied.
            Application.StatusBar = "Permission denied."
            MsgBox "You can't open " & sFilename & _
                ". It requires a password or is in use by " & _
                    "another application."
            iOpenFile = 0
            On Error GoTo 0
            Exit Function
        Case 71 ' Disk not ready.
            ' Keep track of the number of tries.
            iTries = iTries + 1
            ' Let the user try twice, but don't beat them
            ' over the head.
            If iTries < 3 Then
                Application.StatusBar = "Can't read from drive."
                MsgBox "Make sure the disk is inserted and " & _
                    "the drive door is closed."
            ' Fail after second try -- maybe the user changed
            ' his/her mind.
            Else
                iOpenFile = 0
                On Error GoTo 0
                Exit Function
            End If
        Case Else
            ' Report the error, so you can fix it.
            MsgBox "An unanticipated error occurred. " & _
            Please report " & _
            "the following information to AppBug: " _
            & Chr$(10) & _
                "Procedure: iOpenFile" & Chr$(10) & _
                "Error: " & Err & Error()
                iOpenFile = 0
                On Error GoTo 0
            Exit Function
    End Select
    ' (6) You must tell Visual Basic to return after handling
    ' the error.
    Resume
End Function
```

1. The first step is to turn on error handling. On Error Goto *label* sets up an error handler—in this case iOpenFileErr.

2. The Open statement might cause any number of errors. If an error occurs, the code jumps immediately to (3); otherwise, it continues straight to (7).

3. This big Select Case statement will handle all the known problems that might occur while opening a file.

4. The most common problems can be solved by asking the user for the right file name. It is a good idea to let users correct problems if at all possible. This block of code uses Excel's Open File dialog box.

5. In some cases, there is no easy solution, so the function may fail. It is a good idea to pass back 0 or False to indicate failure, rather than simply ending the program. This way, the caller can decide what to do (stop or continue on).

6. After the error is handled, Resume returns execution to line (2) to open the file. Resume Next would return to line (7).

7. Return values should be meaningful to the caller. In this case, if iOpenFile is not 0, then it's the file handle used to access and close the open file.

Tip
Name error handlers after the procedure they reside in using this form: *procedurename*Err. This way, they will always be unique and you'll avoid naming conflicts.

8. Be sure to exit the procedure before the error handler. Otherwise, execution continues at (3) and so on—in this case, the Case Else would run if Exit was omitted.

Error Handling as a Shortcut

Sometimes it's easier to test for an error rather than making sure an action is valid before performing that action. This is a very common practice in BASIC programming—nothing happens faster than an error, so it's also a way to speed up some operations.

The following code replaces "wombat" with "wallaby" on the active sheet. Several errors might occur: the embedded object might not be a worksheet and therefore not have a UsedRange property, it might be protected, or it might be open for read-only access. Rather than testing each case, the code simply tests for an error after the Replace.

```
Sub ShortCuts()
    On Error Resume Next
    oleSheet.Object.UsedRange.Replace "wombat", "wallaby"
    If Err Then MsgBox "Couldn't perform change."
    Err = 0
    On Error GoTo 0
End Sub
```

From Here...

For more information on OLE objects and applications, see the following chapters:

- Chapter 14, "OLE Container Programming Techniques," contains information on saving OLE objects to files.

- Chapter 16, "Distributing OLE Container Applications," discusses installing OLE container applications.

II

Using OLE

Distributing OLE Container Applications

OLE container applications often have special requirements not normally handled by installation programs, such as those generated by the Setup Wizard. This chapter explains those special requirements.

In this chapter, you learn how to do the following:

- Use the Setup Wizard to generate distribution disks for OLE container applications.

- Check for installed OLE applications used by your container application.

- Determine which files you must distribute with your application.

- Check file versions to install only later-version files.

- Register files with the system registration database during setup.

- Distribute 16- and 32-bit applications on the same distribution disks.

- Check the operating system version at run time to determine which version of your application to install.

- Create projects for both 16- and 32-bit operating systems.

Using the Setup Wizard

Ordinarily, you can use the Setup Wizard shipped with Visual Basic to create distribution disks for your application. The Setup Wizard takes care of these installation tasks:

■ Determining the files your application requires. This includes support .DLLs, .OCXs, and (of course) your .EXE.

■ Compressing and copying those files to distribution disks.

■ Creating an installation program to install those files correctly on the user's system. This includes comparing the version of existing files found on the user's system to files found on the distribution disks.

OLE container applications have additional requirements, however. To correctly install an OLE container application, you may add the following tasks to the installation process:

■ Register your application in the system registration database.

■ Check the user's system for required OLE applications.

Updating the System Registry

The .LST file generated by the Setup Wizard contains information about how to register each file it installed. A typical entry in the .LST file looks like this:

```
File1=2,,COMDLG16.OC_,COMDLG16.OCX,$(WinSysPath), _
    $(DLLSelfRegister),8/23/94,69904,4.0.12.10
```

The sixth argument, $(DLLSelfRegister), indicates what action the Setup program takes when registering the file. Possible values for the sixth argument are as follows:

Value	Meaning
None	File is not registered.
$(DLLSelfRegister)	Use the DllSelfRegister function to register the file.
$(EXESelfRegister)	Use the ExeSelfRegister function to register the file.
filename	Use the Registry Editor (REGEDIT.EXE) to merge the file with the system registration database.

If your application uses an .REG file, be sure to edit the .LST file to register the application at setup. For example, the following lines copy the .REG file and register the OLESTORE application:

```
File3=2,,OLESTORE.RE_,OLESTORE.REG,$(APPPATH),,9/22/94,2364
File4=2,,OLESTORE.EX_,OLESTORE.EXE,$(APPPATH),OLESTORE.REG, _
    9/27/94,18192,1.0.0.0
```

Visual Basic applications that expose OLE Automation objects are automatically flagged as $(EXESelfRegister). If these applications provide an .REG file as well, save the registration information that Visual Basic creates into the application's .REG file, then use that file to register the application at setup.

Checking for Installed OLE Objects

Applications that rely on other applications for objects can be a nightmare to maintain. You should never assume that users have all the object applications required by your application. To check for installed OLE object applications, query the system registration database before you install your application.

The GetRegisteredList procedure (listing 16.1) returns an array containing the names of all the installed OLE applications from the target system's system registration database:

Listing 16.1   Checking for Installed OLE Objects

```
' 16LIST01.TXT
Const HKEY_CLASSES_ROOT = 1

#Const Win32 = 1

#If Win16 Then
Declare Function RegOpenKey Lib "Shell" _
    (ByVal HKeyIn As Long, ByVal LPCSTR As String, _
    HKeyOut As Long) As Long
Declare Function RegCloseKey Lib "Shell" _
    (ByVal HKeyIn As Long) As Long
Declare Function RegEnumKey Lib "Shell" _
    (ByVal HKeyIn As Long, ByVal SubKeyIn As Long, _
    ByVal KeyName As String, ByVal KeyNameLen As Long) As Long
Declare Function RegQueryValue Lib "Shell" _
    (ByVal HKeyIn As Long, ByVal SubKey As String, _
    ByVal KeyValue As String, KeyValueLen As Long) As Long
#ElseIf Win32 Then
Declare Function RegOpenKey Lib "Shell32" _
    (ByVal HKeyIn As Long, ByVal LPCSTR As String, _
    HKeyOut As Long) As Long
Declare Function RegCloseKey Lib "Shell32" _
    (ByVal HKeyIn As Long) As Long
Declare Function RegEnumKey Lib "Shell32" _
    (ByVal HKeyIn As Long, ByVal SubKeyIn As Long, _
    ByVal KeyName As String, ByVal KeyNameLen As Long) As Long
Declare Function RegQueryValue Lib "Shell32" _
    (ByVal HKeyIn As Long, ByVal SubKey As String, _
    ByVal KeyValue As String, KeyValueLen As Long) As Long
#End If
```

(continues)

II

Using OLE

Listing 16.1 Continued

```
Function GetRegisteredList() As Variant
    Dim hkroot As Long, x As Long, lLen As Long
    ReDim strInstalled(99) As String
    Dim strKeyID As String * 80, strKeyDesc As String * 80, _
        iKeyCount As Integer
    x = RegOpenKey(HKEY_CLASSES_ROOT, "", hkroot)
    lLen = 80
    Do
        strKeyID = String(lLen, 0)
        If RegEnumKey(hkroot, iKeyCount, strKeyID, lLen) = 0 Then
            lLen = 80
            If Mid(strKeyID, 1, 1) <> "." Then
                strKeyDesc = String(lLen, 0)
                x = RegQueryValue(hkroot, strKeyID, strKeyDesc, _
                                  lLen)
                strInstalled(iKeyCount) = strKeyDesc
                lLen = 80
            End If
            iKeyCount = iKeyCount + 1
            If iKeyCount > UBound(strInstalled) Then
                ' Add elements if the array gets full.
                ReDim Preserve strInstalled _
                    (UBound(strInstalled) + 100)
            End If
        Else
            Exit Do
        End If
    Loop
    ' Trim off excess array elements.
    ReDim Preserve strInstalled(iKeyCount)
    x = RegCloseKey(hkroot)
End Function
```

To verify that the OLE object applications you need are installed, search for the name of the required application in the array returned by GetRegisteredList. The CheckInstalled procedure (listing 16.2) checks a list of required applications against the list of installed applications.

Listing 16.2 The CheckInstalled Procedure

```
' 16LIST02.TXT
Function CheckInstalled(RequiredList, strNotFound As String) _
    As Variant
    Dim InstalledList As Variant
    Dim InstalledName, RequiredName
    Dim bFound As Boolean
```

```
        Dim AppName As String
        InstalledList = GetRegisteredList()
        For Each RequiredName In RequiredList
            For Each InstalledName In InstalledList
                If InStr(InstalledName, RequiredName) Then
                    bFound = True
                    Exit For
                End If
                bFound = False
            Next InstalledName
            ' Build list of application that weren't found.
            If bFound = False Then
                strNotFound = strNotFound & ", " & RequiredName
            End If
        Next RequiredName
        If Len(strNotFound) Then
            strNotFound = Right(strNotFound, Len(strNotFound) - 2)
            CheckInstalled = False
        Else
            CheckInstalled = True
            strNotFound = ""
        End If
    End Function
```

The following Main procedure shows how to use the GetRegisteredList and CheckInstalled procedures together:

```
Sub Main()
    Dim strNotFound As String
    Dim bWorked As Boolean
    bWorked = CheckInstalled(Array("Microsoft Excel", _
        "Microsoft Word"), strNotFound)
    If bWorked Then
        ' All required applications available — continue.
    Else
        MsgBox "The following required applications & _
                were not found: " & strNotFound
    End If
End Sub
```

Determining Required Files

Depending on the size and complexity of your application, it is quite possible that the Visual Basic support files you must distribute are several times the size of your actual .EXE on disk. Usually, these files are already found on the user's system. However, you must always distribute these files along with your .EXE in case your user's files are out of date or not already installed.

OLE container applications require the following files:

Required by	File Name	Description
Visual Basic	VB40016.DLL	Visual Basic run-time library.
	VB40032.DLL	
	VB4EN16.DLL	Visual Basic English-language
	VB4EN32.DLL	object library. This file name will be different for other national languages.
	SCP.DLL	Code page translation library.
	SCP32.DLL	
OLE	DDEML.DLL	Dynamic data exchange manager.
	COMPOBJ.DLL	OLE support for component objects.
	OLE2.DLL	General OLE functions.
	OLE2.REG	Registration file for OLE.
	OLE2CONV.DLL	Supports converting OLE data types.
	OLE2DISP.DLL	Supports OLE Automation.
	OLE2NLS.DLL	Supports OLE national language support and localization features.
	OLE2PROX.DLL	Supports cross-process invocations.
	STDOLE.TLB	The OLE object library.
	STORAGE.DLL	Supports creating OLE compound documents.
	TYPELIB.DLL	Supports access and creation of object libraries.
Setup Toolkit	SETUP.EXE	Bootstrap setup program. Decompresses the Visual Basic run-time and support files, and launches the Setup1 or Setup132 program.
	SETUP.LST	Listing of files to install.
	SETUP1.EXE	Setup program that installs files.
	SETUPKIT.DLL	Support functions for Setup Wizard and Setup Toolkit.
	VER.DLL	Checks file versions during installation.
	VSHARE.386	Permits file sharing under Windows.
Custom controls	??????16.OCX	As used by your application.
	??????32.OCX	
	OC25.DLL	Run-time DLL for OLE custom controls (.OCX).

Using Other Setup Tools

Because of the difficulties customizing the disk layout or installation procedure generated by the Setup Wizard, you may choose to use other installation tools, such as PKZIP—a popular shareware program from PKWARE, Inc. in Brown Deer, WI. If you are using these other setup tools, or creating your own, be sure to perform the following tasks before copying any of the Visual Basic run-time or OLE support files to users' systems:

- Compare file version numbers and only copy later versions. This is particularly important with the OLE files.

- Register required files in the system registration database.

Comparing File Versions

The VER.DLL (16-bit) and VERSION.DLL (32-bit) support files included in the Setup Toolkit provide functions for comparing file version information. The file COMMON.BAS in the Setup Toolkit provides declarations for the functions in these two .DLLs and demonstrates how to use those functions to compare file versions. Table 16.1 lists the functions you use when comparing file versions.

Table 16.1 Version-Comparison Functions in VER.DLL and VERSION.DLL

Procedure	Found in	Use to
GetFileVersionInfo	VER.DLL (16-bit) VERSION.DLL (32-bit) COMMON.BAS (declared)	Retrieve version information from a file.
GetFileVersionInfoSize	VER.DLL (16-bit) VERSION.DLL (32-bit) COMMON.BAS (declared)	Get the size of the version information to retrieve (required to allocate a string to receive the version information).
lmemcpy	SETUP.DLL (16-bit) STPKIT32.DLL (32-bit) COMMON.BAS (declared)	Copy information retrieved by VerQueryValue into a Visual Basic variable.
VerQueryValue	VER.DLL (16-bit) VERSION.DLL (32-bit) COMMON.BAS (declared)	Extract an item of information out of the version information retrieved by GetFileVersionInfo.
VerFindFile	VER.DLL (16-bit) VERSION.DLL (32-bit)	Locate a file on the user's system before installing.
VerInstallFile	VER.DLL (16-bit) VERSION.DLL (32-bit) COMMON.BAS (declared)	Attempt to install a file based on provided file version information.

The VerFindFile and VerInstallFile are the two main functions you use to install files from distribution disks to a target system. Listing 16.3 shows the declarations and constant values used for VerFindFile and VerInstallFile.

Listing 16.3   Declarations for VerFindFile and VerInstallFile

```
' 16LIST03.TXT
#Const Win32 = 1

#If Win16 Then
Declare Function VerInstallFile Lib "VER.DLL" _
    (ByVal Flags As Integer, _
    ByVal SrcName As String, _
    ByVal DestName As String, _
    ByVal SrcDir As String, _
    ByVal DestDir As String, _
    ByVal CurrDir As Any, _
    ByVal TmpName As String, _
    iTempLen As Integer) As Long
Declare Function VerFindFile Lib "VER.DLL" _
    (ByVal iFlags As Integer, _
    ByVal strFileName As String, _
    ByVal strWinDirectory As String, _
    ByVal strAppDir As String, _
    ByVal strCurDir As String, _
    iCurDirLen As Integer, _
    ByVal strDestDir As String, _
    iDestDirLen As Integer) _
    As Integer
#ElseIf Win32 Then
Declare Function VerInstallFile Lib "VERSION.DLL" _
    (ByVal Flags As Integer, _
    ByVal SrcName As String, _
    ByVal DestName As String, _
    ByVal SrcDir As String, _
    ByVal DestDir As String, _
    ByVal CurrDir As Any, _
    ByVal TmpName As String, _
    iTempLen As Integer) As Long
Declare Function VerFindFile Lib "VERSION.DLL" _
    (ByVal iFlags As Integer, _
    ByVal strFileName As String, _
    ByVal strWinDirectory As String, _
    ByVal strAppDir As String, _
    ByVal strCurDir As String, _
    iCurDirLen As Integer, _
    ByVal strDestDir As String, _
    iDestDirLen As Integer) _
    As Integer
#End If

' VerFind flag (only one).
Const VFFF_ISSHAREDFILE = 1
```

```
' VerFindFile error return codes.
Const VFF_CURNEDEST = 1
Const VFF_FILEINUSE = 2
Const VFF_BUFFTOOSMALL = 4

' VerInstallFile flags.
Const VIFF_FORCEINSTALL% = &h1
Const VIF_TEMPFILE& = &h1
' VerInstallFile error return codes.
Const VIF_SRCOLD& = &h4
Const VIF_DIFFLANG& = &h8
Const VIF_DIFFCODEPG& = &h10
Const VIF_DIFFTYPE& = &h20
Const VIF_WRITEPROT& = &h40
Const VIF_FILEINUSE& = &h80
Const VIF_OUTOFSPACE& = &h100
Const VIF_ACCESSVIOLATION& = &h200
Const VIF_SHARINGVIOLATION = &h400
Const VIF_CANNOTCREATE = &h800
Const VIF_CANNOTDELETE = &h1000
Const VIF_CANNOTRENAME = &h2000
Const VIF_OUTOFMEMORY = &h8000
Const VIF_CANNOTREADSRC = &h10000
Const VIF_CANNOTREADDST = &h20000
Const VIF_BUFFTOOSMALL = &h40000
```

The `InstallFile` procedure in listing 16.3 demonstrates how to use `VerFindFile` and `VerInstallFile` during setup. First, `VerFindFile` checks the user's system for the file to install. If the file is not found, `InstallFile` copies the file to the destination directory using `VerInstallFile`. If the file is found, then `VerInstallFile` compares the file's version numbers, preserving the more up-to-date file.

Listing 16.4   Using `VerFindFile` and `VerInstallFile`

```
' 16LIST04.TXT
Sub InstallFile(strSrcFile, strSrcDir, strDestFile, strDestDir)
    Dim strWinDir As String, strCurDir As String, _
        strAppDir As String, strTmpFile As String
    Dim iWorked As Integer, iLen As Integer
    Dim lWorked As Long
    strSrcDir = "b:\"
    strWinDir = GetWinDir
    strAppDir = "c:\olestore"
    strCurDir = CurDir$
    strDestDir = Space(144)
    iLen = Len(strDestDir)
    iWorked = VerFindFile(VFFF_ISSHAREDFILE, strDestFile, _
        strWinDir, strAppDir, strCurDir, Len(strCurDir), _
        strDestDir, iLen)
```

(continues)

II

Using OLE

Listing 16.4   Continued

```
Select Case iWorked
        ' File not found, so OK to install.
        Case VFF_CURNEDEST
            ' Install file (0& indicates no pre-existing file)
            lWorked = VerInstallFile(0, _
                strSrcFile, _
                strDestFile, _
                strSrcDir, _
                strDestDir, _
                0&, _
                strTmpFile, _
                iLen)
        ' File is locked and can't be overwritten.
        Case VFF_FILEINUSE
            GoTo errInstallFile
        ' Destination directory string not big enough.
        Case VFF_BUFFTOOSMALL
            GoTo errInstallFile
        ' File was found, so compare versions.
        Case Else
            If iLen Then
                strTmpFile = Space(144)
                iLen = Len(strTmpFile)
                lWorked = VerInstallFile(0, _
                    strSrcFile, _
                    strDestFile, _
                    strSrcDir, _
                    strDestDir, _
                    strDestDir, _
                    strTmpFile, _
                    iLen)
                If lWorked And VIF_SRCOLD Then
                'Source file was older, not copied
                ElseIf lWorked And (VIF_DIFFLANG Or _
                        VIF_DIFFCODEPG Or VIF_DIFFTYPE) Then
                ' Retry and force installation.
                ' May want to prompt here in your code...
                    lWorked = VerInstallFile(VIFF_FORCEINSTALL, _
                        strSrcFile, _
                        strDestFile, _
                        strSrcDir, _
                        strDestDir, _
                        strDestDir, _
                        strTmpFile, _
                        iLen)
                Else
                    GoTo errFileInstall
                End If
        End Select
        Exit Sub
errInstallFile:
        ' Error handler for installation errors.
        ' These lines left in template form
```

```
        ' for the sake of brevity here.
        ' VerFindFile errors.
        If iWorked = VF_FILEINUSE Then
            ' Notify user to close application.
        Else
            ' Internal problem (buffer too small).
         Debug.Print "buffer too small"
        End If
        ' VerInstallFile errors.
        If lWorked And VIF_WRITEPROT Then
        ElseIf lWorked And VIF_FILEINUSE Then
        ElseIf lWorked And VIF_OUTOFSPACE Then
        ElseIf lWorked And VIF_ACCESSVIOLATION Then
        ElseIf lWorked And VIF_SHARINGVIOLATION Then
        ElseIf lWorked And VIF_OUTOFMEMORY Then
        Else
            ' For these cases, report the error
            ' and do not install the file
            If lWorked And VIF_CANNOTCREATE Then
            ElseIf lWorked And VIF_CANNOTDELETE Then
            ElseIf lWorked And VIF_CANNOTRENAME Then
            ElseIf lWorked And VIF_CANNOTREADSRC Then
            ElseIf lWorked And VIF_CANNOTREADDST Then
            ElseIf lWorked And VIF_BUFFTOOSMALL Then
            End If
        End If
    End Sub
```

To use InstallFile to copy a file from your distribution disks to the user's system, call the procedure with source and destination arguments, as follows:

```
InstallFile "olestore.ex_", "b:\", "olestore.exe", "c:\olestore"
```

The VerInstallFile function automatically expands the file if it was compressed on the distribution disk.

The preceding procedure uses the GetWinDir utility function (listing 16.5). GetWinDir is a general-purpose function that simply returns the directory where Windows is installed.

Listing 16.5   The GetWinDir Utility Function

```
    ' 16LIST05.TXT
#Const Win32 = 1

#If Win16 Then
Declare Function GetWindowsDirectory Lib "Kernel" _
    (ByVal lpBuffer As String, _
    ByVal nSize As Integer) _
    As Integer
```

(continues)

II

Using OLE

Listing 16.5 Continued

```
#ElseIf Win32 Then
Declare Function GetWindowsDirectory Lib "Kernel32" _
    (ByVal lpBuffer As String, _
    ByVal nSize As Integer) _
    As Integer
#End If


' Returns the Windows directory.
Function GetWinDir() As String
    Dim strWinDirectory As String
    Dim iWorked As Integer
    ' Allocate space for the returned path string.
    strWinDirectory = Space(144)
    ' Get the Windows directory.
    iWorked = GetWindowsDirectory(strWinDirectory, _
    Len(strWinDirectory))
    ' Trim off the excess space.
    GetWinDir = Left(strWinDirectory, iWorked)
End Function
```

Registering Files

The SETUPKIT.DLL (16-bit) and STPKIT32.DLL (32-bit) support files included in the Setup Toolkit provide functions for registering files with the system registration database. Files may register themselves or provide an .REG file which should be merged with the system registration database.

Table 16.2 Registration Functions in SETUP.DLL and STPKIT32.DLL

Procedure	Found in	Use to
FSyncShell	COMMON.BAS	Start an application and wait for it to finish running.
DLLSelfRegister	SETUP.DLL (16-bit) STPKIT32.DLL (32-bit) COMMON.BAS (declared)	Merge registration information stored in a DLL into the system registration database.
ExeSelfRegister	SETUP.DLL (16-bit) STPKIT32.DLL (32-bit) COMMON.BAS (declared)	Merge registration information stored in an .EXE into the system registration database.
RegEdit	SETUP1.BAS	Merge registration information stored in an .REG file into the system registration database.

Creating Distribution Disks for 16- and 32-Bit Systems

When distributing applications on 16- and 32-bit platforms, you have three choices:

- Build and distribute only 16-bit applications. This simplifies development and distribution, but does not take advantage of the new 32-bit operating systems.

- Build both 16-bit and 32-bit applications, and distribute the applications on separate sets of disks. This reduces the number of disks you have to send out, but complicates the installation process for users.

- Build both 16-bit and 32-bit applications, and distribute them on one set of distribution disks. This adds to the total number of disks you need to distribute but it simplifies the installation procedure for users.

> **Note**
>
> The support files for each target system consume about 2M of disk space compressed. Dual-platform installation disks will use at least three disks for support files alone.

Creating Single-Platform Installation Disks

The Setup Wizard comes in 16- and 32-bit versions. Use the 16-bit version to create distribution disks for 16-bit target platforms; and use the 32-bit version to create disks for 32-bit platforms.

Creating Dual-Platform Installation Disks

The Setup Wizard does not directly support creating dual-platform installation disks. In order to create an installation system that automatically switches between 16- and 32-bit file lists, depending on the user's operating system, you need to perform these tasks.

- Modify the Setup Toolkit to test the user's operating system and use the file list that matches the user's operating system.

- Run the Setup Wizard on both the 16- and 32-bit systems and combine the results.

II

Using OLE

The problem with distributing 16- and 32-bit applications on the same disks is that the Setup Toolkit is written in Visual Basic and, therefore, requires the Visual Basic run-time and support .DLLs to be installed by SETUP.EXE before you can use Visual Basic code to determine which operating system is running.

You must install the 16-bit run-time and support files on 32-bit systems if you use the Setup Toolkit to create distribution disks that support both platforms. This cost—several megabytes of disk space—may be enough to convince you to use two sets of installation disks. On the other hand, most of your 32-bit target systems may already have the 16-bit Visual Basic run-time and support files installed, so this issue may be moot.

Testing the User's Operating System during Setup

In the SETUP1.VBP project, make these modifications:

1. In the file COMMON.BAS, change the constant `gstrFILE_SETUP$` to a `Public` variable, as follows:

   ```
   ' Old declaration.
   ' Global Const gstrFILE_SETUP$ = "SETUP.LST
   ' New declaration.
   Public gstrFILE_SETUP$
   ```

2. In the file SETUP1.FRM, add a call to the `CheckOperatingSystem` procedure in the form's `Load` event procedure, as follows:

   ```
   Private Sub Form_Load()
    ' New line.
    CheckOperatingSystem
    ' Remaining lines omitted here...
   ```

3. Add a module to the project containing the `CheckOperatingSystem` procedure. `CheckOperatingSystem` and other support procedures are shown after this procedure.

4. Build the project in the 16-bit version of Visual Basic.

The `CheckOperatingSystem` procedure sets the setup file list to use, based on which operating system the target system is running:

```
Option Explicit
Declare Function GetVersion Lib "Kernel" () As Long

' Lauches the correct 16- or 32-bit Setup .EXE,
' depending on the user's operating system.
Sub CheckOperatingSystem()
    Dim lWinInfo As Long, strWinVer As String
    ' Retrieve Windows version information.
    lWinInfo = GetVersion()
    ' Parse the Windows version number from the returned
    ' Long integer value.
```

```
        strWinVer = LoByte(LoWord(lWinInfo)) & "." & _
            HiByte(LoWord(lWinInfo))
    ' Parse the DOS version number from the returned
    ' Long integer value (shown here for informational purposes
    ' -- not used).
    ' strDOSversion = HiByte(HiWord(lWinInfo)) & "." _
                    & LoByte(HiWord(lWinInfo))
    '
    ' If the version is less than 3.5 (Win NT 3.5)...
    If Val(strWinVer) < 3.5 Then
        gstrFILE_SETUP$ = "setup.lst"    ' Use the 16-bit list.
    Else                                 ' Otherwise,
        gstrFILE_SETUP$ = "setup32.lst" ' use the 32-bit list.
    End If
End Sub
```

The CheckOperatingSystem procedure uses four utility functions to parse version information from the long integer returned by the GetVersion API function. These utility functions are also useful for parsing flags—in fact, the Windows header file (WINDOWS.H) defines C macros with equivalent names.

```
Function HiWord(lArg)
    If lArg > &H7FFFFFFF Then
        HiWord = (lArg And &HFFFF0000) \ &H10000
    Else
        HiWord = ((lArg And &HFFFF0000) \ &H10000) Xor &HFFFF0000
    End If
End Function

Function HiByte(iArg)
    HiByte = (iArg And &HFF00) \ &H100
End Function

Function LoWord(lArg)
    LoWord = lArg And (lArg Xor &HFFFF0000)
End Function

Function LoByte(iArg)
    LoByte = iArg Xor (iArg And &HFF00)
End Function
```

Building the 16- and 32-Bit Distribution Disks

To create the distribution disks for both 16- and 32-bit platforms, follow these steps:

1. Run the 16-bit Setup Wizard for your 16-bit application, and in step 5 of the Wizard, add all of the files used by your 32-bit application (including the Visual Basic 32-bit run-time and support files).

2. Create the distribution disks.

3. Copy the generated SETUP.LST file back to your hard disk.

4. Copy the SETUP.LST file again to the new file name SETUP32.LST.

5. Edit both files, removing the 32-bit application files from SETUP.LST and removing the 16-bit application files from SETUP32.LST. Data files that are common to both installation procedures should appear on both files.

6. Copy both .LST files back to Disk 1 of your distribution disks. You may need to move another file from Disk 1 to another disk in order to create enough space for both .LST files—be sure to edit the appropriate .LST file to accommodate this change (if necessary).

Programming OLE for 16-Bit and 32-Bit Platforms

Visual Basic can create applications that run under the Windows 3.1 (16-bit) operating system, Windows NT 3.5 (32-bit) operating system, or Windows 95 (32-bit) operating system. Visual Basic itself comes in two versions: 16-bit and 32-bit.

For the most part, the same Visual Basic code will compile and run in either version of Visual Basic. However, you must use the appropriate version of Visual Basic for the operating system you are using (16- or 32-bit). You can't run Visual Basic 16-bit under Windows 95, or Visual Basic 32-bit under Windows 3.1. Table 16.3 shows the compatibility between Visual Basic and widely installed Windows operating systems.

Table 16.3	Visual Basic Windows Operating System Compatibility		
Item	**Runs under This Operating System**		
	Windows 3.1	**Windows NT 3.1/3.5**	**Windows NT 3.51**	**Windows 95**
---	---	---	---	---
Visual Basic 16-bit development environment	Y	N	Y	Y
Visual Basic 32-bit development environment	N	N	Y	Y
Visual Basic 16-bit applications	Y	Y	Y	Y
Visual Basic 32-bit applications	N	N	Y	Y

As table 16.3 shows, you can run 16-bit applications created with Visual Basic on some 32-bit platforms. However, you can't run 32-bit applications on any 16-bit platform.

Sharing Code between 16- and 32-Bit .EXEs

To create a 16-bit application in Visual Basic, you must use the 16-bit version of the Visual Basic development environment. Similarly, you must use the 32-bit development environment to create 32-bit .EXEs. You can use the same project (.VPJ) and source files on both platforms, with the exceptions shown in table 16.4.

Table 16.4 Compatibility Problems and Solutions When Sharing Visual Basic Code between 16- and 32-Bit Platforms	
Problem	**Solution**
Old-style custom controls (.VBX) are not supported in Visual Basic 32-bit. Resource files (.RES) are 16-bit and 32-bit specific.	Use OLE custom controls (.OCX). Create duplicate 16- and 32-bit resource files and separate project files for 16- and 32-bit.
Windows API library names and function names may be different between operating systems.	Use the Alias keyword and/or conditional compilation when declaring Windows API functions.
The API function names are case-sensitive on 32-bit systems; they are case-insensitive on 16-bit systems.	Use the Alias keyword when declaring Windows API functions.
Window handles (hWnd) are the Integer data type in 16-bit operating systems and the Long data type in 32-bit systems.	Use conditional compilation statements for all API functions that take hWnd arguments or return hWnd values.
Compiled support file names (.OCX, .DLL, .EXE) are usually different between 16-bit and 32-bit systems. Support files usually embed "16" or "32" in their names to identify their target operating system.	Create separate .VPJ files for 16- and 32-bit and use conditional compilation statements when declaring API functions in DLLs. Create separate 16- and 32-bit Setup disks when distributing applications.
You cannot use the Visual Basic StrConv function in 32-bit Visual Basic. Therefore, you can't access Unicode text strings in data files.	Use only ANSI data files when doing file I/O in code.

II

Using OLE

Calling between 16- and 32-Bit Executables

When using OLE objects in Visual Basic, you may not know whether the application providing the object is a 16- or 32-bit executable. The OLE DLLs support calling between 16- and 32-bit executables any which-way. However, you need to be aware of conversions that may occur as a result.

Container (.EXE)	Object (.EXE)	Automatic OLE Conversion
16-bit	16-bit	None. All strings are ANSI.
16-bit	32-bit	Call: ANSI strings converted to Unicode. Return: Unicode strings converted to ANSI
32-bit	16-bit	Call: Unicode strings converted to ANSI. Return: ANSI strings converted to Unicode.
32-bit	32-bit	None. All strings are Unicode.

Calling between 16- and 32-Bit DLLs

When using OLE objects that are contained in DLLs, a Visual Basic application uses the DLL that matches the mode that the application was compiled in. Sixteen-bit applications use only 16-bit OLE object DLLs; and 32-bit applications use only 32-bit OLE object DLLs.

All Windows DLLs (16- or 32-bit) use ANSI character strings. Visual Basic 32-bit uses Unicode strings internally, but uses ANSI characters when passing or receiving strings from API functions declared in code. If you are using the 32-bit version of Visual Basic, Visual Basic automatically converts arguments to ANSI from Unicode and returns values to Unicode from ANSI.

Container (.EXE)	DLL	Automatic Conversion
16-bit	API 16-bit	None. All strings are ANSI.
16-bit	OLE 16-bit	None. All strings are ANSI.
32-bit	API 32-bit	Call: Arguments converted from Unicode to ANSI. Return: Arguments converted from ANSI to Unicode.
32-bit	OLE 32-bit	None. All strings are Unicode.

From Here...

For more information on related topics, see Chapter 23, "Building and Distributing OLE Objects," which explains how to install OLE server applications.

II

Using OLE

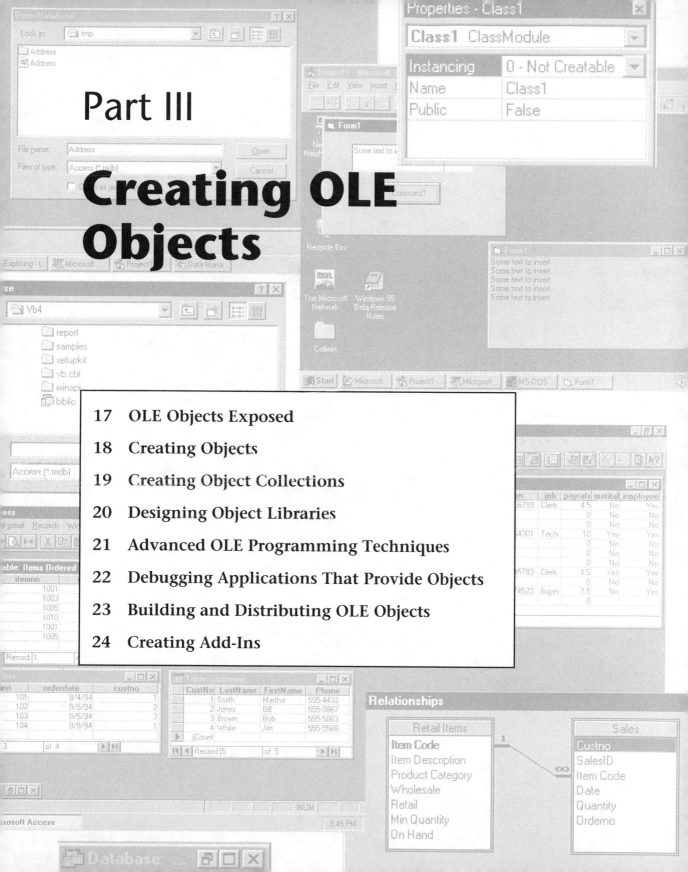

Part III

Creating OLE Objects

Chapter 17

OLE Objects Exposed

A programming language provides a way to accomplish tasks and also a structure for thinking about the tasks that you can accomplish. Visual Basic's new object-oriented language features change the way that you think about what you can accomplish. Not only are the new horizons broader, the landscape is fundamentally different.

This chapter introduces you to object-oriented programming with Visual Basic and readies your thinking for brave new vistas.

In this chapter, you learn about the following:

- How to analyze a programming problem in terms of objects rather than procedures

- How to use objects to solve problems with global data

- How to create and destroy instances of objects

- General rules for programming with objects

- The types of applications that you can create with objects

- The differences between object libraries and dynamic linking libraries (DLLs)

- What you need to create OLE Automation objects and what you *can't* create in Visual Basic

- How to plan an application that uses objects

- How to map the initialization and destruction of objects

- How to determine the methods and procedures that you must create for an object

> **Note**
>
> Visual Basic Standard Edition prevents you from creating `Public` class modules. Therefore, objects that you create with the Standard Edition are available only inside the application in which you define them. To create applications that share objects *across* applications, you need the Professional Edition or Enterprise Edition. The Enterprise edition also enables you to create objects that can be used remotely across the network.

Thinking about Objects

A well-designed object is like a black box; it handles a particular task without exposing the solution's details. The advantage of using "black boxes" is that you can stack an infinite number of them without worrying that some internal quirk within one of them will cause the whole stack to tumble.

The quirks that destabilize large applications are almost always related to global variables. The problem occurs when two unrelated procedures inadvertently use the same variable name for different purposes. If the variable is local to the procedure, no problem occurs. But if the variable is global to the application, you can get completely unpredictable results. This problem is fairly specific to large applications, simply because smaller applications have fewer variables. The fewer variables, the less likely they are to collide.

You have a better chance of avoiding problems with global variables if you observe rigorous variable-naming conventions. Some organizations even have personnel whose sole job is to allocate variable and procedure names. (Although their job may sound trivial, these people are actually quite powerful within their organizations; if you get on their wrong side, you'll be prefixing all your variable names with `ImSoSorry`.)

Visual Basic 4.0 enables you to keep sensitive variables and procedures inside a black box called an *object*. Objects are more than just another level of scope—they are a programming structure that provides a new form of containment, as shown in figure 17.1.

Objects protect procedures and variables through their instances. Calling procedures must get an instance of the object from another procedure or create a new instance of the object themselves to have access to items in the object. Each instance of an object provides its own private storage, which other instances of the same object do not affect.

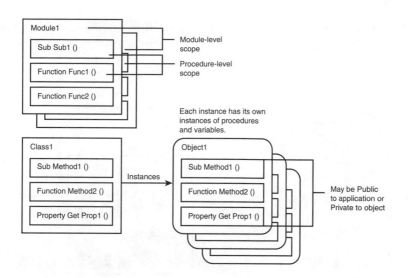

Fig. 17.1
Visual Basic adds objects to its traditional programming structures.

Objects also benefit programmers by molding the design process around things rather than processes. Windows applications tend to promote nonlinear user interaction. Object-oriented design focuses on creating self-contained objects that manage nonlinear tasks better than applications that you create using structured programming techniques, as shown in figure 17.2.

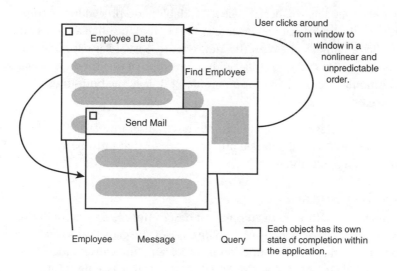

Fig. 17.2
Object-oriented programming focuses on "what" rather than "how."

III

Creating OLE Objects

Objects in Visual Basic

For most Visual Basic programmers, forms are the best visible example of objects. Each form has a definition that the programmer creates at design time and stores in a form module (.FRM). At run time, Visual Basic creates an *instance* of the form, and that instance has predefined methods and properties. Methods and properties always apply to a single instance of the form, as shown in figure 17.3.

Fig. 17.3
The Move method applies to a single instance of a form, no matter how many instances of the same form exist.

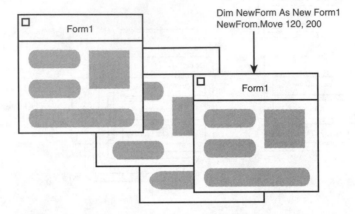

Until Visual Basic 4.0, forms were *not* considered full objects, because you couldn't add methods or properties to them. All data and procedures in a form module were local to that form—you had to use global variables or built-in Form properties to get data in or out of a form.

Visual Basic 4.0 lets you declare Public variables and procedures within a form module. Items that you declare as Public look just like a form's built-in properties and methods. With this new feature, Visual Basic forms are now true objects. Visual Basic 4.0 also adds a new type of file, the *class module*. Class modules are similar to form modules, but lack the built-in user interface.

Use form modules to define objects that have a user interface. Use class modules to define objects that lack a user interface or that must be available outside of an application.

Creating Instances

You create the definition of an object at design time as a form module or a class module. The actual object is an *instance* of the class that Visual Basic creates at run time. This distinction is important, and causes much confusion among people learning object-oriented programming (see fig. 17.4).

Another important detail is that form modules are self-instantiating, but class modules are not. In other words, Visual Basic automatically creates an instance of a form when you refer to the form's properties or methods in code.

You've probably run into this as a bug in your code—inadvertently referencing a form's `Visible` property loads the form invisibly, as shown in figure 17.5.

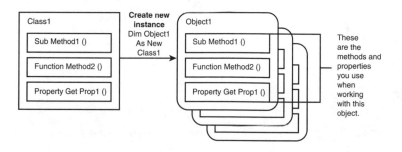

Fig. 17.4
A *class* defines an object; an *object* is an instance of a class.

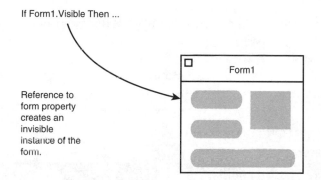

Fig. 17.5
Referring to a form property automatically creates a "ghost" instance of the form.

This self-instantiation doesn't happen with class modules. To create an instance of a class module, You must use the `New` keyword in a declaration as shown in figure 17.6.

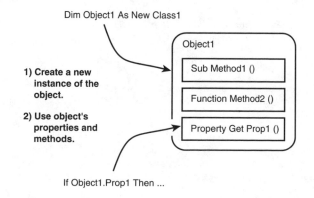

Fig. 17.6
You must declare a variable as a `New` class to create an object from a class module.

III

Creating OLE Objects

Destroying Instances

Objects that you create from form modules exist until you call the Unload statement on the form. Objects that you create from class modules exist as long as one or more variables refer to the object. Visual Basic objects follow the same reference-counting conventions as all OLE objects:

- Each new variable reference to an object adds one to the reference count.

- Each time that a referencing object variable is set to Nothing or loses scope, the object's reference count deincrements by one.

- When the object's reference count equals zero, Visual Basic destroys the object.

Listing 17.1 demonstrates reference counting. When Proc1 runs, Visual Basic creates a new object based on the Class1 class module (references = 1). At the end, Proc1 sets the vModule module-level variable to refer to the new object (references = 2). When clsProcedure loses scope, Visual Basic does not destroy the object (references = 1). Later, Proc2 shows that the object still exists by displaying its IExist property. Setting vModule to Nothing finally destroys the object (references = 0).

Listing 17.1   A Demonstration of Reference Counting

```
' Declare a module-level
' generic variable.
Dim vModule As Variant

Private Sub Proc1()
    ' Create a new instance of an object
    ' (references = 1).
    Dim clsProcedure As New Class1
    ' Set a property in the object.
    clsProcedure.IExist = True
    ' Establish another reference
    ' to the object (references = 2).
    Set vModule = clsProcedure
    ' clsProcedure loses scope.
    ' (references = 1).
End Sub

Private Sub Proc2()
    ' Displays True -- object still exists!
    MsgBox vModule.IExist
    ' Destroy object (references = 0).
    vModule.IExist = Nothing
End Sub
```

Creating and Destroying Objects That Display Forms

An object that displays forms or controls does not automatically unload those forms or controls when Visual Basic destroys the object. If you hide a form or control, you can create a "lost reference" that stays around as long as the application is running—consuming memory and resources. Figure 17.7 shows the flow of control that can create a lost reference to a loaded form.

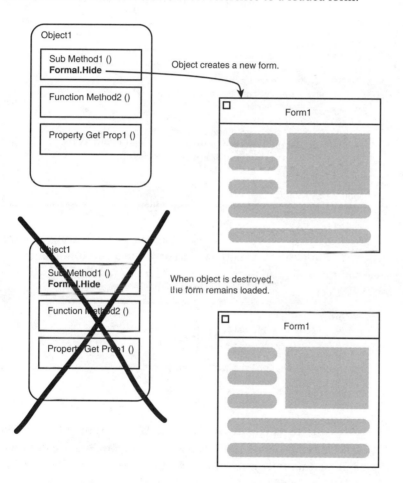

Fig. 17.7
Object1 creates a new, hidden Form1. After Object1 loses scope, Form1 remains in memory.

Classes that create forms or controls should use the class module Initialize and Terminate events to create and delete those objects. Listing 17.2 shows the Initialize and Terminate event procedures for a simple class that displays a form. The Initialize event procedure creates a new instance of a form. The Terminate method unloads the form and sets the newForm variable to Nothing.

III

Creating OLE Objects

Listing 17.2   **The** `Initialize` **and** `Terminate` **Event Procedures for a Simple Class**

```
' Module-level variable.
Private newForm

Public Function Class_Initialize()
    ' Create a new instance of a form.
    Set newForm = New Form1
    ' Display the new form.
    newForm.Show
End Function

Public Sub Class_Terminate()
    ' Destroy the instance of the form
    ' created by Create.
    Unload newForm
    ' Invalidate the reference to the form
    ' This prevents other class members from
    ' reinstantiating the form without going
    ' through Initialize.
    Set newForm = Nothing
End Sub
```

The following code creates and then deletes a new object by using the preceding methods. Although `Delete` correctly unloads the form from memory, you still must set the object variable to `Nothing` or let the variable lose scope to destroy the object.

```
Sub Main()
    ' Create the new object and establish
    ' a reference to is.
    Dim objForm As New Class1
    ' Destroy the object (or simply let the
    ' variable lose scope -- same effect).
    Set objForm = Nothing
End Sub
```

The `Initialize` and `Terminate` events in listing 17.2 are similar to C++ constructor and destructor functions. However, C++ constructor and destructor functions can take arguments to initialize data in the object. The Visual Basic `Initialize` and `Terminate` events do not take arguments; you must initialize data by using methods and properties that you define in the class or form module.

Rules of Thumb

Objects in themselves don't solve any of your programming problems. For objects to be helpful, you must observe some general rules. Because programming is a subjective and creative process, the rules aren't absolute or immutable. They give you a starting point from which you can work to develop your own style and preferences.

The following two rules of thumb are adapted from *The C++ Programming Language* by Bjarne Stroustrup, the father of object-oriented programming. The following adaptation modifies some rules to use terms familiar to Visual Basic programmers, and others have been changed or omitted because of limitations in Visual Basic's approach to objects (Visual Basic is not yet fully object-oriented):

- Use classes to represent the concrete aspects of your application in the following circumstances:

    If you can think of the aspect as a separate idea, make it a class.

    If you can think of the aspect as a separate entity within a class, create a separate class for the entity.

    If two classes have something in common, define a separate class for those common items.

- Restrict access to variables and procedures as much as possible:

    Avoid Public variables in code modules (global variables).

    Avoid Public procedures in code modules (global procedures).

    Don't access Public variables in another class directly. Instead, use the class's Property procedures to get and set values.

The Future of Visual Basic Objects

The previous section mentioned that Visual Basic is not yet fully object-oriented. That isn't an excuse for C++ or SmallTalk programmers to dismiss the language; Visual Basic is still the most productive tool for creating Windows programs. The limitations bear mentioning, however, because they are the language features that you can expect Microsoft to add in future releases:

- *Inheritance.* Currently, Visual Basic doesn't enable you to derive new classes from base classes. You must redefine common methods and properties within each class. Also, you can't base classes on objects with built-in capabilities, such as forms. However, you can control forms and other objects from within a class.

- *Default members.* Forms, controls, and most OLE Automation objects have default properties or methods. For instance, Text1.Text = "Some text" is the same as Text1 = "Some text". You can't define such behavior in a Visual Basic class.

■ *Friend properties and methods.* Classes and their members are either Public or Private; currently you cannot share some properties and methods in a Public class with just a few other classes.

■ *Name overloading.* Visual Basic still reserves many keywords, such as Select and Print, which you can't use as method or property names in a class.

Applications That You Can Create with Objects

Applications that use objects can be large or small. They can be completely stand-alone or used as components in other applications. Table 17.1 lists the types of applications that you can create with Visual Basic's new object-oriented features.

Table 17.1   Types of Applications Creatable with Visual Basic 4.0's Object-Oriented Features

Type of Application	Example(s)	Chapter in Which Discussed
New general-purpose data types, such as extended Integer or recursive types.	TYPES.VBP, OUTLINE.VBP	21
OLE components for use in other applications as add-ins.	SYSTEM.VBP	18, 21
Stand-alone applications that provide services and data sharing to other applications.	CDPLAYER.VBP	17
Components to run in separate processes for performance reasons.	VBTERMINAL.VBP	18
Internal components used as a structuring technique within an application.	CDPLAYER.VBP, WINDOWS.VBP	17, 19

Type of Application	Example(s)	Chapter in Which Discussed
Extensions to the Visual Basic programming environment.	REGADDIN.VBP	24

OLE Automation and Object Libraries

Objects can be used internally in a single application or externally among multiple applications. Objects available for external use are sometimes called *OLE Automation objects*, because they are available through the OLE 2.0 Automation interfaces.

Applications that include one or more OLE Automation objects are called *object libraries*. Object libraries are similar to conventional dynamic link libraries (DLLs), except that object libraries provide their features through objects rather than functions. Also unlike DLLs, object libraries use the Visual Basic data types, not C-specific types like null-terminated strings and pointers.

To create internal or external objects, you use the same programming techniques. The settings of two class module properties determine whether an object is available to other applications: Instancing and Public. For this reason, most of the procedures and examples in this book apply equally well to internal and external objects.

OLE Automation Requirements

To create applications that multiple applications can use, you must use Visual Basic 4.0 Professional Edition. The Standard Edition does not enable you to create class modules that have their Public property set to True. Therefore, Standard Edition objects are visible only within the project that defines them.

The Standard Edition also doesn't let you create Visual Basic *add-ins,* which are OLE Automation objects that enable you to extend the Visual Basic programming system. For example, an add-in might provide templates and wizards for certain types of applications that are commonly created in Visual Basic. These objects contain some special methods for loading and registering the add-in in Visual Basic.

You can create internal objects using Visual Basic Standard Edition. To use any of the object samples in this book with existing Standard Edition projects, simply add the desired class, form, and code module files to the existing project.

What You Cannot Create

You *can't* create OLE objects that support in-place editing with Visual Basic. Visual Basic applications display information only in the context of forms, which are separate windows or dialog boxes in an application. You can use Visual Basic to insert text, graphics, and other OLE objects into documents in OLE container applications, however.

Planning an Application with Objects

The CD Player sample application (CDPLAYER.VBP) demonstrates how to build an application out of objects. Analyzing the task to be performed—playing an audio CD—yields three features that you can represent as objects:

- A CD player

- A CD disk or title

- Tracks on the CD title

In addition, the application has a user interface, or control panel, to the CD player. You can represent this interface or control panel as a form object. You can represent all these objects graphically as shown in figure 17.8.

Fig. 17.8
Your code can represent the physical aspects of a CD player as objects.

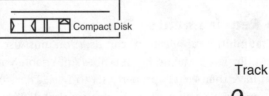

Mapping an application's initialization, termination, and interaction graphically, as shown in figures 17.9 and 17.10, is helpful when building applications with objects. As you sketch your application, don't worry about the

details of *how* you will do something; object-oriented design focuses on identifying *what* each object represents and which objects control other objects.

Mapping Object Initialization

A separate class or form module in Visual Basic defines each of the preceding
objects. Objects can create or destroy each other as events occur. When
CDPLAYER.VBP runs, the Application object creates ControlPanel and Title
objects. The Title object creates an instance of the Track object for each track
on the CD. Figure 17.9 shows the flow of initialization when CDPLAYER.VBP
starts.

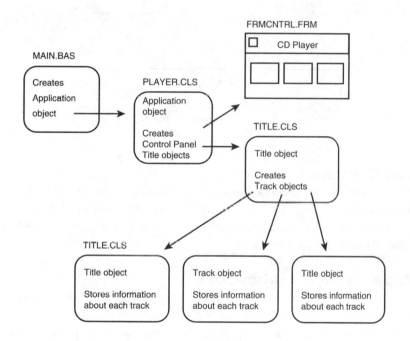

Fig. 17.9
The Application
class creates the
initial objects,
which in turn
create others.

Figure 17.9 indicates that the Application object and Title object both need
Initialize event procedures to create subordinate objects: the Application
object's Initialize event procedure creates the ControlPanel and Title objects; the Title object's Initialize event procedure creates a collection of
Track objects.

Mapping Object Termination

When CDPLAYER.VBP shuts down, the Title and Track objects lose scope
and are destroyed automatically. The Application object, however, must unload the ControlPanel object because it is a form and does not otherwise go
away. Figure 17.10 shows how the application destroys its objects when it
terminates.

III

Creating OLE Objects

Fig. 17.10
The Application object must unload the form before terminating; other objects are unloaded as they lose scope.

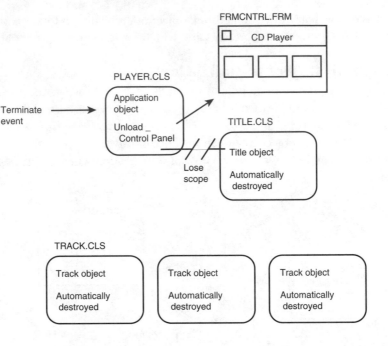

Figure 17.10 indicates that only the Application object needs a Terminate event procedure. The Application object's Terminate event procedure unloads the ControlPanel that it creates on initialization. Other objects don't require Terminate event procedures, because Visual Basic unloads them as they lose scope when the application ends.

Mapping Object Interaction

The CDPLAYER.VBP responds to events through its objects. The ControlPanel object receives all user events, because it is the only visible part of the application. The Application object responds to all programmatic requests through its Public methods and properties, as shown in figure 17.11.

These interactions help determine the various navigational properties and methods that you must create to move among objects. The next section discusses how you create these properties and methods.

Identifying Methods and Properties to Create

After mapping the objects in a cleanly organized way, you can identify the methods and properties for each class. The best way to do so is in two passes:

■ First list the navigational methods and properties. These are the items that create and track subordinate objects and forms. Navigational items also include standard items, like Application and Parent, that Microsoft recommends that you create for all Public classes.

■ Next list the functional methods and properties. These are the unique aspects that make the object useful within your application.

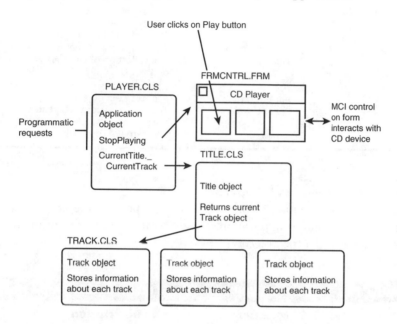

Fig. 17.11
User events go directly from the form to the device; OLE Automation requests go through the Application object.

Sometimes this process requires that you add or rename objects. The software design process is unavoidably iterative. (You hope that it doesn't become an infinite loop.)

Navigational Methods and Properties

Table 17.2 lists the navigational methods and properties for each class in the CDPLAYER.VBP sample application. The members in bold are unique to this application. The other members are standard navigational items that Microsoft recommends for all Public objects. The standard navigational items are especially useful when debugging an object application. For this reason, you should always include them, even though they are a little boring to cut and paste between classes.

Table 17.2 CDPLAYER.VBP's Navigational Methods and Properties

Object	Member	Return Value
Application	Application	Application object
	Parent	Application object
	Name	"CD Player"
	Title	Title object of the current CD
Title	Application	Application object
	Parent	Application object
	Name	The name of the CD
	CurrentTrack	The Track object that is playing
	Tracks	The collection of all Track objects on the CD
Track	Application	Application object
	Parent	The Title object that created the track
	Name	The name of the track

Functional Methods and Properties

Table 17.3 shows the functional methods and properties for each class in the CDPLAYER.VBP sample application. These are the methods and properties that do the work for the objects.

Table 17.3 CDPLAYER.VBP's Functional Methods and Properties

Object	Member	Description
Application	Play	Starts playing the CD
	PlayNext	Skips to the next track
	PlayPrevious	Skips to the previous track
	StopPlaying	Stops playing the CD
	Eject	Ejects the CD
	Quit	Exits the application
	Visible	Sets or returns the visible state of the application
	ElapsedTime	Returns the minutes and seconds that the CD has been playing
frmControlPanel	CurrentTitle	Keeps track of the name of the CD currently playing
	ElapsedMinutes	Returns the minutes that the CD has been playing
	ElapsedSeconds	Returns the seconds that the CD has been playing
	CurrentTrack	Returns the index of the track that currently is playing
	Tracks	Returns the number of tracks on the CD
	Track	Sets the tracks about which to get information

Object	Member	Description
	TrackPosition	Returns the start position of a track on the CD
	TrackLength	Returns the length of a track on the CD
	Command	Executes a string command on the MCI control
Title	None	Provides a way to organize tracks; doesn't contain functional members
Track	StartPosition	Returns the track's starting position on the CD
	Length	Returns the length of the track

The following are some interesting aspects of table 17.3:

- The frmControlPanel object is actually just a front end for the MCI custom control. The object's methods and properties simply repackage the MCI control's methods and properties, sometimes with a few changes to make them easier to use for playing CD audio.

- The Application object repackages the frmControlPanel members so that other applications can access them. Methods and properties in a form are Private to an application, but items in a class module can be Public.

- The Title object is simply a container for Track objects. Using one object to contain a collection of other objects is a common technique when working with objects. Title actually contains a private collection of Track objects that it returns with the Tracks method.

Creating an application using objects is a subjective, creative endeavor. In the CDPLAYER.VBP sample, you could have applied the Play method to the Title object just as well as to the Application object. By placing the method in the Application object, however, you make the syntax that you use from other applications a little simpler (Application.Play rather than Application.Title.Play).

CDPLAYER.VBP is not complete. Like all software, it awaits new features. Ideally, it should store CD titles and song names in a data file, then retrieve those names when the appropriate CD is loaded. It should also support play lists, shuffle, and other standard CD player features. Using objects and the framework provided, it's relatively easy to imagine many ways to enhance the sample application by providing all these features.

The challenge of object-oriented programming is to think in terms of objects rather than procedures. Whether you are creating a new PlayList object or serializing the Title object to a file, objects give you a new way to tackle programming problems.

In the words of Brian Kernighan, "The only way to learn a programming language is by writing programs in it." So let's get started!

From Here...

For more information on the following topics, see the following chapters:

- Chapter 18, "Creating Objects," explains how to begin programming with objects.

- Chapter 19, "Creating Object Collections," explains how to manage groups of objects within an application.

- Chapter 20, "Designing Object Libraries," describes design approaches that you need to consider when creating applications that provide objects to other applications.

- Chapter 22, "Debugging Applications That Provide Objects," gives you important insight into solving the many new problem areas that crop up as you program with objects.

Chapter 18
Creating Objects

Packaging your modules as objects with properties and methods is a natural way to expand Visual Basic's capabilities. You can create objects for use within a single project, or make those objects available to other applications through OLE Automation.

In this chapter, you learn how to do the following:

- Choose the correct type of module to use when creating an object

- Create OLE Automation objects to use across applications

- Use an OLE Automation object from another application

- Create objects to use within a single project

- Name objects meaningfully

- Create methods and read/write, read-only, and object properties

- Add OLE Automation objects to existing applications

- Extend Visual Basic's form properties

- Document your new objects, properties, and methods

- Avoid name conflicts with built-in Visual Basic keywords

> **Note**
>
> To create OLE Automation objects, you first must have Visual Basic Professional or Enterprise Edition. Although you can create objects with the Standard Edition, you can use those objects only within the current project.

Overview of Objects

With Visual Basic, you can create your own objects that have properties and methods. Each object is contained in a module, the name of which identifies the object. Visual Basic now has three types of modules: code modules, form modules, and class modules.

Code modules now support object-style syntax. For example, the following line calls the Average function in Module1:

```
x =  Module1.Average(98, 22, 45, 67, 876)
```

MODULE1.BAS defines the Average function as a procedure, as follows:

```
' MODULE1.BAS
' Average method, returns the average of a series of numbers.
' Note the use of the ParamArray argument -- this procedure takes
' any number of arguments.
Function Average(ParamArray x())
    ' Using each element in the array x()...
    For Each vCount In x
        ' Add the value to a running total.
        temp = temp + vCount
    Next vCount
    ' Return the average.
    Average = temp / (UBound(x) + 1)
End Function
```

Module1.Average's syntax looks just like that of an object reference, with one significant difference: instances. Code modules have one static instance that the application creates on startup. Form and class modules can have multiple instances with separate storage for each.

You can use objects within a single project, or across projects as OLE Automation objects. You use different types of modules to define different types of objects, as shown in table 18.1.

Table 18.1	Module Types and Their Uses	
Module Type	**Default Name**	**Use**
Code module	Module*n*	Defines procedures, variables, and constants for use within the current project. Code modules don't usually have a visual interface.
Form module	Form*n*	Defines a visible object for use within the current project.
Class module	Class*n*	Defines an object for use by the current application or other applications and projects. Class modules enable other applications to control the current application as an OLE Automation object.

Objects that you define in code modules and form modules are called *internal objects*, because you use them within the project in which you defined them. Objects that you define in class modules are called *OLE Automation objects*, because they are available to other projects and applications through OLE Automation.

Creating and Using OLE Automation Objects

Class modules are perhaps the most interesting type of module for creating objects, because they are available to other projects and applications through OLE Automation. Class modules enable you to create compiled libraries of code that you can use in the current project or other applications. Class modules have two properties not found in code and form modules:

- The `Instancing` property determines whether other applications can start the object's application by using the `CreateObject` or `GetObject` functions on the object. The property also determines whether multiple applications can use the application at the same time.

- The `Public` property determines whether other applications can view the object in the Object Browser. Even if the object is not `Public`, other applications can still use it—it simply is hidden from general view.

You set the `Instancing` and `Public` properties in the class module's Properties window, as shown in figure 18.1.

III

Creating OLE Objects

Fig. 18.1
Use the class module's Instancing and Public properties to make an object available to other applications.

Creating Your First OLE Automation Object

To create an OLE Automation object, follow these steps:

1. Create a new project.

2. Choose Insert, Class Module. Visual Basic adds a new class module to your project.

3. Create a simple method by adding the following lines of code to the class module:

```
Sub AddText(Text)
      Form1.Print Text
End Sub
```

4. Right-click on the class module window and choose Properties. You should change the Instancing property to Creatable SingleUser and the Public property to True.

5. Choose Tools, Options. In the Project tab of the Options dialog box, set Startmode to be OLE Server.

6. Choose File, Make EXE File. Visual Basic compiles the project.

7. From Windows, run the .EXE file that you just created. Running the file outside of Visual Basic registers the application with your system registration database to make it available to other applications.

Using the Object from Another Application

To use the OLE Automation object that you created in the preceding section, follow these steps:

1. Create a new project in Visual Basic.

2. Add a text box and a command button to Form1.

3. Add the following lines of code to the command button's Click event procedure:

```
Private Sub Command1_Click()
        Dim x As Object
         Set x = CreateObject("Project1.Class1")
         x.AddText Text1
End Sub
```

4. Press F5 to run the project in Visual Basic.

> **Note**
>
> If your OLE Automation object doesn't recognize methods and properties that you've just defined, check to ensure that you are running the right version of the object. When debugging, you can easily load the .EXE version accidentally rather than the new version that Visual Basic hasn't yet compiled. To avoid this, be sure to use GetObject in your container application and start the OLE Automation application in the other instance of Visual Basic *before* calling the object from the container application.

When you click the Command1 button on Form1, the CreateObject function starts the OLE Automation object application, PROJECT1.EXE, and returns a reference to the Class1 object. The AddText method then places the text in the Text1 text box on the OLE Automation object's form, as shown in figure 18.2.

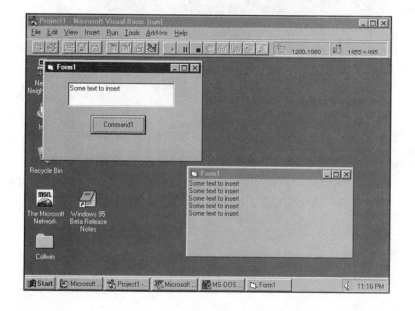

Fig. 18.2
Running the simple OLE Automation object from another application.

III

Creating OLE Objects

Finding the String That Works with *CreateObject* and *GetObject*

To identify OLE Automation objects to other applications, you use a string called a *programmatic identifier* or *ProgID*. The CreateObject and GetObject functions use this string to query the system registration database to find the application.

For OLE Automation objects, the programmatic identifier consists of the name that you enter in the Project Options dialog box's Project Name text box and the name of the class module that defines the object. Figure 18.3 shows this relationship.

Fig. 18.3
The string that you use with CreateObject and GetObject consists of the project name and the class module name.

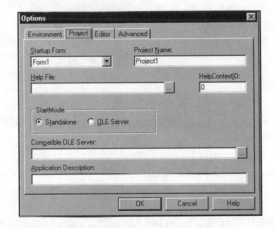

Visual Basic registers programmatic identifiers for all class modules that have their Instancing property set to Creatable Single Use or Creatable MultiUse. Therefore, a project with more than one creatable class has multiple entries in the registration database.

Visual Basic *doesn't* register applications permanently until you run the application outside of the programming environment. When you run the application within Visual Basic, it creates a registration entry in a temporary area that Visual Basic controls. Figure 18.4 shows the difference between permanent and temporary entries in the system registration database.

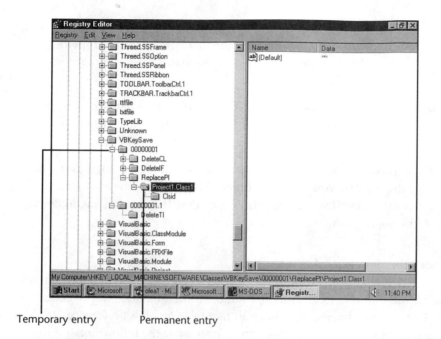

Temporary entry   Permanent entry

Fig. 18.4
Visual Basic adds a temporary registration entry when you debug an OLE Automation object. After you build the .EXE file and run the application, the entry becomes permanent.

Creating and Using Internal Objects

Objects defined in forms, procedures, and code modules are available only within the current project. Using a method from an internal object isn't any different from using a procedure defined in the module. The following code lines show alternative syntax for calling the Average() procedure in Module1:

```
' Object syntax: call Average as method.
MsgBox Module1.Average(12, 3, 4, 54)
' Old-style syntax: call Average as function.
MsgBox Average(12, 3, 4, 54)
```

Both object and old-style syntax display the same result. However, using object syntax gives you a few advantages over the old syntax:

■ Using the object syntax is explicit. You might store in different modules procedures with the same name. If so, calling the procedure without the module name results in an "Ambiguous name detected" error.

III

Creating OLE Objects

- You can use properties. Properties provide a convenient way to set and return internal variables that you use in a module. Also, properties, unlike global variables, enable you to validate values and perform actions when the values change.

- Properties and methods enable you to add features to a form. When you define properties and methods in a form module, new instances of the form also have those properties and methods.

- Objects help you organize your code into logical groupings. You don't really organize your code any differently—you can always organize modules logically—you simply now can use the object name to describe the logical grouping.

Code Modules versus Form Modules

Code modules aren't truly objects. However, objects defined in a form module are full-blown objects. Thus you can use form modules, but not code modules, in any statement or function that takes an object reference. Examples of such statements and functions include the following:

- `Dim`, `New`, `Public`, and `Private` declarations

- The `With...End With` flow-control statement

- The `TypeName` function

Another major difference is that forms have a built-in visual interface (the form) and modules don't. Use form modules for objects that have an appearance or that you need to use as objects with the preceding statements. Use code modules to perform general support tasks, such as mathematical operations.

Code and Form Modules versus Class Modules

Class modules provide the external interface that a project exposes to other applications. Code and form modules define the properties and methods used internally in the project. Without the class modules to act as the connection point, different programs could not communicate.

Naming Objects

You identify objects by their module name. By default, Visual Basic names modules based on their module type—Form1, Module1, Module2, Class1, and so on. Instead of relying on these default names, you should carefully choose descriptive names for your objects, just as you would for the procedures, variables, and other symbols in your project.

The object names that you choose should be as obvious as possible. For instance, an application that provides one OLE Automation object might name the object "Application." A project that uses many internal objects might have its own object-naming convention, using such prefixes as *mod*, *frm*, and *cls* to identify the type of object. Although naming objects is a subjective process, there are a few OLE conventions to follow. Chapter 20, "Designing Object Libraries," discusses OLE naming guidelines for objects.

To change the name of a module, follow these steps:

1. In the project window (fig. 18.5), double-click on the module that you want to rename. For form modules, Visual Basic displays the form. For code and class modules, Visual Basic displays the module's code windows.

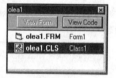

Fig. 18.5
Select the module to rename in the project window.

2. Press F4. Visual Basic displays the module's Properties window as shown in figure 18.6.

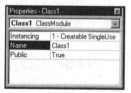

Fig. 18.6
Use the Properties window to rename a module.

3. Type the new module name in the Name property box.

Creating Methods and Properties

As mentioned previously, you can use module names when calling procedures in Visual Basic. For example, the following code line displays the result of the Average() function in Module1:

```
MsgBox Module1.Average(1, 12, 31, 44, 15)
```

This line is syntactically identical to the `Pmt` method in the Visual Basic for Applications (VBA) object library:

```
MsgBox VBA.Pmt(.07 / 12, 360, -70000, 0, True)
```

In fact, a module's `Sub` and `Function` procedures are equivalent to an object's methods. Like `Function` procedures, methods that return values enclose their arguments in parentheses, as in the preceding example. Like `Sub` procedures, methods that don't return values omit the parentheses. The following two lines demonstrate methods that don't return values:

```
Module1.Swap arg1, arg2
Form1.Move 1, 1, 90, 90
```

You use special `Property` procedures to create properties for an object. Table 18.2 describes the different types of procedures that you use when creating objects.

Table 18.2 Types of Procedures That Objects Use

Procedure Type	Use
Sub	Defines methods that don't return a value
Function	Defines methods that return a value
Property Get	Returns a property's value
Property Let	Assigns a property's value
Property Set	Sets the property to a reference to an object

Creating Read/Write Properties

Properties can have one or all three types of property procedures. Usually, properties have both a `Property Get` and `Property Let` procedure. Listing 18.1 shows a pair of property procedures that define the `NumLock` property:

Listing 18.1 Two Property Procedures That Define the `NumLock` Property

```
' Module Keyboard
' File: 18LIST01.TXT
' Declare Windows API calls used to get and set keyboard states.
Declare Sub GetKeyboardState Lib "USER32" (lpKeyState As Any)
Declare Sub SetKeyboardState Lib "USER32" (lpKeyState As Any)
```

```
' The index for the NumLock key in the 256-byte lpKeyState array.
Const VK_NUMLOCK = vbKeyNumLock

' Returns the state of the NumLock key: True = on, False = Off
Property Get NumLock() As Boolean
    ' Create an array to hold key states
    ' (256 bytes = 128 integers)
    Dim lpbKeyState(128) As Integer
    ' Get key state settings.
    GetKeyboardState lpbKeyState(0)
    ' Check the VK_NUMLOCK element of the array.
    If (lpbKeyState(VK_NUMLOCK / 2)) Then
        NumLock = True
    Else
        NumLock = False
    End If
End Property

' Changes the state of the NumLock key: True = on, False = off
Property Let NumLock(bState As Boolean)
    ' Create an array to hold key states
    ' (256 bytes = 128 integers)
    Dim lpbKeyState(128) As Integer
    ' Get key state settings.
    GetKeyboardState lpbKeyState(0)
    ' If the current state is the same as the bState,
    ' then no change needed.
    If lpbKeyState(VK_NUMLOCK / 2) And bState Then Exit Property
    ' Otherwise, set the correct value in the array.
    If bState Then
        lpbKeyState(VK_NUMLOCK / 2) = 1
    Else
        lpbKeyState(VK_NUMLOCK / 2) = 0
    End If
    ' Set the keyboard state.
    SetKeyboardState lpbKeyState(0)
End Property
```

You use a property procedure the same way that you use object properties.
The following code lines display the Num Lock key state and then turn on
the Num Lock key:

```
Sub UseNumLock()
    ' Get property
    MsgBox Keyboard.NumLock
    ' Set property.
    Keyboard.NumLock = True
End Sub
```

Creating a Read-Only or Write-Only Property

To create a read-only property, create a Property Get procedure for the property and omit the Property Let procedure. The following code shows a read-
only SystemDirectory property that returns the Windows system directory:

```
' Environmental Windows functions
Declare Function GetSystemDirectory Lib "KERNEL" (ByVal _
    lpBuffer As String, ByVal nSize As Integer) As Integer

Property Get SystemDirectory() As String
    Dim lpBuffer As String * 256
    iLen = GetSystemDirectory(lpBuffer, 256)
    If iLen Then
        SystemDirectory = Mid$(lpBuffer, 1, iLen)
    Else
        SystemDirectory = ""
    End If
End Property
```

You can read the new `SystemDirectory` property, but you cannot set it. The following assignment statement causes a "Procedure type mismatch" error:

```
Sub TestSystemDirectory()
    ' Display SystemDirectory
    MsgBox SystemDirectory
    ' Set SystemDirectory (causes procedure type mismatch error)
    SystemDirectory = "c:\win\system"
End Sub
```

"Procedure type mismatch" is not a trappable error; that is, you cannot handle such an error in code. To be a little kinder to your application's users, define a `Property Let` procedure that triggers an error, as in the following example:

```
Property Let SystemDirectory(s As String)
    ' Error 383 is the same error that VB displays
    ' when you try to set a read-only property.
    Err.Raise 383
End Property
```

You can trigger any error value with the `Error` statement. `Error 383` is the error code that Excel returns when you try to assign a value to one of its read-only properties.

To create a write-only property, define a `Property Let` procedure and omit (or return an error for) the `Property Get` procedure. Write-only properties are far less common than read/write and read-only properties.

Creating Object Properties

Properties that contain objects have `Property Get` and `Property Set` procedures. As you might expect, working with objects is more complicated than setting or returning simple values. Listing 18.2 shows procedures that demonstrate four common operations:

- `Create()` shows how to create an embedded Word document. The function calls the `Basic()` `Property Set` procedure to initialize the `Basic` property.

- `Property Set SetBasic()` sets the `mobjBasic` object variable. Both the variable and the `Property Set` procedure are private and thus unavailable to other modules. If you want to enable users to set the object variable, remove the `Private` keyword.

- `Property Get Basic()` returns the `mobjBasic` object variable. You commonly use `Property Get` functions to provide access to private variables like `mobjBasic`. This procedure provides a level of control over the variable.

- `Property Let Basic()` enables users to set the object variable by using assignment syntax rather than `Set`. You can omit this procedure, which equates to the private `SetBasic()` procedure.

Listing 18.2   Creating Object Properties

```
' Document form module.
' File: 18LIST02.TXT
'    This is the code for a form named "Document" containing an
'    OLE container control named oleWord.
'
' Internal variable for WordBasic object.
Private mobjBasic As Object

Function Create(x1, y1, x2, y2) As Object
     ' Add a Word object to an OLE container object on a form.
    With Me.oleWord
         ' Create the embedded object
        .CreateEmbed "", "Word.Document"
         ' Set the position and size.
        .top = x1
        .left = y1
        .Width = x1 - x2
        .Height = y2 - y1
         ' Set the Basic property of the Word object
        Set Document.SetBasic = _
             oleWord.OLEObjects(.Index) _
                   .Object.Application.WordBasic
         ' Return the object that was created
         ' (same behavior as Excel's Add methods)
        Set Create = oleWord.OLEObjects(.Index)
    End With
End Function
```

(continues)

III

Creating OLE Objects

Listing 18.2   Continued

```
Private Property Set SetBasic(obj As Object)
    ' Check if this is a WordBasic object.
    If TypeName(obj) = "wordbasic" Then
        Set mobjBasic = obj
    Else
        Err.Raise 1005
    End If
End Property

Property Get Basic() As Object
    ' If there is an object in mobjBasic.
    If IsEmpty(mobjBasic) = False Then
        ' Return the WordBasic object.
        Set Basic = mobjBasic
    Else
        ' No current object, trigger
        ' "Unable to get property" error (same as Excel uses).
Err.Raise 1006
    End If
End Property

' Optional, let users assign an object to the object variable.
Property Let Basic(obj As Object)
    ' Delegates to SetBasic().
    Set SetBasic = obj
End Property
```

The `TestObject()` procedure demonstrates how to use the `Property Get Basic` procedure:

```
Sub TestObject()
    Basic.Activate
    ' Create an embedded document.
    With Document.Create(1, 1, 100, 100)
        .Activate
        ' Get the Basic property and call Word's Insert method.
        .Basic.Insert "Some text"
    End With
End Sub
```

The `AssignObject()` procedure demonstrates how to use the `Property Let Basic` procedure to set an object reference with assignment rather than using the `Set` statement:

```
Sub AssignObject()
    ' Set an object reference using property assignment.
    Basic = Me.oleWord.Object.Application.WordBasic
End Sub
```

You might not want to let users create object references by using assignment. You simply determine which is clearer: allowing assignment, requiring the `Set` statement, or prohibiting the setting of references altogether.

Adding OLE Automation Objects to Existing Projects

One of the fastest ways to get up and running with OLE Automation is to add a class module to an existing application. To do so, follow these steps:

1. Change to `Public` the declarations of selected event procedures in an application.

2. Create a set of methods and properties in a class module that call the newly `Public` event procedures.

3. Change the Project Property settings to generate an OLE server.

4. Compile the application and run the .EXE file to register the application in the system registration database.

The following sections describe each of these steps in greater detail, using the VB Terminal (VBTERM.VBP) sample application included on the Visual Basic distribution disks.

Making Form Event Procedures *Public*

To make the VB Terminal sample application an OLE Automation object that you can use from other applications, you must change event procedure declarations in VBTERM.FRM from `Private` to `Public`. This change enables you to call the event procedures from the class module that provides the OLE Automation object that other applications use.

To change the VB Terminal event procedure declarations to `Public`, follow these steps:

1. Load the project VBTERM.VBP in Visual Basic.

2. In the project window, select the form file VBTERM.FRM and click the View Code button.

3. Change each of the `Private` declarations to `Public`, as follows:

```
Public Sub MDial_Click()

Public Sub MHangup_Click()
```

For now, you need only change these declarations. The other event procedures can remain `Private`.

4. Save the project.

You use these `Public` event procedures in the next section.

Calling Form Events from a Class Module

After making it possible to call the crucial event procedures from outside a form, you can create a class module to repackage those procedures as methods. To create a class module for VB Terminal, follow these steps:

1. Choose Insert, Class Module. Visual Basic displays a new class module and adds it to the project.

2. Press F4. Visual Basic displays the Properties window for the class module.

3. Change the instancing to Creatable SingleUse, the Name property to Application, and the Public property to True, as shown in figure 18.7.

Fig. 18.7
Change the
Name and Public
properties of the
new class.

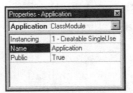

4. Select the code window for the class module and enter the following lines:

```
' Dial method -- same as clicking the Dial Phone Number
' menu item in the user interface.
Sub Dial()
    Form1.MDial_Click
End Sub

' Hangup method -- same as clicking the Hangup Phone menu
' item in the user interface.
Sub HangUp()
    Form1.MHangup_Click
End Sub
```

Tip
If you have Visual
Basic Professional
Edition but get an
error message
when you try to
create a Public
class module, your
installation might
be corrupt. Try
reinstalling the
Visual Basic
development
environment.

5. Save the project.

Running and Using the New OLE Automation Object

After making event procedures Public and creating a class module to call those event procedures, you can run and test VB Terminal as an OLE Automation object. To run VB Terminal as an OLE Automation object, follow these steps:

1. Choose Tools, Options. Visual Basic displays the Options dialog box. Choose the Project tab as shown in figure 18.8.

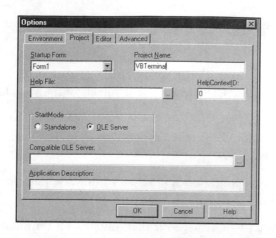

Fig. 18.8
The Project tab of
the Options dialog
box enables you to
change the project
name and select
the StartMode.

2. In the Project Options dialog box, change the entry in the Project Name text box to VBTerminal and select the OLE Server option button in the StartMode group. The project name identifies the application through OLE Automation. The StartMode tells Visual Basic to watch for OLE Automation requests from another instance of Visual Basic. Click OK to close the Options dialog box.

3. Save the project.

4. Run the project.

5. Start another instance of Visual Basic. You need to have two instances of Visual Basic running at the same time so that you can step through code in both the OLE Automation object application and the container application that uses the object.

6. In the new instance of Visual Basic, write some code to test the VB Terminal OLE Automation object. The following code is a sample of a simple test:

```
' Declare a module-level variable for the OLE Automation
' object being tested.
Dim objVBTerm As Object

Private Sub Command1_Click()
    ' Get a reference to the VB Terminal application
    Set objVBTerm = GetObject("", "VBTerminal.Application")
    ' Call the Dial method.
    objVBTerm.Dial
End Sub
```

7. Run the test code. You might want to step through the test procedure and use the Immediate window to test the other methods.

When you are satisfied with the VB Terminal OLE Automation object, you can build it as an .EXE file and test it outside of the Visual Basic environment.

To build and test the VB Terminal application as an .EXE file, follow these steps:

1. Stop the test application and the VB Terminal application in both instances of Visual Basic.

2. In the instance of Visual Basic that contains VB Terminal, choose File, Make EXE File. Visual Basic displays the Make EXE File dialog box (see fig. 18.9).

Fig. 18.9
Building an OLE Automation .EXE file is the same as for any other project.

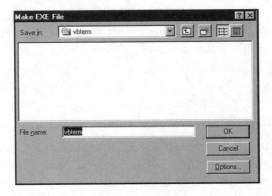

3. Click OK to compile the project into an .EXE file.

4. In the Windows File Manager, run the .EXE file that you just created. You must run the application to register it with the system registration database.

5. Close the VB Terminal application.

6. Change the test code that you used previously so that it ensures that the VB Terminal application is registered. The following code runs VB Terminal from the .EXE file:

```
' Declare a module-level variable for the OLE Automation
' object being tested.
Dim objVBTerm As Object
```

```
Private Sub Command1_Click()
    ' Start the VB Terminal application
    ' and get a reference.
    Set objVBTerm = CreateObject("VBTerm.Application")
    ' Call the Dial method.
    objVBTerm.Dial
End Sub
```

7. Run the test code. The CreateObject method starts the VB Terminal application if it is not already running. This differs from the previous example, which used GetObject to get the VB Terminal application running in another instance of Visual Basic.

Running the .EXE file reregisters the application in the system registration database. This reregistration maintains the registration entry even if the user moves or renames the file. In some cases, you must rerun the application outside of Visual Basic to get CreateObject to work after changes to the OLE Automation object.

Refining the OLE Automation Object

The methods defined so far for VB Terminal are quite simple: they merely repackage existing event procedures without adding any more logic. The limitation of defining such simple methods is that the interface is not as programmable as you might want it to be. For instance, the Dial method displays an input box to get the phone number, whereas a more useful technique is to enable Dial to accept a phone number argument.

The next few sections refine the VB Terminal OLE Automation object by adding or modifying the following features:

- You modify the Dial method to receive a phone number argument.

- You add a PortOpen property that can open and close the comm port.

- You add a SendLine method to send command lines and text to the VB Terminal window.

- You add TrapText and Text properties to detect comm port events and to get the text displayed in the VB Terminal window.

With these additional or modified features, VB Terminal becomes quite useful to other applications.

III

Creating OLE Objects

Adding a Phone Number Argument to the *Dial* Method

The Dial method calls the MDial_Click event procedure in VBTERM.FRM, which displays an input box. This call isn't necessary if Dial has a phone number argument. To add a phone number argument to Dial, you must modify the VBTERM.FRM and APPLICAT.CLS files.

The first change is to split the MDial_Click event procedure into two procedures, as shown in listing 18.3.

Listing 18.3   Splitting the MDial Click Event Procedure

```
' 18LIST03.TXT
Public Sub MDial_Click()
    On Local Error Resume Next
    Static Num$

    ' Get a number from the user.
    Num$ = InputBox$("Enter Phone Number:", "Dial Number", Num$)
    If Num$ = "" Then Exit Sub

    ' Call new DialNumber procedure.
    DialNumber Num$

    ' Move to new DialNumber procedure. -- comment out here.
    ' Open the port if it isn't already open.
    'If Not MSComm1.PortOpen Then
    '    MOpen_Click
    '    If Err Then Exit Sub
    'End If

    ' Dial the number.
    'MSComm1.Output = "ATDT" + Num$ + Chr$(13) + Chr$(10)
End Sub

' New procedure bypasses user input for Dial method.
Public Sub DialNumber(Num$)
On Local Error Resume Next
    ' Open the port if it isn't already open.
    If Not MSComm1.PortOpen Then
        MOpen_Click
        If Err.Number <> 0  Then Exit Sub
    End If

    ' Dial the number.
    MSComm1.Output = "ATDT" + Num$ + Chr$(13) + Chr$(10)
End Sub
```

Next, change the Dial method in APPLICAT.CLS to take an optional argument. If the user omits the argument, call MDial_Click as before; if the user includes the argument, call the new `DialNumber` procedure. The following code lines show the new `Dial` method:

```
Sub Dial(Optional PhoneNumber As Variant)
    If IsMissing(PhoneNumber) Then
        Form1.MDial_Click
    Else
        Form1.DialNumber Cstr(PhoneNumber)
    End If
End Sub
```

Adding a *PortOpen* Property

Knowing whether the comm port is open is important to any application that wants to send a command string directly to VB Terminal. The port's status is also useful if other applications can open or close the port. To provide these features, you should add a read/write `PortOpen` property to the VB Terminal OLE Automation object.

> **Note**
>
> Deciding whether to provide an item as a property or as a method is often difficult. Usually, properties represent the *state* of an object and methods represent an *action* that the object takes.

The following `PortOpen` property enables other applications to get and set the `PortOpen` property for the `MSComm` control on the VB Terminal form:

```
' PortOpen property
' Read/Write, Boolean
'    True if Comm port is open.
'    False if Comm port is closed.
Property Get PortOpen() As Boolean
    PortOpen = Form1.MSComm1.PortOpen
End Property

Property Let PortOpen(bSetting As Boolean)
    Form1.MSComm1.PortOpen = bSetting
End Property
```

Adding a *SendLine* Method

Another useful feature to provide is away to send command strings directly to the VB Terminal application. This feature enables another application to configure the modem by using standard modem commands and to send strings for logging on to services, exchanging data, and so on.

The SendLine method sends a string of characters to the comm port. If the VB Terminal Echo flag is on, the characters echo in the Terminal window; otherwise, the window does not display the characters. The following code is the SendLine method:

```
' SendLine method.
' Sends a command string to the VB Terminal window.
Sub SendLine(strText As String)
    If Form1.MSComm1.PortOpen Then
        ' Send the line to the comm port.
        Form1.MSComm1.Output = strText & Chr$(13)
        ' If Echo is on, send the string to the
        ' text box on the VB Terminal form.
        If Echo Then
            Form1.Term.Text = Form1.Term.Text _
                & strText & Chr(13)
        End If
    End If
End Sub
```

Adding *TrapText* and *Text* Properties

If you want to send commands to VB Terminal, you probably also want it to return information. For these purposes, you must define two related properties: TrapText and Text.

Normally, when VB Terminal receives data from the comm port, that data triggers the OnComm event procedure in VBTERM.FRM. This procedure retrieves the data and clears the buffer. To retrieve this data from another application, you must delay the OnComm event by increasing the threshold value that triggers the event. As listing 18.4 shows, if you set the TrapText property to True, you increase the MSComm control's threshold value to its maximum setting. This setting enables you to retrieve the data in the buffer from another application by using the Text property, which is described next.

Listing 18.4   The TrapText Property

```
' TrapText property
' Read/write
'    True turns on trapping -- Text property
'    returns the text from the comm port.
'    False turns off trapping -- data received
'    from the comm port is passed through to the
'    Terminal window via the OnComm event.
Property Let TrapText(bSetting As Boolean)
    ' If True, set to the current buffer size.
    If bSetting Then
        Form1.MSComm1.RThreshold = Form1.MSComm1.InBufferSize
```

```
        Else
            Form1.MSComm1.RThreshold = 0
        End If
End Property

Property Get TrapText() As Boolean
    If Form1.MSComm1.RThreshold <> 0 Then
        TrapText = True
    Else
        TrapText = False
    End If
End Property
```

The Text property (listing 18.5) returns the text that was in the comm port's input buffer. It also echos the received text in the VB Terminal window if Echo is on.

Listing 18.5 The Text Property

```
' Text property
' Read only.
'     Returns the text waiting in the comm port
'     input buffer. Display the text in the VB
'     Terminal window if Echo is on.
Property Get Text() As String
    ' Set InputLen to 0 so all data is retrieved.
    Form1.MSComm1.InputLen = 0
    ' Get the data.
    Text = Form1.MSComm1.Input
    ' If Echo is on, display the data in the
    ' Terminal window.
    Form1.Term.Text = Form1.Term.Text _
                & Text
End Property
```

Extending Form Properties

Property procedures provide a good way to extend form display attributes. For instance, you can display a Help window on top of all other windows by choosing Help, Always On Top. To display the window this way with a Visual Basic form, you must call the Windows API function SetWindowPos. This technique isn't elegant, because SetWindowPos takes seven arguments, most of which the function doesn't even use when setting the window to display always on top of all others. A more natural (or BASIC-like) technique is to repackage the SetWindowPos function in an OnTop property.

III

Creating OLE Objects

Listing 18.6 shows the declarations and property procedures that you use to create the OnTop property. When you set the form's OnTop property to True, the form appears on top of all other windows. When set to False, the form displays as it normally does.

Listing 18.6   Setting the OnTop Property

```
' 16-bit Win API declaration and constants used by OnTop property.
Private Declare Sub SetWindowPos Lib "User" _
    (ByVal hWnd As Integer, _
    ByVal hWndInsertAfter As Integer, _
    ByVal X As Integer, ByVal Y As Integer, _
    ByVal cx As Integer, ByVal cy As Integer, _
    ByVal wFlags As Integer)

' 32-bit Win API declaration and constants used by OnTop property.
Private Declare Function SetWindowPos Lib "user32" _
    (ByVal hwnd As Long, _
    ByVal hWndInsertAfter As Long, _
    ByVal x As Long, _
    ByVal y As Long, _
    ByVal cx As Long, _
    ByVal cy As Long, _
    ByVal wFlags As Long) As Long

Const SWP_NOACTIVATE = &h10
Const SWP_SHOWWINDOW = &h40
Const SWP_NOSIZE = &h1
Const SWP_NOMOVE = &h2
Const HWND_TOPMOST = -1
Const HWND_NOTOPMOST = -2

' Flag used by OnTop property to track window state.
Dim mbOnTop As Boolean

' Assigns the OnTop property.
Property Let OnTop(bSetting As Boolean)
    ' If True, Form is displayed as always on top.
    If bSetting Then
        SetWindowPos Me.hWnd, _
            HWND_TOPMOST, _
            0, 0, 0, 0, _
            SWP_NOSIZE Or SWP_NOMOVE _
            Or SWP_NOACTIVATE Or SWP_SHOWWINDOW
        ' Set flag to keep track of window state.
        mbOnTop = True
    ' If False, Form is displayed normally.
    Else
```

```
        SetWindowPos Me.hWnd, _
            HWND_NOTOPMOST, _
            0, 0, 0, 0, _
            SWP_NOSIZE Or SWP_NOMOVE _
            Or SWP_NOACTIVATE
        ' Set flag to keep track of window state.
        mbOnTop = False
    End If
End Property

' Returns True if the form is displayed as always on top,
' otherwise returns false.
Property Get OnTop() As Boolean
    ' Return the value of the flag set by Property Let.
    OnTop = mbOnTop
End Property
```

> **Caution**
>
> You need only one version of the declare for the SetWindowPos API. Choose the one
> that you need based on whether you are writing a 16- or 32-bit application.

To see the OnTop property at work, add the preceding code to a form, then set
the form's property in code. The following Click event procedure demonstrates turning OnTop on and off:

```
Private Sub Command1_Click()
    Form1.OnTop = Not Form1.OnTop
End Sub
```

Documenting Objects, Properties, and Methods

You can document your objects, properties, and methods at two levels:

- In the Description line of the Object Browser

- In a Help file that accompanies your application

Figure 18.10 shows how to use the Object Browser to display Help for your
object, properties, and methods.

Fig. 18.10
The Object Browser.

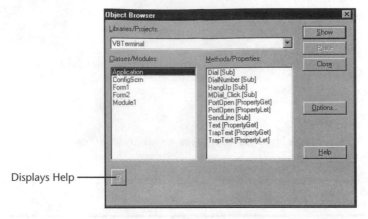

Displays Help ——

To document the object's properties and methods in a project, follow these steps:

1. Choose Tools, Options, and select the Project tab. Visual Basic displays the Project page of the Options dialog box (fig. 18.11).

Fig. 18.11
To find Help for a project's objects, properties, and methods, you can use the Object Browser to search for the file name in the Help File text box of the Project page of the Options dialog box.

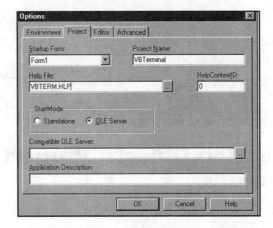

2. Enter the name of the project's Help file in the Help File text box. The same Help file that lists items related to your project's user interface also lists more technical items, such as programming with objects, properties, and methods.

3. Choose View, Object Browser. Visual Basic displays the Object Browser dialog box.

4. Select the item that you want to document and then choose the Options button. Visual Basic displays the Member Options dialog box (see fig. 18.12).

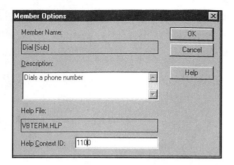

Fig. 18.12
Enter the description and Help context ID in the Member Options dialog box.

5. In the Description text box, enter the description to display in the Object Browser. In the Help Context ID text box, enter the Help context ID number.

6. Repeat steps 4 and 5 for each item that you want to document.

> **Note**
>
> To document a class or module, click on the class or module name in the Object Browser in step 4. This deselects the properties and methods in the class or module.

Help for a project's objects, properties, and methods resides in the same Help file as for the rest of the project. When designing your Help file, you should be careful not to confuse users by including highly technical programming topics in the same table of contents used by people seeking Help on your application's user interface.

Restricted Names

You cannot redefine any existing form properties or methods. Therefore, you cannot create Property procedures that use the same name as any form property, and you cannot create any Sub or Function procedures that use the same name as any form method.

This prevents you from changing a form's built-in behavior. For instance, preventing a form's window state from changing in code is sometimes useful. The following Property procedure prevents other procedures from changing a form's window state:

```
' Intercept calls to the form's WindowState property.
Property Let WindowState(Value)
     ' Do nothing
End Property
```

Visual Basic enables you to add this procedure to a form, but when you try to run the project, it causes the error message "Member already exists on this form." The following names are restricted within a form module:

ActiveControl	FontStrikethru	Point
Auto3D	FontTransparent	PopupMenu
AutoRedraw	FontUnderline	PrintForm
BackColor	ForeColor	PSet
BorderStyle	hDC	Refresh
Caption	Height	Scale
Circle	HelpContextID	ScaleHeight
ClipControls	Hide	ScaleLeft
Cls	hWnd	ScaleMode
ControlBox	Icon	ScaleTop
Controls	Image	ScaleWidth
Count	KeyPreview	ScaleX
CurrentX	Left	ScaleY
CurrentY	Line	SetFocus
DrawMode	LinkMode	Show
DrawStyle	LinkTopic	Tag
DrawWidth	MaxButton	TextHeight
Enabled	MDIChild	TextWidth
FillColor	MinButton	Top
FillStyle	MouseIcon	Visible
Font	MousePointer	Width
FontBold	Move	WindowState
FontItalic	Name	ZOrder
FontName	PaintPicture	
FontSize	Picture	

Similarly, Visual Basic reserves about 100 names for its own use. If you try to use these names as identifiers in any module, you get an error with the form "Expected: *description*," where *description* is some text describing the keyword's usual use. The following are the names that Visual Basic restricts within any module:

Abs	Declare	Format
And	DefBool	FreeFile
Any	DefCur	Function
As	DefDate	Get
Boolean	DefDbl	Global
ByRef	DefInt	Go
ByVal	DefLng	GoSub
Call	DefObj	GoTo
Case	DefSng	If
CBool	DefStr	Imp
CCur	DefVar	In
CDate	Dim	Input
CDbl	Dir	InputB
CDecl	Do	Instr
CInt	Double	InstrB
Circle	Each	Int
CLng	Else	Integer
Close	ElseIf	Is
Command	Empty	LBound
Const	End	Len
CSng	EndIf	LenB
CStr	Environ	Let
CurDir	Eqv	Like
Currency	Erase	Line
CVar	Error	Load
CVDate	Exit	LoadPicture
CVErr	False	Local
Date	Fix	Lock
Debug	For	Long

III

Creating OLE Objects

Loop	Private	StrComp
LSet	Property	String
Me	PSet	Sub
Mid	Public	Tab
MidB	Put	Then
Mod	QBColor	To
Name	ReDim	True
New	Rem	Type
Next	Resume	TypeOf
Not	Return	UBound
Nothing	RSet	Unload
Null	SavePicture	Unlock
Object	Scale	Until
On	Seek	Variant
Open	Select	Wend
Option	Set	While
Optional	Sgn	Width
Or	Shared	With
ParamArray	Single	Write
Point	Spc	Xor
Preserve	Static	
Print	Stop	

From Here...

In this chapter, you learned about creating objects and the many different facets of using them. You learned about their properties and how to create and use OLE objects from other processes.

To learn more about related topics, see Chapter 19, "Creating Object Collections," which discusses in more detail how to create collections of objects. Collections can be very useful and time saving from a programming point of view.

Chapter 19

Creating Object Collections

Object libraries that contain multiple objects organize their objects by using collections. If you use these libraries or intend to create your own, you must understand how collections work and how to use them in your code.

In this chapter, you learn how to do the following:

- Identify uses for collections in your code

- Understand how collections work and how they differ from arrays

- Create simple collections to perform actions on groups of objects

- Create collections that contain a single type of object, called *type safe* collections

- Use collections to create an object hierarchy within your application

What Is a Collection?

A *collection* is a group of objects that is itself a type of object. Visual Basic has two built-in collection objects: the Forms collection and the Controls collection. You can use these collections with the For Each...Next statement to perform actions on all the objects that they contain. For example, the following MinimizeAll procedure minimizes each loaded form in an application:

```
' Minimizes all loaded forms.
Sub MinimizeAll()
    Dim frmElement As Form
    ' For each loaded form.
    For Each frmElement In Forms
        ' Minimize the form.
        frmElement.WindowState = vbMinimized
    Next frmElement
End Sub
```

For Each...Next statements provide a way to repeat an action on each item in a collection. Unlike For...Next, For Each...Next doesn't use an index or counter variable. Instead, a For Each...Next statement simply gets each object in a collection, one after the other. The collection determines the order in which the statement retrieves the objects. A collection does not store the objects in a fixed order; instead, the order can vary based on the order of the objects' display or user access. This is the major difference between arrays of data and collections of objects (see fig. 19.1).

Fig. 19.1

The differences between arrays of data and collection objects.

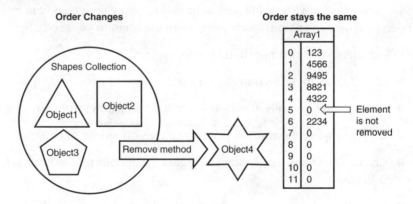

Why Aren't Collections Stored in a Fixed Order?

Objects often have a visual interface and are subject to the whims of users. For instance, a user might unload a form in an application by closing it. This action removes the form from the application's Forms collection and automatically reorders the collection.

This scenario doesn't happen with arrays; to add or remove items from an array, you must use the Redim or Redim Preserve statement in the code. The indices of an array are always contiguous, so you cannot, for example, remove the third element in a seven-element array. Of course, you can set the third element to zero, but that element still exists.

Because objects consume much more memory than simple numeric variables, Visual Basic must recover the memory of removed objects. You can have an array of integers with many unused elements, but a `Forms` collection with many unused forms would quickly exhaust your system resources.

Why Use a Collection?

Collections solve the following three problems, which most programmers face when working with objects:

- Provide a standardized way to create and track multiple instances of an object

- Group similar objects for fixed tasks, such as changing color properties or dragging to a new location

- Organize large systems of objects into a hierarchy

The following sections describe each of these aspects of using collections when creating object-oriented applications in Visual Basic.

Standard Collection Properties and Methods

Collections share a common set of properties and methods. Some collections may have additional properties and methods, but all collections have at least the set described in table 19.1.

Table 19.1	Properties and Methods Common to All Collections
Item	**Use**
`Count` property	Finds the number of objects in a collection
`Item` method	Gets a single object from a collection
`NewEnum` property	Iterates over the items in a Visual Basic collection from another language, such as C++

You can use `Count` and `Item` together to do the same sorts of tasks that you might perform with `For...Each Next`. The following is the `MinimizeAll` procedure using `For...Next` with `Count` and `Item` rather than `For Each...Next`, as shown earlier:

```
' Minimizes all loaded forms.
Sub MinimizeAll()
    Dim iCount As Integer
    ' For each loaded form.
    For iCount = 0 to Forms.Count - 1
        ' Minimize the form.
      Forms.Item(iCount).WindowState = vbMinimized
    Next iCount
End Sub
```

This `MinimizeAll` procedure and the earlier one do exactly the same thing. If you work on projects developed in Visual Basic 3.0, you probably will see such code as the preceding, because Visual Basic 4.0 introduces the `For Each...Next` statement.

The `Item` method is the default method for Visual Basic's built-in collections. Therefore, you can omit the keyword `Item` when using the method. The following two lines are equivalent:

```
Forms.Item(iCount).WindowState = vbMinimized
Forms(iCount).WindowState = vbMinimized
```

The second version is more common because it is shorter. Be aware that when you see this form, the `Item` method is in use.

The `NewEnum` property is private, so you cannot use it directly in Visual Basic code. The property enables Visual Basic's `For Each...Next` statement and programmers using other languages to iterate over the elements in collections. Under the OLE 2.0 standard, each collection provides its own function that `For Each...Next` statements use to iterate over the collection. `NewEnum` returns a handle to that function in the object.

Methods That Most Collections Provide

In addition to providing the preceding items, collections usually provide two more methods. The methods in table 19.2 are common to *most* collections.

Table 19.2 Methods Common to Most Collections

Method	Use
Add	Adds an object to a collection
Remove	Deletes an object from a collection

`Add` and `Remove` provide programmers with a standard way to create and delete items in a collection. Visual Basic maintains the Visual Basic `Forms` and

`Controls` collections, therefore you cannot add or remove them. `Add` and `Remove` are quite common in object libraries such as those provided by Microsoft Excel and Project.

Collection Inconsistencies

Some inconsistencies that Microsoft introduced in its own products undermine the standardization of collections somewhat. These differences prove that not all great minds think alike:

- `Forms` and `Controls` collections and data access object (DAO) collections start indexing from 0. The `Collection` object and most OLE Automation collections start indexing from 1. In the following code, `colForms(1)` and `Forms(0)` refer to the same form:

```
Sub CollectionIndexes()
    Dim colForms As New Collection
    colForms.Add Form1
    ' Collection object starts at 1.
    colForms(1).Print "Needless consistency is the"
    ' Forms collection starts at 0!
    Forms(0).Print "hobgoblin of small minds."
End Sub
```

- The process for removing objects is rarely consistent in collections. The `Collection` object supplies a `Remove` method, but most OLE Automation objects remove themselves from collections by using a `Delete` method on the singular object. The `Forms` collection removes items by using the `Unload` statement on a `Form` object. The following code shows three different ways to remove an object from a collection:

```
' In Excel, Delete is common.
ActiveWorkbook.Sheets(3).Delete
' In VB Collection objects, it is Remove.
colForms.Remove 1
' In VB built-in collections,
' it depends on the object...
Unload Forms(0)
```

With both of these inconsistencies, the problem is not that one system is significantly better than the other, but rather that a diverse set of rules is simply more difficult to remember than a consistent set. In your own code, you can choose to be consistent—and should do so.

III

Creating OLE Objects

Creating a New Collection for Grouped Actions

You can create new collections to contain forms, controls, classes, and OLE Automation objects from other applications. Use the `Collection` object data type when creating a new collection. The following declaration creates a new collection, `colSelected`:

```
Dim colSelected As New Collection
```

Declaring a variable as a `Collection` object gives you five built-in properties and methods, which are listed in table 19.3.

Table 19.3 `Collection` **Objects' Built-In Properties and Methods**

Item	Use
Count property	Returns the number of objects in the collection.
NewEnum property (Private)	Supports `For Each...Next` with the collection. You cannot use this property directly.
Add method	Adds an object to the collection.
Item method	Gets a single object from the collection.
Remove method	Deletes an object from the collection.

The following code creates a new collection, `colTextBoxes`, and adds all the text boxes on a form to the new collection:

```
Option Explicit

' Create a new collection to contain all the
' text boxes on a form
Dim colTextBoxes As New Collection

Private Sub Form_Initialize()
    ' Variable used in For Each to get controls.
    Dim cntrlItem As Control
    ' Loop through the controls on the form.
    For Each cntrlItem In Me.Controls
        ' If the control is a text box, add it to the
        ' collection of text boxes.
        If TypeName(cntrlItem) = "TextBox" Then
            colTextBoxes.Add cntrlItem
        End If
    Next cntrlItem
End Sub
```

The following code uses the collection `colTextBoxes` to clear all the text entered on the form:

```
Sub cmdClear_Click()
    ' Variable used in For Each to get controls.
    Dim cntrlItem As Control
    ' Clear each of the text boxes in the collection.
    For Each cntrlItem In colTextBoxes
        cntrlItem.Text = ""
    Next cntrlItem
End Sub
```

One problem with the `colTextBoxes` collection as used in the preceding code is that the collection can contain any type of object, not just text box controls. Using the `Text` property on each of the collection's elements, as in the preceding example, isn't really safe. If another procedure inadvertently adds a command button to the collection, the `Text` property assignment fails when the `For Each` loop encounters it.

To solve this problem, you must create a class to contain the collection and check the type of the object before you add it to the collection. This solution is called *type-safe* programming.

Creating Collections of a Single Object Type

Ideally, a collection should check whether items that you add to it are of the correct type. The Visual Basic `Collection` object doesn't provide any built-in feature that does this. To create a type-safe collection, you must create a new class.

Listing 19.1 shows the code in a class module that defines a type-safe collection. The `Add` method mimics that of the Visual Basic's `Collection` object, but adds a step for checking the type of object to add. If the type doesn't match, `Add` triggers a "Type Mismatch" error.

III

Creating OLE Objects

Listing 19.1   A Class Module Defining a Type-Safe Collection

```
'    Class TextBoxes -- TXTBOXES.CLS
'    A type-safe collection for text box controls.
Option Explicit

' Private collection contains the objects --
' Add, Item, Remove, and Count members control
' access to this collection.
```

(continues)

Listing 19.1   Continued

```
Private colTextBoxes As New Collection
Public Const PROJECTNAME = "TextBoxCollection"

' Modified Add method -- verifies object type
' before adding an object to the collection.
Sub Add(TextBox As Control, Optional Key, Optional Before, _
                            Optional After)
    ' If the object is a text box, add it to
    ' the collection.
    If TypeName(TextBox) = "TextBox" Then
        colTextBoxes.Add TextBox, Key, Before, After
    ' Cause a type mismatch error.
    Else
        Err.Raise 13, PROJECTNAME & "." _
            & Typename(Me), "Object is not a text box."
    End If
End Sub
```

The Remove, Item, and Count members of the TextBoxes class simply delegate
to the built-in properties and methods of the private Collection object
colTextBoxes (to *delegate* is to use an object's built-in functionality and then
repackage it in a similar method):

```
' Standard Remove method.
Sub Remove(Index)
    colTextBoxes.Remove Index
End Sub

' Standard Item method.
Function Item(Index) As Object
    ' Use the Set statement to return an object
    ' reference. Simple assignment would return
    ' the default property for the object
    Set Item = colTextBoxes.Item(Index)
End Function

' Standard Count property.
Property Get Count() As Integer
    Count = colTextBoxes.Count
End Property
```

Using a Type-Safe Collection

Using a type-safe collection seems to be the same as using any other type of
collection. A version of the code in listing 19.2 appeared earlier in this chapter with the Visual Basic Collection object. To use the type-safe collection
TextBoxes, you need only modify one word.

Listing 19.2   Using a Type-Safe Collection

```
Option Explicit

' Create a new collection using the
' type-safe TextBoxes collection.
Dim colTextBoxes As New TextBoxes
    ' <- Changed "Collection" to "TextBoxes"

Private Sub Form_Initialize()
    ' Variable used in For Each to get controls.
    Dim cntrlItem As Control
    ' Loop through the controls on the form.
    For Each cntrlItem In Me.Controls
        ' If the control is a text box, add it to the
        ' collection of text boxes.
        If TypeName(cntrlItem) = "TextBox" Then
            colTextBoxes.Add cntrlItem
        End If
    Next cntrlItem
End Sub
```

Now if you try to add an object other than a text box object to the collection, you get a "Type Mismatch" error. To see the result, try entering the following line of code:

```
colTextBoxes.Add Form1
```

Reasons to Use Type-Safe Collections

Type-safe collections verify the type of objects that you are adding to a collection. This verification is a good first-line defense against bugs. But type-safe collections also enable you to extend the object by adding properties and methods that the Visual Basic Collection object does not provide.

The following code shows an Arrange method added to the Windows collection in the sample application WINDOWS.VPJ. Arrange is a logical extension of the Windows collection, because the method's task is common to most multiple-document interface (MDI) applications.

```
' Arrange all of the child windows in the
' MDI parent.
Sub Arrange(arrangement As Integer)
    ' Delegate to the MDI window's Arrange method.
    mdiApplication.Arrange arrangement
End Sub
```

The Arrange method and the rest of the WINDOWS.VPJ application are described in detail later in this chapter.

Limitations of Type-Safe Collections

A big drawback of type-safe collections is that you cannot use them with the `For Each...Next` statement. Visual Basic and other applications provide a special, private `NewEnum` property for their collections. The `NewEnum` property returns a pointer to a function in the collection that supports the `For Each...Next` statement. You cannot add this capability to a class that you create in Visual Basic.

To repeat actions on items in a type-safe collection, use the `For...Next` statement rather than `For Each...Next`. The following code uses the collection `colTextBoxes` to clear all the text that the `For...Next` statement enters on the form:

```
Sub cmdClear_Click()
    ' Variable used in For Next as counter.
    Dim Item As Integer
    ' Clear each of the text boxes in the collection.
    ' WARNING: Must start from 1 rather than 0 since this
    ' is really a Collection object rather than the Controls
    ' collection (which starts at 0).
    For Index = 1 to colTextBoxes.Count
        colTextBoxes.Item(Index).Text = ""
    Next cntrlItem
End Sub
```

Another limitation is that you cannot define a default property or method in a Visual Basic class. Therefore, you must always specify the `Item` method explicitly when working with a type-safe collection. The following lines are *not* equivalent:

```
colTextBoxes.Item(iCount).Text = ""
colTextBoxes(iCount).WindowState = ""               ' Causes error!
```

Using Collections to Organize Objects

Object hierarchies are necessary when an application defines many classes that relate to each other. The hierarchy defines an understandable way for users to choose from among the many objects. You use collections to create a hierarchical organization of classes. The Excel object library is a good example of a large class hierarchy, part of which is shown in figure 19.2.

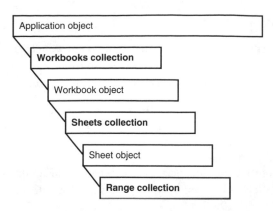

Fig. 19.2
Excel uses collections to form a hierarchy of objects.

In figure 19.2, you can use Excel collections to find individual objects. For instance, the following code line makes a cell in a worksheet bold:

```
Application.Workbooks("stock.xls").Sheets("Portfolio). _
    Range(1,1).Font = xlBold
```

The following table describes the action that each method or property takes in the preceding line of code:

Item	Action
Application	Returns the top-level object in Excel.
Workbooks	The `Application` object's `Workbooks` method returns the collection of all loaded workbooks in Excel.
("stock.xls")	The default method for the `Workbooks` collection is the `Item` method, so `"stock.xls"` returns the STOCK.XLS `Workbook` object within the `Workbooks` collection.
Sheets	The `Workbook` object's `Sheets` method returns a collection of all the sheets in a workbook. These sheets include worksheets, dialog sheets, and chart sheets.
("Portfolio")	Again, the implicit `Item` method returns a single `Sheets` object from within the `Sheets` collection.
Range	The `Worksheet` object's `Range` method returns the collection of cells on a worksheet.
(1,1)	The `Range` object's `Item` method returns a single cell from the `Range` collection.
Font = xlBold	The `Range` object's `Font` property sets the cell's font to appear bold.

III

Creating OLE Objects

This example has a few noteworthy aspects:

- Each object defines a method that returns the collection of objects the next level down in the hierarchy. You use this mechanism to navigate downward from the top-level object to the individual cell.

- Not all collections are homogeneous. For instance, the Sheets collection can contain objects of these different types: Worksheet, Chart, Module, and DialogSheet objects.

- The bottom-level object (Range) is a collection of items, not a collection of objects. The Excel object library does not include a Cell object.

The rest of this chapter shows you how to use collections to create a class hierarchy in Visual Basic. The example uses simple Window objects, based on forms.

The WINDOWS.VPJ sample defines three classes in its object hierarchy. You can create the top-level Application object from other applications. All classes are available to other applications through OLE Automation, as shown in table 19.4.

Table 19.4 WINDOWS.VPJ Class Module Property Settings		
Class Name	**Creatable**	**Public**
Application	True	True
Windows	False	True
Window	False	True

The *Application* Object

The Application class (APPLICAT.CLS) defines the WINDOWS.VPJ Application object. This class controls an MDI form that contains all the child windows. The Application object has the following methods and properties:

Property/Method	Description
ActiveWindow property	Returns the Window object within the application that currently has focus. (Read-only.)
Windows method	Returns the application's Windows collection object. The Windows collection consists of all the child windows that the application displays.

Property/Method	Description
Top and Left properties	Set or return the application window's position. These properties repackage the MDI form's Top and Left properties. (Read/write.)
Height and Width properties	Set or return the application window's dimensions. These properties repackage the MDI form's Height and Width properties. (Read/write.)

The *ActiveWindow* Property

The Application object's ActiveWindow property uses the variable modDeclares.gActiveWindow to return the window that has focus within the application. By placing global variables in a code module, you make them available internally to the application, but not externally to other applications. ActiveWindow is a read-only property, so access to the variable gActiveWindow must be limited to the current application. Listing 19.3 defines the ActiveWindow property in the Application class.

Listing 19.3   Definition for the ActiveWindow Property in the Application Class

```
' Application ActiveWindow property (read only)
Public Property Get ActiveWindow() As Window
    Set ActiveWindow = modDeclares.gActiveWindow
End Property
```

The *Windows* Method

The Application object's Windows method uses the modDeclares.Windows variable to return the application's Windows collection. You could just as easily define this method as a read-only property. There is no real difference between a read-only property and a method that takes no arguments. Listing 19.4 defines the Windows property in the Application class.

Listing 19.4   Definition of the Windows Property of the Application Class

```
' Application Windows method.
Public Function Windows() As Object
    ' Return the Windows variable from the
    ' modDeclares module.
    Set Windows = modDeclares.Windows
End Function
```

III

Creating OLE Objects

The *Height*, *Width*, *Top*, and *Left* Properties

This section discusses the Application object's Height, Width, Top, and Left properties together because they are all so similar. Each of these properties simply repackages one of the MDI form's properties. To define a read/write property, you need a pair of Property procedures (Let and Get). Listing 19.5 defines the Windows property in the Application class.

Listing 19.5 Definition of the Windows Property in the Application Class

```
' Application window height property (read/write).
Public Property Let Height(iVal As Integer)
    mdiApplication.Height = iVal
End Property

Public Property Get Height() As Integer
    Height = mdiApplication.Height
End Property

' Application window width property (read/write).
Public Property Let Width(iVal As Integer)
    mdiApplication.Width = iVal
End Property

Public Property Get Width() As Integer
    Width = mdiApplication.Width
End Property

' Application window top property (read/write).
Public Property Let Top(iVal As Integer)
    mdiApplication.Top = iVal
End Property

Public Property Get Top() As Integer
    Top = mdiApplication.Top
End Property

' Application window left property (read/write).
Public Property Let Left(iVal As Integer)
    mdiApplication.Left = iVal
End Property

Public Property Get Left() As Integer
    Left = mdiApplication.Left
End Property
```

The *Windows* Collection

The Windows class (WINDOWS.CLS) defines WINDOWS.VPJ's Windows collection object. The class maintains a type-safe collection that contains all the child windows. WINDOWS.VPJ creates its own Windows collection. The application could instead use its Forms collection, except that the Visual Basic Forms collection includes the MDI parent form as well as all the child forms. Working around this parent inclusion behavior is less than straightforward.

Creating a special Windows collection and a separate Windows class requires more code than using the built-in Forms collection, but makes the class hierarchy more easy to understand and modify. To compare this technique to using the Forms collection for a similar purpose, see the example WINALT.VPJ.

The Windows collection object in WINDOWS.VPJ has the following methods and properties:

Property/Method	Description
Add method	Adds a Window object to the collection.
Remove method	Removes a Window object from the collection.
Item method	Returns a single Window object from the collection by using a numeric or string index.
Count property	Returns the number of child windows in the application. (Read-only.)
Arrange method	Tiles the child windows within the MDI parent window.

You should include this table's first four items in every collection that you create. By being consistent, you make it easier for your object library's users to use your objects correctly.

The *Add* Method

The Windows object's Add method checks the type of objects before adding them to the colWindows collection. You declare the collection colWindows as Private at the module level, as you should *always* use the Add method to add items. Enabling programmers to add items directly by making colWindows a Public variable could result in the collection storing the wrong object types.

The Add method also enables programmers to create an object simply by omitting the first argument. This is a common syntactic practice in the Excel object library. Listing 19.6 defines the Add method in the Windows class.

Listing 19.6 Definition for the Add Method of the Windows Class

```
' Create a Windows collection
Private colWindows As New Collection

' Windows Add method -- verifies object type
' before adding an object to the collection.
Sub Add(Optional winVal, Optional Key, Optional Before, _
        Optional After)
    ' If no form is specified, create a new form.
    If IsMissing(winVal) Then
        ' Create a new instance of the Window class.
        Dim Window As New Window
        ' Tell the window to create itself and
        ' add it to the collection.
        colWindows.Add _
            Window.Create(SOURCE_INTERNAL), _
            Window.Index
        Exit Sub
    End If
    ' If the object is a form, add it to
    ' the collection.
    If TypeName(winVal) = "Window" Then
        ' Make sure object has been initialized.
        If Len(winVal.Index) Then
            colWindows.Add winVal, Key, Before, After
        ' If it hasn't, use the Create function to create it.
        Else
            colWindows.Add _
                winVal.Create(SOURCE_INTERNAL), _
                winVal.Index
        End If
    ' Cause a type mismatch error.
    Else
      Err.Raise 13, PROJECTNAME & "." _
            & Typename(Me), "Object is not a window."
    End If
End Sub
```

The *Remove* Method

The Windows object's Remove method deletes a Window object and removes it from the Windows collection. If you don't delete the object before removing it from the collection, you lose the reference to the object without recovering the memory that it consumes. In WINDOWS.VPJ, the Window object's Delete method unloads the form that it displays. Listing 19.7 defines the Remove method in the Windows class.

Listing 19.7   Definition for the Remove Method of the Windows Class

```
' Standard Remove method.
Sub Remove(Index)
    ' Delete the form -- SOURCE_INTERNAL argument
    ' indicates that Delete is used internally, so
    ' Remove is not called to remove the Window from
    ' the collection (causing infinite loop).
    colWindows.Item(Index).Delete SOURCE_INTERNAL
    ' Remove the object from the collection.
    colWindows.Remove Index
End Sub
```

The *Item* Method

The Windows object's Item method returns a Window object from the Windows collection. Because Item returns an object reference rather than a simple data type, you must use the Set statement when returning the object. Listing 19.8 defines the Item method in the Windows class.

Listing 19.8   Definition of the Item Method in the Windows Class

```
' Standard Item method.
Function Item(Index) As Object
    ' Use the Set statement to return an object
    ' reference. Simple assignment would return
    ' the default property for the object
    Set Item = colWindows.Item(Index)
End Function
```

The *Count* Property

The Windows object's Count property returns the number of Window objects in the Windows collection. Other procedures that must iterate over the collection use Count; you cannot use a For Each...Next statement when iterating over a type-safe collection. Listing 19.9 defines the Count property in the Windows class.

Listing 19.9   Definition of the Count Property in the Windows Class

```
' Standard Count property.
Property Get Count() As Integer
    Count = colWindows.Count
End Property
```

III

Creating OLE Objects

The *Arrange* Method

The Windows object's Arrange method tiles all the Window objects within the Application window. Arrange demonstrates how you can extend a collection object to include methods and properties other than the standard four: Add, Remove, Item, and Count.

Because the MDI form already provides an Arrange method, you can simply delegate to that method. To control access to an aspect of the application that should remain private (such as the MDI form), you should delegate, rather than expose, the MDI form directly. Listing 19.10 defines the Arrange method of the Windows object.

Listing 19.10   Definition of the Arrange Method in the Windows Object

```
' Arrange all of the child windows in the
' MDI parent.
Sub Arrange(arrangement As Integer)
    ' Delegate to the MDI window's Arrange method.
    mdiApplication.Arrange arrangement
End Sub
```

The *Window* Object

The Window class (WINDOW.CLS) defines the Window object in WINDOWS.VPJ. The class creates and controls a child form (frmWindow) object. Objects that are part of a collection have these requirements that you must consider:

- Objects that are part of a collection should provide an Index property so that programmers can remove the object from its collection. By convention, the collection's Remove method takes the object's Index (not the object itself) as its argument.

- Objects that you can create or delete at run time should include Create and Delete methods in their classes. Keeping these methods within the object's class instead of putting them in the collection object's Add and Remove methods makes the code easier to maintain, because the object encapsulates the object-specific tasks.

The Window object's methods and properties include the following:

Property/Method	Description
Create method	Creates and displays a new child form. The Windows collection's Add method uses Create, but the method is also available to other applications through OLE Automation.
Delete method	Unloads a child form. The Windows collection's Add method uses Delete, but the method is also available to other applications through OLE Automation.
Index property	Returns the key value (in WINDOWS.VPJ, the form caption) that identifies the object in the Windows collection. (Read-only.)
Top and Left properties	Set or return the position of the child form. These properties repackage the form's Top and Left properties. (Read/write.)
Height and Width properties	Set or return the dimensions of the child form. These properties repackage the form's Height and Width properties. (Read/write.)

The *Create* Method

The Window object's Create method creates a new child form and returns the Window object that controls that form. The Windows collection's Add method uses Create, which leads to a problem: You can't assume that the user knows to use the Add method when creating objects, and you can't hide Create from other applications because it is a member of a Public class. Therefore, you must make Windows.Add and Window.Create essentially interchangable in code.

The Create method in listing 19.11 uses an internal flag, SOURCE_INTERNAL, to determine whether the Windows object's Add method called Create. If Add did not call the Create method, Create calls Add anyway, to maintain the Windows collection correctly.

If the SOURCE_INTERNAL flag is set, Create assumes that the Add method called it and proceeds to create the new form, set its index, and return the created object. SOURCE_INTERNAL is hidden from other applications because it is defined in a code module rather than a class or form module. Therefore, the flag is like a private key that you can use to unlock behavior that you should restrict from the outside world.

Listing 19.11 defines the Create method in the Window class.

Tip
If you encounter a
"Duplicate Defini-
tion" error when
trying to add an
object to a collec-
tion, make sure
that the key argu-
ment is unique
within the
collection.

Listing 19.11 Definition of the Create Method in the Window Class

```
Private Window As New frmWindow
Private mstrIndex As String

Public Function Create(Optional iCode) As Object
    If IsMissing(iCode) Then
        Windows.Add Me
    ' If source was within this project, don't
    ' delegate to Windows.Remove.
    ElseIf iCode = SOURCE_INTERNAL Then
        ' Keep track of the total number of windows
        ' ever created for Window Index property.
        ' Can't use Windows.Count, since deleting
        ' windows yields a nonunique number.
        giWindowsCount = giWindowsCount + 1
        mstrIndex = "Window" & giWindowsCount
        Window.Caption = mstrIndex
        ' Register as the active window
        Set modDeclares.gActiveWindow = Me
        ' Return this object as the result of Create.
        Set Create = Me
    ' Otherwise, an invalid argument was used.
    Else
        ' Invalid procedure call error.
     Err.Raise 5, PROJECTNAME & "." _
            & Typename(Me), "Invalid argument."
    End If
End Function
```

The *Delete* Method

The Window object's Delete method unloads the child form that the Window object controls. Delete, the companion to the Create method, is available for internal use by the Windows collection and for external use by other applications.

The Windows object's Remove method uses Delete, which uses the SOURCE_INTERNAL internal flag to determine whether the Windows object's Delete method called it. If the Delete method did not call Remove, Delete simply calls Remove anyway to maintain the Windows collection correctly. If the SOURCE_INTERNAL flag is set, Delete assumes that the Remove method called it and unloads the child form.

Listing 19.12 defines the Delete method in the Window class.

Listing 19.12   Definition of the Delete Method in the Window Class

```
' Window Delete method, unloads the form.
Public Function Delete(Optional iCode)
    ' Check source of Delete call -- if omitted,
    ' delegate to Windows.Remove.
    If IsMissing(iCode) Then
        Windows.Remove Me
    ' If source was within this project, don't
    ' delegate to Windows.Remove.
    ElseIf iCode = SOURCE_INTERNAL Then
        Unload Window
    ' Otherwise, an invalid argument was used.
    Else
        ' Invalid procedure call error.
    Err.Raise 13, PROJECTNAME & "." _
        & Typename(Me), "Invalid argument."
    End If
End Function
```

The *Index* Property

The Window object's Index property returns the key name that you use to store the Window object in the Windows collection. In WINDOWS.VPJ, the key name is the caption that the form displays. You should maintain the Index property internally and make it available for read-only access. If you change the Index property outside of the application, you lose the object in its collection. Listing 19.13 defines the Count property in the Windows class.

Listing 19.13   Definition of the Count Property in the Windows Class

```
' Windows index property (read only).
Public Property Get Index() As String
    Index = mstrIndex
End Property
```

The *Height, Width, Top,* and *Left* Properties

This section discusses the Window object's Height, Width, Top, and Left properties together because they are all so similar. Each of these properties simply repackages one of the child form's properties. To define a read/write property, you need a pair of Property procedures (Let and Get). Listing 19.14 defines these properties for the Window class.

III

Creating OLE Objects

Listing 19.14 **Definition of the** Height, Width, Top, **and** Left **Properties in the** Window **Class**

```
' Window Height property (read/write).
Public Property Let Height(iVal As Integer)
    Window.Height = iVal
End Property

Public Property Get Height() As Integer
    Height = Window.Height
End Property

' Window Width property (read/write).
Public Property Let Width(iVal As Integer)
    Window.Width = iVal
End Property

Public Property Get Width() As Integer
    Width = Window.Width
End Property

' Window Top property (read/write).
Public Property Let Top(iVal As Integer)
    Window.Top = iVal
End Property

Public Property Get Top() As Integer
    Width = Window.Top
End Property

' Window Left property (read/write).
Public Property Let Left(iVal As Integer)
    Window.Left = iVal
End Property

Public Property Get Left() As Integer
    Width = Window.Left
End Property
```

The *frmWindow* Form

You must ensure that your system of objects reflect user actions correctly, particularly when you are maintaining a collection. The frmWindow form (FRMWIN.FRM) in WINDOWS.VPJ contains two event procedures that affect the objects defined in the application:

User Action	Event Procedure	Description
Switch focus between windows	`Form_GotFocus`	Updates the `Application` object's `ActiveWindow` property to reflect the window that has focus
Close a window by using the form's Control menu	`Form_QueryUnload`	Remove the associated `Window` object from the `Windows` collection

The *Form_GotFocus* Event Procedure

The `frmWindow` forms's `Form_GotFocus` event procedure is triggered when the form receives focus. Because the `Application` object provides a property that returns the currently active form, you must maintain that property setting from within `Form_GotFocus`.

The `Application` object's `ActiveWindow` property is read-only externally, and uses the internal variable `gActiveWindow` to maintain the active `Window` object internally. `Form_GotFocus` sets this variable by using its `Caption` property to retrieve its controlling object from within the `Windows` collection.

> **Note**
>
> You should return object references for properties with object-related names, such as `ActiveWindow`. By returning such names, you create a more natural syntax, such as `ActiveWindow.Print` or `ActiveWindow.Delete`.

Listing 19.15 defines the `Form_GotFocus` event procedure in the `frmWindow` form.

Listing 19.15   Definition of the `Form_GotFocus` Event Procedure in the `frmWindow` Form

```
' Register that this is the active window.
Private Sub Form_GotFocus()
    Set modDeclares.gActiveWindow = Windows.Item(Me.Caption)
End Sub
```

The *Form_QueryUnload* Event Procedure

The frmWindow form's Form_QueryUnload event procedure is triggered just before the form unloads, while form properties are still available. Because the Windows collection object contains all the Window objects displayed on-screen, you must remove the form's controlling Window object from its collection when the user closes the form. Listing 19.16 defines the Form_QueryUnload event procedure in the frmWindow form.

Listing 19.16   Definition for the Form_QueryUnload Event Procedure in the frmWindow Form

```
Private Sub Form_QueryUnload(Cancel As Integer, _
                    UnloadMode As Integer)
    ' If the user closes the form manually,
    ' be sure to remove it from the collection.
    If UnloadMode = vbFormControlMenu Then
        Windows.Remove Me.Caption
    End If
End Sub
```

The *modDeclares* Module

The modDeclares module (DECLARES.BAS) in WINDOWS.VPJ contains Public variables that you use throughout the application. The modDeclares module also defines a counter, giWindowsCount, that the Window class uses to create a unique title and key value that you use when storing the Window object in the Windows collection.

Code modules are not available to other applications through OLE Automation, so programmers often use them to declare application-wide internal variables that Public class modules use. Visual Basic provides no other way to share variables between classes without also making them Public to other applications. The variables and the constant that the modDeclares module defines are as follows:

Item	Description
Application	The instance of the Application class used throughout the application.
Windows	The instance of the Windows class used throughout the application.
giWindowsCount	A counter that creates unique key names and form captions in the Windows class' Add method.

Item	Description
gActiveWindow	An internal variable that tracks the currently active window. You can set this variable within the application, but you expose it to other applications as the Application object's read-only ActiveWindow property.
SOURCE_INTERNAL	An internal flag that the Windows class' Add and Remove methods use to call the Window class' Create and Delete methods. This flag prevents other applications from calling Create or Delete without first calling Add or Remove.

Listing 19.17 shows the modDeclares module's declarations.

Listing 19.17 The modDeclares Module's Declarations

```
' Classes used throughout the application.
Public Application As New Application
Public Windows As New Windows

' Unique number to use in Window Index and caption.
Public giWindowsCount As Integer

' Internal variable that tracks active window.
Public gActiveWindow As Window

' Internal flag used when calling the Delete and
' Create Window methods.
Public Const SOURCE_INTERNAL = &h20
```

The *mdiApplication* Form

The mdiApplication form (MDIWIN.FRM) in WINDOWS.VPJ contains menu event procedures that demonstrate how to use the application's objects in code. The mdiApplication form responds to the following user actions:

User Action	Event Procedure	Description
Choose Window, Add	mnuAdd_Click	Invokes the Add method on application's Windows collection
Choose Window, Arrange	mnuArrange_Click	Invokes the Arrange method on the application's Windows collection
Choose Window, Delete	mnuDelete_Click	Retrieves the Application object's ActiveWindow property, then invokes the Delete method on the returned object

III

Creating OLE Objects

The *mnuAdd_Click* Event Procedure

The mdiApplication form's mnuAdd_Click event procedure adds a window to the application. Listing 19.18 defines the mnuAdd_Click event procedure in the mdiApplication form.

Listing 19.18   Definition of the mnuAdd_Click **Event Procedure in the** mdiApplication **Form**

```
Private Sub mnuAdd_Click()
    Windows.Add
End Sub
```

This procedure could just as easily use the Window object's Create method, but it must first create a new instance of the object, as follows:

```
Private Sub mnuAdd_Click()
    Dim Window As New Window
    Window.Create
End Sub
```

This method isn't as obvious as that of Windows.Add, so the first method is preferable.

The *mnuArrange_Click* Event Procedure

The mdiApplication form's mnuArrange_Click event procedure tiles the child windows in the application window. Listing 19.19 defines the mnuArrange_Click event procedure in the mdiApplication form.

Listing 19.19   Definition of the mnuArrange_Click **Event Procedure in the** mdiApplication **Form**

```
Private Sub mnuArrange_Click()
    Windows.Arrange
End Sub
```

This procedure demonstrates the essence of object-oriented programming: Objects know how to do what they are told. You consign the complexities of arranging the windows on-screen to the Windows object itself. The object's users don't have to worry about the details.

The *mnuDelete_Click* Event Procedure

The mdiApplication form's mnuDelete_Click event procedure deletes the active child window. Listing 19.20 defines the mnuDelete_Click event procedure in the mdiApplication form.

Listing 19.20   Definition of the `mnuDelete_Click` **Event Procedure in the** `mdiApplication` **Form**

```
Private Sub mnuDelete_Click()
    Application.ActiveWindow.Delete
End Sub
```

The following code uses the `Windows` collection's `Remove` method to do the same thing. Because `Remove` takes the `Window` object's index as an argument, this code is a little less obvious than the preceding version:

```
Private Sub mnuDelete_Click()
    Windows.Remove Application.ActiveWindow.Index
End Sub
```

As you can see from the `mnuDelete_Click` and `mnuAdd_Click` event procedures, creating objects from the collection object and deleting objects from the individual object are usually more convenient. This practice is exhibited throughout the Excel object library—the collection object's `Add` method creates new objects, and the individual object's `Delete` method removes them.

From Here...

In this chapter, you learned about object collections and how to manipulate them. For more information on creating and using objects, see the following chapters:

- Chapter 18, "Creating Objects," explains how to begin programming with objects.

- Chapter 20, "Designing Object Libraries," describes design approaches that you need to consider when creating applications that provide objects to other applications.

- Chapter 22, "Debugging Applications That Provide Objects," gives you important insight into solving the many new problem areas that crop up as you program with objects.

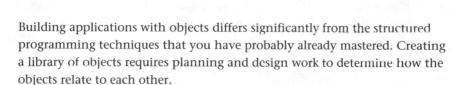

Chapter 20

Designing Object Libraries

Building applications with objects differs significantly from the structured programming techniques that you have probably already mastered. Creating a library of objects requires planning and design work to determine how the objects relate to each other.

In this chapter, you learn how to do the following:

- Choose between the two major ways of organizing your object library

- Compare the advantages and disadvantages of broad and deep organizations

- Structure your object library so that users can navigate among the objects that it contains

- Use collections to organize multiple instances of objects

- Name objects, properties, and methods so that they are understandable

- Provide standard objects, properties, and methods as described in the OLE 2 standard

Exploring Broad versus Deep Organization

The two basic ways to organize the objects that an application provides are the following:

- A *broad* organization provides all objects at the top level. You can create each object outside the application. Objects in a broad organization can be related, but aren't dependent on each other. Therefore, objects in a broad organization tend to have more methods and properties per object than those objects in a deep organization.

- A *deep* organization provides for the creation of one or more objects at the top level and subordinate objects under each top-level object. Superordinate objects depend on their subordinate objects for services, so each object tends to have fewer methods and properties than those objects in a broad organization.

Microsoft Word and Microsoft Excel are two extreme examples of both object library organizations. The broad Word object library provides one creatable object, WordBasic, and hundreds of properties and methods. The deep Excel object library provides three creatable objects and almost a hundred subordinate objects. Figures 20.1 and 20.2 illustrate the two approaches to designing object libraries.

Fig. 20.1

The Word object library is so broad that it is flat.

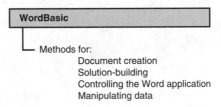

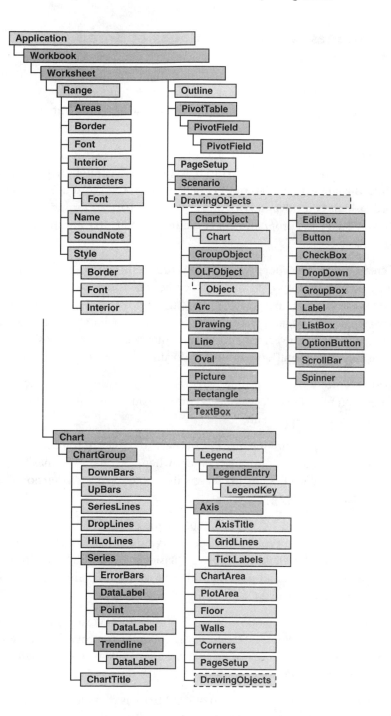

Fig. 20.2
The Excel object
library is as deep as
an ocean.

Advantages and Disadvantages of Broad Organization

Offhand, broad organizations like Word's might seem poorly planned. In fact, Word's object library is what Microsoft calls "opportunistic." Microsoft added the library to Word 6.0 near the end of the development cycle by using the OLE 2.0 CreateDispatch helper functions.

In practice, however, the Word object library is quite useful and understandable. This is because the Word object library accurately reproduces the WordBasic language, which itself closely matches the Word user interface. WordBasic has the advantage of an existing user base and some familiarity among Visual Basic programmers. It is already BASIC-like and thus fits well in Visual Basic code.

To create WordBasic code, you use the Word menu, dialog box, and field names. If you want to open a Word document by using Word's object library, you use the FileOpen method; to change the style of a paragraph, you use the FormatStyle method; and so on. These names are obvious to users, because users see the names every day in the user interface, and the WordBasic programming documentation has already documented the names.

Broad organizations can accurately reproduce an existing interface, which enables you to create objects quickly. Also, broad organizations are simple and thus easy to understand.

The disadvantage of linking an object library to names in the user interface is that you must change your object library when you change names in your user interface. Word has already faced this problem with two version changes of WordBasic.

When updating Word 1.0 to Word 2.0, Microsoft added a macro translation utility that converted Word 1.0 macros to Word 2.0 macros. However, this utility didn't work well within the WordBasic programming environment, and would not work at all now that other programming environments, such as Visual Basic and Visual C++, can use WordBasic code.

To accommodate changes from Word 2.0, Microsoft Word 6.0 includes support for all the old Word 2.0 language. Therefore, two programmers can be doing the same thing in the same environment while using completely different languages—which is not a good idea.

Another disadvantage of the Word object library is that all methods and properties operate on the currently active selection or document rather than an actual object. Unfortunately, the selection can easily change because of user actions. To avoid this problem, you can use objects, because the object variable to which you apply methods and properties always points to the same object. Figure 20.3 shows how WordBasic methods act on the currently active document rather than a document object.

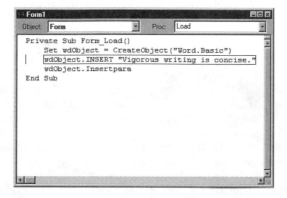

Active document

Intended document

Fig. 20.3
Changing the active document affects code written with the Word object library.

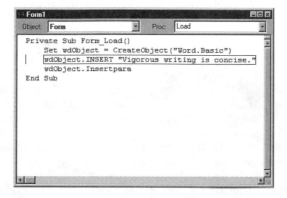

Summary

The following lists summarize the features, advantages, and disadvantages of a broad organization. The features include the following:

- You can create all objects by using Visual Basic's `CreateObject` or GetObject functions.

- Each object has many methods and properties.

(continues)

(continued)

- Method and property names often match the menu and dialog box names of the user interface.

- Objects don't provide methods that return subordinate objects.

The advantages of a broad organization include the following:

- Adding such an organization to existing applications is quick and relatively easy.

- Method and property names are understandable and easy to remember because they derive from the user interface.

- When documenting methods and properties, you can draw from existing documentation from the user interface.

- Alphabetic ordering of method and property names in the Object Browser works well because the organization groups together File menu, Edit menu, and other menu-specific items.

Disadvantages of a broad organization include the following:

- Code written with the object library is vulnerable to user actions, because methods and properties tend to act on the currently active selection, which the user can change.

- Changes to the user interface affect method and property names, making the object library difficult to maintain.

- Changes to the object library can break code from existing applications that use the object library.

- The number of properties and methods for a single object can be overwhelming, requiring a lot of scrolling in the Object Browser.

Advantages and Disadvantages of a Deep Organization

Deep object libraries, such as Excel's, require much more planning than broad organizations. A team of product managers at Microsoft wrote hundreds of pages of specifications before Microsoft wrote any code to implement the Excel objects. By the end of the process, the team used an Access database to keep the specifications up to date.

Excel is about as complex as the human brain. Excel's full potential, like that of the human brain, is seldom tapped; 90 percent of Excel's users never use more than 10 percent of the program's capabilities. Still, the Excel object library manages to include every feature and capability of Excel, and makes them all available from Visual Basic.

In all, the Excel object library defines about 4,200 items, including 1,943 properties, 1,385 methods, 756 constants, and 130 objects. This is much too large a chunk of knowledge for anyone to swallow whole, so Excel's object hierarchy breaks it down into smaller bites. The 130 objects include both individual objects and their collections. If you count objects and collections together, you have only 80 unique items. If you learn the purposes of these 80 objects, you can use the Excel object library effectively.

For example, performing calculations on a range of cells in Excel involves only four objects: Application, Workbook, Worksheet, and Range. Understanding this, you can focus on the relatively smaller number of properties and methods that those objects provide. Deep organizations of objects break the complexity of large object libraries into manageable pieces.

However, deep organizations can get too deep. Some Excel objects are nine levels down in the hierarchy. For example, the following code line changes the marker in the legend of a chart embedded on an Excel worksheet:

```
Application.Workbooks("stock.xls").Sheets("sheet1") _
    .ChartObjects(1).Chart.ChartGroups(1).Legend _
    .LegendEntries(1).LegendKey.MarkerStyle = xlTriangle
```

The preceding line requires nine object references to navigate down to the object to act on. Excel ameliorates this problem slightly by providing Application object properties such as ActiveWorkbook, ActiveSheet, and Selection, which act as shortcuts through the object hierarchy.

Another disadvantage to deep organizations of objects is that users might have trouble finding the object that they want to use for a specific task. You can address this problem by documenting your object library adequately; you not only must define *what* your objects are, you also must tell users *how* to use them.

Making objects easy to find and understand is not much of a problem for broad organizations, in which the method and property names mirror the user interface. Because of this mirroring, users can simply mimic their user-interface actions in code.

III

Creating OLE Objects

Summary

The following lists summarize the features, advantages, and disadvantages of a deep organization. The features include the following:

- You can create a few top-level objects by using Visual Basic's `CreateObject` or `GetObject` functions.

- Objects have methods that return subordinate and superordinate objects for navigation among objects.

- Each object has relatively few methods and properties.

- Methods and properties apply to specific instances of objects in the application rather than the current selection.

- Method and property names describe the actions that they perform or data that they represent rather than mirroring names on menus and dialog boxes.

Here are the advantages of a deep organization:

- If you have a complex, large library of objects, you can break it down into manageable pieces.

- Code written with the object library tends to be safe from user actions, because methods and properties act on references to specific objects.

- Changes to the user interface do not affect the object library.

- Object, property, and method names can describe more abstract items and tasks than the user interface can represent directly.

Disadvantages of a deep organization include the following:

- Users can have trouble understanding the relationships among objects or remembering which object to use for a specific task.

- Creating deep object libraries requires careful planning and a good understanding of object-oriented design.

- You must write documentation for object, properties, and methods from scratch.

- Having too many levels of objects can lead to awkward lines of code.

Recommendations

You must amortize the time that you spend planning the organization of your objects against the lifetime of your application. Creating a broad organization is faster and requires less planning, but misses out on the advantages of a well-designed deep organization.

Use broad organizations when implementing OLE Automation objects on top of an existing, widely installed application that is stable. Don't use a broad organization for an application that you often revise, particularly if you expect the user interface to change.

Use deep organizations of objects for new applications that you are building from the ground up, particularly if they are complex applications that you are building with object-oriented programming techniques.

Combine the two approaches when you want to compromise between effort and value. Not all features offer equal value to your users, so you should concentrate your design effort on the most-used features in your application. Don't use this as an excuse to be messy or inconsistent; just know where the value of your application lies.

Designing an Object Hierarchy

In an object hierarchy, superordinate objects provide methods that return subordinate objects. This enables users to create a top-level object, then navigate down to the object that they need, as shown in figure 20.4.

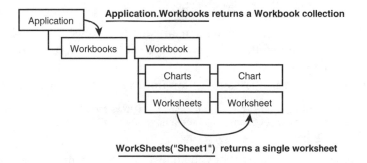

Fig. 20.4
Each object provides methods that return the next object down in the hierarchy.

If an object supports multiple instances of a subordinate object, the method returns a collection object. In figure 20.4, the Excel Application object supports multiple open files, represented by the Workbooks collection.

Not all subordinate objects have multiple instances. In Excel, charts can have only one legend, so the Chart object's Legend method returns a singular Legend object.

Subordinate objects should provide a way to navigate back up the object hierarchy. Microsoft decrees that all objects should have a Parent property that returns the next object up in the hierarchy, and an Application property that returns the top-level object in the hierarchy. Figure 20.5 shows how you use the Application and Parent property to navigate up an object hierarchy.

Fig. 20.5

The Application property jumps to the top of the hierarchy; Parent moves up one step.

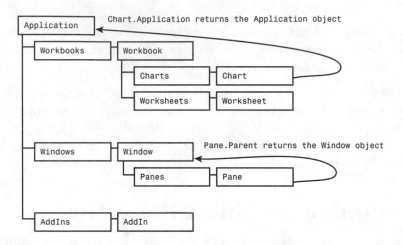

The Application and Parent properties skip over collections. For instance, Pane.Parent returns the Window object, not the Panes collection. Similarly, the Panes.Parent returns the Window object.

Because a single object can belong to many different collections, Visual Basic provides no standard method for returning an object's collection. You usually can get the object's collection from its parent object. The following code shows how to get a Worksheets collection from a Worksheet object in Excel:

```
Function GetCollection(objWorksheet As Worksheet) As Worksheets
    Set GetCollection = objWorksheet.Parent.Worksheets
End Function
```

The preceding code requires that you know that a Worksheets method for the Worksheet object's parent exists. Parent objects *usually* include a method for the child object's collection, but you should check the object library's documentation to make sure.

Why Is Navigation Important?

Applications usually expose only a few objects that `CreateObject` or `GetObject` can create. This limits the number of external entry points into the application and ensures that objects are correctly initialized before access.

Navigating downward through objects enables users to access the objects that are subordinate to those objects that `CreateObject` or `GetObject` can create. The methods that provide this downward mobility can create the object, initialize data, or lock access to data depending on the object's needs. In other words, navigation controls the flow through your application's objects.

Upward navigation is important to procedures that receive objects. You often have to know not only the type of an object, but which instance of another object owns it. `Parent` and `Application` properties help identify objects wherever they may roam.

Used together, upward and downward navigation enables you to move between any two objects in an object library, as shown in figure 20.6.

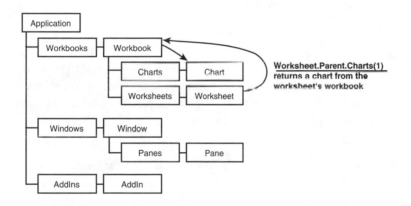

Fig. 20.6
Using navigation to move around in an object library.

Rules for Navigating Down

The method name and the name of the object that the method returns should be the same. This blurs the distinction between the method and the object, but makes code easier to read and understand. The following code uses the `Application` object's `Windows` method to display the number of `Window` objects in an application:

```
MsgBox Application.Windows.Count
```

III

Creating OLE Objects

> **Note**
>
> You could just as easily define the Application object's Windows method as a read-only property. In this case, choosing between a method and a property is a matter of taste.

The following code shows the definition for the Application object's Windows method. The variable that stores the application-wide Windows collection is defined in a code module so that other applications cannot modify the variable's setting.

```
' MODDECL.BAS -- DECLARES code module.
' Classes used throughout the application.
Public Application As New Application
Public Windows As New Windows

' APPLICAT.CLS -- APPLICATION Class.
' Application Windows method.
Public Function Windows() As Object
    ' Return the Windows variable from the
    ' modDeclares module.
    Set Windows = modDeclares.Windows
End Function
```

You also should provide Application object properties to return currently active objects in the application. This provides a shortcut to the object that has focus. Active object properties should be read-only. If you want to control focus from outside an application, provide an Activate method for the object.

The following code shows the definition for the Application object's ActiveWindow property. Because a code module defines the variable that stores the Window object that has focus, other applications cannot modify the variable's setting.

```
' MODDECL.BAS -- DECLARES code module.
' Internal variable that tracks active window.
Public gActiveWindow As Window

' APPLICAT.CLS -- APPLICATION Class.
' Application ActiveWindow property (read only)
Public Property Get ActiveWindow() As Window
    Set ActiveWindow = modDeclares.gActiveWindow
End Property
```

The following code shows the definition for the Window object's Activate method. The method sets the focus of a form within the application, and the form's GotFocus event procedure updates the internal variable (gActiveWindow) that stores the currently active Window object.

```
' WINDOW.CLS -- Window class module.
' Window Activate method.
Public Sub Activate()
    frmWindow.SetFocus
End Sub

' FRMWIN.FRM -- frmWindow form module.
' When form receives focus, update the ActiveWindow property.
Private Sub Form_GotFocus()
    ' Register the Window object
    ' that controls this form as the active object.
    Set modDeclares.gActiveWindow = Windows.Item(Me.Caption)
End Sub
```

Rules for Navigating Up

All objects in the hierarchy should define Application and Parent properties. Microsoft states this as a rule in the *OLE Programmer's Reference, Volume 2* (Microsoft Press). The Application property returns the top-level object in the object library's hierarchy. The Parent property returns the object that "owns" the current object. Both properties are read-only.

The Application and Parent properties for the Application object return the Application object itself. The following code defines the Application and Parent properties for an Application object:

```
' APPLICAT.CLS -- APPLICATION Class.
' Application object Application property
Public Property Get Application()
    Set Application = Me
End Property

' Application object Parent property
Public Property Get Parent()
    Set Parent = Me
End Property
```

The following code shows the definition for the Window object's Parent property. Because a code module defines the variable that stores the Application object, other applications cannot modify the variable's setting.

```
' WINDOW.CLS -- WINDOW Class.
' Window object Application property
Public Property Get Application()
    Set Application = modDeclares.Application
End Property
```

The Parent property of each object reflects the hierarchy of objects in the library. For each object, the property should return the object that created the object or otherwise owns control of the object. For objects that only one type of object can create, the object to return is easy to determine. For objects that many other objects can create, determining the object that Parent should return is more difficult.

Listing 20.1 shows how an object that many other objects can create and use maintains the Parent property. The DialogBox object's Create method displays the DialogBox object and registers the object that created the object as the newly created object's parent by using a Private variable, miParent. The object's Parent property returns a reference to that object.

Listing 20.1   Use a Private Object Variable to Keep Track of an Object's Parent

```
' DIALOG.CLS -- DialogBox Class.
Private miParent As Object

' DialogBox Create method.
Public Function Create(Owner As Object) As DialogBox
    ' Set the Parent of this object.
    Set miParent = Owner
    ' Create a new instance of the form.
    Dim NewDlg As New frmDialog
    ' Display the form
    NewDlg.Show
    ' Return a reference to this object.
    Set Create = Me
End Function

' DialogBox Parent property
Public Property Get Parent()
    ' Return reference to module-level variable
    ' set by Create.
    Set Parent = miParent
End Property
```

The Parent property of an object should stay within the bounds of the application that provides the object. In other words, if another application uses CreateObject to create an object, that object's Parent is *not* the calling application. The Parent and Application properties are intended for navigation within a single object library.

When Should You Create a Collection?

Collections organize multiple instances of objects within your application. Collections can be *homogeneous*—made up of objects of the same type—or *heterogeneous*—made up of objects of different types.

Homogeneous collections help you control multiple instances of objects that the application creates. For instance, an application that supports multiple open files might want to provide access to those files through a Documents collection. Each time that the user opens a new file, the application adds to the Documents collection the object that controls that file. When the application closes, it can check each document to see whether the application needs to save it, by using code similar to the following:

```
For Index = 1 to Documents.Count
    If Documents(Index).IsDirty Then
        Documents(Index).Save
    End If
Next Index
```

Without a container for all the Document objects, you cannot easily check which files need to be saved.

Heterogeneous collections provide a way to create multiple selections and to group diverse objects as a single unit for general operations, such as moving or sizing. For example, a Document object might provide a Selection method that returns a collection of all the objects currently selected in the document. The objects that the user can select provide the Selected property to add them to the collection.

> **Note**
>
> A Select method might seem like a more natural way to add objects to a Selection collection, but Visual Basic reserves the keyword Select, so you cannot use it as a method name.

Listing 20.2 shows the Selected property that selects an object. This read/write property should exist for each object that the user can select. A code module, modDeclares, stores the actual collection, so outside applications cannot change the property's setting directly.

Listing 20.2   The Selected Property Should Exist for Each Object That the User Can Select

```
' MODDECL.BAS -- modDeclares module.
Public Selection As Collection

' Object class -- this code belongs in each class module of
' objects that can be selected.
' Selected property (read/write)
```

(continues)

Listing 20.2 Continued

```
Public Property Get Selected() As Boolean
    Selected = mbSelected
End Sub

Public Property Let Selected(bVal As Boolean)
    mbSelected = bVal
    If bVal = True Then
        ' Add this object to the private Selection
        ' collection
        modDeclares.Selection.Add Me
        ' Indicate the item is selected by
        ' highlighting it.
        Me.BackColor = HIGHLIGHT
    End If
End Sub
```

The Document object provides a Selection method that returns the collection of objects stored in modDeclares.Selection. This provides a way to get the objects that the user selects, but prevents direct changes to the collection. The following is the Selection method:

```
' Document object Selection method.
Public Function Selection() As Collection
    Set Selection = modDeclares.Selection
End Sub
```

Using Sensible Names for OLE Automation Objects

Like all symbols in your code, objects, properties, and methods should have names that clearly describe what they are or what they do. Objects, properties, and methods that are visible outside your application should have English-like, readable names. Therefore, OLE Automation objects might not follow the same naming conventions that you use for other symbols in your application. Table 20.1 shows the names in an application that appear to other applications.

Table 20.1   Application Names and Where They Appear

Item	Location of Appearance
Project name	First part of the programmatic ID in the system registration database, and the first part of the Libraries/Projects name in the Object Browser

Item	Location of Appearance
Project description	The library description in the References dialog box and the second part of the Libraries/Projects name in the Object Browser
Class module name for system-creatable objects	Second part of the programmatic ID in the registration database
Class module name for `Public` objects	Name in the Classes/Modules list of the Object Browser
Class module name for `Private` objects	Nowhere outside the application
Form module name	Nowhere outside the application
Code module name	Nowhere outside the application
`Public` procedure and variable names in a `Public` class module	Methods/Properties names in the Object Browser
`Private` procedure and variable names in a `Public` class module	Nowhere outside the application

Programmatic IDs

A class module with an `Instancing` property set to `True` has a programmatic ID. Visual Basic creates the programmatic ID by combining the project name and the class name. The programmatic ID is registered in the system registration database and used in the `CreateObject` or `GetObject` function to create the object from another application. For example, the following line of code starts the VB Terminal application and returns a reference to its `Application` object:

```
Set objVBTerm = CreateObject("vbterminal.application")
```

Project names should not include any of the following special characters:

```
~!@#$%^&*()_+'-=<>?/.,
```

Visual Basic removes these characters when creating the programmatic ID. For example, the project name `My_Project` becomes `MyProject` in the registration database.

Project names should not start with a number. Visual Basic appends `vb4` when creating class names that begin with a numeric digit. For example, the project name `1234` becomes `vb41234` in the registration database.

The application's project name also appears in the Object Browser along with the project description. The application's description appears in the References dialog box, as shown in figure 20.7. Including a description for your application is very important if it provides `Public` classes; otherwise, the References dialog box simply displays the application name.

Fig. 20.7
Applications that don't have project descriptions appear as "mystery" applications in the References dialog box.

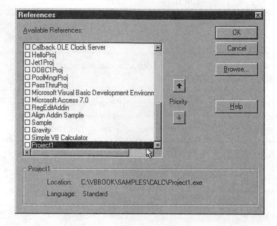

You set project names and descriptions in the Project page of the Options property pages (fig. 20.8).

Fig. 20.8
Choose Tools, Options to display the Options property pages.

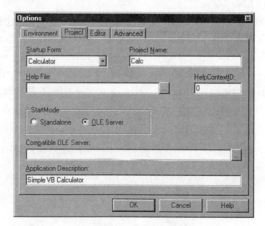

Public Class, Procedure, and Variable Names

A class module is visible from other applications if you set its `Public` property to `True`. All the procedures and variables declared as `Public` in that module are also visible from other applications.

The name of `Public` class modules appears in the Classes/Modules list of the Object Browser. The `Public` procedures and variables appear in the Methods/ Properties list, as shown in figure 20.9.

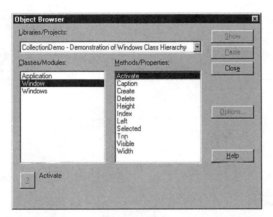

Fig. 20.9
The Object Browser displays all the `Public` procedures and variables in a `Public` class module.

> **Note**
>
> Inside the application that defines them, `Public` variables don't appear in the Object Browser. Outside the application, however, you can view them in the Object Browser's Methods/Properties list.

The names of `Public` classes, procedures, and variables should follow the rules listed in table 20.2.

Table 20.2   Class, Procedure, and Variable Naming Rules

Rule	Use	Don't Use
Use entire words or syllables whenever possible.	Application Window Document Selection	App Wnd NewDoc SelObjects

(continues)

III

Creating OLE Objects

Table 20.2 Continued		
Rule	**Use**	**Don't Use**
Use mixed case to separate words.	ActiveWindow BasedOn IsDirty	activewindow based_on Is_Dirty
Use the same word as you use in the application's interface.	Toolbar ProjectOptions SelectAll	ToolsCollection UserPrefs HighlightAll
Use the plural of the singular object for collection names.	Windows TextBoxes Axis	colWindows TextBoxCollection Axes
For plurals that are the same as the singular form, append Collection.	SheepCollection SeriesCollection	Sheeps CollectionSeries

Standard Objects, Properties, and Methods

When creating an object library, you must be as consistent as possible with similar object libraries. That is, you must use the same or similar names for like objects, properties, and methods. If you maintain such consistency, you save users from having to relearn names for common objects, properties, and methods.

You do not have to be so slavishly consistent that you can't take advantage of the unique capabilities that your application provides. The guidelines in this section should help you create object libraries that enable users to become quickly familiar with its objects, properties, and methods; the guidelines should not limit what your application can do.

As this chapter previously mentioned, all objects should provide Application and Parent properties. These properties return values of the Object data type, as shown in table 20.3.

Table 20.3   Properties and Methods That All Collections Should Provide

Property	Return Type	Description
Application	Object	Returns the top-level object in the object hierarchy. (Read-only.)
Parent	Object	Returns the object that created or owns the object. (Read-only.)

All collection objects should provide additional properties and methods that enable users to add, remove, and manipulate the objects contained in the collection. Table 20.4 lists the objects that are required for collection objects as well as those that are recommended.

Table 20.4   Properties That All Collections Should Provide

Item	Return Type	Description
Required Properties		
Count property	Long	Returns the number of objects in the collection. (Read-only.)
Item method	Object	Returns one object from the collection. Item might require a numeric index or a string argument to identify the object to retrieve from the collection.
Recommended Properties		
Add method	Object	Adds an object to the collection.
Remove method	None	Removes an item from the collection. Remove might require a numeric index or a string argument to identify the object to remove from the collection.

According to the *OLE 2 Programmer's Reference, Volume 2* (Microsoft Press), applications that create documents should provide the following standard objects:

- An Application object

- A Document object

■ A Documents collection

■ A Font object

Microsoft identifies these objects as "standard" because they were the ones that the Microsoft Excel and Microsoft Word product groups could agree on before Microsoft released OLE 2.0. Although these objects might not apply to your application, they are useful to examine for their approach to some common properties and methods, such as Left, Top, and Quit. The following sections describe the properties and methods for these standard objects.

The *Application* Object

The Application object should have the following properties and methods. Table 20.5 shows items that are required for the Application object as well as those that are recommended.

Table 20.5	Application **Object Properties and Methods**	
Item	**Return Type**	**Description**
Required Properties		
Application property	Object	Returns the Application object. (Read-only.)
Name property	String	Returns the name of the application, such as Microsoft Excel. (Read-only.)
Parent property	Object	Returns the Application object. (Read-only.)
Quit method	None	Exits the application and closes all open documents.
Recommended Properties		
Active *Document* property	Object	Returns the active document object. In this property name, you should use the name of the document object. For example, ActiveWindow or ActiveWorkbook are appropriate names. (Read-only.)
Caption property	String	Sets or returns the title of the application window. (Read/write.)

Item	Return Type	Description
DefaultFilePath property	String	Sets or returns the default path specification that the application uses for opening files. (Read/write.)
Documents property	Object	Returns a collection object for the open documents. The name of this property should match the name that you use for your Documents collection. (Read-only.)
FullName property	String	Returns the file specification for the application, including the path. Example: C:\DRAWDIR\SCRIBBLE.EXE. (Read-only.)
Height property	Single	Sets or returns the distance between the top and bottom edge of the main application window. (Read/write.)
Help method	None	Displays online Help for the application.
Interactive property	Boolean	Sets or returns whether the application accepts actions from the user. (Read/write.)
Left property	Single	Sets or returns the distance between the left edge of the physical screen and the main application window. (Read/write.)
Path property	String	Returns the path specification for the application's executable file. Example: C:\DRAWDIR if the executable is C:\DRAWDIR\SCRIBBLE.EXE. (Read-only.)
Repeat method	None	Repeats the previous action in the user interface.
StatusBar property	String	Sets or returns the text displayed in the status bar. (Read/write.)

(continues)

III

Creating OLE Objects

Table 20.5   Continued

Item	Return Type	Description
Top property	Single	Sets or returns the distance between the top edge of the physical screen and main application window. (Read/write.)
Undo method	None	Reverses the previous action in the user interface.
Visible property	Boolean	Sets or returns whether the application is visible to the user. (Read/write.)
Width property	Single	Sets or returns the distance between the left and right edges of the main application window. (Read/write.)

The *Document* Object

If your application is document-based, you should provide a Document object. You should use the name Document for this object unless you have used a different name, such as Drawing, within your application. Table 20.6 lists items that are required for the Document object as well as those that are recommended.

Table 20.6   Document Object Properties and Methods

Item	Return Type	Description
Required Properties		
Application property	Object	Returns the Application object. (Read-only.)
Close method	None	Closes all windows associated with a given document and removes the document from the Documents collection.
Name property	String	Returns the file name of the document, not including the file's path specification. (Read-only.)
Parent property	Object	Returns the parent of the Document object. (Read-only.)

Item	Return Type	Description
Recommended Properties		
Activate method	None	Activates the first window associated with a given document.
Author property	String	Sets or returns summary information about the document's author. (Read/write.)
Comments property	String	Sets or returns summary information comments for the document. (Read/write.)
FullName property	String	Returns the file specification of the document, including the path. (Read/write.)
Keywords property	String	Sets or returns summary information keywords associated with the document. (Read/write.)
NewWindow method	None	Creates a new window for the given document.
Path property	String	Returns the path specification for the document, not including the file name or file name extension. (Read-only.)
PrintOut method	None	Prints the document.
PrintPreview method	None	Previews the pages and page breaks of the document. Equivalent to choosing File, Print Preview.
ReadOnly property	Boolean	Returns True if the file is read-only and False otherwise. (Read-only.)
RevertToSaved method	None	Reverts to the last saved copy of the document, discarding any changes.
Save method	None	Saves changes to the file specified in the document's FullName property.

(continues)

Table 20.6	Continued	
Item	**Return Type**	**Description**
Saved property	Boolean	Returns True if the document has never been saved or changed since its creation. Returns True if the document was saved and has not changed since the last save. Returns False if the document was never saved but was changed since its creation, or if the document was saved but has changed since the last save. (Read-only.)
SaveAs method	None	Saves changes to a file. Takes one optional argument, *filename* (VT_BSTR). The *filename* argument can include a path specification.
Subject property	String	Sets or returns the summary information about the subject of the document. (Read/write.)
Title property	String	Sets or returns summary information about the document's title. (Read/write.)

The *Documents* Collection

If your application is document-based, you should provide a Documents collection object. You should use the name Documents for this collection unless that name is inappropriate for your application. Table 20.7 lists the items required for the Documents collection as well as those that are recommended.

Table 20.7	Documents **Collection Properties and Methods**	
Item	**Return Type**	**Description**
Required Properties		
Add method	Object	Creates a new document and adds it to the collection. Returns the document that the method created.
Application property	Object	Returns the Application object. (Read-only.)

Item	Return Type	Description
Count property	Long	Returns the number of items in the collection. (Read-only.)
Item method	Object	Returns a Document object from the collection. Takes an optional argument, index, which can take a String indicating the document's Name property, an Integer indicating the ordered position within the collection, or either (Variant).
Parent property	Object	Returns the parent of the Documents collection object. (Read-only.)
Recommended Properties		
Close method	None	Closes all documents in the collection.
Open method	Object	Opens an existing document and adds it to the collection. Returns the document that the method opened or Empty if the method could not open the object.

The *Font* Object

Table 20.8 lists the items required for Font object as well as those that are recommended.

Table 20.8	Font **Object Properties and Methods**	
Item	**Return Type**	**Description**
Required Properties		
Application property	Object	Returns the Application object. (Read-only.)
Name property	String	Returns the name of the font. (Read-only.)
Parent property	Object	Returns the parent of the Font object. (Read-only.)
Recommended Properties		
Bold property	Boolean	Sets or returns whether the font is boldface. (Read/write.)

III

Creating OLE Objects

(continues)

Table 20.8 Continued

Item	Return Type	Description
Recommended Properties		
Color property	Long	Sets or returns the RGB color of the font. (Read/write.)
Italic property	Boolean	Sets or returns whether the font is italic. (Read/write.)
OutlineFont property	Boolean	Sets or returns whether the font is scaleable. For example, bitmapped fonts are not scaleable, but TrueType fonts are. (Read/write.)
Shadow property	Boolean	Sets or returns whether the font appears with a shadow. (Read/write.)
Size property	Single	Sets or returns the size of the font in points. (Read/write.)
Strikethrough property	Boolean	Sets or returns whether the font appears with a line running through it. (Read/write.)
Subscript property	Boolean	Sets or returns whether the font is subscripted. (Read/write.)
Superscript property	Boolean	Sets or returns whether the font is superscripted. (Read/write.)

From Here...

For more information on the following topics, see the indicated chapters:

- Chapter 22, "Debugging Applications That Provide Objects," gives you important insight into solving the many new problem areas that crop up as you program with objects.

- Chapter 23, "Building and Distributing OLE Objects," tells you how to compile and build installation programs for applications that provide objects to other applications. It also discusses how to maintain applications so future versions don't break compatibility with previous versions.

Chapter 21

Advanced OLE Programming Techniques

Advanced topics should always be slightly shocking. Fortunately, Visual Basic enables you to do many startling things with objects. The topics in this chapter range from the esoteric (extending data types) to the downright practical (extending Excel). All, however, are eye-openers.

In this chapter, you learn about the following:

- Extending fundamental data types with objects

- Storing data in tree structures by creating recursive objects

- Creating write-once, read-always properties

- Organizing multideveloper projects using object libraries

- Using Visual Basic 4.0 object libraries from the Visual Basic Applications Edition

- Creating object libraries for use in Excel

- Extending the VBA language with code-only object libraries

- Invoking object library properties and methods from Excel menus and toolbars

- Creating and modifying Excel menus and toolbars in code

- Using Excel add-ins to distribute object libraries written for Excel

Creating Extended Data Types

Objects are a type of data, so you can use them just like any other data type in Visual Basic. This can lead to some interesting and surprising applications. For example, many DLLs return flag settings as bytes within a long integer. To extract the information from the returned long integer, you must read the various parts of the integer, as shown in figure 21.1.

Fig. 21.1
Reading the bytes from a long integer.

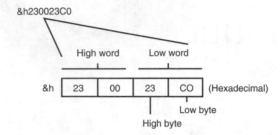

The procedural approach to this problem is to create four functions that return the various parts of the long integer: HiWord, LoWord, HiByte, and LoByte. But you can also tackle this problem by using objects. By creating classes for Long and Integer types, you can have the object parse itself by using its own methods. The TYPES.VBP sample defines two classes, as shown in table 21.1.

Table 21.1 TYPES.VBP Class Module Property Settings		
Class Name	**Instancing**	**Public**
clsLong	True	True
clsInteger	True	True

The *clsLong* Object

TYPES.VBP defines its clsLong object in the clsLong class (LONG.CLS). The clsLong object has the following property and methods:

Property/Method	Description
Value property	Sets or returns the value that the object contains. (Read/write.)
HiWord method	Returns a clsInteger object that contains the value of the high word of the clsLong object.
LoWord method	Returns a clsInteger object that contains the value of the low word of the clsLong object.

The HiWord and LoWord methods return an object rather than a value, so you can easily use the subsequent methods in clsInteger to get the high and low bytes. Listing 21.1 shows the clsLong class that contains the Value property and HiWord and LoWord methods.

Listing 21.1   The clsLong Class

```
' Long class -- LONG.CLS
'    Parses Long integers into integers (words)
'
'    Properties
'        Value
'
'    Methods
'        LoWord
'        HiWord
'
Option Explicit

' Value property (read/write)
Public Value

Public Function HiWord() As Object
    ' Create a new object to return.
    Dim intReturn As New clsInteger
    ' Get the high word and set the inReturn object's
    ' Value property.
    If Me.Value > &H7FFFFFFF Then
        intReturn.Value = (Me.Value And &HFFFF0000) \ &H10000
    Else
        intReturn.Value = ((Me.Value And &HFFFF0000) / _
                    &H10000) Xor &HFFFF0000
    End If
    ' Return the intReturn object as the result.
    ' Note that you must use Set, since this is object
    ' assignment.
    Set HiWord = intReturn
End Function

Public Function LoWord() As Object
    ' Create a new object to return.
    Dim intReturn As New clsInteger
    ' Get the low word and set the inReturn object's
    ' Value property.
    intReturn.Value = Me.Value And (Me.Value Xor &HFFFF0000)
    ' Return the intReturn object as the result.
    ' Note that you must use Set, since this is object
    ' assignment.
    Set LoWord = intReturn
End Function
```

III

Creating OLE Objects

The *clsInteger* Object

The clsInteger class (LONG.CLS) defines TYPES.VBP's clsInteger object. The object has the following property and methods:

Property/Method	Description
Value property	Sets or returns the value that the object contains. (Read/write.)
HiByte method	Returns a Byte that contains the value of the high byte of the clsInteger object.
LoByte method	Returns a Byte that contains the value of the low byte of the clsInteger object.

The HiByte and LoByte methods return a fundamental type (Byte) rather than an object. You can easily extend this example to return a bits collection that contains the eight bits of the byte. Listing 21.2 shows the clsInteger class that contains the Value property and HiByte and LoByte methods.

Listing 21.2   The clsInteger Class

```
' clsInteger class -- INTEGER.CLS
'    Parses integers (words) into bytes.
'
'    Properties:
'        Value
'
'    Methods:
'        LoByte
'        HiByte
'
Option Explicit

' Value property.
Public Value

' HiByte method.
Public Function HiByte()
    ' Return the high byte from an integer.
    HiByte = (Me.Value And &HFF00) \ &H100
End Function

' LoByte method.
Public Function LoByte()
    ' Return the low byte from an integer.
    LoByte = Me.Value Xor (Me.Value And &HFF00)
End Function
```

Using *clsLong* and *clsInteger* Objects

Using the clsLong and clsInteger objects in code is the same as using any
other object. First, declare a variable as a new instance of the object; then, use
the object's properties and methods. The following code demonstrates how to
use the two objects to parse a long integer:

```
Sub Main()
    ' Create an object variable.
    Dim lngValue As New clsLong
    ' Set the object's Value property.
    lngValue.Value = &h1020304
    ' Display the value of
    ' the least significant byte.
    MsgBox lngValue.LoWord.LoByte
End Sub
```

You cannot create default properties for objects in Visual Basic, so you must
remember to use a Value property when assigning a value to an object of an
extended type.

Creating Recursive Data Types

One of the most interesting applications of an extended data type is a recursive type. *Recursive types* contain elements of their own type, creating a tree of
data. You can use tree structures to solve many programming problems, such
as sorting data, storing directory structures, and creating outlines.

The OUTLINE.VBP sample provides a Topic object that you can use as a general data type to store any tree-structured information. The Topic object provides an AddSubtopic method to create more instances of itself, as shown in
figure 21.2.

You can create the same type of structure by using user-defined data types
(Type...End Type) and arrays, but objects give you the advantage of automatic
garbage-collection. If you delete Topic3 from the structure shown in figure
21.2, you also automatically destroy TopicA and TopicB because their reference (contained in Topic3) no longer exists.

The OUTLINE.VBP sample defines a single class, as shown in table 21.2.

Fig. 21.2
The Topic object can create subordinate objects of its own type to store tree-structured data.

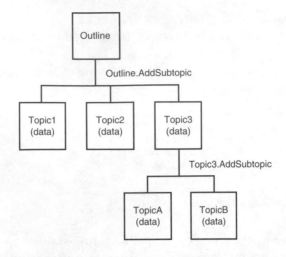

Table 21.2 TYPES.VBP Class Module Property Setting		
Class Name	**Instancing**	**Public**
Topic	True	True

Most of the properties and methods of the Topic object are navigational; that is, they deal with the creation and placement of the object in a hierarchy (tree) of objects. Only the Value property is functional. It sets or returns the actual data that you want to store in the hierarchy. Of course, you can expand the Topic object to contain more functional methods and properties. Methods for printing the data or storing it to disk are some enhancements that you might consider. Table 21.3 describes the properties and methods that Topic provides.

Table 21.3 Topic **Object Properties and Methods**	
Property/Method	**Description**
Parent property	Returns the creator of this object. For the top-level object, returns itself (which is an OLE convention). (Read/write once.)
Index property	Returns a numeric index that stores the object in its containing collection. The Delete method uses this property to remove the object. (Read/write once.)

Property/Method	Description
Value property	Sets or returns the value that the object contains. The Value property can receive any data type, so it has Property Get, Let, and Set procedures. (Read/write.)
AddSubtopic method	Creates a new, subordinate Topic object and adds it to the current object's collection. AddSubtopic sets the new Topic object's Index and Parent properties for the first (and only) time.
Delete method	Deletes the Topic object from its Parent object's collection, destroying the current object and all of its contained objects (subtopics).
SubTopics method	Returns the collection of Topic objects that this object contains.

Module-Level *Private* Variables

The Topic class uses Private variables to store the settings of Parent, Index, and Value properties. The Property procedures for these properties control access to the variables. Topic also uses a Private collection variable, colSubTopics, to contain the object's subtopics. The AddSubtopics and Delete methods maintain the colSubTopics variable, and the Topics method returns the variable. The following lines show the module-level comments and declarations for the Topic class:

```
' Topic class -- TOPIC.CLS
'    Recursive data type -- stores any type of
'    tree-structured information.
'
'    Properties
'        Parent
'        Index
'        Value
'
'    Methods
'        AddSubtopic
'        Delete
'        Topics
'
Option Explicit

' Internal variables used to store information
' used by various methods and properties.
Private mParent As Topic
Private mIndex As Integer
Private mValue As Variant
Private colSubTopics As New Collection
```

The *Parent* and *Index* Properties

The Parent and Index properties are the primary navigational properties for the Topic class. The AddSubtopic method initializes both properties once; thereafter, the properties are read-only. They demonstrate how to implement write-once, read-always properties, which are useful in a variety of contexts.

You use the Parent property to move up in the object hierarchy. The Delete method uses the property to get the collection object from which to remove the object. Listing 21.3 is the definition of the Parent property for the Topic class.

Listing 21.3   Definition of the Parent Property for the Topic Class

```
' Parent property (write-once, read-always).
Public Property Get Parent() As Topic
    ' If parent is not set, then the object
    ' is the top-level topic, so Parent is Me.
    If TypeName(mParent) = "Nothing" Then
        Set Parent = Me
    End If
    ' Return the parent object.
    Set Parent = mParent
End Property

Public Property Set Parent(objSetting As Topic)
    ' Initialize this property only once. Afterward, return
    ' an error.
    If TypeName(mParent) = "Nothing" Then
        Set mParent = objSetting
    Else
        ' Can't reset.
        Err.Raise 383, "Topic object", _
            "Parent property is read-only."
    End If
End Property
```

You use the Index property to select an item from the collection that the Topics method returns. The Delete method uses this property to identify which object to delete from the Parent object's collection. Usually, objects that belong to a collection must provide some kind of Index property to enable specific objects to be selected and deleted. Listing 21.4 shows the definition of the Index property for the Topic class.

Listing 21.4   Definition of the Index **Property for the** Topic **Class**

```
' Index property (write-once, read-always).
Public Property Get Index() As Integer
    ' Return the internal Index variable
    ' initialized when Name is first set.
    Index = mIndex
End Property

Public Property Let Index(iSetting As Integer)
    ' Check if property has already been set.
    If mIndex = 0 Then
        ' Set index on first call.
        mIndex = iSetting
    Else
        ' Can't reset.
        Err.Raise 383, "Topic object", _
            "Index property is read-only."
    End If
End Property
```

The *Value* Property

The Value property is an example of a property that can receive or return any type of value—fundamental type or object reference. The property has all three types of Property procedure: Get, Let, and Set. The property invokes the appropriate procedure, depending on the data that Value stores. The Property Let procedure is *polymorphic*—that is, it returns a value if the stored data is a fundamental type; it returns an object reference using Set if the stored data is an object. Listing 21.5 is the definition of the Value property for the Topic class.

Listing 21.5   Definition of the Value **Property for the** Topic **Class**

```
' Value property (read/write).
' May contain object data or fundamental type
' (get/let/set).
Public Property Get Value() As Variant
    ' If the data is an object, use Set.
    ' Otherwise, use regular assignment.
    If IsObject(mValue) Then
        ' Return the internal Data variable.
        Set Value = mValue
    Else
        ' Return the internal Data variable.
        Value = mValue
    End If
End Property
```

(continues)

Listing 21.5 Continued

```
Public Property Let Value(vSetting As Variant)
    ' Update the internal Data variable.
    mValue = vSetting
End Property

Public Property Set Value(objSetting As Object)
    ' Update the internal Data variable.
    Set mValue = objSetting
End Property
```

The *AddSubtopic* Method

The AddSubtopic method adds a Topic object to the current object's colSubtopics collection. This behavior makes the Topic object *recursive*—that is, you can add as many levels to the object hierarchy as you want, using just one class. AddSubtopic initializes the new object's write-once properties, Index and Parent, ensuring that the user cannot change them and disrupt the hierarchy. Listing 21.6 is the definition of the AddSubtopic method for the Topic class.

Listing 21.6 Definition of the AddSubtopic Method for the Topic Class

```
' AddSubTopic method.
Public Function AddSubtopic() As Topic
    ' Create a new subtopic.
    Dim NewTopic As New Topic
    ' Use a static Index to create a unique key
    ' for each subtopic to add to the collection.
    Static Index As Integer
    Index = Index + 1
    NewTopic.Index = Index
    ' Set Parent property (creator is parent).
    Set NewTopic.Parent = Me
    ' Add the topic to the collection of
    ' subtopics (NewTopic.Index is unique).
    colSubTopics.Add NewTopic, Str(NewTopic.Index)
    ' Return this object as the result of function.
    Set AddSubtopic = NewTopic
End Function
```

The *Delete* Method

The Delete method deletes the current object by calling the Remove method on the Parent object's collection. Remove takes a numeric index or string key value as its argument. Because a collection's order can change, you must use the object's Index property to delete the appropriate object. Delete requires special code to handle being called on the hierarchy's top-level object. In this case, Delete clears the object's collection when called on the top-level object. Listing 21.7 is the definition of the Delete method for the Topic class.

Listing 21.7   Definition of the Delete Method for the Topic Class

```
Public Sub Delete()
    ' If this is the top-level object, then
    ' clear the collection, destroying all
    ' subtopics.
    If (Me Is Me.Parent) Then
        ' Remove first item from the collection
        ' until it is empty
        Do Until colSubTopics.Count = 0
            colSubTopics.Remove 1
        Loop
    ' This object isn't the first topic, so
    ' remove it from its parent's collection.
    Else
        Me.Parent.Topics.Remove Me.Index
        ' Subtopics under this topic are automatically
        ' destroyed when they go out of scope.
    End If
End Sub
```

The *Topics* Method

The Topics method returns the collection of Topic objects contained in the private colSubtopics variable. You use the Topics method to navigate down in the object hierarchy. Listing 21.8 is the definition of the Topics method for the Topic class.

Listing 21.8   Definition of the Topics Property for the Topic Class

```
Public Function Topics() As Collection
    Set Topics = colSubTopics
End Function
```

Using the *Topics* Object

You traverse recursive data structures by using recursive procedures. A *recursive procedure* is one that calls itself to solve a problem. Listing 21.9 is a Main procedure that uses two recursive procedures: AddLevel creates new Topic objects from tab-delineated lines of text, and SearchTree traverses the object hierarchy to find a Topic object with a specific Value setting.

III

Creating OLE Objects

Listing 21.9   A `Main` Procedure with Two Recursive Procedures

```
Option Explicit
' Create a new Topic object variable.
Dim Outline As New Topic

Sub Main()
    Dim strLine As String, strName As String
    Dim Topic As Topic
    Open "org.txt" For Input As #1
    Do Until EOF(1)
        Line Input #1, strLine
        AddLevel strLine, Outline
    Loop
    Close 1
    strName = InputBox("Enter your name")
    Set Topic = SearchTree(strName, Outline)
    MsgBox "Your boss is " & Topic.Parent.Value
    Set Outline = Nothing
    End
End Sub
```

The `AddLevel` procedure adds topics to the object hierarchy based on a passed-in string argument, `strLine`. `AddLevel` uses the number of tab characters in the string to determine the level in the hierarchy for the new object. Listing 21.10 shows the `AddLevel` procedure.

Listing 21.10   The `AddLevel` Procedure

```
Sub AddLevel(strLine As String, objTopic As Topic)
    ' If the line starts with a tab...
    If Mid(strLine, 1, 1) = Chr$(9) Then
        ' Trim off the character and call again.
        AddLevel Right(strLine, Len(strLine) - 1), _
            objTopic.Topics.Item(objTopic.Topics.Count)
    Else
        objTopic.AddSubtopic.Value = strLine
    End If
End Sub
```

The `SearchTree` procedure searches down each branch of the object hierarchy, checking for a match between `strName` and the passed-in object's `Value` property. `SearchTree` keeps searching downward until it finds the bottom-level object in each branch (when `Topics.Count = 0`). If the procedure finds a match before reaching the bottom, it returns that object. Otherwise, `SearchTree` bubbles back up and searches down the next branch. Listing 21.11 shows the `SearchTree` procedure.

Listing 21.11   The SearchTree Procedure

```
Function SearchTree(strName As String, objTopic As Topic) As Topic
    Dim Item As Topic
    If objTopic.Topics.Count > 0 Then
        For Each Item In objTopic.Topics
            If Item.Value = strName Then
                Set SearchTree = Item
            Else
                Set SearchTree = SearchTree(strName, Item)
            End If
        Next Item
    End If
End Function
```

Using Object Libraries during Development

You can use extended data types like clsLong and Topic within an application by copying their class modules to the application's project, or you can compile them and use them as object libraries across multiple applications.

If you use these objects across applications, you incur some overhead from using OLE objects. Sometimes, this overhead might not be a problem. However, if you use many extended fundamental types, such as clsLong, you might consider developing your application by using the class as an OLE .DLL and then creating your release-version application with the class compiled into the project's .EXE file.

This solution enables you to distribute the development of your application among programmers, but optimizes the performance in your released .EXE file. By using object libraries during development, you restrict the changes to those libraries and draw clearer lines of responsibility among developers. Using object libraries in this way is similar to using .LIB files when developing applications in the C programming language. Figure 21.3 illustrates this approach to developing projects.

Compiling an object library as a .DLL rather than an .EXE improves the performance of applications that use the object library. Accessing a method or property from a .DLL is 10 to 100 times faster than accessing a method or property from an .EXE.

III

Creating OLE Objects

Fig. 21.3
Use compiled ob-
ject libraries during
development, then
optimize by com-
piling the classes
into the release
.EXE file.

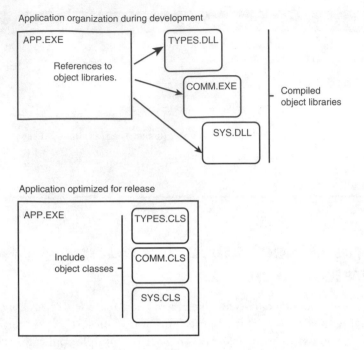

Creating Object Libraries for Other Applications

Any application that includes Visual Basic Applications Edition (VBA) can use object libraries that you compile in Visual Basic. Currently, only two applications fit this description: Microsoft Excel and Microsoft Project. The next release of Microsoft Access is supposed to include VBA, and Microsoft Word 7.0 probably will provide access to VBA objects through its language, WordBasic.

Other companies, such as Borland International, are working on support for OLE objects in their applications and development tools. But currently it is unclear what depth those features will have.

For now, the primary clients for Visual Basic object libraries are Microsoft Excel and applications created in Visual Basic. The process of creating an object library is the same regardless of the application for which you intend it. Chapter 18, "Creating Objects," demonstrates how to build an .EXE file that provides objects to other applications.

Using an object library from another application varies slightly from application to application. For instance, VBA in Excel and Project does not provide a

New keyword, so you cannot declare a variable as a new object (Dim obVar As New Class), as you can in Visual Basic 4.0.

VBA itself is an object library, but you can't "switch out" the VBA 1.0 library in Excel or Project from the VBA 2.0 library. Therefore, when writing code within Excel or Project, you must limit yourself to language supported in VBA 1.0. Table 21.4 lists the VBA 2.0 features unavailable from within VBA in Excel or Project.

Table 21.4   Language Features Unavailable in Microsoft Excel and Project

VBA 2.0 Feature	VBA 1.0 Substitute
Dim...As New...	Use the CreateObject function.
Specific object types	Use generic Object data type for objects created in Visual Basic 4.0.
Collection objects	Pass Excel or Project collections to VBA 2.0 procedures. You cannot create new collections in VBA 1.0.
Class modules	Pass Excel or Project objects to VBA 2.0 procedures. You cannot create new classes of objects in VBA 2.0.

Using Visual Basic Object Libraries from Excel

You can use object libraries created in Visual Basic 4.0 to extend Excel's features. These extensions take two general forms:

- Extensions to the VBA programming language in Excel
- New user-interface components, such as new menu items and dialog boxes

The following sections describe how to add to the Microsoft Excel application some features created in Visual Basic 4.0. Because these sections deal with VBA in Excel, the code examples show you how to write the code in a VBA code module within Excel. You can actually run these lines in either Excel or Visual Basic 4.0 (VB4). However, in VB4, you must first establish a reference to the Excel object, because this reference is implicit from within Excel.

The following code lines demonstrate how to initialize commonly used Excel object references from within VB4:

```
' Microsoft Excel commonly used object variables.
Public Application As Object
Public ActiveWorkbook As Object
Public ActiveSheet As Object

Sub Main()
' Initialize objects.
    ' Starts Microsoft Excel and establishes a reference to the
    ' Excel application object.
    Set Application = CreateObject("Excel.Application")
    ' Excel starts invisibly, so make it visible as a first step.
    Application.Visible = True
    ' Microsoft Excel starts with no loaded workbook,
    ' so create one.
    Application.Workbooks.Add
    Set ActiveWorkbook = Application.ActiveWorkbook
    Set ActiveSheet = Application.ActiveSheet
End Sub
```

Adding New Objects to VBA in Excel

Object libraries that you create in VB4 are automatically available from VBA in Excel if they meet the following criteria:

- They must contain classes with Instancing and Public properties set to True.

- Their .EXE files must be registered in the system registration database or be running in the Visual Basic programming environment as object applications.

From VBA in Excel, use the CreateObject or GetObject functions to establish a reference to an object in a VB4 object library. The following Microsoft Excel VBA code line establishes a reference to the WinAPI application object in the SYSTEM.VBP sample included on the companion CD:

```
Set WinAPI = CreateObject("WinAPI.Application")
```

After establishing a reference to the object, you can use the object's methods and properties just as you can within VB4. The following code line uses the preceding WinAPI object to get the path of the Windows directory:

```
strWinDir = WinAPI.Information.WindowsDirectory
```

Browsing VB4 Object Libraries in Excel

You don't have to establish a reference to a VB4 object library to use it from Excel. However, establishing a reference enables you to view the object library using Excel's Object Browser, which is identical to the VB4 Object Browser.

To establish a reference to a VB4 object library in Excel, follow these steps:

1. Display a code module in Excel. Choose <u>T</u>ools, <u>R</u>eferences. Excel displays the References dialog box (see fig. 21.4).

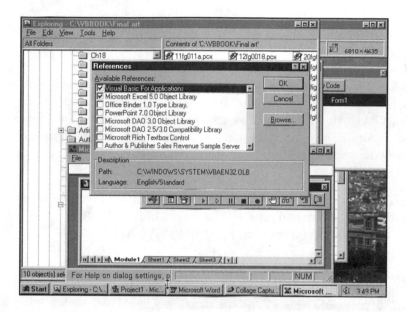

Fig. 21.4
Excel's References
dialog box.

2. The References dialog box's <u>A</u>vailable References list displays all the object libraries registered with the system registration database. If the list does not display the library that you want, choose the <u>B</u>rowse button. Excel displays the Object Browser (fig. 21.5), in which you can select a VB4 .EXE file that contains the object library.

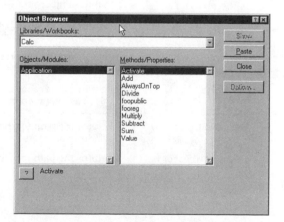

Fig. 21.5
Excel's Object
Browser.

III

Creating OLE Objects

3. Select a file to reference and click Close. Excel adds the file to the References dialog box and marks with an X the check box to the file name's left. This mark indicates that you have a reference to that object library.

After you have a reference to a VB4 object library, you can use the Excel Object Browser to view its Public object, methods, and properties.

A Code-Only Object Library

The SYSTEM.VBP sample on the companion CD is a good example of a code-only object library that you might want to use from VBA in Excel or any other VBA client. SYSTEM.VBP repackages some popular Windows API calls as objects. Although you can call Windows DLLs directly from VBA in Excel, getting the declarations right is often difficult, and the argument lists are long and complicated.

SYSTEM.VBP simplifies calling some of the Window API functions by providing them as methods and properties of various objects. Table 21.5 lists the objects, properties, and methods provided in SYSTEM.VBP.

Table 21.5   The SYSTEM.VBP Sample's Object, Properties, and Methods

Object	Property/Method	Description
Application	FileIO	Returns the FileIO object that this object library provides.
	Help	Returns the Help object that this object library provides.
	Information	Returns the Information object that this object library provides.
	Keyboard	Returns the Keyboard object that this object library provides.
	Registration	Returns the Registration object that this object library provides.
	Version	Returns the Version object that this object library provides.
FileIO	WindowsDirectory	Returns the path for the Windows directory.
	SystemDirectory	Returns the path for the Windows system directory.
	TempFileName	Returns the path and file name for a new temporary file.
Help	hWnd	Sets the window handle of the application that controls the Help window.

Object	Property/Method	Description
	FileName	Sets the name of the Help file to open.
	Context	Sets the context ID for which to search the Help file.
	Keyword	Sets the keyword for which to search the Help file.
	Show	Displays Help for the appropriate keyword or context ID.
	OnTop	Displays the Help window on top of all other windows.
Information	Memory	Returns the amount of physical memory installed.
	Processor	Returns the series number of the installed microprocessor (386 or 486).
	GetTasks	Returns a list of the running Windows applications, including those that are not visible on-screen.
	IsRunning	Checks whether an application is currently running.
	MakeVisible	Makes a hidden application window visible.
	FindWindow	Finds the handle of a given window.
	WindowsVersion	Returns the version number of the running Windows operating system.
Keyboard	NumLock	Sets or returns the Num Lock key state.
Registration	CheckRegistrationEntry	Checks whether an application is correctly registered.
	GetRegisteredList	Returns the system registration database's list of applications.
	CheckInstalled	Checks whether an application is registered in the system registration database.
Version	InstallFile	Installs the latest version of a file on the system.

Adding Menu Items in Excel

Use Excel's Menu Editor to modify the menus Excel displays. To start the Excel Menu Editor, follow these steps:

   1. Select or add a VBA code module sheet.

2. Choose <u>T</u>ools, <u>M</u>enu Editor. Excel displays the Menu Editor only when a module sheet is active, as shown in figure 21.6.

Fig. 21.6
Excel's Menu
Editor.

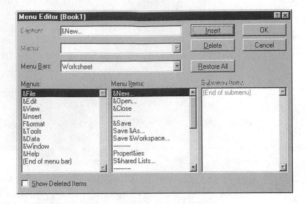

Excel menus have four parts, as shown in figure 21.7.

Fig. 21.7
Parts of an Excel
menu (menu
objects).

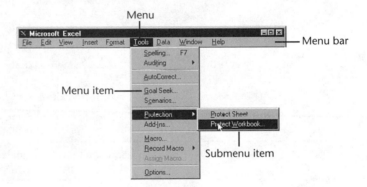

Menu bars change depending on Excel's current context. While a worksheet is active, Excel displays the Worksheet menu bar; when you switch to a module, the Visual Basic Module menu bar replaces the Worksheet menu bar; and so on.

Menu bars contain menus. In Excel, *menus* organize related tasks, which the *menu items* indicate. Each menu item performs a specific action when the user selects it. The action might be a task, such as sorting, or a step toward a task, such as displaying a dialog box.

Submenu items subordinate a task one more level. For example, <u>R</u>ecord Macro presents the submenu choices of recording a new macro, using relative references, or recording at a mark. Applications display submenu items when a dialog box would be obtrusive to a task.

Attaching Procedures to Menu Items

You can assign VBA procedures to run when a user clicks a menu item. To display a VB4 object after an Excel menu click, you must create a VBA procedure to call that object. For example, the following VBA procedure starts the VB4 CDPlayer application when the user clicks on the menu item assigned to CDPlay:

```
Sub CDPlay()
     ' Create an object reference to the VB4 object library.
     Dim CD As Object
     Set CD = CreateObject("CDPlayer.Application")
     ' Invoke the Play method on the VB4 object.
     CD.Play
End Sub
```

> **Note**
>
> You can assign procedures only to menu items and submenu items that you have added. You cannot attach procedures to menus or to built-in menu items.

To attach a procedure to a custom menu item, follow these steps:

1. From the Menu Editor, select the menu item by clicking its name in the Menu Items or Submenu Items list box.

2. In the Macro list box, type the name of the procedure to attach. Then click OK.

Saving and Distributing Menus

Menu changes are saved with files. The changes last while the file is open. When you save a menu with a workbook, the menu is *local* to that workbook; that is, the menu goes away as soon as you close the workbook. To make the changes available to all workbooks, save the changes to a workbook template.

Excel defines two types of templates: the default template BOOK.XLT, and custom templates, which can have any base name other than CHART and end with .XLT. To make templates available automatically, you must save them in Excel's startup directory (\EXCEL\XLSTART).

To create a template, follow these steps:

1. Choose File, New.

2. Enter data, formats, and menu changes as appropriate.

3. Choose File, Save As. Select Template from the Save File as Type list box and select Excel's startup directory from the Directories list box (usually \EXCEL\XLSTARTUP).

4. Type the file's base name in the File Name text box. New files that you create from this template will use the base name as the default name. For example, if you specify BOOK as the default template, the default names will be BOOK1.XLS, BOOK2.XLS, and so on.

5. Click OK to save the file.

The new template is not automatically available until you restart Excel. After you restart Excel, it displays the New dialog box (see fig. 21.8) and lists the template types if you have multiple template files in the startup directory.

Fig. 21.8
Excel's New dialog box.

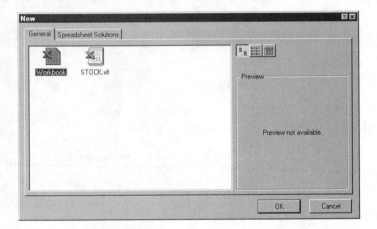

To distribute a template to other users, simply copy the template file to their startup directory and restart Excel on their machines.

Creating and Displaying Menu Bars Dynamically

Excel changes its menu bars when you activate various types of sheets and windows. The Excel MenuBars collection contains all these built-in menu bars. Use the constants in table 21.6 to get to a specific menu. (Shortcut menus use strings rather than constants.)

Table 21.6 Excel's Built-In Menu Bar Constants	
Constant	**Menu Bar Returned**
xlWorksheet	Worksheet, macro sheet, and dialog sheet

Constant	Menu Bar Returned
`xlChart`	Chart
`xlModule`	Visual Basic module
`xlNoDocuments`	No documents open
`xlInfo`	Info Window
`"Shortcut Menus 1"`	General worksheet, module, and toolbar shortcut
`"Shortcut Menus 2"`	Drawing object and dialog sheet shortcut
`"Shortcut Menus 3"`	Charting shortcut
`xlInfo`	Info window
`xlInfo`	Info window
`xlWorksheet4`	Excel 4.0 worksheet
`xlChart4`	Excel 4.0 chart
`xlWorksheetShort`	Excel 3.0 short worksheet
`xlChartShort`	Excel 3.0 short chart

The following line returns a reference to the worksheet menu bar:

```
Set mnubrWorksheet = Application.MenuBars(xlWorksheet)
```

Once you have a reference to a menu bar, you can get the menus that the menu bar contains or add new menus to the menu bar. For instructions on adding menus to a menu bar, see the section "Creating and Displaying Menus Dynamically," on the next page.

Excel also enables you to create your own menu bars in code. The following line creates a new menu bar:

```
Application.MenuBars.Add("New Menu Bar")
```

To display a menu bar, use the Excel `MenuBar` object's `Activate` method. The following line displays the new menu bar:

```
Application.MenuBars("New Menu Bar").Activate
```

If you just ran the preceding line without looking ahead, you might have been surprised that you just wiped out the menu bar. The new menu bar is blank and it replaced the built-in menu bar when you activated it.

Tip
While Excel displays the Debug window, you cannot see the changes that you make to the menu bar. You cannot modify the Debug menu bar.

III

Creating OLE Objects

To restore the built-in menu bar, activate it. The following line activates the module menu bar:

```
Application.MenuBars(xlModule).Activate
```

Creating and Displaying Menus Dynamically

You can use Visual Basic to create Excel menus dynamically at run time. This capability is useful when installing and removing add-in components and when creating systems that make menus available at the appropriate times within a workbook.

Use the Excel MenuBar object's Add method to add menus to a menu bar. The following line adds a Procedures menu to the Worksheet menu bar:

```
Application.MenuBars(xlWorksheet).Menus.Add "&Procedures", _
    "&Window"
```

Use the Excel MenuBar object's Delete method to remove menus from a menu bar. The following line deletes the Help menu:

```
Application.MenuBars(xlWorksheet).Menus("Help").Delete
```

Use the Excel MenuBar object's Reset method to restore the default settings of a built-in menu. The following line restores the Help menu, previously de-leted from the menu bar:

```
Application.MenuBars(xlWorksheet).Reset
```

Adding Items to Menus

You can use Visual Basic to create menu items dynamically at run time. This capability is useful when updating lists on a menu. Excel's Window list is an example of a use for dynamic menu items.

Use the Excel MenuItems object's Add method to add menu items to a menu. The following line adds an item to the Window menu:

```
Application.MenuBars(xlWorksheet).Menus("Window").MenuItems.Add "_
    &Locator Map"
```

Use the Add method with a hyphen to add a separator bar to a menu. This line adds a separator bar to the Window menu:

```
Application.MenuBars(xlWorksheet).Menus("Window").MenuItems.Add _
    "-"
```

Use the Excel MenuItems object's Delete method to remove items from a menu. The following line deletes the menu item that the previous line added:

```
Application.MenuBars(xlWorksheet).Menus("Window"). _
    MenuItems("Locator Map").Delete
```

Use the Excel `MenuItems` object's `Reset` method to restore the default settings of a built-in menu. The following line restores the <u>W</u>indow menu:

```
Application.MenuBars(xlWorksheet).Menus("Window").Reset
```

Creating and Editing Toolbars

You can customize the Excel workspace by creating new toolbars and by changing existing, built-in toolbars. Changes are saved with your system and remain in effect until you delete or reset the toolbars. Figure 21.9 displays the Excel toolbar objects.

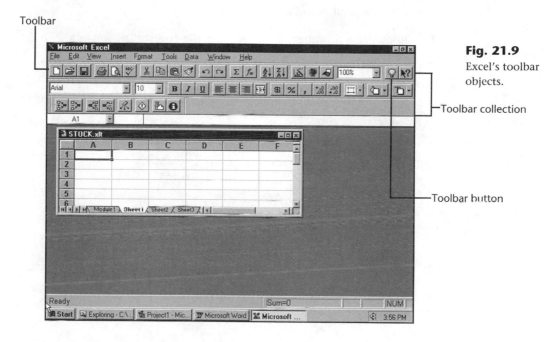

Fig. 21.9
Excel's toolbar objects.

From within Excel, you can do the following:

- Create new toolbars

- Add buttons to new and existing toolbars

- Change the image displayed on a button

- Change the procedure assigned to a button

- Distribute custom toolbars to others

To display a VB4 object after an Excel toolbar button click, you must create a VBA procedure to call that object. For example, the following VBA procedure starts the VB4 CDPlayer application when the user clicks on the menu item assigned to `CDPlay`:

```
Sub CDPlay()
    ' Create an object reference to the VB4 object library.
    Dim CD As Object
    Set CD = CreateObject("CDPlayer.Application")
    ' Invoke the Play method on the VB4 object.
    CD.Play
End Sub
```

The following sections describe how to perform these tasks manually from within Excel.

Creating New Toolbars

To create a new toolbar in Excel, follow these steps:

1. Choose View, Toolbars. Excel displays the Toolbars dialog box (see fig. 21.10).

Fig. 21.10

Excel's Toolbars dialog box.

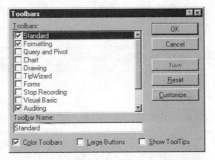

2. Type the name of the toolbar to create in the Toolbar Name text box.

3. Click the New button. Excel displays the Customize dialog box (see fig. 21.11).

Fig. 21.11

Excel's Customize dialog box.

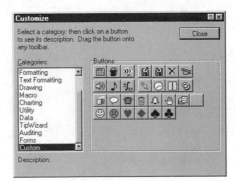

Adding Buttons to Toolbars

To add a button to a toolbar, follow these steps:

1. Drag a button from the Customize dialog box's Buttons palette to the destination toolbar.

2. If the button is from the Custom category, Excel displays the Assign Macro dialog box (see fig. 21.12).

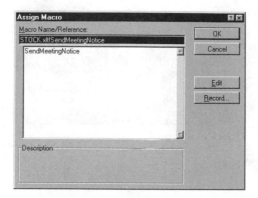

Fig. 21.12

Excel's Assign Macro dialog box.

3. In the Macro Name/Reference text box, type the name of a procedure to run when the user clicks the button. Click OK.

Changing the Procedure Assigned to a Button

To change the assigned procedure name, follow these steps:

1. Display the Customize dialog box.

2. Choose Tools, Assign Macro. (The Tools and shortcut menus display Assign Macro only while the Customize dialog box is open.) Excel displays the Assign Macro dialog box.

3. Type the new procedure name in the the Macro Name/Reference text box and click OK.

Changing a Button Image

To edit a button image, follow these steps:

1. Display the Customize dialog box.

2. Left-click on the button that you want to edit. Excel displays a shortcut menu.

3. Choose Edit Button Image. (The shortcut menu displays Edit Button Image only while the Customize dialog box is open.) Excel then displays the Button Editor (see fig. 21.13).

Fig. 21.13
Excel's Button
Editor.

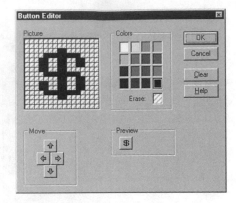

4. Edit the image and click OK.

Distributing Toolbars with Excel Files

You can distribute custom toolbars to other users by attaching them to a file. When they open the file, the toolbar is installed on their system. A user has to open the file only once to install the toolbar.

To attach a toolbar to a file, follow these steps:

1. Open or create the file to which to attach the toolbar.

2. Display a module sheet.

3. Choose Tools, Attach Toolbars. Excel displays the Attach Toolbars dialog box (see fig. 21.14).

Fig. 21.14
Excel's Attach
Toolbars dialog
box.

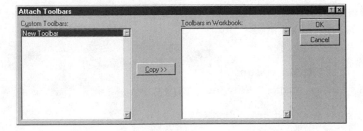

4. Choose the toolbar to attach and then choose <u>C</u>opy. You can attach to a file as many toolbars as you want.

5. Click OK and save the file. Excel defines the .XLB file extension for toolbars, but you can use any file extension that you want.

Tip

If the buttons on the toolbar run Visual Basic procedures, you must ensure that the file containing those procedures is on the user's path or in Excel's library directory (\EXCEL\LIBRARY by default).

Creating and Displaying Toolbars Dynamically

You can use Visual Basic to create toolbars dynamically at run time. This capability is useful when installing and removing add-in components and when creating systems that make tools available at the appropriate times (Excel itself creates toolbars dynamically in that the menus change as you switch between contexts.)

Use the Add method of the Toolbars collection to add toolbars dynamically. The following line adds a new, custom toolbar:

```
Application.Toolbars.Add "Budget Tools"
```

Adding a toolbar automatically displays it. You can hide the toolbar by using its Visible property. The following line adds a toolbar, but does not display it:

```
Application.Toolbars.Add ("Invoicing Tools").Visible = False
```

The Position, Top, and Left properties control a toolbar's position. Position determines whether the toolbar floats or is attached to the window's edge. The following line makes the Standard toolbar a floating toolbar:

```
Application.Toolbars("Standard").Position = xlFloatingToolbar
```

You remove a custom toolbar by using the Delete method. You cannot delete built-in toolbars, but you can restore their default setting by using the Reset method.

Using VB4 Objects with Excel Add-Ins

Add-ins extend Excel's capabilities by adding features, menus, and toolbars as if they were built in. Add-ins are a good way to distribute VB4 object libraries written for Excel, because the add-in can contain all the menus, toolbars, and VBA procedures that call the VB4 object library, as shown in figure 21.15.

As shown in figure 21.15, the Excel add-in contains a compiled version of the VBA "wrapper" procedures that access the VB4 object library. The add-in can also include toolbars and menu bars, so making the new features available in the user interface is easy.

Fig. 21.15
Create Excel add-ins when distributing VB4 object libraries written for Excel.

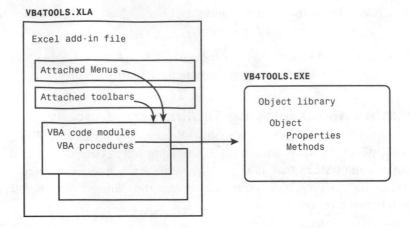

Loading Add-Ins

You must load an add-in in Excel before you can use the functions that the add-in provides.

To load an add-in in Excel, follow these steps:

1. Choose Tools, Add-Ins. Excel displays the Add-Ins dialog box (see fig. 21.16).

Fig. 21.16
Excel's Add-Ins dialog box.

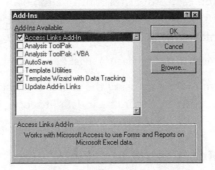

2. If the Add-Ins Available list box lists the add-in, click the check box beside the add-in name to load the add-in. When an add-in is loaded, the corresponding check box is marked.

3. If the list box does not list the add-in, choose Browse. Excel displays the Browse dialog box (see fig. 21.17).

4. Double-click the file name of the add-in to load. Excel adds the add-in to the Add-Ins dialog box's Add-Ins Available list box and loads the add-in.

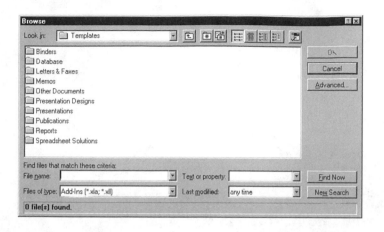

Fig. 21.17
Excel's Browse
dialog box.

To make an add-in's procedures available to another Visual Basic procedure, you must add a reference to the add-in. To add a reference to an add-in, follow these steps:

1. Display a VBA code module.

2. Choose Tools, References. Excel displays the References dialog box.

3. In the Available References list, click the check box beside the add-in name to establish a reference to that add-in. Then click OK to close the dialog box.

Creating Add-Ins in Excel

Add-ins created from workbook files (.XLS) do not create a new workbook when loaded. However, add-ins created from template files (.XLT) create a new workbook based on the source template when the add-in is loaded. SLIDES.XLT is an example of a template add-in.

To create an add-in from a workbook or template file, follow these steps:

1. Open the file in Excel and display a VBA code module.

2. Choose Tools, Make Add-In. Excel displays the Make Add-In dialog box (see fig. 21.18).

3. Click OK.

4. Save the file as the source for the add-in. You cannot edit .XLA files, so you must keep the .XLS or .XLT file if you want to modify the add-in in the future.

Tip

Each add-in consumes memory and takes time to load. Loading more than three or four add-ins can cause significant problems running Excel.

III

Creating OLE Objects

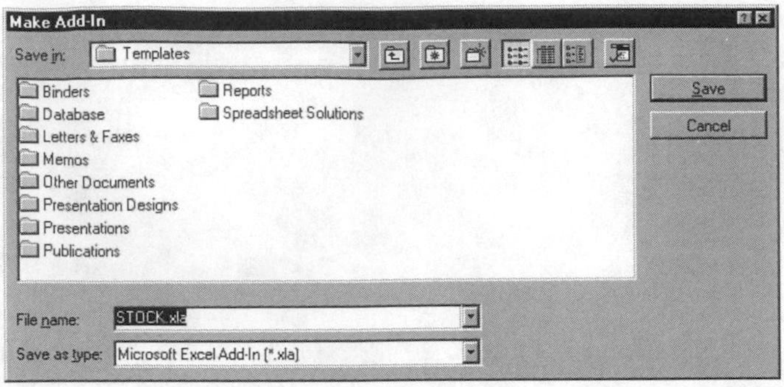

Fig. 21.18
Excel's Make Add-In dialog box.

Distributing Add-In Files

When you distribute add-ins to other users, you must copy the files to the user's machine and load the add-in in Excel. If you are providing functions that will be called from VBA, you also must add a reference to the add-in.

The procedures that you follow to install an add-in differ depending on whether the add-in consists of a single file or multiple files.

Single-File Add-Ins

Single-file add-ins can contain VBA procedures, toolbars, menus, and templates. They do not call VB4 object libraries, DLLs, or other add-ins.

To install a single-file add-in on a machine, follow these steps:

1. Copy the add-in to the user's machine. The following line uses the Excel Addins object's Add method to copy an add-in to a local machine from a network location:

   ```
   Application.Addins.Add _
       "\\public\tools\excel\addins\demo.xla", True
   ```

   Add copies the add-in file to Excel's \LIBRARY directory and adds the add-in's title to the add-in list.

2. Load the add-in in Excel. The following line loads the add-in:

   ```
   Application.Addins("Demo").Installed = True
   ```

3. If the add-in must be available to procedures in Visual Basic, add a reference to the add-in. You cannot add this reference directly in code. You must instruct users how to do this manually, or provide a template file with a reference to the add-in.

Listing 21.12 demonstrates how to install an add-in and install a template with a reference to the add-in. sPath can be a network drive or a floppy drive.

Listing 21.12   Installing an Add-In and a Template with a Reference to the Add-In

```
' Installs an add-in.
Sub InstallAddin(sPath As String, sAddinName As String)
     ' Copy file to the \EXCEL\LIBRARY directory.
     With Application.Addins.Add(sPath & sAddinName, True)
          ' Load the add-in.
          .Installed = True
     End With
End Sub

' Copies a Template file to the user's XLSTART directory.
' The Template file must be created manually and
'  have a reference to the add-in.
Sub InstallTemplate(sPath As String, sTemplateName As String)
     ' Copy file to the directory where EXCEL.EXE is installed.
     ' Save the file as a template in the user's
     ' Excel startup directory.
     FileCopy sPath & sTemplateName, Application.StartupPath
     ' Set make the template read/write.
     SetAttr Application.StartupPath & "\" & sTemplateName, _
          vbNormal
End Sub
```

Add-Ins That Use Other Files

Add-ins that use VB4 object libraries, DLLs, or other files present two problems that you don't encounter with single-file add-ins:

- You must ensure that the add-in can find its dependent files.

- You must check the versions of the dependent files before installing over existing files.

When you compile an add-in, Excel writes the paths of any dependent files into the add-in. When you install your add-in on other machines (or if you move the add-in on your own machine), the add-in must search for any DLLs, templates, or other files that it uses. The search follows this order:

1. Absolute build path. *Build* refers to the path on which the files were installed when you compiled the add-in.

2. Relative build path.

3. Current directory.

4. Windows directory.

5. Windows system directory.

6. DOS path.

III

Creating OLE Objects

Tip

If an add-in uses a .DLL, you should install both the .XLA file and the .DLL in the user's Windows system directory. This ensures that the add-in can find its .DLL.

Excel's LIBRARY directory typically is not on the DOS path, so you should not rely on the Addins collection's Add method to copy multifile add-ins to new systems. Instead, use the FileCopy statement.

Listing 21.13 installs a multifile add-in in the user's Windows system directory and then loads the add-in on the user's machine.

Listing 21.13   Installing and Loading a Multifile Add-In

```
' Declarations
#If Win16 Then
Declare Function GetSystemDirectory Lib "KERNEL" (ByVal _
     lpBuffer As String, ByVal nSize As Integer) As Integer
#ElseIf Win32 Then
Declare Function GetSystemDirectory Lib "KERNEL32" (ByVal _
     lpBuffer As String, ByVal nSize As Integer) As Integer
#End If

' Demonstrates calling InstallFiles
Sub CopyDemo()
     ' Copy the files to the Windows System directory.
     InstallFiles "b:\", Array("DEMO.XLA", "DEMO.DLL")
     ' Load the addin in Excel.
     With Application.Addins.Add "DEMO.XLA"
          .Installed = True
     End With
End Sub

' Copies files to Windows System directory, compares file dates.
Sub InstallFiles(sSourceDirectory As String, _
     vFileInstall As Variant)
     Dim sTemp As String * 144
     Dim sSysDirectory As String
     Dim iCopy As Integer
     ' Turn on error checking (for file/drive-related errors)
     On Error GoTo errInstallFiles
     ' Get the Windows system directory.
     iWorked = GetSystemDirectory(sTemp, 144)
     ' If the previous API call worked,
     ' then trim the returned string.
     If iWorked Then
          sSysDirectory = Mid(sTemp, 1, InStr(sTemp, _
               Chr(0)) - 1) & "\"
     ' Otherwise, return an error to the user.
     Else
          MsgBox _
          "Couldn't get system directory. Operation cancelled."
          End
     End If
     ' For each file in the vFileInstall array.
     For Each sNewFile In vFileInstall
          ' Check if the file exists.
          If Len(Dir(sSysDirectory & sNewFile)) = 0 Then
```

```
        ' If it doesn't, copy the new file.
        FileCopy sSourceDirectory & sNewFile, _
            sSysDirectory & sNewFile
    Else
        ' Otherwise, compare the date stamps on the files.
        dtExisting = FileDateTime(sSysDirectory & sNewFile)
        dtNew = FileDateTime(sSourceDirectory & sNewFile)
        ' If the new file is more recent,
        ' copy over the old file.
        If dtExisting < dtNew Then
            FileCopy sSourceDirectory & sNewFile, _
                sSysDirectory & sNewFile
        ' Otherwise, ask the user what to do.
        Else
            iCopy = MsgBox ("A newer version of " _
            & sNewFile & _
          " exists on your system. Keep newer version?", _
            vbYesNoCancel)
            Select Case iCopy
                Case vbYes
                    ' Don't copy file.
                Case vbNo
                    ' Copy file anyway.
                    If iCopy Then FileCopy _
                        sSourceDirectory & sNewFile, _
                        sSysDirectory & sNewFile
                Case vbCancel
                    ' End this procedure.
                    MsgBox _
        "Operation cancelled, installation is not complete."
                    End
                End Select
        End If
    End If
Next sNewFile
Exit Sub

' Error handler
errInstallFiles:
    Select Case Err
        ' Disk full
        Case 61
            MsgBox _
            "Your disk is full. Free some space and try again."
            End
        ' Disk drive not ready or path not found.
        Case 71, 76
            iCopy = MsgBox("Drive " & sSourceDirectory & _
          " is not ready or could not be found. Try again?", _
            vbOKCancel)
            Select Case iCopy
                ' User chose OK, so try again.
                Case vbOK
                    Err = 0
                    Resume
                ' User chose Cancel, so end.
```

(continues)

Listing 21.13   Continued

```
                Case vbCancel
                    ' End this procedure.
                    MsgBox _
         "Operation cancelled, installation is not complete."
                    End
                End Select
        ' Unknown error.
        Case Else
                MsgBox "Error " & Err & _
                       " occurred. Installation is not complete."
                End
        End Select
End Sub
```

Working with the Excel *Addin* Object

The Addins collection and Addin object enable you to load, unload, and get information about add-ins. You cannot use the Addin object to create an add-in or establish a reference to an add-in. You can perform those tasks only through Excel's user interface.

To install a new add-in in Excel, use the Add method. The following line, for example, copies an add-in file from drive B to the Excel LIBRARY directory:

```
Application.Addins.Add "B:\DEMO.XLA", True
```

To load an add-in in Excel, use the Installed property. The following line loads the add-in installed in the preceding line:

```
Application.Addins("DEMO").Installed = True
```

Tip

Most Excel collections use the object's Name property to identify items. For add-ins, Name returns the add-in's file name.

You identify add-ins by their Title property. The Addins collection uses an add-in's index or Title to return a specific add-in. The following line installs the Analysis Toolpak:

```
Application.Addins("Analysis Toolpak").Installed = True
```

From Here...

For more information on the following topics, see the indicated chapters:

■ Chapter 22, "Debugging Applications That Provide Objects," gives you important insight into solving the many new problem areas that crop up as you program with objects.

■ Chapter 23, "Building and Distributing OLE Objects," tells you how to compile and build installation programs for applications that provide objects to other applications. It also discusses how to maintain applications so that future versions don't break compatibility with previous versions.

■ Chapter 24, "Creating Add-Ins," explains how to create add-in applications that you can use to extend the Visual Basic programming system.

III

Creating OLE Objects

Chapter 22

Debugging Applications That Provide Objects

Designing and writing code is only a portion of the process of creating an application. Debugging prior to release can take more time and effort than most programmers are willing to admit—or schedule. Applications that provide objects can be especially problematic, because they expose a whole new (programmatic) interface with a whole new set of problems. This chapter discusses those problems and supplies approaches for solving them.

In this chapter, you learn how to do the following:

- Anticipate problems before they occur when building applications that provide objects

- Determine the instance of an object using watch expressions while debugging

- Correctly initialize objects for multiple instances

- Identify the problems that global data can cause when an object's application provides objects to multiple applications

- Avoid conflicts among applications that share access to a single object

- Keep an object's application loaded in memory invisibly

- Understand how Visual Basic locates an object's application

- Debug applications that provide objects

- Debug objects as they run in-process, interacting with one or more other applications

- Test objects before final release

- Maintain released objects without breaking compatibility

- Avoid bugs through careful coding

Problems Unique to Objects

Debugging an application that uses objects internally or provides objects to other applications presents these new problems:

- Visual Basic cannot watch object variables, so determining which instance of an object class is causing a problem is difficult.

- If an application that provides objects is already running, the application's objects might not get properly initialized.

- If an application that provides objects is loaded in memory more than once, you cannot predict which instance will provide an object.

- Applications that use objects from the same object application can affect each other through the object application's global variables or procedures.

- Objects might leave invisible instances in memory.

- Multiple applications can access the same object, causing problems with concurrency.

- Problems in the application's registration database entries can cause the wrong version of an object's executable file to run.

The following sections discuss these problems in greater detail and explain how you solve them.

Finding the Instance of an Object

When you try to place a watch on an object variable, Visual Basic displays the value "Object doesn't support this property" in the Watch window, as shown in figure 22.1.

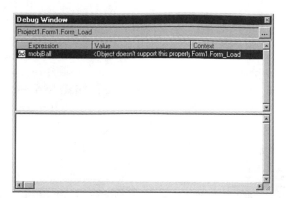

Fig. 22.1
Visual Basic
cannot watch
object variables
directly.

This is a huge problem, because objects might have multiple instances and
you often must know which instance you are dealing with when a bug occurs. To find an instance of an object, you must use a watch expression on
some property of the object. When debugging objects, it helps if you've
defined two standard properties:

■ The Name property uniquely identifies the instance of the object.

■ The Parent property identifies the object that created the object.

Placing a watch expression on Object.Name tells you whether you're looking
at the correct object. Checking Object.Parent helps you look backward in
code to discover how the object was created. Figure 22.2 shows how to use
the Name and Parent properties in the Watch window when tracing execution.

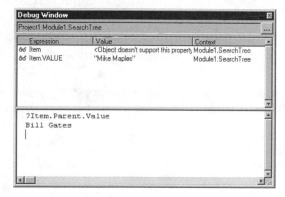

Fig. 22.2
Use object
properties to
determine the
instance of an
object.

The Name and Parent properties aren't automatic for all objects. Programmers
must define the properties in code. Although defining these properties for *all*
objects might seem like extra work, the properties can save you much trouble
when tracing through complex object interactions.

III

Creating OLE Objects

Multiple Instances of Object Applications

Visual Basic applications can have multiple instances of the same application loaded in memory at the same time. Visual Basic's OLE Automation features, however, deal with only a *single* instance of any application. If you have multiple instances of an executable file, you can't accurately predict from which instance Visual Basic will get an object, as shown in figure 22.3.

Fig. 22.3
CreateObject
and GetObject
functions don't
discern among
multiple instances
of an object's
application.

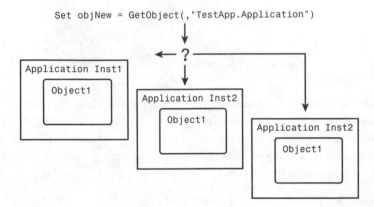

After getting an object from multiple instances of an application, Visual Basic always seems to use the same instance. Therefore, you can't enumerate through the instances until you find the one that you want.

The only sure way to avoid bugs from connecting to the wrong instance of an object's application is to limit the object's application to a single instance. Listing 22.1 shows how to use objects provided in the SYSTEM.VPJ, from this book's companion CD, to check whether an application is already loaded in memory. Using these lines as the startup procedure of an application that provides objects prevents more than one instance of the application from loading.

Listing 22.1 SYSTEM.VBP Checking for Loaded Applications

```
Sub Main()
    ' Use the WinAPI object in SYSTEM.VPJ
    Dim WinAPI As Object
    Set WinAPI = CreateObject("WinAPI.Application")
    ' Check if application is running.
    If WinAPI.Information.IsRunning("Object Application") Then
        ' If it is, switch to that application.
        AppActivate "Object Application"
        ' And end...
        End
    End If
    ' Otherwise, start as normal...
End Sub
```

> **Note**
>
> You can't depend on AppActivate returning an error if an application is not running;
> OLE Automation can start applications invisibly. You must use the Windows API calls
> contained in SYSTEM.VBP to detect applications started for OLE Automation reliably.

Problems with Multiple Initialization

If you are already running an application that provides objects, Visual Basic's
CreateObject function might not start a new instance of the application.
Instead, the function calls the code in the running instance of the executable
file to create the new object. This can cause problems if the application initializes global object variables at startup. Figure 22.4 illustrates how this
problem can occur.

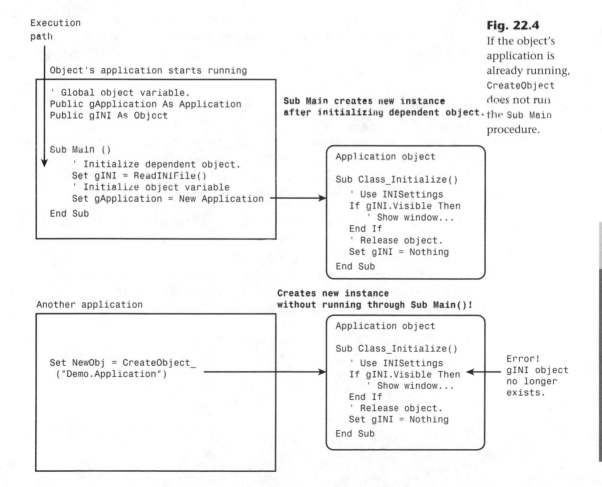

Fig. 22.4
If the object's application is already running, CreateObject does not run the Sub Main procedure.

In figure 22.4, the CreateObject function causes an error in the object's application, because the object's first Initialize event procedure released the gINI object the first time that it ran. The second Initialize event procedure can no longer get gINI, so an "Object variable not set" error occurs.

This problem isn't limited to the use of CreateObject. Visual Basic actually has four ways to create a new instance of a Public, Instancing object within an already running application:

■ Use the Dim *objVar* As New *ClassName* statement and then access the object's properties and methods.

■ Use the Set *objVar* = New *ClassName* statement.

■ Use the CreateObject function.

■ Use the GetObject function, omitting the first argument.

To avoid problems with initializing objects, *don't* initialize an object's dependent data outside of its Initialize event procedure unless you preserve that data for the life of the application. If possible, make each Public, Instancing object in your application self-contained.

Multiple Applications Can Access Global Data

In figure 22.4, both Application objects share the same address space. This can lead to other bugs, because both objects have access to the same global variables and functions. You can't see from the other applications the global data in the object's application, but you can affect the data through the object's methods and properties, as shown in figure 22.5.

By causing Object1 to change a global variable that Object2 uses, Application1 can inadvertently affect Application2. This problem underscores the importance of not using global variables or procedures in applications that provide objects. Objects that must share data with their subordinate objects should do so through instances of a Private object. Figure 22.6 illustrates how you use a Private object to share data among subordinate objects.

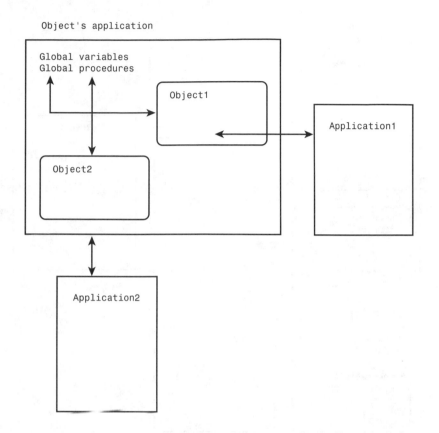

Object's application

Global variables
Global procedures

Object1

Object2

Application1

Application2

Using a Private data object ensures that each new top-level object has its own, private data that other top-level objects created by other applications will not affect.

An Application Can Remain Loaded Invisibly

Sometimes an object's application can remain loaded invisibly in memory. This sometimes happens when a CreateObject or GetObject function succeeds in starting the application but fails before returning the reference to the object. This can result in a lost reference to the object; you can't destroy the reference, because your object variable isn't Set.

III

Creating OLE Objects

Fig. 22.6

Create a Private data object instead of using global variables.

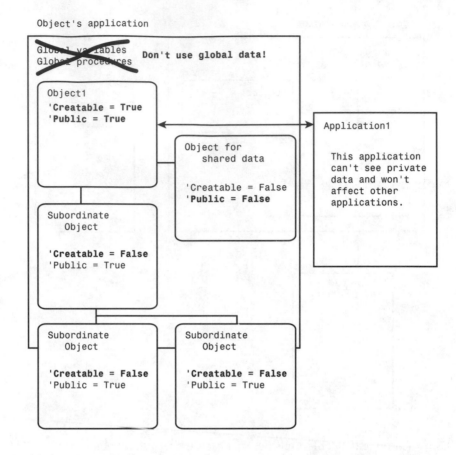

Object's application

Global variables
Global procedures

Don't use global data!

Object1
'**Creatable = True**
'**Public = True**

Object for
shared data

'Creatable = False
'**Public = False**

Application1

This application
can't see private
data and won't
affect other
applications.

Subordinate
Object

'**Creatable = False**
'Public = True

Subordinate
Object

'**Creatable = False**
'Public = True

Subordinate
Object

'**Creatable = False**
'Public = True

If a CreateObject or GetObject function fails while you are debugging an application, check the Windows Task List to make sure that the object's application isn't left in memory. If it is, you can close the application from the Task List.

In compiled code, you should *not* call CreateObject or GetObject again when handling errors from these functions. Doing so might simply create more lost references and, eventually, fill available memory.

Multiple Applications Can Access the Same Object

If you use the following form of GetObject, Visual Basic returns a reference to an existing instance of an object:

```
Set objvar = GetObject(,"projectname.objectname")
```

The object can't detect that more than one application has access to it, although OLE increments its reference count and keeps the object from being destroyed until the last reference goes out of scope or is set to Nothing.

Therefore, one application can affect another through a shared object. Sometimes you want this to happen. However, in other instances, it causes unexpected results.

Because an object has no built-in knowledge of which application will use it, you either need to trust that other programmers will be careful when getting running instances of objects, or you must limit access to subordinate objects through some sort of password mechanism. The following code shows a method that returns a subordinate object only when the appropriate KeyValue argument is provided:

```
Const ACCESS_KEY = &h1234
Public Function Secure(KeyValue As Integer) As Object
    If KeyValue = ACCESS_KEY Then
        Dim SubordinateObject As New clsSubObj
        Set Secure = SubordinateObject
    End If
End Function
```

Problems with the Registration Database

When creating OLE Automation objects during debugging, Visual Basic seems to prefer compiled versions of the object over the object's project loaded in another instance of Visual Basic. During debugging, an application might actually have two entries in the system registration database, as shown in figure 22.7.

Fig. 22.7
The compiled
version of the
object exists at the
root level; the
debug version
exists under the
VBKeySave entry.

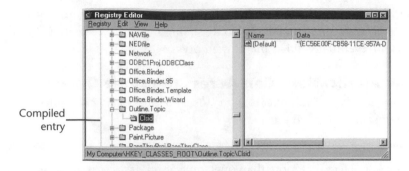

Compiled
entry

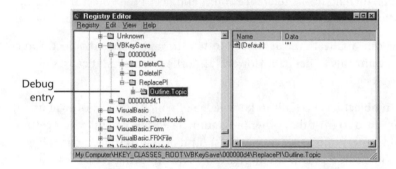

Debug
entry

When attempting to create the object, another application searches for the object in this order:

1. In memory. If the object is already running, Visual Basic creates a new instance of the running object.

2. At the root level of the registration database. Visual Basic uses the object's programmatic ID to find the object's class ID, then finds the path to the executable file from the class ID's entry.

3. In the VBKeySave entry of the registration database.

To ensure that you are using the right object when debugging, close all instances of the object's application. Make sure to check the Windows Task List to ensure that no hidden instances of the application are running. Then start the correct version of the object's application in another instance of Visual Basic.

As an added precaution, avoid creating an executable file for an object until you have completely debugged it. This saves you much work maintaining correct system registration database entries on your system.

Strategies for Debugging Objects

Approaches to debugging are as varied and personal as driving habits. Some programmers debug their applications defensively and others are more aggressive. The following list constitutes the "rules of the road" for debugging applications that provide objects, but, like the rules of the paved road, they are subject to interpretation:

1. Debug objects in-process.

2. Debug objects cross-process. Use each of the following start modes:

   The object is not running.

   The object is already running, create a new object.

   The object is already running, get an existing object.

3. Debug multiple access cross-process, using each of the preceding start modes.

4. Test the application before release by running through the preceding three steps, using the compiled executable on systems that simulate each of your target platforms.

Debugging In-Process

When designing an application that provides objects, consider starting it from a Sub Main procedure rather than from a form. In addition to helping you think clearly about how the application starts up, this technique gives the application a place to add some conditional code that tests the application in-process, whether it has a visual interface or not.

Because applications that provide objects shouldn't use global variables or procedures or initialize dependent objects outside of a class' Initialize event procedure, you should dedicate almost all the code in your Sub Main procedures to debugging the application in-process, as shown in listing 22.2, which is from the companion CD's OUTLINE.VPJ sample.

Listing 22.2   Use a Main Procedure for In-Process Testing

```
#Const DebugBuild = -1
Option Explicit
' Module-level variable.
Dim Outline As New Topic
```

(continues)

III

Creating OLE Objects

Listing 22.2 Continued

```
Sub Main()
    #If DebugBuild Then
    Dim strLine As String, strName As String
    Dim Topic As Topic
    Open "org.txt" For Input As #1
    Do Until EOF(1)
        Line Input #1, strLine
        AddLevel strLine, Outline
    Loop
    Close 1
    strName = InputBox("Enter your name")
    Set Topic = SearchTree(strName, Outline)
    MsgBox "Your boss is " & Topic.Parent.Value
    Set Outline = Nothing
    #End If
End Sub

#If DebugBuild Then
Sub AddLevel(strLine As String, objTopic As Topic)
    ' If the line starts with a tab...
    If Mid(strLine, 1, 1) = Chr$(9) Then
        ' Trim off the character and call again.
        AddLevel Right(strLine, Len(strLine) - 1), _
            objTopic.Topics.Item(objTopic.Topics.Count)
    Else
        objTopic.AddSubtopic.Value = strLine
    End If
End Sub
#End If

#If DebugBuild Then
Function SearchTree(strName As String, objTopic As Topic) As Topic
    Dim Item As Topic
    If objTopic.Topics.Count > 0 Then
        For Each Item In objTopic.Topics
            If Item.Value = strName Then
                Set SearchTree = Item
            Else
                Set SearchTree = SearchTree(strName, Item)
            End If
        Next Item
    End If
End Function
#End If
```

The #Const DebugBuild = -1 setting at the beginning of the module includes all the subsequent debugging code. The code in Sub Main and the AddLevel and SearchTree procedures are designed to go through all the possible code paths for the Topic object. Placing this code in Sub Main rather than doing ad hoc testing builds a consistent debugging path that you can use cross-process and for platform testing later.

When you compile the release version of the executable file, change the DebugBuild option to 0. This prevents the debug code from being built in to the executable file, and thus saves code space.

Debugging Cross-Process

To debug an object for cross-process access, follow these steps:

1. Check the Windows Task List and end any running instances of the object's application.

2. Load the object's application project (.VBP) in Visual Basic.

3. Choose <u>T</u>ools, <u>O</u>ptions. Visual Basic displays the Options properties pages (see fig. 22.8).

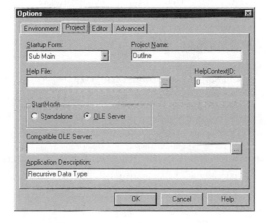

Fig. 22.8
The StartMode options of the Options properties pages have an effect only while debugging an application within Visual Basic.

4. In the Options Project property page, select the <u>O</u>bject Application from the StartMode group. Click OK.

5. Start the application.

6. Start another instance of Visual Basic and load the project that tests cross-process access to the previous application.

7. Choose <u>T</u>ools, <u>O</u>ptions. Visual Basic displays the Options property pages (see fig. 22.9).

Fig. 22.9

The Error Trapping options of the Advanced Options property page determine which application Visual Basic stops in if an error occurs.

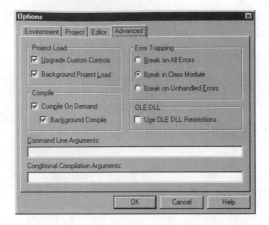

8. In the Advanced Options property page, deselect the Break on All Errors check box and select the Break in Class Module check box. This selection enables you to step from the current application to the object's application if an error occurs.

9. Run the application loaded in step 6.

As you debug an object's application, test the logic of your objects under different access paths. One of the most critical areas for objects is their initialization. Therefore, it is important to test the different forms of access that can result in different types of initialization.

In addition to run-time errors, you must watch for unexpected results that can occur due to uninitialized data or multiple initialization of the same object. Comparing expected results to actual results is important.

Creating New Objects from a Running Application

If you created debug code in Sub Main while debugging in-process, you can use very similar code to debug cross-process access. Listing 22.3 contains procedures that show the modifications made to the in-process debug code for OUTLINE.VBP.

Listing 22.3   Debugging OUTLINE.VBP Cross-Process

```
Option Explicit

Sub Main()
Dim strLine As String, strName As String
    Dim Outline As Object, Topic As Object
                ' << changed to generic Object type
```

```
        Set Outline = CreateObject("outline.topic")
                    ' << added CreateObject
        Open "org.txt" For Input As #1
        Do Until EOF(1)
            Line Input #1, strLine
            AddLevel strLine, Outline
        Loop
        Close 1
        strName = InputBox("Enter your name")
        Set Topic = SearchTree(strName, Outline)
        MsgBox "Your boss is " & Topic.Parent.Value
        Set Outline = Nothing
    End Sub

    Sub AddLevel(strLine As String, objTopic As Object)
                    ' << Changed to Object type
    ' If the line starts with a tab...
        If Mid(strLine, 1, 1) = Chr$(9) Then
            ' Trim off the character and call again.
            AddLevel Right(strLine, Len(strLine) - 1), _
                objTopic.Topics.Item(objTopic.Topics.Count)
        Else
            objTopic.AddSubtopic.Value = strLine
        End If
    End Sub

    Function SearchTree(strName As String, objTopic As Object) _
        As Object           ' << Changed to Object type
        Dim Item As Object  ' << Changed to Object type
        If objTopic.Topics.Count > 0 Then
            For Each Item In objTopic.Topics
                If Item.Value = strName Then
                    Set SearchTree = Item
                Else
                    Set SearchTree = SearchTree(strName, Item)
                End If
            Next Item
        End If
    End Function
```

The test code in listing 22.3 uses the generic Object data type and CreateObject to avoid having to establish a reference to the object's application. References to the object's application type library aren't available until the application is compiled. You should not compile object applications before debugging them for cross-process access, because creating an executable file results in registering with your system two versions of the applications.

Getting Existing Objects from a Running Application
To ensure that the way that you get an existing object from a running application works correctly, add a new procedure call before the end of your

cross-process-debug Sub Main. The new procedure, GetRunningObject (see listing 22.4), should use GetObject to manipulate the object that you created earlier.

Listing 22.4   The GetRunningObject Procedure

```
Sub Main()
    ' Code omitted here...
    ' Call procedure that debugs GetObject access
    GetRunningObject
    Set Outline = Nothing
End Sub

Sub GetRunningObject()
    Dim RunningObject As Object
    ' Get a reference to the Outline object created earlier.
    Set RunningObject = GetObject(,"outline.topic")
    ' Add a new topic to the outline.
    RunningObject.AddSubtopic.Value = "New Name"
    ' Search the outline for the topic.
    Set RunningObject = SearchTree("New Name", RunningObject)
    ' Display the result
    MsgBox "New name's boss is " & RunningObject.Name
End Sub
```

The GetRunningObject procedure uses the GetObject function, rather than a passed-in variable, to get an existing object reference. This tests the code path for returning and modifying an existing object.

Starting the Object's Application

You should test starting the application by using CreateObject, because by doing so you run the object application's Sub Main procedure. Using CreateObject with the object already running doesn't test this path for cross-process access.

The Visual Basic documentation implies that you can start an object's application for cross-process debugging by using CreateObject. Currently, that technique doesn't work. You must first start the object's application in Visual Basic before attempting to use CreateObject.

If the documentation is correct, and the product is fixed by release time, you should be able to simply stop the application started in step 5 in the preceding section, then run the cross-process test again.

However, if the documentation is wrong, you must use a compiled version of the object's application to test whether CreateObject correctly starts the object's application. Be sure to register the object's application before testing with the compiled application.

Debugging Multiple Access to Objects

You can run as many instances of Visual Basic as your machine's memory can hold. Therefore, you can debug an object's application using two or more accessing applications at the same time. You can't have more than two object applications running in instances of Visual Basic, however. This is because the VBKeySave entry that Visual Basic creates in the system registration database is limited to two applications.

You can use the same debug code that you used for cross-process debugging when debugging multiple access, although it is better to change the order in which objects are used among the accessing projects. Having different orders of access is more likely to uncover conflicts among objects running multiple cross-process access down parallel paths.

Testing on Target Platforms

After completing the preceding steps, you can build your debug executable file to start testing for errors on target platforms. You should not rely on debugging performed on developers' machines as a final test, because developers tend to have more available memory and faster processors than many of the users for whom they develop.

Try to get a couple of unused machines that are representative of those used by the users for whom you develop. You might be surprised at the diversity of problems that can reveal themselves when running the same code on computers from different manufacturers. Some manufacturers are more fastidious than others at following standards and doing quality checks. You'll soon learn which types of machines, video cards, and disk drives are "tolerant" and which ones aren't.

If you've followed the steps in this chapter to this point, you probably have a pretty good code base for creating some automated testing on these platforms. If not, you should return to the section "Strategies for Debugging Objects" and start over. When testing on target platforms, you should use compiled objects and test code. If a problem develops on a particular machine, you can install Visual Basic and step through the code to find the error.

Testing on target platforms also gives you a good chance to test your Setup procedure. Object applications must be properly registered in the system registration database. As this book has frequently mentioned, getting the registration right can pose problems.

III

Creating OLE Objects

Maintaining Compatibility with Released Versions

After releasing an application that provides objects, you have a whole new problem: maintenance. Some applications just keep chugging away like old Volvos. Others seem more like MGs. Whichever type of application you're responsible for, you don't want to kill the driver every time that you make a few changes under the hood.

Visual Basic gives you a handy feature for maintaining compatibility with released object libraries: the Compatible OLE Server text box on the Options properties pages (see fig. 22.10).

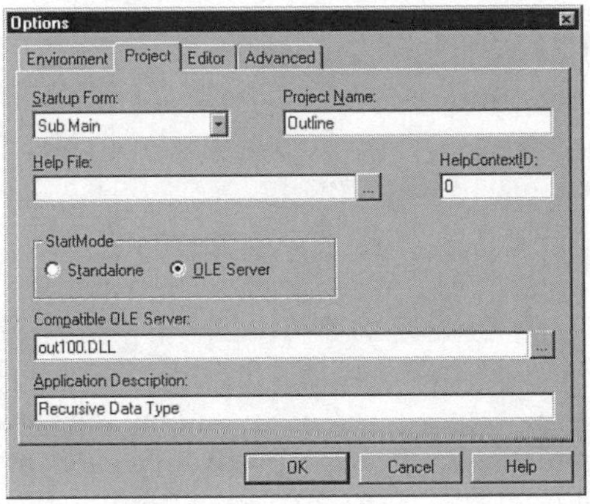

Fig. 22.10
Type the name of the released executable file to which to maintain compatibility in the Compatible OLE Server text box.

Entering a name in the Compatible OLE Server text box compares the loaded application to the existing executable file's object library when you run or compile your application. If you've broken compatibility with the released version, you get a warning message.

These types of changes cause a warning to occur, because they break compatibility with released object libraries:

- Changing the name of a released project, class, method, or property

- Changing a `Public` class, method, or property to `Private`

- Changing a property from read/write to read-only or write-only

- Removing arguments or changing the order of arguments in a method

- Changing an optional argument to a required one in a method

These aren't the only types of changes that can break compatibility with released object libraries. Changes in behavior, memory requirements, or software requirements can be just as deadly.

Guidelines for Avoiding Bugs

You should maintain guidelines for naming variables, procedures, constants, and other user-created items in the code that you write. Naming these items in a consistent way helps you distinguish among Visual Basic keywords and items defined somewhere in code. Such guidelines are especially useful in large programs or those in which more than one user uses the code.

At first, following a set of guidelines seems to require much extra work. It quickly becomes second-nature, however. Style guidelines not only make it easier for other programmers to read your code, they also make it easier for you to remember what you wrote. Also, following guidelines can give your work a professional-looking polish. Other programmers will be jealous when they see how consistently you can produce bug-free software by doing some simple housekeeping.

The guidelines that this section presents are a good starting point and are used throughout this book in the sample code. You might choose to develop your own or follow someone else's. Only a couple of rules are absolute:

- Declare all variables before use.

- Use prefixes to identify scope and data type.

- Use descriptive names where possible.

- Indent related blocks of code.

- Precede blocks of code with descriptive comments.

- Note all assumptions in comments at the beginning of procedures.

Requiring Variable Declarations (*Option Explicit*)

Visual Basic enables you to work in a very free-form way. You can start writing code without ever worrying about reserving space for variables or assigning the correct data types. This is a great way to start learning and enables you to begin doing useful work almost immediately. However, it also means that typos in variable names are very hard to catch.

III

Creating OLE Objects

For example, the following code does not display the message box, because the If statement misspells bAnswer. Visual Basic considers Anwser a new variable and initializes it to an empty value.

```
Sub SpellingError()
    bAnswer = True
    If bAnwser = True Then MsgBox("True")
                ' Oops! Message box never displays.
End Sub
```

If you add an Option Explicit statement to the beginning of each module, form, and class, Visual Basic checks to ensure that you have declared each variable that you use. This is an effective way to check the spelling of variable names throughout your code.

Here's the same code with an Option Explicit statement:

```
Option Explicit

Sub SpellingError()
    Dim bAnswer As Boolean          ' This line is now required.
    bAnswer = True
    If bAnwser = True Then MsgBox("True")
                        ' This line causes an error when run!
End Sub
```

You can still have typos, but Visual Basic alerts you when you try to run the code.

Using Option Explicit is more than good form; many contracts that request software written in Visual Basic require the use of the statement.

Identifying Scope with Prefixes

Scope is the range within code where you can use a variable, constant, or procedure. Visual Basic has three levels of scope:

Scope	Description	Prefix
Local	The variable or constant is valid only within the procedure that defines it.	None
Module	The variable or constant is valid only within the module that defines it.	m
Global	The variable or constant is valid within any module in a project.	g

Local Scope

Any variable or constant defined in a procedure has local scope by default, as in the following example:

```
Sub LocalScope()
    ' Define a local variable of data type integer.
    Dim iCount As Integer
    For iCount = 0 to 200
        ' Do something...
    Next iCount
End Sub
```

If another procedure uses the variable iCount, the variable is new and doesn't reflect the value from the procedure LocalScope. You cannot change local variables outside the procedure.

Constants behave the same way, except that their values never change (hence their name). Note the following example:

```
Sub LocalScope()
    ' Local constants for RGB colors.
    Const RED = &HFF, GREEN = &HFF00, BLUE = &HFF0000
    ' Following code would cause an error, so it's commented out.
    ' RED = 32
End Sub
```

Again, other procedures can't see the value of RED defined in the procedure LocalScope.

When using local variables, the Dim statement is optional. Visual Basic automatically creates a variable whenever you use a word that it does not recognize, as in the following example.

```
Sub AutomaticVariable()
    ' Create a local variable that contains a string.
    vAutoString = "This variable was not explicitly declared"
    ' Create a local variable that contains a number.
    vAutoNumber = 10
End Sub
```

When creating a variable automatically, Visual Basic uses the default data type. Visual Basic uses the Variant data type as the default unless you change it by using the Deftype statement.

Tip

The names of constants are usually typed in uppercase characters. The exception to this rule is a product-defined constant that begins with a product prefix, as in xlMaximize.

III

Creating OLE Objects

Caution

Automatic variables make it hard to catch variable name spelling errors. It is safer to turn off this feature by using the Option Explicit statement.

Module Scope

Any variable or constant defined outside a procedure has module scope by default. Listing 22.5 shows such a procedure.

Listing 22.5   A Procedure with Module Scope

```
' Define a module-level variable of data type Boolean (true/false)
Dim mbFlag As Boolean

' Run this procedure to see how module-level variables work.
Sub ModuleVariable()
    ' Assign a value to the module-level variable.
    mbFlag = True
    ' Call another procedure to display the value of the variable
    DisplayVariable
    ' Displays False in a message box.
    MsgBox bFlag
End Sub

' This procedure is called by ModuleVariable.
Sub DisplayFlag()
    ' Displays True in a message box.
    MsgBox mbFlag
    ' Change the value to False.
    mbFlag = False
End Sub
```

The `ModuleVariable` and `DisplayFlag` procedures can see and change the `mbFlag` variable. If you move `DisplayFlag` to another module, however, this is no longer true; the procedures can see the value `mbFlag` only within the module that declares it.

Constants behave the same way. If you declare them outside a procedure, every procedure in that module can see them.

Global Scope

Variables and constants defined outside a procedure with the `Public` keyword have global scope, as in the following examples:

```
' Define a global variable of data type Boolean (true/false).
Public gbFlag As Boolean

' Define a global constant for the RGB color red.
Public Const gRED = &HFF
```

The variable `gbFlag` and the constant `gRED` are available to all procedures in all modules. Notice that you can't use `Public` inside a procedure; this keeps global and module scope declarations together at the beginning of each module.

Identifying Data Types with Prefixes

Data type indicates the kinds of data that a variable can contain. Visual Basic has 12 built-in data types, which table 22.1 lists.

Table 22.1 Recommended Visual Basic Fundamental Type Prefixes

Data Type	Prefix
Boolean	b
Byte	by
Currency	c
Date/time	dt
Double	d
Error	err
Integer	i
Long	l
Object	obj
Single	s
String	str
User-defined type	u
Variant	v

In addition to the built-in data types, Visual Basic has many types for objects and collections. It is important to use a set of prefixes for these object types and for the types of objects that you create in your own application. Table 22.2 lists recommended prefixes for the Visual Basic object types.

Table 22.2 Recommended Visual Basic Object Variable Prefixes

Object Type	Object Prefix
Form	frm
MDIForm	mdi
CheckBox	chk

III

Creating OLE Objects

(continues)

Table 22.2   Continued

ComboBox	cbo
CommandButton	cmd
CommonDialog	dlg
Data	dat
DBCombo	dbc
DBList	dbl
DBGrid	dbg
DirListBox	dir
DriveListBox	drv
FileListBox	fil
Frame	fra
HScrollBar	hsb
Image	img
Label	lbl
Line	lin
ListBox	lst
Menu	mnu
OLE	ole
OptionButton	opt
PictureBox	pic
Shape	shp
TextBox	txt
Timer	tmr
VScrollBar	vsb

Choosing Descriptive Names

The names of variables, constants, and procedures should tell you something about them. This is especially important for procedures and for variables that refer to objects or have module or global scope.

For example, if you have a variable that refers to a button with the caption OK, you should name the variable cmdOK. A procedure that sorts arrays should be named SortArray.

Using shorter names for frequently used items is convenient. For example, iCount is a convenient name for a counter in a For...Next loop. Many programmers simply use i or j for counters in For...Next loops.

If a name seems too long, being less descriptive is better than using a series of abbreviations. Wherever you declare the item, you can always add comments to describe fully the item's use.

Difficulty naming a procedure is sometimes a good tip-off that the code is too general or complex. You might consider breaking a procedure into several smaller ones if you can't come up with a descriptive name.

Table 22.3 presents some guidelines for naming procedures.

Table 22.3   Procedure-Naming Guidelines

Good Name	Poor Name	Reason
iCount, i, j,	IndexvCounter, LoopCounter	Counters that you use in For...Next and Do...Loop statement blocks should be easy to type and identify. Using Integer variables makes loops execute faster.
SortArray, DisplayResult, AdjustMargins	DoThings, ShowIt, FormatOutputForPrinting	Procedure names should be descriptive and specific. Using "It" or "Thing" is far too general. Try to use verb/noun pairs.
butOK, chrtInventory, rngSourceData	Button1, chrtInv, rMyData	You should name object variables consistently and clearly identify what they represent. If an object has a descriptive caption or name, use that name as part of the variable name.

Formatting Code

Use tabs to indicate the relationships among blocks of code. For constructions with a beginning and end, such as loops, indent the contents of the construction once for each level of nesting. Listing 22.6 shows a well-indented code block.

Listing 22.6   A Well-Indented Code Block

```
' Takes a string and reverses it.
Sub ReverseString(vInput)
    ' Begin body of Sub..End Sub, so indent once.
    If TypeName(vInput) = "String" Then
        ' Begin body of If...Then, so indent again.
        Dim sOutput As String, iCount As Integer
        For iCount = Len(vInput) To 1 Step -1
            ' Begin body of For...Next loop, so indent again.
            sOutput = sOutput & Mid$(vInput, iCount, 1)
        Next iCount
        vInput = sOutput
    End If
End Sub
```

In listing 22.6, you can easily see where loops and conditional statements begin and end. This is critical in long passages of conditional code, such as long `Select Case` statements or a series of `If...Then` statements.

Commenting Code

Good comments are the most important step to writing code that other programmers can understand and maintain. This practice is extremely important if you want to take occasional vacations from work. Try writing comments one procedure at a time, using the following general form:

■ The *procedure description* explains what the procedure does, mentions any global or module-level variables that it uses, and describes the arguments and return value (if any). You might also consider including the name of the author and the revision history.

■ *Variable declarations* describe the key variables that the procedure uses.

■ *Descriptive comments* narrate what the code is doing. You need not explain in English what every line of code does; simply indicate the actions that the code performs and the decisions that the code makes.

■ *Assumptions and Undones* are flags that indicate that you haven't finished your work yet. You might want to get a procedure up and running before making it bulletproof. If you do so, try to flag the assumptions that you are making (you might type these assumptions in all uppercase letters). These flags make it easier to get back to work after demonstrating the software to your boss.

Listing 22.7 shows a block of code that demonstrates these commenting guidelines.

Listing 22.7   A Well-Commented Code Block

```
' (1) Procedure Description
' Adds a button to the Standard toolbar
' when this workbook is opened.
' Use this command line to install button:
'    EXCEL.EXE VISIO.XLS
' Make sure "InsertVisioDrawing" macro is
' available (see VISIO.XLA).
' Written by: A. Wombat
' Revisions: None.
' The bitmap picture embedded on Sheet 1 determines
' the picture that appears on the button.
Sub Auto_Open()
    ' (2) Variable Declarations
    Dim tbutCount As ToolbarButton, tbutVisio As ToolbarButton
    Application.ScreenUpdating = False
    ' (3) Descriptive Comments (from here on)
    ' Check if toolbar button already exists
    For Each tbutCountIn Toolbars("Standard").ToolbarButtons
        If tbutCount.Name = "Insert Visio drawing" Then Exit Sub
    Next tbutCount
    ' Add a blank toolbar button to the Standard toolbar.
    Toolbars("Standard").ToolbarButtons.Add Button:=231
    ' Create an object variable for the button
    ' (it is the last button on the toolbar).
    Set tbutVisio = Toolbars("Standard"). _
        ToolbarButtons(Toolbars("Standard").ToolbarButtons.Count)
    ' Set the macro the toolbar button will run.
    tbutVisio.OnAction = "InsertVisioDrawing"
    ' Give the button a name to display in the Tool Tip balloon.
    tbutVisio.Name = "Insert Visio drawing"
    ' Copy the bitmap.
    Sheets("Sheet1").DrawingObjects("Visio Toolbar Button"). _
        CopyPicture
    ' Paste it into the button.
    tbutVisio.PasteFace
    Application.ScreenUpdating = True
    ' Close this workbook.
    ' (4) Assumptions and Undones.
    ' UNDONE: Uncomment this line to cause
    ' workbook to automatically close.
    ' Makes it hard to edit this macro, though!
    'ActiveWorkbook.Close
End Sub
```

From Here...

For more information on the following topics, see the indicated chapters:

- Chapter 23, "Building and Distributing OLE Objects," tells you how to compile and build installation programs for applications that provide objects to other applications. It also discusses how to maintain applications so that future versions don't break compatibility with previous versions.

- Chapter 24, "Creating Add-Ins," explains how to create add-in applications that you can use to extend the Visual Basic programming system.

Chapter 23

Building and Distributing OLE Objects

Other applications use object libraries, so you must take special care when installing them. Objects must be registered with the system and you must distribute subsequent versions of your objects in a way that does not break existing, dependent applications.

In this chapter, you learn how to do the following:

- Identify the files that you need to distribute with your application

- Manage versions and editions of your application during installation

- Install and register objects based on the version and edition

- Create registration (.REG) files for your objects

- Deinstall your objects

Required Files

You cannot safely assume that anyone using objects that you create in Visual Basic already has a current version of the OLE 2.0 DLLs. Applications that use earlier versions of OLE 2.0 can create and use objects that you create in Visual Basic 4.0 (VB4). These applications include the following:

- Visual Basic 3.0

- Microsoft Excel 5.0

- Microsoft Project 3.0

These three applications permit programmatic access to objects through the CreateObject and GetObject functions. However, for CreateObject and GetObject to use VB4 objects, you must distribute the newest versions of the OLE 2.0 DLLs along with your objects. The earlier versions of the OLE 2.0 DLLs are not compatible with VB4 objects.

Unfortunately, this requirement adds a lot of extra stuff that you must distribute every time that you send out an application. Your .EXE file might be as small as 18K, but you'll need at least two high-density disks for every copy that you distribute. Table 23.1 lists the files required for applications that provide objects.

Table 23.1 Files Required by Applications That Provide Objects	
File Name	**Description**
VB40016.DLL	Visual Basic run-time library
VB40032.DLL	Visual Basic run-time library
VB4EN16.DLL	Visual Basic English-language object library
VB4EN32.DLL	This file name differs for other national languages
SCP.DLL	Code page translation library
SCP32.DLL	Code page translation library
DDEML.DLL	Dynamic Data Exchange (DDE) manager
COMPOBJ.DLL	OLE support for component objects
OLE2.DLL	General OLE functions
OLE2.REG	Registration file for OLE
OLE2CONV.DLL	Support for converting OLE data types
OLE2DISP.DLL	Support for OLE Automation
OLE2NLS.DLL	Support for OLE national languages and localization features
OLE2PROX.DLL	Support for cross-process invocations
STDOLE.TLB	The OLE object library
STORAGE.DLL	Support for creating OLE compound documents
TYPELIB.DLL	Support for accessing and creating object libraries

The OLE 2.0 files that table 23.1 lists are 16-bit versions. Windows 95 ships with current versions of the OLE 2.0 DLLs, so you should not have to worry about distributing 32-bit OLE 2.0 DLLs unless either of the following conditions exist:

- Your target platform is Windows NT 3.51, and Visual Basic breaks compatibility between the Windows NT release DLLs and the Visual Basic final release.

- Problems arise with the OLE 2.0 DLLs released in Windows 95, and Visual Basic must issue updated DLLs.

Either of these conditions is impossible to foresee at this point. Check the Visual Basic README.TXT if you have concerns, or call Microsoft's Product Support Services to verify compatibility.

Versioning Objects

Applications that provide objects have two levels of versioning:

- File version
- File edition

The *file version* differentiates between files with the same name. For instance, you might distribute an updated version of an object library that contains bug fixes. In this case, the new file would have a later file version and simply replace the earlier file when installed.

The file name itself includes the *file edition*. You must issue a new edition of an application if it breaks compatibility with the previous edition. New editions of an application must not overwrite prior editions.

Creating New Versions

If you are distributing an application that replaces a previous version, the new version must be code-compatible with the previous version. That is, other programs written using objects in the previous version should not break when the users install the new version. There are many ways that you can break compatibility with previous versions of an application, but the ones that OLE defines as critical are all related to the syntax of the objects, properties, and methods that your application provides. Any of the following changes breaks compatibility with previous versions:

- Changing the name of a `Public` project, class, method, or property
- Changing the declaration of a `Public` class, method, or property to `Private`
- Changing the `Instancing` property of a class
- Changing `Public` property access from read/write to read-only or write-only
- Removing arguments or order of arguments in a `Public` method
- Changing data types of arguments or values returned by `Public` methods or properties
- Changing an optional argument to a required one in a `Public` method

To have Visual Basic check for compatibility, you can enter the name of the previous version of your released application in the Compatible OLE Server text box on the Project page of the Options property pages.

If you do not make any of the changes in the preceding list, you can safely overwrite the previous version of your application according to the OLE 2.0 rules. The Setup program created by the Setup Wizard automatically determines whether a file should be overwritten, by checking the file's version information. To add version information to a Visual Basic application, follow these steps:

1. Choose File, Make EXE File or File, Make OLE DLL File. Visual Basic displays a dialog box (see fig. 23.1).

Fig. 23.1
Choose the Options button on the Make EXE File or Make OLE DLL dialog box to add version information to an executable file.

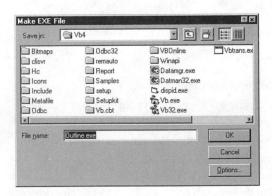

2. Choose the Options button. Visual Basic displays the executable options dialog box (see fig. 23.2).

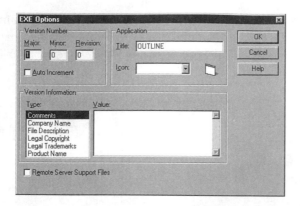

Fig. 23.2
The EXE Options
and DLL Options
dialog boxes en-
able you to write
version informa-
tion into the exe-
cutable file that
the functions in
VER.DLL can read.

3. Enter new version numbers in the Version Number frame. Then click OK.

4. Click OK to build the executable file.

In the EXE and DLL Options dialog boxes, you can choose from three version number fields:

Field	Increment If
Major	You are releasing a new edition of your application with significant new features.
Minor	You are releasing an updated version of your application with new features and bug fixes.
Revision	You are revising an existing Minor version with bug fixes. You can also use the Revision field to track builds of your application prior to release.

Each time that you update a field, you should reset the less-significant fields to 00. The accepted convention for prerelease software is to keep Major revision set to 00 until the initial release; this limits you to only 99,999,999 iterations before you have to ship it.

Creating New Editions

If an application that provides objects is not compatible with the previous version, you must release it as a new edition. Application editions have unique file names, such as OUT0100.DLL. The new edition must not overwrite the previous edition, or you risk breaking other, dependent applications on the user's system.

Applications that use editions must include edition information in the system registration database. You must create registration entries that append the edition number to the programmatic ID for each creatable object, as shown in figure 23.3.

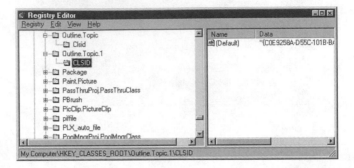

Applications can also register an entry in the registration database that indicates the most current edition. This entry does not include an edition number. Figure 23.3 shows both edition-specific and general entries for OUT0100.DLL. Both programmatic IDs (`Outline.Topic` and `Outline.Topic.1`) share the same class ID number. OLE uses the class ID to locate the executable file, so both programmatic IDs start the same application when used with `CreateObject` or `GetObject`. The following two lines have equivalent results:

```
Set Outline = CreateObject("outline.topic")
Set Outline = CreateObject("outline.topic.1")
```

The only difference between the preceding two lines is compatibility. If a new edition of the OUTLINE.VBP application is released, the first line might cause subsequent code to break. The second line, however, always starts the original edition of the application.

Installing Objects

Visual Basic writes registration information into each application that provides public, creatable objects. During installation, you can write this information to the system registration database by running the application with the /REGSERVER switch. For example, the following line registers the OUTLINE.EXE application:

```
Shell "outline.exe /REGSERVER"
```

If your executable is a .DLL, you can't use the `Shell` function to register the executable's objects, because .DLLs cannot run by themselves. Instead, you must use the `DLLSelfRegister` API function included in the Setup Toolkit .DLL. The following code shows the declarations and use of the function:

```
Public gstrPath = "c:\windows\system"
    ' Change this to get the right path at install time.
Public gstrDLLName = "OUT100.DLL"

#If Win16
    Declare Sub DLLSelfRegister Lib _
      "STKIT416.DLL" (ByVal lpDllName As String)
#Else
    Declare Sub DLLSelfRegister Lib _
      "STKIT432.DLL" (ByVal lpDllName As String)
#End If

Sub RegisterMe()
    DLLSelfRegister(gstrPath & gstrDLLName)   ' Register the DLL.
End Sub
```

The Setup Wizard automatically registers an application file if you add the `$(EXESelfRegister)` flag as the sixth argument for the file's entry in the SETUP.LST file. The following line shows the .LST file line that registers OUTLINE.EXE during setup:

```
File12=2,,OUTLINE.EX_, ,$(WinSysPath),$(EXESelfRegister), _
    8/23/94,69904,1.0.0.0
```

To register .DLLs, use the `$(DLLSelfRegister)` flag, as in the following example:

```
File12=2,,OUTLINE.DLL, ,$(WinSysPath),$(DLLSelfRegister), _
    8/23/94,69904,1.0.0.0
```

If your application needs to register a new edition, you must create a separate .REG file that registers both the current version and the edition-specific entries for your application.

Creating an .REG File

To create an .REG file that contains edition information, follow these steps:

1. Build your application on your system.

2. Run the application to register it in your system registration database.

3. Run the Registry Editor (see fig. 23.3) by entering **REGEDIT /V**.

4. Select the registration entry of the application that you just registered and choose File, Save Registration File.

5. Locate the matching entry for the class ID registered for the application that you just registered. You can locate the key by copying the value of the CLSID entry into the Find dialog box, as shown in figure 23.4. To display the dialog box, choose Edit, Find.

Fig. 23.4

To locate the class ID entry, copy the value of the CLSID key into the Find dialog box.

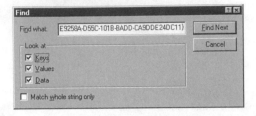

6. Select the CLSID entry and choose File, Save Registration File. Figure 23.5 shows a key selected for the CLSID entry before being saved.

Fig. 23.5

The CLSID entry contains the location and name of the executable file for the object.

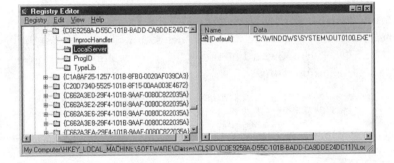

7. Repeat steps 4 through 6 for each creatable object that your application provides.

8. Merge all the saved files by using a text editor.

9. Add edition information to the programmatic ID for each object.

The following lines show the .REG file entries for OUT0100.EXE. The file contains edition-specific entries and general entries indicating the current edition.

```
REGEDIT
; General entry -- indicates current edition.
HKEY_CLASSES_ROOT\Outline.Topic\CLSID =
➥ {C0E9258A-D55C-101B-BADD-CA9DDE24DC11}
HKEY_CLASSES_ROOT\CLSID\{C0E9258A-D55C-101B-BADD-CA9DDE24DC11}
➥\TypeLib = {C0E92535-D55C-101B-BADD-CA9DDE24DC11}
```

```
HKEY_CLASSES_ROOT\CLSID\{C0E9258A-D55C-101B-BADD-CA9DDE24DC11}
➥\InprocHandler = OLE2.DLL
HKEY_CLASSES_ROOT\CLSID\{C0E9258A-D55C-101B-BADD-CA9DDE24DC11}
➥\LocalServer = C:\WINDOWS\SYSTEM\OUT0100.EXE
HKEY_CLASSES_ROOT\CLSID\{C0E9258A-D55C-101B-BADD-CA9DDE24DC11}
➥\ProgID = Outline.Topic
; Edition-specific entry.
HKEY_CLASSES_ROOT\Outline.Topic.1\CLSID =
➥{C0E9258A-D55C-101B-BADD-CA9DDE24DC11}
HKEY_CLASSES_ROOT\CLSID\{C0E9258A-D55C-101B-BADD-CA9DDE24DC11}
➥\TypeLib = {C0E92535-D55C-101B-BADD-CA9DDE24DC11}
HKEY_CLASSES_ROOT\CLSID\{C0E9258A-D55C-101B-BADD-CA9DDE24DC11}
➥\InprocHandler = OLE2.DLL
HKEY_CLASSES_ROOT\CLSID\{C0E9258A-D55C-101B-BADD-CA9DDE24DC11}
➥\LocalServer = C:\WINDOWS\SYSTEM\OUT0100.EXE
HKEY_CLASSES_ROOT\CLSID\{C0E9258A-D55C-101B-BADD-CA9DDE24DC11}
➥\ProgID = Outline.Topic.1
```

The preceding .REG file includes the file path (\WINDOWS\SYSTEM) where the
Setup program installed the application. During Setup, you must modify this
information to indicate the actual installed path and file name.

Note

The Registry Editor differs in Windows 95 and Windows 3.x. Windows 3.x requires
the /V command-line switch to view full listings. The Windows 95 version ignores
this switch. Also, some commands and menus differ in the two versions.

Registering an .REG File

To register an .REG file during setup, modify the SETUP.LST file generated by
the Setup Wizard to include the application's .REG file name, as follows:

```
File12=2,,OUT0100.EX_, ,$(WinSysPath),OUT0100.REG,8/23/94,69904, _
    1.0.0.0
```

Be sure to include the .REG file in the list of files to be installed. The Setup
program generated by the Setup Wizard decompresses all files before registering them, so you need not worry about the order of .REG and executable files
in SETUP.LST.

To register an .REG file without using the Setup Wizard, run the Registry
Editor with the /S switch, as follows:

```
Shell "REGEDIT /S out0100.reg"
```

The /S switch runs the Registry Editor silently, without displaying a confirmation message after the application is registered.

III

Creating OLE Objects

Uninstalling Objects

Most Windows 3.x applications do not provide a facility for removing themselves from the system. This capability is a new feature that Windows 95 provides. If you are distributing your applications for Windows 95, you need not worry about uninstalling because the process is built in to the system. However, on earlier versions of Windows, you *do* need to concern yourself with uninstalling.

The Windows 3.x system registration database (REG.DAT) can fill up. Once the file exceeds 110K, it may be too big to edit in the Registry Editor. This can also cause problems within Visual Basic when loading and reading entries from REG.DAT. If REG.DAT becomes too big on your system, you get "Not enough memory" errors when you try to load the database in the Registry Editor.

When such errors occur, you can only delete the file and run SETUP.REG from your Windows system directory. This reregisters the applications that come with Windows. You must rerun each of your other Windows applications to reregister them.

You can run your application with the /UNREGSERVER switch to remove its registration database entries before you remove the executable file from disk. The following lines show how you might remove the OUTLINE.VBP sample:

```
Shell "outline.exe /UNREGSERVER"
Kill "outline.exe"
```

The /UNREGSERVER switch removes only the OLE Automation entries for an application. If you created associations among file types and your application in the registry, you must use the Windows registration APIs to delete the keys. The SYSTEM.VBP sample includes a Registration object to provide methods that invoke these functions. The following code shows how to use the Registration object to delete the registration entry for the OUT0100.EXE application:

```
Sub DeRegister()
    Dim Registration As Object
    Set Registration = CreateObject(""System.Application""). _
        Registration
    ' Delete .cdc file type from Registration database.
    Registration.DeleteKey ".cdc"
End Sub
```

From Here...

For more information on the following topics, see the indicated chapters:

- Chapter 22, "Debugging Applications That Provide Objects," gives you important insight into solving the many new problem areas that crop up as you program with objects.

- Chapter 24, "Creating Add-Ins," explains how to create add-in applications that you can use to extend the Visual Basic programming system.

III

Creating OLE Objects

Chapter 24

Creating Add-Ins

Visual Basic 4.0 introduces add-ins. Add-ins are to the Visual Basic programming environment what custom controls are to your applications: pieces of compiled functionality that you can simply plug in and use. Unlike custom controls, however, add-ins can be created by the programmer right in Visual Basic. This chapter explains how to create add-ins in Visual Basic.

In this chapter, you learn about the following:

- How the Add-In Manager loads add-ins and how Visual Basic interacts with them

- Which objects to use when creating an add-in

- What Visual Basic events add-ins can detect and respond to

- How to detect Visual Basic events from within your add-in

- How to navigate among Visual Basic's add-in objects

- How to create an add-in in Visual Basic

- How to install the add-in

- How to add and remove items on the Visual Basic Add-Ins menu

- How to debug the add-in

Overview

The Visual Basic Add-In Manager loads add-in files into the Visual Basic programming environment. Once loaded, an add-in can extend Visual Basic in three ways: by providing new items on the Add-Ins menu; by providing custom templates for new forms; or by adding special features, such as automatic source control.

You can create add-ins using Visual Basic Professional or Enterprise Editions. Add-ins created in Visual Basic include special methods in a public, creatable class. When you load an add-in, Visual Basic starts the add-in's .EXE file and connects it to specific Visual Basic events. Classes in the add-in's executable can respond to these events and interact with Visual Basic through objects that the Visual Basic programming environment provides.

The add-in's executable file stays loaded in memory until Visual Basic quits or the user unloads the add-in from the Add-In Manager. During this time, the add-in can respond to certain user events as they occur in Visual Basic. These events include saving files, adding new forms, and clicking on certain menu items. Figure 24.1 shows how an add-in interacts with Visual Basic.

Fig. 24.1
Once loaded, add-ins can use Visual Basic add-in objects and respond to events in the programming environment.

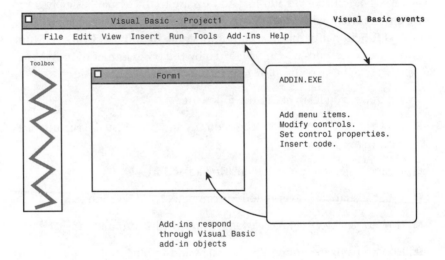

Loading an Existing Add-In

To load an add-in in Visual Basic, follow these steps:

1. Choose Add-Ins, Add-In Manager. Visual Basic displays the Add-In Manager dialog box (see fig. 24.2).

2. Select the check box next to the name of the add-in to load. Then click OK. Visual Basic loads the selected add-in.

After you select add-ins in the Add-In Manager, they load each time that you start Visual Basic. The [add-ins16] or [add-ins32] section of the VB.INI file stores these selections, as follows:

```
[add-ins16]
RegEditAddin.Application=1
```

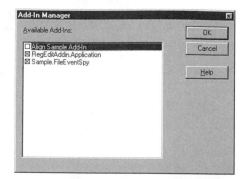

Fig. 24.2
The Add-In Manager displays the available add-ins.

The name of the add-in (`RegEditAddin.Application`) shown in the preceding example is the programmatic ID of the add-in as it is registered in the system registration database. The setting for each add-in (0 or 1) indicates whether the add-in is loaded.

An add-in might be registered in the system registration database, but if the add-in is not listed in the add-ins section of VB.INI, it does not appear in the Add-In Manager.

Objects That Add-Ins Use

Visual Basic provides an object library, VBEXT.OLB, that you can use to extend the Visual Basic programming environment. Figure 24.3 shows the hierarchy of the objects that Visual Basic provides. Table 24.1 describes the tasks that you perform with each of the objects.

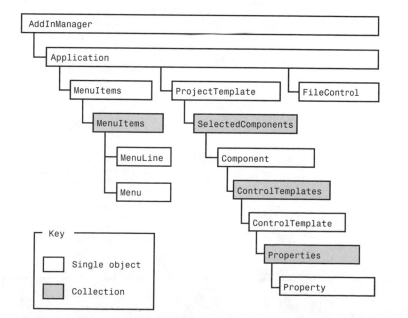

Fig. 24.3
The Visual Basic add-in object hierarchy.

Creating OLE Objects

Table 24.1 VBEXT Objects by Task

Task	Object	Description
Load an add-in	AddInManager	Triggers ConnectAddin and DisconnectAddin methods in your add-in. You use these events to activate and deactivate your add-in when loaded in Visual Basic.
	Application	Provides access to all the subordinate objects. You get a reference to the Application object from the ConnectAddin method in your add-in.
Add items to the Add-Ins menu	Menu	Controls the display of items in the Add-Ins menu.
	MenuItems	Adds or removes menu items or menus from the Add-Ins menu.
	MenuLine	Controls the text displayed for a menu item in the Add-Ins menu. Also defines the action taken when the user clicks the menu item.
Control the active project	ProjectTemplate	Controls the active project by providing access to all the subordinate objects.
	SelectedComponents	Provides access to all the form, class, and code modules in the active project.
	Component	Controls a form, class, or code module.
	FormTemplate	Provides access to the controls on a form.
	ControlTemplates	Adds new controls to a form; returns ControlTemplate objects for each of the controls on a form.
	ControlTemplate	Provides access to the Properties collection of a control on a form.
	Properties	Provides access to each of a control's property settings.
	Property	Sets or returns the setting of a control's property.
Respond to File menu events	FileControl	Triggers methods in your add-in when the user chooses any of the items from the Visual Basic File menu.

Add-In Object Events

Three add-in objects expose events that you can detect:

■ The AddInManager object events occur when Visual Basic loads or unloads your add-in. Use these events to initialize and deinitialize your add-in and to get the current instance of the Visual Basic Application object.

■ The MenuLine object event occurs when a user clicks on the menu item. This event applies only to the items that you have added to the Add-Ins menu.

■ The FileControl object events occur when the user clicks on items in the File menu and when Visual Basic performs file actions. The main purpose of the FileControl object is to provide a way to connect to these events in Visual Basic.

Table 24.2 lists the add-in object events and describes when each occurs.

Table 24.2 Add-In Object Events		
Object	**Event**	**Trigger**
AddInManager	ConnectAddIn	Visual Basic loads the add-in.
	DisConnectAddIn	Visual Basic unloads the add-in or Visual Basic quits.
MenuLine	AfterClick	The user clicks on the menu item.
FileControl	AfterAddFile	The user adds a form, code, class, resource, or .VBX file to a project.
	AfterChangeFileName	Visual Basic saves a file, renames a file, or creates an .EXE file.
	AfterCloseFile	The project file closes. This includes a project file closing because Visual Basic is quitting.
	AfterRemoveFile	The user removes a form, code, class, resource, or .VBX file from a project.
	AfterWriteFile	A project, form, code, or class file is written to disk.
	BeforeLoadFile	Visual Basic loads a project, form, code, class, resource, .FRX, or .VBX file.

(continues)

Table 24.2 Continued

Object	Event	Trigger
FileControl	DoGetAddFileName	The user chooses File, Add.
	DoGetNewFileName	The user chooses File, Save File or File, Save Project for a new file; or the user chooses the File menu's Save File As, Save Project As, or Make EXE File for an existing file.
	DoOpenProjectName	The user chooses File, Open Project.
	RequestChangeFileName	Visual Basic prepares to rename a project, form, class, or code module file to disk.
	RequestWriteFile	Visual Basic prepares to save a project, form, class, or code module file to disk.

Connecting to an Object's Event

The AddInManager object automatically associates two special method names with its events: ConnectAddIn and DisconnectAddIn. If you provide methods with these names in a public, creatable class, the Add-In Manager creates an instance of that object and invokes the ConnectAddIn method when the add-in is loaded. The ConnectAddIn method has the following form:

```
Public Sub ConnectAddIn(Application As Object)
    ' Your initialization code goes here.
End Sub
```

The Application argument is a passed-in reference to the current instance of the Visual Basic Application object. This reference is your one opportunity to access the Application object, so you must use this reference to derive all subsequent object references in your add-in.

The Add-In Manager invokes the DisconnectAddIn method just before it unloads the add-in. The add-in might unload if a user deselects the add-in in the Add-In Manager or if Visual Basic quits. The DisconnectAddIn method has the following form:

```
Public Sub DisconnectAddIn(Mode As Integer)
    ' Your deinitialization code goes here.
End Sub
```

The Mode argument indicates why the add-in is unloading: 0 indicates that
Visual Basic is quitting, and 1 indicates that the user deselected the add-in in
the Add-In Manager. Use the DisconnectAddIn method to unload any forms
that your add-in uses and to save any settings that you want to preserve.

To detect the events for MenuLine or FileControl objects, you must create an
association between the event and the object that you've created to respond
to the event. The add-in object's ConnectEvents method creates this association. The following code shows how to use the ConnectAddIn event to add
a line to the Add-Ins menu. The code associates the new line with the
AfterClick method in this object.

```
' Initialize the add-in.
Public Sub ConnectAddIn(Application As Object)
    ' Create a new MenuLine object.
    Set mnuitCreateDirectory = Application. _
        AddInMenu.MenuItems.Add("Create Directory")
    ' Associate the MenuLine AfterClick event
    ' with this object.
    mnuitCreateDirectory.ConnectEvents Me
End Sub

' The AfterClick event procedure for the
' Create Directory menu item.
Public Sub AfterClick()
    ' Display the Create Directory form.
    frmCreateDirectory.Show vbModal
End Sub
```

The object that you associate with an event must exist before you call
ConnectEvents. The following code shows how to create an instance of an
object before associating the object with a FileControl event:

```
' Application class -- APLICAT.CLS
'
'    Creatable = Tru
'    Public = True

' Initialization method.
Public Sub ConnectAddIn(Application As Object)
    ' Create a new instance of an object
    ' to receive file control events.
    Dim objFileControl As New clsFileControl
    ' Connect the VB FileControlEvents to the object.
    Application.FileControl.ConnectEvents objFileControl
End Sub
```

Listing 24.1 shows the class definition for the clsFileControl object. This
object simply displays a message box indicating when a file event occurs in
Visual Basic. You can use this class as a template for your own file control
object.

III

Creating OLE Objects

Listing 24.1 The Class Definition for the `clsFileControl` Object

```
' clsFileControl class -- FILEVENTS.CLS
'
'   Creatable = False
'   Public = True
Option Explicit

Public Sub AfterAddFile(FileName As String)
    MsgBox "AfterAddFile"
End Sub

Public Sub AfterChangeFileName(FileType As String, _
    NewName As String, OldName As String)
    MsgBox "AfterChangeFileName"
End Sub

Public Sub AfterFileClose(FileNames() As String)
    MsgBox "AfterChangeFileName"
End Sub

Public Sub AfterRemoveFile(FileNames() As String)
    MsgBox "AfterRemoveFile"
End Sub

Public Sub AfterWriteFile(FileName As String, Success As Integer)
    MsgBox "AfterWriteFile"
End Sub

Public Sub BeforeLoadFile(FileNames() As String)
    MsgBox "BeforeLoadFile"
End Sub

Public Sub DoGetAddFileName(FileNames() As String, _
    Cancel As Boolean)
    MsgBox "DoGetAddFileName"
End Sub

Public Sub DoGetNewFileName(FileType As Integer, _
    NewName As String, OldName As String, Cancel As Boolean)
    MsgBox "DoGetNewFileName"
End Sub

Public Sub DoGetOpenProjectName(ProjectName As String, _
    NewName As String, OldName As String, Cancel As Boolean)
    MsgBox "DoGetOpenProjectName"
End Sub

Public Sub DoRequestChangeFileName(FileType As Integer, _
    NewName As String, OldName As String, Cancel As Boolean)
    MsgBox "DoRequestChangeFileName"
End Sub

Public Sub RequestChangeFileName(FileType As Integer, _
    NewName As String, OldName As String, Cancel As Boolean)
    MsgBox "RequestChangeFileName"
End Sub
```

```
Public Sub RequestWriteFile(FileName As String, Cancel As Boolean)
    MsgBox "RequestWriteFile"
End Sub
```

Navigating the Add-In Object Hierarchy

The add-in objects don't closely follow the OLE naming conventions for collections. Therefore, you sometimes must use nonobvious method and property names when navigating down the add-in object hierarchy. Table 24.3 shows the properties and methods that you use to navigate down each level in the add-in object hierarchy.

Table 24.3 Properties and Methods Used to Navigate down the Add-In Object Hierarchy

From Object	To Object	Use This Property/ Method
AddInManager	Application	None; an Application object is passed in as the argument to the ConnectAddin method
Application	Menu	AddInMenu property
Menu	MenuItems	MenuItems method
MenuItems	MenuLine	Item method (default method)
MenuItems	Menu	Item method (default method)
Application	ProjectTemplate	ActiveProject property
ProjectTemplate	SelectedComponents	SelectedComponents property
SelectedComponents	Component	ActiveForm property or Item method (default method)
Component	ControlTemplates	ControlTemplates method or SelectedControlTemplates property
ControlTemplates	ControlTemplate	Item method (default method)
ControlTemplate	Properties	Properties method
Properties	Property	Item method (default method)
Application	FileControl	FileControl property

To navigate up the add-in object hierarchy, use the Parent or Application properties. All add-in objects provide these properties.

Creating an Add-In

To create an add-in, write code to perform the following actions:

1. Add the add-in's programmatic ID to the VB.INI file so that it is available from the Add-In Manager.

2. Initialize the add-in when Visual Basic loads it.

3. Respond to menu and file events in Visual Basic.

4. Deinitialize the add-in when it is unloaded or when Visual Basic quits.

The following sections explain each of these steps in greater detail.

Installing the Add-In

Add-ins must have at least one class with Creatable and Public properties set to True. Typically this class is called Application and provides the programmatic ID that you install in the VB.INI file. Visual Basic doesn't provide a built-in way to add entries to the .INI files, so you must use the Windows API function WritePrivateProfileString to perform this task.

Listing 24.2 shows a Main procedure that installs the add-in in the VB.INI file if you run the add-in .EXE file with the /install switch. This procedure demonstrates a handy way to distribute your add-ins, although it increases the code size slightly. You can use this Main procedure in your own add-ins simply by modifying the module-level constants and making it the startup procedure for your add-in.

Listing 24.2   Registering an Add-In with Visual Basic

```
' Adds an entry to VB.INI that will add an add-in to
' VB's Add-Ins dialog box when VB is started.
Option Explicit

' Win API declaration used to write to VB.INI
#If Win16 Then
Declare Function WritePrivateProfileString Lib "Kernel" _
    (ByVal lpApplicationName As String, _
    ByVal lpKeyName As String, _
    ByVal lpString As Any, _
    ByVal lplFileName As String) _
```

```
        As Integer
#ElseIf Win32 Then
Declare Function WritePrivateProfileString Lib "Kernel32" _
    (ByVal lpApplicationName As String, _
    ByVal lpKeyName As String, _
    ByVal lpString As Any, _
    ByVal lplFileName As String) _
    As Integer
#End If
' Change to ProgID of your add-in's Application class.
Const AddIn = "RegEditAddin.Application"
' Change to "add-ins32" for 32-bit systems.
Const INISection = "add-ins16"
Const INIFile = "vb.ini"

Sub Main()
    Dim strAddIn As String, strSetting As String
    ' If the add-in was launched with the \install
    ' switch, install the add-in in the VB.INI file.
    If InStr(LCase(Command$), "install") Then
        ' Name of add-in = applicationname.classname
        ' 1 loads add-in, 0 does not load
        strSetting = "1"
        ' Add entry to VB.INI.
        If WritePrivateProfileString(INISection, AddIn, _
            strSetting, INIFile) Then
            ' Success.
        Else
            ' Notify user that add-in couldn't be registered.
            MsgBox "Addin could not be registered in VB.INI. " & _
            "Add these lines to VB.INI and " & _
                restart Visual Basic: " & _
            Chr(13) & _
            INISection & Chr(13) & _
            "[" & AddIn & "]" & "=" & strSetting, _
            vbExclamation, "Install Addin"
        End If
    End If
End Sub
```

Initializing the Add-In

The Application class that provides the programmatic ID that you install in
the VB.INI file must contain the ConnectAddIn and DisconnectAddIn methods.
These methods initialize the add-in when it is loaded, and deinitialize it
when it is unloaded or when Visual Basic quits.

The ConnectAddIn has one argument, Application, which passes in a reference
to the instance of Visual Basic that is loading the add-in. You use this object
reference in all subsequent access to Visual Basic objects, so you must preserve its value before the ConnectAddIn procedure ends and the argument
loses scope. The best way to save the value of Application is as the Parent

III

Creating OLE Objects

property of the add-in's `Application` object. This is consistent with the OLE standard for object navigation and enables you to get the Visual Basic `Application` object from all the other objects in your add-in.

Listing 24.3 shows the `ConnectAddIn` method for the `Application` class of the REGADDIN.VBP sample, a simple add-in that adds the Registry Editor to the Visual Basic <u>A</u>dd-Ins menu.

Listing 24.3   The `ConnectAddIn` Method for REGADDIN.VBP's `Application` Class

```
' Application class -- APLICAT.CLS
'    Creatable = True
'    Public = True
Option Explicit
' Declaration for the menu line object to add.
Private mnuitRegedit As Object

' ConnectAddIn method
' Initializes the add-in
Public Sub ConnectAddIn(Application As Object)
' Set the Parent of this add-in
    Set Me.Parent = Application
    ' Add a menu item to the Add-Ins menu
    Set mnuitRegedit = Application.AddInMenu.MenuItems _
    .Add("Registration Info Editor")
    ' Connect the menu item to this object.
    mnuitRegedit.ConnectEvents Me
End Sub
```

The `Parent` property of the `Application` class is a write-once, read-always property. After initializing `Parent`, the `ConnectAddIn` method is effectively read-only. Listing 24.4 shows the definition for the `Parent` property of the `Application` class in the REGADDIN.VBP sample.

Listing 24.4   The `Parent` Property for REGADDIN.VBP's `Application` Class

```
' This variable declaration must appear at the beginning
' of the module (before executable code). Stores a private
' copy of the parent object.
Private mParent As Object

' Parent property (read always/write once).
Public Property Get Parent() As Object
    ' Return the parent object.
    Set Parent = mParent
End Property
```

```
Public Property Set Parent(objSetting As Object)
    If TypeName(mParent) = "Nothing" Then
        Set mParent = objSetting
    Else
        ' Can't reset.
        Err.Raise 383, "Application object", _
            "Parent property is read-only."
    End If
End Property
```

Responding to Menu and File Events

After you use the ConnectEvents method to connect an object to a Visual
Basic menu or file control events, Visual Basic runs the appropriate method
in that object when an event occurs. The method name and parameter count
and type must match the definition that Visual Basic expects for the particular method.

Listing 24.5 shows the AfterClick method included in the REGADDIN.VBP
sample. This method resides in the Application class, which also contains the
ConnectAddIn method that creates the association between the menu item and
the current object.

**Listing 24.5   The AfterClick Method for REGADDIN.VBP's
Application Class**

```
' This line must occur before executable code.
' Retains the handle used to shut down the application on exit.
Private mAppHandle As Integer

Public Sub AfterClick()
    ' Run the Registry Editor.
    mAppHandle = Shell ("REGEDIT /V", 1)
End Sub
```

The AfterClick method is a very simple application of an add-in. It merely
shells another application—in this case, one that you use quite often when
working with OLE: the Registry Editor.

Listings 24.6 and 24.7 are the definitions for the menu and file control events
in Visual Basic. You can change the name of the arguments that these definitions use, but not their number, order, or type.

III

Creating OLE Objects

Listing 24.6   Add-In Event Definitions for the `MenuLine` Object

```
Public Sub AfterClick()
End Sub
```

Listing 24.7   Add-In Event Definitions for the `FileControl` Object

```
Public Sub AfterAddFile(FileName As String)
End Sub

Public Sub AfterChangeFileName(FileType As String, _
    NewName As String, OldName As String)
End Sub

Public Sub AfterFileClose(FileNames() As String)
End Sub

Public Sub AfterRemoveFile(FileNames() As String)
End Sub

Public Sub AfterWriteFile(FileName As String, Success As Integer)
End Sub

Public Sub BeforeLoadFile(FileNames() As String)
End Sub

Public Sub DoGetAddFileName(FileNames() As String, _
    Cancel As Boolean)
End Sub

Public Sub DoGetNewFileName(FileType As Integer, _
    NewName As String, OldName As String, Cancel As Boolean)
End Sub

Public Sub DoGetOpenProjectName(ProjectName As String, _
    NewName As String, OldName As String, Cancel As Boolean)
End Sub

Public Sub DoRequestChangeFileName(FileType As Integer, _
    NewName As String, OldName As String, Cancel As Boolean)
End Sub

Public Sub RequestChangeFileName(FileType As Integer, _
    NewName As String, OldName As String, Cancel As Boolean)
End Sub

Public Sub RequestWriteFile(FileName As String, Cancel As Boolean)
End Sub
```

Use the `DisconnectEvents` method to remove the association between a menu or `FileControl` object and an object in your application. The `DisconnectEvents` method suspends event trapping for the specified object.

Deinitializing the Add-In

The `DisconnectAddIn` method in the add-in's `Application` class undoes the actions taken in the `ConnectAddIn` method. Before Visual Basic unloads the add-in, you want your add-in to remove any items that it added to the Add-Ins menu and unload any forms that it displayed.

Listing 24.8 is the `DisconnectAddIn` method in the REGADDIN.VBP sample's `Application` class. The method closes the Registry Editor before the add-in unloads and removes the Add-Ins menu item if the user deselected the add-in in the Add-In Manager.

Listing 24.8   The `DisconnectAddIn` Method in the REGADDIN.VBP Sample's `Application` Class

```
' Declarations for functions used by DisconnectAddIn
#If Win16 Then
Private Declare Function PostAppMessage Lib "User" _
    (ByVal htask As Integer,
    ByVal wMsg As Integer, _
    ByVal wParam As Integer, _
    lParam As Any) _
    As Integer
Private Declare Function IsTask Lib "KERNEL"
     (ByVal htask As Integer) _
     As Integer
Const WM_QUIT = &H12
#Else
' Under Win32, ending an application is very different.
Private Declare Function OpenProcess Lib "KERNEL32" _
    (ByVal dwDesiredAccess As Long, _
    ByVal bInheritHandle As Long, _
    ByVal dwProcessId As Long) As Long
Private Declare Function TerminateProcess Lib "KERNEL32" _
    (ByVal hProcess As Long, _
    ByVal uExitCode As Long) As Long
Const TERMINATE_PROCESS = &H1
#End If

Public Sub DisconnectAddIn(iConnect As Integer)
    ' Check if RegEdit is still running.
    #If Win16 Then
    Dim iWorked As Integer
    If IsTask(mAppHandle) Then
        ' Tell RegEdit to close
        iWorked = PostAppMessage(mAppHandle, _
```

(continues)

Listing 24.8   Continued

```
        WM_QUIT, 0, 0)
    End If
#Else
    Dim iWorked As Long
    iWorked = OpenProcess(TERMINATE_PROCESS, _
        0, mAppHandle)
    If iWorked Then
        iWorked = TerminateProcess(iWorked, 0)
    End If
#End If
Select Case iConnect
    ' Addin disconnected because VB closed.
    Case 0
        ' No extra work.
    ' Addin disconnected because user deselected its
    ' check box in the Addin Manager.
    Case 1
        ' Remove menu item.
        mnuitRegedit.Parent.Remove mnuitRegedit
End Select
' End AddIn
End
End Sub
```

Adding a Menu Item

Use the MenuItems collection's Add method to add an item to the Add-Ins menu. Visual Basic enables you to add items only to the Add-Ins menu. Other menus are off-limits for now.

The Add method returns a reference to the MenuLine object that you just added. You can use this reference in subsequent lines to associate the menu item with an object that detects the item's AfterClick event. The following line shows how to add a line displaying the text "Registration Info Editor" to the Add-Ins menu:

```
Set mnuitRegedit = Application.AddInMenu.MenuItems. _
    Add("&Registration Info Editor")
```

After adding the MenuLine object, you can connect it to an object that contains the AfterClick method to respond to click events on the MenuLine object. The following line connects the current object to the MenuLine object's AfterClick event:

```
mnuitRegedit.ConnectEvents Me
```

You can also add submenus to the Add-Ins menu. A *submenu* is a menu that displays other menu items, which cascade downward as shown in figure 24.4.

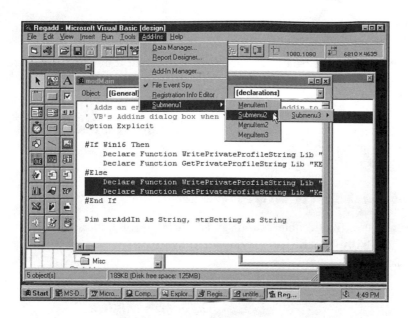

Fig. 24.4
You can add cas-
cading submenus
to the Add-Ins
menu.

Use the MenuItems collection's AddMenu method to add a submenu to the Add-Ins menu. The AddMenu method returns a reference to the Menu object that you just added. You can use this reference in subsequent lines to add MenuLines or additional submenus. The following line shows how to add to the Add-Ins menu a submenu that displays the text "Submenu1":

```
Set mnuSub1 = Application.AddInMenu.MenuItems.AddMenu("&Submenu1")
```

Submenus can't detect click events the same way that MenuLine objects can. To add menu lines to a submenu, use the Add method on the Menu object's MenuItems collection. The following line shows how to add the line "MenuLine1" to the submenu Submenu1, which the previous line added:

```
Set mnuitLine1 = mnuSub1.MenuItems.AddMenu("&MenuLine1")
```

Removing a Menu Item

Use the MenuItems collection's Remove method to delete an item from the Add-Ins menu. Deleting an item automatically removes all its subitems if the removed item is a submenu. The following line shows how to remove the Registration Info Editor line that you added in the previous section:

```
mnuitRegedit.Parent.MenuItems.Remove mnuitRegedit
```

If you want to disable a menu line without removing it, set its Enabled property. The following line disables (grays) the Registration Info Editor line:

```
mnuitRegedit.Enabled = False
```

III

Creating OLE Objects

To disable a menu line without graying it or to associate a menu item with an `AfterClick` method in another object, use the `DisconnectEvents` method. The following line disassociates the <u>R</u>egistration Info Editor line from the current object:

```
mnuitRegedit.DisconnectEvents
```

After using `DisconnectEvents`, you can associate the menu line with a new object by using the `ConnectEvents` method.

Debugging an Add-In

If Visual Basic has trouble locating an add-in or running the `ConnectAddIn` method, it displays the message shown in figure 24.5 when you try to load the add-in.

Fig. 24.5
This error indicates a problem with the registration or `ConnectAddIn` event of an add-in.

If the add-in is correctly registered and its programmatic ID matches the one installed in VB.INI, the `ConnectAddIn` method probably has a problem.

You can debug an add-in by using two instances of Visual Basic. This is similar to the way that you debug any object library cross-process, but it involves a couple extra steps.

To debug an add-in, follow these steps:

1. Check the Windows Task List and end any running instances of the add-in's application.

2. Load the add-in application's project (.VBP) in Visual Basic.

3. Choose <u>T</u>ools, <u>P</u>roject Options. Visual Basic displays the Project Options dialog box.

4. In the Project Options dialog box's StartMode group, select the <u>O</u>bject Application option. Click OK.

5. Start the application.

6. Edit the VB.INI file to include an entry in the [add-ins16] or [add-ins32] section for the programmatic ID of the add-in's Application class. The following lines show an example of the entry for REGADDIN.VBP:

```
[add-ins16]
RegEditAddIn.Application = 1
```

7. Start another instance of Visual Basic. The new instance automatically connects to the add-in application running in the other instance of Visual Basic.

8. Choose Tools, Environment Options. Visual Basic displays the Environment Options dialog box.

9. In the Environment Options dialog box, deselect the Break on All Errors check box and select the Break in Object Application check box, then click OK. This enables you to step from the current application into the add-in if an error occurs.

You might want to set a breakpoint on the ConnectAddIn method within the add-in application to trace through initialization. After you set this breakpoint, you can rerun ConnectAddIn by unloading and reloading the add-in in the other instance of Visual Basic.

From Here...

For more information on the following topics, see the indicated chapters:

■ Chapter 22, "Debugging Applications That Provide Objects," gives you important insight into solving the many new problem areas that crop up as you program with objects.

■ Chapter 23, "Building and Distributing OLE Objects," tells you how to compile and build installation programs for applications that provide objects to other applications. It also discusses how to maintain applications so that future versions don't break compatibility with previous versions.

III

Creating OLE Objects

Part IV

Integrating with Office Applications

Chapter 25

Understanding VBA and Other Microsoft Basic Languages

On May 20, 1991, Microsoft announced Visual Basic at Windows World '91 in Atlanta, and the programming world hasn't been the same since. Windows programmers finally had a very powerful programming language that was simple to use and very intuitive. Visual Basic for Applications takes the success of Visual Basic one step further, and in this chapter you learn how VBA helps make your job as a programmer much easier.

In this chapter, you learn more about the following:

- The origin of Visual Basic for Applications and how it relates to Visual Basic (VB)

- How to use similar code in all the Microsoft Basic languages for Windows

- What type libraries are and why they are useful

- How to access database files directly with Visual Basic using data access objects (DAO)

- Determining when to use Access rather than Visual Basic

- The Word Insertable Object Control

- Using OLE Automation and the OLE container control with Word

Introducing Visual Basic for Applications (VBA)

Visual Basic for Applications (VBA) is Microsoft's attempt to create a common macro language for its products. VBA is based on the highly successful Visual Basic (VB) product. This second generation version of Visual Basic is as easy to use as VB and includes many new enhancements to the language. Some of its major enhancements include the following:

- Close integration with OLE 2.0 (including enhanced OLE Automation support)

- Additions to the language (line continuation character, optional arguments, and so on)

- A stronger emphasis on object oriented concepts (encapsulation, objects, classes, and so on)

- Consistency across different implementations (a common VBA type library for basic features)

Most of the improvements help to make VBA a more robust language for its most important feature, OLE Automation.

> **Note**
>
> For a more exhaustive discussion on VBA, read *Using Visual Basic for Applications, Excel Edition,* by Jeff Webb. This book contains useful information for using VBA with the most powerful OLE 2.0 server, Microsoft Excel.

Understanding the Differences between VB and VBA

Although VB and VBA are very similar, they differ in some important ways. Perhaps the most important difference is the definition of the two languages. Table 25.1 provides these definitions.

Table 25.1 Definitions of VB and VBA	
Language	**Definition**
Visual Basic	As of Visual Basic 4.0, this version is actually VBA 2.0. It differs from VBA in that it enables you to create a stand-alone executable that you can distribute to users who do not own a Microsoft application.
Visual Basic for Applications	Introduced in the fall of 1993 as a replacement for Microsoft Excel's XLM macro language, VBA 1.0 is currently included in Excel 5.0 and Project 4.0, and its applications require the product in which they were created.

All this stuff is rather confusing, but there's a simple way to differentiate between the two: VB is a separate programming product that enables you to make executables, and VBA is a new macro language for Microsoft's applications. As of VB 4.0, both products can share elements (type libraries) through the Object Browser. Currently only Excel 5.0 and Project 4.0 have VBA, but eventually all Microsoft languages will adopt VBA as a common macro language.

Using Visual Basic for Applications

You are probably wondering whether you can simply look at a code sample and automatically distinguish VB code from VBA code. You cannot; instead, you must look at the editor in which the code was written. For example, the following procedure could appear in either VB or VBA:

```
Sub Greetings(YourName As String)
Dim Reply As Integer

    Reply = MsgBox("Hello " & YourName & _
    ", are you ready to compute?", vbQuestion + vbYesNo)

    If Reply = vbYes Then
        MsgBox "Well then, let's get busy!", vbInformation
    Else
        MsgBox "I'm sorry to hear that, but you must.", _
               vbInformation
    End If

End Sub
```

By looking at this code in its editor, you can tell which language was used. Figure 25.1 shows an example of VBA in Microsoft Excel, and figure 25.2 shows an example of Visual Basic 4.0. Viewing the editor makes a difference because all VBA editors conform to the same basic rules.

Fig. 25.1

VBA code in Microsoft Excel 5.0.

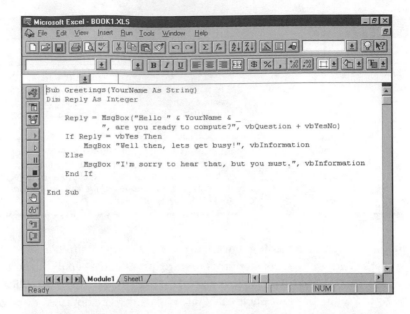

Fig. 25.2

The same code in Visual Basic 4.0.

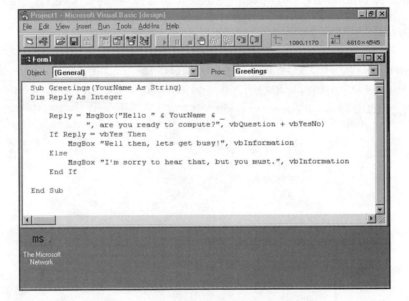

Type Libraries and the Object Browser

How can one language meet all the needs of three separate products? That's where type libraries enter the picture. A type (or object) library is a file that each variation of Visual Basic provides to add product-specific features (for example, accessing a range of cells in Excel). In fact, all products with VBA share a common VBA type library. What's more, any variation of VBA can use type libraries from other applications to perform OLE Automation.

Type libraries are managed by a program, the Object Browser, that is built in to VBA. Object Browser (see fig. 25.3) provides the user with a list of the available libraries and their elements.

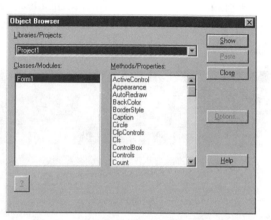

Fig. 25.3
The Object Browser in Visual Basic 4.0 provides easy access to type libraries.

> **Note**
>
> Visual Basic 4.0's version of the Object Browser (VBA 2.0) is slightly enhanced from VBA 1.0's, but their purposes are identical.

Other Basic Languages from Microsoft

New programmers often complain that they are confused by all the "Basics" found in Microsoft products. This section clears up the confusion for you.

Currently, Microsoft has four versions of BASIC floating around in Windows: Visual Basic, Visual Basic for Applications, WordBasic, and Access Basic. You have already seen the two Visual Basic forms, so this section introduces the other two forms.

WordBasic

You can trace the origin of Visual Basic back to the macro language in Microsoft Word for Windows 1.0. This macro language, WordBasic, included many of the elements found in Visual Basic today. In fact, WordBasic is still the macro language used in Word for Windows 7.0.

> **Note**
>
> This chapter focuses only on Microsoft BASIC development in Windows. Other forms
> of Microsoft BASIC (for example, QuickBasic) are not discussed.

You can run the Greetings sample in WordBasic, with some slight modifications. As you can see in figure 25.4, Visual Basic inherited its MsgBox function from WordBasic.

Fig. 25.4

Some features of WordBasic are identical to their Visual Basic counterparts.

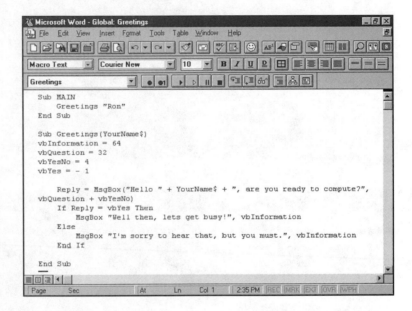

```
Sub MAIN
    Greetings "Ron"
End Sub

Sub Greetings(YourName$)
vbInformation = 64
vbQuestion = 32
vbYesNo = 4
vbYes = - 1

    Reply = MsgBox("Hello " + YourName$ + ", are you ready to compute?",
vbQuestion + vbYesNo)
    If Reply = vbYes Then
        MsgBox "Well then, lets get busy!", vbInformation
    Else
        MsgBox "I'm sorry to hear that, but you must.", vbInformation
    End If

End Sub
```

Tip

For the greatest compatibility between Word and VB code, consider using Visual Basic 1.0, or using OLE Automation with the WordBasic type library from VB4.

> **Caution**
>
> Usually Visual Basic code is *not* interchangeable with WordBasic. For a detailed
> description of WordBasic's syntax, consult the Microsoft WordBasic Help file
> (WRDBASIC.HLP) in the directory in which you installed Microsoft Word for
> Windows.

At this point, you might be jumping for joy at the idea that WordBasic and Visual Basic are similar. However, here's the bad news: Although Visual Basic derives partially from WordBasic, the languages have several differences. In fact, almost every line of code ported between the two products requires some modification. However, all is not lost.

After the tremendous success of Visual Basic, Microsoft realized that it needed a way to enable Visual Basic programmers to customize or control other applications (for example, Word) from VB. Although Word has always exposed WordBasic through Dynamic Data Exchange (DDE), this method was too cumbersome and links were easily broken. Microsoft's solution was to make WordBasic an OLE Automation object. This means that almost any method performed in WordBasic can be executed directly in Visual Basic. Listing 25.1 demonstrates this point.

Listing 25.1   Using WordBasic from Visual Basic

```
Sub Command1_Click()
'****************************************************
' Create an object variable using the name of
' your choice.
'****************************************************
Dim Word As Object
    '****************************************************
    ' Don't stop for errors.
    '****************************************************
    On Error Resume Next
    '****************************************************
    ' Assign a WordBasic object to your variable.
    '****************************************************
    Set Word = CreateObject("Word.Basic")
    '****************************************************
    ' Create a new document and insert some text.
    '****************************************************
    With Word
        .AppShow
        .FileNew
        .Insert "It Works!"
        .MsgBox "See, it works!"
    End With
    '****************************************************
    ' If error = 440, then Word couldn't process
    ' your commands.
    '****************************************************
    If Err = 440 Then
        MsgBox "That command is unavailable", vbCritical
    End If
    '****************************************************
    ' When you are done with your object, you can
    ' reclaim used memory by using the Nothing
    ' keyword. In this case, the next line really
    ' isn't necessary because the memory will
    ' be recovered when your object goes out of
    ' scope (at the End Sub).
    '****************************************************
    Set Word = Nothing
```

Tip
For a complete listing of the WordBasic's OLE Automation syntax, use the WordBasic Type Library with the Object Browser.

For more information about using WordBasic from within Visual Basic, see "Integration with Microsoft Word" later in this chapter.

Access Basic

In late 1992, over a year after the release of Visual Basic, Microsoft released yet another version of BASIC. This version, Access Basic, is the macro language that enables you to customize Microsoft Access. Although there are some subtle differences, Access Basic is about 90-percent compatible with Visual Basic.

> **Note**
>
> Microsoft Access 7.0 includes VBA 2.0, so your Access code must be 100-percent compatible with Visual Basic 4.0. Use the information in this chapter if you want to integrate Access 2.0 with Visual Basic 4.0.

If you declare your constants and remove the line continuation character from your VB code, you can successfully run the Greetings example in Access. Figure 25.5 shows the modified Greetings example in Microsoft Access 2.0.

Fig. 25.5
Code that conforms to the Visual Basic 3.0 syntax is virtually interchangeable with Access Basic.

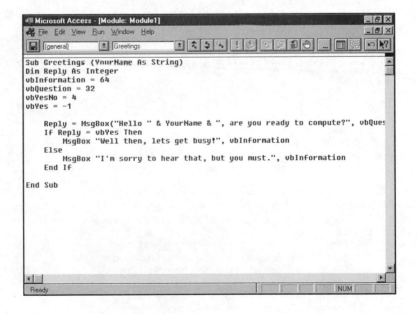

> **Caution**
>
> Visual Basic 4.0 includes major enhancements to its language that make its code much less compatible with Access Basic 2.0. Although you can create functions that work with either product, you must be more careful when doing so. Be sure to avoid VBA enhancements (for example, line continuation characters, optional arguments, and so on) when writing code for both products, unless you intend to use Access 7.0.

If you want to distribute an application that you have created in Access Basic, Microsoft provides the Access Development Kit (ADK). This product includes additional documentation about Access Basic, and includes everything that you need to distribute your Access application legally to users who do not own Access.

> **Tip**
>
> For the best compatibility between Visual Basic 4.0 (VB4) and Access, you should develop your code in VB4, using the DAO 2.5/3.0 Compatibility layer, and port it to the next version of Access when it becomes available.

When to Use Macros Rather Than VB

When should you use any one of these versions of BASIC? Although there is no one answer, you can use table 25.2 as a guide to help decide which is best for you.

Table 25.2   Choosing the Right Language

Language	Usage
Access Basic	If you are creating a database application, consider using Access along with the ADK. This solution gives you an enormous amount of "free" functionality, and the users do not have to own Microsoft Access. In addition, Access Basic can control other applications through OLE Automation, so you can do a lot with this powerful product.
Visual Basic	If your application requires a tremendous amount of flexibility, or if your application's users do not own any Microsoft products, Visual Basic is right for you.
Visual Basic for Applications	If your application depends on an application that uses VBA as its macro language (such as Excel Project or Access 95), use VBA. Unless your users do not have one of these products, VBA is probably the right choice for your application. Remember that VBA includes support for OLE Automation, so your possibilities are virtually endless. (For more advice, see the note that follows this table.)
WordBasic	If your application is completely specific to Microsoft Word, use WordBasic. Otherwise, use one of the other three choices and control Word through OLE Automation. Microsoft eventually will update Word to include VBA, so you will have to rewrite any serious development in the future.

Note

If you're developing a custom application and the customer doesn't have Excel or Project, consider buying them a copy. Even the smallest custom projects can cost several thousand dollars, so including one of these products (which you can typically purchase for less than $150) can save you weeks or months of development time.

Integration with Other Microsoft Applications

To harness the full power of Visual Basic, you should take advantage of the existing Microsoft applications installed on your user's computer. This approach saves you from the burden of reinventing the wheel, and enables you to take advantage of the robust features that these products offer.

Communication with Access

At the heart of most custom applications is a database, and Microsoft Access has quickly become one of the most popular programs for database management. This section describes how you can tap the power of Access for use in your Visual Basic applications.

Programmers often ask how their program can control Access. However, this question is rather silly due to the nature of Access. If you own a copy of Visual Basic 3.0 or greater, you already have most of the power of Access. The only part of Access over which you don't have control is its user interface. However, that part of Access isn't very important for custom applications because you create your own user interface with Visual Basic. To help clarify, the next few sections describe some of the components of Access and how you can access them.

Jet Database Layer 2.5

The real power behind Microsoft Access (MSACCESS.EXE) is its database engine, Jet. Everything else in Access is basically a user interface for the Jet. This concept is very important to you as a Visual Basic programmer because you also have control of the Jet Database Layer (also referred to as data access objects, or DAO). Consider the following scenarios:

■ Suppose that your application needs the titles of all books in a database file created in Microsoft Access. Because Visual Basic has access to the Jet Database Layer, you can directly retrieve this information using Visual Basic code.

- Suppose that your application needs to create, modify, and compact database files created in Access. Again, Visual Basic has access to the Jet Database Layer, so you can perform these actions directly using Visual Basic code.

- Suppose that your application needs to perform actions on SQL Server or some other foreign database format. Because the Jet Database Layer supports many database formats (through ODBC), you can directly access these files using Visual Basic code.

These scenarios show some of the most common uses of Access, but your copy of VB.EXE already has much of the power of MSACCESS.EXE to perform these tasks. In most cases, if you *really* need the Access interface, you shouldn't use Visual Basic.

Communicating with Access through DDE

If you absolutely must communicate with Access directly, you can perform a wealth of operations by using DDE. To connect to an application through DDE, your application must know an application (or service) name, a LinkTopic, and a LinkItem. Access always uses the MSAccess application name. Table 25.3 lists the available topics and items.

Table 25.3   DDE Methods for Microsoft Access 2.0

Topics	Items
System	Formats
	Status
	SysItems
	Topics
<Database>	FormList
To retrieve available database names, use	QueryList
LinkTopic = MSAccess¦System	MacroList
LinkItem = Topics	ModuleList
	ReportList
	TableList
<Database>;<TABLE¦QUERY> <TableName¦QueryName>	All
To retrieve available tables' names, use	Data
LinkTopic = MSAccess¦<database>	FieldCount
LinkItem = TableList	FieldNames
	FieldNames;T
	FirstRow
	LastRow
	NextRow
	PrevRow
	SQLText
	SQLText;<1 - 255>

(continues)

IV

Integrating with Office

Table 25.3 Continued	
Topics	**Items**
<Database>;<SQL> [SQL Statement]	All
	Data
	FieldCount
	FieldNames
	FieldNames;T
	FirstRow
	LastRow
	NextRow
	PrevRow
	SQLText
	SQLText;<1 - 255>

In addition to the previously mentioned DDE methods, Access also can receive the following commands through LinkExecute:

- The name of any macro in an open database

- [DoCmd [<same as Access Basic>]]

- [OpenDatabase <database filename>]

- [CloseDatabase]

Using DDE with Microsoft Access 2.0

To demonstrate the power of DDE with Access, this section presents a small application (shown in fig. 25.6) that performs many of the DDE methods previously described.

Fig. 25.6

An example of a DDE tester for Microsoft Access 2.0.

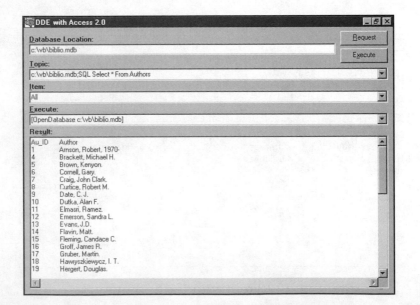

This program is very helpful for testing DDE commands to ensure that they work with Access, before you write a single line of implementation code. Listing 25.2 shows this handy utility's code, which demonstrates how to implement many of the DDE methods in VB.

Listing 25.2   FRMODE.FRM, an Access 2.0 DDE Test Application

```
'*****************************************************************
' FRMDDE.FRM: User interface for DDE with Access 2.0.
'*****************************************************************
Option Explicit
'*****************************************************************
' This is the DDE topic name that is used by all DDE connects
' in this demonstration program.
'*****************************************************************
Const DDE_APPLICATION = "MSAccess"
'*****************************************************************
' These are the indexes of the cbo control array.
'*****************************************************************
Const DDE_TOPIC = 0      'cbo(0)
Const DDE_ITEM = 1       'cbo(1)
Const DDE_EXECUTE = 2    'cbo(2)
'*****************************************************************
' Arbitrary constants which are used to populate the cbo(1)
' list with valid commands.
'*****************************************************************
Const ITEMS_SYSTEM = 0
Const ITEMS_LISTS = 1
Const ITEMS_DATA = 2
'*****************************************************************
' This variable stores the path to BIBLIO.MDB file.
'*****************************************************************
Private DatabaseName As String
'*****************************************************************
' When cbo(0) loses its focus, cbo(1) needs to be updated
' with valid DDE commands.
'*****************************************************************
Private Sub cbo_LostFocus(Index As Integer)
    Select Case Index
        Case DDE_TOPIC
            If InStr(cbo(DDE_TOPIC), "System") Then
                LoadItems ITEMS_SYSTEM
            ElseIf InStr(cbo(DDE_TOPIC), ";TABLE") Then
                LoadItems ITEMS_DATA
            ElseIf InStr(cbo(DDE_TOPIC), ";QUERY") Then
                LoadItems ITEMS_DATA
            ElseIf InStr(cbo(DDE_TOPIC), ";SQL") Then
                LoadItems ITEMS_DATA
            Else
                LoadItems ITEMS_LISTS
            End If
        Case DDE_ITEM
        Case DDE_EXECUTE
    End Select
End Sub
```

(continues)

Listing 25.2 Continued

```
'*****************************************************************
' Either request data, or execute a command.
'*****************************************************************
Private Sub cmd_Click(Index As Integer)
    Select Case Index
        '*******************************************************
        ' Request Data.
        '*******************************************************
        Case 0
            '***************************************************
            ' Get the data from Access and close the link.
            '***************************************************
            DDERequest DDESource, DDE_APPLICATION, _
                    (cbo(DDE_TOPIC).Text), (cbo(DDE_ITEM).Text)
            '***************************************************
            ' If the data returned doesn't contain a line
            ' feed, then replace tabs with carriage returns.
            '***************************************************
            If InStr(DDESource, Chr$(10)) = 0 Then
                txtResult = Replace(DDESource, Chr$(9), _
                                Chr$(13) & Chr$(10))
            '***************************************************
            ' Otherwise display the data as it was received.
            '***************************************************
            Else
                txtResult = DDESource
            End If
        '*******************************************************
        ' Execute a Command.
        '*******************************************************
        Case 1
            txtResult = ""
            DDEExecute DDESource, DDE_APPLICATION, _
                            (cbo(DDE_EXECUTE).Text)
    End Select
End Sub
'*****************************************************************
' Load cbo(0) with some valid topics for Access.
'*****************************************************************
Private Sub LoadTopics()
    With cbo(DDE_TOPIC)
        .Clear
        .AddItem "System"
        .AddItem DatabaseName
        .AddItem DatabaseName & ";TABLE Authors"
        .AddItem DatabaseName & ";QUERY [By State]"
        .AddItem DatabaseName & ";SQL Select * From Authors"
        .ListIndex = 0
    End With
End Sub
'*****************************************************************
' Load cbo(1) with some valid items for Access, based on a
' specific type of topic.
'*****************************************************************
Private Sub LoadItems(TypeOfTopic As Integer)
```

```
        With cbo(DDE_ITEM)
            .Clear
            Select Case TypeOfTopic
                Case ITEMS_SYSTEM
                    .AddItem "Status"
                    .AddItem "Topics"
                    .AddItem "SysItems"
                    .AddItem "Formats"
                Case ITEMS_LISTS
                    .AddItem "TableList"
                    .AddItem "QueryList"
                    .AddItem "FormList"
                    .AddItem "ReportList"
                    .AddItem "MacroList"
                    .AddItem "ModuleList"
                Case ITEMS_DATA
                    .AddItem "All"
                    .AddItem "Data"
                    .AddItem "FieldNames"
                    .AddItem "FieldNames;T"
                    .AddItem "FieldCount"
                    .AddItem "NextRow"
                    .AddItem "PrevRow"
                    .AddItem "LastRow"
                    .AddItem "FirstRow"
                    .AddItem "SQLText"
                    .AddItem "SQLText;5"
                Case Else
                    LoadItems ITEMS_SYSTEM
            End Select
            .ListIndex = 0
        End With
End Sub
'***************************************************************
' Loads cbo(2) with some valid Access LinkExecute commands.
'***************************************************************
Private Sub LoadExecutes()
    With cbo(DDE_EXECUTE)
        .Clear
        .AddItem "[OpenDatabase " & DatabaseName & "]"
        .AddItem "[CloseDatabase]"
        .ListIndex = 0
    End With
End Sub
'***************************************************************
' Prepares the form for use.  This function is also called
' by txtDatabase_LostFocus to refresh the form.
'***************************************************************
Private Sub Form_Load()
    #If Win32 Then
        MsgBox "This sample is for Win16 only!", vbCritical
        End
    #End If
    DatabaseName = txtDatabase
    LoadTopics
    LoadItems ITEMS_SYSTEM
```

(continues)

Listing 25.2 Continued

```
        LoadExecutes
        txtResult = ""
        DDESource = ""
End Sub
'****************************************************************
' Resizes the controls to the size of the form. This function
' is not foolproof, so don't try to break it.
'****************************************************************
Private Sub Form_Resize()
Static Border%
Dim i%
        '****************************************************************
        ' If the form is minimized, then break out.
        '****************************************************************
        If WindowState = 1 Then Exit Sub
        '****************************************************************
        ' Load the border variable, once.
        '****************************************************************
        If Not Border Then Border = txtDatabase.Left * 2
        '****************************************************************
        ' Adjust the combo boxes and command buttons.
        '****************************************************************
        For i = 0 To 2
            cbo(i).Width = ScaleWidth - Border
            If i < 2 Then cmd(i).Left = cbo(i).Width + _
                        cbo(i).Left - cmd(i).Width
        Next
        '****************************************************************
        ' Adjust the text boxes.
        '****************************************************************
        txtDatabase.Width = cmd(0).Left - (txtDatabase.Left * 2)
        txtResult.Move txtResult.Left, _
            txtResult.Top, ScaleWidth - Border, _
            ScaleHeight - txtResult.Top - (Border / 2)
End Sub
'****************************************************************
' Updates the database variable and reloads the combo boxes
' to reflect any changes.
'****************************************************************
Private Sub txtDatabase_LostFocus()
    DatabaseName = txtDatabase
    Form_Load
End Sub
'****************************************************************
' DDE.BAS: An application-independent, reusable module that
'           performs DDEExecute and DDERequest methods.
'****************************************************************
'****************************************************************
' Require variable declaration, make text comparisons case-
' insensitive, and declare API functions.
'****************************************************************
Option Explicit
Option Compare Text
#If Win16 Then
Private Declare Function GetModuleHandle Lib "Kernel" _
                    (ByVal ModuleName As String) As Integer
#End If
```

```
'*****************************************************************
' Execute one DDE Command.
'*****************************************************************
Public Sub DDEExecute(Source As Control, DDEApplication$, _
                      DDECommand$, Optional DDETopic)

    On Error GoTo DDEExecute_Error
    '*************************************************************
    ' If the program isn't running, then exit.
    '*************************************************************
    If GetModuleHandle(DDEApplication) = 0 Then
        MsgBox "This feature requires " & _
                UCase$(DDEApplication) & _
                ".EXE to be running!", vbCritical
        Exit Sub
    End If
    '*************************************************************
    ' If the optional argument wasn't provided, then assume
    ' System.
    '*************************************************************
    If IsMissing(DDETopic) Then DDETopic = "System"
    '*************************************************************
    ' Manual connect, execute the command, and close the link.
    '*************************************************************
    Source.LinkTopic = DDEApplication & "¦" & DDETopic
    Source.LinkMode = 2                 'Open the Link
    Source.LinkExecute DDECommand       'Send the Command
    Source.LinkMode 0                   'Close the Link
    Exit Sub

DDEExecute Error:
    Resume Next
End Sub
'*****************************************************************
' Execute a DDE Command.
'*****************************************************************
Public Sub DDERequest(Source As Control, DDEApplication$, _
                      DDETopic$, DDEItem$)

    On Error GoTo DDERequest_Error
    '*************************************************************
    ' If the program isn't running, then exit.
    '*************************************************************
    If GetModuleHandle(DDEApplication) = 0 Then
        MsgBox "This feature requires " & _
                UCase$(DDEApplication) & _
                ".EXE to be running!", vbCritical
        Exit Sub
    End If
    '*************************************************************
    ' Manual connect, request the data, and close the link.
    '*************************************************************
    Source.LinkTopic = DDEApplication & "¦" & DDETopic
    Source.LinkItem = DDEItem
    Source.LinkMode = 2
    Source.LinkRequest
    Source.LinkMode = 0
```

(continues)

Listing 25.2 Continued

```
'****************************************************************
' WARNING: If you wish to use a topic such as NextRow,
'          you will have to rewrite this program so that
'          the link is not broken. NextRow and PrevRow
'          require a consistent link in order to cycle
'          through the database.
'****************************************************************
    Exit Sub

DDERequest_Error:
    Resume Next
End Sub
'****************************************************************
' Locate a string within Source, and replace it with
' ReplaceStr.
'****************************************************************
Public Function Replace(ByVal Source$, FindStr$, _
                        ByVal ReplaceStr$) As String
Dim res%, retStr$
    '****************************************************************
    ' See if the search string exists.
    '****************************************************************
    res = InStr(Source, FindStr)
    '****************************************************************
    ' While FileStr is in Source, continue to replace it with
    ' ReplaceStr.
    '****************************************************************
    Do While res <> 0
        retStr = retStr & Left$(Source, res - 1) & ReplaceStr
        Source = Mid(Source, res + 1)
        res = InStr(Source, FindStr)
    Loop
    '****************************************************************
    ' Don't forget to return whatever is left over in source.
    '****************************************************************
    Replace = retStr & Source
End Function
```

This sample demonstrates how easily you can communicate with Access 2.0 through DDE. After this book is published, you might find yourself purchasing a copy of Access 7.0. Although the preceding technique should work with Access 7.0, you should consider using OLE Automation instead. For more information on using OLE Automation, see the next section and Chapter 26, "Integration with Microsoft Excel."

Integration with Microsoft Word 6.0

Microsoft Word for Windows 6.0 includes a vast amount of functionality that would take a tremendous amount of time to rewrite in Visual Basic. Fortunately, with the release of OLE 2.0 Automation, you can tap into Word's power with relative ease. This section explains how you can make Word work for you.

DDE, the Origin of Communication with Word

Traditionally, if you wanted to tap the power of Microsoft Word, you either wrote a custom application in WordBasic or you used DDE. DDE links are easily broken, so most developers were reluctant to use the power of Word. This problem forced many programmers to rewrite Word's features in Visual Basic, or they simply purchased custom controls with similar functionality.

Today, programmers no longer need to use DDE with Word because Visual Basic 4.0 can access Word with OLE Automation. For this reason, this book doesn't discuss this dated technology in detail.

Caution

You should avoid using DDE, because its future is uncertain. Currently, almost every application that uses DDE is being rewritten to support OLE Automation instead. Therefore, you should use DDE only as a last resort.

OLE Automation with Microsoft Word 6.0

In late 1993, Microsoft released Word for Windows 6.0 with the entire WordBasic engine exposed as an OLE Automation object. Therefore, Visual Basic programmers can now depend on stable connections with Word, and the barriers of the past have been removed. The Speller program shown in figure 25.7 demonstrates the power of this new feature. Listing 25.3 shows the program's code.

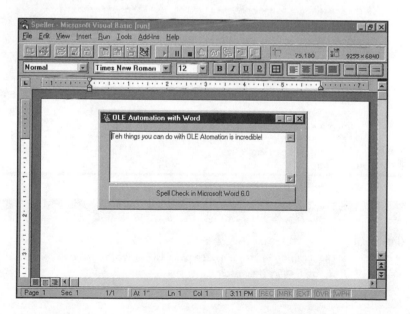

Fig. 25.7
Speller demonstrates the power of OLE Automation with Word.

Listing 25.3   OLE Automation with Word Can Save You Hours of Work

```
Public Function SpellCheck(ByVal IncorrectText$) As String
Dim Word As Object, retText$
    '****************************************************
    ' OLE Automation always returns errors which can
    ' usually be ignored.
    '****************************************************
    On Error Resume Next
    '****************************************************
    ' Create the Object (Word will be opened if it not
    ' currently running).
    '****************************************************
    Set Word = CreateObject("Word.Basic")
    '****************************************************
    ' Change the active window to Word, and insert
    ' the text from Text1 into Word.
    '****************************************************
    Word.AppShow
    Word.FileNew
    Word.Insert IncorrectText
    '****************************************************
    ' Perform a spell check.
    '****************************************************
    ' NOTE: Visual Basic will not regain control and
    '        execute the next line until the spell
    '        check is complete.
    '****************************************************
    Word.ToolsSpelling
    Word.EditSelectAll
    '****************************************************
    ' Trim the trailing character from the returned text.
    '****************************************************
    retText = Word.Selection$()
    SpellCheck = Left$(retText, Len(retText) - 1)
    '****************************************************
    ' Close Word and return to Visual Basic.
    '****************************************************
    Word.FileClose 2
    Show
    '****************************************************
    ' Recover the memory being used by the Word object.
    '****************************************************
    Set Word = Nothing
End Function
```

Note

Unfortunately, not all WordBasic features are available from Visual Basic. For a complete listing of the unsupported features, see page 167 of *Programming Integrated Solutions with Microsoft Office* (Microsoft Press, 1993).

> **Caution**
>
> OLE Automation requires that your application, the server application, and the OLE 2.0 dynamic link libraries (DLL) be loaded. Consequently, OLE Automation applications consume a great deal of random-access memory (RAM) and system resources. You should prepare your program for low-memory situations, which could prevent the program from running under 16-bit Windows. Under 32-bit Windows, low-memory situations rarely occur, but you should still trap for them.

The SpellCheck function provides an easy way to spell check text in your application with only a few lines of code, but this is only the beginning. You can find a listing of all the methods that WordBasic supports in the "Microsoft Word Object" chapter of the ODK's *Programming Integrated Solutions* book.

> **Caution**
>
> To use WordBasic's named arguments in OLE Automation, you *must* use Visual Basic 4.0 or VBA. Earlier versions of Visual Basic do not support named arguments.

Tips for OLE Automation with Word

When you use OLE Automation with Word 6.0, you should remember the following tips:

- Creating an OLE Automation object variable with Word automatically launches Word and makes it visible to your user. This might distract or confuse the user, so be prepared to handle this problem. However, this behavior does not exist in Word 7.0.

- If creating your object variable (for example, Word in the Speller example) starts Word, Word closes when that variable loses scope. You then lose any unsaved changes because OLE Automation does not cause Word to mark documents as dirty.

- When you use CreateObject with it, Word 6.0, unlike other applications, does *not* launch a new instance. Therefore, you can use CreateObject without determining whether Word is already running.

- If you start Word with OLE Automation, no documents are open on startup. Therefore, your application must always use .FileNew or .FileOpen before performing any actions.

- If multiple instances of Word are running, Word uses the most recently run instance that is visible.

Using Word with Custom Controls

By now you should be quite familiar with the reasons that custom controls can be helpful, but with OLE's in-place activation, such controls are an absolute necessity. A tremendous amount of work has gone into making in-place activation usable by Visual Basic programmers, so you certainly want to take advantage of it. In VB 4.0, you can support two types of in-place activation for Word:

■ Using Word directly as an OLE custom control

■ Using the OLE container control

Each of these methods has advantages and disadvantages. The next few sections demonstrate the power of each tool so that you can decide which is right for you.

Word as an OLE Custom Control

One of the most exciting new features of Visual Basic 4.0 is the capability to use OLE objects as controls on your forms. This capability enables you to use any OLE server as a control in your application. Because Word is such a powerful OLE server, you will certainly want to use this capability.

To experience the simplicity of this powerful feature, just follow these 10 steps:

1. If it is not already running, start Visual Basic and create a new project.

2. Choose Tools, Custom Controls.

3. In the list of available controls in the Custom Controls dialog box (shown in fig. 25.8), click on the Microsoft Word 6.0 Document check box.

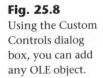

Fig. 25.8
Using the Custom Controls dialog box, you can add any OLE object.

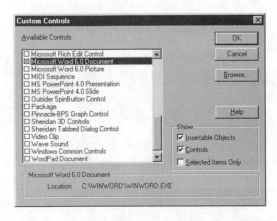

4. Click OK and Visual Basic adds the Word control to your Toolbox. Your Toolbox should now look similar to that shown in figure 25.9.

Word document custom control

Fig. 25.9
The Toolbox with a Word 6.0 document custom control.

5. Click the Word control, then click the upper-left corner of Form1. Drag your mouse to the lower-right corner and release the mouse button.

6. Click the bottom border of your form and increase the height of the form by about half an inch.

7. Add a new command button to the form and resize it as it is shown in figure 25.10.

Fig. 25.10
This application demonstrates the power of in-place activating OLE custom controls.

8. With Form1 still active, choose Tools, Menu Editor.

9. From the Menu Editor, add an invisible top-level menu item called "x" (or whatever else you want). Figure 25.11 shows the properties for this menu item.

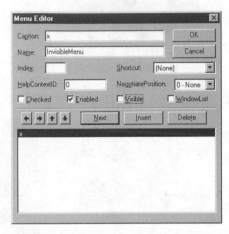

Fig. 25.11

The Menu Editor with an invisible menu entry.

10. Run the application and double-click on the Word object. Your application should look similar to that shown in figure 25.10.

Note

After you activate an OLE object in place, you can deactivate (or close) it only after it loses the focus. The only purpose of the codeless command button in figure 25.10 is to provide an easy way to change the focus.

Caution

The form in which you place the control must have either a visible or invisible menu. If it does not, the activated object cannot display its menu in your application.

In addition to the functionality shown earlier, the Word document control supports the following properties and events:

DragDrop event	LostFocus event
DragIcon property	Name property
DragMode property	TabIndex property

DragOver event	TabStop property
GotFocus event	Tag property
Height property	Top property
HelpContextID property	Visible property
Index property	WhatsThisHelpID property
Left property	Width property

As you can see, the Word document control (and any other OLE controls) support a wealth of events and properties. In some cases, this method possesses all the functionality that you need.

> **Caution**
>
> Your application fails if the destination system does not have Microsoft Word 6.0, or if Word is not registered in the system registry properly.

OLE Container Control with Microsoft Word 6.0

One of the major enhancements for Visual Basic 3.0 was its support for OLE 2.0. Unfortunately, because no major OLE 2.0 applications existed at that time, Visual Basic 3.0's OLE container control shipped with several limitations.

Now that people are starting to use OLE 2.0, Microsoft has released a more advanced version of this control. Some of the benefits of this updated control are the following:

- Many new events, methods, and properties, which provide an enormous amount of flexibility and control over the object

- The capability to print the contents of an embedded OLE object at design time

- Data-binding with OLE fields in your Access database

The container control gives you the power to create the program shown in figure 25.10, and you also have more control of your inserted object. Figure 25.12 and listing 25.4 show a sample application that adds a full-featured word processor to your application with very little code (except for comments).

Tip

If you plan to use only Word in your application, the Word document control is a great choice. However, if your users need to insert objects at run time, consider using the OLE container control.

IV

Integrating with Office

Fig. 25.12
OLECONT.VBP
demonstrates in-
place activation.

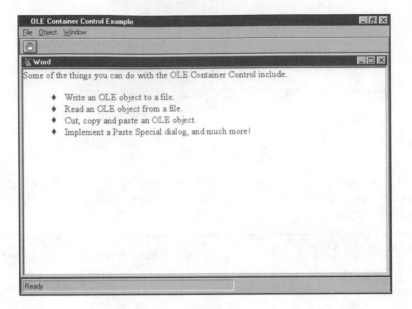

The first file in the OLECONT.VBP is PUBLIC.BAS. It keeps track of all the
Public (or Global) constants, variables, and functions for this project. Because
this application uses a multiple document interface, you have to store your
variables that keep track of the open forms in a module that all the project's
forms can access. This module also contains a public function, UpdateStatus,
that gives any procedure in the project the capability to update the status bar.

**Listing 25.4   OLECONT.VBP, an OLE Container Control with Word
Embedded**

```
'******************************************************************
' PUBLIC.BAS - Global constants, functions, and variables
'******************************************************************
Option Explicit
'******************************************************************
' These globals keep track of the new instances of frmWord
'******************************************************************
Public Const MAX_WINDOWS = 4
Public WinWord(MAX_WINDOWS) As New frmWord
Public WordWindows As Integer
'******************************************************************
' Generic update status bar routine
'******************************************************************
Public Sub UpdateStatus(StatusBar As Label, Optional StatusText)
    If IsMissing(StatusText) Then
        StatusBar = "Ready"
    Else
        StatusBar = StatusText
    End If
End Sub
```

The second file in this project is the MDI parent form, `mdiOLE`. This form is responsible for controlling the status bar, toolbar, and its menu.

```
'**********************************************************************
' MDIOLE.FRM - MDI Parent Form
'**********************************************************************
Option Explicit
'**********************************************************************
```

The application stores the toolbar buttons in a image control array, `imgTools`. You set the picture's property and the control's position in the array at design time. The odd controls in the array contain the up picture, and the even (odd number + 1) controls contain the down picture. The `imgHold` image control is a temporary location to store the toolbar picture when the user clicks a toolbar button.

When an odd-numbered image control receives a `Mouse_Down` event, the application stores its image in a holding image control, `imgHold`. Next, the application sets the `imgTools(Index)` picture property to the picture of the next control in the array (index + 1), which should be its down picture. Finally, when the control receives a `Mouse_Up` event, the application restores the control's up picture by setting `imgTools(Index)` to the picture currently stored in `imgHold`. The following code shows how to accomplish this:

```
' Saves the button image in imgHold, and inserts the down picture
'**********************************************************************
Private Sub imgTools_MouseDown(Index As Integer, _
            Button As Integer, Shift As Integer, X As Single, _
            Y As Single)
    imgHold.Picture = imgTools(Index).Picture
    imgTools(Index).Picture = imgTools(Index + 1).Picture
End Sub
'**********************************************************************
' Restores the graphic, and closes the application
'**********************************************************************
Private Sub imgTools_MouseUp(Index As Integer, _
        Button As Integer, Shift As Integer, _
        X As Single, Y As Single)
    imgTools(Index).Picture = imgHold.Picture
    Unload Me
End Sub
```

Placing Action Code

Because this toolbar has only one tool, you place its code in the `Mouse_Down` event. If this toolbar had more than one button, you would place the *action code* for the `imgTools` control array in a large `Select` statement in the `Click` event.

Every time that the user moves the mouse over a toolbar button, you should update the status bar to reflect the action that the tool performs. Listing 25.5 demonstrates how to do this.

Listing 25.5   Updating the Status Bar

```
'*********************************************************************
' Updates the status bar
'*********************************************************************
Private Sub imgTools_MouseMove(Index As Integer, _
                               Button As Integer, _
                               Shift As Integer, X As Single, _
                               Y As Single)
    UpdateStatus lblStatus, "Closes " & Caption
End Sub
```

As listing 25.6 demonstrates, the MDIForm_Load procedure maximizes the window and tiles all open child windows, and the MouseMove procedures set the caption of lblStatus equal to "Ready" whenever the user moves the mouse over the MDI form.

Listing 25.6   Preparing OLECONT.VBP for Use

```
'*********************************************************************
' Prepares the application for use
'*********************************************************************
Private Sub MDIForm_Load()
    WindowState = 2
    frmWord.Show
    Arrange vbTileHorizontal
End Sub
'*********************************************************************
' Updates the status bar with the default text
'*********************************************************************
Private Sub MDIForm_MouseMove(Button As Integer, _
                              Shift As Integer, _
                              X As Single, Y As Single)
    UpdateStatus lblStatus
End Sub
'*********************************************************************
' Updates the status bar with the default text
'*********************************************************************
Private Sub Toolbar_MouseMove(Button As Integer, _
                              Shift As Integer, _
                              X As Single, Y As Single)
    UpdateStatus lblStatus
End Sub
'*********************************************************************
' Updates the status bar with the default text
'*********************************************************************
```

```
Private Sub StatusBar_MouseMove(Button As Integer, _
                               Shift As Integer, _
                               X As Single, Y As Single)
    UpdateStatus lblStatus
End Sub
```

To make this code application-independent, you create separate procedures for `Highlight` and `HighlightBar`. You can then use these procedures in this project, but also copy and paste them into another project.

Listing 25.7 adds a three-dimensional appearance to the status bar and the toolbar.

Listing 25.7   Adding a Three-Dimensional Appearance to the Status Bar and Toolbar

```
'*********************************************************************
' Adds a 3-D appearance to the status bar
'*********************************************************************
Private Sub StatusBar_Paint()
    HighlightBar StatusBar
    Highlight lblStatus
End Sub
'*********************************************************************
' Adds a 3-D appearance to the toolbar
'*********************************************************************
Private Sub Toolbar_Paint()
    HighlightBar Toolbar
End Sub
```

Listing 25.8 shows two functions that demonstate how to use a series of line methods to create a three-dimensional effect around controls.

Listing 25.8   Adding a Three-Dimensional Appearance to Controls

```
'*********************************************************************
' Adds a 3-D effect to a picture box
'*********************************************************************
Private Sub HighlightBar(Bar As PictureBox)
    Bar.Line (0, 5)-(Bar.ScaleWidth, 5), vb3DLite
    Bar.Line (0, Bar.ScaleHeight - 15)-(Bar.ScaleWidth, _
                      Bar.ScaleHeight - 15), vb3DShadow
End Sub
'*********************************************************************
' Adds a 3-D border around a control
'*********************************************************************
Private Sub Highlight(Object As Control)
Const HORIZONTAL_OFFSET = 50
Const VERTICAL_OFFSET = 70
```

(continues)

Listing 25.8 Continued

```
'*******************************************************
' Top
'*******************************************************
StatusBar.Line (Object.Left - HORIZONTAL_OFFSET, _
                Object.Top - HORIZONTAL_OFFSET)- _
                (Object.Width, _
                Object.Top - HORIZONTAL_OFFSET), _
                vb3DShadow
'*******************************************************
' Left
'*******************************************************
StatusBar.Line (Object.Left - HORIZONTAL_OFFSET, _
                Object.Top - HORIZONTAL_OFFSET)- _
                (Object.Left - HORIZONTAL_OFFSET, _
                Object.Height + VERTICAL_OFFSET), _
                vb3DShadow
'*******************************************************
' Bottom
'*******************************************************
StatusBar.Line (Object.Left - HORIZONTAL_OFFSET, _
                Object.Height + VERTICAL_OFFSET)- _
                (Object.Width, _
                Object.Height + VERTICAL_OFFSET), _
                vb3DHiLight
'*******************************************************
' Right
'*******************************************************
StatusBar.Line (Object.Width, _
                Object.Top - HORIZONTAL_OFFSET)- _
                (Object.Width, _
                Object.Height + VERTICAL_OFFSET + 15), _
                vb3DHiLight
End Sub
```

Listing 25.9 shows FRMWORD.FRM, an MCI child form with an OLE container control.

Listing 25.9 FRMWORD.FRM, an MCI Child Form with an OLE Container Control

```
'*************************************************************************
' FRMWORD.FRM - MDI Child form with an OLE container control.
'*************************************************************************
Option Explicit
'*************************************************************************
' This ensures that the Word object is always the same size as the
' client area of the window.
'*************************************************************************
Private Sub Form_Resize()
    Word.Move 0, 0, ScaleWidth, ScaleHeight
End Sub
```

```
'*********************************************************************
' Handles clicks from the File submenu
'*********************************************************************
Private Sub mnuFileItems_Click(Index As Integer)
    On Error Resume Next
    Select Case Index
        Case 1 'New
            If WordWindows <= MAX_WINDOWS Then
                WordWindows = WordWindows + 1
                WinWord(WordWindows - 1).Caption = Me.Caption _
                        & " -" & Str$(WordWindows + 1)
            End If
        Case 2 'Open...
            mdiOLE!cdlg.InitDir = App.Path
            mdiOLE!cdlg.Flags = cdlOFNFileMustExist + _
                cdlOFNHideReadOnly + cdlOFNNoChangeDir
            mdiOLE!cdlg.ShowOpen
            If Err = cdlCancel Then Exit Sub
            Open (mdiOLE!cdlg.FileName) For Binary As #1
                Word.ReadFromFile 1
            Close #1
        Case 3 'Save As...
            mdiOLE!cdlg.Flags = cdlOFNOverwritePrompt + _
                            cdlOFNNoChangeDir
            mdiOLE!cdlg.ShowSave
            If Err = cdlCancel Then Exit Sub
            Open (mdiOLE!cdlg.FileName) For Binary As #1
                Word.SaveToFile 1
            Close #1
        Case 5
            mdiOLE!cdlg.Flags = cdlPDDisablePrintToFile + _
                cdlPDNoPageNums + cdlPDNoSelection
            mdiOLE!cdlg.ShowPrinter
            If Err = cdlCancel Then Exit Sub
            With Word
                .DoVerb vbOLEShow
                Printer.PaintPicture .picture, 0, 0
                .Close
                Printer.EndDoc
            End With
        Case 7 'Exit
            Unload mdiOLE
    End Select
End Sub
'*********************************************************************
' Updates the Object submenu's enabled status
'*********************************************************************
Private Sub mnuObject_Click()
    mnuObjectItems(1).Enabled = Not (Word.OLEType = vbOLENone)
    mnuObjectItems(2).Enabled = Not (Word.OLEType = vbOLENone)
    mnuObjectItems(3).Enabled = Word.PasteOK
    mnuObjectItems(4).Enabled = Word.PasteOK
    mnuObjectItems(5).Enabled = Not (Word.OLEType = vbOLENone)
End Sub
'*********************************************************************
' Handles clicks from the Object Submenu
```

(continues)

Listing 25.9 Continued

```
'************************************************************************
Private Sub mnuObjectItems_Click(Index As Integer)
    Select Case Index
        Case 1 'Cut
            With Word
                .DoVerb vbOLEShow
                .Copy
                .Close
                .Delete
            End With
        Case 2 'Copy
            With Word
                .DoVerb vbOLEShow
                .Copy
            End With
        Case 3 'Paste
            Word.Paste
        Case 4 'Paste Special...
            Word.PasteSpecialDlg
        Case 5 'Delete
            Word.Delete
        Case 7 'Close Object
            Word.Close
    End Select
End Sub
'************************************************************************
' Updates the status bar
'************************************************************************
Private Sub Word_MouseMove(Button As Integer, Shift As Integer, _
                            X As Single, Y As Single)
UpdateStatus mdiOLE!lblStatus, _
                    "Double click to edit this object in Word"
End Sub
'************************************************************************
' Handles clicks from the Window submenu
'************************************************************************
Private Sub mnuWindowItems_Click(Index As Integer)
    mdiOLE.Arrange Index - 1
End Sub
'************************************************************************
' Displays an Open dialog, and loads the file into an OLE container
'************************************************************************
Private Sub OLEOpenFile(OLEObject As OLE)
Dim iFile%
    mdiOLE!cdlg.InitDir = App.Path
    mdiOLE!cdlg.Flags = cdlOFNFileMustExist + cdlOFNHideReadOnly _
                        + cdlOFNNoChangeDir
    mdiOLE!cdlg.ShowOpen
    If Err = cdlCancel Then Exit Sub
    iFile = FreeFile
    Open (mdiOLE!cdlg.FileName) For Binary As iFile
        OLEObject.ReadFromFile iFile
    Close iFile
```

```
End Sub
'**********************************************************************
' Displays a Save As dialog and saves contents of an OLE container
'**********************************************************************
Private Sub OLESaveFile(OLEObject As OLE)
Dim iFile%
    mdiOLE!cdlg.Flags = cdlOFNOverwritePrompt + NoChangeDir
    mdiOLE!cdlg.ShowSave
    If Err = cdlOFNCancel Then Exit Sub
    iFile = FreeFile
    Open (mdiOLE!cdlg.FileName) For Binary As iFile
        OLEObject.SaveToFile iFile
    Close iFile
End Sub
```

As this application demonstrates, the power of the OLE container control can yield some amazing results. In addition, you can spare yourself from hundreds of hours of coding by using this powerful feature.

From Here...

This chapter demonstrated how powerful Visual Basic can be when you integrate Office applications, so now it is time to explore more ways to use Microsoft Office products in your programs. The next chapter looks in detail at the most powerful Office product, Microsoft Excel, and demonstrates how easily you can use a VBA-aware application such as Excel with Visual Basic 4.0 to create world-class applications.

To learn more about related topics, see the following sections:

■ Your copy of the Microsoft Developer's Network Starter Kit CD. This compact disk contains much great information on OLE and more. It also includes excellent tips and workarounds for Visual Basic in the KnowledgeBase articles.

■ The *Guide to Data Access Objects* in the Professional Features Book 1 is a source of information about data access. This document also includes many helpful example programs.

■ The Access Software Development Kit (available separately from Microsoft) is essential if you intend to write any serious applications with Access Basic.

■ The WordBasic Developer's Kit (available from Microsoft Press) is a great source for understanding WordBasic. If you need to know what a particular WordBasic command does, this book is a must.

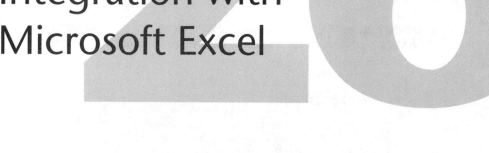

Chapter 26

Integration with Microsoft Excel

No discussion of custom applications or Visual Basic for Applications (VBA) is complete without discussing Microsoft Excel. This product is arguably the most powerful single application ever written for Windows, so you'll certainly want to take advantage of it. In this chapter, you see how to exploit the power of Excel so that you can develop world-class custom applications.

In this chapter, you learn more about the following:

- The power of OLE Automation with Excel
- How to use Excel as a custom control
- The power of the OLE container control with an Excel object

OLE Automation with Microsoft Excel

In late 1993, Excel for Windows 5.0 became the first Microsoft product to be released with VBA. It introduced new features to the Visual Basic languages, and the concept of shareable OLE type libraries. This release opened up a whole new way to integrate applications with Visual Basic, and this section covers how you can benefit from this feature.

Using Excel's Macro Recorder to Write OLE Automation Code

Because Excel and Visual Basic (VB) both use VBA (albeit different versions), you can paste most of your Excel code directly into VB without encountering errors. What's more, you can take advantage of Excel's macro recorder to get a rough script of what you need to do through OLE Automation, without writing a single line of code. For example, the code in listing 26.1 was recorded in Excel and pasted directly into VB to perform an OLE Automation task.

Listing 26.1   Code Can Be Recorded in Excel and Used with VB

```
Option Explicit
Dim Excel As Object

Sub RecordedForVB4()
'***********************************************************
' This code was unmodified from Excel's recorder,
' except the With Excel...End With statement. This
' statement is required because VB needs to know which
' object it should reference.
'***********************************************************
    With Excel
        .Workbooks.Add
        .Range("A2").Select
        .ActiveCell.FormulaR1C1 = "North"
        .Range("A3").Select
        .ActiveCell.FormulaR1C1 = "South"
        .Range("A4").Select
        .ActiveCell.FormulaR1C1 = "East"
        .Range("A5").Select
        .ActiveCell.FormulaR1C1 = "West"
        .Range("B1").Select
        .ActiveCell.FormulaR1C1 = "Spring"
        .Range("C1").Select
        .ActiveCell.FormulaR1C1 = "Summer"
        .Range("D1").Select
        .ActiveCell.FormulaR1C1 = "Fall"
        .Range("E1").Select
        .ActiveCell.FormulaR1C1 = "Winter"
        .Range("B2").Select
        .ActiveCell.FormulaR1C1 = "100"
        .Range("C2").Select
        .ActiveCell.FormulaR1C1 = "125"
        .Range("D2").Select
        .ActiveCell.FormulaR1C1 = "108"
        .Range("E2").Select
        .ActiveCell.FormulaR1C1 = "97"
        .Range("E3").Select
        .ActiveCell.FormulaR1C1 = "118"
        .Range("D3").Select
        .ActiveCell.FormulaR1C1 = "110"
        .Range("C3").Select
        .ActiveCell.FormulaR1C1 = "109"
        .Range("B3").Select
        .ActiveCell.FormulaR1C1 = "110"
        .Range("B2:E3").Select
```

```
            .Selection.AutoFill Destination:=.Range("B2:E5") _
            .Range("B2:E5").Select
            .Range("A1:E5").Select
            .Calculate
            .Charts.Add
      End With
End Sub

Private Sub Command1_Click()
'**********************************************************
' Create the object, make Excel visible, run the macro,
' then free the object.
'**********************************************************
      Set Excel = CreateObject("Excel.Application")
      Excel.Visible = True
      RecordedForVB4
      Excel.ActiveWorkbook.Saved = True 'Ignore changes
      MsgBox "Macro Complete!"
      Excel.Quit
      Set Excel = Nothing
      Unload Me
End Sub
```

This feature is incredibly powerful, because it's like having an OLE Automation recorder built in to VB. No matter how complex your task might be, you can just turn on Excel's recorder and let Excel write your code for you.

> **Note**
>
> Macro recorder code requires some editing because it records your every keystroke. Therefore, you should examine the recorded code to remove unnecessary elements. You also must surround your recorded code within a With block and prefix each line with a period.

Tips for OLE Automation with Excel

When you use OLE Automation with Excel, you should remember the following:

- Creating an OLE Automation object variable with Excel automatically launches Excel, but does *not* make the object visible to your user. Therefore, you must explicitly enter a .Visible = True statement so that your users can see Excel.

- If creating your object variable (for example, Excel in the RecordedForVB4() example) starts Excel, Excel does *not* close when that variable loses scope. Therefore, you must explicitly close Excel by using its .Quit method.

- Unlike Word, Excel notes any changes that you make to it through OLE Automation. Therefore, Excel prompts the user to save changes when you close a workbook. This could cause your application to hang until the user responds, unless you either save all open workbooks yourself or set their .Saved property equal to True.

- Excel supports GetObject properly, so you should determine whether Excel is already started before creating a new object. If you neglect to do this while Excel is already running, you might get an "Out of Memory" error message. This happens because Excel tries to launch a new instance of itself, and there might not be enough system resources available to complete this task.

- If OLE Automation starts Excel, no workbooks are open on startup. Therefore, your application must always use the .Workbooks.Add or .Workbooks.Open method before performing any actions.

- If multiple instances of Excel are running, GetObject uses the most recently started instance that is visible.

> **Note**
>
> Because Excel includes VBA and support for custom forms, you can easily create powerful custom applications using Excel alone. In many cases, you might want to choose Excel as your primary application environment and expose your VB application (or its classes) as an OLE object. This enables Excel to use some of the powerful features of VB without creating an application entirely in VB. In this sense, you can use VB's exposed objects the same way that a C programmer uses a dynamic linking library (DLL).

Tip

As a general rule, make sure that you are using the latest updates of any applications that you are using with OLE Automation. At the time that this chapter was completed, the latest version of Excel was 5.0c, and Word's was 6.0c.

> **Caution**
>
> Excel 5.0 and Word 6.0 are almost opposites in the way that they behave toward OLE Automation. Until you get used to the differences, you might want to consult this book (or some other source) before writing any code. Failing to do so could lead to unexpected results, and possibly even a General Protection Fault.

Leveraging the Power of Excel in Your Applications

After the previous chapter's discussion of Word, you should be very familiar with the reasons that an OLE server's custom control can be helpful. However, with OLE's in-place activation, a custom control is a lifesaver. Microsoft has done a tremendous amount of work to make in-place activation usable by Visual Basic programmers, so you'll certainly want take advantage of it. In Visual Basic 4.0 (VB4), you can support two types of in-place activation for Excel:

- Using Excel directly as an OLE insertable object control

- Using the OLE container control

Each of these methods has advantages and disadvantages. The next few sections demonstrate the power of each tool so that you can decide which is right for you.

Excel as an OLE Insertable Object Control

With the power of Excel's workbooks and graphs, there are few better applications to use as an insertable object control. If you have ever used the Graph or Grid .VBX controls in previous versions of VB, you know that it requires a great deal of work simply to enter data and create charts. With an Excel insertable object control, this functionality is so easy that you might find yourself including it in the simplest of applications.

> **Note**
>
> Instead of using both Excel's chart and worksheet OLE insertable object controls in a project, you can use either one individually because your data is stored in a workbook. Therefore, you can have a workbook containing a chart sheet and a worksheet, to display the same information in two different ways with the same control.

The following example program uses the Excel Worksheet OLE insertable object control to view and edit data in a grid and in a worksheet by exploiting the power of workbooks. Figure 26.1 shows the program displaying formatted data in a worksheet, and figure 26.2 shows the same data in a chart.

The capability to use the same control to display data in both a grid and chart is unheard of for Visual Basic users, so this is certainly a powerful feature. Figure 26.3 shows the simplicity of switching from either view.

Fig. 26.1
Excel worksheet controls can display data in worksheets.

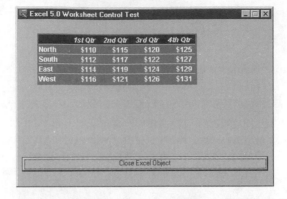

Fig. 26.2
Excel worksheet controls can also display data in charts.

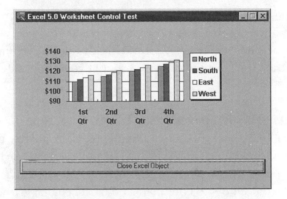

Fig. 26.3
Using Excel's powerful workbooks, you can switch between different views.

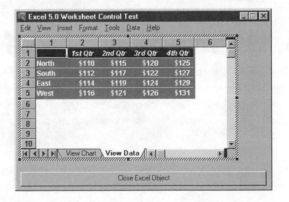

Note

Because creating this application is almost identical to the steps listed in the previous chapter, they are not listed here. However, you can use the steps shown in the Word chapter to create this application. In addition, you can find this program on the companion CD as EXCELWBK.VBP.

In addition to the functionality that the preceding figures depict, the Excel insertable object control supports the following events, methods, and properties:

Drag method	Name property
DragDrop event	Object property
DragIcon property	Parent property
DragMode property	SetFocus method
DragOver event	TabIndex property
GotFocus event	TabStop property
Height property	Tag property
HelpContextID property	Top property
Index event	Visible property
Left property	WhatsThisHelpID property
LostFocus property	Width property
Move method	ZOrder method

As you can see, the Excel Worksheet insertable object control (and any other OLE controls) support a wealth of events and properties. In most cases, this method possesses all the functionality that you will ever need.

Caution

Your application fails to run if the destination system does not have Microsoft Excel, or if Excel.Worksheet is not properly registered in the system registry.

Tip

If you plan to use only Excel in your application, the Excel worksheet control is a great choice. However, if your users need to insert objects at run time, you should consider using the OLE container control.

> **Note**
>
> If you are unsure whether your users have a copy of Excel properly installed on their system, you should consider using the Grid control (GRID.OCX) with either the Graph control (GRAPH.OCX) or a Microsoft Graph (GRAPH5.EXE) OLE object control. This way, you can ensure that the user has the correct products installed.

Using the OLE Container Control with Excel

Before I began writing this section, I never realized how much the OLE container control could do. I found myself doing things that I never dreamed were possible. What's more, I saw VB and Excel handle these incredibly difficult tasks with the greatest of ease. After seeing this section's code example at work, you also will appreciate the power that these two products possess.

The sample program in this section is an MDI application that presents information from Excel in chart and table form. The user can switch between the two views, shown in figures 26.4 and 26.5, by using tabs.

Fig. 26.4

By using tabs with the OLE container control, you can view data in a chart.

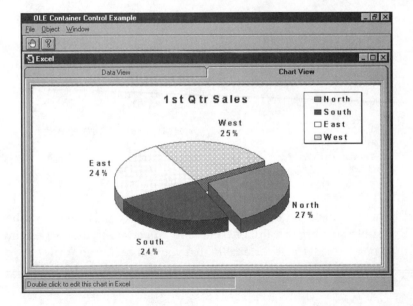

It is a good programming practice to build a set of "helper functions" for use with large-scale applications. Listing 26.2 contains code that must be accessible to two or more modules in the project at run time. Placing this code in a separate module prevents you from having to maintain the identical code in several modules.

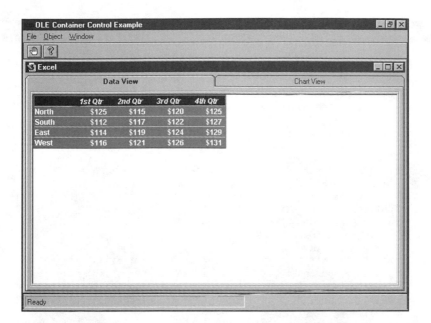

Fig. 26.5
Using tabs with
the OLE container
control also
enables you to
view data in a
spreadsheet table.

**Listing 26.2   Shared Procedures and Declarations Should
Be Stored in Modules**

```
'***********************************************************************
' PUBLIC.BAS - Global constants, functions, and variables.
'***********************************************************************
Option Explicit
'***********************************************************************
' API Declarations for this module.
'***********************************************************************
#If Win32 Then
Private Declare Function GetPrivateProfileString Lib _
    "kernel32" Alias "GetPrivateProfileStringA" _
    (ByVal lpApplicationName As String, lpKeyName As Any, ByVal _
    lpDefault As String, ByVal lpRetStr As String, ByVal nSize _
    As Long, ByVal lpFileName$) As Long
Private Declare Function FindWindow Lib "user32" _
    Alias "FindWindowA" (ByVal lpClassName As Any, _
    ByVal lpWindowName As Any) As Long
Private Declare Function PostMessage Lib "user32" Alias _
    "PostMessageA" (ByVal hWnd As Long, ByVal wMsg As Long, _
    ByVal wParam As Long, lParam As Any) As Long
Private Declare Function ShowWindow Lib "user32" (ByVal hWnd&, _
    ByVal nCmdShow As Long) As Long
#Else
Private Declare Function GetPrivateProfileString Lib "Kernel" _
    (ByVal lpAppName$, ByVal lpKeyName$, ByVal lpDefault$, _
    ByVal lpReturnStr$, ByVal nSize%, ByVal lpFileName$) _
    As Integer
```

(continues)

Listing 26.2 Continued

```
Private Declare Function FindWindow Lib "User" _
    (ByVal lpClassName$, ByVal lpWindowName As Long) As Integer

Private Declare Function PostMessage Lib "User" (ByVal hWnd%, _
    ByVal wMsg As Integer, ByVal wParam%, lParam&) As Long

Private Declare Function ShowWindow Lib "User" _
    (ByVal hWnd As Integer, ByVal nCmdShow As Integer) As Integer
#End If
'*********************************************************************
' These globals keep track of the new instances of frmExcel.
'*********************************************************************
Public Const MAX_WINDOWS = 4
Public Excels(MAX_WINDOWS) As New frmExcel
Public ExcelWindows As Integer
Public ActiveIndex%
'*********************************************************************
' Generic update status bar routine.
'*********************************************************************
Public Sub UpdateStatus(StatusBar As Label, Optional StatusText)
    If IsMissing(StatusText) Then
        StatusBar = "Ready"
    Else
        StatusBar = StatusText
    End If
End Sub
'*********************************************************************
' Start an OLE Server, if it is not already running.
'*********************************************************************
Public Function StartServer(ClassName$, Program$) As Long
Const SW_SHOWNA = 8
#If Win32 Then
Dim hWnd As Long
#Else
Dim hWnd As Integer
#End If
    '*************************************************************
    ' Prevent any error messages from interrupting the program.
    '*************************************************************
    On Error Resume Next
    '*************************************************************
    ' Check to see if it's already running.
    ' If so, then activate it.
    '*************************************************************
    hWnd = FindWindow(ClassName, 0&)

    If hWnd Then
        ShowWindow hWnd, SW_SHOWNA
        '*********************************************************
        ' Return False to indicate that it was already running.
        '*********************************************************
        StartServer = False
    Else
```

```
'**********************************************************
'  Otherwise, start it and return its hWnd.
'**********************************************************
      Shell Program, vbMinimizedNoFocus
      DoEvents
      StartServer = FindWindow(ClassName, 0&)
   End If

End Function
'**********************************************************
' Calls the API to read an .INI file, and return the results.
'**********************************************************
' NOTE: ByVal is used, so you can pass control values such
'        as Text1.Text without surrounding it in parentheses.
'**********************************************************
Public Function GetINI(ByVal Section$, ByVal Key$, ByVal _
                        Default$, ByVal FileName$) As String
Dim res%, retVal$
      retVal = Space$(32400)
      res = GetPrivateProfileString(Section, Key, Default, _
                           retVal, Len(retVal), FileName)
      GetINI = Left$(retVal, res)
End Function
'**********************************************************
' Posts a WM_CLOSE message to an application.
'**********************************************************
Public Sub CloseApp(hWnd As Long)
Const WM_CLOSE = &H10
      #If Win32 Then
          PostMessage hWnd, WM_CLOSE, 0, 0&
      #Else
          PostMessage CInt(hWnd), WM_CLOSE, 0, 0&
      #End If
End Sub
```

Listing 26.3 contains the minimum amount of code needed to display the splash screen. This form (see fig. 26.6) gives the user some "visual candy" during long processing times. A splash screen reassures users that their system has not locked up during heavy processing.

Listing 26.3   Splash Screens Calm the User's Fears

```
'**********************************************************
' FRMSPLASH - This is just a splash form that is used to display
'             messages to the user during long processes.
'**********************************************************
Option Explicit
'**********************************************************
' Declare SetWindowPos so this window can be "AlwaysOnTop".
'**********************************************************
```

(continues)

Listing 26.3 Continued

```
#If Win32 Then
Private Declare Sub SetWindowPos Lib "user32" _
    (ByVal hWnd As Long, ByVal hWndInsertAfter As Long, _
    ByVal X As Long, ByVal Y As Long, ByVal cx As Long, _
    ByVal cy As Long, ByVal wFlags As Long)
#Else
Private Declare Function SetWindowPos Lib "User" (ByVal hWnd%, _
    ByVal hb%, ByVal X%, ByVal Y%, ByVal cx%, ByVal cy%, _
    ByVal FLAGS%) As Integer
#End If
'********************************************************************
' Initialize the form.
'********************************************************************
Private Sub Form_Load()
Const HWND_TOPMOST = -1
Const SWP_NOMOVE = 2
Const SWP_NOSIZE = 1
Const FLAGS = SWP_NOMOVE Or SWP_NOSIZE
    '********************************************************************
    ' Set the mouse pointer.
    '********************************************************************
    Screen.MousePointer = vbHourglass
    '********************************************************************
    ' Set the window to TopMost, and ignore the return value.
    '********************************************************************
    SetWindowPos hWnd, HWND_TOPMOST, 0, 0, 0, 0, FLAGS
    '********************************************************************
    ' Reposition the label to the center of the form.
    '********************************************************************
    lblMessage.Move (ScaleWidth - lblMessage.Width) / 2, _
                    (ScaleHeight - lblMessage.Height) / 2
    Move (Screen.Width - Width) / 2, (Screen.Height - Height) / 2
End Sub
'********************************************************************
' Restore the mouse pointer.
'********************************************************************
Private Sub Form_Unload(Cancel As Integer)
    Screen.MousePointer = vbDefault
End Sub
```

Listing 26.4 contains code to size the form and its command button. This form displays information, gathered through OLE Automation, about the linked OLE object in this application (see fig. 26.7).

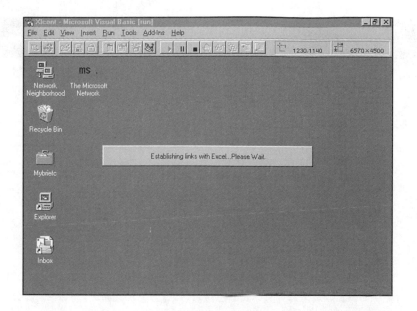

Fig. 26.6
The splash screen provides the user with "visual candy" during long processing times.

Integrating with Office

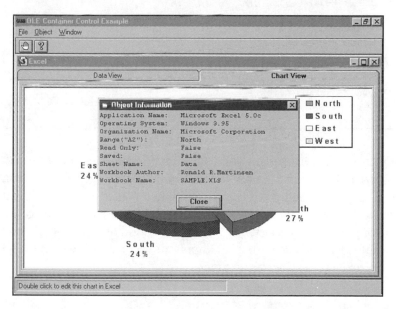

Fig. 26.7
The Object Information dialog box displays data that was gathered by using OLE Automation with the OLE container control's Object property.

Listing 26.4   Information Dialog Boxes Should Contain Little or No Code

```
'*********************************************************************
' FRMINFO.FRM - This is essentially a "stupid" dialog used by
'               frmExcel. Its only purpose is to display
'               information.
'*********************************************************************
Option Explicit
'*********************************************************************
' Initialize the form so that it can hold 10, 40 char lines.
'*********************************************************************
Private Sub Form_Load()
    '*********************************************************************
    ' Get the height and width of a character
    ' to set the form size.
    '*********************************************************************
    Width = TextWidth(String(42, "X"))
    Height = TextHeight("X") * 14
    '*********************************************************************
    ' Move the command button to the bottom center of the form.
    '*********************************************************************
    cmd.Move (ScaleWidth - cmd.Width) / 2, _
             ScaleHeight - cmd.Height - 10
    Move (Screen.Width - Width) / 2, (Screen.Height - Height) / 2
End Sub
'*********************************************************************
' Always unload this form, since it loads so fast.
'*********************************************************************
Private Sub cmd_Click()
    Unload Me
End Sub
```

Listing 26.5 is the MDI parent. This form contains code that starts Excel (if necessary) and maintains the toolbar and the status bar (see fig. 26.8). You develop the toolbar and status bar, shown in figure 26.8, entirely in Visual Basic by using picture boxes and image controls. You use no custom controls, so your application loads faster and your distribution disk is smaller. This is important when you are writing large applications, because every control in your project increases the startup time.

Fig. 26.8
The MDI form
contains only a
minimal menu, a
toolbar, and status
bar.

IV

Integrating with Office

**Listing 26.5   MDI Forms Should Only Manage Themselves and
Load the First Child Form**

```
'*********************************************************************
' MDIOLE.FRM - MDI Parent Form.
'*********************************************************************
Option Explicit
Private StartedExcel As Long
'*********************************************************************
' Saves the button image in imgHold, and inserts the down picture.
'*********************************************************************
Private Sub imgTools_MouseDown(Index As Integer, _
      Button As Integer, Shift As Integer, X As Single, _
      Y As Single)
   imgHold.Picture = imgTools(Index).Picture
   imgTools(Index).Picture = imgTools(Index + 1).Picture
End Sub
'*********************************************************************
' Updates the status bar.
'*********************************************************************
Private Sub imgTools_MouseMove(Index As Integer, _
    Button As Integer, Shift As Integer, X As Single, Y As Single)
    UpdateStatus lblStatus, imgTools(Index).Tag
End Sub
'*********************************************************************
' Restores the graphic, and processes toolbar clicks.
'*********************************************************************
Private Sub imgTools_MouseUp(Index As Integer, _
      Button As Integer, Shift As Integer, X As Single, _
      Y As Single)
```

(continues)

Listing 26.5 Continued

```
'****************************************************************
' Restore the toolbar picture.
'****************************************************************
imgTools(Index).Picture = imgHold.Picture
'****************************************************************
' Execute the appropriate toolbar action.
'****************************************************************
Select Case Index
    Case 0 ' Hand
        Unload Me
    Case 2 ' Question Mark
        '****************************************************************
        ' Bring up the splash form again, because the first OLE
        ' Automation call will require Excel to be started. After
        ' it is started, any subsequent calls will be performed
        ' as fast as they would be in a native Excel macro.
        '****************************************************************
        frmSplash.lblMessage = _
"Gathering OLE Automation information from Excel...Please Wait!"
        frmSplash.Show
        frmSplash.Refresh
        '****************************************************************
        ' Load the info dialog, and start printing to it.
        '****************************************************************
        Load frmInfo
        '****************************************************************
        ' NOTE: Using the OLE Container's Object property, you can
        '          execute OLE Automation statements on the object in
        '          the control.
        '****************************************************************
        ' Using 2 .Parent properties, allows you to access Excel's
        ' Application object.
        '****************************************************************
        PrintMessage "Application Name:", _
          ActiveForm.Excel(0).Object.Parent.Parent.Name & " " & _
          ActiveForm.Excel(0).Object.Parent.Parent.Version

        PrintMessage "Operating System:", _
          ActiveForm.Excel(0).Object.Parent.Parent.OperatingSystem

        PrintMessage "Organization Name:", _
          ActiveForm.Excel(0).Object.Parent.Parent.OrganizationName
        '****************************************************************
        ' By default, the Object property points to a Worksheet.
        '****************************************************************
        PrintMessage "Range(""A2""):", _
          ActiveForm.Excel(0).Object.Range("A2")
        '****************************************************************
        ' Using 1 call to Parent, allows you to access Excel's
        ' Workbook object.
        '****************************************************************
        PrintMessage "Read Only:", _
          ActiveForm.Excel(0).Object.Parent.ReadOnly
```

```
            PrintMessage "Saved:", _
                ActiveForm.Excel(0).Object.Parent.Saved

            PrintMessage "Sheet Name:", _
                ActiveForm.Excel(0).Object.Name

            PrintMessage "Workbook Author:", _
                ActiveForm.Excel(0).Object.Parent.Author

            PrintMessage "Workbook Name:", _
                ActiveForm.Excel(0).Object.Parent.Name
            '**********************************************************
            ' Make sure all activity is complete, before unloading
            ' the splash.
            '**********************************************************
            DoEvents
            Unload frmSplash
            '**********************************************************
            ' Display the information to the user.
            '**********************************************************
            frmInfo.Show 1
    End Select
End Sub
'**************************************************************************
' Print the formatted string to frmInfo.
'**************************************************************************
Private Sub PrintMessage(Item As String, Result As Variant)
Dim LeftStr As String * 20, RightStr As String * 30
    LeftStr = Item
    RightStr = Result
    frmInfo.Print LeftStr & RightStr
End Sub
'**************************************************************************
' Prepares the application for use.
'**************************************************************************
Private Sub MDIForm_Load()
Dim XLPath$
    '******************************************************************
    ' Always use the system defined backcolor.
    '******************************************************************
    BackColor = vb3DFace
    StatusBar.BackColor = vb3DFace
    Toolbar.BackColor = vb3DFace
    '******************************************************************
    ' If necessary, start Excel to prevent annoying message boxes.
    '******************************************************************
    XLPath = GetINI("Microsoft Excel", "cbtlocation", _
            "c:\excel\excelcbt", "excel5.ini")
    XLPath = Left(XLPath, Len(XLPath) - 8) & "excel.exe"
    StartedExcel = StartServer("XLMAIN", XLPath)
    WindowState = 2 'Maximized
    frmExcel.Show
    Arrange vbTileHorizontal
End Sub
```

(continues)

Listing 26.5 Continued

```
'***********************************************************************
' Updates the status bar with the default text.
'***********************************************************************
Private Sub MDIForm_MouseMove(Button As Integer, _
        Shift As Integer, X As Single, Y As Single)
    UpdateStatus lblStatus
End Sub
'***********************************************************************
' If you had to start Excel, close it. Otherwise, leave it alone.
'***********************************************************************
Private Sub MDIForm_Unload(Cancel As Integer)
    If StartedExcel <> False Then
        CloseApp StartedExcel
    End If
End Sub
'***********************************************************************
' Terminates the application.
'***********************************************************************
Private Sub mnuFileItems_Click(Index As Integer)
    Unload Me
End Sub
'***********************************************************************
' Updates the status bar with the default text.
'***********************************************************************
Private Sub StatusBar_MouseMove(Button As Integer, _
        Shift As Integer, X As Single, Y As Single)
    UpdateStatus lblStatus
End Sub
'***********************************************************************
' Adds a 3-D appearance to the status bar.
'***********************************************************************
Private Sub StatusBar_Paint()
    HighlightBar StatusBar
    Highlight lblStatus
End Sub
'***********************************************************************
' Updates the status bar with the default text.
'***********************************************************************
Private Sub Toolbar_MouseMove(Button As Integer, _
        Shift As Integer, X As Single, Y As Single)
    UpdateStatus lblStatus
End Sub
'***********************************************************************
' Adds a 3-D appearance to the toolbar.
'***********************************************************************
Private Sub Toolbar_Paint()
    HighlightBar Toolbar
End Sub
'***********************************************************************
' Adds a 3-D effect to a picture box.
'***********************************************************************
```

```
   Private Sub HighlightBar(Bar As PictureBox)
       Bar.Line (0, 5)-(Bar.ScaleWidth, 5), vb3DHighlight
       Bar.Line (0, Bar.ScaleHeight - 15)-(Bar.ScaleWidth, _
                        Bar.ScaleHeight - 15), vb3DShadow
   End Sub
   '*****************************************************************
   ' Adds a 3-D border around a control.
   '*****************************************************************
   Private Sub Highlight(Object As Control)
   Const HORIZONTAL_OFFSET = 50
   Const VERTICAL_OFFSET = 70
       '*************************************************************
       ' Top
       '*************************************************************
       StatusBar.Line (Object.Left - HORIZONTAL_OFFSET, _
                    Object.Top - HORIZONTAL_OFFSET)- _
                    (Object.Width, _
                    Object.Top - HORIZONTAL_OFFSET), _
                    vb3DShadow
       '*************************************************************
       ' Left
       '*************************************************************
       StatusBar.Line (Object.Left - HORIZONTAL_OFFSET, _
                    Object.Top - HORIZONTAL_OFFSET)- _
                    (Object.Left - HORIZONTAL_OFFSET, _
                    Object.Height + VERTICAL_OFFSET), _
                    vb3DShadow
       '*************************************************************
       ' Bottom
       '*************************************************************
       StatusBar.Line (Object.Left - HORIZONTAL_OFFSET, _
                    Object.Height + VERTICAL_OFFSET)- _
                    (Object.Width, _
                    Object.Height + VERTICAL_OFFSET), _
                    vb3DHighlight
       '*************************************************************
       ' Right
       '*************************************************************
       StatusBar.Line (Object.Width, _
                    Object.Top - HORIZONTAL_OFFSET)- _
                    (Object.Width, _
                    Object.Height + VERTICAL_OFFSET + 15), _
                    vb3DHighlight
   End Sub
```

Listing 26.6 is the child form. This form is the heart of the application because it contains all the code necessary to display the data and tabs. It also keeps the status bar up to date when the user moves the mouse around the screen.

Listing 26.6   In an MDI Application, a Majority of Your Code Should Reside in the Child Form

```
'*********************************************************************
' FRMEXCEL.FRM - MDI Child form with an OLE container control.
'*********************************************************************
Option Explicit
'*********************************************************************
' The RECT and GetClientRect decs are required for PositionFrame.
'*********************************************************************
#If Win32 Then
Private Type RECT
    rLEFT As Long
    rTOP As Long
    rWIDTH As Long
    rHEIGHT As Long
End Type
Private Declare Sub GetClientRect Lib "user32" _
    (ByVal hWnd As Long, lpRect As RECT)
#Else
Private Type RECT
    rLEFT As Integer
    rTOP As Integer
    rWIDTH As Integer
    rHEIGHT As Integer
End Type
Private Declare Sub GetClientRect Lib "User" _
    (ByVal hWnd As Integer, lpRect As RECT)
#End If
'*********************************************************************
' Gets the client area of a frame, and sizes an object to it.
'*********************************************************************
Private Sub PositionFrame(SourceFrame As Frame, _
    ChildObject As Control)
Dim Client As RECT, X As RECT
    GetClientRect SourceFrame.hWnd, Client
    X.rLEFT = (Client.rLEFT * Screen.TwipsPerPixelX) + 50
    X.rTOP = (Client.rTOP * Screen.TwipsPerPixelY) + 150
    X.rWIDTH = (Client.rWIDTH * Screen.TwipsPerPixelX) - 90
    X.rHEIGHT = (Client.rHEIGHT * Screen.TwipsPerPixelY) - 190
    ScaleMode = vbTwips
    ChildObject.Move X.rLEFT, X.rTOP, X.rWIDTH, X.rHEIGHT
    ScaleMode = vbPixels
End Sub
'*********************************************************************
' Initializes this form instance. This code is also called
' every time a new form is created.
'*********************************************************************
Private Sub Form_Load()
    '*****************************************************************
    ' Establishing links takes a few minutes, so give the user
    ' something to look at.
    '*****************************************************************
    frmSplash.lblMessage = _
        "Establishing links with Excel...Please Wait."
```

```vb
        frmSplash.Show
        frmSplash.Refresh
        '*****************************************************************
        ' Always create your recreate links in case the program is
        ' moved. In a real program, you should NEVER hard-code
        ' your links.
        '*****************************************************************
        Excel(0).CreateLink App.Path & "\" & "SAMPLE.XLS!R1C1:R5C5"
        Excel(1).CreateLink App.Path & "\" & "SAMPLE.XLS!Pie"
        '*****************************************************************
        ' Call DoEvents to process the links, and to prevent
        ' the splash screen from disappearing prematurely.
        '*****************************************************************
        DoEvents
        Unload frmSplash
End Sub
'*********************************************************************
' Updates the status bar with the default text.
'*********************************************************************
Private Sub Form_MouseMove(Button As Integer, Shift As Integer, _
                                    X As Single, Y As Single)
        UpdateStatus mdiOLE.lblStatus
End Sub
'*********************************************************************
' This procedure controls the tab redrawing to handle switching.
'*********************************************************************
Private Sub Form_MouseUp(Button As Integer, Shift As Integer, _
                                    X As Single, Y As Single)
Dim res%
        res = Abs(DrawTabs(Me, X, Y) - 1)
        If res < 2 Then Tabs(res).ZOrder
End Sub
'*********************************************************************
' Reposition the frames and resize the tabs.
'*********************************************************************
Private Sub Form_Resize()
Dim ActivateTab!
        '*****************************************************************
        ' When the form is resized, the tabs must be rescaled to fit.
        '*****************************************************************
        SetupTabs Me, 2
        '*****************************************************************
        ' Position the OLE Containers to fit inside the frames.
        '*****************************************************************
        PositionFrame Tabs(0), Excel(0)
        PositionFrame Tabs(1), Excel(1)
        '*****************************************************************
        ' SetupTabs will make the first tab active. Determine which
        ' tab should be active, and MouseUp it.
        '*****************************************************************
        ActivateTab = IIf(ActiveIndex = 0, 10, _
                ((ScaleWidth - 2) / 2) + 100)
        Form_MouseUp 0, 0, ActivateTab, 20
End Sub
```

(continues)

Listing 26.6 Continued

```
'*******************************************************************
' Automatically saves any changes to the data.
'*******************************************************************
Private Sub Form_Unload(Cancel As Integer)
    Excel(0).Object.Parent.RunAutoMacros (xlAutoClose)
End Sub
'*******************************************************************
' Handles clicks from the File submenu.
'*******************************************************************
Private Sub mnuFileItems_Click(Index As Integer)
    On Error Resume Next
    Select Case Index
        Case 1 'New
            If ExcelWindows <= MAX_WINDOWS Then
                ExcelWindows = ExcelWindows + 1
                '***************************************************
                ' Create a new form, and set its caption.
                '***************************************************
                Excels(ExcelWindows - 1).Caption = "Excel -" _
                                        & Str$(ExcelWindows + 1)
                '***************************************************
                ' Remove the caption from both frames.
                '***************************************************
                Excels(ExcelWindows - 1).Tabs(0) = ""
                Excels(ExcelWindows - 1).Tabs(1) = ""
            End If
        Case 3 'Exit
            Unload mdiOLE
    End Select
End Sub
'*******************************************************************
' Handles clicks from the Object submenu.
'*******************************************************************
Private Sub mnuObjectItems_Click(Index As Integer)
    Select Case Index
        Case 1 'Update Links
            Excel(0).Update
            Excel(1).Update
        Case 2 'Close Object
            Excel(ActiveIndex).Close
    End Select
End Sub
'*******************************************************************
' Updates the status bar.
'*******************************************************************
Private Sub Excel_MouseMove(Index As Integer, Button As Integer, _
                    Shift As Integer, X As Single, Y As Single)
    UpdateStatus mdiOLE!lblStatus, Excel(Index).Tag
End Sub
'*******************************************************************
' Handles clicks from the Window submenu.
'*******************************************************************
```

```
Private Sub mnuWindowItems_Click(Index As Integer)
    mdiOLE.Arrange Index - 1
End Sub
'**********************************************************************
' Set the ActiveIndex. This isn't foolproof, but it works for this
' demonstration. In the "real world," this wouldn't be enough.
'**********************************************************************
Private Sub Tabs_MouseMove(Index As Integer, Button As Integer, _
                    Shift As Integer, X As Single, Y As Single)
    ActiveIndex = Index
End Sub
```

In addition to all the code and forms in Visual Basic, this application also includes some code inside of Excel that enables the user to return to your application. Listing 26.7 includes the key Excel macros.

Listing 26.7   Supporting Code in Excel Can Help in Two-Way Communication between Your Applications

```
'**********************************************************************
' Returns control to your VB Program, and minimizes Excel.
'**********************************************************************
Sub ReturnToExample()
    On Error Resume Next
    AppActivate Title:="OLE Container Control Example"
    If Err Then MsgBox "The example program isn't open.", _
        vbInformation
    Application.WindowState = xlMinimized
End Sub
'**********************************************************************
' Turns off errors and saves the workbook.
' This code is VITAL to prevent the user from being bothered
' by unnecessary message boxes.
'**********************************************************************
Sub Auto_Close()
    Application.DisplayAlerts = False
    ThisWorkbook.Save
End Sub
```

The ReturnToExample() procedure enables you to add a macro button to the worksheet (as shown in fig. 26.9). Such a button shows users clearly what they are supposed to do to return to your application. In addition, you can modify your menus (shown in fig. 26.10) to prevent users from closing the file or Excel. Notice how the Exit menu item has been removed.

Fig. 26.9
When using linked objects, you usually should give the user a visible way to return to your application.

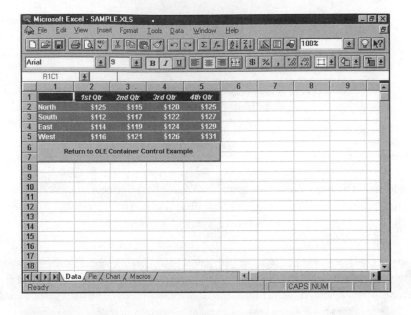

Fig. 26.10
Modifying Excel's menus can be helpful to ensure that users can't do anything that they shouldn't.

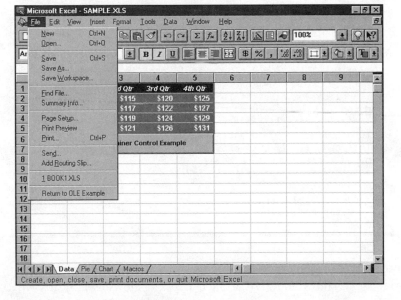

Using Your VB Application as a DLL for Excel

Most programmers would love to create DLLs in Visual Basic so that they can share common code among applications. Although you can't write a traditional DLL in Visual Basic, you *can* write a class that you can expose to other applications (for example, Excel) to achieve the same effect. In fact, this section shows you how OLE Automation servers that you create with VB are more useful and easier to use than any traditional DLL could ever be.

The Useful Class Object

Before reading this section, you should have already read about classes and OLE Automation servers, including how to write an OLE Automation server. However, this project is rather lengthy, so it does require some additional explanation.

The project's first file is the About dialog box form. External applications use this form to display a professional-looking About dialog box easily. This form (shown at design time in fig. 26.11) includes only the minimum code necessary to initialize the form. Listing 26.8 demonstrates how to create a generic About box.

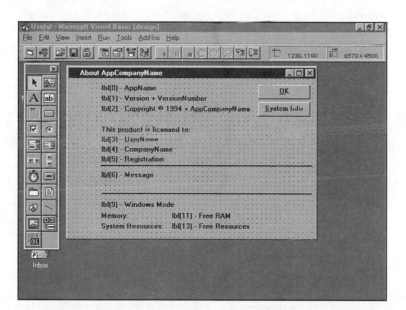

Fig. 26.11
The generic About box at design time differs significantly from its run-time counterpart.

Listing 26.8   A Generic About Box Is Useful to Give Your Applications a Consistent Look and Feel

```
'******************************************************************
' ABOUTBOX.FRM - This form contains a generic About dialog
'                box which is accessed by the About class.
'                You should never use this form directly.
'******************************************************************
```

(continues)

Listing 26.8 Continued

```vb
Option Explicit
'*******************************************************************
' API calls for use by this form only.
'*******************************************************************
#If Win32 Then
Private Type MEMORYSTATUS
        dwLength As Long
        dwMemoryLoad As Long
        dwTotalPhys As Long
        dwAvailPhys As Long
        dwTotalPageFile As Long
        dwAvailPageFile As Long
        dwTotalVirtual As Long
        dwAvailVirtual As Long
End Type
Private Declare Sub GlobalMemoryStatus Lib "kernel32" _
    (lpBuffer As MEMORYSTATUS)
#Else
Private Declare Function GetFreeSpace Lib "Kernel" (ByVal _
    wFlags%) As Long

Private Declare Function GetFreeSystemResources Lib "User" _
    (ByVal wSysResource%) As Integer

Private Declare Function GetWinFlags Lib "Kernel" () As Long
#End If
'*******************************************************************
' Form level variables for preserving the pointer, and creating
' an About object.
'*******************************************************************
Private OrigPointer As Integer
'*******************************************************************
' Form Initialization
'*******************************************************************
Private Sub Form_Load()
#If Win32 Then
Dim MemoryStat As MEMORYSTATUS
#Else
Const WF_ENHANCED = &H20
Const GFSR_SYSTEMRESOURCES = &H0
#End If
    '*******************************************************
    ' Remember the current pointer, and change it to an hrglass
    '*******************************************************
    OrigPointer = Screen.MousePointer
    Screen.MousePointer = vbHourglass
    '*******************************************************
    ' If this form isn't being displayed as a splash screen
    '*******************************************************
    If Not bSplashScreen Then
    '*******************************************************
    ' Set the visible property of the button based on the
    ' existences of msinfo.exe (from Microsoft).
    '*******************************************************
```

```
            #If Win32 Then
            cmdSysInfo.Visible = FileExists(GetWinDir(True) _
                            & "msapps\msinfo\msinfo32.exe")
            #Else
            cmdSysInfo.Visible = FileExists(GetWinDir(True) _
                            & "msapps\msinfo\msinfo.exe")
            #End If
        '**************************************************************
        ' NOTE: You CANNOT distribute MSINFO.EXE, so this is the
        '          next best thing.
        '**************************************************************
        End If
    '**************************************************************
    ' Set the label to reflect the environment mode
    '**************************************************************
#If Win32 Then
    lbl(9) = "Windows (32-bit)"
#Else
    lbl(9) = IIf(GetWinFlags() And WF_ENHANCED, _
                "386 Enhanced Mode", "Standard Mode")
#End If
    '**************************************************************
    ' Call the API, and format the responses
    '**************************************************************
#If Win32 Then
    GlobalMemoryStatus MemoryStat
    lbl(10) = "Physical Memory"
    lbl(11) = Format(MemoryStat.dwTotalPhys \ 1024, _
        "###,###,##0") & " KB"
    lbl(12) = "Memory Load"
    lbl(13) = Format(MemoryStat.dwMemoryLoad) & "%"
#Else
    lbl(11) = Format$(GetFreeSpace(0) \ 1024, _
        "###,###,##0") & " KB"
    lbl(13) = Format$(GetFreeSystemResources _
        (GFSR_SYSTEMRESOURCES)) & "%"
#End If
    '**************************************************************
    ' Center the form
    '**************************************************************
    Move (Screen.Width - Width) \ 2, (Screen.Height - Height) \ 2
    '**************************************************************
    ' Set the pointer to default, so the user doesn't see
    ' an hourglass on the About box.
    '**************************************************************
    Screen.MousePointer = vbDefault
End Sub
'**************************************************************
' Restore the pointer to its previous state, and free memory
'**************************************************************
Private Sub Form_Unload(Cancel As Integer)
    Screen.MousePointer = OrigPointer
    Set AboutBox = Nothing
End Sub
```

(continues)

Listing 26.8   Continued

```
'****************************************************************
' Dismiss the dialog box, and run Form_Unload
'****************************************************************
Private Sub cmdOk_Click()
    Unload Me
End Sub
'****************************************************************
' If this button is visible, then this will work. Since we
' ignore the return value, you don't need parentheses or
' variable = .
'****************************************************************
Private Sub cmdSysInfo_Click()
    #If Win32 Then
        Shell GetWinDir(True) & "msapps\msinfo\msinfo32.exe", _
                            vbNormalFocus
    #Else
        Shell GetWinDir(True) & "msapps\msinfo\msinfo.exe"
    #End If
End Sub
```

Listing 26.9 is the private, noncreatable About class. This class contains all the
code required to display the About dialog box. To prevent exposing multiple
classes for a single project, you expose only the Application class and hide
the About class.

**Listing 26.9   Noncreatable Classes Are Useful for Creating
an Object Hierarchy**

```
'****************************************************************
' ABOUT.CLS - This is the About class which is used to display
'             the About dialog. Its Instancing and Public
'             properties have been set so that it is only
'             visible to this project.
'****************************************************************
Option Explicit
'****************************************************************
' Declare private variables for your properties as Variant so
' you can take advantage of IsEmpty(). Remember that Variants
' are very inefficent because they are the largest data type,
' so you should try to limit your use of them.
' I included variants just to demonstrate a variety of
' techniques, but I normally avoid variants at all costs.
'****************************************************************
Private App, AppCompany, VerNum, User, Company
Private RegNum, AboutMsg
'****************************************************************
' NOTE: For all of the following properties, if a Get is
'       performed before a Let, then a default value will be
'       returned. However, this value is NOT stored in its
'       related private variable.
'****************************************************************
```

```
'*****************************************************************
' This is a Read/Write property which should be set with the
' name of the program that is using this object.
'*****************************************************************
Public Property Let AppName(str As String)
    App = str
End Property

Public Property Get AppName() As String
    AppName = IIf(IsEmpty(App), "AppName  Default", App)
End Property
'*****************************************************************
' This is a Read/Write property which should be set with the
' name of the company who wrote the application that is
' calling this object.
'*****************************************************************
Public Property Let AppCompanyName(str As String)
    AppCompany = str
End Property

Public Property Get AppCompanyName() As String
    AppCompanyName = IIf(IsEmpty(AppCompany), _
                        "AppCompanyName Default", AppCompany)
End Property
'*****************************************************************
' This is a Read/Write property which should be set with the
' version number of the application which is using this object.
'*****************************************************************
Public Property Let VersionNumber(str As String)
    VerNum = str
End Property

Public Property Get VersionNumber() As String
   VersionNumber = IIf(IsEmpty(VerNum), "1.00", VerNum)
End Property
'*****************************************************************
' This is a Read/Write property which should be set with the
' name of the end user who is using your application.
'*****************************************************************
Public Property Let UserName(str As String)
    User = str
End Property

Public Property Get UserName() As String
    UserName = IIf(IsEmpty(User), "UserName Default", User)
End Property
'*****************************************************************
' This is a Read/Write property which should be set with the
' user's (see above) company name.
'*****************************************************************
Public Property Let CompanyName(str As String)
    Company = str
End Property
```

(continues)

Listing 26.9 Continued

```
Public Property Get CompanyName() As String
    CompanyName = IIf(IsEmpty(Company), "CompanyName Default", _
                      Company)
End Property
'****************************************************************
' This is a Read/Write property which should be set with a
' registration or serial number of the product that called
' this object.
'****************************************************************
Public Property Let Registration(str As String)
    RegNum = str
End Property

Public Property Get Registration() As String
    Registration = IIf(IsEmpty(RegNum), "Registration Default", _
                       RegNum)
End Property
'****************************************************************
' This is a Read/Write property which can contain up to 2
' lines of text to display in the About box. The text will
' automatically wrap, so carriage returns aren't required.
'****************************************************************
Public Property Let Message(str As String)
    AboutMsg = str
End Property

Public Property Get Message() As String
    Message = IIf(IsEmpty(AboutMsg), "Message Default", AboutMsg)
End Property
'****************************************************************
' This method determines how the dialog box should be displayed,
' then it loads it with the appropriate values and displays it.
'****************************************************************
Public Sub ShowAbout(AsSplash As Boolean)
    '****************************************************************
    ' Set the variable so the About box knows how to
    ' display itself.
    '****************************************************************
    bSplashScreen = AsSplash
    '****************************************************************
    ' Set the common elements used by the splash screen and
    ' About box.
    '****************************************************************
    With AboutBox
        .lbl(0) = AppName
        .lbl(1) = "Version " & VersionNumber
        .lbl(2) = "Copyright © " & Year(Now) & " " _
                & AppCompanyName
        .lbl(3) = UserName
        .lbl(4) = CompanyName
        .lbl(5) = Registration
        .lbl(6) = Message
    End With
```

```
        If AsSplash Then
            '**********************************************************
            ' Show About Box as splash screen by removing its
            ' caption, hiding the OK button, and displaying it as
            ' modeless.
            '**********************************************************
            With AboutBox
                .cmdOk.Visible = False
                .Caption = ""
                .Show
                '**********************************************************
                ' NOTE: This refresh is required, because splash
                '        screens are usually shown during peak
                '        processing times. If you don't refresh,
                '        then you'll just display a white form.
                '**********************************************************
                .Refresh
            End With
            '**********************************************************
            ' Set the About box on top to prevent it from
            ' disappearing during event processing.
            '**********************************************************
            AlwaysOnTop AboutBox.hwnd, False
        Else
            With AboutBox
                .cmdOk.Visible = True
                .Caption = "About " & AppCompanyName
                .Show 1
            End With
        End If
End Sub
'**********************************************************
' Unloads the about box
'**********************************************************
Public Sub HideSplash()
    Unload AboutBox
End Sub
```

Listing 26.10 is the common module that contains elements that all objects in the class share. However, because this is a module, you cannot expose it.

Listing 26.10   Modules Are Helpful When Two or More Files in a Project Need Access to the Same Procedure or Declaration

```
'**********************************************************
' COMMON.BAS - This module contains declarations and
'              procedures that are needed by more than one
'              form or class in this project. It also includes
'              the required starting point for the project by
'              declaring a public Sub Main().
'**********************************************************
```

(continues)

Listing 26.10 Continued

```vb
Option Explicit
'****************************************************************
' API calls that are only used by this module don't need to
' be public.
'****************************************************************
#If Win32 Then
Private Declare Function SetWindowPos Lib "user32" (ByVal _
    hwnd As Long, ByVal hWndInsertAfter As Long, ByVal x _
    As Long, ByVal y As Long, ByVal cx As Long, ByVal cy _
    As Long, ByVal wFlags As Long) As Long
Private Declare Function GetWindowsDirectory Lib "kernel32" _
    Alias "GetWindowsDirectoryA" (ByVal lpBuffer As String, _
    ByVal nSize As Long) As Long
Public Declare Function GetVersion Lib "kernel32" () As Long
Public Declare Function SendMessage Lib "user32" Alias _
    "SendMessageA" (ByVal hwnd As Long, ByVal wMsg As Long, _
    ByVal wParam As Long, lParam As Any) As Long
Public Declare Function PostMessage Lib "user32" Alias _
    "PostMessageA" (ByVal hwnd As Long, ByVal wMsg As Long, _
    ByVal wParam As Long, lParam As Any) As Long
#Else
Private Declare Function SetWindowPos Lib "User" (ByVal hwnd%, _
    ByVal hb%, ByVal x%, ByVal y%, ByVal cx%, ByVal cy%, _
    ByVal FLAGS%) As Integer
Private Declare Function GetWindowsDirectory Lib "Kernel" _
    (ByVal retStr$, ByVal bufferLen%) As Integer
'****************************************************************
' API calls used by other modules, forms, or classes should
' be exposed via Public.
'****************************************************************
Public Declare Function GetVersion Lib "Kernel" () As Long
Public Declare Function SendMessage Lib "User" (ByVal hwnd As _
    Integer, ByVal wMsg As Integer, ByVal wParam As Integer, _
    lParam As Any) As Long
Public Declare Function PostMessage Lib "User" (ByVal hwnd As _
    Integer, ByVal wMsg As Integer, ByVal wParam As Integer, _
    lParam As Any) As Long
#End If
'****************************************************************
' This Boolean keeps track of the way the About box should
' be displayed.
'****************************************************************
Public bSplashScreen As Boolean
'****************************************************************
' This procedure will set or restore a window to the topmost
' position above all open windows.
'****************************************************************
#If Win32 Then
Public Sub AlwaysOnTop(ByVal hwnd&, ResetWindow As Boolean)
#Else
Public Sub AlwaysOnTop(ByVal hwnd%, ResetWindow As Boolean)
#End If
Const HWND_TOPMOST = -1
```

```
Const HWND_NOTOPMOST = -2
Const SWP_NOMOVE = 2
Const SWP_NOSIZE = 1
Const FLAGS = SWP_NOMOVE Or SWP_NOSIZE
Dim success%

    On Error GoTo AlwaysOnTop_Err

    If ResetWindow Then
        success = SetWindowPos(hwnd, HWND_NOTOPMOST, 0, 0, _
                    0, 0, FLAGS)
    Else
        success = SetWindowPos(hwnd, HWND_TOPMOST, 0, 0, 0, _
                    0, FLAGS)
    End If

    Exit Sub

AlwaysOnTop_Err:
    ErrHandler Err, "AlwaysOnTop" & str$(ResetWindow)
    Exit Sub
End Sub
'**************************************************************
' This is a generic error handler which will display a message,
' close any open files, and restore the pointer and Err.
'**************************************************************
Public Sub ErrHandler(ErrType%, FromWhere$)
    '**************************************************************
    ' We wouldn't be here if there wasn't an error, so be sure
    ' to turn error handling off.
    '**************************************************************
    On Error Resume Next
    '**************************************************************
    ' ErrType = 32755 is Cancel button was selected
    ' ErrType = 3197 Then Data has changed when 2 users
    ' accessing one record
    '**************************************************************
    If ErrType = 32755 Or ErrType = 3197 Then Exit Sub
    '**************************************************************
    ' This statement prevents an error message if this function
    ' was accidentally called.
    '**************************************************************
    If ErrType <> 0 Then
        '**************************************************************
        ' Set Err so we can get Error
        '**************************************************************
        Err = ErrType
        '**************************************************************
        ' Restore the mouse, and display a descriptive message
        '**************************************************************
        Screen.MousePointer = vbDefault
        MsgBox "An error of type" & str(Err) & " occurred in " _
                & FromWhere & ".", vbExclamation, Error
```

(continues)

Listing 26.10   Continued

```
        '**********************************************************
        ' Restore Err, and close any open files to prevent
        ' corrupting files.
        '**********************************************************
        Err = 0
        Close
    End If
End Sub
'**************************************************************
' Uses the Dir command to see if a file exists. Resume Next is
' required in case FileName contains an invalid path.
'**************************************************************
Public Function FileExists(FileName$) As Boolean
    On Error Resume Next
    FileExists = IIf(Dir(FileName) <> "", True, False)
End Function
'**************************************************************
' Returns the path to the Windows directory with or without
' a trailing backslash.
'**************************************************************
Public Function GetWinDir(WithSlash As Boolean) As String
Dim lpBuffer$, res%, GetWin$
    '**********************************************************
    ' Turn on error handling
    '**********************************************************
    On Error GoTo GetWinDir_Err
    '**********************************************************
    ' Initialize a buffer that is large enough to hold the
    ' result, otherwise you'll get a GPF.
    '**********************************************************
    lpBuffer = Space$(2048)
    '**********************************************************
    ' Call the function, and strip the null terminator using
    ' the return value.
    '**********************************************************
    res = GetWindowsDirectory(lpBuffer, Len(lpBuffer))
    GetWin = LCase$(Left$(lpBuffer, res))
    '**********************************************************
    ' Add or Remove the slash depending on what was returned,
    ' and the value of WithSlash.
    '**********************************************************
    If Right$(GetWin, 1) <> "\" And WithSlash Then
        GetWinDir = GetWin & "\"
    ElseIf Right$(GetWin, 1) = "\" And Not WithSlash Then
        GetWinDir = Left$(GetWin, Len(GetWin) - 1)
    Else
        GetWinDir = GetWin
    End If
    '**********************************************************
    ' Don't forget to exit, otherwise you'll fall into the
    ' error handler.
    '**********************************************************
    Exit Function
```

```
'***************************************************************
' If error, call the error handler, and tell it where the
' error occurred. This is useful for distributed apps.
'***************************************************************
GetWinDir_Err:
    ErrHandler Err, "GetWinDir"
    Exit Function
End Function
'***************************************************************
' All projects must have an entry point (either a startup form
' or Sub Main()). This one just initializes our variables.
'***************************************************************
Sub Main()
    '***********************************************************
    ' If this program is started manually, then show the
    ' About box.
    '***********************************************************
    If App.StartMode = vbSModeStandalone Then
        Dim thisApp As New Application
        thisApp.ShowAboutBox False, App:="Martinsen's Software", _
            AppCompany:="Martinsen's Software", _
            VerNum:="1.00.01",
            User:="John Doe", Company:="XYZ Incorporated", _
            AboutMsg:="This OLE object was started manually.", _
            RegNum:="Registration Number: 12345"
    End If
End Sub
```

Listing 26.11 is the Application class. This public, creatable class is this
project's exposed interface. It contains a routine to display the About box and
includes some other helpful functions that your calling application might
need.

Listing 26.11   An Exposed Class Provides an Interface for Your OLE Server

```
'***************************************************************
' APP.CLS - This is the application class which is exposed
'           to other OLE Automation clients. It provides some
'           handy routines that aren't included in VB, and it
'           is a good demonstration on how to write an OLE server
'           that can be used with other Office apps.
'***************************************************************
Option Explicit
'***************************************************************
' Hidden API functions for private use only
'***************************************************************
#If Win32 Then
Private Declare Function GetPrivateProfileInt Lib "kernel32" _
    Alias "GetPrivateProfileIntA" (ByVal lpApplicationName$, _
    ByVal lpKeyName As String, ByVal nDefault As Long, ByVal _
    lpFileName As String) As Long
```

(continues)

Listing 26.11   Continued

```
Private Declare Function GetPrivateProfileString Lib "kernel32" _
    Alias "GetPrivateProfileStringA" (ByVal lpApplicationName$, _
    lpKeyName As Any, ByVal lpDefault As String, ByVal _
    lpReturnedString As String, ByVal nSize As Long, ByVal _
    lpFileName As String) As Long

Private Declare Function WritePrivateProfileString Lib _
    "kernel32" Alias "WritePrivateProfileStringA" (ByVal _
    lpApplicationName As String, lpKeyName As Any, lpString _
    As Any, ByVal lplFileName As String) As Long

Private Declare Function GetShortPathName Lib "kernel32" Alias _
    "GetShortPathNameA" (ByVal lpszLongPath As String, ByVal _
    lpszShortPath As String, ByVal cchBuffer As Long) As Long
#Else
Private Declare Function GetPrivateProfileInt Lib "Kernel" _
        (ByVal lpApplicationName As String, ByVal lpKeyName _
        As String, ByVal nDefault As Integer, ByVal lpFileName _
        As String) As Integer

Private Declare Function GetPrivateProfileString Lib "Kernel" _
        (ByVal lpAppName As Any, ByVal lpKeyName As Any, _
        ByVal lpDefault As String, ByVal lpReturnedString _
        As String, ByVal nSize As Integer, ByVal lpFileName _
        As String) As Integer

Private Declare Function WritePrivateProfileString% Lib "Kernel" _
        (ByVal lpAppName As Any, ByVal lpKeyName As Any, ByVal _
        lpString As Any, ByVal lpFileName As String)
#End If
'****************************************************************
' Hidden variable for this class
'****************************************************************
Private thisAbout As New About
'****************************************************************
' Description: This procedure displays an About box
'
' Arguments:
' AsSplash  (Boolean)- Display as splash screen?
' App       (String) - The name of your application
' AppCompany(String) - The name of your company
' VerNum    (String) - The version number of your app
' User      (String) - The name of the registered user
' Company   (String) - The user's company name
' RegNum    (String) - The user's registration number
' AboutMsg  (String) - Your About box message that goes
'                      between the 2 black lines
' IconProg  (String) - The file name (without an extension)
'                      of the running app that contains
'                      the icon you would like to use.
'                      The default is Progman
'                      (for Program Manager)
'
```

```
' IconIdx   (Long)   - The 1 based index of the icon
'                      stored in IconProg. The default
'                      is 1
'****************************************************************
Public Sub ShowAboutBox(AsSplash As Boolean, _
                        Optional App, _
                        Optional AppCompany, _
                        Optional VerNum, _
                        Optional User, _
                        Optional Company, _
                        Optional RegNum, _
                        Optional AboutMsg)

    '****************************************************************
    ' You should only set the properties if the argument was
    ' provided. Otherwise, just let the default values appear.
    '****************************************************************
    If Not IsMissing(App) Then thisAbout.AppName = App
    If Not IsMissing(AppCompany) Then _
                        thisAbout.AppCompanyName = AppCompany
    If Not IsMissing(VerNum) Then thisAbout.VersionNumber = VerNum
    If Not IsMissing(User) Then thisAbout.UserName = User
    If Not IsMissing(Company) Then thisAbout.CompanyName = Company
    If Not IsMissing(RegNum) Then thisAbout.Registration = RegNum
    If Not IsMissing(AboutMsg) Then thisAbout.Message = AboutMsg
    '****************************************************************
    ' Show it using the About object
    '****************************************************************
    thisAbout.ShowAbout AsSplash
End Sub
'****************************************************************
' Returns a reference to an About object so that its properties
' may be accessed individually.
'****************************************************************
Public Property Get CreateAbout() As Object
    Set CreateAbout = thisAbout
End Property
'****************************************************************
' Unload via the About object
'****************************************************************
Public Sub UnloadSplash()
    thisAbout.HideSplash
End Sub
'****************************************************************
' This method is just a wrapper for the global function which
' the About object needs too. This demonstrates how you can
' expose nonclass objects.
'****************************************************************
' NOTE: You may be wondering why I didn't just put the code
'       in here, and require other modules to just call this
'       one. The reason is that this is a class. If another
'       module wants to use a class method, then they must
'       create an object which consumes a great deal of
'       memory. This method exposes our object, but it also
'       leaves it available to all forms by putting it into
'       a module. This duplication is actually an optimization.
'****************************************************************
```

(continues)

Listing 26.11   Continued

```
#If Win32 Then
Public Sub AlwaysOnTop(ByVal hwnd&, ResetWindow As Boolean)
#Else
Public Sub AlwaysOnTop(ByVal hwnd%, ResetWindow As Boolean)
#End If
    Common.AlwaysOnTop hwnd, ResetWindow
End Sub
'*****************************************************************
' This method is a wrapper for Common.FileExists.
'*****************************************************************
Public Function FileExists(FileName$) As Boolean
    FileExists = Common.FileExists(FileName)
End Function
'*****************************************************************
' This method is a wrapper for Common.GetWinDir.
'*****************************************************************
Public Function GetWinDir(WithSlash As Boolean) As String
    GetWinDir = Common.GetWinDir(WithSlash)
End Function
#If Win32 Then
'*****************************************************************
' This function converts a long file name into a DOS-compatible
' short file name.
'*****************************************************************
Private Function GetShortName(LongFileName As String) As String
Dim strFileName As String
    strFileName = Space(2048)
    GetShortName = Left(strFileName, GetShortPathName _
        (LongFileName, strFileName, Len(strFileName)))
End Function
#End If
'*****************************************************************
' This method extracts the file name (with extension) from a
' fully qualified path. If path = "c:\autoexec.bat", then
' this method returns "autoexec.bat".
'*****************************************************************
' NOTE: This method is not used by any modules or forms in this
' project, so its code belongs here.
'*****************************************************************
'*****************************************************************
' WARNING: This function modifies Path, so ByVal is required.
'*****************************************************************
Public Function ExtractFileName(ByVal Path As String) As String
Dim res%
    '*********************************************************
    ' One of the few uses for GoTo is as an error handler, and
    ' this is a great example of how to use them.
    '*********************************************************
    On Error GoTo ExtractFileName_Err
    '*********************************************************
    ' Since a file name (with extension) in DOS can only be
    ' a maximum of 13 chars (8 + 1 + 3), get rid of the rest.
    '*********************************************************
```

```
        #If Win32 Then ' Convert LFN's to SFN's
            Path = GetShortName(Path)
        #End If
        If Len(Path) > 13 Then Path = Right(Path, 13)
        res = InStr(Path, "\")
        '*************************************************************
        ' Get rid of the rest of the garbage by looking for slashes.
        '*************************************************************
        Do While res <> 0
            Path = Mid$(Path, res + 1, Len(Path))
            res = InStr(Path, "\")
        Loop
        '*************************************************************
        ' Return the result, and exit the function to prevent
        ' executing the error handler.
        '*************************************************************
        ExtractFileName = Path
        Exit Function
'*****************************************************************
' Our error handler calls an external module's generic error
' handler, and exits to prevent further damage.
'*****************************************************************
ExtractFileName_Err:
    ErrHandler Err, "ExtractFileName"
    Exit Function
End Function
'*****************************************************************
' Calls the API to read an .INI file, and return the results.
' A large buffer is used so that this function can be used
' in any app without causing a GPF.
'*****************************************************************
' NOTE: ByVal is used, so you can pass control values such
'       as Text1.Text without surrounding it in parentheses.
'*****************************************************************
Public Function GetINI(ByVal Section$, ByVal Key$, ByVal _
                       Default$, ByVal FileName$) As String
Dim res&, retVal$
    retVal = Space$(32400)
    res = GetPrivateProfileString(Section, Key, Default, _
                          retVal, Len(retVal), FileName)
    GetINI = Left$(retVal, res)
End Function
'*****************************************************************
' Same as above, but it returns an integer.
'*****************************************************************
Public Function GetINIInt(ByVal Section$, ByVal Key$, ByVal _
                       Default%, ByVal FileName$) As Integer
    GetINIInt = GetPrivateProfileInt(Section, Key, Default, _
                       FileName)
End Function
'*****************************************************************
' This function is useful with SendMessage and GetVersion
' so you can get the low order word.
'*****************************************************************
Public Function GetLoWord(ByVal DWORD&) As Long
    GetLoWord = DWORD And &HFFFF&
End Function
```

(continues)

Listing 26.11   Continued

```
'*********************************************************************
' Same as above, but returns the high order word.
'*********************************************************************
Public Function GetHiWord(ByVal DWORD As Long) As Long
    GetHiWord = DWORD \ &H10000
End Function
#If Win16 Then
'*********************************************************************
' This function is EXTREMELY useful under Win16 for making
' a DWORD which is sometimes required by SendMessage's lParam
' argument.
'*********************************************************************
Public Function MakelParam(LoWord%, HiWord%) As Long
    MakelParam = CLng(HiWord) * &H1000& Or LoWord
End Function
#End If
'*********************************************************************
' This method returns the Windows version as a variant so you
' can use it as text or as a number.
'*********************************************************************
Public Function WindowsVersion() As Variant
Dim WinVer As Long
    WinVer = GetLoWord(GetVersion())
    WindowsVersion = Format((WinVer Mod 256) + ((WinVer \ 256) _
                            / 100), "Fixed")
End Function
'*********************************************************************
' This method accepts alphanumeric settings to write to an
' .INI file. In addition, you can delete a section or key by
' passing the special "_DELETE_" string.
'*********************************************************************
Public Sub WriteINI(ByVal Section$, ByVal Key$, ByVal Setting _
                    As Variant, ByVal FileName$)
    '*************************************************************
    ' If key is set to _DELETE_, then delete the section
    '*************************************************************
    If Key = "_DELETE_" Then
        WritePrivateProfileString Section, 0&, 0&, FileName
    '*************************************************************
    ' If setting is set to _DELETE_, then delete the key
    '*************************************************************
    ElseIf Setting = "_DELETE_" Then
        WritePrivateProfileString Section, Key, 0&, FileName
    '*************************************************************
    ' Otherwise, convert the setting to a string and write it
    ' to the .INI file.
    '*************************************************************
    Else
        WritePrivateProfileString Section, Key, CStr(Setting), _
                                FileName
    End If
End Sub
#If Win32 Then
```

```
'****************************************************************
' This method demonstrates how you can expose API calls. Since
' you can't use As Any with functions, SendMessage requires
' type-safe versions.
'****************************************************************
Public Function SendMessageAsLong(hwnd As Long, wMsg As _
            Integer, wParam As Long, lParam As Long) As Long
    SendMessageAsLong = Common.SendMessage(hwnd, wMsg, wParam, _
                                    lParam)
End Function
'****************************************************************
' See above.
'****************************************************************
Public Function SendMessageAsStr(hwnd As Long, wMsg As _
            Integer, wParam As Long, lParam As String) As Long
    SendMessageAsStr = Common.SendMessage(hwnd, wMsg, wParam, _
        lParam)
End Function
'****************************************************************
' See above.
'****************************************************************
Public Function PostMessage(ByVal hwnd As Long, ByVal wMsg _
    As Integer, ByVal wParam As Long, lParam As Long) As Long
    PostMessage = Common.PostMessage(ByVal hwnd, wMsg, wParam, _
                                    lParam)
End Function
#Else
'****************************************************************
' This method demonstrates how you can expose API calls. Since
' you can't use As Any with functions, SendMessage requires
' type-safe versions.
'****************************************************************
Public Function SendMessageAsLong(hwnd As Integer, wMsg As _
            Integer, wParam As Integer, lParam As Long) As Long
    SendMessageAsLong = Common.SendMessage(hwnd, wMsg, wParam, _
                                    lParam)
End Function
'****************************************************************
' See above.
'****************************************************************
Public Function SendMessageAsStr(hwnd As Integer, wMsg As _
            Integer, wParam As Integer, lParam As String) As Long
    SendMessageAsStr = Common.SendMessage(hwnd, wMsg, wParam, _
        lParam)
End Function
'****************************************************************
' See above.
'****************************************************************
Public Function PostMessage(ByVal hwnd As Integer, ByVal wMsg _
    As Integer, ByVal wParam As Integer, lParam As Long) As Long
    PostMessage = Common.PostMessage(ByVal hwnd, wMsg, wParam, _
                                    lParam)
End Function
#End If
```

The net result of this project is an exposed class that other VBA applications (such as Excel) can use to display a dialog box (see fig. 26.12) and access some helpful routines. It also demonstrates how you can create reusable objects that are more useful than DLLs, without having to learn C.

Fig. 26.12
You can call this generic About box from any OLE Automation client, including Access, Excel, and Project.

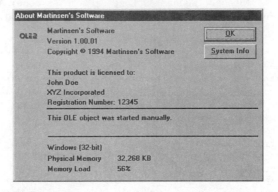

To use this handy OLE Server from Excel, you need only to create an object variable of this type and access its member functions. Listing 26.12 demonstrates how to use the ShowAboutBox method, but the same method applies for all its member functions.

Listing 26.12   OLE Servers Created in VB Can Be Used with External Applications Such as Excel

```
Sub ShowAbout()
Dim Helpful As Object
    Set Helpful = CreateObject("Useful.Application")
    Helpful.ShowAboutBox AsSplash:=False, _
      App:="My Excel Workbook", _
      AppCompany:="Martinsen's Software", VerNum:="1.00", _
      User:="Ronald R. Martinsen", Company:="", _
      RegNum:="1234-567", _
      AboutMsg:="My AboutMessage Goes Here!"
End Sub
```

Note

Because Visual Basic can create OLE Automation servers, you might find that other applications (for example, Access, Excel, or Project) are better source programs for your application code. You will also find that you can save yourself a lot of work without giving up the power of Visual Basic 4.0.

Using DDE with Microsoft Excel

As the previous chapter mentioned, no VB programmer should ever have any valid reason to use DDE with an application that supports OLE Automation. Because Excel has an outstanding type library exposed, you should take advantage of it through OLE Automation. For this reason, this book intentionally does not cover this topic.

From Here...

Unfortunately, this chapter could cover only a few of the amazing things that you can do when integrating VB with Excel. However, the following are some great, highly recommended resources:

- *Using Visual Basic for Applications, Excel Edition.* This book, written by Jeff Webb, is a valuable aid for understanding VBA 1.0 with Excel. Because Visual Basic 4.0 and Project 4.0 are based on VBA, you'll also find some tips that apply to non-Excel projects.

- *Microsoft Developers Network CD* (available directly from Microsoft). The compact disks that this service provides are priceless. In most cases, if you have a problem, this CD has the answer.

Chapter 27

Integration with Other OLE Applications

Access, Excel, and Word are the most powerful Microsoft Office applications, so this book dedicates two informative chapters to each of these products. However, Microsoft also offers other powerful applications that you might want to incorporate into your custom programs. None of these applications possesses enough power to warrant its own chapter, but collectively they warrant a brief discussion.

In this chapter, you learn how to do the following:

- Connect to OLE Automation servers

- Take advantage of OLE miniservers

- Use OLE objects as Visual Basic (VB) controls

- Communicate with applications that don't support dynamic data exchange (DDE) or object linking and embedding (OLE).

Connecting to OLE Automation Servers

You might think that once you've seen one OLE Automation server, you've seen them all. For the most part, this is true. Connecting to any OLE Automation server requires the same basic steps, but using the server and disconnecting isn't so easy. Every server has its own way of doing things, so you have to be careful. To demonstrate this point, this chapter introduces a simple text editor written in MFC (Microsoft Foundation Classes), called TextServer, that supports OLE Automation (see fig. 27.1). This chapter also introduces Talker, a sample Visual Basic program, to demonstrate the communication between a VB application and TextServer (see fig. 27.2).

Fig. 27.1
TextServer is a useful program that can serve as an OLE Automation testing tool for Visual Basic.

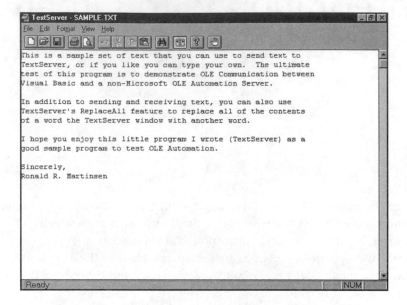

Fig. 27.2
Talker demonstrates that OLE Automation with TextServer is similar to Microsoft applications.

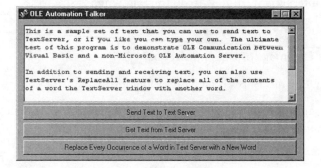

To demonstrate OLE Automation between a VB application and a typical non-Microsoft application (TextServer), this section discusses the steps required to write Talker. To begin this project, you first create an object variable that does not go out of scope. By doing so, you prevent yourself from accidentally losing your OLE Automation connection. Next, use `CreateObject` to establish a connection with TextServer. Listing 27.1 shows how you begin building Talker.

Listing 27.1   Establishing a Connection with TextServer

```
'******************************************************************
' Create an object that won't go out of scope too early.
'******************************************************************
Option Explicit
Private TextServer As Object
'******************************************************************
' Loads the form and establishes a connection with TextServer.
'******************************************************************
Private Sub Form_Load()

    On Error Resume Next

    Move (Screen.Width - Width) / 2, (Screen.Height - Height) / 2
    '**************************************************************
    ' As this line demonstrates, all objects are created
    ' the same way.
    '**************************************************************
    Set TextServer = CreateObject("Text.Document")

    If Err Then
        '**********************************************************
        ' TextServer is not properly registered in the system
        ' registry, so register it.
        '**********************************************************
        RegisterTextServer
        MsgBox "Please restart Talker now!", vbInformation
        Unload Me
    End If
LoadText
    '**************************************************************
    ' Show is one of TextServer's OLE Automation commands.
    ' It causes TextServer to be activated and visible.
    '**************************************************************
    ' NOTE: TextServer (and most OLE Automation apps) are
    '       invisible by default, so you must make them visible
    '       by some method if you want the user to see the
    '       application. If the user doesn't need to see the
    '       application, then it isn't necessary to make it
    '       visible.
    '**************************************************************
    TextServer.Show
End Sub
```

The first two buttons in the cmd control array simply send or receive text to or from TextServer. Listing 27.2 shows the OLE Automation calls needed to accomplish this task.

Listing 27.2   Sending and Receiving Text to and from TextServer

```
'*******************************************************************
' Process command button clicks.
'*******************************************************************
Private Sub cmd_Click(Index As Integer)
Dim FindText$, ReplaceWith$

    Select Case Index
        Case 0 'Send Text to TextServer
            '*******************************************************
            ' SetEditText takes 1 argument (a string). TextServer
            ' uses this string to populate its text box.
            '*******************************************************
            TextServer.SetEditText Text1
            TextServer.Show
        Case 1 'Get Text from TextServer
            '*******************************************************
            ' GetEditText returns a string that contains
            ' the contents of TextServer's text box.
            '*******************************************************
            Text1 = TextServer.GetEditText()
        ...
```

The last button in the control array prompts the user for a word to find in TextServer's text window, and replaces every occurrence of that word with another user-provided word. Next, the button calls TextServer's ReplaceAll function and displays TextServer to show the user the results of ReplaceAll. Listing 27.3 shows how to use TextServer's ReplaceAll method.

Listing 27.3   Using TextServer's ReplaceAll Method

```
        ...
        Case 2 'Replace Every Occurrence of a Word
            '*******************************************************
            ' ReplaceAll finds every occurrence of a word,
            ' and replaces it with a new word. After the replace
            ' is complete, the TextServer text box is updated to
            ' reflect the changes.
            '*******************************************************
            FindText = InputBox("Find What?")
            If FindText = "" Then Exit Sub
            ReplaceWith = InputBox("Replace With?")
            If FindText = "" Then Exit Sub
            TextServer.ReplaceAll FindText, ReplaceWith
            TextServer.Show
    End Select

End Sub
```

`LoadText` (see listing 27.4) simply opens SAMPLE.TXT from the directory in which the project or executable resides, loads all the file's text, and inserts the text into the text box.

Listing 27.4   The `LoadText` Procedure

```
'*********************************************************************
' This procedure just loads the text box with some sample text.
'*********************************************************************
Private Sub LoadText()
Dim Source%, res$

    Source = FreeFile

    Open App.Path & "\sample.txt" For Input As Source
        res = Input(LOF(Source), Source)
        Text1 = res
    Close Source

End Sub
```

When writing applications that depend on certain OLE applications being properly registered, you usually should write a procedure that automatically registers those applications. Your application need only run REGEDIT.EXE (included with Windows) with the OLE server's .REG file as the command-line argument.

The `RegisterTextServer` procedure (see listing 27.5) goes a step further by inserting the .REG file into a new procedure so that the application can customize and create the file while running. By doing so, `RegisterTextServer` ensures that a valid .REG file exists, even if the user accidentally deletes his or her own.

Listing 27.5   The `RegisterTextServer` Procedure

```
'*********************************************************************
' This procedure demonstrates how you can automatically register
' (or reregister) an application without any interaction
' from the user.
'*********************************************************************
Private Sub RegisterTextServer()
Dim sTemp$, Source%, RegFile$
    '*************************************************************
    ' Since you'll need a bunch of hard returns, you'll want
    ' to cache them in a variable.
```

(continues)

Listing 27.5   Continued

```
'*****************************************************************
'*****************************************************************
' The entire contents of sTemp were created by opening an.REG
' file in Notepad, and inserting text before and after each
' line. That text was then pasted into VB, and Notepad was
' closed without saving. In addition, any of the lines that
' pointed to the .EXE were updated to reflect the path to
' the program (in this case App.Path).
'*****************************************************************
sTemp = "REGEDIT" & vbCrLf
sTemp = sTemp & "; This .REG file is used to properly register
➥TextServer." & vbCrLf
sTemp = sTemp & "COleObjectFactory::UpdateRegistryAll." & _
    vbCrLf
sTemp = sTemp & "" & vbCrLf
sTemp = sTemp & "HKEY_CLASSES_ROOT\.txt = Text.Document" & _
    vbCrLf
'*****************************************************************
' The next 2 lines are combined into one line in the file that
' points to the path where TEXTSVER.EXE is stored. If the
' system registry doesn't point to a vaild path, DDE
' connections will always fail unless TextServer is already
' running.
'*****************************************************************
sTemp = sTemp & _
    "HKEY_CLASSES_ROOT\Text.Document\shell\open\command = "
sTemp = sTemp & App.Path & "\TEXTSVER.EXE %1" & vbCrLf
sTemp = sTemp & _
    "HKEY_CLASSES_ROOT\Text.Document\shell\open\ddeexec
    ➥= [open(""%1"")]" & vbCrLf
sTemp = sTemp & _
    "HKEY_CLASSES_ROOT\Text.Document\shell\open\ddeexec
    ➥\application = TEXTSVER" & vbCrLf
sTemp = sTemp & "" & vbCrLf
sTemp = sTemp & _
    "HKEY_CLASSES_ROOT\Text.Document = Text Document" & vbCrLf
sTemp = sTemp & "HKEY_CLASSES_ROOT\Text.Document\CLSID =
➥{F15017A0-8245-101B-95FE-00AA0030472F}" & vbCrLf
sTemp = sTemp & "" & vbCrLf
sTemp = sTemp & "HKEY_CLASSES_ROOT\CLSID\{F15017A0-8245-
➥101B-95FE-00AA0030472F} = Text Document" & vbCrLf
'*****************************************************************
' Once again, the next two lines point to the path where
' TEXTSVER.EXE is stored. If the system registry doesn't point
' to a vaild path, CreateObject will always fail unless
' TextServer is already running.
'*****************************************************************
sTemp = sTemp & "HKEY_CLASSES_ROOT\CLSID\{F15017A0-8245-101B-
➥95FE-00AA0030472F}\LocalServer = "
sTemp = sTemp & App.Path & "\TEXTSVER.EXE" & vbCrLf
sTemp = sTemp & "HKEY_CLASSES_ROOT\CLSID\{F15017A0-8245-101B-
➥95FE-00AA0030472F}\ProgId = Text.Document" & vbCrLf
'*****************************************************************
```

```
' Create the .REG file on the end user's hard drive.
'****************************************************************
Source = FreeFile
RegFile = App.Path & "\TEXTSVER.REG"
'****************************************************************
' Clear the file
'****************************************************************
Open RegFile For Output As Source
Close Source
'****************************************************************
' Create the .REG file
'****************************************************************
Open RegFile For Binary As Source
    Put Source, , sTemp
Close Source
'****************************************************************
' Run RegEdit with the .REG file to automatically register it.
' If the app was already registered, your file will update the
' registry with any changes.
'****************************************************************

Shell "regedit.exe /s " & RegFile, vbMinimizedNoFocusEnd Sub
```

> **Note**
>
> The RegisterTextServer procedure in listing 27.5 demonstrates how you can create and register an OLE application on the fly. Even if the user doesn't have the .REG file, your application will run because it creates its own. If your OLE application doesn't have an .REG file, it probobly can register itself, so the preceding step is unnecessary.

> **Note**
>
> You can access all OLE Automation servers in a manner similar to that demonstrated in the Talker example. This is important to know, because new OLE Automation servers are being released every month.

For a more detailed discussion on communicating with OLE Automation servers, see Chapter 18, "Creating Objects."

Using Microsoft's OLE Miniservers

You might have noticed that Microsoft has several programs in the MSAPPS subdirectory of your Windows directory. One or more Microsoft applications use these programs to provide some special feature such as a ClipArt manager. However, if you ever try to run one of these programs directly, you get a message that tells you that you can run the program only from within a host application. This is because these small programs are OLE miniservers, which run only if an OLE host application (such as Word or your Visual Basic application) calls them. This section explains how you can use these handy miniservers in your Visual Basic applications.

Caution

You cannot redistribute these miniservers. Therefore, your programs should use them only if they are already installed on the user's system. Otherwise, your application must handle this situation gracefully.

Although the exact number is always changing, Microsoft currently distributes seven OLE miniservers. Table 27.1 lists each miniserver, along with the application with which it is bundled.

Table 27.1 Microsoft's OLE Miniservers

Miniserver	Path from the MSAPPS Directory	Application
ClipArt Gallery	..\ARTGALRY\ARTGALRY.EXE	Publisher
Draw	..\MSDRAW\MSDRAW.EXE	Works, Publisher
Equation Editor	..\EQUATION\EQNEDIT.EXE	PowerPoint, Word
Graph	..\MSGRAPH5\GRAPH5.EXE	Access, Word
Note-It	..\NOTE-IT\NOTE-IT.EXE	Works
Organization Chart	..\ORGCHART\ORGCHART.EXE	PowerPoint
WordArt	..\WORDART\WORDART2.EXE	PowerPoint, Publisher, Word

Note

Table 27.1 refers only to the 1994 versions of each application, so earlier versions might not include the listed miniserver. For more information on which miniserver the applications include, contact Microsoft Product Support Services.

To demonstrate how easy it is to use these miniservers in your applications, listing 27.6 presents a portion of the code for MINISERV.VBP, a program that uses the currently installed OLE miniservers in the OLE container control. This program contains seven OLE container controls on the form, with a miniserver embedded in each of the controls. When you run the program, it adds an item to a drop-down list box for each miniserver that exists on the system. This drop-down list box enables you to navigate between the available miniservers so that you can view and edit an object of each type of available miniserver.

Listing 27.6   Determining Which Miniservers Are Available

```
'********************************************************************
' Only load miniservers that exist.
'********************************************************************
Private Sub LoadList()
Dim MSAppsRoot$

    With cboServers
        .Clear

        MSAppsRoot = Space(256)
        MSAppsRoot = Left(MSAppsRoot, _
            GetWindowsDirectory(MSAppsRoot, Len(MSAppsRoot)))

        If Win05UI() Then
            MSAppsRoot = _
            "C:\Program Files\Common Files\Microsoft Shared\"
        Else
            MSAppsRoot = MSAppsRoot & "\msapps\"
        End If

        If FileExists(MSAppsRoot & "artgalry\artgalry.exe") Then
            .AddItem "MS ClipArt"
            .ItemData(.NewIndex) = 0
        End If
#If Win16 Then
        If FileExists(MSAppsRoot & "equation\eqnedit.exe") Then
#Else
        If FileExists(MSAppsRoot & "equation\eqnedt32.exe") Then
#End If
            .AddItem "MS Draw"
            .ItemData(.NewIndex) = 1
        End If

        If FileExists(MSAppsRoot & "msdraw\msdraw.exe") Then
            .AddItem "MS Equation Editor"
            .ItemData(.NewIndex) = 2
        End If
```

(continues)

Listing 27.6 Continued

```
            If FileExists(MSAppsRoot & "msgraph5\graph5.exe") Then
                .AddItem "MS Graph"
                .ItemData(.NewIndex) = 3
            End If

            If FileExists(MSAppsRoot & "note-it\note-it.exe") Then
                .AddItem "MS Note-It"
                .ItemData(.NewIndex) = 4
            End If

            If FileExists(MSAppsRoot & "orgchart\orgchart.exe") Then
                .AddItem "MS Organization Chart"
                .ItemData(.NewIndex) = 5
            End If

            #If Win16 Then
            If FileExists(MSAppsRoot & "wordart\wordart2.exe") Then
            #Else
            If FileExists(MSAppsRoot & "wordart\wrdart32.exe") Then
            #End If
                .AddItem "MS WordArt"
                .ItemData(.NewIndex) = 6
            End If
    End With
End Sub
'*********************************************************************
' Check to see if a file exists.
'*********************************************************************
Private Function FileExists(FileName$) As Boolean
    On Error Resume Next
    FileExists = IIf(Dir(FileName) = "", False, True)
End Function
'*********************************************************************
' Check to see if the user is running the Windows 95 shell.
'*********************************************************************
Private Function Win95UI() As Boolean
Dim lngWinVer As Long
    lngWinVer = GetVersion() And &HFFFF&
    Win95UI = IIf((lngWinVer And &HFF) + _
                ((lngWinVer And &HFF00) / 256) > 3.5, True, _
                False)
End Function
```

Caution

Don't let the name fool you: miniservers are full-blown graphical applications. They consume as much memory and resources as most large-scale applications. If you do run out of system resources, you will get "Unable to Activate Object" or "Object Not Properly Registered" errors when you try to activate a miniserver.

Although listing 27.6 contains a fair amount of code, most of it is for cosmetic purposes. The most important element of this project occurs at design time, when you load your OLE custom controls from the available miniservers installed on your system.

Using Other Microsoft Applications in Your Applications

You've seen plenty of information about integration with Access, Excel, and Word, but you may wonder about integration with other Microsoft applications. This section puts together a quick application that demonstrates how to use the OLE container control to display objects from five other Microsoft applications—Paintbrush, PowerPoint, Project, Sound Recorder, and Video for Windows (see fig. 27.3–27.7).

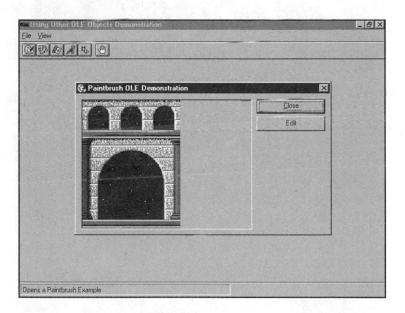

Fig. 27.3
Paintbrush is another Microsoft application that you can embed in your applications.

Fig. 27.4
PowerPoint is
another Microsoft
application that
you can embed in
your applications.

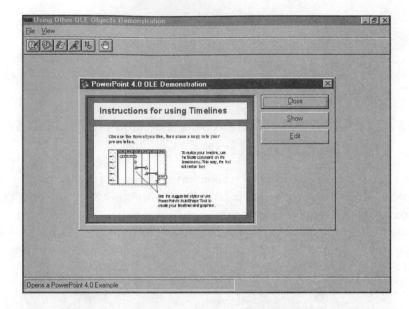

Fig. 27.5
Project is another
Microsoft appli-
cation that you
can embed in your
applications.

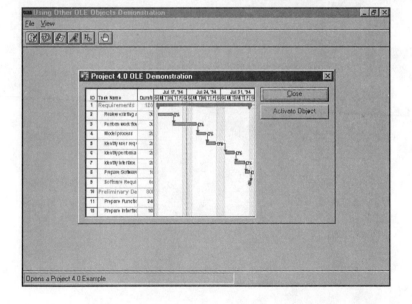

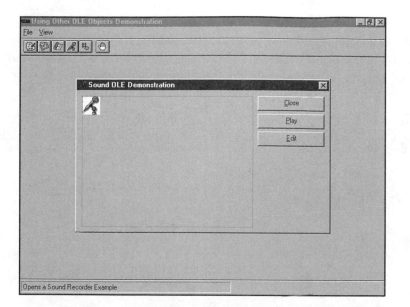

Fig. 27.6
Sound Recorder is another Microsoft application that you can embed in your applications.

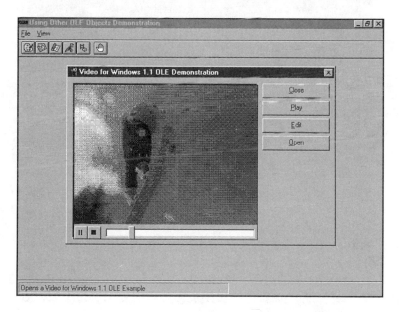

Fig. 27.7
Video for Windows is another Microsoft application that you can embed in your applications.

This application's code (listing 27.7) is rather simple, because the OLE container control does most of the work. This application demonstrates how advantageous it is to own applications that support OLE, because you can easily use them to enhance your application's functionality.

Listing 27.7   FRMOBJ.FRM Takes Advantage of Some Available OLE Servers

```
'**********************************************************************
' FRMOBJECT.FRM: Used to display an object and its verbs.
'**********************************************************************
Option Explicit
Private OLEObject As OLE
. . .
'**********************************************************************
' Execute a verb (verbs are from 1 to x, so you need to add 1).
'**********************************************************************
Private Sub cmdVerbs_Click(Index As Integer)
    On Error Resume Next
    OLEObject.DoVerb (Index + 1)
    If Err Then MsgBox "Err = " & Format(Err) & ": " _
        & Error, vbCritical
End Sub
'**********************************************************************
' This public method is used to display the form
' and to call necessary loading routines.
'**********************************************************************
Public Sub Display(obj As OLE)
    Set OLEObject = obj
    OLEObject.Visible = True
    PrepareForm
    Show vbModal
End Sub
'**********************************************************************
' Center the form and load the command buttons for its verbs.
'**********************************************************************
Public Sub PrepareForm()
Dim i As Integer
    '**********************************************************************
    ' Center the dialog.
    '**********************************************************************
    Move (Screen.Width - Width) / 2, _
    (Screen.Height - Height) / 2
    '**********************************************************************
    ' Create and label a command button on the form for each verb.
    '**********************************************************************
    For i = 1 To OLEObject.ObjectVerbsCount - 1
        '**********************************************************************
        ' cmdVerbs(0) already exists, so skip it.
        '**********************************************************************
        If i > 1 Then Load cmdVerbs(i - 1)
        With cmdVerbs(i - 1)
            If i > 1 Then
```

```
                        .Top = cmdVerbs(i - 2).Top _
                            + cmdVerbs(i - 2).Height + 75
                End If
                .Caption = OLEObject.ObjectVerbs(i)
                .Visible = True
            End With
        Next i
    End Sub
```

Listing 27.7 includes three important procedures: the PrepareForm procedure, the Display method, and the cmdVerbs_Click event.

The PrepareForm procedure uses the .ObjectVerbCount property of the OLE container control to determine how many command buttons are to appear on the form. PrepareForm also uses the .ObjectVerbs property to set the button's caption. When the user clicks one of these buttons, the application invokes the DoVerb method.

The Display method enables a function from another form to specify which OLE container control should be used when displaying the form. By knowing which control to use, the form can then prepare itself (through PrepareForm) for use and display itself modally.

The cmdVerbs_Click event invokes a verb for the object in the visible OLE container control. This invocation is important because it enables the user to display, open, or edit the object.

Using Other Microsoft Applications That Don't Support OLE or DDE

If you want to use a Microsoft application that doesn't support OLE or DDE, your choices are limited to the following:

- Use "brute force" to control the application with the Windows API.

- Run the application with Shell, give control to the user, and then work on the file after the user exits the application.

- Use Visual Basic's SendKeys method.

- Rewrite the application in Visual Basic and do whatever you want.

The next example program, shown in figures 27.8 and 27.9, demonstrates how to accomplish the first three alternatives. (I'll leave the last as an exercise for you.)

Fig. 27.8
The Stubborn
program high-
lights the client
area of any
window on the
screen.

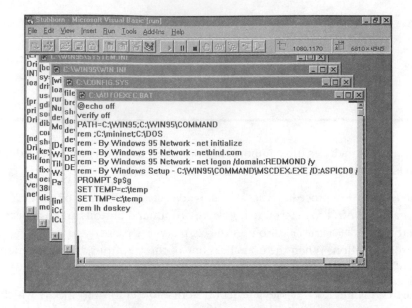

Fig. 27.9
After you click
on the desired
window, the text
from that window
is inserted into the
Stubborn program.

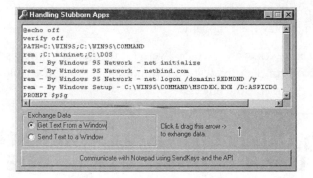

Figure 27.8 shows the 32-bit user interface of Stubborn, but figure 27.9
shows a totally different interface for the 16-bit version. Why? In Win32, the
SetCapture API call requires the user to hold down the mouse while moving it
over different processes. To force the user to do so, you design the user interface so that the user must drag an up-arrow pointer across the screen. When
the user releases the mouse button, the operating system automatically calls
ReleaseCapture for you.

In Win16, the behavior of SetCapture is exactly the opposite. SetCapture
requires the user to press the mouse button and then release it before the
mouse pointer is captured. Once in "capture mode," the user can move the
mouse around the screen without holding down the mouse button. After
the user clicks on something, the operating system automatically calls

`ReleaseCapture` for you. Figure 27.10 shows how you must design the 16-bit user interface to accommodate the 16-bit version of `SetCapture`.

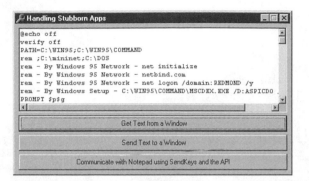

Fig. 27.10
The 16-bit version of Stubborn requires a different user interface.

EXCHANGE.BAS (listing 27.8) is a good exercise in using the 16- and 32-bit Windows API to extend Visual Basic. The functions in this module enable an application to send or grab text to or from any window on the screen. The module starts by declaring the necessary API stuctures (or user-defined types) and function calls.

Listing 27.8   EXCHANGE.BAS, a Module for Exchanging Data Manually with Other Windows

```
'********************************************************************
' EXCHANGE.BAS: Used to manually exchange data with other windows.
'********************************************************************
Option Explicit
Option Compare Text
'********************************************************************
' The API functions we are using in this module require
' us to define two new types.
'********************************************************************
#If Win32 Then
Private Type PointAPI
    x As Long
    y As Long
End Type

Private Type RECT
    Left As Long
    Top As Long
    Right As Long
    Bottom As Long
End Type

#Else
```

(continues)

Listing 27.8 Continued

```
Private Type PointAPI
    x As Integer
    y As Integer
End Type

Private Type RECT
    Left As Integer
    Top As Integer
    Right As Integer
    Bottom As Integer
End Type
#End If
'********************************************************************
' Mouse Capture
'********************************************************************
#If Win32 Then
Private Declare Function SetCapture& Lib "user32" _
    (ByVal hWnd As Long)
Public Declare Function GetCapture Lib "user32" () As Long
Private Declare Sub ReleaseCapture Lib "user32" ()
#Else
Private Declare Function SetCapture Lib "User" (ByVal hWnd%) _
    As Integer
Public Declare Function GetCapture Lib "User" () As Integer
Private Declare Sub ReleaseCapture Lib "User" ()
#End If
'********************************************************************
' Window Information
'********************************************************************
#If Win32 Then
Private Declare Function GetClassName Lib "user32" _
    Alias "GetClassNameA" (ByVal hWnd&, ByVal lpClassName$, _
    ByVal nMaxCount As Long) As Long
#Else
Private Declare Function GetClassName Lib "User" _
    (ByVal hWnd%, ByVal lpClassName$, ByVal nMaxCount%) As Integer
#End If
'********************************************************************
' Window Coordinates, Points and Handles
'********************************************************************
#If Win32 Then
Private Declare Sub ClientToScreen Lib "user32" _
    (ByVal hWnd As Long, lpPoint As PointAPI)
Private Declare Sub GetWindowRect Lib "user32" _
    (ByVal hWnd As Long, lpRect As RECT)
Private Declare Function WindowFromPoint Lib "user32" (ByVal _
    ptScreenX As Long, ByVal ptScreenY As Long) As Long
#Else
Private Declare Sub ClientToScreen Lib "User" _
    (ByVal hWnd%, lpPoint As PointAPI)
Private Declare Sub GetWindowRect Lib "User" (ByVal hWnd%, _
    lpRect As RECT)
Private Declare Function WindowFromPoint% Lib "User" _
    (ByVal ptScreen&)
#End If
```

```
'********************************************************************
' Window Device Contexts
'********************************************************************
#If Win32 Then
Private Declare Function GetWindowDC& Lib "user32" _
    (ByVal hWnd As Long)
Private Declare Function ReleaseDC Lib "user32" _
    (ByVal hWnd As Long, ByVal hdc As Long) As Long
#Else
Private Declare Function GetWindowDC Lib "User" _
    (ByVal hWnd%) As Integer
Private Declare Function ReleaseDC% Lib "User" _
    (ByVal hWnd%, ByVal hdc%)
#End If
'********************************************************************
' Brushes and Painting
'********************************************************************
#If Win32 Then
Private Declare Function GetStockObject& Lib "gdi32" _
    (ByVal nIndex&)
Private Declare Function CreatePen Lib "gdi32" (ByVal nPenStyle&, _
    ByVal nWidth&, ByVal crColor&) As Long
Private Declare Function SetROP2 Lib "gdi32" (ByVal hdc As Long, _
    ByVal nDrawMode As Long) As Long
Private Declare Function Rectangle Lib "gdi32" _
    (ByVal hdc&, ByVal X1&, ByVal Y1&, ByVal X2&, _
    ByVal Y2&) As Long
Private Declare Function SelectObject Lib "gdi32" _
    (ByVal hdc As Long, ByVal hObject As Long) As Long
Private Declare Function DeleteObject& Lib "gdi32" _
    (ByVal hObject&)
#Else
Private Declare Function GetStockObject% Lib "GDI" (ByVal nIndex%)
Private Declare Function CreatePen Lib "GDI" (ByVal nPenStyle%, _
    ByVal nWidth%, ByVal crColor&) As Integer
Private Declare Function SetROP2 Lib "GDI" (ByVal hdc As Integer, _
    ByVal nDrawMode As Integer) As Integer
Private Declare Function Rectangle Lib "GDI" _
    (ByVal hdc%, ByVal X1%, _
    ByVal Y1%, ByVal X2%, ByVal Y2%) As Integer
Private Declare Function SelectObject Lib "GDI" (ByVal hdc%, _
    ByVal hObject%) As Integer
Private Declare Function DeleteObject% Lib "GDI" (ByVal hObject%)
#End If
'********************************************************************
' Misc. API Functions
'********************************************************************
#If Win32 Then
Private Declare Function SendMessage Lib "user32" _
    Alias "SendMessageA" (ByVal hWnd As Long, _
    ByVal wMsg As Long, ByVal wParam As Long, lParam As Any) _
    As Long
Private Declare Function SetFocusAPI Lib "user32" Alias _
    "SetFocus" (ByVal hWnd As Long) As Long
```

(continues)

Listing 27.8 Continued

```
Private Declare Sub InvalidateRect Lib "user32" (ByVal hWnd&, _
    lpRect As Any, ByVal bErase As Long)
Private Declare Function GetSystemMetrics& Lib "user32" _
    (ByVal nIndex&)
#Else
Private Declare Function GetSystemMetrics% Lib "User" _
    (ByVal nIndex%)
Private Declare Function SendMessage Lib "User" (ByVal hWnd%, _
    ByVal wMsg As Integer, ByVal wParam%, lParam As Any) As Long
Private Declare Function SetFocusAPI Lib "User" Alias "SetFocus" _
    (ByVal hWnd%) As Integer
Private Declare Sub InvalidateRect Lib "User" _
    (ByVal hWnd%, lpRect As Any, ByVal bErase%)
#End If
'*********************************************************************
' Private API Constants
'*********************************************************************
Private Const WM_USER = &H400
Private Const WM_SETTEXT = &HC
```

CaptureWindows (listing 27.9) is the most important function in the module because it contains the interface that enables the user to point and capture or exchange text from any window on the screen. The function gets the calling form's window handle (hWnd) and handles the Start, Move, and End events.

Listing 27.9 CaptureWindows Enables Users to Point to the Window of Their Choice

```
'*********************************************************************
' This function communicates with the main form to send or receive
' text to or from a window.
'*********************************************************************
Public Function CaptureWindows(Mode$, FormName As Form, x!, y!, _
                                    ByVal SendText$) As String
#If Win32 Then
    Dim res&, retStr$, pt As PointAPI, wrd&, FormHwnd&, CurHwnd&
    Static PrevScaleMode%, LasthWnd&
#Else
    Dim res%, retStr$, pt As PointAPI, wrd&, FormHwnd%, CurHwnd%
    Static PrevScaleMode%, LasthWnd%
#End If

    FormHwnd = FormName.hWnd

    Select Case Mode
```

Start (listing 27.10) performs some initialization steps and uses SetCapture to capture MouseMove events over the entire Windows desktop to the calling form.

Listing 27.10   The Start Event

```
...
Case "Start"
        '***************************************************************
        ' Set the scalemode to pixels.
        '***************************************************************
        PrevScaleMode = FormName.ScaleMode
        FormName.ScaleMode = vbPixels
        '***************************************************************
        ' Turn on the PointMode and mouse capture.
        '***************************************************************
        FormName.Visible = False
        If SetCapture(FormHwnd) Then Screen.MousePointer = _
            vbUpArrow
        CaptureWindows = "Start"
```

Move (listing 27.11) uses WindowFromPoint to determine the handle of the window under the mouse pointer. If the handle of the window differs from that of the last window, Move draws an inverted box around the window.

Listing 27.11   The Move Event

```
...
Case "Move"
        If GetCapture() Then
                '*********************************************************
                ' Store the current points into a POINTAPI struct.
                '*********************************************************
                pt.x = x
                pt.y = y
                '*********************************************************
                ' Change coordinates in pt into screen coordinates.
                '*********************************************************
                ClientToScreen FormHwnd, pt
        #If Win32 Then
                '*********************************************************
                ' Get the window that is under the mouse pointer.
                '*********************************************************
                CurHwnd = WindowFromPoint(pt.x, pt.y)
        #Else
                '*********************************************************
                ' Convert the points into a WORD,
                ' so they may be used later
                '*********************************************************
```

(continues)

Listing 27.11   Continued

```
                    wrd = CLng(pt.y) * &H10000 Or pt.x
                    '********************************************************
                    ' Get the window that is under the mouse pointer.
                    '********************************************************
                    CurHwnd = WindowFromPoint(wrd)
            #End If
                    '********************************************************
                    ' Only redraw if there is a new active window.
                    '********************************************************
                    If CurHwnd <> LasthWnd Then
                        '****************************************************
                        ' If there is a LasthWnd, then restore it.
                        '****************************************************
                        If LasthWnd Then InvertTracker LasthWnd
                        '****************************************************
                        ' Draw a border around the current window, and
                        ' remember the last hWnd.
                        '****************************************************
                        InvertTracker CurHwnd
                        LasthWnd = CurHwnd
                    End If
                End If
```

The most important part of this procedure is End (listing 27.12), which restores the screen back to normal and either grabs or sends text to or from the
window under the cursor.

Listing 27.12   The End Event

```
        ...
        Case "End"
                '************************************************************
                ' Restore the last window's border, and refresh the screen
                ' to remove any ghosts that may have appeared.
                '************************************************************
                RefreshScreen
                '************************************************************
                ' Exchange the data, and return a result.
                '************************************************************
                CaptureWindows = ExchangeData(LasthWnd, SendText)
                '************************************************************
                ' Clear the public variable to indicate that there is
                ' no LasthWnd because ALL windows are restored.
                '************************************************************
                LasthWnd = 0
                '************************************************************
                ' If the form has the capture, then release it.
                '************************************************************
                If GetCapture() = FormHwnd Then ReleaseCapture
                '************************************************************
```

```
                        ' Restore ScaleMode and the MousePointer.
                        '**********************************************************
                        FormName.ScaleMode = PrevScaleMode
                        FormName.Visible = True
                        Screen.MousePointer = vbDefault
              End Select
        End Function
```

The ExchangeData function (listing 27.13) performs the physical data exchange between your application and another application. The function
begins by declaring some API constants and determining the type of control
to which the user is pointing. After determining the control's type,
ExchangeData sends a message requesting text from the control.

Listing 27.13   The ExchangeData Function

```
'****************************************************************************
' This is the magic cookie of this module. It takes a handle and
' sends or receives text to and from standard windows controls.
'****************************************************************************
Public Function ExchangeData(ByVal TaskHandle&, PasteText$) _
      As String
#If Win32 Then
      Dim i&, res&, buffer$, retStr$, LastIdx&, CtrlType$
      Const LB_GETTEXT = &H189
      Const LB_GETTEXTLEN = &H18A
      Const LB_GETCOUNT = &H18B
      Const CB_GETLBTEXT = &H148
      Const CB_GETLBTEXTLEN = &H149
      Const CB_GETCOUNT = &H146
      Const WM_GETTEXT = &HD
#Else
      Dim i%, res%, buffer$, retStr$, LastIdx%, CtrlType$
      Const LB_GETTEXT = WM_USER + 10
      Const LB_GETTEXTLEN = WM_USER + 11
      Const LB_GETCOUNT = WM_USER + 12
      Const CB_GETLBTEXT = WM_USER + 8
      Const CB_GETLBTEXTLEN = WM_USER + 9
      Const CB_GETCOUNT = WM_USER + 6
      Const WM_GETTEXT = &HD
#End If
      '****************************************************************
      ' Find out the class type of the control.
      '****************************************************************
      CtrlType = GetClass(TaskHandle)
```

Although the way that you communicate with each window's control type is
similar, subtle differences exist that require that you handle each type of
control separately. You handle combo and list boxes in the same way, except

that they use different API constants. The key to capturing a list is to find out how many items are in it (using ?B_GETCOUNT) and capture each line individually (using GETTEXT) by iterating through the list. The code in listing 27.14 demonstrates how you determine this number.

Listing 27.14   Capturing Text from a List

```
...
'*****************************************************************
' If it is a combo box, use combo functions to communicate.
'*****************************************************************
If InStr(CtrlType, "Combo") Then
    '*****************************************************************
    ' Find out how many items are in the combo box.
    '*****************************************************************
    LastIdx = SendMessage(TaskHandle, CB_GETCOUNT, 0, 0&) - 1
    '*****************************************************************
    ' Iterate through the combo to retrieve every item.
    '*****************************************************************
    For i = 0 To LastIdx
        '*****************************************************************
        ' Find out how long the current item is, and build a
        ' buffer large enough to hold it.
        '*****************************************************************
        buffer = Space(SendMessage(TaskHandle, _
            CB_GETLBTEXTLEN, i, 0&) + 1)
        '*****************************************************************
        ' Prevent overflow errors.
        '*****************************************************************
        If Len(retStr) + Len(buffer) - 1 > 32000 Then Exit For
        '*****************************************************************
        ' Get the item from the combo box.
        '*****************************************************************
        res = SendMessage(TaskHandle, CB_GETLBTEXT, i, _
                        ByVal buffer)
        '*****************************************************************
        ' Trim the null terminator, and append it to retStr.
        '*****************************************************************
        retStr = retStr & Left(buffer, res) & vbCrLf
    Next i
    '*****************************************************************
    ' Return your results to the calling procedure, and exit.
    '*****************************************************************
    ExchangeData = retStr
    Exit Function
'*****************************************************************
' If it is a list box, then use list functions.
'*****************************************************************
ElseIf InStr(CtrlType, "List") Then
    '*****************************************************************
    ' Find out how many items are in the list box.
    '*****************************************************************
    LastIdx = SendMessage(TaskHandle, LB_GETCOUNT, 0, 0&) - 1
```

```
'***********************************************************
' Iterate through the list to retrieve every item.
'***********************************************************
For i = 0 To LastIdx
    '***********************************************************
    ' Find out how long the current item is, and build a
    ' buffer large enough to hold it.
    '***********************************************************
    buffer = Space(SendMessage(TaskHandle, _
                LB_GETTEXTLEN, i, 0&) + 1)
    '***********************************************************
    ' Prevent overflow errors.
    '***********************************************************
    If Len(retStr) + Len(buffer) - 1 > 32000 Then Exit For
    '***********************************************************
    ' Get the item from the list box.
    '***********************************************************
    res = SendMessage(TaskHandle, LB_GETTEXT, i, _
            ByVal buffer)
    '***********************************************************
    ' Trim the null terminator, and append it to retStr.
    '***********************************************************
    retStr = retStr & Left(buffer, res) & vbCrLf
Next i
'***********************************************************
' Return your results to the calling procedure, and exit.
'***********************************************************
ExchangeData = retStr
Exit Function
```

If the control isn't a combo or list box, then try WM_GETTEXT or WM_SETTEXT (see listing 27.15). These messages work on most standard Windows controls and some nonstandard controls.

Listing 27.15   Using the WM_GETTEXT or WM_SETTEXT Messages

```
...
'*********************************************************************
' Otherwise, try WM_GETTEXT and WM_SETTEXT.
'*********************************************************************
Else
    '***********************************************************
    ' If paste text is empty, then retrieve text.
    '***********************************************************
    If PasteText = "" Then
        '***********************************************************
        ' Build a huge buffer, and get it.
        '***********************************************************
        retStr = Space(32000)
        res = SendMessage(TaskHandle, WM_GETTEXT, _
            Len(retStr), ByVal retStr)
        '***********************************************************
```

(continues)

```
Listing 27.15   Continued
                    ' Keep all text to the left of the null terminator.
                    '********************************************************
                    ExchangeData = Left(retStr, res)
                    Exit Function
            '********************************************************
            ' Otherwise, send text to the window.
            '********************************************************
            Else
                    '********************************************************
                    ' If the window is an edit box, then paste text to it.
                    ' Otherwise don't. This prevents you from changing the
                    ' captions of labels, buttons, etc...
                    '********************************************************
                    If InStr(CtrlType, "Edit") Or _
                             InStr(CtrlType, "Text") Then
                            '********************************************************
                            ' Put the text into the window, and activate it.
                            '********************************************************
                            SendMessage TaskHandle, WM_SETTEXT, 0, _
                                    ByVal PasteText
                            SetFocusAPI TaskHandle
                            '********************************************************
                            ' Return the num of chars pasted.
                            '********************************************************
                            ExchangeData = Format(Len(PasteText))
                    Else
                            ExchangeData = Format(0)
                    End If
                    Exit Function
            End If
    End If
```

The next code segment is only called if ExchangeData cannot communicate with the control to which the user was pointing. Send the calling function some flaky error message so it can be distinguished from a valid return string.

```
    ...
    '****************************************************************
    ' If you got here, then this function is unsuccessful.
    '****************************************************************
    ' I use an obscure return string that I'll recognize, to keep
    ' my code from getting confused with valid return values.
    '****************************************************************
    ExchangeData = "Error:" & String(10, "~")

End Function
```

GetClass simply returns the class name of a window:

```
'****************************************************************
' Returns the class name of a window.
'****************************************************************
Private Function GetClass(ByVal TaskHandle&) As String
Dim res&, Classname$
```

```
'*********************************************************
' Get the class name of the window.
'*********************************************************
    Classname = Space$(32000)
    res = GetClassName(TaskHandle, Classname, Len(Classname))
    GetClass = Left$(Classname, res)
End Function
```

The InvertTracker procedure (listing 27.16) draws an inverted box around a window to indicate visually to the user the window with which he or she is about to communicate. This procedure simply gets a handle to the window's device context (an hDC) and draws the inverted box around it.

Listing 27.16   The InvertTracker Procedure

```
'************************************************************************
' Draws an inverted hatched line on two sizes of a window.
'************************************************************************
#If Win32 Then
Private Sub InvertTracker(hwndDest As Long)
    Dim hdcDest&, hPen&, hOldPen&, hOldBrush&
    Dim cxBorder&, cxFrame&, cyFrame&, cxScreen&, cyScreen&
#Else
Private Sub InvertTracker(hwndDest As Integer)
    Dim hdcDest%, hPen%, hOldPen%, hOldBrush%
    Dim cxBorder%, cxFrame%, cyFrame%, cxScreen%, cyScreen%
#End If
Const NULL_BRUSH = 5
Const R2_NOT = 6
Const PS_INSIDEFRAME = 6
Dim rc As RECT
    '********************************************************************
    ' Get some windows dimensions.
    '********************************************************************
    cxScreen = GetSystemMetrics(0)
    cyScreen = GetSystemMetrics(1)
    cxBorder = GetSystemMetrics(5)
    cxFrame = GetSystemMetrics(32)
    cyFrame = GetSystemMetrics(33)
    '********************************************************************
    ' Get the device context for the current window.
    '********************************************************************
    hdcDest = GetWindowDC(hwndDest)
    '********************************************************************
    ' Get the size of the window.
    '********************************************************************
    GetWindowRect hwndDest, rc
    '********************************************************************
    ' Create a new pen and select it (and a stock brush) into the
    ' device context.
    '********************************************************************
```

(continues)

```
Listing 27.16   Continued

      SetROP2 hdcDest, R2_NOT
      hPen = CreatePen(PS_INSIDEFRAME, 3 * cxBorder, RGB(0, 0, 0))
      '*************************************************************
      ' Get the size of the window.
      '*************************************************************
      hOldPen = SelectObject(hdcDest, hPen)
      hOldBrush = SelectObject(hdcDest, GetStockObject(NULL_BRUSH))
      '*************************************************************
      ' Draw a box around the selected window.
      '*************************************************************
      Rectangle hdcDest, 0, 0, rc.Right - rc.Left, _
          rc.Bottom - rc.Top
      '*************************************************************
      ' Restore the old brush and pen.
      '*************************************************************
      SelectObject hdcDest, hOldBrush
      SelectObject hdcDest, hOldPen
      '*************************************************************
      ' Release the device context back to its owner.
      '*************************************************************
      ReleaseDC hwndDest, hdcDest
      '*************************************************************
      ' Delete the hatched brush.
      '*************************************************************
      DeleteObject hPen
  End Sub
```

A call to InvalidateRect with null parameters results in repainting the entire screen. CaptureWindows does this repainting just in case it left any ghost lines. Here is the call to InvalidateRect:

```
      '*************************************************************
      ' Force the entire screen to be repainted immediately.
      '*************************************************************
      Private Sub RefreshScreen()
          InvalidateRect 0, 0&, True
      End Sub
```

FRMSTUB.FRM, the user interface for STUBBORN.VBP, provides the command buttons' functional code. It begins by setting up some necessary declarations and doing some form initialization routines. Next, the program lists a helper function, FileExists, followed by the Text1_Change event, which enables or disables the Send Text to a Window button. Listing 27.17 shows FRMSTUB.FRM.

Listing 27.17 FRMSTUB.FRM, the User Interface for STUBBORN.VBP

```
'*******************************************************************
' FRMSTUB.FRM: This program demonstrates how to communicate
'                with apps that don't respond via DDE or OLE.
'*******************************************************************
Option Explicit
'*******************************************************************
' Form-level 16- & 32-bit API declarations.
'*******************************************************************
#If Win32 Then
Private Const PROCESS_QUERY_INFORMATION = &H400
Private Const STILL_ACTIVE = &H103
Private Declare Function OpenProcess& Lib "kernel32" (ByVal _
    dwDesiredAccess&, ByVal bInheritHandle&, ByVal dwProcessId&)
Private Declare Function GetExitCodeProcess Lib "kernel32" (ByVal _
    hProcess As Long, lpExitCode As Long) As Long
Private Declare Function LoadCursor Lib "user32" Alias _
    "LoadCursorA" (ByVal hInstance&, ByVal lpCursor&) As Long
Private Declare Function DrawIcon Lib "user32" _
    (ByVal hdc As Long, ByVal x As Long, ByVal y As Long, _
    ByVal hIcon As Long) As Long
Private Const IDC_UPARROW = 32516&
#Else
Private Declare Function GetModuleUsage% Lib "Kernel" _
    (ByVal hModule%)
#End If
'*******************************************************************
' Form-level variables.
'*******************************************************************
Private SendIt As Boolean, PointMode As Boolean
'*******************************************************************
' Form Initialization.
'*******************************************************************
Private Sub Form_Load()
'*******************************************************************
' Exchanging data is totally different in Win32, so readjust the
' visual appearance of the form for it.  Win16 uses the default
' configuration set at design time.
'*******************************************************************
#If Win32 Then
Dim iX%, iY%, iDrawX%
    '*************************************************************
    ' Change the ScaleMode to pixels and turn on AutoRedraw
    '*************************************************************
    ScaleMode = vbPixels
    AutoRedraw = True
    '*************************************************************
    ' Hide controls for use with Win16 and display Win32 controls.
    '*************************************************************
    cmd(0).Visible = False
    cmd(1).Visible = False
    Frame1.Visible = True
    '*************************************************************
    ' Build positioning variables and set CurrentX & CurrentY
```

(continues)

Listing 27.17   Continued

```
    '***************************************************************
    iX = Frame1.Left + Frame1.Width
    CurrentX = iX
    iDrawX = iX + ((ScaleWidth - iX) / 2) + 10
    iY = Text1.Top + Text1.Height
    iY = iY + ((ScaleHeight - (Frame1.Top + Frame1.Height)) _
        / 2) + 5
    CurrentY = iY
    '***************************************************************
    ' Draw MousePointer vbUpArrow
    ' into the form's persistent bitmap.
    '***************************************************************
    DrawIcon hdc, iDrawX, iY, LoadCursor(0, IDC_UPARROW)
    '***************************************************************
    ' Give the user some instructions
    ' about why the arrow is painted
    ' on the form.
    '***************************************************************
    Print "  Click & drag this arrow ->"
    CurrentX = iX
    Print "  to exhange data."
#End If
    '***************************************************************
    ' Hide controls for use with Win32 and display Win16 controls.
    '***************************************************************
    cmd(0).Visible = True
    cmd(1).Visible = True
    Frame1.Visible = False
    '***************************************************************
    ' Centers the form to the screen
    '***************************************************************
    Move (Screen.Width - Width) / 2, (Screen.Height - Height) / 2
End Sub
'***************************************************************
' This function checks to see if a file exists.
'***************************************************************
Private Function FileExists(FileName$) As Boolean
    On Error Resume Next
    FileExists = IIf(Dir(FileName) <> "", True, False)
End Function
'***************************************************************
' Only enable cmd(1) when it contains text.
'***************************************************************
Private Sub Text1_Change()
    cmd(1).Enabled = IIf(Text1 = "", False, True)
End Sub
```

cmd_Click processes command-button clicks. The action code for the first two buttons is in EXCHANGE.BAS's CaptureWindows function, which contains the code for cmd(2):

```
'******************************************************************
' Process command-button clicks.
'******************************************************************
Private Sub cmd_Click(Index As Integer)
Dim hNotepad&, Source%, FileName$, msg$, Handle&, ExitCode&
    Select Case Index
        Case 0 ' Get
            SendIt = False
            PointMode = True
            CaptureWindows "Start", Me, 0, 0, ""
        Case 1 ' Send
            SendIt = True
            PointMode = True
            CaptureWindows "Start", Me, 0, 0, ""
```

The SendKeys button (listing 27.18) starts Notepad, enters some text, and
waits for the user to save the file and close Notepad. After Notepad stops
running, the function continues by opening the data file and inserting it into
Text1. Although not the best way to communicate with an application, the
scheme certainly presents a valid, possible solution.

Listing 27.18   Handling the SendKeys Button

```
        ...
    Case 2 ' Use SendKeys
            '******************************************************
            ' Build a temporary file name.
            ' Kill it if it already exists.
            '******************************************************
            FileName = App.Path & "\~test~.txt"
            If FileExists(FileName) Then Kill FileName
            '******************************************************
            ' Run Notepad maximized with the new file
            ' and store its task handle into a variable
            ' for later use.
            '******************************************************
            hNotepad = Shell("notepad.exe " & FileName, _
                            vbNormalFocus)
            '******************************************************
            ' This statement hits Enter to create the new file.
            '******************************************************
            SendKeys "~", True
            '******************************************************
            ' Build an instruction screen and insert it
            ' into Notepad.
            '******************************************************
            msg = "Enter your text in here." & vbCrLf
            msg = msg & "When you are done, quit "
            msg = msg & "Notepad and save your changes."
            SendKeys msg, True
            '******************************************************
            ' Finally, highlight the instructions so the user can
            ' easily delete them.
```

(continues)

Listing 27.18 Continued

```
'*******************************************************
        SendKeys "^+{Home}", True
'*******************************************************
        ' Wait while Notepad is still open.
'*******************************************************
#If Win32 Then
        Handle = OpenProcess(PROCESS_QUERY_INFORMATION, _
                             False, hNotepad)
        Do
            GetExitCodeProcess Handle, ExitCode
            DoEvents
        Loop While ExitCode = STILL_ACTIVE
#Else
        Do While GetModuleUsage(hNotepad)
            DoEvents
        Loop
#End If
'*******************************************************
        ' Once Notepad is unloaded, open the file and insert
        ' it into Text1.
'*******************************************************
        Source = FreeFile
        Open FileName For Input As Source
            Text1 = Input(LOF(Source), Source)
        Close Source
'*******************************************************
        ' Kill the temporary file.
'*******************************************************
        Kill FileName
    End Select
End Sub
```

The next two procedures, MouseDown and MouseMove, execute only while the application is capturing the mouse. During this time, the application draws a box around the window to which the user is pointing. When the user chooses a window, the program calls ExchangeData. Listing 27.19 shows the code for these two procedures.

Listing 27.19 The MouseDown and MouseMove Events

```
'***********************************************************************
' Win32 version of SetCapture requires the left mouse button to be
' depressed in order to capture data from other processes and the
' MouseUp event automatically does a ReleaseCapture.
' This difference requires totally different code
' (and a different UI).
'***********************************************************************
#If Win32 Then
    Private Sub Form_MouseDown(Button As Integer, Shift%, x!, y!)
```

```
'****************************************************************
' If opt(0) is checked, then send the text from Text1
' using the code already in cmd(0)'s click event.
' Otherwise, get text from another window using
' cmd(1)'s code.
'****************************************************************
    If opt(0) Then
        cmd_Click 0
    Else
        cmd_Click 1
    End If
End Sub
'****************************************************************
' Stop capturing and exchange the text
' on the Form_MouseUp event.
'****************************************************************
    Private Sub Form_MouseUp(Button As Integer, Shift%, x!, y!)
        HandleMouse Button, Shift, x, y
    End Sub
'****************************************************************
' 16-bit version of MouseDown. MouseUp is ignored.
'****************************************************************
#Else
'****************************************************************
' Stop capturing and exchange the text
' on the Form_MouseDown event
'****************************************************************
    Private Sub Form_MouseDown(Button As Integer, Shift%, x!, y!)
        HandleMouse Button, Shift, x, y
    End Sub
#End If
'****************************************************************
' Mouse code is the same for Win16 & Win32, but it's called in
' different locations on the two platforms. Rather than repeating
' code, this code is entered once and called from the appropriate
' event.
'****************************************************************
Private Sub HandleMouse(Button As Integer, Shift%, x!, y!)
Dim errStr$, retStr$
'****************************************************************
' Build a string that matches the return error value.
'****************************************************************
    errStr = "Error:" & String(10, "~")
'****************************************************************
' Get text from a window.
'****************************************************************
    If PointMode And SendIt = False Then
        retStr = CaptureWindows("End", Me, x, y, "")
        If retStr = errStr Then
            MsgBox "Sorry, but that control didn't respond!", 48
        Else
            Text1 = retStr
        End If
        PointMode = False
'****************************************************************
```

(continues)

Listing 27.19   Continued

```
    ' Send text to a window.
    '*****************************************************************
    ElseIf PointMode And SendIt Then
        retStr = CaptureWindows("End", Me, x, y, Text1)
        If retStr = "0" Or retStr = errStr Then
            MsgBox _
            "Sorry, but that control will not accept text!", 48
        End If
        PointMode = False
    End If
End Sub
'*****************************************************************
' During the PointMode, this window receives a mouse move
' for the entire desktop. This function causes a new highlight
' to be drawn.
'*****************************************************************
Private Sub Form_MouseMove(Button As Integer, Shift%, x!, y!)
    If GetCapture() Then CaptureWindows "Move", Me, x, y, ""
End Sub
'*****************************************************************
' Only enable cmd(1) when it contains text.
'*****************************************************************
Private Sub Text1_Change()
    cmd(1).Enabled = IIf(Text1 = "", False, True)
End Sub
```

Stubborn is a good sample program to use to test whether you can communicate with other applications. If Stubborn can't enable you to communicate with another application, you should contact the application's vendor to see whether you can try anything else. Finally, if all else fails, consider rewriting the application yourself. Although this isn't a great solution, it is necessary sometimes.

From Here...

Unfortunately, few resources are available that cover communications with other Microsoft applications. Of those that exist, however, the best include the following:

■ *Microsoft Windows SDK Programmer's Guide,* Volumes 1, 2, and 4 (Microsoft Press), contains important information on several key libraries, API calls, and file formats. Although these books are difficult to understand, if you dig long enough you often can find helpful information.

- *Visual Basic Programmer's Guide to the Windows API* (Ziff-Davis, 1994), by Daniel Appleman, will be your bible if you decide to explore extensive API programming with Visual Basic. In fact, I used this reference as I wrote the Stubborn sample application.

Chapter 28

Integration with Multiple Office Applications

Eventually you will need to build an application that uses more than one Microsoft Office application. This project will probably involve a large programming team and will require weeks (or even months) to complete.

In this chapter, you learn how to do the following:

- Use a generic database class that simplifies how to use data access objects (DAO)

- Use a rectangle class that eliminates the need for three-dimensional (3-D) controls and improves performance

- Create an application-independent way of returning to your main form from another application

- Perform OLE Automation on an embedded chart so that it reflects the changes in a database

- Play .WAV files from a resource file

- Draw pictures from a resource by using PaintPicture

- Create your own 3-D buttons using graphics methods and a picture box

- Create shareable and reusable objects

Creating a Large-Scale Integrated Application

This chapter's example, UseAll, is an integrated application that encompasses the most common obstacles to developing large-scale programs. This relatively small application doesn't do anything particularly useful except demonstrate some powerful techniques. Also, by using application-independent objects, the application demonstrates the importance of reusability.

Before viewing this application's code, this section presents the UseAll application's user interface. Figures 28.1 through 28.8 display the elements of this application's user interface. The figure captions describe the purpose of each element. This interface is designed to help a program manager accomplish the following:

- Plan the amount of time and resources that it will take to complete the project

- Analyze bugs that have been reported on the company's products

- Provide a consistent method for entering these bug reports into a bug database

- Edit and view a PowerPoint presentation that communicates your project's progress to upper management

Fig. 28.1
The interface's main window provides access to all the application's features.

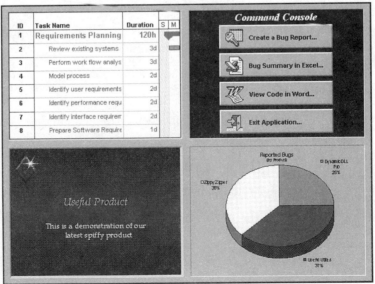

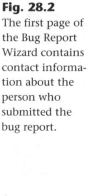

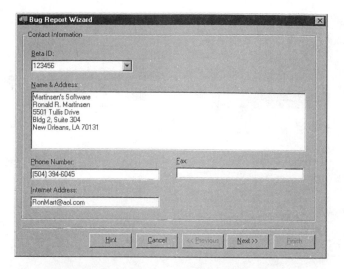

Fig. 28.2

The first page of the Bug Report Wizard contains contact information about the person who submitted the bug report.

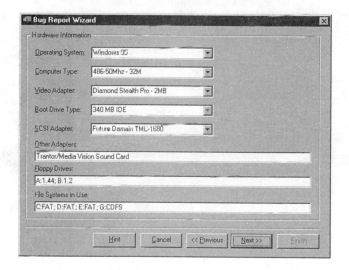

Fig. 28.3

The second page of the Bug Report Wizard contains system information about the person who submitted the bug report.

Fig. 28.4
The final page of
the Bug Report
Wizard is the
actual bug-
reporting form
used by all the
applications that
this company
distributes.

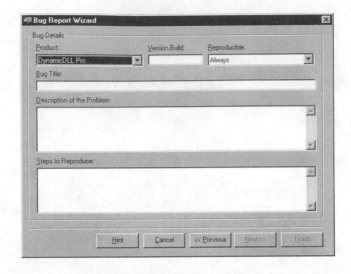

Fig. 28.5
UseAll sends a bug
summary to Excel
for further
analysis.

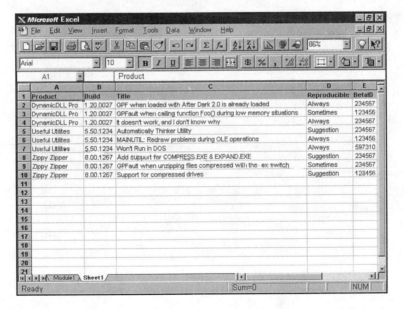

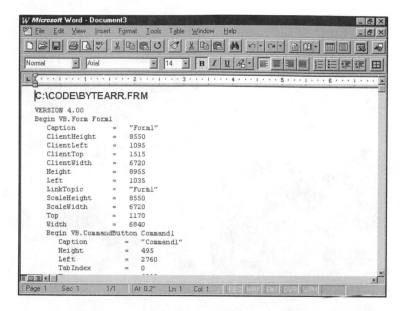

Fig. 28.6
Instead of viewing code as text, UseAll formats the text in Word for easy viewing.

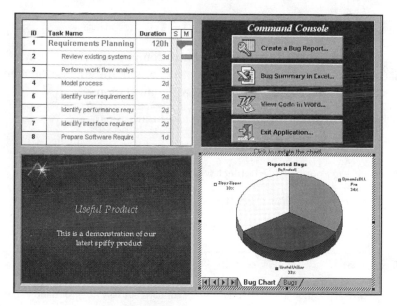

Fig. 28.7
When a user clicks the embedded chart, UseAll automatically updates the chart by using OLE Automation and in-place activation.

Integrating with Office

IV

Fig. 28.8
The user can edit Project and PowerPoint objects by right-clicking on the object and then choosing a verb.

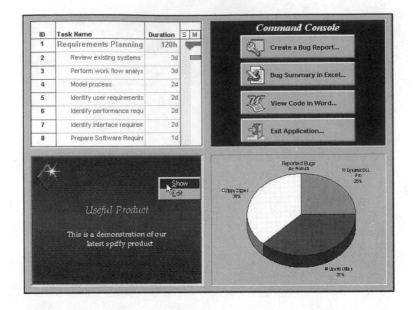

Putting It All Together

This small application encompasses the most common obstacles of such projects. Although it doesn't do anything very useful, the application demonstrates how you can accomplish the following integration tasks:

- Using OLE Automation with Word for Windows 6.0

- Using OLE Automation to analyze data from an Excel database

- Updating an embedded object with external data

- Using embedded PowerPoint and Project objects

- Creating a wizard for entering database data

Caution

The sample application in this chapter, UseAll, contains virtually no error handling, in the interest of keeping the example simple. However, you should *never* release an application without extensive error handling. Chapter 29, "Distributing Integrated Applications," demonstrates proper error-handling techniques.

> **Note**
>
> Don't panic when you see code listing for this example. Although the listing is rather long, most of the code is relatively simple. Also, previous chapters have already discussed about 80 percent of the techniques that this example demonstrates. If you just take the application one file at a time, you shouldn't have any trouble understanding the material that the code presents.

SHARED.BAS—a Common Module

SHARED.BAS (listing 28.1) contains code that two or more files in this project use. The code provides a way for this project's files to set a window's AlwaysOnTop status and enables the application to show or hide a splash form.

> **Caution**
>
> The SetWindowPos API call used by the AlwaysOnTop routine in SHARED.BAS does not work while you are running this sample within the Visual Basic 4.0 IDE. However, when you compile your application and run it outside of the IDE, it will work as expected.

Listing 28.1   SHARED.BAS: Common Modules Are Useful for Application-Independence and Code Sharing

```
'*****************************************************************
' SHARED.BAS - This module contains code that is shared
'              by two or more modules.
'*****************************************************************
Option Explicit
'*****************************************************************
' Declare SetWindowPos for AlwaysOnTop.
'*****************************************************************
#If Win32 Then
Private Declare Function SetWindowPos Lib "user32" (ByVal hWnd&, _
     ByVal y As Long,ByVal cx As Long, ByVal cy As Long, _
     ByVal wFlags As Long) As Boolean
#Else
Private Declare Function SetWindowPos Lib "User" (ByVal hWnd%, _
        ByVal hb%, ByVal x%, ByVal y%, ByVal cx%, ByVal cy%, _
        ByVal FLAGS%) As Integer
#End If
'*****************************************************************
' Forces a window to stay in front of all other windows.
'*****************************************************************
Public Sub AlwaysOnTop(FormName As Form, TopMost As Boolean)
Const HWND_TOPMOST = -1
```

(continues)

Listing 28.1 Continued

```
Const HWND_NOTOPMOST = -2
Const SWP_NOSIZE = &H1
Const SWP_NOMOVE = &H2
Const FLAGS = SWP_NOMOVE Or SWP_NOSIZE
    '******************************************************************
    ' Set the window to TopMost, and ignore the return value.
    '******************************************************************
    If TopMost Then
        SetWindowPos FormName.hWnd, HWND_TOPMOST, 0, 0, 0, 0, _
        FLAGS
    '******************************************************************
    ' Otherwise, return the window to its normal nontopmost state.
    '******************************************************************
    Else
        SetWindowPos FormName.hWnd, HWND_NOTOPMOST, 0, 0, 0, 0, _
            FLAGS
    End If
End Sub
'**********************************************************************
' Displays and unloads the splash form.
'**********************************************************************
Public Sub SplashVisible(bState As Boolean, _
                         Optional ByVal sCaption)
    If bState Then
        sCaption = IIf(IsMissing(sCaption), _
        "Loading...Please Wait!", sCaption)
        With frmSplash
            .lblMessage = sCaption
            .Show
            .Refresh
        End With
    Else
        DoEvents
        Unload frmSplash
    End If
End Sub
'**********************************************************************
' This procedure draws a 3-D button (in either an up
' or down state), draws a picture, and prints a caption.
'**********************************************************************
Public Sub DrawButton(pBox As PictureBox, IsDown As Boolean, _
            IsResource As Boolean, Optional ByVal sCaption, _
            Optional ByVal sIcon)
Dim Offset%, where%, sTag$
    '******************************************************************
    ' If the button is supposed to be down, offset it by 2 pixels.
    '******************************************************************
    On Error Resume Next
    If IsDown Then Offset = 2
    '******************************************************************
```

```
' The tag can contain a caption and a name of an sIcon.
' The format is "sCaption¦sIcon". If a caption and icon were
' provided, then the tag is ignored.
'****************************************************************
sTag = Trim(pBox.Tag)
where = InStr(sTag, "¦")
If sTag <> "" Then
    sCaption = IIf(IsMissing(sCaption), _
    Left(sTag, where - 1), sCaption)
    sIcon = IIf(IsMissing(sIcon), Mid(sTag, where + 1), sIcon)
Else
    sCaption = IIf(IsMissing(sCaption), "", sCaption)
    sIcon = IIf(IsMissing(sIcon), "", sIcon)
End If
'****************************************************************
' Clear the picture box, and redraw the 3-D effect.
'****************************************************************
pBox.Cls
Draw3DPicBorder pBox, IsDown
'****************************************************************
' Paint the picture from a file, or icon resource, then
' vertically center position for the caption.
'****************************************************************
With pBox
    If IsResource Then
        .PaintPicture LoadResPicture(sIcon, vbResIcon), 10, _
            ((pBox.Height / 2) - 16) + Offset
    Else
        .PaintPicture LoadPicture(sIcon), 10, 4 + Offset
    End If
    .CurrentY = (pBox.Height / 2) - _
                (pBox.TextHeight("X") / 2) + Offset
    .CurrentX = 52
End With
'****************************************************************
' Draw the caption.
'****************************************************************
pBox.Print sCaption
End Sub
```

QUADRANT.BAS—Creating and Manipulating a Form's Region

QUADRANT.BAS manipulates one of four regions on a form. The module starts with GetQuadrants, which divides the form into four equal regions, starting from the upper-left corner and incrementing the regions from left to right and top to bottom. The drawing functions that follow simply enable you to perform drawing methods (some of which are predefined) on any of a form's four regions. Table 28.1 describes the remaining helper functions and their purpose. Listing 28.2 is the code for QUADRANT.BAS.

Table 28.1 QUADRANT.BAS Helper Functions

Helper Function	Description
EqualToQuadClient	Checks whether a given control is equal to the client area of a rectangle
GetQuad	Sets a given RECT variable to the value of an existing quadrant
GetRectWidth	Returns a rectangle's width
GetRectHeight	Returns a rectangle's height
MoveRect	Changes the left and top values of a rectangle without changing the right and bottom values
ResizeRect	Inflates or deflates a rectangle from all sides or from the bottom
SizeToRectClient	Resizes a control into the client area of a given rectangle

Listing 28.2 QUADRANT.BAS Is Helpful for the Cosmetics of USEALL.VBP

```
'********************************************************************
' QUADRANT.BAS - This is a special rectangle module that performs
'                several rectangle functions.
'********************************************************************
Option Explicit
'********************************************************************
' Exposé a new rectangle data type.
'********************************************************************
#If Win32 Then
Public Type RECT
    rL As Long 'Left
    rT As Long 'Top
    rR As Long 'Right (This is NOT equal to Width)
    rB As Long 'Bottom (This is NOT equal to Height)
End Type
Public Type PointAPI
        x As Long
        y As Long
End Type
#Else
Public Type RECT
    rL As Integer 'Left
    rT As Integer 'Top
    rR As Integer 'Right (This is NOT equal to Width)
    rB As Integer 'Bottom (This is NOT equal to Height)
End Type
Public Type PointAPI
        x As Integer
        y As Integer
End Type
```

```
#End If
'*********************************************************************
' API Declarations.
'*********************************************************************
#If Win32 Then
Public Declare Sub GetClientRect Lib "user32" _
    (ByVal hWnd As Long, lpRect As RECT)
Public Declare Sub InflateRect Lib "user32" (lpRect As RECT, _
    ByVal x As Long, ByVal y As Long)
Public Declare Function PtInRect Lib "user32" (lpRect As RECT, _
    ByVal ptScreenX As Long, ByVal ptScreenY As Long) As Long
Public Declare Function ClientToScreen Lib "user32" _
    (ByVal hWnd&, lpPoint As PointAPI) As Long
#Else
Public Declare Sub GetClientRect Lib "User" (ByVal hWnd%, _
    lpRect As RECT)
Public Declare Sub InflateRect Lib "User" (lpRect As RECT, _
    ByVal iX%, ByVal iY%)
Public Declare Sub ClientToScreen Lib "User" (ByVal hWnd%, _
    lpPoint As PointAPI)
Public Declare Function PtInRect Lib "User" (lpRect As RECT, _
    ByVal ptScreenY As Integer, ByVal ptScreenX As Integer) _
    As Integer
'       ptRect As PointAPI) As Integer
#End If
'*********************************************************************
' Private Module Variables
'*********************************************************************
Private Quad1 As RECT, Quad2 As RECT, Quad3 As RECT, Quad4 As RECT
'*********************************************************************
' Divides a form into 4 quadrants, starting with the upper left
' corner (Q1), and continuing clockwise.
'*********************************************************************
Public Sub GetQuadrants(FormName As Form, Q1 As RECT, _
    Q2 As RECT, Q3 As RECT, Q4 As RECT)
Dim FormWidth%, FormHeight%
    '*************************************************************
    ' The form ScaleMode MUST be in pixels!
    '*************************************************************
    FormName.ScaleMode = vbPixels
    '*************************************************************
    ' Determine the height & width of the form's client area.
    '*************************************************************
    FormWidth = FormName.ScaleWidth
    FormHeight = FormName.ScaleHeight
    '*************************************************************
    ' Set the 4 quad arguments and the module-level quads.
    '*************************************************************
    With Quad1
        .rL = 0
        .rT = 0
        .rR = FormWidth / 2
        .rB = FormHeight / 2
    End With
```

(continues)

Listing 28.2   Continued

```
        Q1 = Quad1

        With Quad2
            .rL = FormWidth / 2
            .rT = 0
            .rR = FormWidth - 1
            .rB = FormHeight / 2
        End With

        Q2 = Quad2

        With Quad3
            .rL = 0
            .rT = FormHeight / 2
            .rR = FormWidth / 2
            .rB = FormHeight - 1
        End With

        Q3 = Quad3

        With Quad4
            .rL = FormWidth / 2
            .rT = FormHeight / 2
            .rR = FormWidth - 1
            .rB = FormHeight - 1
        End With

        Q4 = Quad4
End Sub
'*********************************************************************
' Draw either a solid or hollow rectangle on a form.
'*********************************************************************
Public Sub DrawRect(FormName As Form, rRect As RECT, _
                    Solid As Boolean, Optional RectColor)
    '*************************************************************
    ' If no color is provided, then use black.
    '*************************************************************
    RectColor = IIf(IsMissing(RectColor), RGB(0, 0, 0), RectColor)
    '*************************************************************
    ' Draw the rectangle on the form.
    '*************************************************************
    If Solid Then
        FormName.Line (rRect.rL, rRect.rT)-(rRect.rR, rRect.rB), _
                                                RectColor, BF
    Else
        FormName.Line (rRect.rL, rRect.rT)-(rRect.rR, rRect.rB), _
                                                RectColor, B
    End If
End Sub
'*********************************************************************
' Draw a hollow 3-D rectangle. (Similar to the SSPanel3D control.)
'*********************************************************************
Public Sub Draw3DRect(FormName As Form, rRect As RECT, _
    Inset As Boolean)
```

```
    Dim LT&, BR&
    '***************************************************************
    ' Set the L(eft)T(op) and B(ottom)R(ight) line colors.
    '***************************************************************
    LT = IIf(Inset, vb3DShadow, vb3DHighlight)
    BR = IIf(Inset, vb3DHighlight, vb3DShadow)
    '***************************************************************
    ' Draw the 4 lines.
    '***************************************************************
    FormName.Line (rRect.rL, rRect.rT)-(rRect.rL, rRect.rB), LT
    FormName.Line (rRect.rL, rRect.rT)-(rRect.rR, rRect.rT), LT
    FormName.Line (rRect.rR, rRect.rT)-(rRect.rR, rRect.rB), BR
    FormName.Line (rRect.rL, rRect.rB)-(rRect.rR + 1, rRect.rB), _
        BR
End Sub
'*******************************************************************
' Draw a hollow 3-D rectangle. (Similar to the SSPanel3D control.)
'*******************************************************************
Public Sub Draw3DPBRect(pBox As PictureBox, rRect As RECT, _
    Inset As Boolean)
Dim LT&, BR&
    '***************************************************************
    ' Set the L(eft)T(op) and B(ottom)R(ight) line colors.
    '***************************************************************
    LT = IIf(Inset, vb3DShadow, vb3DHighlight)
    BR = IIf(Inset, vb3DHighlight, vb3DShadow)
    '***************************************************************
    ' Draw the 4 lines.
    '***************************************************************
    pBox.Line (rRect.rL, rRect.rT)-(rRect.rL, rRect.rB), LT
    pBox.Line (rRect.rL, rRect.rT)-(rRect.rR, rRect.rT), LT
    pBox.Line (rRect.rR, rRect.rT)-(rRect.rR, rRect.rB), BR
    pBox.Line (rRect.rL, rRect.rB)-(rRect.rR + 1, rRect.rB), BR
End Sub
'*******************************************************************
' Draw a hollow 3-D rectangle around the edge of the picture box.
'*******************************************************************
Public Sub Draw3DPicBorder(pBox As PictureBox, Inset As Boolean)
Dim rRect As RECT
    '***************************************************************
    ' Get the client rect of the form.
    '***************************************************************
    GetClientRect pBox.hWnd, rRect
    '***************************************************************
    ' Deflate the right & bottom of the rect by 1 pixel.
    '***************************************************************
    ResizeRect rRect, -1, -1, True
    '***************************************************************
    ' Draw the 3-D rect, and repeat again.
    '***************************************************************
    Draw3DPBRect pBox, rRect, Inset
    ResizeRect rRect, -1, -1, False
    Draw3DPBRect pBox, rRect, Inset
End Sub
'*******************************************************************
```

(continues)

Listing 28.2 Continued

```
' Draw a hollow 3-D rectangle around the edge of the form.
'******************************************************************
Public Sub Draw3DFormRect(FormName As Form, Inset As Boolean)
Dim rRect As RECT
    '******************************************************************
    ' Get the client rect of the form.
    '******************************************************************
    GetClientRect FormName.hWnd, rRect
    '******************************************************************
    ' Deflate the right & bottom of the rect by 1 pixel.
    '******************************************************************
    ResizeRect rRect, -1, -1, True
    '******************************************************************
    ' Draw the 3-D rect.
    '******************************************************************
    Draw3DRect FormName, rRect, Inset
End Sub
'******************************************************************
' Inflates or deflates a rectangle from all sides or the bottom.
'******************************************************************
Public Sub ResizeRect(rRect As RECT, iX%, iY%, _
    KeepSameLT As Boolean)
    '******************************************************************
    ' If KeepSameL(eft)T(op), then only operate on .rR & .rB.
    '******************************************************************
    If KeepSameLT Then
        rRect.rR = rRect.rR + iX
        rRect.rB = rRect.rB + iY
    '******************************************************************
    ' Otherwise inflate or deflate all 4 sides.
    '******************************************************************
    Else
        InflateRect rRect, iX, iY
    End If
End Sub
'******************************************************************
' Changes the left & top values of a rectangle.
'******************************************************************
Public Sub MoveRect(rRect As RECT, ByVal iX%, ByVal iY%)
    rRect.rL = rRect.rL + iX
    rRect.rT = rRect.rT + iY
End Sub
'******************************************************************
' Draws a 3-D grid on a form with 4 child quadrants.
'******************************************************************
Public Sub Draw3DGrid(FormName As Form, Inset As Boolean, _
                    Optional ByVal Offset)
Dim InsideOffset%, OutsideOffset%
    '******************************************************************
    ' Set the offset values.
    '******************************************************************
    On Error Resume Next
    Offset = IIf(IsMissing(Offset), 10, Offset)
    InsideOffset = Offset
```

```
    OutsideOffset = Abs(IIf(IsMissing(Offset), 5, (Offset / 2)) _
        - 1)
    '******************************************************************
    ' This is a bit redundant, but it's necessary.
    '******************************************************************
    GetQuadrants FormName, Quad1, Quad2, Quad3, Quad4
    '******************************************************************
    ' Draw the 4 3-D quadrants.
    '******************************************************************
    MoveRect Quad1, InsideOffset + 1, InsideOffset + 1
    ResizeRect Quad1, -InsideOffset, -InsideOffset, True
    Draw3DRect FormName, Quad1, Inset

    MoveRect Quad2, OutsideOffset, InsideOffset + 1
    ResizeRect Quad2, -InsideOffset - 1, -InsideOffset, True
    Draw3DRect FormName, Quad2, Inset

    MoveRect Quad3, InsideOffset + 1, OutsideOffset
    ResizeRect Quad3, -InsideOffset, -InsideOffset, True
    Draw3DRect FormName, Quad3, Inset

    MoveRect Quad4, OutsideOffset, OutsideOffset
    ResizeRect Quad4, -InsideOffset - 1, -InsideOffset, True
    Draw3DRect FormName, Quad4, Inset
    '******************************************************************
    ' Draw a 3-D border around the form.
    '******************************************************************
    Draw3DFormRect FormName, False
End Sub
'******************************************************************
' Set a given RECT (Quad) to the value of a quadrant.
'******************************************************************
Public Sub GetQuad(Quadrant%, Quad As RECT)
    Select Case Quadrant
        Case 1
            Quad = Quad1
        Case 2
            Quad = Quad2
        Case 3
            Quad = Quad3
        Case 4
            Quad = Quad4
    End Select
End Sub
'******************************************************************
' Get the Width & Height of a rectangle.
'******************************************************************
Public Function GetRectWidth(rRect As RECT) As Integer
    GetRectWidth = rRect.rR - rRect.rL
End Function

Public Function GetRectHeight(rRect As RECT) As Integer
    GetRectHeight = rRect.rB - rRect.rT
End Function
'******************************************************************
```

(continues)

Listing 28.2 Continued

```
' Size a control into the client area of a rectangle.
'**********************************************************************
Public Sub SizeToRectClient(Cntl As Control, rSourceRect As RECT)
Dim rRect As RECT
    rRect = rSourceRect
    ResizeRect rRect, -1, -1, False
    Cntl.Move rRect.rL, rRect.rT, GetRectWidth(rRect), _
                                  GetRectHeight(rRect)
End Sub
'**********************************************************************
' Check to see if a control is equal to the client area of a rect.
'**********************************************************************
Public Function EqualToQuadClient(Cntl As Control, _
                                  rSourceRect As RECT) As Boolean
Dim rRect As RECT
    '**********************************************************************
    ' Since you can't pass rects by value, then create a new copy.
    '**********************************************************************
    rRect = rSourceRect
    '**********************************************************************
    ' Resize the copy.
    '**********************************************************************
    ResizeRect rRect, -1, -1, False
    '**********************************************************************
    ' If any are true, then return false.
    '**********************************************************************
    If Cntl.Left <> rRect.rL Then GoSub ReturnFalse
    If Cntl.top <> rRect.rT Then GoSub ReturnFalse
    If Cntl.Width <> GetRectWidth(rRect) Then GoSub ReturnFalse
    If Cntl.Height <> GetRectHeight(rRect) Then GoSub ReturnFalse
    '**********************************************************************
    ' If you got this far, then they are indeed equal.
    '**********************************************************************
    EqualToQuadClient = True
    Exit Function
'**********************************************************************
' Save yourself some typing by using a GoSub to here.
'**********************************************************************
ReturnFalse:
    EqualToQuadClient = False
    Exit Function
End Function
'**********************************************************************
' Converts a rectangle to screen coordinates.
'**********************************************************************
Public Sub ConvertRectToScreen(FormName As Form, _
    rSourceRect As RECT)
Dim ptLT As PointAPI, ptRB As PointAPI
    ptLT.x = rSourceRect.rL
    ptLT.y = rSourceRect.rT
    ptRB.x = rSourceRect.rR
    ptRB.y = rSourceRect.rB
    ClientToScreen FormName.hWnd, ptLT
    ClientToScreen FormName.hWnd, ptRB
End Sub
```

BASWAVE.BAS—Playing .WAV Files

BASWAVE.BAS (listing 28.3) plays sound files from a resource file. The magic
of this module lies in the API call to sndPlaySound in the multimedia library
(MMSYSTEM.DLL) that comes with Windows 3.1.

**Listing 28.3   BASWAVE.BAS Plays Wave Files from a File or
Resource**

```
'*******************************************************************
' BASWAVE.BAS - Plays a wave file from a resource.
'*******************************************************************
Option Explicit
#If Win32 Then
Private Declare Function PlaySound Lib "winmm.dll" Alias _
    "PlaySoundA" (lpszName As Any, ByVal hModule&, _
    ByVal dwFlags As Long) As Long
Private Declare Function sndPlaySound& Lib "winmm" Alias _
    "sndPlaySoundA" (lpszSoundName As Any, ByVal uFlags As Long)
'*******************************************************************
' Flag values for uFlags parameter.
'*******************************************************************
Public Const SND_SYNC = &H0      ' Play synchronously (default)
Public Const SND_ASYNC = &H1     ' Play asynchronously
                                 ' **SEE NOTE IN PlayWavRes!!!!
Public Const SND_NODEFAULT = &H2 ' No default sound event is used
Public Const SND_MEMORY = &H4    ' lpszSoundName points to a
                                 ' memory file.
Public Const SND_ALIAS = &H10000 ' Name is a WIN.INI [sounds] entry
Public Const SND_FILENAME = &H20000 ' Name is a file name
Public Const SND_RESOURCE = &H40004
                                 ' Name is a resource name or atom
Public Const SND_ALIAS_ID = &H110000  ' Name is a WIN.INI [sounds]
                                      ' entry identifier.
Public Const SND_ALIAS_START = 0 ' Must be > 4096 to keep strings
                                 ' in same section of resource file.
Public Const SND_LOOP = &H8
                             ' Loop the sound until next sndPlaySound
Public Const SND_NOSTOP = &H10
                             ' Don't stop any currently playing sound
Public Const SND_VALID = &H1F    ' Valid flags
Public Const SND_NOWAIT = &H2000' Don't wait if the driver is busy
Public Const SND_VALIDFLAGS = &H17201F ' Set of valid flag bits.
                                 ' Anything outside this range
                                 ' will raise an error.
Public Const SND_RESERVED = &HFF000000
                             ' In particular these flags are reserved
Public Const SND_TYPE_MASK = &H170007
Public Const SND_PURGE = &H40  ' Purge nonstatic events for task
Public Const SND_APPLICATION = &H80
                    'Look for application-specific association
```

(continues)

Listing 28.3 Continued

```
#Else
Private Declare Function sndPlaySound Lib "MMSYSTEM" ( _
    lpszSoundName As Any, ByVal wFlags%) As Integer
'*********************************************************************
'  Flag values for wFlags parameter.
'*********************************************************************
Public Const SND_SYNC = &H0          ' Play synchronously (default)
Public Const SND_ASYNC = &H1         ' Play asynchronously
                                     ' **SEE NOTE IN PlayWavRes!!!!
Public Const SND_NODEFAULT = &H2     ' Don't use default sound
Public Const SND_MEMORY = &H4
                                 ' lpszSoundName points to a memory file
Public Const SND_LOOP = &H8
                                 ' Loop the sound until next sndPlaySound
Public Const SND_NOSTOP = &H10
                                 ' Don't stop any currently playing sound
#End If
'*********************************************************************
' Plays a wave file from a resource.
'*********************************************************************
Public Sub PlayWaveRes(vntResourceID As Variant, _
                        Optional vntFlags)
    Dim bytSound() As Byte
                        ' Always store binary data in byte arrays!
    bytSound = LoadResData(vntResourceID, "WAVE")
    '*********************************************************************
    ' If no flags were provided, then set the defaults.
    '*********************************************************************
    If IsMissing(vntFlags) Then
        vntFlags = SND NODEFAULT Or SND_SYNC Or SND_MEMORY
    End If
    '*********************************************************************
    ' Make sure the SND_MEMORY bit is set.
    '*********************************************************************
    If (vntFlags And SND_MEMORY) = 0 Then
        vntFlags = vntFlags Or SND_MEMORY
    End If
    '*********************************************************************
    ' WARNING:  If you want to play sound files asynchronously in
    '           Win32, you MUST change bytSound() from a local
    '           variable to a module-level or static variable.
    '           Doing this prevents your array from being
    '           destroyed before sndPlaySound is complete.
    '           If you fail to do this, you will pass an invalid
    '           memory pointer, which will cause a GPF in MCI.
    '*********************************************************************
    If (vntFlags And SND_ASYNC) Then
                ' Turn off SND_ASYNC if present
        vntFlags = vntFlags Xor SND_ASYNC
    End If
    '*********************************************************************
    ' Pass the address of the first element in the byte array
    ' to play the wave file.
    '*********************************************************************
    If sndPlaySound(bytSound(0), vntFlags) = False Then
        MsgBox "PlayWaveRes failed!", vbCritical
```

```
            End If
    End Sub

    Public Sub PlayWaveFile(strFileName As String, Optional vntFlags)
        '****************************************************************
        ' If no flags were provided, then set the defaults.
        '****************************************************************
        If IsMissing(vntFlags) Then
            vntFlags = SND_NODEFAULT Or SND_SYNC
        End If
        '****************************************************************
        ' Turn off SND_MEMORY if present.
        '****************************************************************
        If (vntFlags And SND_MEMORY) Then
            vntFlags = vntFlags Xor SND_MEMORY
        End If
        '****************************************************************
        ' Play the wave (BE SURE TO USE ByVal!!!!).
        '****************************************************************
        If sndPlaySound(ByVal strFileName, vntFlags) = False Then
            MsgBox "PlayWaveFile failed!", vbCritical
        End If
    End Sub
```

GENERIC.CLS—a Simple Database Class

GENERIC.CLS (listing 28.4) is a useful database class that you can use in any
project. Its purpose is to simplify the data-access features of Visual Basic 4.0
by making them easier to use. The class begins by declaring some necessary
variables and initialization and continues by performing some extensive data-
access functions.

Caution

GENERIC.CLS requires your project to have a reference to the Microsoft DAO 2.5/3.0
Compatibility Object Library. If you attempt to run this example without this reference, you get an error.

Listing 28.4   GENERIC.CLS: A Reusable Generic Database Class

```
    '****************************************************************
    ' GENERIC.CLS - A database class with a set of common routines.
    '****************************************************************
    Option Explicit
    '****************************************************************
    ' Class data members
    '****************************************************************
```

(continues)

```
Listing 28.4   Continued

      Private WSpace As Workspace      ' Class Workspace
      Private DBase As Database        ' Class Database
      Private RecSet As Recordset      ' Main Class RecordSet
      Private DBFileName As String     ' File name of the database
      Private TBDef As TableDef        ' For creating new tables
      Private FieldName As Field        ' For creating new fields
      '****************************************************************
      ' This procedure creates the default workspace
      '****************************************************************
      Private Sub Class_Initialize()
          Set WSpace = DBEngine.Workspaces(0)
      End Sub
      '****************************************************************
      ' The recordset, database, and workspace are closed when
      ' the object goes out of scope to prevent corrupting the database.
      '****************************************************************
      Private Sub Class_Terminate()
          On Error Resume Next
          RecSet.Close
          DBase.Close
          WSpace.Close
      End Sub
      ...
```

GENERIC.CLS provides six read-only properties—GetWorkspace, GetDatbase, Data, NewTable, NewField, and Filename—that enable calling functions to manipulate the database directly in ways that the class itself does not provide. Listing 28.5 shows the code for these properties.

```
Listing 28.5   Helpful Properties Provided by the OpenDB Class

      ...
      '****************************************************************
      ' Returns a reference to the workspace.
      '****************************************************************
      Public Property Get GetWorkspace() As Workspace
          Set GetWorkspace = WSpace
      End Property
      '****************************************************************
      ' Returns a reference to the database.
      '****************************************************************
      Public Property Get GetDatabase() As Database
          Set GetDatabase = DBase
      End Property
      '****************************************************************
      ' Returns a reference to the currently open recordset.
      '****************************************************************
      Public Property Get Data() As Recordset
          Set Data = RecSet
      End Property
      '****************************************************************
```

```
' Returns a reference to the open TableDef.
'*********************************************************************
Public Property Get NewTable() As TableDef
    Set NewTable = TBDef
End Property
'*********************************************************************
' Returns a reference to the currently open field definition.
'*********************************************************************
Public Property Get NewField() As Field
    Set NewField = FieldName
End Property
'*********************************************************************
' Returns the file name of the database that is currently open.
'*********************************************************************
Public Property Get FileName() As String
    FileName = DBFileName
End Property
```

The most common data-access method is OpenDatabase, which makes data access easier and more reliable. The method first ensures that the file exists; if it does, OpenDatabase tries to open the file. If the method cannot open the database, it prompts the user to repair the possibly corrupt database. Listing 28.6 shows a custom OpenDatabase method called OpenDB.

Listing 28.6   The OpenDB Method

```
'*********************************************************************
' Opens a database for use with this class.
'*********************************************************************
Public Sub OpenDB(File$, Optional OpenExclusive, _
                  Optional OpenReadOnly)
Dim res%
    '*************************************************************
    ' If any arguments are missing, add default values.
    '*************************************************************
    On Error Resume Next
    If Not IsMissing(File) Then DBFileName = File
    If IsMissing(OpenExclusive) Then OpenExclusive = False
    If IsMissing(OpenReadOnly) Then OpenReadOnly = False
    '*************************************************************
    ' Convert the arguments into valid Booleans.
    '*************************************************************
    OpenExclusive = CBool(OpenExclusive)
    OpenReadOnly = CBool(OpenReadOnly)
    '*************************************************************
    ' Open the database.
    '*************************************************************
    Set DBase = WSpace.OpenDatabase(DBFileName, OpenExclusive, _
                                    OpenReadOnly)
    '*************************************************************
    ' If the database is corrupted, then prompt to repair it.
    '*************************************************************
```

(continues)

Listing 28.6 Continued

```
      If Err = 3049 Then
          res = MsgBox(Error & vbLf & vbLf & _
            "Would you like to attempt to repair this database?", _
            vbQuestion + vbYesNo)
          '*********************************************************
          ' If no, then bug out.
          '*********************************************************
          If res = vbNo Then Exit Sub
          '*********************************************************
          ' Otherwise repair it, clear the error flag,
          ' and try again.
          '*********************************************************
          Repair DBFileName: Err = 0
          Set DBase = WSpace.OpenDatabase(DBFileName, _
                                    OpenExclusive, OpenReadOnly)
          '*********************************************************
          ' If there is another error, then give up.
          '*********************************************************
          If Err Then
              MsgBox "An attempt to open the database failed!", _
                  vbCritical
          End If
      '*************************************************************
      ' If some other error, then just report it.
      '*************************************************************
      ElseIf Err <> 0 And Err <> 3049 Then
          MsgBox Error, vbExclamation
      End If
End Sub
```

CreateRecordset (listing 28.7) creates a recordset for use with the methods in this class. If you don't specify a recordset type, the procedure assumes a dynaset.

Listing 28.7 The CreateRecordset Method

```
'*****************************************************************
' Creates a recordset for use with this class.
'*****************************************************************
Public Sub CreateRecordSet(Source$, Optional ViewType, _
                          Optional Options)
      '*********************************************************
      ' If any arguments are missing, add default values.
      '*********************************************************

      If IsMissing(ViewType) Then ViewType = dbOpenDynaset
      If IsMissing(Options) Then
          Set RecSet = DBase.OpenRecordset(Source, CInt(ViewType))
      Else
```

```
          Set RecSet = DBase.OpenRecordset(Source, CInt(ViewType), _
                                        CInt(Options))
      End If
End Sub
```

The methods in listing 28.8—Create, MakeTable, AddTable, MakeField, AddField, and MakeIndex—simplify the process of creating a database and appending fields and indexes to a database.

Listing 28.8   Database and Table Creation Methods

```
'********************************************************************
' Creates a new database.
'********************************************************************
Public Sub Create(File$)
    If Not IsMissing(File) Then DBFileName = File
    Set DBase = WSpace.CreateDatabase(DBFileName, dbLangGeneral)
End Sub
'********************************************************************
' Creates a TableDef.
'********************************************************************
Public Sub MakeTable(TableName As String)
    Set TBDef = DBase.CreateTableDef(TableName)
End Sub
'********************************************************************
' Writes the TableDef to the table, so a new table can be created.
'********************************************************************
Public Sub AddTable()
    DBase.TableDefs.Append TBDef
    Set TBDef = Nothing
End Sub
'********************************************************************
' Creates a new field definition. Other attributes
' should be set by obtaining the NewField reference,
' and making the changes directly.
'********************************************************************
Public Sub MakeField(FName$, FType%, Optional FSize)
    Set FieldName = TBDef.CreateField(FName, FType)
    If Not IsMissing(FSize) Then FieldName.Size = CInt(FSize)
End Sub
'********************************************************************
' Writes the field definition to the current TableDef.
'********************************************************************
Public Sub AddField()
    TBDef.Fields.Append FieldName
    Set FieldName = Nothing
End Sub
'********************************************************************
' Writes an index to a TableDef.
'********************************************************************
Public Sub MakeIndex(FldName$, PrimaryKey As Boolean, _
                  UniqueKey As Boolean)
```

(continues)

Listing 28.8 Continued

```
Dim NewIndex As New Index        ' For creating new indexes
    With NewIndex
        .Name = "idx" & FldName
        .Fields = FldName
        .Primary = PrimaryKey
        .Unique = IIf(PrimaryKey, True, UniqueKey)
    End With
    TBDef.Indexes.Append NewIndex
End Sub
```

The next three methods—GetData, GetArrayData, and GetControlData—provide an easy way to return all the records in a field either as a string or in an array or control. The key to the success of these functions is to start at the first record in the table and iterate through to the last. Listing 28.9 shows these three methods.

Listing 28.9 Methods That Return a Field's Records

```
'*****************************************************************
' Returns all (up to ~32k) of the records of a field
' in a delimited string. This is a useful feature
' for inserting data into a text box.
'*****************************************************************
Public Function GetData(FName$, ByVal Delimiter$) As String
Dim res$, retStr$
    '*************************************************************
    ' Move to the first record.
    '*************************************************************
    On Error Resume Next
    RecSet.MoveFirst
    '*************************************************************
    ' Build a large (<=~32k) delimited string of the records.
    '*************************************************************
    Do While Not RecSet.EOF
        res = Trim(RecSet(FName))
        If Len(res) + Len(retStr) > 32001 Then Exit Do
        retStr = retStr & res & Delimiter
        RecSet.MoveNext
    Loop
    '*************************************************************
    ' Return to the first record, and return the results.
    '*************************************************************
    RecSet.MoveFirst
    GetData = retStr
End Function
'*****************************************************************
' Same as GetData, but the data is stored in an array.
'*****************************************************************
Public Sub GetArrayData(FName$, retArray() As String)
```

```
        Dim res$, retStr$, i%
            On Error Resume Next
            Erase retArray
            RecSet.MoveFirst
            Do While Not RecSet.EOF
                res = Trim(RecSet(FName))
                If Len(res) + Len(retStr) > 32001 Then Exit Do
                If Not IsNull(res) Then
                    retStr = retStr & res
                    ReDim Preserve retArray(i + 1)
                    retArray(i) = res
                    i = i + 1
                End If
                RecSet.MoveNext
            Loop
            RecSet.MoveFirst
        End Sub
        '*********************************************************************
        ' Same as GetData, but the data is loaded into a control.
        ' The control MUST either be a list or combo box in order
        ' for this method to work.
        '*********************************************************************
        Public Sub GetControlData(FName$, CtrlName As Control)
        Dim res$, retStr$
            On Error Resume Next
            RecSet.MoveFirst
            Do While Not RecSet.EOF
                res = Trim(RecSet(FName))
                If Len(res) + Len(retStr) > 32001 Then Exit Do
                If Not IsNull(res) Then
                    retStr = retStr & res
                    CtrlName.AddItem res
                End If
                RecSet.MoveNext
            Loop
            CtrlName.ListIndex = 0
            RecSet.MoveFirst
        End Sub
```

AddOrEditRecord adds a new record or edits an existing one. Its first argument determines whether to add or edit the data that the FieldPipeValue parameter array stores. The second parameter, FieldPipeValue, is a parameter array that contains values delimited by the pipe character (¦), in the form *Field Name¦Value*.

This function begins by ensuring that the parameter array isn't empty, and then sets the current recordset's .Add or .Edit property based on the action specified by the AddRec parameter. Next, AddOrEditRecord iterates through the parameter array, determines the data type, and updates the recordset. Listing 28.10 shows the AddOrEditRecord method.

Listing 28.10 The `AddOrEditRecord` Method Manipulates Data at the Record Level

```
'*********************************************************************
' Adds a new record, or edits an existing one.
' This method should not be used when adding or
' editing > 20 records (for performance reasons).
'*********************************************************************
Public Sub AddOrEditRecord(ByVal AddRec As Boolean, _
                           ParamArray FieldPipeValue())
Dim NumItems%, i%, where%, FName$, FValue
    '*************************************************************
    ' Find out how many parameters were passed.
    ' If none, then exit.
    '*************************************************************
    On Error Resume Next
    NumItems = UBound(FieldPipeValue)
    If IsEmpty(FieldPipeValue(0)) Then Exit Sub
    '*************************************************************
    ' Determine whether to add or edit the record.
    '*************************************************************
    If AddRec Then
        RecSet.AddNew
    Else
        RecSet.Edit
        '*********************************************************
        ' If there was no current record, then notify the user.
        '*********************************************************
        If Err = 3021 Then
            MsgBox "Since there is no current record,
            ➥it cannot be edited.", vbCritical
            Exit Sub
        End If
    End If
    '*************************************************************
    ' If loop through each parameter.
    '*************************************************************
    For i = 0 To NumItems
        '*********************************************************
        ' Separate the field name from its value.
        '*********************************************************
        FName = FieldPipeValue(i)
        where = InStr(FName, "¦")

        If where = 0 And i > 1 Then
            Exit For
        ElseIf where = 0 And i < 1 Then
            Exit Sub
        End If

        FValue = Mid(FName, where + 1)
        FName = CStr(Left(FName, where - 1))
        '*********************************************************
        ' Determine the record type, and convert the value.
        '*********************************************************
```

```
            Select Case RecSet(FName).Type
                Case dbBoolean
                    RecSet(FName) = CBool(FValue)
                Case dbByte, dbInteger
                    RecSet(FName) = CInt(FValue)
                Case dbLong
                    RecSet(FName) = CLng(FValue)
                Case dbCurrency
                    RecSet(FName) = CCur(FValue)
                Case dbSingle
                    RecSet(FName) = CSng(FValue)
                Case dbDouble
                    RecSet(FName) = CDbl(FValue)
                '*****************************************************
                ' Otherwise it must be a dbDate, dbText,
                ' dbLongBinary, & dbMemo.
                '*****************************************************
                Case Else
                    where = RecSet(FName).Size
                    '*************************************************
                    ' If the record is too long, then clip it.
                    '*************************************************
                    If where And (Len(FValue) > where) Then
                        FValue = Left(FValue, where)
                    ElseIf Len(FValue) > 32000 Then
                        FValue = Left(FValue, 32000)
                    End If
                    RecSet(FName) = FValue
            End Select
        Next i
        '*********************************************************
        ' Complete the transaction.
        '*********************************************************
        RecSet.Update
End Sub
```

The next four methods—MFirst, MLast, MNext, and MPrev—navigate through the recordset and return the current record. The last two methods—FindRecord and GetRecord—provide methods for searching for a specific record and retrieving the current record. Listing 28.11 contains all six of these methods.

Listing 28.11   GENERIC.CLS Recordset Navigation Methods

```
'*********************************************************************
' Move to the first record.
'*********************************************************************
Public Function MFirst(Optional FName) As String
    On Error Resume Next
    If RecSet.Type = 2 Then Exit Function
    RecSet.MoveFirst
```

(continues)

Listing 28.11 Continued

```
        If Not IsMissing(FName) Then
            MFirst = Trim(RecSet(CStr(FName)))
        End If
End Function
'********************************************************************
' Move to the last record.
'********************************************************************
Public Function MLast(Optional FName) As String
        On Error Resume Next
        RecSet.MoveLast
        If Not IsMissing(FName) Then
            MLast = Trim(RecSet(CStr(FName)))
        End If
End Function
'********************************************************************
' Move to the next record.
'********************************************************************
Public Function MNext(Optional FName) As String
        On Error Resume Next
        RecSet.MoveNext
        If RecSet.EOF Then RecSet.MoveLast
        If Not IsMissing(FName) Then
            MNext = Trim(RecSet(CStr(FName)))
        End If
End Function
'********************************************************************
' Move to the previous record.
'********************************************************************
Public Function MPrev(Optional FName) As String
        On Error Resume Next
        If RecSet.Type = 2 Then Exit Function
        RecSet.MovePrevious
        If RecSet.BOF Then RecSet.MoveFirst
        If Not IsMissing(FName) Then
            MPrev = Trim(RecSet(CStr(FName)))
        End If
End Function
'********************************************************************
' Locates a record, and returns its result.
'********************************************************************
Public Function FindRecord(FName$, FindWhat, Optional ByVal _
                            ExactMatch) As Variant
        '********************************************************************
        ' Determine whether to find a similar or exact match.
        '********************************************************************
        On Error Resume Next
        ExactMatch = IIf(IsMissing(ExactMatch), True, ExactMatch)
        '********************************************************************
        ' Start at the beginning, and find the record.
        '********************************************************************
        RecSet.MoveFirst
        If ExactMatch Then
            RecSet.FindFirst FName & " = '" & FindWhat & "'"
        Else
```

```
            RecSet.FindFirst "[" & FName & "] LIKE '" & FindWhat & "'"
        End If
        '*****************************************************************
        ' If no match, then return "".
        '*****************************************************************
        FindRecord = IIf(RecSet.NoMatch, "", _
            FindRecord = RecSet(FName))
    End Function
    '*****************************************************************
    ' Returns a record from a specific field.
    '*****************************************************************
    Public Function GetRecord(FName$) As Variant
        On Error Resume Next
        GetRecord = RecSet(FName)
    End Function
```

Databases sometimes become damaged, so the `Repair` method (listing 28.12) provides a cleaner way to repair and compact a corrupted database.

Listing 28.12   The `Repair` Method

```
    '*****************************************************************
    ' Repairs and compacts a damaged database.
    '*****************************************************************
    Public Sub Repair(FileName$)
    Dim BakFileName$, res%
        '*****************************************************************
        ' Make a copy of the database to work on.
        '*****************************************************************
        On Error Resume Next
        BakFileName = Left(FileName, InStr(FileName, ".")) & "BAK"
        FileCopy FileName, BakFileName
        DBEngine.RepairDatabase BakFileName
        '*****************************************************************
        ' If it was successfully repaired, then kill the original.
        '*****************************************************************
        If Err = 0 Then
            Kill FileName
            '*****************************************************************
            ' Repaired databases should be compacted, so do it now.
            '*****************************************************************
            DBEngine.CompactDatabase BakFileName, FileName
            '*****************************************************************
            ' If it succeeded, ask users if they want to delete
            ' the backup copy.
            '*****************************************************************
            If Err = 0 Then
              If MsgBox("Would you like to delete the backup file?", _
                    vbYesNo + vbQuestion) = vbYes Then Kill BakFileName
            End If
        End If
    End Sub
```

PRETTY.CLS—Creating Word-Formatted Copies

PRETTYPR.CLS (listing 28.13) is a class that shows off the power of OLE Auto-mation with Microsoft Word, by performing several methods to create a for-matted copy of a given Visual Basic code file. The class begins by declaring some useful constants and properties.

Listing 28.13   The PRETTYPR.CLS Class Formats VB Code in Word

```
'*********************************************************************
' PRETTYPR.CLS: Reads a Visual Basic file and displays a formatted
'               copy in Microsoft Word 6.0 or 7.0.
'*********************************************************************
Option Explicit
Option Compare Text
'*********************************************************************
' Private Member Variables
'*********************************************************************
Private ColorDeclare%, ColorComment%, ColorFunction%
Private ColorSub%, ColorContinueChar%, ColorDefault%
Private Word As Object, SourceFile As Integer
Private DocFileName As String, ErrValue%, bRestore As Boolean
'*********************************************************************
' Private Member Constants
'*********************************************************************
Private Const FIND_CONTINUE_CHAR = " _"
Private Const FIND_COMMENT = "'"
Private Const FIND_DECLARE = "Declare"
Private Const FIND_FUNCTION = "Function"
Private Const FIND_PROPERTY = "Property"
Private Const FIND_SUB = "Sub"
'*********************************************************************
' Private Member Color Constants
'*********************************************************************
Private Const wordAutomatic = 0
Private Const wordBlack = 1
Private Const wordBlue = 2
Private Const wordCyan = 3
Private Const wordGreen = 4
Private Const wordMagenta = 5
Private Const wordRed = 6
Private Const wordYellow = 7
Private Const wordWhite = 8
Private Const wordDarkBlue = 9
Private Const wordDarkCyan = 10
Private Const wordDarkGreen = 11
Private Const wordDarkMagenta = 12
Private Const wordDarkRed = 13
Private Const wordDarkYellow = 14
Private Const wordDarkGray = 15
Private Const wordLightGray = 16
'*********************************************************************
' The following 6 properties are used to change the colors used to
' display certain elements.
'*********************************************************************
```

```
            Public Property Let clrContinueChar(iColor As Integer)
                ColorContinueChar = iColor
            End Property

            Public Property Let clrComment(iColor As Integer)
                ColorComment = iColor
            End Property

            Public Property Let clrDeclare(iColor As Integer)
                ColorDeclare = iColor
            End Property

            Public Property Let clrDefault(iColor As Integer)
                ColorDefault = iColor
            End Property

            Public Property Let clrFunction(iColor As Integer)
                ColorFunction = iColor
            End Property

            Public Property Let clrSub(iColor As Integer)
                ColorSub = iColor
            End Property
            '******************************************************************
            ' Expose the Word object in case the user wants to perform
            ' additional file processing.
            '******************************************************************
            Public Property Set GetWord(obj As Object)
                Set obj = Word
            End Property
            '******************************************************************
            ' This property lets you set the visible state of Word.
            '******************************************************************
            Public Property Let Visible(bShowWindow As Boolean)
                If bShowWindow Then
                    Word.AppHide
                    Word.AppShow
                Else
                    Word.AppHide
                End If
            End Property

            Public Property Get Errors() As Integer
                Errors = ErrValue
            End Property
```

The application calls the Initialize event (shown in listing 28.14) for this class when you first access any member or method in the clsPrettyPrint class. This event displays a splash screen while attempting to create a Word object. In addition, the procedure initializes class variables with default values. When the class is destroyed, the Terminate event sets the Word object equal to Nothing to free up the memory that the Word object is using. Listing 28.14 shows both of these events.

```
┌─────────────────────────────────────────────────────────────────────┐
│ Listing 28.14  The Initialize and Terminate Events                    │
└─────────────────────────────────────────────────────────────────────┘
' *********************************************************************
' Initialize all member variables.
' *********************************************************************
Private Sub Class_Initialize()
    On Error Resume Next
    frmProgress.Update 0, "Establishing a connection with Word..."
    frmProgress.Refresh
    ColorDefault = wordAutomatic
    ColorContinueChar = wordRed
    ColorFunction = wordDarkBlue
    ColorDeclare = wordDarkCyan
    ColorComment = wordDarkGreen
    SourceFile = FreeFile
    OLEConnect Word, "Word.Basic"
End Sub
' *********************************************************************
' Release the memory use by Word.
' *********************************************************************
' WARNING: If Word wasn't already running, then all changes
'          will be lost. If you want to save the changes,
'          you must access the Word object and save them manually.
' *********************************************************************
Private Sub Class_Terminate()
    On Error Resume Next
    If bRestore Then Word.ToggleFull
    Unload frmProgress
    Set Word = Nothing
End Sub
```

PrettyPrint (listing 28.15) is the key method in the clsPrettyPrint class.
It provides an interface for the calling module to format the document and
display the results. The method begins by displaying a splash screen while
opening a new document based on the PRETTYPR.DOT template. PrettyPrint
then prints a header and reads the code from the file. The method reads each
line and inserts and formats it into Word. On reaching the end of the file,
PrettyPrint displays the results for the user.

```
┌─────────────────────────────────────────────────────────────────────┐
│ Listing 28.15  The PrettyPrint Method                                 │
└─────────────────────────────────────────────────────────────────────┘
' *********************************************************************
' Inserts a formatted copy of a VB file into Word.
' *********************************************************************
Public Sub PrettyPrint(FileName As String, Optional Header)
Dim Look$
    ' *********************************************************************
    ' Change the pointer, open a new file, and print the header.
    ' *********************************************************************
    On Error GoTo PrettyPrint_Err
```

```
        frmProgress.Update 0, "Initializing..."
        Screen.MousePointer = vbHourglass
        Word.FileNew Template:=App.Path & "\prettypr.dot"
        PrintHeader IIf(IsMissing(Header), FileName, Header)
        '**********************************************************************
        ' Open the file as READ ONLY, and examine every line.
        '**********************************************************************
        Open FileName For Input Access Read As SourceFile
            Do While Not EOF(SourceFile)
                Line Input #SourceFile, Look
                frmProgress.Update (Seek(SourceFile) / _
                    LOF(SourceFile)) * 100, "Reading " & _
                    LCase(FileName) & "..."
                ExamineLine Look
            Loop
        Close SourceFile

        frmProgress.Update 100, "Complete!"
        '**********************************************************************
        ' Change the margins, and view it at 90% in Normal mode.
        '**********************************************************************
        DisplayResults IIf(MsgBox( _
          "Would you like to view your results in full-screen mode?", _
          vbQuestion + vbYesNo) = vbYes, True, False)
        With Word
            .FilePageSetup TopMargin:="0.25", BottomMargin:="0.25", _
                           LeftMargin:="0.25", RightMargin:="0.25"
            .ViewNormal
            .ViewZoom ZoomPercent:="90%"
        End With
        '**********************************************************************
        ' When you are done, restore the pointer and create
        ' a Word file name.
        '**********************************************************************
        DocFileName = Left(FileName, InStr(FileName, ".")) & "DOC"
        Screen.MousePointer = vbDefault
        Unload frmProgress
        Exit Sub

PrettyPrint_Err:
        Unload frmProgress
        MsgBox Error, vbCritical
        Screen.MousePointer = vbDefault
        ErrValue = Err
        Exit Sub
End Sub
```

The next two procedures are responsible for formatting the document.
PrintHeader inserts a formatted header line at the top of the first page. The
procedure prints this line to describe which file the document contains.
ExamineLine determines how to format the line and sends the line to the
appropriate procedure for processing. Listing 28.16 shows both of these
procedures.

Listing 28.16 The `PrintHeader` and `ExamineLine` **Procedures**

```
'*******************************************************************
' This is the first line printed before the file is inserted.
'*******************************************************************
Private Sub PrintHeader(Header As String)
    '*******************************************************************
    ' Change the current font, and insert the header.
    '*******************************************************************
    ChangeFont sFont:="Arial", bBold:=1, sPoints:="14"
    With Word
        .Insert Header
        .FormatParagraph After:="6 pt"
        .InsertPara
        .FormatParagraph After:="0 pt"
    End With
End Sub
'*******************************************************************
' Determine how the line should be formatted.
'*******************************************************************
Private Sub ExamineLine(Source As String)
Dim where%
    '*******************************************************************
    ' Check for a Sub, Function, Property, and regular line,
    ' respectively.
    '*******************************************************************
    where = InStr(Source, FIND_SUB)
    If where Then
        FormatProceedure where, Source
    Else
        where = InStr(Source, FIND_FUNCTION)
        where = IIf(where, where, InStr(Source, FIND_PROPERTY))
        If where Then
            FormatProceedure where, Source
        Else
            FormatDefault Source
        End If
    End If
End Sub
```

The next four procedures—FormatProcedure, FormatDefault, FormatComment, and FormatDeclaration—actually format and insert the line into Word. Each of these functions looks for a specific keyword (such as Sub, Function, or neither) and formats the line appropriately. If any of the lines contain comment characters, the function handles them appropriately as well. Listing 28.17 shows the code for these four functions. This code isn't actually as complicated as it looks. The key is to take each line and formatting option separately.

Listing 28.17   PRETTYPR.CLS' Functions for Formatting Lines in Word through OLE Automation

```
'*******************************************************************
' This procedure handles the formatting of properties, subs, and
' functions.
'*******************************************************************
Private Sub FormatProcedure(where%, Source$)
Dim CommentPresent%, DeclarePresent%
    '***************************************************************
    ' Search for comments and external declarations.
    '***************************************************************
    CommentPresent = InStr(Source, FIND_COMMENT)
    DeclarePresent = InStr(Source, FIND_DECLARE)
    '***************************************************************
    ' If this line is really a procedure and not a Exit Sub, Exit
    ' Function, or API declaration, then continue.
    '***************************************************************
    If where And InStr(Source, _
        "Exit ") = 0 And DeclarePresent = 0 Then
        '***********************************************************
        ' Change the font.
        '***********************************************************
        ChangeFont bBold:=1, iColor:=ColorFunction
        '***********************************************************
        ' If a comment is present, split the line for formatting.
        '***********************************************************
        If CommentPresent Then
            Word.Insert Left(Source, CommentPresent - 1)
            FormatComment CommentPresent, Source
        '***********************************************************
        ' If there is a line-continuation char, then...
        '***********************************************************
        ElseIf Right(Source, 2) = FIND_CONTINUE_CHAR Then
            '*******************************************************
            ' Loop while the current line has line-continue char.
            '*******************************************************
            Do While Right(Source, 2) = FIND_CONTINUE_CHAR
                Word.Insert Left(Source, Len(Source) - 2)
                '***************************************************
                ' Format the continuation char, so it sticks out.
                '***************************************************
                ChangeFont bBold:=1, iColor:=ColorContinueChar
                Word.Insert Right(Source, 2)
                Word.InsertPara
                ChangeFont bBold:=1, iColor:=ColorFunction
                '***************************************************
                ' Read the next line.
                '***************************************************
                Line Input #SourceFile, Source
                frmProgress.Update (Seek(SourceFile) \ _
                            LOF(SourceFile)) * 100
            Loop
            Word.Insert Source
```

(continues)

Listing 28.17   Continued

```
                Word.InsertPara
            Else
                Word.Insert Source
                Word.InsertPara
            End If
        '****************************************************************
        ' If it is an external declartion, then process it.
        '****************************************************************
        ElseIf DeclarePresent Then
            FormatDeclaration Source
        '****************************************************************
        ' Otherwise, it must be a normal line.
        '****************************************************************
        Else
            FormatDefault Source
        End If
End Sub
'********************************************************************
' Formats a line with the default formatting.
'********************************************************************
Private Sub FormatDefault(ByVal Source$)
Dim where%
        '****************************************************************
        ' If there is a line continuation char,
        ' then loop and format each continued line.
        '****************************************************************
        If Right(Source, 2) = FIND_CONTINUE_CHAR Then
            Do While Right(Source, 2) = FIND_CONTINUE_CHAR
                ChangeFont
                Word.Insert Left(Source, Len(Source) - 2)
                ChangeFont bBold:=1, iColor:=ColorContinueChar
                Word.Insert Right(Source, 2)
                Word.InsertPara
                Line Input #SourceFile, Source
                frmProgress.Update (Seek(SourceFile) \ _
                            LOF(SourceFile)) * 100
            Loop
            ChangeFont
            Word.Insert Source
            Word.InsertPara
        '****************************************************************
        ' Otherwise use the default format and check for comments.
        '****************************************************************
        Else
            ChangeFont
            where = InStr(Source, FIND_COMMENT)
            If where Then
                Word.Insert Left(Source, where - 1)
                FormatComment where, Source
            Else
                Word.Insert Source
                Word.InsertPara
            End If
```

```
        End If
End Sub
'*********************************************************************
' Formats a comment in italics.
'*********************************************************************
Private Sub FormatComment(where%, Source)
    '*********************************************************************
    ' Change the font to italics, and print the rest of the line.
    '*********************************************************************
    ChangeFont bItalic:=1, iColor:=ColorComment
    Word.Insert Mid(Source, where)
    Word.InsertPara
End Sub
'*********************************************************************
' Formats a declare statement like the default, but it's colored.
'*********************************************************************
Private Sub FormatDeclaration(Source$)
Dim CommentPresent%
    '*********************************************************************
    ' Search for a comment char, and change the font.
    '*********************************************************************
    CommentPresent = InStr(Source, FIND_COMMENT)
    ChangeFont iColor:=ColorDeclare
    '*********************************************************************
    ' If a comment is present, then print up to the comment.
    '*********************************************************************
    If CommentPresent Then
        Word.Insert Left(Source, CommentPresent - 1)
        FormatComment CommentPresent, Source
    '*********************************************************************
    ' If there is a line-continuation char,
    ' then loop and format each continued line.
    '*********************************************************************
    ElseIf Right(Source, 2) = FIND_CONTINUE_CHAR Then
        Do While Right(Source, 2) = FIND_CONTINUE_CHAR
            Word.Insert Left(Source, Len(Source) - 2)
            ChangeFont bBold:=1, iColor:=ColorContinueChar
            Word.Insert Right(Source, 2)
            Word.InsertPara
            ChangeFont iColor:=ColorDeclare
            Line Input #SourceFile, Source
            frmProgress.Update (Seek(SourceFile) \ _
                        LOF(SourceFile)) * 100
        Loop
        Word.Insert Source
        Word.InsertPara
    '*********************************************************************
    ' Otherwise, just print it with the new font settings.
    '*********************************************************************
    Else
        Word.Insert Source
        Word.InsertPara
    End If
End Sub
```

The next three procedures—DisplayResults, Save, and PrintResults—display, save, or print the results of the formatting. The last procedure, ChangeFonts, is a helper procedure that the three previous procedures use to change the formatting of the current font in Word. Listing 28.18 shows all four of these functions.

Listing 28.18   Displaying, Printing, and Saving Formatting Results

```
'**********************************************************************
' Displays Word in Full Screen Word.
'**********************************************************************
Public Sub DisplayResults(FullScreenMode As Boolean)
    '**********************************************************************
    ' Return to the start of the document.
    '**********************************************************************
    Word.StartOfDocument
    '**********************************************************************
    ' If the user wants full screen mode, then make sure the Full
    ' Screen toolbar is visible.
    '**********************************************************************
    If FullScreenMode Then
        With Word
            .ToggleFull
            .ViewToolbars Toolbar:="Full Screen", Show:=1
            .MoveToolbar "Full Screen", 5, 595, 43
        End With
        bRestore = True
    End If
    '**********************************************************************
    ' Let the system catch up, then show Word.
    '**********************************************************************
    DoEvents
    Word.AppHide
    Word.AppShow
End Sub
'**********************************************************************
' Saves the file. If no file name is provided, then a default is
' provided by using the original name with a .DOC extension.
'**********************************************************************
Public Sub Save(Optional FileName)
    Word.FileSaveAs IIf(IsMissing(FileName),DocFileName,FileName)
End Sub
'**********************************************************************
' Prints the results of the formatting to the current printer.
'**********************************************************************
Public Sub PrintResults()
    Word.FilePrintDefault
End Sub
'**********************************************************************
' Changes the current font in Word. If an argument is omitted,
' a default value is used.
'**********************************************************************
```

```
Private Sub ChangeFont(Optional sPoints, Optional iColor, _
               Optional sFont, Optional bBold, Optional bItalic)
    Word.FormatFont Points:=IIf(IsMissing(sPoints), "10", _
            sPoints), Color:=IIf(IsMissing(iColor), _
            ColorDefault, iColor), _
            Font:=IIf(IsMissing(sFont), "Courier New", _
            sFont), Bold:=IIf(IsMissing(bBold), 0, bBold), _
            Italic:=IIf(IsMissing(bItalic), 0, bItalic)
End Sub
```

The OLEConnect function establishes an OLE Automation connection with
Word, whether it is running or not. You write this function to be generic so
that you can easily insert the same code into your own project without making any modifications.

```
'*********************************************************************
' OLEConnect takes a pointer to an object variable and class name.
' If this function is successful, then the function returns true
' and the obj argument points to a valid OLE Automation object.
'*********************************************************************
Private Function OLEConnect(obj As Object, sClass As String) _
    As Boolean
    '*****************************************************************
    ' Temporarily turn off error handling
    '*****************************************************************
    On Error Resume Next
    Set obj = GetObject(, sClass)
    '*****************************************************************
    ' If GetObject failed, then try Create
    '*****************************************************************
    If Err = 429 Then
        '*************************************************************
        ' Resume error handling
        '*************************************************************
        On Error GoTo OLEConnect_Err
        Set obj = CreateObject(sClass)
    '*****************************************************************
    ' If any other error, then display & exit
    '*****************************************************************
    ElseIf Err <> 0 Then
        GoSub OLEConnect_Err
    End If
    '*****************************************************************
    ' If this line is executed, then the function succeeded
    '*****************************************************************
    OLEConnect = True
    Exit Function
'*********************************************************************
' Display error message and abort
'*********************************************************************
OLEConnect_Err:
    MsgBox Err.Description, vbCritical
    Exit Function
End Function
```

REPRT2XL.CLS—Creating Bug Reports from a Database

REPRT2XL.CLS (listing 28.19) is a class that shows off the power of OLE Automation and data access with Microsoft Excel by performing several methods to create a report from a database query. The class begins by declaring some variables and exposing a read-only pointer to the object that this class uses. When initialized, the class displays a splash screen while trying to create an Excel object. When destroyed, the class sets the Excel object equal to nothing to close Excel and free up the memory that the object is using.

Listing 28.19   REPRT2XL.CLS Sends Report Data to Excel

```
'*******************************************************************
' REPRT2XL.CLS - Sends data from a bug report database
' to Excel.
'*******************************************************************
Option Explicit
Private Excel As Object, CloseExcel As Boolean
Private BugDBase As New GenericDB
'*******************************************************************
' Expose the Excel object for further processing.
'*******************************************************************
Public Property Set GetExcel(obj As Object)
    Set obj = Excel
End Property
'*******************************************************************
' Set the Excel object, if possible.
'*******************************************************************
Private Sub Class_Initialize()
    On Error Resume Next
    SplashVisible True, "Establishing a connection with Excel..."
    OLEConnect Excel, "Excel.Application"
    SplashVisible False
End Sub
'*******************************************************************
' Close the workbook (or Excel) without saving any changes.
'*******************************************************************
Private Sub Class_Terminate()
    On Error Resume Next
    Excel.ActiveWorkbook.Saved = True
    If CloseExcel Then
        Excel.Quit
    Else
        Excel.ActiveWorkbook.Close saveChanges:=False
        Excel.WindowState = -4140 'xlMinimized
    End If
    SplashVisible False
    Set Excel = Nothing
End Sub
```

The ReportToExcel method (listing 28.20) retrieves data from BUGS.MDB and inserts it into USEALL.XLS. After inserting the data, the procedure formats it to make it easier to read and removes the splash screen.

Listing 28.20   ReportToExcel Demonstrates OLE Automation with Excel

```
'******************************************************************
' Create a summary report in Excel from a database file.
'******************************************************************
Public Sub ReportToExcel(Optional ByVal FileName)
Dim XLSFile$
    '**************************************************************
    ' Open the default or create a new workbook,
    ' then open the database.
    '**************************************************************
    On Error Resume Next
    SplashVisible True, "Sending data to Excel..."
    XLSFile = App.Path & "\useall.xls"
    If Dir(XLSFile) = "" Then
        Excel.Workbooks.Add
    Else
        Excel.Workbooks.Open XLSFile
    End If
    BugDBase.OpenDB IIf(IsMissing(FileName), _
                        App.Path & "\bugs.mdb", FileName)
    '**************************************************************
    ' Set the current cell to bold blue with a gray background.
    '**************************************************************
    With Excel.Range("A1")
        .Font.Bold = True
        .Font.ColorIndex = 11
        .Interior.ColorIndex = 15
        .Interior.Pattern = 1
    End With
    '**************************************************************
    ' Autofill to the adjacent cells
    '**************************************************************
    Excel.Selection.AutoFill Destination:=Excel.Range("A1:E1"), _
        Type:=0
    '**************************************************************
    ' Write the data to Excel.
    '**************************************************************
    LoadColumn "Bug Details", "Product", "A"
    LoadColumn "Bug Details", "Build", "B"
    LoadColumn "Bug Details", "Title", "C"
    LoadColumn "Bug Details", "Reproducible", "D"
    LoadColumn "Bug Details", "BetaID", "E"
    '**************************************************************
    ' Select all of the data, and format it.
    ' Make XL visible when done.
    '**************************************************************
    With Excel
```

(continues)

Listing 28.20 Continued

```
            .Range("A2").Select
            .Selection.End(-4121).Select
            .Selection.End(-4161).Select
            .Range(Excel.Selection.Address, "A1").Select
            .ActiveWindow.Zoom = 86
            .Selection.Columns.AutoFit
            .Selection.Sort Key1:=Excel.Range("A2"), Order1:=1, _
            Header:=0, OrderCustom:=1, MatchCase:=False, _
            Orientation:=1
            .Visible = True
            .Range("A1").Select
        End With
        SplashVisible False
    End Sub
```

The key to the ReportToExcel method is the LoadColumn procedure (listing 28.21). LoadColumn requires that the caller provide a table name, a field name, and the column in which to insert the data from the field. The procedure queries the database and prints the results in Excel.

Listing 28.21 The LoadColumn Procedure

```
'******************************************************************
' Load a column in Excel with the values from the bug database.
'******************************************************************
Private Sub LoadColumn(TableName$, FieldName$, XLColumn$)
Dim i%, NumItems%, retArray() As String
    '**************************************************************
    ' Create a dynaset and load an array with its values.
    '**************************************************************
    On Error Resume Next
    BugDBase.CreateRecordSet TableName
    BugDBase.GetArrayData FieldName, retArray()
    '**************************************************************
    ' Determine how many items were returned.
    '**************************************************************
    NumItems = UBound(retArray)
    '**************************************************************
    ' Print a column heading, then continue.
    '**************************************************************
    Excel.Range(XLColumn & "1").Select
    Excel.ActiveCell.FormulaR1C1 = FieldName
    Excel.Range(XLColumn & "2").Select
    '**************************************************************
    ' Iterate through the array and write its value to Excel.
    '**************************************************************
    For i = 0 To NumItems
        Excel.ActiveCell.FormulaR1C1 = retArray(i)
        Excel.Range(XLColumn & Format(i + 3)).Select
    Next i
End Sub
```

FRMSPL.CLS—Displaying a Splash Screen

Any large project such as UseAll inevitably performs certain tasks that take several minutes to complete. Because long intervals with no apparent activity can scare users into prematurely rebooting their computers, a splash screen provides a reassuring visual effect. For this project, FRMSPL.FRM (listing 28.22) provides the code for presenting the splash screen.

Listing 28.22 FRMSPL.FRM Presents a Splash Form

```
'*********************************************************************
' FRMSPL.FRM - This is just a splash form that is used to display
'              messages to the user during long processes.
'*********************************************************************
Option Explicit
'*********************************************************************
' Initialize the form.
'*********************************************************************
Private Sub Form_Load()
    '*************************************************************
    ' Set the mouse pointer, and put the window on top.
    '*************************************************************
    Screen.MousePointer = vbHourglass
    AlwaysOnTop Me, True
    '*************************************************************
    ' Reposition the label to the center of the form.
    '*************************************************************
    lblMessage.Move (ScaleWidth - lblMessage.Width) / 2, _
                    (ScaleHeight - lblMessage.Height) / 2
    Move (Screen.Width - Width) / 2, (Screen.Height - Height) / 2
End Sub
'*********************************************************************
' Restore the mouse pointer.
'*********************************************************************
Private Sub Form_Unload(Cancel As Integer)
    Screen.MousePointer = vbDefault
End Sub
```

FRMRET.FRM—Enabling the User to Return to UseAll

The clsPrettyPrint and clsReportToXL classes leave the user in different applications when they finish processing. FRMRET.FRM (listing 28.23) is a form that looks like a button in the screen's upper-right corner. The form provides the user an easy (and safe) way to return to your application. FRMRET.FRM also closes the current program (either Excel or Word) by setting its objects equal to nothing.

Listing 28.23   FRMRET.FRM Presents a Button That Enables Users to Return to Your Application

```
'******************************************************************
' FRMRET.FRM - This form is a picture button that provides a
'               generic way to return to your app from Excel & Word.
'******************************************************************
Option Explicit
Option Compare Text
'******************************************************************
' Position the form and button to the same size in the upper-right
' corner so they block the Minimize & Maximize buttons.
'******************************************************************
Private Sub Form_Load()
Dim XTwips%, YTwips%
    XTwips = Screen.TwipsPerPixelX
    YTwips = Screen.TwipsPerPixelY
    '**************************************************************
    ' Size the control, THEN move it to the upper-right corner.
    '**************************************************************
    Move Left, Top, 200 * XTwips, 43.4 * YTwips
    Move Screen.Width - Width, 0
    picReturn.Move 0, 0, 200, 43.4
    '**************************************************************
    ' Prevent the window from being covered up,
    ' and draw the button.
    '**************************************************************
    AlwaysOnTop Me, True
    Handle_MouseUpDown False
End Sub
'******************************************************************
' When the form is unloaded, close the app by examining the form's
' .Tag property. This property was set by the calling function.
'******************************************************************
Private Sub Form_Unload(Cancel As Integer)
    If Tag = "Excel" Then
        Set frmMain.clsR2XL = Nothing
    Else
        Set frmMain.clsPPrint = Nothing
    End If
End Sub
'******************************************************************
' Handle drawing the button in its various states.
' Notice how we use the DrawButton routine from frmMain.
'******************************************************************
Private Sub Handle_MouseUpDown(bState As Boolean)
    frmMain.DrawButton picReturn, IsDown:=bState, _
                sCaption:="Return to " & App.Title & "...", _
                sIcon:="RETURN", IsResource:=True
End Sub
'******************************************************************
' Simulate a button click via graphics methods.
'******************************************************************
Private Sub picReturn_MouseDown(Button%, Shift%, x As Single, _
    y As Single)
```

```
        Handle_MouseUpDown True
    End Sub

    Private Sub picReturn_MouseUp(Button%, Shift%, x As Single, _
                                  y As Single)
        Handle_MouseUpDown False
    End Sub
    '*******************************************************************
    ' Show the main form, and unload this window.
    '*******************************************************************
    Private Sub picReturn_Click()
        frmMain.Show
        Unload Me
    End Sub
```

FRMBUGS.FRM—Writing Data to an Access Database

FRMBUGS.FRM (listing 28.24) is a bug-reporting wizard that you use to store information into an Access database. The form begins by declaring some form-level constants. Next, the SetupForm procedure initializes the form by positioning all the controls, loading the combo boxes, and playing an opening tune. Listing 28.24 also includes the LoadCombos procedure, which uses the GetControlData function from the GenericDB class to load all the combo boxes on the form.

Listing 28.24 FRMBUGS.FRM Shows How to Create a "Bugbase" Wizard

```
'*******************************************************************
' FRMBUGS.FRM - This is a bug reporting form that writes
'               to an Access database via direct calls
'               to the Jet database layer.
'*******************************************************************
Option Explicit
Private DBase As New GenericDB
Private FrameIndex%, BetaID$
'*******************************************************************
' Create more descriptive names for the cmd array indexes.
'*******************************************************************
Private Const CMD_HINT = 0
Private Const CMD_CANCEL = 1
Private Const CMD_PREV = 2
Private Const CMD_NEXT = 3
Private Const CMD_FINISH = 4
Private Const MAX_FRAMES_INDEX = 2
'*******************************************************************
' Position everything, open the database, load the combos,
' and play an opening tune.
'*******************************************************************
Private Sub Form_Load()
```

(continues)

Listing 28.24 Continued

```
'*****************************************************************
' Show the splash form, and set up the form.
'*****************************************************************
SplashVisible True
SetupForm
LoadFrames
'*****************************************************************
' Open the database, and load the combos from its contents.
'*****************************************************************
DBase.OpenDB App.Path & "\bugs.mdb"
LoadCombos
'*****************************************************************
' Play an introductory tune, and unload the splash form.
'*****************************************************************
PlayWaveRes "Game"
SplashVisible False
End Sub
'*****************************************************************
' Load all of the combo boxes with data from the database.
'*****************************************************************
Private Sub LoadCombos()
    DBase.CreateRecordSet "List Defaults"

    DBase.GetControlData "OS", cboHardware(0)
    DBase.GetControlData "Computer", cboHardware(1)
    DBase.GetControlData "Video", cboHardware(2)
    DBase.GetControlData "Boot", cboHardware(3)
    DBase.GetControlData "SCSI", cboHardware(4)

    DBase.GetControlData "Products", cboBugs(0)
    DBase.GetControlData "Repro", cboBugs(1)
    DBase.Data.Close

    DBase.CreateRecordSet fra(0)
    DBase.GetControlData "BetaID", cboContact
End Sub
'*****************************************************************
' Position the buttons, form, and frames.
'*****************************************************************
Private Sub SetupForm()
Const CMD_TOP = 5350
Const CMD_WIDTH = 1095
Const CMD_HEIGHT = 375

    cmd(0).Move 1880, CMD_TOP, CMD_WIDTH, CMD_HEIGHT
    cmd(1).Move 3095, CMD_TOP, CMD_WIDTH, CMD_HEIGHT
    cmd(2).Move 4310, CMD_TOP, CMD_WIDTH, CMD_HEIGHT
    cmd(3).Move 5480, CMD_TOP, CMD_WIDTH, CMD_HEIGHT
    cmd(4).Move 6695, CMD_TOP, CMD_WIDTH, CMD_HEIGHT

    Width = 8125
    Height = 6300
    Move (Screen.Width - Width) / 2, (Screen.Height - Height) / 2
```

```
        LoadFrames
        Draw3DLine
End Sub
'********************************************************************
' Draw a 3-D line above the command buttons.
'********************************************************************
Private Sub Draw3DLine()
Dim iXStart%, iXEnd%, iYStart%, iPixel%
        '********************************************************************
        ' Calculate where the line should be drawn.
        '********************************************************************
        iPixel = Screen.TwipsPerPixelY
        iXEnd = cmd(4).Left + cmd(4).Width
        iXStart = fra(0).Left + iPixel
        iYStart = cmd(0).Top - (iPixel * 10)
        '********************************************************************
        ' Draw the gray line, then the white line underneath.
        '********************************************************************
        Line (iXStart, iYStart)-(iXEnd, iYStart), vb3DShadow
        iYStart = iYStart + iPixel
        Line (iXStart, iYStart)-(iXEnd, iYStart), vb3DHilight
End Sub
'********************************************************************
' Initializes the frames.
'********************************************************************
Private Sub LoadFrames()
        '********************************************************************
        ' Position the frames.
        '********************************************************************
        fra(0).Move 135, 135, 7665, 4875
        fra(1).Move 135, 135, 7665, 4875
        fra(2).Move 135, 135, 7665, 4875
        '********************************************************************
        ' Change the captions.
        '********************************************************************
        fra(0) = "Contact Information"
        fra(1) = "Hardware Information"
        fra(2) = "Bug Details"
End Sub
```

The NavigatePages procedure (listing 28.25) handles the navigation between different pages in the wizard by hiding and displaying the appropriate frames.

Listing 28.25 The NavigatePages Procedure

```
'********************************************************************
' Handles changing frames.
'********************************************************************
Private Sub NavigatePages(ByVal bMoveNext As Boolean)
        '********************************************************************
```

(continues)

Listing 28.25   Continued

```
    ' If you can't update the data, then exit.
    '****************************************************************
    If bMoveNext And Not UpdateData(FrameIndex) Then Exit Sub
    '****************************************************************
    ' Hide the current frame, increment FrameIndex,
    ' then show the new frame.
    '****************************************************************
    fra(FrameIndex).Visible = False
    FrameIndex = IIf(bMoveNext, FrameIndex + 1, FrameIndex - 1)
    fra(FrameIndex).Visible = True
    '****************************************************************
    ' Open the table for the current page, and load the data.
    '****************************************************************
    DBase.Data.Close
    DBase.CreateRecordSet fra(FrameIndex)
    LoadPage
    '****************************************************************
    ' Change the enabled status of the command buttons.
    '****************************************************************
    If FrameIndex = 0 Then
        cmd(CMD_PREV).Enabled = False
    ElseIf FrameIndex = MAX_FRAMES_INDEX Then
        cmd(CMD_NEXT).Enabled = False
    Else
        cmd(CMD_PREV).Enabled = True
        cmd(CMD_NEXT).Enabled = True
    End If
End Sub
```

As UseAll changes each page, it calls `UpdateData` (listing 28.26) to write the data to the database. This function calls either the `VerifyRequiredField` function, to verify that required fields are filled, or the `AddOrEditRecord` function, to write data to the database.

Listing 28.26   The `UpdateData` Function

```
'****************************************************************
' Write the changes or additions to the database.
'****************************************************************
Private Function UpdateData(Index%, Optional AddRec) As Boolean
Static Iterations As Integer
    '****************************************************************
    'AddRec determines whether to add or update a record.
    '****************************************************************
    AddRec = IIf(IsMissing(AddRec), True, AddRec)
    '****************************************************************
    ' Iterations are used to prevent uncontrolled recursive loops.
    '****************************************************************
    Iterations = Iterations + 1
    '****************************************************************
```

```
' Clear the error handler (for recursive calls only).
'**********************************************************************
If Iterations > 0 Then Err = 0
'**********************************************************************
' Update the appropriate page.
'**********************************************************************
Select Case Index
        '************************************************************
        ' Contact Information
        '************************************************************
        Case 0
            '********************************************************
            ' Verify required fields.
            '********************************************************
            If Not VerifyRequiredField(txtMultiContact(0)) _
                Then Exit Function
            If Not VerifyRequiredField(txtContact(0)) _
                Then Exit Function
            DBase.AddOrEditRecord AddRec, _
                "NameAddress¦" & txtMultiContact(0), _
                "Phone¦" & txtContact(0), _
                "Fax¦" & txtContact(1), _
                "InternetAddress¦" & txtContact(2), _
                "BetaID¦" & cboContact
        '************************************************************
        ' Hardware Information
        '************************************************************
        Case 1
            If Not VerifyRequiredField(cboHardware(0)) _
                Then Exit Function
            If Not VerifyRequiredField(cboHardware(1)) _
                Then Exit Function
            If Not VerifyRequiredField(cboHardware(2)) _
                Then Exit Function
            If Not VerifyRequiredField(cboHardware(3)) _
                Then Exit Function
            DBase.AddOrEditRecord AddRec, _
                "OperatingSystem¦" & cboHardware(0), _
                "ComputerType¦" & cboHardware(1), _
                "VideoAdapter¦" & cboHardware(2), _
                "BootDiskType¦" & cboHardware(3), _
                "SCSI¦" & cboHardware(4), _
                "OtherDiskTypes¦" & txtHardware(0), _
                "Floppies¦" & txtHardware(1), _
                "FileSystems¦" & txtHardware(2), _
                "BetaID¦" & BetaID
        '************************************************************
        ' Bug Details
        '************************************************************
        Case 2
            If Not VerifyRequiredField(txtBugs(0)) _
                Then Exit Function
            If Not VerifyRequiredField(txtBugs(1)) _
                Then Exit Function
```

(continues)

Listing 28.26 Continued

```
                If Not VerifyRequiredField(txtMultiBugs(0)) _
                    Then Exit Function
                If Not VerifyRequiredField(txtMultiBugs(1)) _
                    Then Exit Function
                DBase.AddOrEditRecord AddRec, _
                    "Product¦" & cboBugs(0), _
                    "Build¦" & txtBugs(0), _
                    "Reproducible¦" & cboBugs(1), _
                    "Title¦" & txtBugs(1), _
                    "Problem¦" & txtMultiBugs(0), _
                    "Steps¦" & txtMultiBugs(1), _
                    "BetaID¦" & BetaID
        End Select
        '****************************************************************
        ' If Index is 2 and duplicate key error, then notify the user
        ' that the title is invalid.
        '****************************************************************
        If Index = MAX_FRAMES_INDEX And Err = 3022 Then
            PlayWaveRes "Ring"
            MsgBox "A report with the same name has already
            ➥been reported.", vbExclamation
            Iterations = 0
            UpdateData = False
        '****************************************************************
        ' If less than 2 iterations, then recursively call.
        '****************************************************************
        ElseIf Iterations < 2 And Err Then
            UpdateData = UpdateData(Index, False)
            Iterations = 0
        '****************************************************************
        ' Otherwise return true and reset the iterations variable.
        '****************************************************************
        Else
            UpdateData = True
            Iterations = 0
        End If
End Function
```

As the cboContact drop-down combo box loses its focus, the cboContact procedure (listing 28.27) checks whether the combo box is blank. If it is, the procedure displays a message and returns the focus to the combo box. If not, the user information (if any) that is already in the database fills the page.

Listing 28.27 The cboContact Procedure

```
    '****************************************************************
    ' Make sure a Beta ID is listed.
    '****************************************************************
Private Sub cboContact_LostFocus()
    '****************************************************************
    ' Set the global variable.
    '****************************************************************
```

```
        BetaID = Trim(cboContact)
        '****************************************************************
        ' If one wasn't entered, then alert the user and halt.
        '****************************************************************
        If BetaID = "" Then
            PlayWaveRes "Ding"
            MsgBox "This field can not be blank!", vbCritical
            cboContact.SetFocus
        '****************************************************************
        ' Otherwise load the other controls with data from that id.
        '****************************************************************
        Else
            LoadPage
        End If
End Sub
```

The cmd_Click procedure handles click events from the command buttons on the wizard. The only control with any significant code is the Finish button. This button writes the bug report to the database and then asks the user if he or she wants to enter another bug. If not, the procedure dismisses the form. Otherwise, the procedure clears the page and returns the focus to the first drop-down combo box. The txtMultiBugs_Change event handles the enabled status of the Finish button to prevent users from finishing prematurely. Listing 28.28 shows these event-handling routines.

Listing 28.28   FRMBUGS Event-Handling Routines

```
'****************************************************************
' Process command-button clicks.
'****************************************************************
Private Sub cmd_Click(Index As Integer)
    Select Case Index
        '****************************************************************
        ' Display a hint (from the frame's .Tag) in a message box.
        '****************************************************************
        Case CMD_HINT
            PlayWaveRes "Chimes"
            MsgBox fra(FrameIndex).Tag, vbInformation
        '****************************************************************
        ' Cancel is used to quit without filing a report.
        '****************************************************************
        Case CMD_CANCEL
            If MsgBox("Are you sure you want to Quit?" _
                        , vbQuestion + vbYesNo) = vbYes Then
                PlayWaveRes "Hasta"
                Unload Me
            End If
        '****************************************************************
        ' The next two are used to navigate between frames.
        '****************************************************************
```

(continues)

Listing 28.28 Continued

```
                Case CMD_PREV
                    NavigatePages False
                Case CMD_NEXT
                    NavigatePages True
            '********************************************************
            ' File the bug report.
            '********************************************************
                Case CMD_FINISH
                    '********************************************************
                    ' If UpdateData failed, the title must have already
                    ' appeared in the database. Set the focus to the title
                    ' text box, and exit. If users want to quit without
                    ' fixing the problem, they'll have to use Cancel.
                    '********************************************************
                    If Not UpdateData(FrameIndex) Then
                        txtBugs(1).SetFocus
                        Exit Sub
                    End If
                    '********************************************************
                    ' If the report was successfully filed, then ask users
                    ' if they want to file another. If so, clear the page.
                    '********************************************************
                    If MsgBox("Would you like to report another bug?" _
                                , vbQuestion + vbYesNo) = vbYes Then
                        txtBugs(1) = ""
                        txtMultiBugs(0) = ""
                        txtMultiBugs(1) = ""
                        txtBugs(1).SetFocus
                    '********************************************************
                    ' Otherwise tell the user goodbye, and unload.
                    '********************************************************
                    Else
                        PlayWaveRes "ItsBeen"
                        MsgBox "Thank you for completing this report.", _
                                                        vbInformation

                        Unload Me
                    End If
            End Select
        End Sub
        '********************************************************
        ' If the "Steps" text box is empty, disable the Finish button.
        '********************************************************
        Private Sub txtMultiBugs_Change(Index As Integer)
            If Index = 1 Then
                cmd(CMD_FINISH).Enabled = IIf(txtMultiBugs(1) <> "", _
                    True, False)
            End If
        End Sub
```

The LoadPage procedure loads a page with data from the database.
The next procedure, ClearAll, clears all the form's controls. Finally, the
VerifyRequiredField procedure verifies that the field isn't null. If it is, the

procedure displays an error message and adds a space to the field to prevent multiple errors. Listing 28.29 shows all three of these procedures.

Listing 28.29   The `LoadPage`, `ClearAll`, **and** `VerifyRequiredField`
Procedures

```
'******************************************************************
' Loads the data from the database into the controls.
'******************************************************************
Private Sub LoadPage()
    '**************************************************************
    ' Find the record based on its BetaID value.
    '**************************************************************
    If DBase.FindRecord("BetaID", BetaID) = "" Then
        ClearAll
        Exit Sub
    End If
    '**************************************************************
    ' Use the public FrameIndex value to determine
    ' which frame to load.
    '**************************************************************
    Select Case FrameIndex
        Case 0
            '******************************************************
            'NOTE: & "" is appended to each line to prevent
            '       triggering an error if the return value
            '       from the record is NULL.
            '******************************************************
            txtMultiContact(0) = DBase.GetRecord("NameAddress") _
                & ""
            txtContact(0) = DBase.GetRecord("Phone") & ""
            txtContact(1) = DBase.GetRecord("Fax") & ""
            txtContact(2) = DBase.GetRecord("InternetAddress") _
                & ""
        Case 1
            cboHardware(0) = DBase.GetRecord("OperatingSystem") _
                & ""
            cboHardware(1) = DBase.GetRecord("ComputerType") & ""
            cboHardware(2) = DBase.GetRecord("VideoAdapter") & ""
            cboHardware(3) = DBase.GetRecord("BootDiskType") & ""
            cboHardware(4) = DBase.GetRecord("SCSI") & ""
            txtHardware(0) = DBase.GetRecord("OtherDiskTypes") _
                & ""
            txtHardware(1) = DBase.GetRecord("Floppies") & ""
            txtHardware(2) = DBase.GetRecord("FileSystems") & ""
    End Select
End Sub
'******************************************************************
' Clear and reset selected controls.
'******************************************************************
Private Sub ClearAll()
    txtMultiContact(0) = ""
    txtContact(0) = ""
```

(continues)

Listing 28.29   Continued

```
        txtContact(1) = ""
        txtContact(2) = ""
        cboHardware(0).ListIndex = 0
        cboHardware(1).ListIndex = 0
        cboHardware(2).ListIndex = 0
        cboHardware(3).ListIndex = 0
        cboHardware(4).ListIndex = 0
        txtHardware(0) = ""
        txtHardware(1) = ""
        txtHardware(2) = ""
End Sub
'*********************************************************************
' If the field is required, then make sure it isn't blank.
'*********************************************************************
Private Function VerifyRequiredField(Cntl As Control) As Boolean
    If Cntl.Text = "" Then
        MsgBox "This is a required field!", vbExclamation
        '*********************************************************************
        ' Put blank space in control to prevent another error.
        '*********************************************************************
        Cntl.Text = " "
        Cntl.SetFocus
        VerifyRequiredField = False
        Exit Function
    End If
    '*********************************************************************
    ' If its data is valid, then return True.
    '*********************************************************************
    VerifyRequiredField = True
End Function
```

FRMMAIN.FRM—Combining Modules to Create an Interface

FRMMAIN.FRM (listing 28.30) ties all the previous modules together in one central user interface. The beginning of this form contains some necessary declarations, followed by the form initialization tasks. The Form_Load procedure draws the 3-D effect of the form and its four graphical buttons. In addition, the procedure positions the controls on the form to fit each individual quadrant. These tasks can be rather time consuming, so FRMMAIN.FRM displays a splash screen during startup processing.

Listing 28.30   FRMMAIN.FRM Is USEALL.VBP's Central User Interface

```
'*********************************************************************
' FRMMAIN.FRM - This is command central where everything begins.
'*********************************************************************
```

```vb
Option Explicit
Public clsR2XL As New clsReportToXL
Public clsPPrint As New clsPrettyPrint
#If Win32 Then
Private Declare Function GetDeviceCaps Lib "gdi32" (ByVal hDC As _
    Long, ByVal nIndex As Long) As Long
#Else
Private Declare Function GetDeviceCaps Lib "GDI" (ByVal hDC%, _
    ByVal nIndex%) As Integer
#End If
'*****************************************************************
' This is a form-level conditional compilation constant. It's used
' to prevent performing certain time-consuming tasks
' during debugging.
'*****************************************************************
#Const DEBUG_MODE = False
'*****************************************************************
' Position and size all objects on the form.
'*****************************************************************
Private Sub Form_Load()
Dim Quad2 As RECT, Quad4 As RECT, NewQuad As RECT, i%

    '*****************************************************************
    ' Since these are time consuming to display, hide them during
    ' debugging.
    '*****************************************************************
    #If DEBUG_MODE Then
        oleExcel.Visible = False
        olePower.Visible = False
        oleProject.Visible = False
    #End If
    '*****************************************************************
    ' Change Backcolor and display the splash screen.
    '*****************************************************************
    On Error Resume Next
    picButton(0).BackColor = vb3DFace
    BackColor = vb3DFace
    SplashVisible True
    '*****************************************************************
    ' Size the form to the screen.
    '*****************************************************************
    Move 0, 0, Screen.Width, Screen.Height
    '*****************************************************************
    ' Draw a 3-D grid on the form.
    '*****************************************************************
    Draw3DGrid Me, True
    '*****************************************************************
    ' Position a label above the oleExcel control.
    '*****************************************************************
    GetQuad 2, Quad2
    GetQuad 4, Quad4
    With NewQuad
        .rL = Quad2.rL
        .rT = Quad2.rB
        .rR = Quad2.rR
```

(continues)

Listing 28.30 Continued

```
                 .rB = Quad4.rT
        End With
        SizeToRectClient lblStatus, NewQuad
        '***************************************************************
        ' Draw a DkBlue background in Quad2 & position lbl
        ' and picButtons.
        '***************************************************************
        ResizeRect Quad2, -1, -1, False
        DrawRect Me, Quad2, Solid:=True, RectColor:=RGB(0, 0, 64)
        SizeToRectClient lbl, Quad2
        lbl.top = Quad2.rT + 2
        lbl.Height = GetRectHeight(Quad2) * 0.1
        picButton(0).Move lbl.Left + 50, lbl.top + lbl.Height, _
                         lbl.Width - 100, GetRectHeight(Quad2) * 0.2
        '***************************************************************
        ' Load 3 more buttons 5 pixels apart.
        '***************************************************************
        For i = 1 To 3
            Load picButton(i): picButton(i).Visible = True
            picButton(i).top = picButton(i - 1).top + _
                             picButton(i - 1).Height + 5
        Next i
        '***************************************************************
        ' Create the button effect, and label them.
        '***************************************************************
        picButton(0).Tag = "Create a Bug Report..." & "¦ADD_BUGS"
        Handle_MouseUpDown 0, False
        Handle_MouseUpDown 1, False
        Handle_MouseUpDown 2, False
        Handle_MouseUpDown 3, False
        '***************************************************************
        ' Make sure everything is positioned,
        ' then remove the splash form.
        '***************************************************************
        VerifyControlPositions
        Visible = True
        SplashVisible False
    End Sub
```

The VerifyControlPositions routine (listing 28.31) verifies that the controls are placed properly. If the screen resolution is anything other than 640 by 480, the routine must resize the controls. Every time that you size an OLE container control, you must open the OLE server object and redraw the control's picture. Because this process is time consuming, the routine resizes the controls only if necessary.

Listing 28.31   The `VerifyControlPositions` Routine

```
'*******************************************************************
' Resizing OLE controls can be VERY time consuming, so only
' do it if they have moved, or if resolution is <> 640x480.
'*******************************************************************
Sub VerifyControlPositions()
Const HORZRES = 8   '  Horizontal width in pixels
Const VERTRES = 10  '  Vertical width in pixels
Dim hRes%, vRes%, Quad1 As RECT, Quad3 As RECT, Quad4 As RECT
    '*******************************************************************
    ' Get the size of the quadrants.
    '*******************************************************************
    GetQuad 1, Quad1
    GetQuad 3, Quad3
    GetQuad 4, Quad4
    '*******************************************************************
    ' Get the screen resolution,
    '*******************************************************************
    hRes = GetDeviceCaps(hDC, HORZRES)
    vRes = GetDeviceCaps(hDC, VERTRES)
    '*******************************************************************
    ' If not 640x480, then resize the OLE controls.
    '*******************************************************************
    If hRes <> 640 Or vRes <> 480 Then
        SizeToRectClient oleProject, Quad1
        SizeToRectClient olePower, Quad3
        SizeToRectClient oleExcel, Quad4
    '*******************************************************************
    ' If ole??? has moved or been resized, then fix it.
    '*******************************************************************
    ElseIf Not EqualToQuadClient(oleProject, Quad1) Then
        SizeToRectClient oleProject, Quad1

    ElseIf Not EqualToQuadClient(olePower, Quad3) Then
        SizeToRectClient olePower, Quad3

    ElseIf Not EqualToQuadClient(oleExcel, Quad4) Then
        SizeToRectClient oleExcel, Quad4
    End If
    '*******************************************************************
    ' Process the delays caused by resizing OLE controls.
    '*******************************************************************
    DoEvents
End Sub
```

When unloading the form, the Form_Unload procedure ensures that the application doesn't continue displaying the frmReturn form. The next procedure, Form_MouseMove, ensures that the lblStatus label is no longer visible. The lblStatus label displays when the user moves the mouse over the oleExcel control to display a status message. The message informs users that they update the control by clicking on it. Listing 28.32 shows both of these procedures.

Listing 28.32 The `Form_Unload` and `MouseMove` Procedures

```
'**********************************************************************
' Make sure there are no orphan forms.
'**********************************************************************
Private Sub Form_Unload(Cancel As Integer)
    Unload frmReturn
End Sub
'**********************************************************************
' If the mouse is over the form, then hide lblStatus.
'**********************************************************************
Private Sub Form_MouseMove(Button%, Shift%, x As Single, _
                          y As Single)
    lblStatus.Visible = False
End Sub
'**********************************************************************
' Update the chart whenever the user clicks on it.
'**********************************************************************
Private Sub oleExcel_Click()
    UpdateChart
End Sub
'**********************************************************************
' If the mouse is over the control, then show the label.
'**********************************************************************
Private Sub oleExcel_MouseMove(Button%, Shift%, x As Single, _
                             y As Single)
    lblStatus.Visible = True
End Sub
```

All the following procedures in listing 28.33 paint the graphical buttons that appear on the form. The buttons are actually picture boxes with a 3-D border and a caption and graphic painted on them. The resource file stores the pictures, and `PaintPicture` paints them on the control.

Listing 28.33 The 3-D Graphical Buttons That Use Picture Boxes

```
'**********************************************************************
' Performs the appropriate action for the picButton
' that was clicked.
'**********************************************************************
Private Sub picButton_Click(Index As Integer)
    '**********************************************************************
    ' Since a Click event only occurs when an object gets
    ' a Mouse_Down AND a Mouse_Up event, all command processing
    ' should be here.
    '**********************************************************************
    On Error Resume Next
    Select Case Index
        Case 0
            frmBugs.Show vbModal
        Case 1
```

```
                    '********************************************************
                    ' Display frmReturn by calling its Display method,
                    ' instead of using the Show method. This allows
                    ' frmReturn to know which form is requesting
                    ' that frmReturn is displayed. This is important
                    ' because frmReturn needs to know which form it
                    ' should activate when it is unloaded.
                    '********************************************************
                    frmReturn.Display Me
                    clsR2XL.ReportToExcel App.Path & "\bugs.mdb"
                Case 2
                    '********************************************************
                    ' Display a common file open dialog.
                    '********************************************************
                    cdlg.FLAGS = cdlOFNFileMustExist + _
                                cdlOFNHideReadOnly +cdlOFNPathMustExist
                    cdlg.ShowOpen
                    If Err <> cdlCancel Then
                        frmReturn.Display Me
                        clsPPrint.PrettyPrint cdlg.FileName
                    End If
                Case 3
                    Unload Me
            End Select
        End Sub
        '********************************************************************
        ' These two events simulate the button-clicking effect.
        '********************************************************************
        Private Sub picButton_MouseDown(Index%, Button%, Shift%, x!, y!)
            Handle_MouseUpDown Index, True
        End Sub

        Private Sub picButton_MouseUp(Index%, Button%, Shift%, x!, y!)
            Handle_MouseUpDown Index, False
        End Sub
        '********************************************************************
        ' A single procedure is used so that the code appears in only one
        ' place. This prevents errors from duplicate code.
        '********************************************************************
        Private Sub Handle_MouseUpDown(Index%, bState As Boolean)
            '****************************************************************
            ' Here's where all of buttons are drawn. Any changes here will
            ' affect all other procedures that operate on picButtons.
            '****************************************************************
            Select Case Index
                Case 0
                    DrawButton picButton(Index), IsDown:=bState, _
                                                IsResource:=True
                Case 1
                    DrawButton picButton(1), IsDown:=bState, _
                                sCaption:="Bug Summary in Excel...", _
                                sIcon:="VIEW_BUGS", _
                                IsResource:=True
                Case 2
                    DrawButton picButton(2), IsDown:=bState, _
                                sCaption:="View Code in Word...", _
```

(continues)

```
Listing 28.33   Continued

                         sIcon:="VIEW_CODE", _
                         IsResource:=True
        Case 3
            DrawButton picButton(3), IsDown:=bState, _
                         sCaption:="Exit Application...", _
                         sIcon:="EXIT", _
                         IsResource:=True

    End Select
End Sub
```

Finally, the UpdateChart procedure (listing 28.34) gets bug data from the
database and uses OLE Automation methods on the object inside the OLE
container control to update the Excel chart.

```
Listing 28.34   The UpdateChart Procedure

    Private Sub UpdateChart()
    Dim BugDBase As New GenericDB, retArray() As String

        BugDBase.OpenDB App.Path & "\bugs.mdb"
        BugDBase.CreateRecordSet "qryBugsByProduct"
        BugDBase.GetArrayData "BugCount", retArray()

        oleExcel.DoVerb 0
        With oleExcel.Object.Parent.Parent.ActiveWorkbook
            .Sheets("Bugs").Range("B2").FormulaR1C1 = retArray(0)
            .Sheets("Bugs").Range("B3").FormulaR1C1 = retArray(1)
            .Sheets("Bugs").Range("B4").FormulaR1C1 = retArray(2)
        End With
        oleExcel.Close

        Set BugDBase = Nothing
    End Sub
```

Note

To help you understand the UseAll application components better, the companion
CD includes six small projects that use each major component separately. If you have
difficulties understanding any of the information presented in this chapter, try opening one of these smaller projects. You might understand the information better if you
focus on a smaller code sample.

From Here...

Although this chapter presents many solutions to integrated application problems, it omits thousands of other solutions. You might find the solutions to some of your integration problems in the following sources:

- *Microsoft Windows SDK.* All the documentation of the Software Development Kit (SDK) contains useful information for manipulating stubborn Windows applications. Although this documentation is sometimes difficult to understand, you might be surprised at the information that it provides.

- *Visual Basic Programmer's Guide to the Windows API* (Ziff-Davis, 1994), by Daniel Appleman. This book will be your bible if you decide to explore extensive API programming with Visual Basic. If you program with the API, make sure that you have this book handy.

Chapter 29

Distributing Integrated Applications

After you finish building and testing your integrated application, you're ready to distribute it—right? Wrong. Before distributing any integrated application, there are several things that you must know. This chapter guides you through the distribution process.

In this chapter, you learn more about the following:

- Preventing distribution embarrassments
- Distributing your applications
- Handling performance considerations
- Understanding the importance of documentation and online Help
- Planning development and handling errors

Preventing Distribution Embarrassments

You've just completed your program and tested it for several hours (or days) on your system. You're convinced that you have a "bug-free" application, so you copy your executable to a floppy and take it to your friend's computer. You spend 20 minutes telling him how awesome your program is, just to arouse his curiosity. After he is so excited that he has declared you a "Computer Genius," you copy your program to his hard disk. You double-click on your program in File Manager, and a big error message comes up on the screen.

Your face turns red, and you begin to sweat. You try to handle the situation by reading the message to yourself and trying to run your program again. Nothing happens. After trying everything you know, with no success, you look to your friend and say, "What the heck is wrong with your stinking computer?"

Has this happened to you? If not, then you better read this chapter to prevent it from happening. If it has, you already know the importance of this chapter.

This chapter discusses some of the important distribution-related issues that will help you to maintain your status as a computer genius, and keep you from jumping off a bridge in embarrassment. Read this chapter carefully and refer to it often, or else you'll be the next victim of a poor distribution attempt.

Distributing Your Applications

The first and most important part of a successful distribution is to ensure that you have the correct files in the correct place. If you forget one file, or if you put it in the wrong directory, your application will not run. Forgetting distribution files also shows sloppiness on the part of your company, so it's something that you should avoid at all costs. See Chapter 30, "Distributing Your Applications," in the *Visual Basic Programmers Guide* for a complete listing of the supporting files that Visual Basic and its custom controls require.

> **Note**
>
> Even if you write your own setup program, you should use the Setup Wizard. The Setup Wizard searches your application for all the required distribution files and copies them to a floppy disk. After Setup Wizard finishes, you can look on the disk to see which files your application requires (ignore the SETUP*.* files) and copy them to your setup disk.

Tip
Play it safe and distribute only those files that you have a legal right to distribute. When in doubt, contact the company that wrote the software or contact Microsoft.

Licensing Considerations

When making your distribution disk, you should copy only those files that you have a license to distribute. Distributing unlicensed files can lead to severe legal action against you and your company, as well as extreme embarrassment. Even if you don't realize that you are illegally distributing a file, you can still get into big trouble.

Even if a file comes with a program that you own (for example, clip art from CorelDRAW! or certain Visual Basic files), you don't necessarily have the legal right to distribute the file.

Handling Missing Files That Can't Be Licensed

If you can't purchase a license to distribute a file, you have to require that your users own the program or file on which your application depends. Because you are likely to write an application that depends on one or more Microsoft Office applications (which you *can't* distribute), you will have to notify the user of which Office applications (and versions) that he or she must have installed before running your program.

Ensuring Proper Installations—Setup Programs

Copying all the proper files to your disk doesn't mean that they will get copied to the correct directory on the user's system. If your application doesn't have a setup program that does *everything* necessary to run your application, the odds of it working on another computer are very poor. You should *always* write a good setup and uninstall program.

The advantages of a good setup and uninstall program are many, because it does the following:

- Provides a more professional appearance for your product

- Ensures that your application will be successfully installed on your customer's computer

- Saves you the expense of support calls regarding setup and removal of your product

- Protects you and your company from embarrassment

Because you purchased Visual Basic 4.0, you have no excuse not to have a setup program, because VB4 includes the Setup Wizard. The Setup Wizard is a great utility that creates a setup/uninstall disk for your Visual Basic application and makes sure that all the files that your application requires are on it.

If your application requires a more robust setup program, you can always modify the source code that Setup Wizard creates and add your application-specific features. If you need even more advanced features and you don't know how to code them, you can always purchase one of the many prewritten setup programs on the market.

A good setup program pays for itself after you sell your first five to ten applications (depending on the product cost), so you have no excuse not to write one (no matter how small your application is).

> **Note**
>
> All Windows 95 certified applications will be required to have a setup program that installs and uninstalls all of its files, so now is the time to learn how to write a good setup program. If you have the Windows 95 SDK, you also can consider using the InstallShield 95 setup and uninstall program that comes with the SDK.

> **Note**
>
> If possible, set up a single system with only your target operating system installed. If your application can run on a system that has only the operating system installed, the odds are that your setup disk is good.

Handling Missing Components—Gracefully

When creating integrated applications that depend on multiple programs being present, you must ensure that your program is prepared to handle a missing component. For example, suppose that you want to create an About box that has a System Info button like the ones in the Office applications, as shown in figure 29.1.

Fig. 29.1
You can add
Microsoft's System
Info button to
your applications.

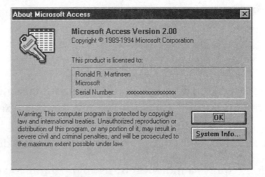

You can't legally distribute the System Information program, so your program can show or hide that button depending on whether that component is present. Listing 29.1 demonstrates how to accomplish this task.

Listing 29.1   This Example Shows How Your Application Can Handle Missing Components Gracefully

```
'******************************************************************
' FRMABOUT.FRM - Demonstrates how to handle a missing component.
'******************************************************************
Option Explicit
Private WinDir As String
#If Win32 Then
Const SYSINFO = "msapps\msinfo\msinfo32.exe"
Private Declare Function GetWindowsDirectory& Lib "Kernel32" _
    Alias "GetWindowsDirectoryA" (ByVal buffer$, ByVal bufLen&)
#Else
Const SYSINFO = "msapps\msinfo\msinfo.exe"
Private Declare Function GetWindowsDirectory% Lib "Kernel" _
    (ByVal buffer$, ByVal bufLen%)
#End If
'******************************************************************
' Unload the form.
'******************************************************************
Private Sub cmdOk_Click()
    Unload Me
End Sub
'******************************************************************
' Start the Microsoft System Information program.
'******************************************************************
Private Sub cmdSysInfo_Click()
    Shell WinDir & SYSINFO, vbNormalFocus
End Sub
'******************************************************************
' Load the form and determine if the System Info button should
' be visible.
'******************************************************************
Private Sub Form_Load()
    '**********************************************************
    ' Always use system colors.
    '**********************************************************
    Lines(0).BorderColor = vb3DHighlight
    Lines(1).BorderColor = vb3DShadow
    Lines(2).BorderColor = vb3DHighlight
    Lines(3).BorderColor = vb3DShadow
    BackColor = vb3DFace
    '**********************************************************
    ' Change the picture displayed in the image control.
    '**********************************************************
    img.picture = Me.Icon
    '**********************************************************
    ' Center the form.
    '**********************************************************
    Move (Screen.Width - Width) \ 2, (Screen.Height - Height) \ 2
    '**********************************************************
    ' Get the path to the Windows directory.
    '**********************************************************
```

(continues)

Listing 29.1   Continued

```
        WinDir = Space(2048)
        WinDir = Left(WinDir, GetWindowsDirectory(WinDir, _
                Len(WinDir))) & "\"
        '****************************************************************
        'Set visible status depending on the existence of the file.
        '****************************************************************
        cmdSysInfo.Visible = FileExists(WinDir & SYSINFO)
End Sub
'****************************************************************
' Determine if the file exists, and return the result.
'****************************************************************
Private Function FileExists(sFileName As String) As Boolean
    On Error Resume Next
    FileExists = IIf(Dir(sFileName) <> "", True, False)
End Function
```

The key element of this program is determining whether the file exists. If MSINFO.EXE is present, the button's Visible property changes to True. Otherwise, the program sets its Visible property to False and hides the button. Figure 29.2 shows how the sample program looks when MSINFO.EXE exists.

Fig. 29.2
The System Info button displays only if MSINFO.EXE exists.

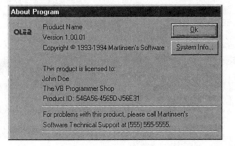

You might think that it is much more difficult to handle a missing Office application, but it really isn't. Listing 29.2 shows how easy it is to determine whether an Office application is present.

Listing 29.2   Checking for an Application's Existence Is Easy

```
'****************************************************************
' FRMEXISTS.FRM - Lists the existence of several Office apps.
'****************************************************************
Option Explicit
#If Win16 Then
Private Declare Function GetProfileString% Lib "Kernel" (ByVal _
    sSection$, ByVal sKey$, ByVal sDef$, ByVal sRetStr$, _
    ByVal iSize%)
#End If
```

```
'*********************************************************************
' Checks to see if a file exists.
'*********************************************************************
Function FileExists(sFileName$) As Boolean
    On Error Resume Next
    FileExists = IIf(Dir(Trim(sFileName)) <> "", True, False)
End Function
#If Win32 Then
'*********************************************************************
' This function determines if an application is present by seeing
' if there is any text in the Registry for the provided SubKey.
'*********************************************************************
Public Function IsAppPresent(strSubKey$, strValueName$) As Boolean
    IsAppPresent = CBool(Len(GetRegString(HKEY_CLASSES_ROOT, _
                        strSubKey, strValueName)))
End Function
#Else
'*********************************************************************
' This function determines if an application is present.
' The sExtension arg is the 3-letter extension of its data files.
' The sDefaultPath is where you think the app might be installed.
'*********************************************************************
Public Function IsAppPresent(sExtension$, sDefaultPath$) _
    As Boolean
Dim sAppPath As String
    '*********************************************************************
    ' Check the [Extensions] section of the WIN.INI to see where
    ' the app is located. If the extension is not found, then
    ' the default EXE path (sDefaultPath) is checked.
    '*********************************************************************
    sAppPath = Space(4098)
    GetProfileString "Extensions", sExtension, sDefaultPath _
        & " ^" & sExtension, sAppPath, Len(sAppPath)
    '*********************************************************************
    ' [Extensions] section stores info in the following format:
    '        <extension>=<application path> ^<extension>
    ' To get the application path, you'll need to take everything
    ' to the left of the caret (^).
    '*********************************************************************
    sAppPath = Left(sAppPath, InStr(sAppPath, "^") - 1)
    '*********************************************************************
    ' Return whether or not the application is present.
    '*********************************************************************
    IsAppPresent = FileExists(sAppPath)
End Function
#End If
'*********************************************************************
' Unloads the form.
'*********************************************************************
Private Sub cmdExit_Click()
    Unload Me
End Sub
'*********************************************************************
' Performs some initialization steps, and lists the existence of
' certain Office apps.
'*********************************************************************
```

(continues)

Listing 29.2 Continued

```
Private Sub Form_Load()
    Move (Screen.Width - Width) / 2, (Screen.Height - Height) / 2
    Print 'Print blank line
    '****************************************************************
    ' Call the appropriate version of IsAppPresent, depending on
    ' the current platform.
    '****************************************************************
#If Win32 Then
    Print " Access", IsAppPresent("Access.Database\CurVer", "")
    Print " Excel", IsAppPresent("Excel.Sheet\CurVer", "")
    Print " PowerPoint", IsAppPresent("PowerPoint.Slide\CurVer", _
        "")
    Print " Word", IsAppPresent("Word.Document\CurVer", "")
#Else
    Print " Access", IsAppPresent("mdb", "c:\access\msaccess.exe")
    Print " Excel", IsAppPresent("xls", "c:\excel\excel.exe")
    Print " PowerPoint", IsAppPresent("ppt", _
        "c:\powerpnt\powerpnt.exe")
    Print " Word", IsAppPresent("doc", "c:\winword\winword.exe")
#End If
End Sub
```

The key feature in this application is the IsAppPresent function. In the 16-bit version of Windows, all you need to do to find out whether an application exists is to check whether its executable is present. Because the WIN.INI file contains the location of most executables in the [Extensions] section, locating the application is easy. Figure 29.3 shows the program in listing 29.2 running.

Fig. 29.3
The APPEXIST.VBP project determines which Office applications exist.

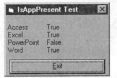

In the 32-bit version of Windows, you will want to search the Registry to make sure that an application is present. The following module, REGISTRY.BAS, retrieves a string from anywhere in the Registry (unlike VB4's GetSetting function):

```
'****************************************************************
' REGISTRY.BAS - Contains the code necessary to access the Windows
'                registration database.
'****************************************************************
#If Win32 Then
Option Explicit
```

```vb
'********************************************************************
' The minimal API calls required to read from the Registry.
'********************************************************************
Private Declare Function RegOpenKey Lib "advapi32" Alias _
    "RegOpenKeyA" (ByVal hKey As Long, ByVal lpSubKey As String, _
    phkResult As Long) As Long
Private Declare Function RegQueryValueEx Lib "advapi32" Alias _
    "RegQueryValueExA" (ByVal hKey As Long, ByVal lpValueName As _
    String, lpReserved As Long, lptype As Long, lpData As Any, _
    lpcbData As Long) As Long
Private Declare Function RegCloseKey& Lib "advapi32" (ByVal hKey&)
'********************************************************************
' The constants used in this module for the Registry API calls.
'********************************************************************
Private Const REG_SZ = 1          ' Unicode null terminated string
Private Const REG_EXPAND_SZ = 2 ' Unicode null terminated string
                                  ' with environment variable
                                  ' references.
Private Const ERROR_SUCCESS = 0
'********************************************************************
' The numeric constants for the major keys in the Registry.
'********************************************************************
Public Const HKEY_CLASSES_ROOT = &H80000000
Public Const HKEY_CURRENT_USER = &H80000001
Public Const HKEY_LOCAL_MACHINE = &H80000002
Public Const HKEY_USERS = &H80000003
Public Const HKEY_PERFORMANCE_DATA = &H80000004
'********************************************************************
' GetRegString takes three arguments. A HKEY constant
' (listed above), a subkey, and a value in that subkey.
' This function returns the string stored in the strValueName
' value in the Registry.
'********************************************************************
Public Function GetRegString(hKey As Long, strSubKey As String, _
                             strValueName As String) As String
Dim strSetting As String
Dim lngDataLen As Long
Dim lngRes As Long
    '************************************************************
    ' Open the key. If success, then get the data from the key.
    '************************************************************
    If RegOpenKey(hKey, strSubKey, lngRes) = ERROR_SUCCESS Then
        strSetting = Space(255)
        lngDataLen = Len(strSetting)
        '********************************************************
        ' Query the key for the current setting. If this call
        ' succeeds, then return the string.
        '********************************************************
        If RegQueryValueEx(lngRes, strValueName, ByVal 0, _
            REG_EXPAND_SZ, ByVal strSetting, lngDataLen) = _
            ERROR_SUCCESS Then
            If lngDataLen > 1 Then
                GetRegString = Left(strSetting, lngDataLen - 1)
            End If
        End If
        '********************************************************
        ' ALWAYS close any keys that you open.
        '********************************************************
```

```
            If RegCloseKey(lngRes) <> ERROR_SUCCESS Then
                MsgBox "RegCloseKey Failed: " & strSubKey, vbCritical
            End If
        End If
    End Function
    #End If
```

Application Performance Considerations

Another major pitfall that you face when distributing an integrated application is performance considerations. If the target system doesn't have enough random-access memory (RAM) or is low on system resources, your application can fail. In this section, you learn how to ensure that your application thrives on its targeted system.

System Requirements

After you create your integrated application, you need to gather the system requirements of all products that your applications use. Using these system requirements, you can take the highest requirements from each to determine what your application requires.

Next, you should take the following steps to determine what minimum free system resources your application requires:

1. Exit and restart Windows.

2. From Notepad's About box, check the available amount of system resources. Write this number down.

3. Close Notepad's About box and run your application.

4. Test every feature of your application (except any that terminate it).

5. While your application is still running, return to Notepad's About box to see what the System Resources line reads now.

6. Subtract the amount in step 5 from the amount in step 2. This is the amount of system resources your application consumes.

Now you're ready to build your system requirements list. Your system requirements should include the following information:

■ Operating system requirements (for example, Windows 3.1 or greater)

■ Minimum and recommended random-access memory (RAM) requirements

- Disk space required (which you calculate from the uncompressed size of all your files on your setup disk)

- Monitor requirements (usually VGA or higher)

- Pointing device requirements (for example, whether the application requires a mouse or pen tablet)

- Office applications (with version) required (for example, Excel 5.0, Word 6.0, and so on)

- Networking software required, if any (for example, whether Windows for Workgroups is required)

Most integrated applications have the following system requirements:

- Windows 3.1, Windows for Workgroups 3.11, or Windows NT 3.51 or greater

- 8M RAM required, 12M or more recommended

- 2M of free disk space or more

- VGA (640×480×16) or higher

- A mouse is optional but strongly recommended

- Microsoft Office Professional 4.3c or greater

After establishing your user requirements, you should put them in the front of your product manual, in your README.TXT file, and on your product packaging (if any). This is important because the customer must know what your product requires before purchasing it.

Hardware Performance Considerations

Because you're reading this book, you're probably a real "power user." You probably have at least a 486–50 or greater system with 16M or more RAM. This means that your application really flies when you use it, but what happens when you install it on a wimpy machine (for example, a 486-25 with 8M of RAM)? If your answer is that "it croaks," you must reconsider how you have written your application.

Handling Wimpy Machines

Writing a program for a system that is less powerful than your own is difficult, but important if you want your program to succeed. Because most institutions (businesses, government, schools, and so on) are usually two or more years behind in technology, you neglect a big market by writing applications that run only on systems that are as fast (or faster) than your own.

Of course, you can't target systems that don't meet your system requirements, but your program should run (at least partially) on any 486 (or higher) system with at least 8M of RAM.

The most important thing about handling a wimpy machine is to ensure that your program doesn't perform unexpectedly during any of the following stressful situations:

- Low memory or system resources

- Low or insufficient disk space

- Printing to dot-matrix printers

- Video resolution is set to 640×480×16

Each of these situations can cause your program to fail miserably, so you must prepare to handle them.

> **Note**
>
> If possible, you should always try to test your application on a 386-33 with 4M of RAM that is running its video at 640×480×16 and prints to a dot-matrix printer. This test will indicate how your program responds to wimpy machines.

Handling Low Memory Situations

No matter how much RAM a system has, your application will eventually face a low memory or low system resource situation. By handling the situation gracefully, you show your customer that you thought of everything when you developed your application, and keep the technical support calls to a minimum.

When a Visual Basic application gets low on memory, the value of Err is either 7 (a standard out-of-memory error) or 31001 (an OLE out-of-memory error). Therefore, your application should always watch for these error messages. It's also useful if your application can do something internally to try to free up some more memory. Listing 29.3 demonstrates some of the steps that your application can take to handle low memory situations.

Listing 29.3   Every Application Should Be Prepared to Handle Low Memory Situations

```
'************************************************************
' FRMLOMEM.FRM - Demonstrates good error-handling techniques.
'************************************************************
Option Explicit
'************************************************************
' Centers the form
'************************************************************
Private Sub Form_Load()
    '********************************************************
    ' Tell your app where to go when an error occurs.
    '********************************************************
    On Error GoTo Form_Load_Err
    '********************************************************
    ' Center the form and the label.
    '********************************************************
    Move (Screen.Width - Width) / 2, (Screen.Height - Height) / 2
    lblMsg.Move (ScaleWidth - lblMsg.Width) / 2, _
            (ScaleHeight - lblMsg.Height) / 2
    '********************************************************
    ' Raise an error to simulate a low memory situation.
    '********************************************************
    Err.Raise InputBox("Enter a error number:", Default:=7)
    Exit Sub

Form_Load_Err:
    '********************************************************
    ' When an error is triggered, jump to the error handler.
    '********************************************************
    ErrHandler Err.Number, "Form_Load"
    End
End Sub
```

This program prompts the user for an error number and passes that number to Err.Raise to simulate an error. After the error is triggered, the program transfers control to the following error-handling routine:

```
'************************************************************
' A generic error handler.
'************************************************************
Sub ErrHandler(iErr%, sCallingProc$)
Dim msg$, res%
    '********************************************************
    ' Prevent crashes in your error handler with Resume Next
    '********************************************************
    On Error Resume Next
    '********************************************************
    ' If out of memory error, then tell user to free memory
    '********************************************************
    If iErr = 7 Or iErr = 31001 Then
```

```
'*******************************************************
' Here is a good place to unload any picture boxes,
' hide unnecessary controls, close DDE links or OLE
' objects, erase arrays, and set object variables
' = Nothing.
'*******************************************************
    msg = "Your system is extremely low on memory, so "
    msg = msg & "please close any applications "
    msg = msg & "that you (or this application) are "
    msg = msg & "not using."
'*******************************************************
' Otherwise tell the user what error occurred, and where
' it was triggered. (This is useful during tech support
' calls.)
'*******************************************************
Else
    msg = "A """ & Error(iErr) & """ error has occurred "
    msg = msg & "in this applications " & sCallingProc
    msg = msg & " procedure. " & vbLf & vbLf & "Please "
    msg = msg & "consult ""Appendix E: Error Messages"" "
    msg = msg & "for instructions on how to correct "
    msg = msg & "this error."
End If
'*******************************************************
' Display the appropriate error message.
'*******************************************************
    MsgBox msg, vbExclamation
End Sub
```

After the error has been triggered, the error handler displays an appropriate error message for the user. If the error was an out-of-memory error, the message says to close any unnecessary applications to free up some more memory. Figure 29.4 shows the error message.

Fig. 29.4
A good error message tells the user what to do to fix the error.

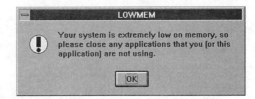

Low or Insufficient Disk Space

Because they usually have large hard disks, programmers can easily forget that others aren't so fortunate. You must prepare your application (especially your setup program) for the dreaded Err 61 (Disk Full) error.

Whenever you create or copy a file, you should always check whether the available disk space is greater than the size of the file that you want to copy or create. If there isn't enough room, you should notify the user to free up some disk space and provide the option of either aborting or trying again.

If there is enough room, you should copy your file, but still include an error handler for Err 61. Listing 29.4 is an example of a function that returns the available disk space.

Listing 29.4   The GetDiskSpaceFree Function Returns the Available Disk Space

```
Option Explicit
#If Win32 Then
Private Declare Function DiskSpaceFree Lib "STKIT432.DLL" Alias _
    "DISKSPACEFREE" () As Long
#Else
Private Declare Function DiskSpaceFree Lib "STKIT416.DLL" () _
    As Long
#End If
'****************************************************************
' Get the disk space free for a specific drive
'****************************************************************
Public Function GetDiskSpaceFree(sDrive As String)
Dim res As Long
    On Error Resume Next
    '****************************************************************
    ' Change to the drive that you wish to check.
    '****************************************************************
    ChDrive sDrive
    res = DiskSpaceFree()
    '****************************************************************
    ' If STKIT4*.DLL or drive can't be found, then return -1.
    '****************************************************************
    GetDiskSpaceFree = IIf(Err, -1, Format(res, _
                        "###,###,###,##0"))
End Function
'****************************************************************
' Get the disk space free for the current drive
'****************************************************************
Private Sub Command1_Click()
    Caption = GetDiskSpaceFree(Left(CurDir, 1))
End Sub
```

Note

If you use the GetDiskSpaceFree function, you must make sure that you install STKIT416.DLL or STKIT432.DLL. You can find this file on any disk created by Setup Wizard.

Handling Different Resolution Printers

Beginning programmers often forget that not every user prints to printers that have the same resolution as theirs. Such a mistake can render your program's printing feature useless to some of your customers, and cause you to lose business.

The only good way to handle printing to different printers is to test your printing features on the following printers:

- A 9- and 24-pin dot-matrix printer at draft and proof quality resolutions

- A 300-dpi and 600-dpi laser printer

- A 600-dpi postscript printer

When your program can successfully print to each of these types of printers, your printing feature is ready to ship. The new printer object in Visual Basic 4.0 provides a wealth of new methods and properties to help take advantage of almost any printer that you can install on Windows. Before calling the Windows API printing functions, make sure that you look closely at the new `Printer` object in VB4.

Developing the UI in 640×480×16

One of the biggest mistakes that a Windows programmer can make is to neglect developing your user interface in 640×480×16 resolution. You might spend over a week developing the perfect user interface, only to discover that your interface is useless on anything less than 800×600×256. Some of the problems that you face by not developing user interface in 640×480×16 are the following:

- Your nonsizable forms are either too tall or too wide.

- If Paint saves its bitmaps in the highest resolution that your video can display, your toolbar bitmaps are accidentally saved as 256-color bitmaps. This causes systems that run in 16 colors either to display the bitmaps in black or generate a General Protection Fault in the video driver.

- Some of your message boxes might contain so much text that the OK button isn't visible to users running at 640×480.

To make matters worse, if you then try to fix your forms, you might discover that there isn't enough room on your existing forms to hold all of your controls. You could wind up spending another two weeks fixing your user interface because you have to double the number of forms in your application. You might have to delay your perfectly debugged product just because you forgot to plan for a lower resolution.

Note

Before you decide to require your users to run your application in 800×600×256, remember that an estimated 90 percent of all Windows users have their video resolution set to 640×480×16. Because most users don't know how to change their video resolution, it is vital that your application support this common video resolution. Windows 95 might alleviate this problem, but you should still consider 640×480×16 as a target resolution.

As you can see in listing 29.5, you don't even have to call the API to get the video resolution. However, if you want to find out how many colors the screen supports, you have to make a few API calls.

Listing 29.5   A Demonstration of How to Retrieve the Current Video Resolution

```
'****************************************************************
' VIDEORES.BAS - Displays the current video resolution.
'****************************************************************
Option Explicit
#If Win32 Then
Private Declare Function GetDC& Lib "User32" (ByVal hWnd As Long)
Private Declare Function GetDeviceCaps% Lib "GDI32" (ByVal hDC&, _
                                        ByVal iCapability&)
#Else
Private Declare Function GetDC% Lib "User" (ByVal hWnd As Integer)
Private Declare Function GetDeviceCaps% Lib "GDI" (ByVal hDC%, _
                                        ByVal iCapability%)
#End If
'****************************************************************
' Displays the video resolution in a message box.
'****************************************************************
Sub Main()
    MsgBox GetResolution(True), vbInformation, "Video Resolution"
End Sub
'****************************************************************
' Determines the width, and height of the screen in pixels,
' and the number of colors the screen can display at one time.
'****************************************************************
Function GetResolution(bReturnColors As Boolean) As String
Dim iWidth, iHeight, iColors, ScreenHDC
Const BITSPIXEL = 12
Const PLANES = 14
    '****************************************************************
    ' Get the resolution using standard VB methods.
    '****************************************************************
    iWidth = Screen.Width \ Screen.TwipsPerPixelX
    iHeight = Screen.Height \ Screen.TwipsPerPixelY
```

(continues)

Listing 29.5   Continued

```
'****************************************************************
' Get the device context of the screen, and use GetDeviceCaps
' to find out how many colors the screen supports.
'****************************************************************
ScreenHDC = GetDC(0)
iColors = GetDeviceCaps(ScreenHDC, PLANES) * 2 _
        ^ GetDeviceCaps(ScreenHDC, BITSPIXEL)
'****************************************************************
' Only display the color resolution if the caller wants it.
'****************************************************************
If bReturnColors Then
    GetResolution = iWidth & "x" & iHeight & "x" & iColors
Else
    GetResolution = iWidth & "x" & iHeight
End If
End Function
```

The Importance of Documentation and Help

Tip
The best online
Help is a copy of
your manual.
You can save
yourself a lot of
time if you first
create your Help
file, then save it
under a different
name, and use it
to create your
manual.

No matter how user-friendly you think your program is, plenty of users still won't be able to figure it out. That's why you must provide a well-written user's manual and online Help file.

Before shipping any application, you should make sure that your documentation and online Help discuss every element of your program and its output (printout, files, and so on). After completing both, you can link every control in your project to its corresponding topic in your Help file by using the HelpContextID property. After your product is ready to ship, test what happens when you press the F1 key on every control.

A good manual and Help file separate good applications from bad ones. Even if your product is shareware, you'll benefit greatly from spending time on these valuable accessories to your product. You'll also find that you increase your chances to get free magazine reviews when you take the time to document your product well.

Planning and Error Handling

This chapter has saved the most important two aspects of the development process for last: planning and error handling. If you neglect either one of these elements during the development process, your application is destined to fail (or at least require a quick maintenance release).

The Planning and Development Process

Planning should be the first step in your entire development process. A discussion of all the aspects of the development life cycle is beyond the scope of this book, but you can use the following list as a guide for every development project:

- Talk to your customers or intended audience and find out what features they want to see in the program you are about to develop. Any project built around user feedback is destined for success.

- Create several user-interface prototypes (don't include any feature-specific code) and give them to your intended audience. After you find out what they like and dislike, you can scrap the prototype and build your user interface.

- *Never* use the prototype as your final user interface. If you do so, you'll pay dearly later in the development life cycle (especially during upgrades).

- After deciding which features you want to implement, code them as functions (or subroutines) and make sure that they are application-independent. A good function can be copied, pasted into another project, and used without modification. The best way to ensure that you write good functions is to code them in temporary projects rather than in your user-interface project.

- Comment *every* line of code. Although doing so might seem ridiculous as you are coding, you'll be glad that you add the comments when it comes time to upgrade your product several months (or years) later.

- Consider putting similar code in modules or classes to make them reusable with other projects.

- After you have a solid (and fully debugged) code base, add the code to your user-interface project. After linking the code to your user interface, debug it again to ensure that no new bugs have appeared.

- Make sure that *every* function (and sub) in all your forms has an error handler. You should also ensure that your error handler provides a useful error message for the user and your technical support staff.

- Make sure that your application gives the user something to look at during long processing times. An hourglass is appropriate only if the processing takes less than a minute. If the processing takes longer, consider using a splash screen or a progress bar.

- Begin writing your Help file and manual as soon as you have completed your user interface. Documentation usually takes two to three times longer than development (if you do it properly), so you should get started early. During the beta tests, you also should solicit feedback to find out what users think of the preliminary draft of your documentation.

Tip

If you like to code but hate commenting, you might try the following technique. Code first, then comment every line of code last. You then must reread every line of code, which often can uncover fuzzy logic and dead code that you can change or eliminate.

- Beta test your product. If possible, let at least 25 users at different locations test your product for a month or two. If your product can go two weeks without any of the 25 beta sites reporting a single bug, you're usually ready to ship your product.

This book could go on for pages citing things that you should do during the planning and development stage, but the preceding list should give you a starting point. See the "From Here" section at the end of this chapter for more information about where you can go to learn more about this important process.

Error Handling

Unless you're some sort of programming god, your application is destined to have run-time bugs that you never expected. The key to handling such bugs is a good error-handling mechanism in your project. The following list describes some valuable tips:

- Create good generic error handling, like that shown in listing 29.3. In addition, you might want to add a few lines that perform such tasks as closing all open files and restoring the mouse pointer.

- Add an error handler to every function (or subroutine) in your forms. A good practice is to use the name of the function, followed by _Err (for example, Form_Load_Err, as shown in listing 29.3).

- Present *very* descriptive error messages so that your application's user and technical support staff have a good idea about what caused your application to fail.

From Here...

An entire book could be written on the topics covered in this chapter, but this chapter is a good start on successfully distributing your integrated application. If you are interested in obtaining additional information on the topics mentioned in this section, you should do the following:

- Read programming-related magazines (for example, *Visual Basic Programmer's Journal*) and attend programming-related conferences (for example, Microsoft's TechEd Conference in the spring). Many of the articles in programming magazines and seminars at programming conferences can save you months (or even years) of trial-and-error experiences.

- See Chapter 30, "Distributing Your Applications," in the *Visual Basic Programmers Guide* for a complete listing of the supporting files that Visual Basic and its custom controls require.

- See this book's Chapter 28, "Integration with Multiple Office Applications," for more information about writing a large-scale application in Visual Basic.

- See Chapter 32, "Advanced Code Techniques," in this book for more information about optimizing your code.

IV

Integrating with Office

Part V

Optimization and Techniques

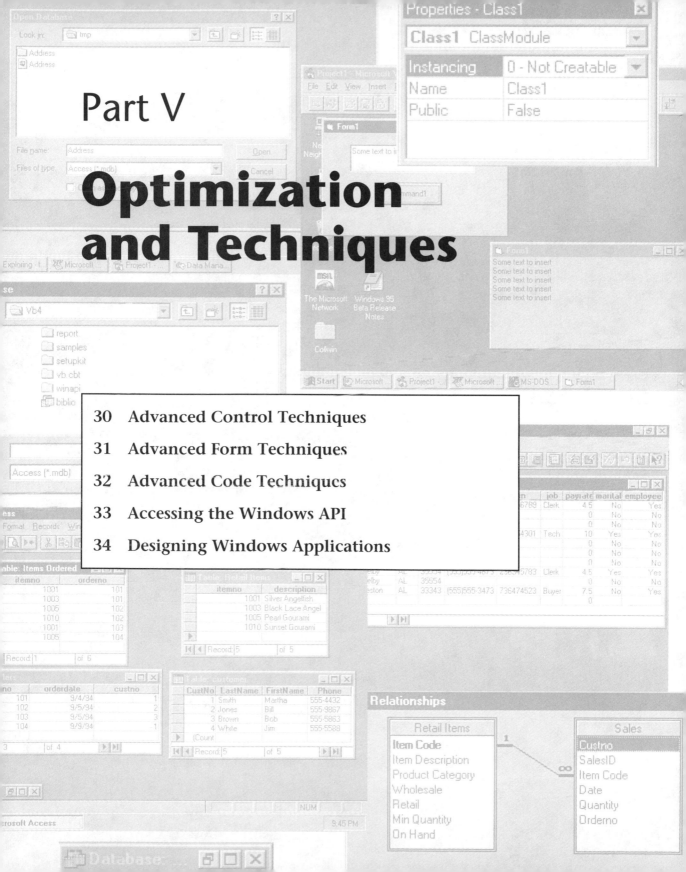

Chapter 30

Advanced Control Techniques

The Visual Basic development environment provides a set of tools for creating Windows applications. Unfortunately, simply having all these controls does not help you to learn to use them effectively and efficiently. Fortunately, sources exist that can help you learn these skills.

Learning how to use a control comes with experience, but you do not have to always wait for that to come. This kind of experience is the usual trial-and-error process of finding out what works for particular situations. There is no substitute for this kind of learning experience. But you don't always have the time and must often depend on the past experience of other programmers.

You cannot expect to memorize every solution that you have ever written. If you tried to do so, you would inevitably forget techniques and constantly find yourself reinventing the wheel. The obvious solution to this problem is to create a central repository of code that you can access as needed. Included with this book are the elements that can serve as the basis of a central repository of code—the basic code for creating new Visual Basic applications. Subsequent chapters explain the different elements of this code.

In this chapter, you learn how to do the following:

- Use Crystal Reports effectively in your applications

- Work with the outline control

- Validate user input with the masked text box

- Create toolbars with the Microsoft "look and feel"

- Make status bars

> **Caution**
>
> Be careful how you reference DOS files in Visual Basic. The path in which you place your files might not be the same path that the application's users have on their own machines. Hard-coded paths to graphics files, data controls, and Help files *will* change. The solution to this problem is to reference a global variable that contains the path in all your code.

Accessing Crystal Reports

Designing reports in Visual Basic used to be a pain. Providing reports used to involve dealing with the small number of methods and properties belonging to the limited `Printer` object. The results were neither professional looking nor easy to work with. Now you can design applications that generate sophisticated, professional-looking reports that you can integrate into your Visual Basic applications.

The process of adding a Crystal Report to an application is easy. Simply place the Crystal control in your project and draw it anyplace on one of your screens. For the sake of simplicity, you get better results when you put the control on the form where the user will invoke the report. Then you need not reference the control's form as well as the control and the properties or methods.

To print an existing report from an application, follow these steps:

1. Create a new project.

2. Change the `name` property of Form1 to `Print`.

3. Add the `Form_Load` event of `Print`.

4. Save the project under the name 30PROJ01.PRJ.

5. Add the CRYSTAL32.OCX to the project.

6. Add a command button to the form.

7. Add the `Command1_Click` event to the command button.

8. Add to the form the code in listing 30.1.

9. Add the `Dim` statement for `DatabasePath$` and `DatabaseName$` to the form's General Declarations section.

10. Get the SHELL.MDB and SHELL.RPT files from the shell code and copy them to the project directory.

Listing 30.1   The 30Proj01 Code Showing a Crystal Report

```
General Declarations

Dim DatabasePath$
Dim DatabaseName$


Form_Load ()
  DatabasePath$ = app.Path
  DatabaseName$ = AddPath$(DatabasePath$, "SHELL.MDB")
End Sub


Function AddPath (Path$, DatabaseName$) As String
  If Mid$(Path$, Len(Path$), 1) <> "\" Then
    Path$ = Path$ & "\"
  End If

  AddPath$ = Path$ & DatabaseName$

End Function


Sub Command1_CLICK ()
  Screen.MousePointer = HOUGLASS
  rptPrint.Destination = 0
  rptPrint.DataFiles(0) = DatabaseName$
  rptPrint.ReportFileName = AddPath(DatabasePath$, "SHELL.RPT")
  rptPrint.Action = 1
  Screen.MousePointer = DEFAULT
End Sub
```

Notice that the Crystal Report displays on top of the calling form. The resulting crystal window, which you can minimize on the screen, displays like a normal window (see fig. 30.1). Also, notice how the `AddPath` function provides a path to use to call the Crystal form. This is a very useful function to add to your projects.

V

Optimization

Fig. 30.1
An example of a Crystal Report displayed as a normal window.

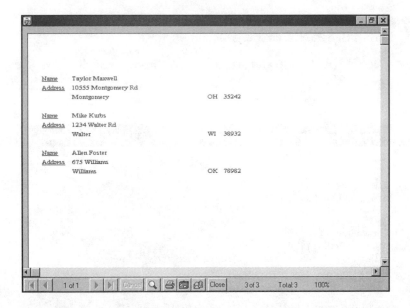

Referencing Forms in Visual Basic

Visual Basic provides many ways to reference forms. In Visual Basic 1.0, you can make references to a text box on form1 by using the following syntax:

```
Form1.Text1.Text
```

Unfortunately, this syntax can confuse those reading the code if the names are unclear, as in Change.ChangeName.Text. Visual Basic 2.0 introduces the solution of using an exclamation point to indicate that you are referencing a form rather than a control, as in Form1!Text1.Text. To make your code more readable, use the exclamation point.

Creating MDI Children

By definition, MDI applications display everything but dialog boxes within the confines of the contain MDI form. Making a form into an MDI child is a simple process of changing the MDIChild property to True. The companion CD's 30Proj02 project provides a simple demonstration of how to create multiple child windows.

> **Caution**
>
> Make sure to format your code properly to make it readable. Don't forget to indent
> your code by pressing the Tab key before each new line of code. Code set within `If-`
> `Then`, `Select Case`, `Do-While`, and similar contructions should be further indented
> one tab stop. Nonindented code is difficult to read, even for the programmer who
> originally wrote it.

Understanding Form Arrays

To begin understanding how the following code listing works, start by study-
ing the code in listing 30.2.

Listing 30.2   The `mnuFileOpen_Click` Event

```
Sub mnuFileOpen_Click()

    Screen.MousePointer = vbHourglass

    ReDim Preview(gNbrPreview% + 1)
    Load Preview(gNbrPreview%)
    Preview(gNbrPreview%).Caption = "Preview"

    Screen.MousePointer = vbDefault

End Sub
```

This event increments the size of the `Preview` form array by one and then
loads the new member of this form array. Notice that the `gNbrPreview` variable stores the size of the form array. Each time that the user chooses the
Open menu choice, this code generates a new member of the form array.

```
ReDim Preview(gNbrPreview% + 1)
    Load Preview(gNbrPreview%)
    Preview(gNbrPreview%).Caption = "SHELL REPORT"
```

To find out where the form arrays `Preview` and `gNbrPreview` are referenced,
look for them in the GLOBAL.BAS under the comment "Print Preview Flag":

```
'Print Preview Flag
Public Preview() As New frmPrintPreview
Public gNbrPreview%
```

Keep four things in mind about this code:

V

Optimization

- Notice the use of the lowercase letter *g* at the beginning of the variable gNbrPreview%. This indicates that the variable is global to the entire application. If a variable does not have this prefix, that variable must be local.

- The gNbrPreview% definition has no value indicating that it has a beginning value of zero.

- The definition of the form array Preview has no value within the parentheses. Therefore, the value can change at run time.

- Note the use of the word New and the reference to frmPreview. This indicates that the members of the Preview form array are to be clones of the frmPreview form. Any code associated with frmPreview form will also belong to any of the members of this form array.

> **Note**
>
> Visual Basic ships with the default tab size set to 4. Code that uses many nested statements is very difficult to read. You can change this default size to 2 and make this code easier to read by choosing Tools, Options. Under the Editor tab, change the Tab Width value to 2. This setting displays more of the code on the screen.

Optimizing Control Arrays

As the user continues to learn more, your programs must become increasingly more configurable at run time. To accommodate user sophistication and to address security concerns, your screens' appearance should change based on different conditions that occur at run time. Controls must be enabled and disabled based on specific criteria. Changing the Enabled property of affected controls has this effect. Unfortunately, however, this solution is not always acceptable, because frustrated users want to know why they cannot access something on the screen. Another possibility is to use the Visible property to make a control appear and disappear at run time. If your application has very few controls, this solution is quite acceptable.

Follow these steps to make a control array:

1. Create a control and draw it on the form.

2. Make the control's Visible property False.

3. Change the Index property to False.

4. At run time, load the control by using the load method and then change the Visible property to True.

Creating Killer Toolbars

Toolbars are an integral part of the current Windows standards (see fig. 30.2). Applications that don't have toolbars are becoming the exception rather than the rule. The reason for this is obvious: Toolbars provide a convenient place on the screen for users to look for frequently used functions. Because the toolbar is normally on the top of the screen, it provides a familiar place for the user to look on almost any application.

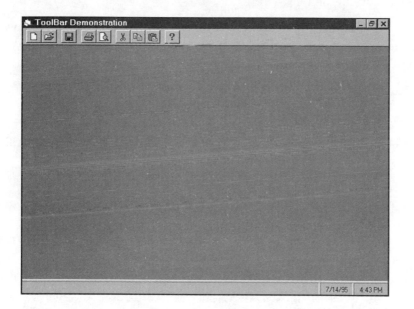

Fig. 30.2
The 30Proj03 application showing the standard colored toolbar.

The earlier versions of applications used monochrome toolbars. Almost all of the current applications have since switched to color toolbars. The bitmaps that ship with Visual Basic are all monochrome. Don't worry, there is an easy method that you can use to create color bitmaps from a monochrome bitmap.

> **Note**
>
> Sheridan Software ships in its Designer Widgets package a Visual Basic .OCX that automates the toolbar-creation process. This product provides another method for creating Visual Basic applications with toolbars.

Color Bitmaps

Standard Visual Basic toolbars consist of bitmaps rather than icons. The standard size of a toolbar icon is 24 pixels wide by 22 pixels high. Around all toolbar icons is a bevel edge that is exactly the same for each icon. Only the interior differs from icon to icon. This interior is 19 pixels wide by 17 pixels high. This is the part that you have to create to make icons in the Visual Basic toolbar custom control.

You can find bitmaps for your toolbars in applications that you already own. The most common application in which to find your icons is Word for Windows. To create your icons from Word for Windows, follow these steps:

1. Display Word for Windows on the screen.

2. Press Print Screen.

3. Open Paint and paste in the resulting screen as shown in figure 30.3.

Fig. 30.3
A Word for Windows screen pasted into Paint.

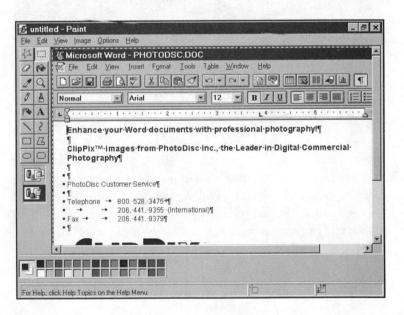

4. Choose <u>V</u>iew, <u>Z</u>oom, <u>L</u>arge Size, as shown in figure 30.4, to change the display size to Large Size.

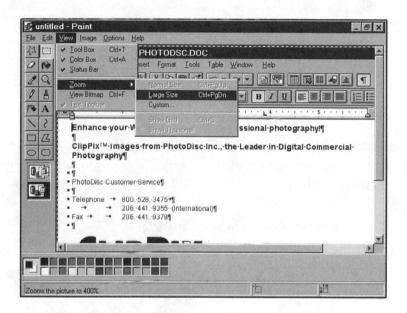

Fig. 30.4
The <u>V</u>iew, <u>Z</u>oom, <u>L</u>arge Size menu choice in Paint.

5. Select the interior of your chosen icon, as shown in figure 30.5.

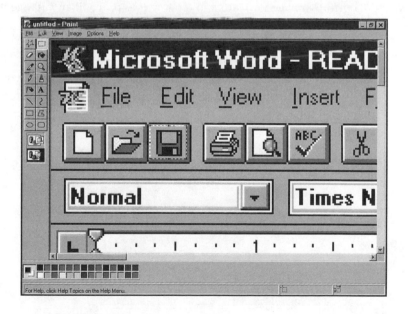

Fig. 30.5
The interior of the Save icon selected in Paint.

6. Choose <u>E</u>dit, C<u>o</u>py To to save the interior of the bitmap to a bitmap file.

The Image List

For each icon that you want to add to your toolbar, you must repeat the icon-creation process. After you have all your icons, you can begin assembling your toolbar in a new project. The steps for this process are as follows:

1. Create a new project and rename it as 30Proj03.

2. Add an MDI form and save it as frmMain with a DOS name of mainMDI.

3. Add a toolbar to frmMain and rename it as ToolBar.

4. Add a status bar to frmMain and rename it as StatusBar.

5. Add a picture box to frmMain and rename it as picToolBar. Change its Visible property to False.

6. Add an image list to picToolBar and rename it as ImageLlst.

7. Add the icons to ImageList using the Custom dialog box as shown in figure 30.6. You can access this by double-clicking on the Custom property on the Properties dialog box.

Fig. 30.6
The Custom dialog box for ImageList.

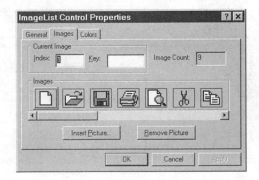

The Toolbar Setup

The next step in the process is to create the code that displays your toolbar buttons. The gSetupToolBar procedure (listing 30.3) is an example of toolbar-creation code for some of the most-often-used icons on a toolbar. Each button appears with the creation of a btn object which you then can use to create each button with the add method. The tbrDefault and tbrSeparator constants are built in, so you need not define them. The lines that use tbrSeparator provide spaces between each icon. Those icons with tbrDefault are the icons with the last number argument identifying the icon to display.

Listing 30.3   The gSetupToolBar Procedure

```
Sub gSetupToolBar(ToolBar As ToolBar, ImageList As ImageList)
Dim btn As Button
   Set ToolBar.ImageList = ImageList

   Set btn = ToolBar.Buttons.Add(, "Sep1", , tbrSeparator, 0)

   Set btn = ToolBar.Buttons.Add(, "New", , tbrDefault, 1)
   btn.ToolTipText = "New"
   btn.Description = "New Object"

   Set btn = ToolBar.Buttons.Add(, "Open", , tbrDefault, 2)
   btn.ToolTipText = "Open"
   btn.Description = "Open Object"

   Set btn = ToolBar.Buttons.Add(, "Sep2", , tbrSeparator, 0)

   Set btn = ToolBar.Buttons.Add(, "Save", , tbrDefault, 3)
   btn.ToolTipText = "Save"
   btn.Description = "Open Object"

   Set btn = ToolBar.Buttons.Add(, "Sep3", , tbrSeparator, 0)

   Set btn = ToolBar.Buttons.Add(, "Print", , tbrDefault, 4)
   btn.ToolTipText = "Print"
   btn.Description = "Print Object"

   Set btn = ToolBar.Buttons.Add(, "Preview", , tbrDefault, 5)
   btn.ToolTipText = "Print Preview"
   btn.Description = "Print Preview"

   Set btn = ToolBar.Buttons.Add(, "Sep4", , tbrSeparator, 0)

   Set btn = ToolBar.Buttons.Add(, "Cut", , tbrDefault, 6)
   btn.ToolTipText = "Cut"
   btn.Description = "Cut Text"

   Set btn = ToolBar.Buttons.Add(, "Copy", , tbrDefault, 7)
   btn.ToolTipText = "Copy"
   btn.Description = "Copy Text"
```

(continues)

Listing 30.3 Continued

```
    Set btn = ToolBar.Buttons.Add(, "Paste", , tbrDefault, 8)
    btn.ToolTipText = "Paste"
    btn.Description = "Paste Text"

    Set btn = ToolBar.Buttons.Add(, "Sep5", , tbrSeparator, 0)
    Set btn = ToolBar.Buttons.Add(, "Help", , tbrDefault, 9)
    btn.ToolTipText = "Help"
    btn.Description = "Context Help"

End Sub
```

Tooltips and Status Bar Text

Help text for tooltips and status bars is becoming a standard feature in Windows applications. The toolbar control supports tooltips and status bar text. To make the tooltips feature work properly, you need only set the ToolTiptext property of each button to the appropriate text. To make the status bar text work, you must add the ToolBar_MouseMove code to your project. This subroutine displays each button's Description property in the status bar when the user moves the mouse over a button.

```
Private Sub ToolBar_MouseMove(Button As Integer, _
Shift As Integer, x As Single, y As Single)

  StatusBar.Panels(1).TEXT = Button.Description

End Sub
```

The ButtonClick event (listing 30.4) enables the program to find which button the user clicked and which action to take. In the example program, you use the buttons' Key property to identify which button the user clicked. Any unique property would work just as well.

Listing 30.4 The ButtonClick Event

```
Private Sub ToolBar_ButtonClick(ByVal Button As Button)

  Select Case Button.KEY
    Case "New"
      frmChild.Show
      frmChild.Caption = "New"
    Case "Open"
      frmChild.Show
      frmChild.Caption = "Open"
    Case "Save"
      StatusBar.Panels(1).TEXT = "Object Saved!"
    Case "Print"
```

```
        StatusBar.Panels(1).TEXT = "Object Printed!"
    Case "Preview"
    Case "Cut"
    Case "Copy"
    Case "Paste"
    Case "Help"
End Select

End Sub
```

Note

Every program has bugs or sometimes just methods of doing things that you do not like. Some programmers prefer to refer to most bugs as features (except for the obvious kinds of bugs, such as those that cause catastrophic General Protection Faults and so on). By thinking of these features in a more positive light, you can begin to take advantage of opportunities that you might not have ever previously considered. As you encounter these features, try to keep this in mind and learn to take advantage of them.

Using the Status Bar

Status bars are another popular element of today's Windows applications. A status bar's main function is to tell the user what is going on. When the user places the mouse over a control for a few seconds, the status bar should give some information about that control. During a very long process, the status bar gives messages about the progress that the program is making. Such messages might use text, graphics, a percentage indicator, or a combination of the three. One of the greatest benefits of a status bar is to give information that indicates to the user that the application has not locked up. Nothing is more frustrating than an application that simply displays an hourglass while you sit and wait. A status bar fixes this problem by letting the user know that something is happening.

V

Optimization

> **Note**
>
> You can shorten If-Then constructions that check whether a variable or property is True. If you omit the = TRUE part of such a construction, Visual Basic assumes it. This technique is very useful for simplifying code on the screen for better readability and faster execution.

Styles

There are as many different types of status bars as there are applications. Status bars are by definition tied to the type of functions performed by the application to which they belong. Microsoft Word for Windows 6.0 displays such information as the page number, the position on the screen, and the time (see fig. 30.7). Microsoft Excel 5.0 shows a "Ready" message to indicate that no processing is taking place (see fig. 30.8). There are also indicators for the Caps Lock, Insert, Scroll Lock, and Number Lock keys. When you design your applications, think carefully and include status bar elements that make sense for that particular program.

Fig. 30.7

Microsoft Word for Windows 6.0 with its status bar.

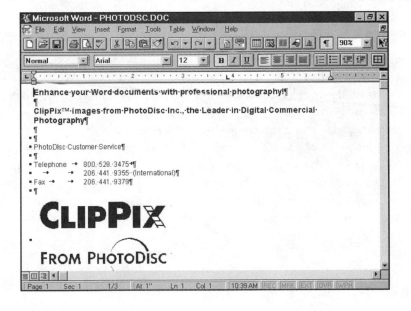

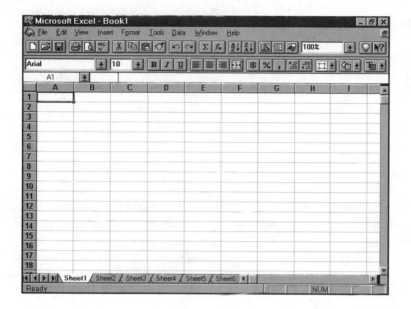

Fig. 30.8
Microsoft Excel 5.0
with its status bar.

Status Bar Controls

Visual Basic 4.0 provides a status bar control. In earlier versions of Visual Basic, you had to create a status bar with code and controls. Now the process of creating a very useful status bar is a simple one:

1. Open the existing main MDI form.

2. Add a status bar control and rename it as StatusBar.

3. Use the Custom property to display the Custom dialog box.

4. Add a panel to the status bar with the style set to Text.

5. Add a panel to the status bar with the style set to Date.

6. Add a panel to the status bar with the style set to Time.

7. Change the AutoSize property of the first panel to Spring.

Using *MaskEdBox* Text Boxes

Databases are only as useful as the data that they contain. One of the most important aspects of a useful, stable database is consistent data-entry practices. A phone number entered inconsistently as either (555) 555-9821 or 555-555-9821 creates problems. If the user doesn't enter a customer's phone numbers using a consistent format, making meaningful searches against this information becomes difficult.

There are two ways to filter the type of information that the user enters. The first method involves the use of the Mask property. Set the Mask property to (###) ###-####, and the user can enter the telephone number only with this format. This method is terrific for quick data-entry that does not redisplay the information after the user enters it. One problem with the method, however, occurs when the contents of the maskEdBox control are blank and the control is bound to a database table. Under these conditions, a blank entry triggers a Visual Basic error.

The second, more useful method of filtering the user's entered data involves the use of the Format property and the KeyPress event. Set the Format property to (###) ###-#### and add the code in listing 30.5 to the KeyPress event of the maskEdBox control. This method prevents the user from entering anything but numbers and then displays the phone number as a valid number afterward.

Listing 30.5   The 30Proj04 Code Showing MaskEdBox Enhancements

```
Private Sub MaskEdBox1_KeyPress(KeyAscii As Integer)
  If KeyAscii = 8 Or KeyAscii > 47 And KeyAscii < 58 Then
    ' Show number
  Else
    KeyAscii = 0
  End If
End Sub
```

To implement the second filtering method, follow these steps:

1. Create a new project and save it as 30Proj02.

2. Add MSMASK32.OCX to the project.

3. Place a MaskEdBox on Form1.

4. Change the Mask property to (###) ###-####.

5. Add the listing 30.5 code to the KeyPress event of MaskEdBox1.

6. Add a text box to Form1 and change its Text property to blank.

7. Adjust form to look like the one shown in figure 30.9.

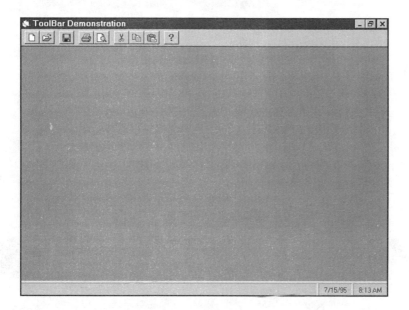

Fig. 30.9
An example
of what your
30Proj04 should
look like showing
MaskEdBox
enhancements.

Outline Enhancements

Many kinds of information take the form of a one-to-many relationship with a single header and many lines of detail. For sales invoices, this relationship is represented with the customer's information as the header and the individual purchases as the detail lines. Visual Basic provides an excellent custom control for displaying this relationship graphically, MSOUTL32.OCX. By displaying information in this fashion, you give the user a high-level view of the information.

The outline control works quite well with some minor code enhancements. Listing 30.6 shows these code enhancements. Unless you use one of the Outline style properties that incorporate the + and – signs, the outline control does not expand and collapse automatically. Many users prefer the Explorer's look and feel (see fig. 30.10), which the outline control supports. The code in listing 30.6 shows how simply you can add this capability.

Fig. 30.10

The Microsoft
Explorer.

Listing 30.6   The 30Proj05 Code Showing Outline Control Enhancements

```
Private Sub Form_Load()
  Outline1.AddItem "Invoice 308912"
  Outline1.PictureType(0) = 0
  Outline1.Indent(0) = 1

  Outline1.AddItem "Alaskan Crab"
  Outline1.PictureType(1) = 2
  Outline1.Indent(1) = 2

  Outline1.AddItem "Ripple"
  Outline1.PictureType(2) = 2
  Outline1.Indent(2) = 2

  Outline1.AddItem "Tossed Salad"
  Outline1.PictureType(3) = 2
  Outline1.Indent(3) = 2

  Outline1.AddItem "Baked Potato"
  Outline1.PictureType(4) = 2
  Outline1.Indent(4) = 2

End Sub

Private Sub Outline1_Click()
Dim Index%

  If Outline1.HasSubItems(Index%) Then
    Index% = Outline1.ListIndex
```

```
        Outline1.Expand(Index%) = Not Outline1.Expand(Index%)
    End If

End Sub

Private Sub Outline1_PictureClick(ListIndex As Integer)

    Outline1.ListIndex = ListIndex%
    Call Outline1_Click

End Sub
```

To create the 30Proj05 application, which demonstrates how to add outline control enhancements, follow these steps:

1. Create a new project and save it as 30Proj05.

2. Add MSOUTL32.OCX to the project.

3. Place an outline on Form1.

4. Change the Style property to 5.

5. Add the listing 30.5 code to Form1.

The key to making the outline control expand and collapse when the user clicks on it lies in the Outline1_Click event. This code uses the HasSubItems property of the outline control to determine whether the current item has subitems. If the currently selected item has subitems, the routine toggles the Expand property by using Not. Figure 30.11 shows what the outline should look like expanded, and figure 30.12 displays the outline collapsed.

Fig. 30.11
An example of 30Proj03 when expanded.

Fig. 30.12
An example of
30Proj03 when
collapsed.

There is one last piece to finish for 30proj03. If the user clicks on the picture of the folder, the outline neither collapses nor expands. There is a separate event for this. To ensure that the same thing happens for clicking on the picture as well as the text, add the code found in Outline1_PictureClick. This code first changes the ListIndex property to the index value of the picture that the user clicked. Then the routine triggers the Outline1_Click event by using the Call method.

> **Note**
>
> Notice the use of the Call method in the Outline1_Click found in listing 30.5. You do not need this method to make the code function properly, but it serves to clarify that the routine triggers an external subroutine. This makes the Outline1_PictureClick event easier to read.

From Here...

Controls are the elements of the screens that your applications' users see. A control's behavior affects how useful your applications are to users. Adding outlines to your applications can give them a graphical view of complex information that users can more easily understand. By preventing the user from entering inappropriate values into a screen, you make your applications less error-prone. Toolbars give users a quick way to access your application's often-used functions. All these control techniques help produce better and more useable applications.

For more information about related topics, see the following chapters:

- Chapter 31, "Advanced Form Techniques," discusses MDI and SDI applications in greater detail.

- Chapter 33, "Accessing the Windows API," provides more information on API calls and window handles.

V

Optimization

Advanced Form Techniques

Forms are much more than containers on which to place your controls. They are the visual glue that binds all an application's controls together. Users focus on the controls that you show them, but a change in the appearance of a form can create a completely different impression.

In this chapter, you learn how to do the following:

- Use new form properties

- Work effectively with form arrays

- Create screen-independent applications

- Use application types to classify your programs

- Position forms effectively on the screen

Exploring New Form Properties

Visual Basic 4.0 includes several new form properties. These properties give you more options for changing the appearance and behavior of your forms. You need these capabilities to create the kind of new forms that you see as part of the growing Windows standard look and feel. Prior to the release of Visual Basic 4.0, you could replicate these capabilities only by using either complicated types of code or third-party controls.

The *Appearance* Property

Users respond positively to forms with a three-dimensional (3-D) look and feel. Visual Basic provides a method for making 3-D forms simply by changing the Appearance property to 1 - 3D.

Tip
Be careful how many controls you place on a form. A form with too many controls can begin to look unpleasant. Forms should contain logical groupings of controls. The most common methods for grouping controls are spacing and using frames.

The *AutoShowChildren* Property

In Visual Basic 4.0, MDI children no longer have to be visible. When the AutoShowChildren property of the MDI parent is True, the Load method does not make the form visible. Sometimes users require that applications work with more forms than can be comfortably displayed on the screen at the same time. The AutoShowChildren property enables you to keep only the currently necessary screens visible while leaving other less necessary screens invisible. With this capability, you can quickly display screens that are already loaded but not visible. This creates the impression of a fast application.

The *NegotiateMenus* Property

Tip

Visual Basic now supports the display of multiple design-time environments. This enables you to access both projects and to move code quickly from one project to another—a vast improvement over the previous version of Visual Basic.

Windows is moving quickly toward OLE technology. You can expect certain features of new applications, including support of OLE 2.0. Until the release of Visual Basic 4.0, programmers had no method for creating Visual Basic applications that fully support OLE 2.0 technology. One of the biggest problems was making the menus of a form match that of the activated OLE object. The NegotiateMenus property provides a means of enabling this transformation to take place automatically. Simply by setting the form's NegotiateMenus property to True, you change all the menus when the user activates an object on that form. This new property enables support for in-place activation (also known as visual editing). This OLE 2.0 technology enables a user to double-click on an object provided by an OLE server. A user can then work with the application without switching to that different application.

Controlling Screen Position

Users want to feel that they are in control of the ways that their applications function. You must strive to look for anything that you can do to give them more control over how your application functions. One obvious place that you can give the user control is the position of the forms on the user's screen.

Dialog Boxes

Positioning dialog boxes is very important, even though users do not need to be able to save the previous positions of dialog boxes. Consider the difference between the dialog box centered in figure 31.1 to that found in figure 31.2. Notice the higher-quality appearance of the dialog box shown in figure 31.2.

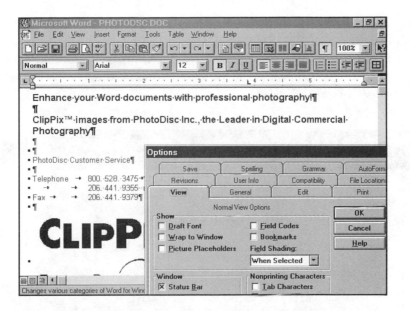

Fig. 31.1
The Options dialog box from Word for Windows is offset on the screen. This kind of problem can happen when a screen is designed on an 800-by-600 screen.

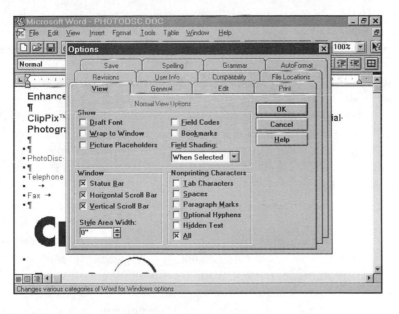

Fig. 31.2
The Options dialog box from Word for Windows is now centered on the screen.

One sign of a badly considered application is one that does not center its dialog boxes on the screen. If you do not enter code in the form's load event, the form appears in the last position that you left it in the design environment. This unacceptable design technique certainly detracts from the program's overall usefulness.

V

Optimization

The `CenterDialogPosition` subroutine, shown in listing 31.1, centers the dialog box over the form. If that form is larger than the main form, the code adjusts itself accordingly to fit over the main form. This ensures that the dialog box does not appear in the incorrect position if the user sizes `frmMain` to smaller than the dialog box.

Listing 31.1 The `CenterDialogPosition` Subroutine Centers the Dialog Box over the Form

```
Sub CenterDialogPosition(WNdName As Form)

  If (WNdName.Height > frmMain.Height) Or _
      (WNdName.Width > frmMain.Width) Then
    WNdName.Top = (Screen.Height - WNdName.Height) \ 2
    WNdName.Left = (Screen.Width - WNdName.Width) \ 2
  Else
    WNdName.Top = frmMain.Top + ((frmMain.Height - _
          WNdName.Height) \ 2)
    WNdName.Left = frmMain.Left + ((frmMain.Width - _
          WNdName.Width) \ 2)
  End If

End Sub
```

Listing 31.1 is an example of how you can make a dialog box appear centered on top of an application's main form. Notice that the code directly references the `Left`, `Top`, `Height`, and `Width` properties of `frmMain`. This code assumes that the main form of your application is named `frmMain`. If you give the main form another name, that name must appear in those places in the code.

The Main Form

As increasingly more users buy computers with higher-resolution monitors, the need for applications that adjust to the size of a screen increases. By default, all Visual Basic forms appear in their last design-time positions on the screen. If you design a screen using an 800-by-600 screen, you must ensure that you position the form properly for lower-resolution monitors. Further, users with higher-resolution monitors probably will want to be able to change the positions of their applications. They also will want to save the last positions or have them appear in a particular position each time that they start their applications.

To make your applications save the last position and size of a form to the Windows Registry, you must declare certain API functions and constants. The necessary API functions and constants appear in listing 31.2. Included with

this code is the error-checking routine gAPIDisplayError. This routine checks
for any errors that might occur when using Registry API calls. For a further
explanation of these constants and API functions, see the section "Understanding Registry APIs" in Chapter 33, "Accessing the Windows API."

**Listing 31.2   The API Functions and Constants Necessary to Save a
Form's Position and Size**

```
Option Explicit

Declare Function RegCloseKey Lib "advapi32" _
    (ByVal hKey As Long) As Long
Declare Function RegCreateKeyEx Lib _
"advapi32" Alias "RegCreateKeyExA"
(ByVal hKey As Long, ByVal lpSubKey As String, _
ByVal Reserved As Long, ByVal lpClass As String, _
ByVal dwOptions As Long, ByVal samDesired As Long, _
lpSecurityAttributes As SECURITY_ATTRIBUTES, _
phkResult As Long, lpdwDisposition As Long) As Long
Declare Function RegOpenKeyEx Lib "advapi32" Alias _
"RegOpenKeyExA" (ByVal hKey As Long, ByVal lpSubKey _
As String, ByVal ulOptions As Long, ByVal samDesired As Long, _
phkResult As Long) As Long
Declare Function RegQueryValueEx Lib "advapi32" Alias _
"RegQueryValueExA" (ByVal hKey As Long, ByVal lpValueName _
As String, lpReserved As Long, lpType As Long, ByVal lpData _
As String, lpchData As Long) As Long
Declare Function RegSetValueEx Lib "advapi32" Alias _
"RegSetValueExA" (ByVal hKey As Long, ByVal lpValueName As _
String, ByVal Reserved As Long, ByVal dwType As Long, _
ByVal lpData As String, ByVal cbData As Long) As Long

'Security Mask constants
Public Const READ_CONTROL = &H20000
Public Const SYNCHRONIZE = &H100000
Public Const STANDARD_RIGHTS_ALL = &H1F0000
Public Const STANDARD_RIGHTS_READ = READ_CONTROL
Public Const STANDARD_RIGHTS_WRITE = READ_CONTROL
Public Const KEY_QUERY_VALUE = &H1
Public Const KEY_SET_VALUE = &H2
Public Const KEY_CREATE_SUB_KEY = &H4
Public Const KEY_ENUMERATE_SUB_KEYS = &H8
Public Const KEY_NOTIFY = &H10
Public Const KEY_CREATE_LINK = &H20
Public Const KEY_ALL_ACCESS = ((STANDARD_RIGHTS_ALL Or _
KEY_QUERY_VALUE Or KEY_SET_VALUE Or KEY_CREATE_SUB_KEY Or _
KEY_ENUMERATE_SUB_KEYS Or KEY_NOTIFY Or KEY_CREATE_LINK) _
And (Not SYNCHRONIZE))
Public Const KEY_READ = ((STANDARD_RIGHTS_READ Or _
KEY_QUERY_VALUE Or KEY_ENUMERATE_SUB_KEYS Or KEY_NOTIFY) _
And (Not SYNCHRONIZE))
```

(continues)

Listing 31.2   Continued

```
Public Const KEY_EXECUTE = ((KEY_READ) And (Not SYNCHRONIZE))
Public Const KEY_WRITE = ((STANDARD_RIGHTS_WRITE Or _
KEY_SET_VALUE Or KEY_CREATE_SUB_KEY) And (Not SYNCHRONIZE))

'Predefined Registry Keys used in hKey Argument
Public Const HKEY_CLASSES_ROOT = &H80000000
Public Const HKEY_CURRENT_USER = &H80000001
Public Const HKEY_LOCAL_MACHINE = &H80000002
Public Const HKEY_USERS = &H80000003
Public Const HKEY_PERFORMANCE_DATA = &H80000004

' Return codes from Registration functions.
Public Const ERROR_SUCCESS = 0&
Public Const ERROR_BADDB = 1009&
Public Const ERROR_BADKEY = 1010&
Public Const ERROR_CANTOPEN = 1011&
Public Const ERROR_CANTREAD = 1012&
Public Const ERROR_CANTWRITE = 1013&
Public Const ERROR_OUTOFMEMORY = 14&
Public Const ERROR_INVALID_PARAMETER = 87&
Public Const ERROR_ACCESS_DENIED = 5&

'Data type Public Constants
Public Const REG_NONE = 0
Public Const REG_SZ = 1
Public Const REG_EXPAND_SZ = 2
Public Const REG_BINARY = 3
Public Const REG_DWORD = 4
Public Const REG_DWORD_LITTLE_ENDIAN = 4
Public Const REG_DWORD_BIG_ENDIAN = 5
Public Const REG_LINK = 6
Public Const REG_MULTI_SZ = 7
Public Const REG_RESOURCE_LIST = 8
Public Const REG_FULL_RESOURCE_DESCRIPTOR = 9
Public Const REG_RESOURCE_REQUIREMENTS_LIST = 10

'Options
Public Const REG_OPTION_VOLATILE = 0
Public Const REG_OPTION_NON_VOLATILE = 1

Type SECURITY_ATTRIBUTES
  nLength As Long
  lpSecurityDescriptor As Variant
  bInheritHandle As Long
End Type

Sub gAPIDisplayError(Code&)

  Select Case Code&
    Case ERROR_BADDB
      MsgBox "Corrupt Registry Database!"
    Case ERROR_BADKEY
      MsgBox "Key name is bad"
```

```
        Case ERROR_CANTOPEN
          MsgBox "Cannot Open Key"
        Case ERROR_CANTREAD
          MsgBox "Cannot Read Key"
        Case ERROR_CANTWRITE
          MsgBox "Cannot Write Key"
        Case ERROR_ACCESS_DENIED
          MsgBox "Access to Registry Denied"
        Case ERROR_OUTOFMEMORY
          MsgBox "Out of memory"
        Case ERROR_INVALID_PARAMETER
          MsgBox "Invalid Parameter"
        Case Else
          MsgBox "Undefined key error code!"
      End Select
End Sub
```

Listing 31.3 is a generic routine that positions the main MDI form of a
project on the screen. First, gSetMainFormPosition checks whether a position
and size are set in the Windows Registry. If no such settings are in the Windows Registry, the main form appears maximized on a 640-by-480 resolution
screen or centered on a higher-resolution screen. If the Registry has saved
settings, gSetMainFormPosition applies them to the main form.

Listing 31.3   An MDI Form-Positioning Routine

```
Sub gSetMainFormPosition(frmMain As Form)
Dim lReturn As Long
Dim hlstrWindowState As String
Dim hlstrTopPosition As String
Dim lTopPosition As Long
Dim hlstrLeftPosition As String
Dim lLeftPosition As Long
Dim hlstrFormWidth As String
Dim lFormWidth As Long
Dim hlstrFormHeight As String
Dim lFormHeight As Long
Dim hWndWindowState As Long
Dim lpcbData As Long

  lpcbData = 255

  lReturn = RegOpenKeyEx(HKEY_LOCAL_MACHINE, "Que\MainForm", 0&, _
KEY_ALL_ACCESS, hWndWindowState)
  If lReturn = 2 Then
    hlstrWindowState = ""
  Else
    hlstrWindowState = Space$(lpcbData)
    lReturn = RegQueryValueEx(hWndWindowState, "WindowState", _
              0&, REG_SZ, hlstrWindowState, lpcbData)
```

                                                              (continues)

Listing 31.3 Continued

```
        If lReturn <> ERROR_SUCCESS Then
          gAPIDisplayError lReturn
          Exit Sub
        End If
      End If

    Select Case Val(hlstrWindowState)
      Case 0
        lpcbData = 255
        hlstrTopPosition = Space$(lpcbData)
        lReturn = RegQueryValueEx(hWndWindowState, "TopPosition", _
                  0&, REG_SZ, hlstrTopPosition, lpcbData)
        lTopPosition = Val(hlstrTopPosition)

        lpcbData = 255
        hlstrLeftPosition = Space$(lpcbData)
        lReturn = RegQueryValueEx(hWndWindowState, "LeftPosition", _
                            0&, REG_SZ,
hlstrLeftPosition, lpcbData)
        lLeftPosition = Val(hlstrLeftPosition)

        lpcbData = 255
        hlstrFormWidth = Space$(lpcbData)
        lReturn = RegQueryValueEx(hWndWindowState, "FormWidth", _
                  0&, REG_SZ, hlstrFormWidth, lpcbData)
        lFormWidth = Val(hlstrFormWidth)

        lpcbData = 255
        hlstrFormHeight = Space$(lpcbData)
        lReturn = RegQueryValueEx(hWndWindowState, "FormHeight", _
                  0&, REG_SZ, hlstrFormHeight, lpcbData)
        lFormHeight = Val(hlstrFormHeight)

        frmMain.Move lLeftPosition, lTopPosition, lFormWidth, _
                lFormHeight
      Case 1
        frmMain.WindowState = vbMinimized
      Case 2
        frmMain.WindowState = vbMaximized
      Case Else
        frmMain.Width = 640 * Screen.TwipsPerPixelX
        frmMain.Height = 480 * Screen.TwipsPerPixelY
        If frmMain.Width + 100 > Screen.Width Then
          frmMain.WindowState = vbMaximized
        Else
          frmMain.Top = (Screen.Height - frmMain.Height) \ 2
          frmMain.Left = (Screen.Width - frmMain.Width) \ 2
        End If
    End Select

    lReturn = RegCloseKey(hWndWindowState)

End Sub
```

`gSetMainFormPosition` uses several Registry API calls to work properly.
`RegOpenKeyEx` identifies the key that contains the setup information.
`RegQueryValueEx` provides the setting found under each value under the key.
You must always remember to use `RegCloseKey` to close a key at the end of a
Registry operation.

`gSaveMainFormPosition` (see listing 31.4) saves the main form's current position, size, and state to the Windows Registry. `RegCreateKeyEx` provides the
window handle of the key that contains the information. Notice that you use
this call whether the key exists or not. This API call simply opens a key in the
same way as `RegOpenKeyEx` if that key already exists. You save the new value
under the key using `RegSetValueEx`. You should never forget to close a
key when you are done with one of these Registry operations that use
`RegCloseKey`.

Listing 31.4   The `gSaveMainFormPosition` Routine

```
Sub gSaveMainFormPosition(frmMain As Form)
Dim hWndQue As Long
Dim hlstrWindowState As String
Dim hlstrTopPosition As String
Dim hlstrLeftPosition As String
Dim hlstrFormWidth As String
Dim hlstrFormHeight As String
Dim lpClass As String
Dim Security As SECURITY_ATTRIBUTES
Dim lpdwDisposition As Long
Dim lReturn As Long

  lpClass = Space$(255)
  lReturn = RegCreateKeyEx(HKEY_LOCAL_MACHINE, "Que\MainForm", _
0&, lpClass, REG_OPTION_NON_VOLATILE, KEY_ALL_ACCESS, Security, _
hWndQue, lpdwDisposition)
  If lReturn <> ERROR_SUCCESS Then
    gAPIDisplayError lReturn
  End If

  hlstrWindowState = Trim$(Str$(frmMain.WindowState))
  lReturn = RegSetValueEx(hWndQue, "WindowState", 0&, REG_SZ, _
hlstrWindowState, Len(hlstrWindowState))
  If lReturn <> ERROR_SUCCESS Then
    gAPIDisplayError lReturn
  End If

  hlstrTopPosition = Trim$(Str$(frmMain.Top))
  lReturn = RegSetValueEx(hWndQue, "TopPosition", 0&, REG_SZ, _
hlstrTopPosition, Len(hlstrTopPosition))
  If lReturn <> ERROR_SUCCESS Then
    gAPIDisplayError lReturn
  End If
```

V

Optimization

(continues)

Listing 31.4 Continued

```
  hlstrLeftPosition = Trim$(Str$(frmMain.Left))
  lReturn = RegSetValueEx(hWndQue, "LeftPosition", 0&, REG_SZ, _
hlstrLeftPosition, Len(hlstrLeftPosition))
  If lReturn <> ERROR_SUCCESS Then
    gAPIDisplayError lReturn
  End If

  hlstrFormWidth = Trim$(Str$(frmMain.Width))
  lReturn = RegSetValueEx(hWndQue, "FormWidth", 0&, REG_SZ, _
hlstrFormWidth, Len(hlstrFormWidth))
  If lReturn <> ERROR_SUCCESS Then
    gAPIDisplayError lReturn
  End If

  hlstrFormHeight = Trim$(Str$(frmMain.Height))
  lReturn = RegSetValueEx(hWndQue, "FormHeight", 0&, REG_SZ, _
hlstrFormHeight, Len(hlstrFormHeight))
  If lReturn <> ERROR_SUCCESS Then
    gAPIDisplayError lReturn
  End If

  lReturn = RegCloseKey(hWndQue)

End Sub
```

The following steps show you how to make this code work together:

1. Open new project and rename this project as 31Proj02.

2. Add a new code module and rename it as WINAPI32.

3. Add the declaration text, constants, and error routine to the General Declarations section of WINAPI32.

4. Add a new code module and rename it as Settings.

5. Add the routines gSetMainFormPosition and gSaveMainFormPosition to the Settings module.

6. Add an MDI form and rename it as frmMain.

```
       Private Sub MDIForm_Load()
         Call gSetMainFormPosition(Me)
       End Sub
       Private Sub MDIForm_Unload(Cancel As Integer)
         Call gSaveMainFormPosition(Me)
       End Sub
```

7. Add the Form_Load code to the load event and the unload code to the unload event of frmMain.

MDI Children

MDI applications can place MDI children anywhere within a form. Exactly where the MDI child appears depends on its purpose—and hopefully the user's choices. Unlike the main form, there is really no all-encompassing default place to put all the MDI children. The only safe default choice is to place a child in the upper-right corner of the MDI parent.

To make your applications save the last position and size of a form to the Windows Registry, you must declare certain API functions and constants. The necessary API functions and constants appear in the WINAPI32 to the MDI form-positioning code. Included with this code is the error-checking routine gAPIDisplayError. This routine checks for any errors that might occur when using Registry API calls. For a further explanation of these constants and API functions, see the section "Understanding Registry APIs" in Chapter 33, "Accessing the Windows API."

gSetChildFormPosition (listing 31.5) positions child windows within the MDI parent. This routine is very similar to gSetMainFormPosition, with a few important differences. First, the default position of frmChild is in the upper-right corner of the MDI parent. Second, gSetChildFormPosition sets only the left and top properties of frmChild. This works quite well for nonresizeable MDI children. This code needs to change for window children with resizeable borders.

Listing 31.5   The gSetChildFormPosition Routine

```
Sub gSetChildFormPosition(frmChild As Form)
Dim lReturn As Long
Dim hlstrWindowState As String
Dim hlstrTopPosition As String
Dim lTopPosition As Long
Dim hlstrLeftPosition As String
Dim lLeftPosition As Long
Dim hWndWindowState As Long
Dim lpcbData As Long

  lpcbData = 255

  lReturn = RegOpenKeyEx(HKEY_LOCAL_MACHINE, "Que\ChildForm", _
                         0&, KEY_ALL_ACCESS, hWndWindowState)
  If lReturn = 2 Then
    hlstrWindowState = ""
  Else
    hlstrWindowState = Space$(lpcbData)
    lReturn = RegQueryValueEx(hWndWindowState, _
            "WindowState", 0&, REG_SZ, hlstrWindowState, lpcbData)
```

(continues)

Listing 31.5 Continued

```
      If lReturn <> ERROR_SUCCESS Then
        gAPIDisplayError lReturn
        Exit Sub
      End If
    End If

    Select Case Val(hlstrWindowState)
      Case 0
        lpcbData = 255
        hlstrTopPosition = Space$(lpcbData)
        lReturn = RegQueryValueEx(hWndWindowState, "TopPosition", _
                  0&, REG_SZ, hlstrTopPosition, lpcbData)
        lTopPosition = Val(hlstrTopPosition)

        lpcbData = 255
        hlstrLeftPosition = Space$(lpcbData)
        lReturn = RegQueryValueEx(hWndWindowState, "LeftPosition", _
                  0&, REG_SZ, hlstrLeftPosition, lpcbData)
        lLeftPosition = Val(hlstrLeftPosition)

        frmChild.Move lLeftPosition, lTopPosition
      Case 1
        frmChild.WindowState = vbMinimized
      Case 2
        frmChild.WindowState = vbMaximized
      Case Else
        frmChild.Top = 0
        frmChild.Left = 0
    End Select

    lReturn = RegCloseKey(hWndWindowState)

  End Sub
```

gSetChildFormPosition uses several Registry API calls to work properly.
RegOpenKeyEx identifies the key that contains the setup information.
RegQueryValueEx provides the setting found under each value under the key.
You must always remember to use RegCloseKey to close a key at the end of a
Registry operation.

gSaveChildFormPosition (listing 31.6) saves the current position of the child
form to the Windows Registry. RegCreateKeyEx provides the window handle
of the key containing the information. Notice that you use this call whether
the key exists or not. This API call simply opens a key in the same way as
RegOpenKeyEx—if that key already exists. You save the new value under the
key by using RegSetValueEx. You should never forget to close a key when you
are done with one of these Registry operations that use RegCloseKey.

Listing 31.6   The `gSetChildFormPosition` **Routine**

```
Sub gSaveChildFormPosition(frmChild As Form)
Dim hWndQue As Long
Dim hlstrWindowState As String
Dim hlstrTopPosition As String
Dim hlstrLeftPosition As String
Dim lpClass As String
Dim Security As SECURITY_ATTRIBUTES
Dim lpdwDisposition As Long
Dim lReturn As Long

  lpClass = Space$(255)
  lReturn = RegCreateKeyEx(HKEY_LOCAL_MACHINE, "Que\ChildForm", _
          0&, lpClass, REG_OPTION_NON_VOLATILE, _
          KEY_ALL_ACCESS, Security, hWndQue, lpdwDisposition)
  If lReturn <> ERROR_SUCCESS Then
    gAPIDisplayError lReturn
  End If

  hlstrWindowState = Trim$(Str$(frmChild.WindowState))
  lReturn = RegSetValueEx(hWndQue, "WindowState", 0&, REG_SZ, _
          hlstrWindowState, Len(hlstrWindowState))
  If lReturn <> ERROR_SUCCESS Then
    gAPIDisplayError lReturn
  End If

  hlstrTopPosition = Trim$(Str$(frmChild.Top))
  lReturn = RegSetValueEx(hWndQue, "TopPosition", 0&, REG_SZ, _
                        hlstrTopPosition, Len(hlstrTopPosition))
  If lReturn <> ERROR_SUCCESS Then
    gAPIDisplayError lReturn
  End If

  hlstrLeftPosition = Trim$(Str$(frmChild.Left))
  lReturn = RegSetValueEx(hWndQue, "LeftPosition", 0&, REG_SZ, _
                        hlstrLeftPosition, Len(hlstrLeftPosition))
  If lReturn <> ERROR_SUCCESS Then
    gAPIDisplayError lReturn
  End If

  lReturn = RegCloseKey(hWndQue)

End Sub
```

The following steps show how to make this code work together:

1. Open new project and rename this project as 31Proj03.

2. Rename Form1 as `frmChild`.

3. Add the code module WINAPI32 from 31Proj02.

4. Add a new code module Settings from 31Proj02.

5. Add the routines `gSetChildFormPosition` and `gSaveChildFormPosition` to the Settings module.

6. Add `frmMain` from 31Proj02, as follows:

```
Private Sub Form_Load()
    Call gSetChildFormPosition(Me)
End Sub
Private Sub Form_Unload(Cancel As Integer)
  Call gSaveChildFormPosition(Me)
End Sub
```

7. Add the `Form_Load` code to the load event and unload code to the unload event of `frmChild`.

Using MDI Design Types

The Windows world has gone MDI (Multiple Document Interface). Most of the applications that you see today use some kind of MDI design. All MDI applications have several common elements. MDI applications consist of a container parent object and children that appear within that parent. Many different kinds of MDI applications have emerged over the years. These different kinds of MDI applications all fall into several general categories: Classic, WorkSpace, WorkBook, Project, and Property Sheet.

The Classic Design

The Classic MDI application works with the members of one data type. Most of the current commercially available Windows applications fit within this category. Applications belonging to this category include programs like Microsoft Word for Windows, Lotus AmiPro, and WordPerfect. Even the MDI example that ships with Visual Basic, MDINote, is an example of this typical MDI design. Figure 31.3 shows what the MDINote application sample looks like.

The most distinguishing characteristic of the Classic MDI design is that it displays only one type of data object. Microsoft Word for Windows 6.0 (WinWord) is a perfect example of a Classic MDI application. Figure 31.4 shows Word on the screen with three open documents. All the MDI children belong to the same data type, the word processing document.

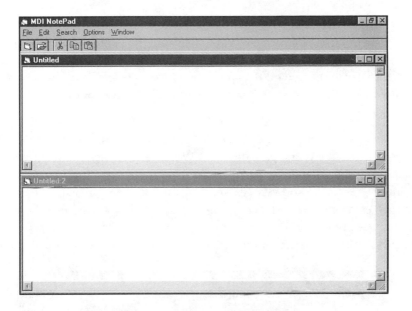

Fig. 31.3
The look and feel of a Classic MDI application.

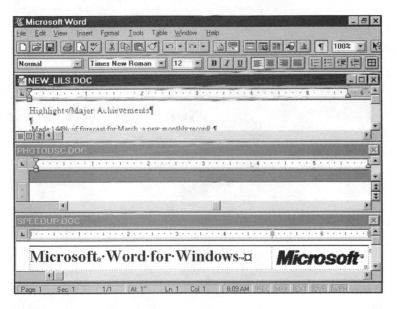

Fig. 31.4
WinWord with three documents open, demonstrating a Classic MDI design.

The WorkSpace Design

For a long time, the Classicdesign was really only one kind of MDI application type. As the Windows environment became more popular, companies started to create their own MDI application types. These applications have requirements that do not all fit into the nice, neat picture of one parent with one child type.

Company programmers began to create applications using a design that Microsoft calls the WorkSpace design. A WorkSpace application distinguishes itself from other MDI designs by displaying multiple data objects in different children. Figure 31.5 shows an example of a WorkSpace application for the Chicago environment. In this case, the application is a word processor. Notice that two types of objects are on the screen. The folder object represents templates. The text document icon stands for a word processing document.

Fig. 31.5

A word processing application that shows the WorkSpace design.

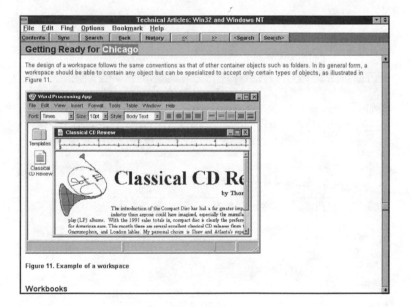

The process for creating a Visual Basic MDI WorkSpace application is simple. Begin with an MDI parent and add two or more MDI children. You must customize the different MDI children to display different kinds of necessary information. For example, you might choose to create one MDI child for displaying the contents of an invoice and a second to display the individual detail items of an invoice.

The WorkBook Design

MDI applications enable the user to view different kinds of information simultaneously. Sometimes so many children are on the parent that the screen becomes confusing to the user. In some cases, the user needs access to different kinds of information, but does not need to see all of it at the same time.

The WorkBook design improves on the WorkSpace design to create an application that uses the notebook metaphor. A WorkBook organizes the different kinds of information into a notebook-like display. This kind of display typically uses folder tabs to provide the user with access to the different kinds of information. Figure 31.6 shows Excel 5.0, which is a perfect example of a WorkBook application design. Notice the tabbed children within the main form.

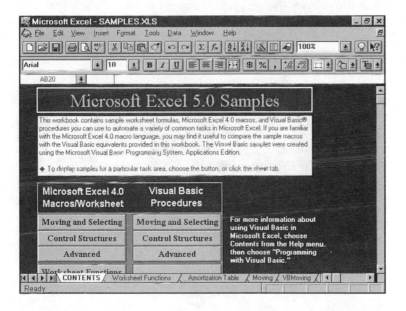

Fig. 31.6
Microsoft Excel 5.0 demonstrating the WorkBook application design.

Some WorkBook designs, like that of Microsoft Excel 5.0, enable the user to work with multiple WorkBooks at the same time. All the user has to do is cycle back and forth between the different WorkBooks. Each of these WorkBooks can contain any of the child objects. In Microsoft Excel 5.0, a WorkBook can contain spreadsheets, pictures, charts, and macro sheets.

The process of creating an effective WorkBook design requires the use of a tab control such as the new 32-bit tab control that ships with Visual Basic 4.0. Several other third-party tab controls are on the market. You can create this kind of design without using a tab control, but such efforts seldom work very effectively in everyday use. The WorkBook design functions better when you need to work with the information as well as organize it.

The Project Design

Another kind of application that works with multiple groupings of information is similar to a WorkBook application but does not use the folder-like tab look and feel. Instead, the presentation looks like a blank screen with a status bar at the bottom. You access the different functions of the application through making choices on this status bar. Windows 95's status bar is the most common example of this Project design.

Figure 31.6 shows what Project applications might look like on the screen. This figure shows Windows 95 using the new interface. Notice the use of the tabs at the bottom of the screen to represent running applications. If you want to organize information instead of working with it, this kind of application style works quite well.

Fig. 31.7
The Windows 95 status bar displaying a Project application.

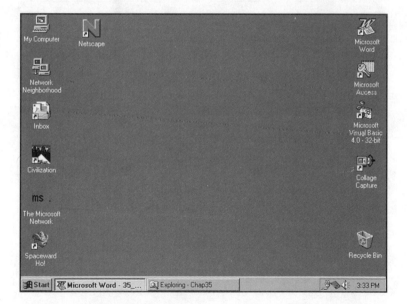

The Property Sheet Design

The Property Sheet design uses the same tabular look and feel as the WorkBook design. Property Sheets are typically modal dialog boxes that contain so much information that they cannot fit on one screen. For this reason, you use the tabbed look and feel to organize the information by categories.

Figure 31.8 shows a dialog box formatted in the Property Sheet design. In this case, the dialog box is Microsoft Word for Windows 6.0's Options dialog box. Notice how the tab names organize the information into distinct groupings based on what the user wants to do. This design has a distinct advantage over putting the names for each of these categories on the menu structure. You do not have to go to multiple screens to modify similar information.

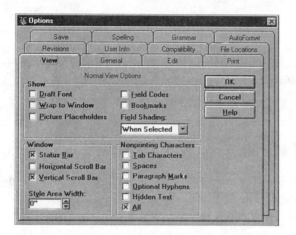

Fig. 31.8
Microsoft Word for Windows 6.0's Options dialog box demonstrating the Property Sheet design.

You save space and simplify the form's appearance by organizing the information in the property sheet design. Consider what this dialog box would look like if you tried to put all the information on the screen at the same time. Such a dialog box probably would not fit on the screen, and also be confusing to read.

Combinations of Styles

The different categories of MDI styles that you have studied in this section are by no means the only ones available. Windows is a living environment that is in a constant state of change based on the needs of users. Toolbars and status bars were not a part of the original versions of Windows applications. Now it is difficult to remember a Windows application that lacks both of these attributes.

Toolbars and status bars became a part of the Windows interface because users wanted them. A programmer came up with the idea, which took off from there. Users liked what they saw and asked for it in the other applications that they used.

V

Optimization

There is no reason that you cannot combine the different elements of the styles of design described in this chapter to create a new one. Each company's needs differ, so if you think that you need a new way to do things, try it. Other users might like your innovation and before you know it, it will become part of the existing style.

Caution

Be careful how you stray from the different styles that you see in other applications. The continuity of Windows interface is what makes many users more comfortable with Windows. When you need to break with the standard, make sure that you do so for good reasons.

From Here...

Forms are the canvases on which you paint your screens. You must be careful to remember that how and where you place your canvases is as important as what you place on them. A form's position on the screen affects whether the user perceives an application as well or poorly constructed. The overall design of how the forms interact with each other affects how easily a user can work with an application. Always keep these factors in mind.

To learn more about related topics, see the following chapters:

- Chapter 30, "Advanced Control Techniques," describes a simplified version of the positioning code, and also discusses toolbars and status bars and how to create them in Visual Basic applications.

- Chapter 33, "Accessing the Windows API," provides more information about Windows API calls.

- Chapter 34, "Designing Windows Applications," explains more about existing Windows standards and discusses screen design issues further.

Chapter 32

Advanced Code Techniques

There is no single way to solve a technical programming problem. Many factors go into choosing a programming solution for a problem. Visual Basic properties, methods, and events define what you can and cannot do. You must find ways to work around bugs when they get in the way of providing a solution. The Windows environment itself presents you with challenges of capabilities and limitations.

When writing code to solve a client's problem, you usually must do so as quickly as possible. Foreknowledge of efficient coding techniques and common technical pitfalls can make writing code a faster process. Being aware of potential resources that provide such knowledge can prepare you to develop such techniques and avoid such pitfalls before difficulties even arise.

In this chapter, you learn how to do the following:

- Work with the Windows Registry

- Design an application's startup code

- Save user preferences at run time

- Position forms on the screen

The MSBASIC Forum on CompuServe Information Services (CIS)

The CompuServe online service provides a wonderful resource for finding solutions to programming problems. Join the MSBASIC forum and talk to other Visual Basic programmers who might have solutions to your current problems. You can obtain a membership copy from most computer software stores, or call 1-800-848-8990 to order a copy directly.

Minimizing CompuServe Charges

CompuServe charges can add up as you increasingly use this valuable resource. One way to reduce your online charges is to use an *auto-navigator*. An auto-navigator reduces your online time by first obtaining the headers of all the new messages; you can then choose which ones you want to read. Then the auto-navigator retrieves your selected messages to enable you to read them offline rather than online—and thus save money. An example of such an auto-navigator is Navcis, which is available in the DVORAK forum, but many other good ones are available. You should try some to discover one that best fits your needs.

Understanding Configuration Options

Visual Basic supports the two most common methods for storing application information: .INI files and the Windows Registry. Support for .INI files exists for compatibility with earlier versions of Windows and Visual Basic. The Windows Registry is the current accepted location for placing application information.

Application .INI Files

Every application should have its own .INI file. This file provides a way to save settings between application sessions. Many Windows applications still store settings in the WIN.INI Windows configuration file. This creates problems when the WIN.INI file grows beyond the 64K limit. Under these circumstances, Windows no longer runs on that machine until someone reduces the .INI files size. Remember to use an application .INI file rather than WIN.INI.

Visual Basic provides no internal functions for creating and maintaining application .INI files. To work with .INI files, you must work directly with the Windows API. Three basic API functions allow access to application .INI files: GetPrivateProfileString, GetPrivateProfileInt, and WritePrivateProfileString. GetPrivateProfileString provides a method for obtaining text or values from an indicated .INI file. The API calls return these settings as a string. GetPrivateProfileInt returns values stored in the indicated .INI file. WritePrivateProfileString saves indicated strings to the indicated .INI file. Chapter 33, "Accessing the Windows API," contains the declarations and syntax for using these routines.

The Windows Registry

Windows 95 and NT place their system configuration information in the Registry database. This is a change from the older .INI system found in Windows 3.x systems. OLE applications like Microsoft Office broke this trend by using the Registry database, but such applications are the exception rather than the rule. Any entries in the old WIN.INI and SYSTEM.INI files are there simply for compatibility reasons. The Registry keeps information in binary files. An application uses the Registry API functions to access data in the Registry.

Visual Basic provides no internal functions for creating and maintaining the Windows Registry. To work with the Windows Registry, you must work directly with the Windows 32 API. Seven API functions allow access to the Windows Registry: `RegOpenKeyEx`, `RegQueryValueEx`, `RegCloseKey`, `RegCreateKeyEx`, `RegSetValueEx`, `RegDeleteKey`, and `RegDeleteValue`. `RegOpenKeyEx` enables you to open a Registry key so that you can work with its contents. Use `RegQueryValueEx` to obtain the settings that belong to a key in the Registry. `RegCreateKeyEx` creates new Registry keys and `RegSetValueEx` assigns settings to a key. `RegDeleteKey` removes keys from the Registry, and `RegDeleteValue` removes a value from a key. Chapter 33 contains the declarations and syntax for using these routines.

Optimizing the Application Startup Process

An application's startup process gives the user a first impression of the entire application. If you design an application that has a long startup, you give the user the impression that your entire application is slow. Unfortunately, at program startup, it is important for an application to make calculations and check settings. Therefore, you are faced with a challenge: to design applications that don't seem slow yet still handle configuration issues at startup. You can use several techniques to avoid this dilemma.

Understanding Pseudo Constants

The following two lines of code define the constants `LINE_FEED` and `TAB_STOP`:

```
' initialize global strings
LINE_FEED = Chr$(10)
TAB_STOP = Chr$(9)
```

V

Optimization

At least these variables *seem* to be formatted as constants. Constants normally appear in the General Declarations sections of modules and, rarely, forms. Unfortunately, you cannot define constants by using functions such as Chr$. The code has to set these variables at run time. These variables are not constants, therefore, but simply behave as constants because you define them only once in the code. For this reason, such variables are called *pseudo constants*. By using such variables, you need only remember a pseudo constant's name instead of having to remember, for example, the ASCII code for the linefeed or tab character.

These pseudo constants allow for carefully formatted message box text throughout your projects. You can now space message text within a text box by placing a space between logical phrases. For example, you can place "Warning, Warning!" at the top of a message and then one line further down "You are about to delete data permanently" by inserting two linefeed constant statements in the string assigned to the message box.

Starting with Code

Visual Basic's Project tab appears on the Options dialog box (which you access by choosing Tools, Options). This dialog box provides a method for identifying the startup form. Along with the names of each of the forms in the current project, you find the strangely out-of-place Sub Main. But you have no form named Sub Main, and when you try to add this subroutine to any of your forms, it does not work properly. The solution is simple: create a new module and place in it a subroutine named Sub Main. Figure 32.1 shows the Options dialog box in which the Sub Main choice appears in the Project tab.

Fig. 32.1
The Options dialog box with Startup Form set to Sub Main.

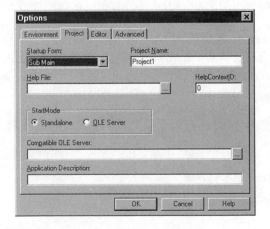

Setup Controls

The project 32Proj01 demonstrates a possible use for Sub Main. To function
properly, Visual Basic applications still must be aware of DOS paths. Users
might not want to place their copy of your applications in the same directories that you intended. How do you discover what path the user wants to use?
The file 32Proj01 on the companion CD includes a rudimentary method for
letting the user indicate the path. Figure 32.2 displays the form that you need
to construct. Use this figure as a model as you proceed through the following
steps:

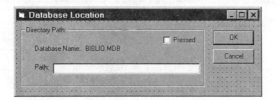

Fig. 32.2
The
frmDataLocation
form at design
time.

1. Create a new form and save it under the DOS name Data Location.

2. Change the Visual Basic name to frmDataLocation.

3. Draw a frame on the form and rename it as fraPath.

4. Make the caption of the new frame "Directory Path."

5. Draw three labels on the frame and rename them lblDatabaseName,
   lblDatabase, and lblPath.

6. Add a command button, rename it cmdOk, and give it the label "OK."

7. Add a comand button, rename it cmdCancel, and give it the label
   "Cancel."

8. Create a new module and rename it STARTUP.BAS.

9. Add to the frame a text box and rename it txtPath.

10. Add to the frame a check box and rename it chkPressed.

11. Add GetDatabasePath, Main, and SaveDatabasePath to STARTUP.BAS.

12. Add cmdOK_Click and cmdCancel_Click to frmDataLocation.

13. Create a new module and rename it WINAPI.BAS.

14. Add the API declarations and code to WINAPI.BAS.

Application Paths

Sub Main contains this project's startup code (see listing 32.1). First this routine loads frmDataLocation and displays the path stored in the Registry or the current application path in the Path text box. Next the code displays frmDataLocation modally and waits for the user to exit from that form. The path placed in the text box on frmDataLocation provides the path for Sub Main to save into the Registry if the user presses the OK command button.

Listing 32.1   The Sub Main Routine

```
Sub Main()

  Load frmDataLocation

  frmDataLocation!txtPath.TEXT = GetDatabasePath

  frmDataLocation.Show vbModal

  If frmDataLocation!chkPressed.VALUE Then
     Call SaveDatabasePath(Trim$(frmDataLocation!txtPath.TEXT))
  End If
End Sub
Unload frmDataLocation

End Sub
```

The *GetDatabasePath* Function

Listing 32.2 shows the GetDatabasePath function. Notice how you use App.Path to provide the database's default path. The reference to App.Path appears to path to the current directory if the Registry doesn't store a database path. Chapter 33, "Accessing the Windows API," features a complete discussion of the API calls for the Registry.

Listing 32.2   The GetDatabasePath Function

```
Private Function GetDatabasePath() As String
Dim lReturn As Long
Dim sClass As String
Dim lDisposition As Long
Dim Security As SECURITY_ATTRIBUTES
Dim sDatabasePath As String
Dim hWndQue As Long
Dim lLength As Long

  'Create or Open Que Registry entry for local machine
  sClass = Space$(255)
```

```
    lReturn = RegCreateKeyEx(HKEY_LOCAL_MACHINE,"QUE",0&,sClass, _
REG_OPTION_NON_VOLATILE, KEY_ALL_ACCESS, Security, hWndQue, _
lDisposition)
    If lReturn <> ERROR_SUCCESS Then
        gAPIDisplayError lReturn
    End If

    lLength = 255
    sDatabasePath = Space$(lLength)
    lReturn = RegQueryValueEx(hWndQue, "DatabasePath", 0&, REG_SZ, _
sDatabasePath, lLength)
    If lReturn <> ERROR_SUCCESS Then
        GetDatabasePath = App.Path
    Else
        GetDatabasePath = Left$(sDatabasePath, lLength - 1)
    End If

    'Close open keys
    lReturn = RegCloseKey(hWndQue)

End Function
```

The *SaveDatabasePath* Function

SaveDatabasePath (listing 32.3) provides a way to save the database path to
the Registry. Chapter 34 includes a complete discussion of the Registry API
database calls.

Listing 32.3   The SaveDatabasePath Function

```
Private Sub SaveDatabasePath(sDatabasePath As String)
Dim lReturn As Long
Dim hWndQue As Long
Dim sClass As String
Dim Security As SECURITY_ATTRIBUTES
Dim lDisposition As Long

    'Create or Open Que Registry entry for local machine
    sClass = Space$(255)
    lReturn = RegCreateKeyEx(HKEY_LOCAL_MACHINE,"QUE",0&,sClass, _
REG_OPTION_NON_VOLATILE, KEY_ALL_ACCESS, Security, hWndQue, _
lDisposition)
    If lReturn <> ERROR_SUCCESS Then
        gAPIDisplayError lReturn
    End If

    'Save Database path in the Registry
    lReturn = RegSetValueEx(hWndQue, "DatabasePath", 0&, REG_SZ, _
sDatabasePath, Len(sDatabasePath))
    If lReturn <> ERROR_SUCCESS Then
        gAPIDisplayError lReturn
    End If
```

(continues)

V

Optimization

Listing 32.3 Continued

```
    'Close open keys
    lReturn = RegCloseKey(hWndQue)

End Sub
```

The *cmdOk_Click* and *cmdCancel_Click* Events

Notice that each of the command-button click events (listing 32.4) hides
frmDataLocation instead of unloading it. This is important because you need
to access the contents of txtPath in the Sub Main routine. Because you display
frmDataLocation modally, none of the code that follows frmDataLocation.Show
vbModal processes until the form unloads or becomes invisible. Using the Hide
method makes frmDataLocation invisible, thus enabling the processing of the
code that follows the Show method in Sub Main.

Listing 32.4 The cmdOk_Click and cmdCancel_Click Events

```
Private Sub cmdOK_Click()

  chkPressed.VALUE = 1
  Me.Hide

End Sub

Private Sub cmdCancel_Click()

  chkPressed.VALUE = False

  Me.Hide

End Sub
```

The Pressed check box on frmDataLocation provides an excellent, easy way to
determine whether the user pressed the Cancel or OK button. Another way
to tell the Sub Main routine which button the user pressed is to use a global
variable.

Global Variables

Several global variables are necessary to operate this project's code. Listing
32.5 shows this project's global variables.

Listing 32.5 The Global Variables

```
Declare Function RegCloseKey Lib "advapi32" _
    (ByVal hKey As Long) As Long

Declare Function RegCreateKeyEx Lib "advapi32" Alias _
"RegCreateKeyExA" (ByVal hKey As Long, ByVal lpSubKey As String, _
ByVal Reserved As Long, ByVal lpClass As String, _
ByVal dwOptions As Long, ByVal samDesired As Long, _
lpSecurityAttributes As SECURITY_ATTRIBUTES, phkResult As Long, _
lpdwDisposition As Long) As Long

Declare Function RegOpenKeyEx Lib "advapi32" Alias _
"RegOpenKeyExA" (ByVal hKey As Long, ByVal lpSubKey As String, _
ByVal ulOptions As Long, ByVal samDesired As Long, _
phkResult As Long) As Long

Declare Function RegQueryValueEx Lib "advapi32" Alias _
"RegQueryValueExA" (ByVal hKey As Long, _
ByVal lpValueName As String, lpReserved As Long, _
lpType As Long, ByVal lpData As String, lpcbData As Long) As Long

Declare Function RegSetValueEx Lib "advapi32" Alias _
"RegSetValueExA" (ByVal hKey As Long, _
ByVal lpValueName As String, ByVal Reserved As Long, _
ByVal dwType As Long, ByVal lpData As String, _
ByVal cbData As Long) As Long

'Security Mask constants
Public Const READ_CONTROL = &H20000
Public Const SYNCHRONIZE = &H100000
Public Const STANDARD_RIGHTS_ALL = &H1F0000
Public Const STANDARD_RIGHTS_READ = READ_CONTROL
Public Const STANDARD_RIGHTS_WRITE = READ_CONTROL
Public Const KEY_QUERY_VALUE = &H1
Public Const KEY_SET_VALUE = &H2
Public Const KEY_CREATE_SUB_KEY = &H4
Public Const KEY_ENUMERATE_SUB_KEYS = &H8
Public Const KEY_NOTIFY = &H10
Public Const KEY_CREATE_LINK = &H20

Public Const KEY_ALL_ACCESS = ((STANDARD_RIGHTS_ALL Or _
KEY_QUERY_VALUE Or KEY_SET_VALUE Or KEY_CREATE_SUB_KEY Or _
KEY_ENUMERATE_SUB_KEYS Or KEY_NOTIFY Or KEY_CREATE_LINK) _
And (Not SYNCHRONIZE))

Public Const KEY_READ = ((STANDARD_RIGHTS_READ Or _
KEY_QUERY_VALUE Or KEY_ENUMERATE_SUB_KEYS Or KEY_NOTIFY) _
And (Not SYNCHRONIZE))

Public Const KEY_EXECUTE = ((KEY_READ) And (Not SYNCHRONIZE))
Public Const KEY_WRITE = ((STANDARD_RIGHTS_WRITE Or _
KEY_SET_VALUE Or KEY_CREATE_SUB_KEY) And (Not SYNCHRONIZE))
```

V

Optimization

(continues)

Listing 32.5 Continued

```
'Predefined Registry Keys used in hKey Argument
Public Const HKEY_CLASSES_ROOT = &H80000000
Public Const HKEY_CURRENT_USER = &H80000001
Public Const HKEY_LOCAL_MACHINE = &H80000002
Public Const HKEY_USERS = &H80000003
Public Const HKEY_PERFORMANCE_DATA = &H80000004

' Return codes from Registration functions.
Public Const ERROR_SUCCESS = 0&
Public Const ERROR_BADDB = 1009&
Public Const ERROR_BADKEY = 1010&
Public Const ERROR_CANTOPEN = 1011&
Public Const ERROR_CANTREAD = 1012&
Public Const ERROR_CANTWRITE = 1013&
Public Const ERROR_OUTOFMEMORY = 14&
Public Const ERROR_INVALID_PARAMETER = 87&
Public Const ERROR_ACCESS_DENIED = 5&

'Data type Public constants
Public Const REG_NONE = 0
Public Const REG_SZ = 1
Public Const REG_EXPAND_SZ = 2
Public Const REG_BINARY = 3
Public Const REG_DWORD = 4
Public Const REG_DWORD_LITTLE_ENDIAN = 4
Public Const REG_DWORD_BIG_ENDIAN = 5
Public Const REG_LINK = 6
Public Const REG_MULTI_SZ = 7
Public Const REG_RESOURCE_LIST = 8
Public Const REG_FULL_RESOURCE_DESCRIPTOR = 9
Public Const REG_RESOURCE_REQUIREMENTS_LIST = 10

'Options
Public Const REG_OPTION_VOLATILE = 0
Public Const REG_OPTION_NON_VOLATILE = 1

Type SECURITY_ATTRIBUTES
  nLength As Long
  lpSecurityDescriptor As Variant
  bInheritHandle As Long
End Type
```

Before proceeding any further, you must declare the API calls. Create a new module and rename it WINAPI32.BAS. Copy the code in listing 32.5 into the General Declarations section of this new module. The API declarations and constants are globally available to the entire application and are necessary to make the code in the remainder of this chapter work. Listing 32.6 shows the API call declarations.

Listing 32.6   Declarations of the API Calls

```
Sub gAPIDisplayError(lCode As Long)

  Select Case lCode
    Case ERROR_BADDB
      MsgBox "Corrupt Registry Database!"
    Case ERROR_BADKEY
      MsgBox "Key name is bad"
    Case ERROR_CANTOPEN
      MsgBox "Cannot Open Key"
    Case ERROR_CANTREAD
      MsgBox "Cannot Read Key"
    Case ERROR_CANTWRITE
      MsgBox "Cannot Write Key"
    Case ERROR_ACCESS_DENIED
      MsgBox "Access to Registry Denied"
    Case ERROR_OUTOFMEMORY
      MsgBox "Out of memory"
    Case ERROR_INVALID_PARAMETER
      MsgBox "Invalid Parameter"
    Case Else
      MsgBox "Undefined key error code!"
  End Select

End Sub
```

Make sure that you add the gAPIDisplayError subroutine to WINAPI32. This
function provides error checking for the Registry calls. Chapter 34 discusses
the API calls and this error-checking routine.

Note

Notice the use of the Visual Basic keyword Public rather than the more familiar
Global. This is a major change that Visual Basic 4.0 introduces. Fortunately, Visual
Basic 4.0 is backward-compatible, so you need not immediately change to using
Public rather than Global. Both keywords behave exactly the same and work prop-
erly in a Visual Basic 4.0 project.

The Application Title

To provide some continuity among the different screens, applications need
to present a consistent title. Sub Main is an excellent location for setting
app.title. By using the Title property of the Visual Basic app object, you
can specify that the same message appear for each screen. This property also
makes changing the title easy, because you need only change the title in one
place to affect each screen. If you had to insert the title text everywhere that
you want it to appear, the process of changing the title would be harder and
possibly less accurate.

V

Optimization

The following code line is the definition of the `app.Title` object:

```
app.Title = Que Publishing
```

The Application Help File

Visual Basic provides a place where you can easily set the name of an application's Help file. Simply set your choice on the Project Options dialog box by choosing the Project tab of the Options dialog box as shown in figure 32.3.

Fig. 32.3

The Project Options dialog box showing the Help File setting.

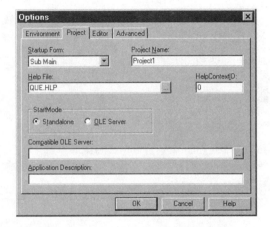

Unfortunately, if you hard-code the path in this dialog box, the user cannot install your application in another directory. If the user chooses another directory, the Help system does not work properly. Fortunately, an alternative to this unacceptable solution exists: Simply use the `app` object's `HelpFile` property to set the path at run time in the `Sub Main` subroutine, as follows:

```
app.HelpFile = app.Path & \QUE.HLP
```

The Splash Form

To create the illusion of a "fast" application, use a splash screen. A splash screen is just a form with a picture showing on-screen something about the application—perhaps a company graphic, descriptive text, or even an entertaining picture—to keep the user's attention while processing takes place in the background. Figure 32.4 shows an example of a splash screen.

To create the splash screen shown in figure 32.4, follow these steps:

1. Create a new form and save it under the DOS name SPLASH.FRM.

2. Change the Visual Basic name to `frmSplash`.

3. Change the `borderstyle` property to `0-None`.

Fig. 32.4
The frmSplash
displayed at run
time.

4. Add THREED.OCX to the project if it does not already exist.

5. Draw a 3D frame and size it to fill the screen.

6. Draw an Image control on the screen and place your own graphic in that image control.

Show versus *Load* **Methods**

You often must choose between using a Show or Load method. Show triggers the form's load event and makes the form visible. Load triggers the same event but leaves the form invisible. To display the form immediately on the screen, simply use Load in Sub Main and change the visible property to True in the form's Load event.

Chapter 31, "Advanced Form Techniques," contains a full discussion of multiple-document interface (MDI) forms.

Creating Common Subroutines

Toolbars and menu choices that trigger the exact same code present you with another problem: how to keep their shared code current. The obvious choice is to create a common subroutine that both the menu choice and the toolbar can call. For the sake of simplicity, you should place these common routines in a separate module. By using separate modules, you can easily port code to other applications simply by copying the module from one project to another.

Saving Settings on Exit

Users perceive customizable applications as user-friendly and enjoy working with them. But consider carefully which parts of your application to make customizable. Features like saving column widths in grids and saving the last object opened are excellent choices for customization. The user sometimes does not want to save the settings from one session to another, so you must enable users to turn this feature on and off. For example, once satisfied with the column widths in grids, a user does not want to overwrite the settings immediately. In these circumstances, the user need only turn on the feature that saves the settings, save the grid's column width, and then simply turn off the feature that saves settings.

The shell's Option menu does not enable the user to save customization choices in an application's executable file. To save settings, you must use the Windows Registry. Place the GetSavedSettings function in MAIN.BAS. This routine checks for any settings in the Windows Registry and creates the defaults if none exist yet. Before any of this code can work, you must add to the project 32Proj01 the 32-bit API code, which appears in the WINAPI32.BAS module.

Using the *gSetValue* Subroutine

Unlike the previous projects in this chapter, saving the different settings associated with forms requires many calls to the Registry. You could make the calls exactly as shown in 32ProjJ01, but the code would be longer and less understandable. Instead, use the gSetValue subroutine to make the Registry calls for you.

gSetValue (see listing 32.7) places a setting in the Registry according to the settings of its arguments: sKey, sKeyValue, and sNewValue. sKey identifies the name of the key to set a value and sKeyValue identifies the name of the value. sNewValue contains the string or number to place under the identified value.

Listing 32.7 The gSetValue Subroutine

```
Sub gSetValue(sKey$, sKeyValue$, sNewValue$)
Dim lReturn As Long
Dim hWndQue As Long
Dim hWnd As Long
Dim sClass As String
Dim Security As SECURITY_ATTRIBUTES
Dim lDisposition As Long

  'Create or open Que Registry entry for local machine
  sClass = Space$(255)
  lReturn = RegCreateKeyEx(HKEY_LOCAL_MACHINE, "QUE", 0&, _
 sClass, REG_OPTION_NON_VOLATILE, KEY_ALL_ACCESS, Security, _
hWndQue, lDisposition)

  sClass = Space$(255)
  lReturn = RegCreateKeyEx(hWndQue, sKey, 0&, sClass, _
REG_OPTION_NON_VOLATILE, KEY_ALL_ACCESS, Security, hWnd, _
lDisposition)
```

```
    'Save value in the Registry
    lReturn = RegSetValueEx(hWnd, sKeyValue, 0&, REG_SZ, _
sNewValue, Len(sNewValue))

    'Close open keys
    lReturn = RegCloseKey(hWndQue)
    lReturn = RegCloseKey(hWnd)

End Sub
```

Using the *gGetValue* Function

gGetValue (listing 32.8) obtains a setting in the Registry according to the settings of the function's arguments: sKey and sKeyValue. sKey identifies the name of the key to set a value, and skeyValue identifies the value's name. The gGetValue function returns the contents of the indicated key's value.

Listing 32.8   The gGetValue **Function**

```
Function gGetValue(sKey$, sKeyValue$) As String
Dim lReturn As Long
Dim sClass As String
Dim lDisposition As Long
Dim Security As SFCURITY_ATTRIBUTES
Dim sValue As String
Dim hWndQue As Long
Dim hWnd As Long
Dim lLength As Long

    'Create or open Que Registry entry for local machine
    sClass = Space$(255)
    lReturn = RegCreateKeyEx(HKEY_LOCAL_MACHINE,"QUE",0&,sClass, _
REG_OPTION_NON_VOLATILE, KEY_ALL_ACCESS, Security, hWndQue, _
lDisposition)

    sClass = Space$(255)
    lReturn = RegCreateKeyEx(hWndQue, sKey, 0&, sClass, _
REG_OPTION_NON_VOLATILE, KEY_ALL_ACCESS, Security, hWnd, _
lDisposition)

    lLength = 255
    sValue = Space$(lLength)
    lReturn = RegQueryValueEx(hWnd, sKeyValue, 0&, REG_SZ, sValue, _
                             lLength)

    'Close open keys
    lReturn = RegCloseKey(hWndQue)
    lReturn = RegCloseKey(hWnd)

    sValue = Trim$(sValue)
    gGetValue = Mid$(sValue, 1, Len(sValue) - 1)

End Function
```

V

Optimization

Using the *gGetSettings* Subroutine

The GetSavedSettings subroutine accommodates all the settings over which you want to give the user control. This routine currently specifies whether the application should save any settings that change.

You want to create a way for the user to turn the Save Settings On Exit option on and off. To do so, simply create a new menu choice named mnuOptions and labeled "&Options," with the submenu mnuOptionsSaveSettings with the label "Save Settings On Exit."

Listing 32.9 contains the code to place in the mnuOptionsSaveSettings_Click event. The code ensures that the user can choose whether to enable or disable the Save Settings On Exit option. To discover the user's choice, note whether a check mark appears next to the menu choice; if the check mark appears, the user enabled the Save Settings On Exit option.

Listing 32.9   The gGetSettings Function

```
Sub gGetSettings()

   giSaveSettings = Val(gGetValue("Preferences", "SaveSettings"))

   frmMain!mnuOptionsSaveSettings.Checked = giSaveSettings

End Sub
```

Positioning the Form

Where a form appears is at least as important as how it appears. Positioning is a frequently overlooked part of Visual Basic programming; many programmers simply let their forms appear in their default design-time positions. The major problem with this approach is that different users have screens with different resolution sizes. A form that appears in the lower-right corner of an 800-by-600 screen disappears completely off a 640-by-480 screen.

This section introduces some routines that help you fine-tune the positioning of your forms. For the sake of simplicity, place all the position routines in a new module named POSITION.BAS.

MDI Form Position

Higher-resolution screens make programming in Visual Basic easier. They provide more room on which you can display different elements of Visual Basic without creating a confusing screen. Unfortunately, not every user has the luxury of an 800-by-600 resolution screen. Be careful to design screens that adjust their size based on the user's screen resolution. Listing 32.10 shows the SetMainFrmPosition subroutine, which sizes and positions frmMain on the screen.

Listing 32.10   The SetMainFrmPosition Subroutine

```
Sub gSetMainFormPosition(frmName As Form)
Dim sWindowState As String
Dim sTopPosition As String
Dim sLeftPosition As String
Dim sFormWidth As String
Dim sFormHeight As String

  sWindowState = gGetValue("Main", "WindowState")
  Select Case sWindowState
    Case "0"
      sTopPosition = gGetValue("Main", "Top")
      sLeftPosition = gGetValue("Main", "Left")
      sFormWidth = gGetValue("Main", "Width")
      sFormHeight = gGetValue("Main", "Height")
      frmName.Move Val(sLeftPosition), Val(sTopPosition), _
Val(sFormWidth), Val(sFormHeight)

    Case "1"
      frmName.WindowState = vbMinimized
    Case "2"
      frmName.WindowState = vbMaximized
    Case Else
      frmName.Width = 640 * Screen.TwipsPerPixelX
      frmName.Height = 480 * Screen.TwipsPerPixelY

      If frmName.Width + 100 > Screen.Width Then
        frmName.WindowState = vbMaximized
      Else
        frmName.TOP = (Screen.Height - frmName.Height) \ 2
        frmName.Left = (Screen.Width - frmName.Width) \ 2
      End If
  End Select

End Sub
```

The gSetMainFormPosition routine changes the appearance of frmMain based on the size of the screen. Therefore, frmMain appears maximized on 640-by-480 resolution screens and centered in 800-by-600 screens.

These choices might be good candidates for a user setting that can save the position of the form so that the next time that the user loads this program, the form appears in exactly the same place. gSaveMainFormPosition (listing 32.11) is a subroutine that gives the user this control.

Listing 32.11   The gSaveMainFormPosition Subroutine

```
Sub gSaveMainFormPosition(frmName As Form)
Dim sWindowState As String
Dim sTopPosition As String
Dim sLeftPosition As String
Dim sFormWidth As String
Dim sFormHeight As String

  If giSaveSettings Then
    sWindowState = Trim$(Str$(frmName.WindowState))
    Call gSetValue("Main", "WindowState", sWindowState)
    sTopPosition = Trim$(Str$(frmName.TOP))
    Call gSetValue("Main", "Top", sTopPosition)
    sLeftPosition = Trim$(Str$(frmName.Left))
    Call gSetValue("Main", "Left", sLeftPosition)
    sFormWidth = Trim$(Str$(frmName.Width))
    Call gSetValue("Main", "Width", sFormWidth)
    sFormHeight = Trim$(Str$(frmName.Height))
    Call gSetValue("Main", "Height", sFormHeight)
  End If

End Sub
```

After users start working with your application, they want to be able to customize its behavior. One user might prefer the main form to appear maximized on a 640-by-480 laptop screen. Another might want to display it in the lower-right corner of a 1,024-by-768 desktop machine. gSaveMainFormPosition puts the left and top coordinates and height and width of the main form into the Registry. This subroutine makes these settings available to gSetMainFormPosition when the main form loads.

The Dialog Box Position

Dialog boxes include any information screens that require a response from the user before the program can continue. Figure 32.5 shows an example of a type of dialog box.

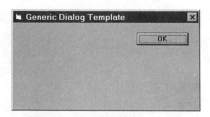

Fig. 32.5
A dialog box can
be positioned in
the center of the
screen.

You can use the gSetDialogPosition subroutine to position all dialog
boxes on the screen. The code for gSetDialogPosition includes all of that
shown in listing 32.12, which shows the code for gCenterDialogPosition.
gCenterDialogPosition centers the indicated dialog box over the MDI form.
For this demonstration, assume that this form's name is frmMain. However,
frmMain could also be an argument of this routine. If the main form is smaller
than the dialog box, gCenterDialogPosition centers the dialog box on the
screen.

Listing 32.12   The gCenterDialogPosition **Subroutine; the Code for**
Is Similar

```
Sub gCenterDialogPosition(WndName As Form)

If (WndName.Height > frmMain.Height) Or _
(WndName.Width > frmMain.Width) Then
  WndName.TOP = (Screen.Height - WndName.Height) \ 2
  WndName.Left = (Screen.Width - WndName.Width) \ 2
Else
  WndName.TOP = frmMain.TOP + _
  ((frmMain.Height - WndName.Height) \ 2)
  WndName.Left = frmMain.Left + _
  ((frmMain.Width - WndName.Width) \ 2)
End If

End Sub
```

MDI Children

There is no right or wrong method for displaying MDI children within an
MDI parent. Every application is different, so you must make any positioning
choices based on the user's needs and the type of application that you are
developing. Figure 32.6 shows where the SetChildWindowPosition subroutine
places the MDI child. This location is an excellent choice for a default. One
good enhancement to this routine is to place the MDI child in the same position as the last time that the user used the form. Listing 32.13 shows the
SetChildWindowPosition subroutine.

V

Optimization

Fig. 32.6
An MDI child
positioned on the
screen.

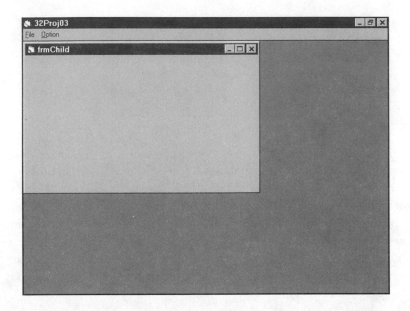

Listing 32.13 The `SetChildWindowPosition` **Subroutine**

```
Sub gSetChildWindowPosition(frmName As Form, sFormTag$)
Dim sWindowState As String
Dim sTopPosition As String
Dim sLeftPosition As String
Dim sFormWidth As String
Dim sFormHeight As String

  sWindowState = gGetValue(sFormTag, "WindowState")
  Select Case sWindowState
    Case "0"
      sFormWidth = gGetValue(sFormTag, "Width")
      sFormHeight = gGetValue(sFormTag, "Height")
      If frmName.BorderStyle = vbSizable Then
        sTopPosition = gGetValue(sFormTag, "Top")
        sLeftPosition = gGetValue(sFormTag, "Left")
        frmName.Move Val(sLeftPosition), Val(sTopPosition), _
                     Val(sFormWidth), Val(sFormHeight)
      Else
        frmName.Move Val(sLeftPosition), Val(sTopPosition)
      End If
    Case "1"
      frmName.WindowState = vbMinimized
    Case "2"
      frmName.WindowState = vbMaximized
    Case Else
      frmName.Move 0, 0
  End Select

End Sub
```

The gSetChildWindow routine is quite similar to the gSetMainFormPosition routine. The only difference lies in the fact that gSetChildWindow requires height and width properties only for sizeable MDI children. This routine checks whether those settings are necessary and, if so, obtains them. Every form differs, so you give this routine a tag name to differentiate it from other child windows. This tag name is normally the form's tag property.

The gSaveChildWindowPosition routine (listing 32.14) performs the exact same function as gSaveMainFormPosition. This routine saves the height, width, left, and top positions of the indicated form. Notice that the giSaveSettings variable indicates whether to save these settings. This variable ensures that the settings do not change after the user sets them to his or her desired choices.

Listing 32.14   The gSaveChildWindowPosition Routine

```
Sub gSaveChildWindowPosition(frmName As Form, sFormTag$)
Dim sWindowState As String
Dim sTopPosition As String
Dim sLeftPosition As String
Dim sFormWidth As String
Dim sFormHeight As String

  If giSaveSettings Then
    sWindowState = Trim$(Str$(frmName.WindowState))
    Call gSetValue(sFormTag, "WindowState", sWindowState)
    sTopPosition = Trim$(Str$(frmName.TOP))
    Call gSetValue(sFormTag, "Top", sTopPosition)
    sLeftPosition = Trim$(Str$(frmName.Left))
    Call gSetValue(sFormTag, "Left", sLeftPosition)
    sFormWidth = Trim$(Str$(frmName.Width))
    Call gSetValue(sFormTag, "Width", sFormWidth)
    sFormHeight = Trim$(Str$(frmName.Height))
    Call gSetValue(sFormTag, "Height", sFormHeight)
  End If

End Sub
```

Creating a Positioning Project

You can fit all these routines into one project to demonstrate how these different routines work. To assemble this project, follow these steps:

1. Create a new project.

2. Save Form1 as frmChild in Visual Basic and Child at the DOS level.

3. Change frmChild's Caption property to 32Proj03.

4. Change frmChild's MDIChild property to True.

5. Save the project as 32Proj03.

6. Add an MDI form to the project and save it as frmMain in Visual Basic and MainMDI at the DOS level.

7. Create a new form and save it as frmDialog in Visual Basic and Dialog at the DOS level.

8. Add a command button to frmDialog and change its caption to "OK."

9. Change the Name property of the command button to cmd_OK.

10. Add the WINAPI32.BAS module from 32Proj01 to this project.

11. Create a new module and rename it POSITION.BAS.

12. Place the following routines in POSITION.BAS: gSetValue, gGetValue, gSetMainFormPosition, gSaveMainFormPosition, gSetChildWindowPosition, and gSaveChildWindowPosition.

13. Put the following declaration into the General Declarations section of POSITION.BAS:

```
Global giSaveSettings As Integer
```

14. Place the following code into the appropriate events for frmChild:

```
Private Sub Form_Load()
  Me.Tag = "frmChild"
  Call gSetChildWindowPosition(Me, Me.Tag)
End Sub
Private Sub Form_Unload(Cancel As Integer)
  Call gSaveChildWindowPosition(Me, Me.Tag)
End Sub
```

15. Include the following code in frmMain's events:

```
Private Sub MDIForm_Load()
   Call gGetSettings
   Call gSetMainFormPosition(Me)
End Sub
Private Sub MDIForm_Unload(Cancel As Integer)
  Call gSaveMainFormPosition(Me)
End Sub
```

16. Include the following code in frmDialog's events:

```
Private Sub cmdOk_Click()
  Unload Me
End Sub
Private Sub Form_Load()
  Call gCenterDialogPosition(Me)
End Sub
```

17. Create the menu File (mnuFile) for frmMain with the Open (mnuOpen), Dialog (mnuFileOpenDialog), Child (mnuFileOpenChild), and Exit (mnuFileExit) submenu choices. Indent Dialog and Child under Open.

18. Create the menu options for frmMain with the Save Settings On Exit submenu option (mnuOptionsSaveSettings).

19. Add the mnuOptionsSaveSettings_Click code to frmMain.

20. Add the following code to frmMain also:

```
Private Sub MDIForm_Load()
  Call gGetSettings
  Call gSetMainFormPosition(Me)
End Sub
Private Sub MDIForm_Unload(Cancel As Integer)
  Call gSaveMainFormPosition(Me)
End Sub
Private Sub mnuFileExit_Click()
  Unload Me
  End
End Sub
```

In Chapter 30, "Advanced Control Techniques," you added the code for controlling whether the toolbar and status bars appear on the main form. See Chapter 30's discussion of how you do this.

Using Copy, Cut, and Paste

In their simplest form, Copy and Paste operations and Cut and Paste operations take highlighted text from one screen, place the text in the Clipboard, and then paste it into a new, compatible location.

The difference between a Copy and Paste operation and a Cut and Paste operation is that the former removes text from the original control. Visual Basic controls support Cut, Copy, and Paste operations without the code, but users like to see the familiar menu and icon choices. To provide these choices, you must add them to frmMain as follows:

1. Create new menu choice Edit and name it mnuEdit with the caption &Edit.

2. Make three submenus: mnuEditCut, mnuEditCopy, and mnuEditPaste.

3. Assign the shortcut key combinations Ctl+C to mnuEditCopy, Ctl+X to mnuEditCopy, and Ctl+V to mnuEditPaste.

V

Optimization

4. Add two text boxes to `frmChild` and make their text properties blank.

5. Save files under the project name 32PROJ04.

The following code shows the `mnuEditCopy_Click` event:

```
Private Sub mnuEditCopy_Click ()
  Call gInitiateCopy(Screen.ActiveControl)
End Sub
```

The `mnuEditCopy_Click` event calls the `InitiateCopy` subroutine and identifies the control by using `Screen.ActiveControl`. The `Screen` object with the related property `ActiveControl` provides a great way to create a generic routine that works for any form in this project.

The `InitiateCopy` subroutine checks which type of control is currently active on the screen:

```
Public Sub gInitiateCopy (Cntl As Control)

  If TypeOf Cntl Is TextBox Then
    Clipboard.SetText Cntl.SelText, vbCFTEXT
  End If

End Sub
```

Notice that some of the controls are commented out. This is because these controls ship with Sheridan Software's DataWidgets and do not work unless you add those VBXs to the project. By examining these references, you can see that you can add any type of control that holds text by referencing the control type with a new `ElseIf` statement. Notice how the routine uses the `SelText` property rather than the `Text` property to obtain only the highlighted text. Also important is the use of the `Clipboard` object and the related `SetText` to place the text on the Clipboard.

The `mnuEditCut_Click` event references the `InitiateCut` subroutine in the same way that `mnuEditCopy` references `InitiateCopy`:

```
Sub mnuEditCut_Click ()
  Call gInitiateCut(Screen.ActiveControl)
End Sub
```

`InitiateCut` identifies the control and its type in exactly the same way that `InitiateCopy` does:

```
Public Sub gInitiateCut (Cntl As Control)

  If TypeOf Cntl Is TextBox Then
    Clipboard.SetText Cntl.SelText, vbCFTEXT
    Cntl.Text = CutText((Cntl.Text), (Cntl.SelText), _
                        (Cntl.SelStart), (Cntl.SelLength))
```

```
    End If

  End Sub
```

Unlike `InitiateCopy`, `InitiateCut` uses the `CutText` function to remove the highlighted text from that control:

```
Function CutText (Text$, SelText$, SelStart&, SelLength&)As String

  If SelStart& > 0 Then
    CutText$ = Mid$(Text$, 1, SelStart&) & Mid$(Text$, _
                    (SelStart& + SelLength& + 1))
  Else
    CutText$ = Mid$(Text$, (SelStart& + SelLength& + 1))
  End If

End Function
```

The `mnuEditPaste_Click` event calls the `InitiatePaste` subroutine in a fashion similiar to that used by `mnuEditCut_Click` and `mnuEditCopy_Click`:

```
Sub mnuEditPaste_Click ()
  Call gInitiatePaste(Screen.ActiveControl)
End Sub
```

The `InitiatePaste` subroutine uses the control and control type to identify where to paste the Clipboard text:

```
Sub gInitiatePaste (Cntl As Control)

  If TypeOf Cntl Is TextBox Then
    Cntl.SelText = Clipboard.GetText(vbCFTEXT)
  End If

End Sub
```

Notice the use of the `SelText` property to identify the text to replace with the new text. If text is highlighted, this routine replaces it. If no text is highlighted, this routine simply pastes the text in the current location on the control. The routine identifies the actual text to paste with the `Clipboard` object and the related `GetText` property.

Look closely at the code lines that reference the `Clipboard` object. Each call includes the word `vbCFTEXT`. This ensures that the format is text. If your program needs to copy and paste or cut and paste something other than text, you need only choose the appropriate argument to identify it.

Chapter 30, "Advanced Control Techniques," includes the code for generating the toolbar and status bar. This discussion includes all the information that you need to know to make toolbars that look like those of Microsoft Office applications.

V

Optimization

Using Icon Sources in Windows Files

A good icon can be the difference between an application making sense or confusing the user. Icons are pictures that represent concepts. If the concepts are unclear to the user, they are less than useless. The user must readily recognize an icon's purpose. In a personal information manager, for example, an icon of a sailboat might have a meaning related to recreation. In another program, such as an inventory system for a boat dealership, the same icon might have another perfectly valid use.

In the shell, you use two types of icons. First are those that ship with Visual Basic. The *Programmer's Guide* that ships with Visual Basic 4.0 includes a list of these icons. They use the .ICO format and appear when the user minimizes a form. Some programmers place such icons on the SSCommand button along with text. However, these icons tend to consume too much space on the screen. The second type of icons are bitmap icons such as those on the frmgraphics form. These icons are smaller than the first type, and look similar to the toolbars that you see in Microsoft products.

Where can you find icons to use in your applications? The primary source of .ICO format icons is the library of icons that ships with Visual Basic 4.0. Another source of these types of icons is on CompuServe, in the WINFUN forum in Library 7. This source offers hundreds of icons that might meet your needs.

The primary source of bitmap icons lies hidden in the Windows DLL files. These icons are those that other applications use. These applications use the DLL files to display various kinds of information. The best method for finding and accessing these bitmaps is to use the AppStudio utility that ships with Microsoft Visual C++ 1.5.

Visual C++'s AppStudio

Microsoft Visual C++ 1.5 ships with a key to the DLL files already installed on your machine. Inside the DLL files that you find listed in AppStudio are a wealth of bitmaps and icons that you can use as the basis for your own icons in your own applications. For copyright reasons, you should not use someone else's icons without permission, but these icons can give you ideas about how to make your own.

Microsoft Paint

If you don't own Visual C++ 1.5, the Paint application that ships with Microsoft Windows can serve as an excellent method for editing and creating useful bitmap icons. Try opening CUSTOM1.BMP, which you can find on this book's companion CD. This file contains a series of commonly used graphics that you can use as the basis for your own icons. Figure 32.7 shows a picture of Microsoft Paint with the CUSTOM1.BMP open.

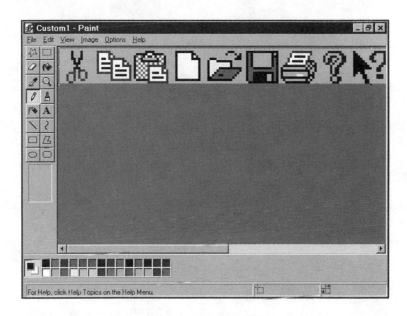

Fig. 32.7
Microsoft
Paint editing
CUSTOM1.BMP.

Designing Install Solutions

Whenever you design an application in Visual Basic, you eventually must install the application on a user's machine. Many of the features that you add to your applications require the addition of certain files besides the compiled executable. These files include .OCX files, OLE support files, and the run-time support files that enable your application to run properly on another machine.

Setup Wizard

Visual Basic ships with a newer version of Setup Wizard that offers several fine enhancements that make the wizard easier to use. Figure 32.8 shows Setup Wizard's enhanced main screen. The wizard now offers an integrated compression utility that does not have to exit to a DOS window to work properly. Setup Wizard also indicates how much space your application will use when installed on a new system.

Fig. 32.8
Microsoft Setup
Wizard's main
screen.

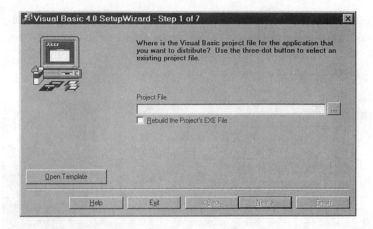

Setup Wizard does not enable you to minimize the compression part of
the setup process so that you can do something else while the wizard is
compressing.

Missing Files

The new Visual Basic Setup Wizard keeps track of all the files that are part of
Visual Basic 4.0. Unfortunately, ensuring that your application will include
any files that you access through API calls or other means (such as database
files or any associated graphics files) is more difficult. As you look through
the files, carefully ensure that such files appear as part of your setup routine.

From Here...

At the heart of all your applications is the code that makes them work and do
what you want. All the advances in technology have not relieved programmers of the need to write code. The more techniques that you have at your
disposal, the easier the process becomes for increasing your arsenal of code.
You can store information from application session to session in configuration files found in the Registry for Window 95 and NT and .INI files in
Windows 3.x. You optimize the startup process by using splash screens and
storing necessary information up front in global variables and the application
object. Finally, you can provide users with more control over the behavior of
an application by enabling them to set the positions of forms and then save
those positions for later sessions. All these techniques make your applications
more useful.

To learn more about related topics, see the following chapters:

- Chapter 30, "Advanced Control Techniques," provides more information about toolbars.

- Chapter 31, "Advanced Form Techniques," discusses multiple-document interface (MDI) and single-document interface (SDI) applications.

- Chapter 33, "Accessing the Windows API," explains more about .INI files, API calls, and window handles.

V

Optimization

Chapter 33

Accessing the Windows API

A programming language establishes boundaries of what can be done based on the different features of the language. If a feature does not exist, you must either create a workaround or do without that feature. If you want to display the extended memory available for a PC in a Visual Basic program, there is no way to do this with native Visual Basic. Fortunately, Visual Basic allows you access to the Windows API, which gives you a method for solving this problem.

API calls add capabilities to your Visual Basic applications. These new capabilities expand the depth of choices available to the Visual Basic programmer. This increase in capabilities comes at the price of forcing you to be more cautious. Visual Basic is inherently a fairly stable language. If you create applications with no API calls, you avoid problems caused by poor code that triggers random GPF errors. A problem with Visual Basic code will normally crash only the program. Problems with API calls will sometimes crash the Windows environment itself.

If API calls make Visual Basic applications potentially less stable, then why use them? You shouldn't use API calls just to use them, but there are several API calls that are very useful for improving the performance and look and feel of your applications. This chapter deals with showing you some of the useful API calls available to Visual Basic.

In this chapter, you learn how to do the following:

- Use Windows API calls in Visual Basic applications

- Wrap your API calls

- Create and access application .INI files

- Manipulate windows

- Find internal Windows configuration information

- Use new 32-bit API calls

- Access and manipulate the Windows Registry

> **Note**
>
> Visual Basic ships with a Help file named WIN31API.HLP. This file contains the declaration statements for most of the 3.1 API calls available within Visual Basic. All you have to do is look up the function or subroutine that you want and paste the appropriate text into one of the modules belonging to your application.

API Call Challenge

Using API calls in Visual Basic presents you with the challenge of how to reduce problems when you work with them. There are two techniques that you can use to reduce the possibility of error. First, jacket all of the API calls that can create problems. Second, create a common code module.

> **Note**
>
> Visual Basic ships with a new feature called the API Text Viewer. This viewer provides a list of Windows API calls that you can search through. You simply have to find the API calls and add them to your project. The major advantage over the WIN31API.HLP file is that you can copy more than one call at the same time. The disadvantage is that there is no explanation text and you cannot see the actual declaration text until you paste it into your project.

Jacket Your Code

Code jacketing involves creating a subroutine or function that calls a specific API function or subroutine. Such a subroutine or function would include any required arguments for that API call. A jacketed API call allows you to shield yourself from any potential landmines that might cause a GPF error. One glaring example lies with the difference between the *fixed-length strings* used by the C-based Windows API calls and those used by Visual Basic. If you try to use a Visual Basic *variable-length string* in an API call, such as `GetPrivateProfileString`, you get a GPF.

The Common BAS File

Every time that you use a new Windows API call, you need to keep the code in a common code module. If you solve a problem once, why keep solving it over and over again? Every time that you start a new project, all you need to do is add this special module to your project and you already have access to all of the API calls and jacketed routines that you have used so far.

Configuration Strategies

Visual Basic 4.0 has the capability to create both 16-bit applications for Windows 3.x and 32-bit applications for Windows 95 and Windows NT. Sixteen-bit Windows 3.x uses .INI files to store application configuration information. 32-bit Windows 95 and NT work with either the newer Registry or .INI files.

The choice of whether to use the Registry or .INI files lies with you. .INI files are more familiar to those of us who programmed for Windows 3.x with Visual Basic 3.0. There is the temptation to stay with the familiar. Use the method that makes the most sense.

Understanding Registry APIs

Windows 95 and NT place their system configuration information in the Registry database. This is a change from the older .INI system found in Windows 3.x systems. Any entries found in the old WIN.INI and SYSTEM.INI files are simply there for compatibility reasons. The Registry keeps information in binary files. An application uses the Registry API functions to access data in the Registry.

Registry Structure

Windows 95 and NT registries store their configuration data in a hierarchically structured tree. Both products ship with a Registry Editor which shows a picture of the Registry for the current computer or other computers on the network. Figure 33.1 shows what the Registry looks like. The Registry Editor does not appear as an icon in the default installation of either Windows 95 or NT. You can access the Registry Editor by running it from either the Run dialog box off of Start in Windows 95 or the Run dialog box from the File menu in Windows NT. The name of the executable is REGEDIT.EXE for Windows 95 and REGEDT32.EXE for Windows NT. You do not need to enter the path to make it work properly.

Each branch of the Registry tree has a text name, which is called a *key*. A key has a text name that consists of one or more printable ANSI characters. This means that only characters with a value between 32 and 127 are eligible. Key names cannot include a backslash, space, or wild-card character (* or ?). You must be sure not to begin a key name with a period.

Fig. 33.1
A view of the hierarchically structured Windows 95 Registry.

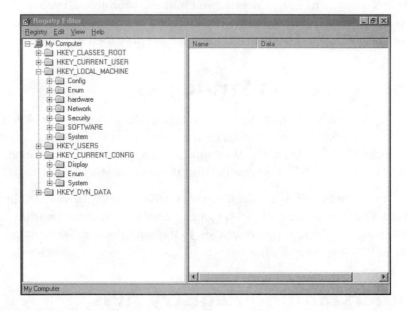

A key can have both *subkeys* and/or *values*. A subkey is a branch of the hierar-chal tree that is connected to another key. For example, figure 33.1 shows Config as a subkey of HKEY_LOCAL_MACHINE. In some cases, the key itself is the data that an application uses. Values are any number of settings given to a key. Figure 33.2 shows the list of values for the Settings subkey.

Fig. 33.2
A view of values of the Settings subkey.

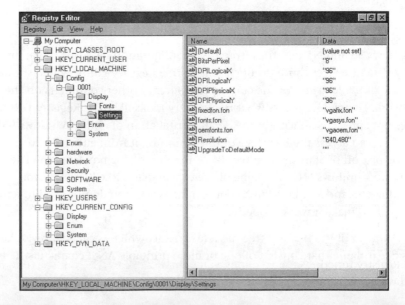

Registry Limits

There are practical limits to how much you should store in the Registry. You should only store configuration information for your applications in the Registry. Registry data consists of the bare outline of what your applications need to function. They answer questions like "Where is the data?" and "What is the valid UserName for this machine?". The list of all the states in the United States would not be a good candidate for the Registry. A better strategy would be to put in the Registry the name and path of the database that contains this information.

Security Mask Constants

Many of the Registry API functions use a security mask that identifies what kind of access a particular call needs. The security mask constants appear in the list of constants shown in listing 33.1. KEY_ALL_ACCESS is the most common setting, and you need to stick with it unless there is a reason to restrict access to the Registry data that you are working with. For example, you might want to use the STANDARD_RIGHTS_READ constant for a user who can view the entries on the Registry but cannot change them. These constants need to be added to the General Declarations section of the WINAPI32.BAS module.

Listing 33.1   Registry Security Mask Constants

```
'Security Mask constants
Public Const READ_CONTROL = &H20000
Public Const SYNCHRONIZE = &H100000
Public Const STANDARD_RIGHTS_ALL = &H1F0000
Public Const STANDARD_RIGHTS_READ = READ_CONTROL
Public Const STANDARD_RIGHTS_WRITE = READ_CONTROL
Public Const KEY_QUERY_VALUE = &H1
Public Const KEY_SET_VALUE = &H2
Public Const KEY_CREATE_SUB_KEY = &H4
Public Const KEY_ENUMERATE_SUB_KEYS = &H8
Public Const KEY_NOTIFY = &H10
Public Const KEY_CREATE_LINK = &H20
Public Const KEY_ALL_ACCESS = ((STANDARD_RIGHTS_ALL Or _
KEY_QUERY_VALUE Or KEY_SET_VALUE Or KEY_CREATE_SUB_KEY Or _
KEY_ENUMERATE_SUB_KEYS Or KEY_NOTIFY Or KEY_CREATE_LINK) And _
(Not SYNCHRONIZE))
Public Const KEY_READ = ((STANDARD_RIGHTS_READ Or KEY_QUERY _
VALUE Or KEY_ENUMERATE_SUB_KEYS Or KEY_NOTIFY) And _
(Not SYNCHRONIZE))
Public Const KEY_EXECUTE = ((KEY_READ) And (Not SYNCHRONIZE))
Public Const KEY_WRITE = ((STANDARD_RIGHTS_WRITE Or KEY_SET_VALUE _
Or KEY_CREATE_SUB_KEY) And (Not SYNCHRONIZE))
```

Registry Error Constants

All Registry functions return a long value that identifies whether the function call was successful. The most common outcome of a function call is

V

Optimization

ERROR_SUCCESS. This indicates that the call worked properly without errors. Any other value returned tells the application that something went wrong. You need to add the following constants in listing 33.2 to the General Declarations section of the WINAPI.BAS module.

Listing 33.2   Registry Return Code Constants

```
' Return codes from Registration functions.
Public Const ERROR_SUCCESS = 0&
Public Const ERROR_BADDB = 1009&
Public Const ERROR_BADKEY = 1010&
Public Const ERROR_CANTOPEN = 1011&
Public Const ERROR_CANTREAD = 1012&
Public Const ERROR_CANTWRITE = 1013&
Public Const ERROR_OUTOFMEMORY = 14&
Public Const ERROR_INVALID_PARAMETER = 87&
Public Const ERROR_ACCESS_DENIED = 5&
```

When an error occurs, you need to know why. Just seeing a blank screen with no data doesn't tell you what went wrong. For this reason, you need some kind of simple error-testing routine to tell you exactly what went wrong. If a Registry API call doesn't work properly and returns something other than ERROR_SUCCESS, then a routine should call this error routine, which in turn displays an error message to tell you exactly what went wrong. This gives you a clue as to where to look for the root of the error. You need to add the gAPIDisplayError to the WINAPI32.BAS module (see listing 33.3).

Listing 33.3   Error-Checking Routine

```
Sub gAPIDisplayError(Code&)

    Select Case Code&
      Case ERROR_BADDB
        MsgBox "Corrupt Registry Database!"
      Case ERROR_BADKEY
        MsgBox "Key name is bad"
      Case ERROR_CANTOPEN
        MsgBox "Cannot Open Key"
      Case ERROR_CANTREAD
        MsgBox "Cannot Read Key"
      Case ERROR_CANTWRITE
        MsgBox "Cannot Write Key"
      Case ERROR_ACCESS_DENIED
        MsgBox "Access to Registry Denied"
      Case ERROR_OUTOFMEMORY
        MsgBox "Out of memory"
      Case ERROR_INVALID_PARAMETER
        MsgBox "Invalid Parameter"
      Case Else
```

```
      MsgBox "Undefined key error code!"
   End Select

End Sub
```

Data Format

When you place values for a key into the Registry, you need to let the API function know the format of the value with which you are working. The most commonly used format is REG_SZ, meaning a simple string value. Listing 33.4 contains a list of the Registry data format constants.

Listing 33.4   Registry Data Format Constants

```
'Data type Public Constants
Public Const REG_NONE = 0
Public Const REG_SZ = 1
Public Const REG_EXPAND_SZ = 2
Public Const REG_BINARY = 3
Public Const REG_DWORD = 4
Public Const REG_DWORD_LITTLE_ENDIAN = 4
Public Const REG_DWORD_BIG_ENDIAN = 5
Public Const REG_LINK = 6
Public Const REG_MULTI_SZ = 7
Public Const REG_RESOURCE_LIST = 8
Public Const REG_FULL_RESOURCE_DESCRIPTOR = 9
Public Const REG_RESOURCE_REQUIREMENTS_LIST = 10
```

The *RegOpenKeyEx* Function

There are two API calls for opening a key from the Windows 95 or NT Registry: RegOpenKeyEx and RegOpenKey. The logical question for you to ask is why there are two functions that do the same thing. RegOpenKeyEx and RegOpenKey do not do the same things. ReOpenKey is included in the current API for compatibility reasons only. Programmers are strongly encouraged to switch their applications to use the newer RegOpenKeyEx and stop using RegOpenKey. Listing 33.5 shows the predefined keys used in RegOpenKeyEx.

Listing 33.5   Predefined Keys Used in RegOpenKeyEx

```
'Predefined Registry Keys used in hKey Argument
Public Const HKEY_CLASSES_ROOT = &H80000000
Public Const HKEY_CURRENT_USER = &H80000001
Public Const HKEY_LOCAL_MACHINE = &H80000002
Public Const HKEY_USERS = &H80000003
Public Const HKEY_PERFORMANCE_DATA = &H80000004
```

V

Optimization

Any application that works with the Registry must begin with an open key. There are several preopened keys including HKEY_CLASSES_ROOT, HKEY_CURRENT_USER, HKEY_LOCAL_MACHINE, HKEY_USERS, and HKEY_PERFORMANCE_DATA. There is a public constant for each of these predefined open keys in the preceding list of constants. You need to place these constants (shown in listing 33.5) in the General Declarations section of the WINAPI32.BAS module. These preopened keys are your starting point for working with the Registry.

```
Declare Function RegOpenKeyEx Lib "advapi32" Alias _
"RegOpenKeyExA"  (ByVal hKey As Long, ByVal lpSubKey As String, _
ByVal ulOptions As Long, ByVal samDesired As Long, _
phkResult As Long) As Long
```

RegOpenKeyEx provides a means for opening additional keys using one of these existing opened keys as a reference point. The syntax for opening a key is relatively simple. It involves identifying any open key with hKey, the key to open in lpSubKey, the security mask in samDesired, and the variable to store the newly opened key's handle in phkResult. The remaining argument, ulOptions, is not used and is always entered as 0&.

The *RegQueryValueEx* Function

Once you open a key, you need to work with that key to get the information to make your application work properly. RegQueryValueEx provides a means to obtain the value of a specified key's stored values. Some programmers use the RegQueryValue API call instead of the RegQueryValueEx function. RegQueryValue is also a 32-bit call included in the current API set for compatibility with Windows 3.x. This older call will return only the default value belonging to a key. If there are any more values, RegQueryValue provides no way to obtain the different values assigned to a key.

```
Declare Function RegQueryValueEx Lib "advapi32" _
Alias "RegQueryValueExA" (ByVal hKey As Long, _
ByVal lpValueName As String, lpReserved As Long, _
lpType As Long, ByVal lpData As String, _
lpcbData As Long) As Long
```

RegQueryValueEx consists of a series of arguments which identify the key and provide a means to obtain one of its values. The key handle, hKey, must be opened with a RegOpenKeyEx call. You need to identify which of a key's values that you need with lpValueName. If there is only one value or you want the default value, leave it blank. You need to indicate the type of value that you are retrieving in lpType with one of the data format constants. REG_SZ represents a string. RegQueryValueEx returns the value in lpData and identifies its expected size with lpcbData. The remaining argument, lpReserved, is not used and is always entered as 0&.

The *RegCloseKey* Function

When you are done working with a key in the Registry, you need to release that key. Make sure that you use this function whether or not a call to do something with a key works properly:

```
Declare Function RegCloseKey Lib "advapi32" _
(ByVal hKey As Long) As Long
```

Failure to remember to close a key can lead to memory loss and possibly make the system less stable.

Listing 33.6 shows the Form_Load event code for project 33Proj01.

Listing 33.6 Form_Load **Event Code for Project 33Proj01**

```
Private Sub Form_Load()
Dim lReturn As Long
Dim hWndSoftware As Long
Dim lpName As String
Dim lpcbName As Long
Dim lpClass As String
Dim lpcbClass As Long
Dim lpData As String
Dim lpcbData As Long

  lpcbName = 255
  lpName = Space$(lpcbName)
  lpcbClass = 255
  lpClass = Space$(lpcbClass)

  lReturn = RegOpenKeyEx(HKEY_LOCAL_MACHINE, _
  "Software\Microsoft\Windows\CurrentVersion\App Paths
➥\IEXPLORE.EXE", 0&, KEY_ALL_ACCESS, hWndSoftware)

  lpcbData = 255
  lpData = Space$(lpcbData)
  lpcbName = 255
  lpName = Space$(lpcbName)
  lReturn = RegQueryValueEx(hWndSoftware, "", 0&, _
REG_SZ, lpData, lpcbData)
  If lReturn <> ERROR_SUCCESS Then
    gAPIDisplayError lReturn
  Else
    Text1.Text = Left$(lpData, lpcbData - 1)
  End If

  lReturn = RegQueryValueEx(hWndSoftware, "Path", 0&, _
REG_SZ, lpData, lpcbData)
  If lReturn <> ERROR_SUCCESS Then
    gAPIDisplayError lReturn
  Else
    Text2.Text = Left$(lpData, lpcbData - 1)
  End If
```

(continues)

Listing 33.6   Continued

```
        lReturn = RegCloseKey(hWndSoftware)

    End Sub
```

The `Form_Load` routine demonstrates the proper usage of the `RegOpenValueEx`, `RegCloseKey`, and `RegQueryValueEx` API functions. This routine is an example of all the concepts about the Registry explained so far. Follow these steps to construct a Visual Basic project that will make this routine work properly.

1. Open a new project and rename this project as 33Proj01.

2. Add a new code module and rename it as WINAPI32.

3. Add the declaration text for `RegOpenKeyEx`, `RegKeyClose`, and `RegQueryValueEx` to the General Declarations section of WINAPI32.

4. Add the Registry Error, Data Format, Predefined Registry Keys, and Security Mask constants to the General Declarations section of WINAPI32.

5. Add the `gAPIDisplayError` routine to WINAPI32.

6. Rename Form1 as frmAPI.

7. Add the `Form_Load` code to the load event of frmAPI.

8. Place two text boxes on the form as shown in figure 33.3.

Fig. 33.3
A view of what frmAPI should look like at design time.

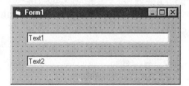

There are a few things for you to notice about the code contained in the `Form_Load` event. The `RegOpenKeyEx` call includes a long string of key names separated by backslashes (\). You do not need to get the key name for each key in between the one that you are working with (EXPLORER.EXE) and the already opened key (`HKEY_LOCAL_MACHINE`). This is a great code saver which saves you from having to call the `RegOpenKeyEx` function five additional times to get the handle for the key that you need.

The string values passed to `RegOpenkeyEx` must be properly formatted for the call to work properly. Notice that `lpName`, `lpClass`, and `lpData` must be filled

with spaces using the String function. If you tried this function call without
this step, RegOpenKeyEx would not work properly.

The *RegCreateKeyEx* Function

Like most of the other Registry functions, there are two functions for creating
new keys: RegCreateKeyEx and RegCreateKey. The recommended function is
RegCreateKeyEx (listing 33.7) because RegCreateKey is in the API only for compatibility with earlier versions.

Listing 33.7   RegCreateKeyEx **Declaration and Constants**

```
Declare Function RegCreateKeyEx Lib "advapi32" _
Alias "RegCreateKeyExA" (ByVal hKey As Long, _
ByVal lpSubKey As String, ByVal Reserved As Long, _
ByVal lpClass As String, ByVal dwOptions As Long, _
ByVal samDesired As Long, _
lpSecurityAttributes As SECURITY_ATTRIBUTES, _
phkResult As Long, lpdwDisposition As Long) As Long

'Options
Public Const REG_OPTION_VOLATILE = 0
Public Const REG_OPTION_NON_VOLATILE = 1

Type SECURITY_ATTRIBUTES
  nLength As Long
  lpSecurityDescriptor As Variant
  bInheritHandle As Long
End Type
```

RegCreateKeyEx creates a new key in the Registry database. The hKey argument
identifies the key that you want to make a new subkey for. lpSubKey contains
the name to give to the new key. lpClass provides the class to which this new
entry belongs. If the specified class does not exist, this function adds it as a
valid entry to the Registry. In the dwOptions argument, then, you decide
whether to make this new key permanent or temporary. This entry has two
valid constant values, REG_OPTION_VOLATILE or REG_OPTION_NON_VOLATILE. The
security mask contains one of the same security mask constants that you used
in RegOpenKeyEx. phkResult returns the window handle of the newly created
key. lpdwDisposition takes a SECURITY_ATTRIBUTES structure. Simply dim a
variable as being part of that type and leave its properties blank. The remaining argument, lpReserved, is not used and is always entered as 0&. The required new constants and new type structure definitions appear along with
the declare statement in listing 33.7.

The *RegSetValueEx* Function

RegSetValue and RegSetValueEx enter a value for a key. RegSetValue is the older version, which is kept in the current API for compatibility reasons. RegSetValueEx has the additional capability of allowing you to create multiple named values under one key, which the older version cannot do.

```
Declare Function RegSetValueEx Lib "advapi32" _
Alias "RegSetValueExA" (ByVal hKey As Long, _
ByVal lpValueName As String, ByVal Reserved As Long, _
ByVal dwType As Long, ByVal lpData As String, _
ByVal cbData As Long) As Long
```

RegSetValueEx creates a new value for the key identified by the hKey argument. The name to give this new key's value appears in lpValueName. dwType identifies the data format and takes one of the data format constants such as REG_SZ. This function places the string in the lpData argument and sets its length at the value in cbData. The remaining argument, lpReserved, is not used and is always entered as 0&.

The following steps include the instructions for assembling project 33Proj02. This project demonstrates the proper use and syntax of the Registry functions RegCreateKeyEx and RegSetValueEx.

1. Open a new project and rename this project as 33Proj02.

2. Add the WINAPI32.BAS file in 33Proj01 to this project.

3. Add the declaration text for RegSetValueEx and RegCreateKeyEx to the General Declarations section of WINAPI32.

4. Add the options constants and SECURITY_ATTRIBUTES type to the General Declarations section of WINAPI32.

5. Rename Form1 as frmLogin.

6. Add two command buttons to frmLogin and rename them cmdOK and cmdCancel.

7. Add the cmdOK_Click (listing 33.8) and cmdCancel code to the Click event of the corresponding command buttons on frmLogin.

8. Place two text boxes and two labels on the form as shown in figure 33.4.

9. Change the captions of the labels to Username: and Password:. Make the names of the labels lblUserName and lblPassword.

10. Change the text of the text boxes to blank. Make the names of the text boxes "txtUserName" and "txtPassword".

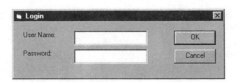

Fig. 33.4
A view of what
frmLogin should
look like at run
time.

Listing 33.8   The `cmdOk_Click()` and `cmdCancel_Click` Procedures

```
Private Sub cmdOk_Click()
Dim lReturn As Long
Dim hlstrUsername As String
Dim hlstrPassword As String
Dim hWndQue As Long
Dim hWndUsername As Long
Dim hWndPassword As Long
Dim lpcbName As Long
Dim lpClass As String
Dim Security As SECURITY_ATTRIBUTES
Dim lpdwDisposition As Long

  'Ensure that username and password are not blank
  hlstrUsername = Trim$(txtUserName.Text)
  hlstrPassword = Trim$(txtPassword.Text)
  If hlstrUsername = "" Or hlstrPassword = "" Then
    MsgBox "Username and Password are required!"
    Unload Me
    End
  End If

  'Create or Open Que Registry entry for local machine
  lpClass = Space$(255)
  lReturn = RegCreateKeyEx(HKEY_LOCAL_MACHINE, "QUE", 0&, _
lpClass,  REG_OPTION_NON_VOLATILE, KEY_ALL_ACCESS, Security, _
  hWndQue, lpdwDisposition)
  If lReturn <> ERROR_SUCCESS Then
    gAPIDisplayError lReturn
  End If

  'Create or Open Username entry for local machine
  lpClass = Space$(255)
  lReturn = RegCreateKeyEx(hWndQue, "UserName", 0&, _
  lpClass, REG_OPTION_NON_VOLATILE, KEY_ALL_ACCESS, _
  Security, hWndUsername, lpdwDisposition)
  If lReturn <> ERROR_SUCCESS Then
    gAPIDisplayError lReturn
  End If

  'Save Username in the Registry
  lReturn = RegSetValueEx(hWndUsername, "", 0&, REG_SZ, _
  hlstrUsername, Len(hlstrUsername))
  If lReturn <> ERROR_SUCCESS Then
    gAPIDisplayError lReturn
  End If
```

V

Optimization

(continues)

Listing 33.8   Continued

```
    'Create or Open Password entry for local machine
    lpClass = Space$(255)
    lReturn = RegCreateKeyEx(hWndQue, "Password", 0&, lpClass, _
    REG_OPTION_NON_VOLATILE, KEY_ALL_ACCESS, Security, _
    hWndPassword, lpdwDisposition)
    If lReturn <> ERROR_SUCCESS Then
      gAPIDisplayError lReturn
    End If

    'Save Username in the Registry
    lReturn = RegSetValueEx(hWndPassword, "", 0&, _
REG_SZ, hlstrPassword, Len(hlstrPassword))
    If lReturn <> ERROR_SUCCESS Then
      gAPIDisplayError lReturn
    End If

    'Close open keys
    lReturn = RegCloseKey(hWndQue)
    lReturn = RegCloseKey(hWndUsername)
    lReturn = RegCloseKey(hWndPassword)

    End

End Sub

Private Sub cmdCancel_Click()

    End

End Sub
```

There are a couple of things to notice about the second project. Notice that the code explicitly closes each of the created handles before the application itself exits. This is very important to remember, or you will receive an error when you exit Windows. Notice that the RegSetValueEx statements have blank entries for lpValueName. This ensures that the setting will appear as the default value. If you need to have multiple values for a key, you simply need to specify a name in this argument.

The *RegDeleteKey* Function

RegDeleteKey provides you with the capability to remove a key from the Registry:

```
Declare Function RegDeleteKey Lib "advapi32" _
Alias "RegDeleteKeyA" (ByVal hKey As Long, _
ByVal lpSubKey As String) As Long
```

The hKey argument identifies an open key and the lpSubKey is the exact path of the subkey to remove. This function will not remove a key with subkeys under it. All subkeys must be removed before you can remove the key itself.

The *RegDeleteValue* Function

RegDeleteValue provides a means for removing value names from a key. The hKey argument identifies the key to remove the value name for, and lpValueName is the name of the value.

```
Declare Function RegDeleteValue Lib "advapi32" _
Alias "RegDeleteValueA" (ByVal hKey As Long, _
ByVal lpValueName As String) As Long
```

Exploring .INI File APIs

Everyone has preferences that dictate how they like to work. Some users like toolbars and status bars and some do not. Your applications need to give users the ability to modify the ways in which they use and view what they see on the screen. Windows provides configuration files that allow an application to store a user's preferences between sessions. These files are known as .INI files, and most Windows applications use at least one .INI file to keep track of user preferences and other application-oriented information.

> **Caution**
>
> Don't use the Windows WIN.INI file to store application parameters and user preferences. There are limits on how big an .INI file can be. When the WIN.INI file grows too large, Windows stops working properly until this problem is fixed manually. Using the WIN.INI file for your application is a sign of bad programming practice that should be avoided.

.INI File Structure

To understand how to work with .INI files, you first must understand their structure. All .INI files consist of three elements of information: *Application*, *KeyName*, and *Value*. The *ApplicationName* (lpApplicationName or lpAppName) identifies the header text that appears between the two brackets "[ ]" in the .INI file. For example, the *Application Name* "Database" would appear as "[Database]". Each *ApplicationName* has a number of *KeyNames* (lpKeyName) with associated *Values* for each. To retrieve or save an .INI file's settings, you need the ApplicationName and KeyName of the information that you want. Further, you need the name of the .INI file that contains the information.

The *WritePrivateProfileString* Function

WritePrivateProfileString stores a string of information in the indicated .INI file name under the ApplicationName and KeyName indicated. This routine

works for both values and strings. The declaration text for
WritePrivateProfileString appears in the following code and needs
to appear in the WINAPI32.BAS module:

```
Declare Function WritePrivateProfileString Lib "kernel32" _
Alias "WritePrivateProfileStringA" (ByVal lpApplicationName _
As String, lpKeyName As Any, lpString As Any, ByVal lplFileName _
As String) As Long
```

The *WriteProfileString* Function

WriteProfileString works in the same way as WritePrivateProfileString
without the naming of the .INI file. In this case, this routine is solely for
changing or adding settings to the WIN.INI file. This routine works for both
values and strings. The declaration text for WriteProfileString appears in the
following code and must appear in the WINAPI32.BAS module:

```
Declare Function WriteProfileString Lib "kernel32" _
Alias "WriteProfileStringA" (ByVal lpApplicationName As String, _
lpKeyName As Any, lpString As Any) As Long
```

The *GetPrivateProfileInt* Function

GetPrivateProfileInt obtains the value stored in the indicated .INI
for the specified ApplicationName and KeyName. If there is a value, the
GetPrivateProfileInt function returns that value as an integer. The declaration text to place in the General Declarations section of WINAPI32.BAS appears in the following code:

```
Declare Function GetPrivateProfileInt Lib "kernel32" _
Alias "GetPrivateProfileIntA" (ByVal lpApplicationName As _
String, ByVal lpKeyName As String, ByVal nDefault As Long, _
ByVal lpFileName As String) As Integer
```

You need not jacket this API call, because it returns a value compatible with
Visual Basic.

The *GetProfileInt* Function

GetProfileInt works in the same way as GetPrivateProfileInt without the
naming of the .INI file. In this function, the .INI file is always the WIN.INI
file. This is an excellent function for obtaining stored Windows settings in
16-bit applications.

```
Declare Function GetProfileInt Lib "kernel32" _
Alias "GetProfileIntA" (ByVal lpAppName As String, _
ByVal lpKeyName As String, ByVal nDefault As Long) As Long
```

The *GetPrivateProfileString* Function

GetPrivateProfileString obtains the value of the indicated ApplicationName and KeyName for the specified .INI file. This .INI file can be any .INI file including the Windows WIN.INI and SYSTEM.INI files. Since this function returns a fixed-length string, you need to use a jacketed function to avoid problems.

```
Declare Function GetPrivateProfileString Lib "kernel32" _
Alias "GetPrivateProfileStringA" (ByVal lpApplicationName _
As String, lpKeyName As Any, ByVal lpDefault As String, ByVal _
lpReturnedString As String, ByVal nSize As Long, _
ByVal lpFileName As String) As Long
```

The following code contains an example of jacketing the GetPrivateProfileString:

```
Function APIGetPrivateProfileString(lpAppName As String, _
lpKeyName As String, lpDefault As String, nSize As Long, _
lpINIFileName) As String
```

The *GetProfileString* Function

GetProfileString works in the same way as GetPrivateProfileString without the naming of the .INI file. Like GetPrivateProfileString, GetProfileString returns the text value in fixed-length string format:

```
Declare Function GetProfileString Lib "kernel32" _
Alias "GetProfileStringA" (ByVal lpAppName As String, _
lpKeyName As Any, ByVal lpDefault As String, ByVal _
lpReturnedString As String, ByVal nSize As Long) As Long
```

You must jacket the call with APIGetProfileString, which is shown in the following code:

```
Function APIGetProfileString(lpAppName As String, _
lpKeyName As String, lpDefault As String, nSize As Long) As String
```

V

Optimization

Going beyond Visual Basic through API Calls

You must always be looking for ways to use the Windows API to help you to go beyond the capabilities of Visual Basic. Visual Basic 4.0 allows you to work with many of the attributes of an application using their properties. There are cases when you need to find out information about a Visual Basic application that is not available with the use of properties. In cases like this, you need to look for API calls to give you the information that you need.

Using *DrawIcon* and *LoadIcon* API Calls

The InputBox method that ships with Visual Basic allows you to display a generic dialog box that prompts the user for information. Figure 33.5 shows what a normal Visual Basic InputBox looks like. Unfortunately, this dialog box is neither very professional looking nor completely useful. You need a more enhanced version of this dialog box that functions much more like the MsgBox dialog box provided by the MsgBox method.

Fig. 33.5
A normal Visual Basic InputBox.

The DrawIcon and LoadIcon API calls provide a way to produce a form that contains the familiar graphics found on Visual Basic message boxes. This provides a continuity between the Visual Basic message box and the new enhanced InputBox. Notice the similarity between the MsgBox in figure 33.6 and the enhanced InputBox in figure 33.7.

Fig. 33.6
A Visual Basic MsgBox.

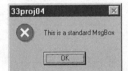

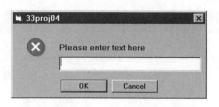

Fig. 33.7
An enhanced
Visual Basic
InputBox.

Listing 33.9 shows the new code for project 33Proj04.

Listing 33.9   New Code for Project 33Proj04

```
Declare Function LoadIcon Lib "user32" Alias "LoadIconA" _
(ByVal hInstance As Long, ByVal lpIconName As Any) As Long
Declare Function DrawIcon Lib "user32" (ByVal hDC As Long, _
ByVal X As Long, ByVal Y As Long, ByVal hIcon As Long) As Long

Option Explicit

Global Const MODAL = 1

'Input Box constants
Global Const OK_BUTTON = 0
Global Const OK_CANCEL = 1
Global Const YES_NO = 2

'Returned Text
Global gInputBoxReturn$

' Standard Icon IDs
Public Const IDI_HAND = 32513&
Public Const IDI_QUESTION = 32514&
Public Const IDI_EXCLAMATION = 32515&
Public Const IDI_ASTERISK = 32516&

Sub Main()
Dim ReturnText$

  MsgBox "This is a demo of Enhanced InputBox", _
vbCritical, App.Title

  ReturnText$ = InputBox("This is a standard Message Box", _
App.Title)

  ReturnText$ = EnhancedInputBox(IDI_HAND, OK_CANCEL, _
"Please enter text here", ReturnText$)
  ReturnText$ = EnhancedInputBox(IDI_QUESTION, OK_CANCEL, _
"Please enter text here", ReturnText$)
  ReturnText$ = EnhancedInputBox(IDI_EXCLAMATION, OK_CANCEL, _
```

(continues)

V

Optimization

Listing 33.9   Continued

```
"Please enter text here", ReturnText$)
  ReturnText$ = EnhancedInputBox(IDI_ASTERISK, OK_CANCEL, _
"Please enter text here", ReturnText$)

  End

End Sub

Sub CenterDialogPosition(WNdName As Form)

  WNdName.Top = (Screen.Height - WNdName.Height) \ 2
  WNdName.Left = (Screen.Width - WNdName.Width) \ 2

End Sub

Function EnhancedInputBox(Icon&, Button%, Label$, Default$) _
    As String
Dim IconhWnd%, ReturnCode%, LeftPosition%, CommandWidth%, _
    ReturnText$
Dim TextLength%, LineLength%, LabelLines%, CommandTop%

  Load frmInputBox

  frmInputBox.Caption = App.Title

  'Display the InputBox icon in picScreenIcon.
  IconhWnd% = LoadIcon(0, Icon&)
  ReturnCode% = DrawIcon(frmInputBox!picScreenIcon.hDC, 0, 0, _
  IconhWnd%)
  frmInputBox!picScreenIcon.Picture = _
      frmInputBox!picScreenIcon.Image

  'Display Proper buttons
  Load frmInputBox!cmdButton(1)
  Select Case Button%
    Case OK_BUTTON
      EnhancedInputBox$ = ""
      Exit Function
    Case OK_CANCEL
      frmInputBox!cmdButton(0).Caption = "OK"
      frmInputBox!cmdButton(0).Default = True
      frmInputBox!cmdButton(1).Caption = "Cancel"
      frmInputBox!cmdButton(1).Cancel = True
    Case YES_NO
      frmInputBox!cmdButton(0).Caption = "YES"
      frmInputBox!cmdButton(0).Default = True
      frmInputBox!cmdButton(1).Caption = "NO"
      frmInputBox!cmdButton(1).Cancel = True
  End Select
```

```
    'Position the command button in center of the form at bottom
    CommandWidth% = frmInputBox!cmdButton(0).Width
    LeftPosition% = ((frmInputBox.ScaleWidth \ 2) - _
        (CommandWidth% + 4))
    frmInputBox!cmdButton(0).Left = LeftPosition%
    frmInputBox!cmdButton(1).Left = LeftPosition% + _
        CommandWidth% + 8
    frmInputBox!cmdButton(1).Visible = True

    'Check length of message and resize form and command buttons
    ' accordingly

    LineLength% = frmInputBox.TextWidth("mmmmmmmmmmmmmmmmmmmmm")
    TextLength% = frmInputBox.TextWidth(Label$)
    If TextLength% > LineLength% Then
      LabelLines% = Int(TextLength% / LineLength%) + 1
      frmInputBox!lblInstructions.Height = _
          (frmInputBox.TextHeight("X")
      * LabelLines%)
      frmInputBox!lblInstructions.Top = _
          frmInputBox!picScreenIcon.Top +
      ((frmInputBox!picScreenIcon.Height - _
      frmInputBox!lblInstructions.Height) / 2)
      frmInputBox!txtInputText.Top = _
          frmInputBox!lblInstructions.Top +
      frmInputBox!lblInstructions.Height + 8
      CommandTop% = frmInputBox!txtInputText.Top + _
      frmInputBox!txtInputText.Height + 16
      frmInputBox!cmdButton(0).Top = CommandTop%
      frmInputBox!cmdButton(1).Top = CommandTop%
      frmInputBox.Height = Screen.TwipsPerPixelY * (CommandTop% + _
      frmInputBox!cmdButton(0).Height + 40)
    End If

    'Show Label
    frmInputBox!lblInstructions.Caption = Label$

    'Show Text box if indicated
    frmInputBox!txtInputText.Text = Default$

    frmInputBox.Show MODAL
    Unload frmInputBox

    'Sets the return text
    ReturnText$ = gInputBoxReturn$
    Select Case ReturnText$
      Case "CANCEL"
        ReturnText$ = ""
      Case "NO"
        ReturnText$ = ""
      Case Else
        EnhancedInputBox$ = ReturnText$
    End Select
End Function
```

Follow these steps to construct project 33Proj04:

1. Create a new project and rename it 33Proj03.

2. Add a new module and insert the code for this module from the code in listing 33.7.

3. Rename Form1 as InputBox at the DOS level and frmInputBox at the Visual Basic level.

4. Change the Appearance property of frmInputBox to 1 - 3D.

5. Add a picture box to frmInputBox and rename it picScreenIcon.

6. Make picScreenIcon's AutoRedraw property True.

7. Create a command button and rename it cmdButton.

8. Change cmdButton's Index property to 0.

9. Draw a text box and rename it txtInputText.

10. Draw a label and rename it lblInstructions.

11. Change lblInstructions' BackStyle property to Transparent.

12. Add the code in listing 33.10 to frmInputBox.

13. Change the Startup form to Sub Main.

Listing 33.10 cmdButton **Code for Project 33Proj04**

```
Private Sub cmdButton_Click(Index As Integer)

    Select Case cmdButton(Index%).Caption
      Case "OK", "Yes"
        gInputBoxReturn$ = Trim$(txtInputText.Text)
      Case "Cancel"
        gInputBoxReturn$ = "CANCEL"
      Case "No"
        gInputBoxReturn$ = "NO"
    End Select

    frmInputBox.Hide

End Sub

Private Sub Form_Load()

    CenterDialogPosition Me

End Sub
```

Module1's General Declarations section supports the constants and variables used in this example. These constants and variables must be included or Project 33Proj04 will not work properly. MODAL is from the CONSTANT.TXT file. The InputBox constants identify which buttons to display on the InputBox. gInputBoxReturn$ contains the text returned by the user. Each of the standard icon IDs gives a text identification key to show which icon to display.

This project begins with the code found in Sub Main. This subroutine demonstrates all of the different message boxes that are used in Visual Basic. Notice the use of the new type of Visual Basic constant, vbCritical, in the MsgBox statement. The most important thing to see is that there is no corresponding constant declaration for vbCritical. This constant is already a part of Visual Basic.

You need to have your enhanced dialog box centered on the screen. The preceding code centers the enhanced InputBox on the screen. Most projects have main forms and need code to center any dialog boxes over that main form. However, this project has no main form, so you don't have to do this.

EnhancedInputBox displays the enhanced input box with the appropriate icon. The LoadIcon API call loads the window handle for the appropriate icon. DrawIcon uses this window handle to draw that icon in the picture box picScreenIcon. The process is very simple and will work for almost any icon graphic.

The remainder of the code formats and displays frmInputBox. This routine checks the size of the text to place in the label and then formats and positions the text box and label appropriately. The argument Default$ identifies whether to place default text in the text box. Button% tells this routine which labels to place on the command button: Yes No, Ok Cancel, or only OK. Based on the text returned in gInputBoxReturn$, this routine returns the text or nothing if the user entered nothing.

EnhancedInputBox also includes a very simple method for returning the user-entered text. You use a MODAL show method to display frmInputBox. This means that you need to return the results of user actions with text. If the user chooses "Yes" or "OK," this is no problem. You simply need to return the entered text in the global variable gInputBoxReturn$. When the user presses "No" or "Cancel," you need to return text that indicates this choice. This normally means that the user does not want to enter this choice of text. You solve this problem by returning "No" or "Cancel."

Using Window APIs

A whole family of API calls work with the different elements of Windows applications, which are all called *windows*.

Windows thinks of everything on the screen as a window. An icon on the screen is not surprisingly called one window. Possibly more surprisingly, the label below the icon is also known as a window. So when you look at an icon and a label, you are really looking at two windows.

The *GetParent* Function

This API call provides a means to obtain the window handle of the parent of the indicated window. This function is especially useful for obtaining the handle of the MDI parent of an MDI child form. You use this function when you need to learn something about the parent of window in another application.

```
Declare Function GetParent Lib "user32" _
Alias "GetParent" (ByVal hWnd As Long) As Long
```

The *GetWindow* Function

This function provides a means to cycle through the different running applications and any of their children. This is a very useful function for finding the window handle of a window which is not readily apparent to the current application. For example, you might need to discover whether Mail is currently running in an application that works with Mail. The GetWindow API call (listing 33.11) is very useful for discovering whether that application is running.

Listing 33.11   GetWindow **Declaration and Constants**

```
Declare Function GetWindow Lib "user32" (ByVal hWnd As Long _
, ByVal wCmd As Long) As Long

' GetWindow() Constants
Public Const GWW_HINSTANCE = (-6)
Public Const GW_HWNDFIRST = 0
Public Const GW_HWNDLAST = 1
Public Const GW_HWNDNEXT = 2
Public Const GW_HWNDPREV = 3
Public Const GW_OWNER = 4
Public Const GW_CHILD = 5
Public Const SW_SHOWNOACTIVATE = 4
```

The code in listing 33.11 shows what is necessary for making the GetWindow API call work properly in your applications. All of this code belongs in the WINAPI32.BAS file. This API call functions differently based on the referenced constant. There is a list of possible constants within this code.

The *GetWindowText* and *GetWindowTextLength* Functions

The GetWindowText and GetWindowTextLength API calls provide a means to obtain the length and text of the indicated window. This function is especially useful for converting the text provided by GetWindowText into a Visual Basic string.

```
Declare Function GetWindowText Lib "user32" _
 Alias "GetWindowTextA" _
  (ByVal hWnd As Long, ByVal lpString As String, _
ByVal aint As Long) As Long
Declare Function GetWindowTextLength Lib "user32" _
Alias "GetWindowTextLengthA" (ByVal hWnd As Long) As Long
```

The *SetParent* Function

The SetParent function offers you the opportunity to move controls from one container object to another at run time. SetParent works in many situations, making it a very valuable function. Using this function, you can move any control from different picture boxes, frames, or forms. You can create highly customizable applications that change appearance based on user input.

```
Declare Function SetParent Lib "user32" Alias "SetParent" _
 (ByVal hWndChild As Long, ByVal hWndNewParent As Long) As Long
```

There are some circumstances in which you need to change the appearance of a form "on the fly" at run time. One way to quickly change a form's appearance is to display the controls on different frames. There will always be controls that are common to both frames. The SetParent function permits you to move buttons such as the OK and Cancel buttons from one frame to another.

There are a couple of things to notice about Project 33.03. First, notice how you use the hWnd property of the command buttons and frames to make this project work properly. Most Visual Basic controls have window handle properties. You use this property when you need to move them or utilize any function that needs its window handle to function properly. Second, note the use of the Unload method before the use of End. This is a cleaner way of closing down an application. You need to always remember to close any open forms with the Unload method prior to using the End method.

Project 33Proj03 demonstrates the use of the GetParent API function. To create this project, use the following steps:

1. Open new project and rename this project as 33Proj03.

2. Add a new module.

3. Add the declaration text for SetParent to module Module1.

4. Draw two frames on Form1 with Frame1 directly over Frame2 as shown in figure 33.8.

Fig. 33.8
A view of what
Form1 should look
like at run time.

5. Place two command buttons on Frame1 and change the caption of Command1 to Exit and Command2 to SetParent.

6. Add the code shown in listing 33.12 to Form1.

Listing 33.12 The Command1_Click **and** Command2_Click **Procedures**

```
Private Sub Command1_Click()

  Unload Me
  End

End Sub

Private Sub Command2_Click()
Dim rc&

If Frame1.Visible Then
  Frame2.Visible = True
  Frame1.Visible = False
  rc& = SetParent(Command1.hWnd, Frame2.hWnd)
  rc& = SetParent(Command2.hWnd, Frame2.hWnd)
Else
  Frame1.Visible = True
  Frame2.Visible = False
  rc& = SetParent(Command1.hWnd, Frame1.hWnd)
  rc& = SetParent(Command2.hWnd, Frame1.hWnd)
End If

End Sub
```

Using File Access APIs

Visual Basic applications are still tied to Windows' underlying operating system. Applications still need to be aware of the locations of required files. You need to be aware that users will not always want to place your applications in the same directory or drive. This means that you need to provide methods for adjusting to these changes. Further, you must be able to perform underlying operating system commands. Because you are now using Windows 95, your applications must work with that underlying operating system. Several Windows APIs make working with files easier.

The *GetSystemDirectory* Function

The GetSystemDirectory function obtains the path of the system directory on the current Windows computer. The system directory contains the specialized Windows files that allow Windows to run properly including the .DLL, .VBX, and .DRV files. You can use this function to discover the path of any of the files that are in this directory.

```
Declare Function GetSystemDirectory Lib "kernel32" _
Alias "GetSystemDirectoryA" (ByVal lpBuffer As String, _
ByVal nSize As Long) As Long
```

Using GetSystemDirectory is very simple. Add the declaration text found to the General Declarations section of WINAPI32.BAS. You need to provide a variable in which to place the return string. This return string must be formatted as a fixed-length string. Additionally, you need an integer variable to store the size of the returned string. Because GetSystemDirectory returns a fixed-length string, you need a means to convert this string to a Visual Basic string.

The *GetWindowsDirectory* Routine

The GetWindowsDirectory routine provides the full path of the current computer's Windows directory. The Windows directory contains the main Windows files that involve the basic inner working of Windows. Each of the executable and Help files of all the basic applications that ship with Windows are here. These files include those for WordPad, Solitaire, Paint, and so on. In addition, there are the .INI configuration files for all of the applications on the current machine including the SYSTEM.INI and WIN.INI files.

```
Declare Function GetWindowsDirectory Lib "kernel32" Alias _
"GetWindowsDirectoryA" (ByVal lpBuffer As String, _
ByVal nSize As Long) As Long
```

There are a couple of secrets to making the GetWindowsDirectory function work properly. The declaration text belongs in the WINAPI.BAS file. You need to use the jacketed form of this function known as APIGetWindowsDirectory. Together, these two things make working with this function an easy process.

From Here...

For more information on related topics, see the following chapters:

- Chapter 31, "Advanced Form Techniques," contains several excellent API examples.

- Chapter 32, "Advanced Code Techniques," contains more API call usage.

Chapter 34

Designing Windows Applications

The root of the Windows operating system lies in a concept of the common user interface. A common "look and feel" assures users that what they learn for one application can be a basis for working with another. Unfortunately, developing the now-familiar Windows "look and feel" requires complex code. Before Visual Basic's release, this complex coding made the Windows development process difficult. You had to concentrate on the underlying code first rather than the interface for which Windows has become so well known.

Visual Basic answers this challenge with its new emphasis on designing the user interface before writing the code. Now you can quickly and easily design the user's screens before writing a single line of code. This important change enables programmers to concentrate on what the user sees rather than how to make the application work in Windows.

Visual Basic now makes it easy for programmers to create Windows applications. Companies all over the world are taking advantage of the flexibility of the Visual Basic environment to provide highly customized internal applications. These applications were almost impossible to create before the release of Visual Basic.

In the years to come, Visual Basic will provide great opportunities. Companies can take advantage of easy interface design to develop applications that precisely fit the needs of users. A dialog between developers and users will result in better applications with smaller periods of time between releases.

These same opportunities, however, also present challenges. All programs that you develop in Visual Basic are subject to all the limitations of the Windows environment. Unfortunately, these limitations are not always apparent to the beginning Visual Basic programmer.

In this chapter, you learn how to do the following:

- Design better Visual Basic applications

- Avoid programming pitfalls

- Write faster applications

- Use Visual Basic constants

- Include helpful comments for readable code

Challenges and Opportunities

Visual Basic's wide range of features is a two-edged sword that creates both opportunities and challenges. The opportunities lie in the flexibility to give the user what he or she needs. The challenges lie in achieving the first goal without creating problems that make the resulting application difficult to use or, worse, unusable. When users ask for so much detail and control that the application becomes unwieldy, you should examine which side of the sword the interface is on. There is always a tension between what a programmer can do and what he or she should do. It is a narrow path, and being aware of the pitfalls makes it easier to avoid them.

When designing a Visual Basic application, you should ask two basic questions:

- Does a desired feature have a performance effect?

- Is the feature likely to confuse the user?

Keep these two questions in mind in the following discussions.

Understanding Controls

One of Visual Basic 3.0's greatest strengths is the wide variety of .VBX controls available from third-party companies. Even with the new .OCX format, Microsoft has provided third-party companies with a lengthy beta cycle. This cycle has enabled many of the major companies to prepare .OCX versions of their popular .VBX controls. When Microsoft releases Visual Basic 4.0, most of the major Visual Basic add-in companies should already have .OCX controls available.

Third-party controls enable programmers to choose solutions for a variety of both specialized and generalized challenges. Such controls include specialized data-bound list and combo boxes, project lists, calendars, and many more. Some programmers might feel that these controls are no longer necessary because of the new ones that ship with Visual Basic 4.0. The reality is that no "magic bullet" control exists that will satisfy every programmer and user. Each situation and need differs, and probably can be addressed by an available control.

Caution

Make sure that you do not become too dependent on fancy controls. Use your head rather than controls to design your applications. Your brain is the most powerful tool that you will ever find to help you design applications. Think about what you want your application to do and how you can do it. If after considering all the possibilities you still decide that you need a custom control, use it. But keep the following in mind: Custom controls are almost always faster than written code, and graphical controls always affect performance. Try to find internal Windows API calls that can accomplish the same thing that you are trying to achieve with controls.

Three-Dimensional Controls

With the release of Windows 95, programmers face the challenge of designing applications with the newer interface. Many of the features of Windows 95 are familiar as part of the growing trends that began long before the release of Windows 95. The most obvious element of the Windows 95 interface is its three-dimensional (3-D) appearance.

For the past few years, developers have been creating applications that feature controls that have a 3-D appearance. Visual Basic 3.0 shipped with several 3-D controls. Many third-party .VBX companies provided methods for creating applications that have a 3-D appearance. A 3-D appearance is nothing new to veteran Visual Basic programmers. Table 34.1 lists upgrades to the 3-D controls that shipped with Visual Basic 3.0. You can find these upgrades in THREED32.OCX.

Table 34.1 The 3-D .OCX Controls in THREED32.OCX

Name	Description
SSCheck	3-D check box
SSCommand	3-D graphical command button
SSFrame	3-D frame

(continues)

Table 34.1 Continued	
Name	**Description**
SSOption	3-D option box
SSPanel	3-D progress indicator and label
SSRibbon	3-D toolbar button

What is new to Visual Basic programmers is a development environment and operating system that have a built-in 3-D appearance. Visual Basic 4.0 includes controls and tools designed to provide an application that looks perfectly at home in the Windows 95 operating system. In fact, Visual Basic 4.0 ships with controls specifically designed for use with Windows 95. Table 34.2 lists these controls, which are available in COMCTL.OCX.

Table 34.2 The 3-D .OCX Controls in COMCTL.OCX	
Name	**Description**
ProgressBar	3-D progress indicator
Slider	3-D slider
StatusBar	3-D status bar
TabStrip	3-D tabs
ToolBar	3-D toolbar
TreeView	3-D outline

Under Windows 3.x and Visual Basic 3.0, 3-D appearance affected performance. Applications that used too many 3-D controls ran slowly. By using 3-D controls, applications tested the limits of Windows 3.x's memory-management system. For this reason, your application's screens must use as few 3-D controls as possible.

With the release of Windows 95 and Visual Basic 4.0, you might think that the 3-D challenge has disappeared. After all, if Microsoft designed both the operating system and development environment for creating applications with a 3-D appearance, surely you no longer need to worry about using 3-D controls in the applications that you develop. But although Microsoft has eliminated or at least loosened the memory and resource limits on 3-D controls, the interface limits still exist.

Even if you could give your applications as many 3-D controls as you want, does that mean that your applications will look better? In the screen shown in figure 34.1, one 3-D frame that fills the entire form contains all the controls.

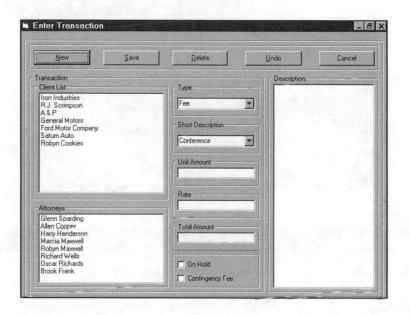

Fig. 34.1
A screen demonstrating a gross overuse of graphical 3-D appearance that degrades an application's performance.

V

Optimization

Such a layout is unnecessary for the interface. All forms start with their Appearance property set to 3D, so putting a frame around the form's controls serves no purpose. Frames are terrific controls for organizing information on the screen to make the screen more readable. However, using too many screens, as in figure 34.1, has the opposite effect of causing more confusion.

Notice in figure 34.1 the overuse of the SSPanel to hold every control on the form. All the command buttons are in one frame. However, each command button has an obvious label directly on it. To indicate that a group of buttons are related, you can simply place them in the same area. Each of the controls would look better if you use a label rather than a frame to differentiate them.

Figure 34.2 shows an appropriate use of 3-D controls. This screen uses frames only to organize similar controls. You save much screen space this way. Notice also how much more easily you can read the information on the screen.

Simplify your screens whenever possible. If you have trouble determining what a screen does, you can't expect the user to understand it. Using many frames just makes the screen more complex and makes it harder for a user to read and understand it.

Fig. 34.2
A screen demon-
strating a much
better implemen-
tation of 3-D
appearance.

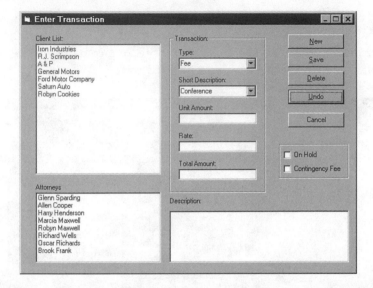

Graphical Controls

Visual Basic Professional Edition ships with three different kinds of graphical
controls: Image, Picture, and Picture Clip. These controls can make a Visual
Basic application much easier to use.

Placing too many Picture controls on one form, however, has a detrimental
effect on Windows resources. One large graphic has the same kind of significant effect on Windows resources. If your application does not require the
use of Picture controls, use an Image control instead. The Image control uses
fewer Windows resources. Don't clutter your screens with too many graphics,
because doing so only confuses users by giving them too much to look at.

List and Combo Boxes

Visual Basic provides two powerful control types: the list box and the combo box. With these controls, the programmer can provide the user with a choice of selections and thus limit user entry problems. Entries that different data-entry people make with these controls appear the same way in the resulting database.

Overusing list boxes and combo boxes can also harm an application's performance. If a list box or combo box lists too many items, the control can increase the load time of the form to which the control belongs. You can reduce the number of items in a list by finding out what the actual limits are. Does a user need all the states in the United States, or only the 10 with which the company normally does business?

Limits on the Number of Controls

There are practical limits to how many controls that you should place on any one screen. This limit is much smaller than the maximum that Visual Basic allows. The actual limit depends on the purpose of the screen that you are designing. As a general rule, try to design each screen with a single purpose in mind; then use only as many controls as are necessary to support that purpose. If any controls stray or detract from that single purpose, remove them.

Designing Forms

Visual Basic makes it easy to add a form to an application. To add a form or module, simply click on the appropriate icon. You need not write any supporting code for forms or modules. Although these icons make it easy to add a screen to an application, they also present challenges.

When users click on an icon, they like to see something happen. Unless the application appears to take some kind of action, some users become confused and begin to suspect that the program doesn't work. Users might perceive an application with many forms as "slow" because it is constantly loading and unloading the forms. This loading and unloading also confuses users and creates a performance problem as well.

Whether an application is "slow" or "fast" is all a matter of the user's perception. If users see something happening on screen while an application is executing, they perceive the application as "fast" rather than "slow." The techniques described in this section help you to create "fast" applications.

> **Note**
>
> Avoid displaying the control box on forms that have command buttons. If the user is to exit from a form by using one or a choice of buttons, the control box provides a tempting alternative. This frequently overlooked problem can have devastating effects on your application and data if it causes your application to miss initiating critical processes connected to the command button.

Load Time

If you load all a program's forms at program startup, they all appear quickly when the application calls them. Although this slows the application's performance at program startup, the application's run-time performance is much faster. Simply load all the forms that belong to an application by using the load method. This method places the forms in memory but invisible.

This technique works well for applications with a small number of forms (2 to 5). For applications with more forms, you might use this technique for similar groupings of forms. For example, an accounting payroll application might load all the forms associated with displaying employee information during an employee data-entry session.

The *Sub Main* Subroutine

The Options dialog box (which you display by choosing Tools, Options), has a Project tab that enables you to change the startup form to Sub Main. Figure 34.3 shows the Options dialog box's Project tab. To take advantage of this setting, you need a module with a Main subroutine. This frees you from having to keep any startup routines within a form's load event.

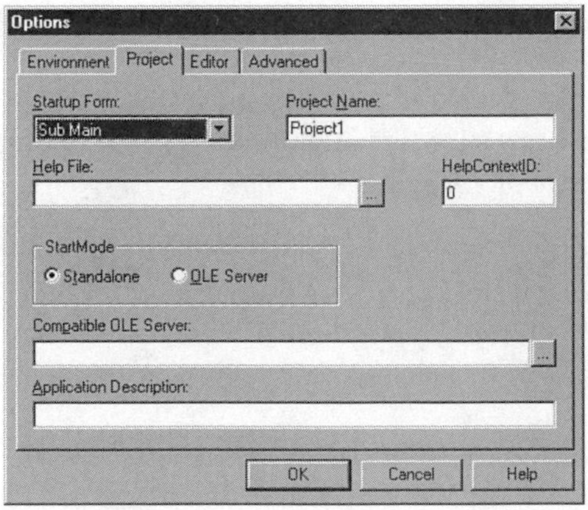

Fig. 34.3

The Project tab of the Options dialog box.

The Sub Main subroutine is an excellent place for all the startup code required at startup time. For example, the Sub Main subroutine might contain code for checking the application's path. You might place a splash screen on the screen while the subroutine checks this path.

Splash Screens

One way to deal with lengthy program startups is to display a splash screen during load time. A splash screen is a borderless form that displays information about the application and its designer. Many commercial applications, including Microsoft Word and Excel, display splash screens at program startup. A splash screen provides the user with visible proof that something is happening. Figure 34.4 shows a typical splash screen.

Fig. 34.4
An example of a splash screen that appears when the application first loads to give the user something to look at while configuration takes place.

Progress Indicators

Applications sometimes must initiate lengthy processes that force the user to wait while they are taking place. (Whether a process is "lengthy" depends on the perception of each individual user, but usually a process that takes more than 10 seconds is considered lengthy.) To most users, simply showing an hourglass or simply leaving the mouse pointer displayed is insufficient. Users like to see some indication that the program is doing something. One of the best ways to provide such an indication is to display a progress indicator on the screen. A progress indicator can be either a modal dialog box or information displayed in the status bar at the bottom of the screen.

Progress Dialog Boxes. A *progress dialog box* (fig. 34.5) usually consists of a borderless modal form with some kind of message and graphical representation of progress. One of the best Visual Basic controls for the graphical display is SSPanel. This control shows the user both a graphical gauge and a percentage indicator, giving the user two kinds of visual information to indicate that the application is doing something. To indicate progress, the control fills with color and displays a percentage.

Fig. 34.5
An example of a progress dialog box, which appears over an application's screen during a process.

Progress Status Bars. Applications with a status bar can change one of the panels to indicate progress. Many applications, including Microsoft Word and Excel, use this method. A bonus benefit of using progress status bars is that you use existing screen controls and thus need not add another form.

Figure 34.6 shows a typical multiple-document interface (MDI) screen with a status bar at the bottom of the screen. Notice the colored portion of the bottom of the status bar and the percentage figure in the center. This figure demonstrates one way to show a percentage indicator in the status bar.

Fig. 34.6
An example of a status bar progress indicator showing at the bottom of the application's screen the percentage of work currently done.

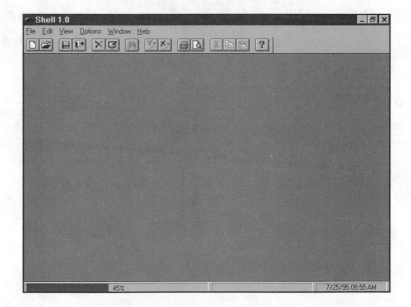

Chapter 30, "Advanced Control Techniques," explains in detail the status bar and its purpose in a Visual Basic application. Also examine the status bar in SHELL.MAK on the companion CD.

About Technical Terms

Remember that other people will use the applications that you write. Most users are not as sophisticated about many of the basic concepts in Windows design. They seldom care about anything except doing their work as quickly and as easily as possible. As a programmer, your job is to design applications that make the user's job easier.

Rethinking 3270 Screens

Many companies are using Visual Basic to replace old 3270 emulation screens. Programmers designing these new screens must be careful not to simply replicate the older 3270 screen in Visual Basic. The screens need not appear exactly the same as they did in the older applications. You can consolidate some screens into one screen; conversely, you might need to divide a screen into multiple ones. Many new techniques are available to the programmer to solve such problems.

List Choices

Visual Basic provides an easy method for displaying list choices to the user. Many older screens required users to know what they had to enter in a particular field. Lists provide users with a choice of items to enter in a field, reducing the chances of the user becoming confused and making entry errors in the field.

The 3270-style screen expects the user to know what to do. Such a screen prompts the user for information, such as the state, but does not specify which format to use. The user must know, for example, exactly which states the company does business in and which format to use when entering that state. Database systems are not very intelligent; for some, "ny" and "NY" are two different states. The 3270-type screens offer few safeguards to prevent users from entering information that confuses the system.

Command Buttons

Command buttons control a screen's basic functions. The names on each of the buttons provide the user a catalog of available actions. If you present command buttons in different places on the same screen in a seemingly random structure, you can confuse the user. Any structure is acceptable; you can place all the buttons along the top, bottom, or (more commonly) right edge of a screen (see fig. 34.7).

Fig. 34.7
A well-constructed screen with all the command buttons placed on its right side.

V

Optimization

Check Boxes and Option Boxes

To present a fixed number of choices,use the check box and option box controls. A check box gives the user two choices only: on or off. For example, you might use a check box to indicate whether to display the current hold status of a sales order. An option box presents the user with a fixed list of choices. For example, you might use an option box to display a list of the states in which a company does business.

Give Users What They Want

Users are focused on the tasks that they want to do. They don't care about how difficult it is for a programmer to produce something for them. They only want what they need to do their job. Sometimes users have trouble articulating what they want, and often what users think they want is not what they actually need. The programmer's job is to get users' required tasks on a screen within an application. Learn to listen to users to discern their underlying requirements. Finally, always be prepared to go through several iterations of screens before you find the right solution for a user.

Sexy versus Usable Interfaces

Be careful not to create application interfaces that are flashy and dazzling, but which actually aren't very usable. Using tabbed screens, for example, might be the latest trend in programming, but if it doesn't help users do their job, try something more practical. Don't force features on users unless they need them.

Technical Jargon

Programmers use terms and concepts that often differ from those familiar to users. Conversely, users work with different concepts and terms with which they are familiar. Your applications should use the concepts and terms that fit the needs of users and avoid using those familiar to programmers (unless your application's users are other programmers). In other words, instead of displaying the phrase "Initiating variables," use the more accessible "Preparing system." Simply by avoiding the use of programmers' jargon, you can make your application more understandable to users.

Breaking Windows Standards

Most Windows applications have a consistent "look and feel," including the now-familiar control boxes and maximize and minimize buttons. Most applications now have the 3-D appearance with a gray background and black text. Most command buttons have either text or icons that indicate the button's function.

You should consider very carefully before you vary from these Windows standards. The purpose of the common user interface is to give users a familiar environment in which knowledge of one application largely applies to another. To the extent that you vary from these standards, you place your application's users into a foreign, unfamiliar environment.

Changing Text Colors

Many Windows users like to change the default colors to those of their preference. Unfortunately, this presents a problem for the programmer. If you change the default colors at design time, those colors might conflict with the user's choices. In such cases, the interface might become unusable. Consider the result, for instance, of the user choosing yellow text against a blue background. If you change the text color to blue, the blue text disappears into the blue background.

Placing Graphics on Command Buttons

Some very popular Windows applications include graphics and text on the same buttons. This style, although quite popular, is inadvisable for several important reasons. Such command buttons take up a great deal of screen real estate and consume a large amount of Windows resources. Avoid using these nonstandard buttons.

MDI versus SDI Considerations

Many different kinds of applications are available for the Windows environment, including word processors, spreadsheets, accounting programs, utilities, presentation software, databases, and many others. With few exceptions, these applications belong to one of two general classes of Windows applications: single-document interface *(SDI)* and multiple-document interface *(MDI)*. Your choice depends on whether your application must display multiple views of data simultaneously.

SDI Interfaces

An SDI application consists of one single screen or a series of single screens (see fig. 34.8). Such applications are typically simple and do not require that the user have multiple views of information simultaneously. Before choosing to create an SDI application, you should carefully consider whether your application will ever require the added functionality of an MDI application.

Fig. 34.8
Notepad is a typical SDI application.

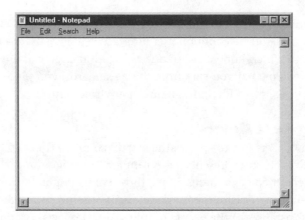

By its very definition, an SDI application consists of a single screen or at most a small number of screens (displayed one at a time). Although you can create an SDI application that displays multiple screens simultaneously, you usually should not. The more forms that appear on the screen, the more the user has to think about what he or she is supposed to do and be looking at. Have you ever run several applications simultaneously and got into trouble because they were all jumbled together? Two of the displayed screens might belong to the same application, but the user might have no easy way of knowing that. In any case, an excellent method exists for avoiding such problems: When your application must display multiple forms at the same time, make it an MDI application.

MDI Interfaces

An MDI application consists of one main screen that serves as a container for all the screens belonging to the application. Within this container, an application can simultaneously show different views of data. Word for Windows and Excel are both MDI applications (see fig. 34.9).

Figure 34.9 includes many screen elements that make up an MDI application. The toolbar at the top contains icons that represent frequently used functions that the user can access without using the application's menus. To make the toolbar always visible, you place it on the application's MDI form.

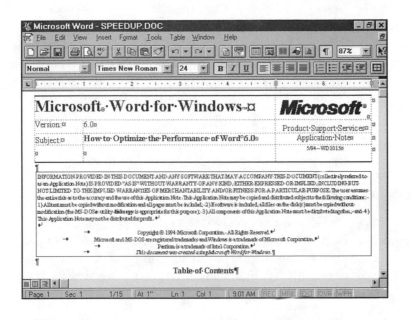

Fig. 34.9
Word for Windows
6.0 is an MDI
application.

Another screen element is the status bar at the bottom of the screen. Status bars contain a wide variety of information including the time and date, comments about the current control, and the last action.

Caution

The choice of MDI versus SDI can be controversial. Programmers on both sides of this issue have very definite, valid opinions. This section has mentioned reasons for leaning toward MDI applications. But always be careful to keep your client's needs in mind when making your decisions about the features that you want to use. Arguments about whether MDI is better than SDI do not solve the client's problems. Remember, you must always base your decisions on your client's or employer's needs.

Programming Readable Code

Your code must be readable not only to you but also to others. If another programmer cannot read your code, he or she must waste precious time figuring out exactly what the program does and how. Readable code becomes very important when someone has to modify your code. No matter how perfectly you write your code, eventually user requirements will change and your code must change as well. Those who have to modify your code will be grateful for the effort you make to ensure that they can read your code.

Using Visual Basic Constants

Visual Basic enables you to write code with numeric values to specify how an object should behave. This capability makes writing code easier, but makes reading the code harder afterwards. The solution is to use global constants that represent these values. Code that uses constants is much easier to read.

Visual Basic 3.0 shipped with a CONSTANT.TXT file that contained the global constants. To use these constants, you only had to add this file to your project. Therefore, you had to load all global constants to your projects whether you needed them or not. The only other solution was to add constants selectively to your projects.

You no longer have to add a CONSTANT.TXT file to your Visual Basic projects. Microsoft included global constants in the support files, so you no longer have to add the constant file to use the constants. Although you can use the older constant files, you should convert your projects to use the new constants and keep up with changes in Visual Basic.

Some programmers are proud that they can read code without the help of constants. Unfortunately, not all programmers are capable of doing so, including some who may need to read your code. By using the Visual Basic global constants, you make your code more readable to all programmers, even those who cannot read code as easily. Even if you are capable of reading code without constants, using constants still makes your code easier to read, especially if you tend to forget what you have done and why. For example, which of the following code lines is more readily understandable?

```
FORM1.SHOW 1

FORM1.SHOW vbModal
```

When you read code that uses the constants, you do not have to remember what each value means. The code is more readable.

Commented Code

Writing commented code is a pain, but reading uncommented code, even code that you wrote just yesterday, can be an even greater pain. Trying to figure out the logic of the code on-screen is time consuming. Taking the time to put in comments, on the other hand, saves you time in the long run. Imagine trying to read and understand the meaning and use of the code in listing 34.1 without the comments.

Listing 34.1   Code from 34List01.BAS, a Program That Searches the Tag Property of Each Control and Displays the Appropriate Database Field Information in Each Control

```
' The following routine searches through all the controls
' on a form and checks each control's TAG property.
' If the tag property is a field name, this routine loads
' the current field's value into that control

Sub LoadFormData (WndName As Form, dyn As Dynaset)
Dim Cntl%, FieldName$, Result$, N%, i%

Screen.MousePointer = vbHOURGLASS

'Search through all the controls on the indicated form
For Cntl% = 0 To WndName.Controls.Count - 1
  FieldName$ = WndName.Controls(Cntl%).Tag
  If TypeOf WndName.Controls(Cntl%) Is OptionButton Then

     ' Find the value of this field and store in the appropriate
     ' option button control
     N% = Abs(dyn(FieldName$))
     If WndName.Controls(Cntl%).Caption = "YES" Then
         WndName.Controls(Cntl%).Value = N%
     ElseIf WndName.Controls(Cntl%).Caption = "NO" Then
         WndName.Controls(Cntl%).Value = Abs(N% - 1)
     End If

  ElseIf TypeOf WndName.Controls(Cntl%) Is ComboBox Then

     If dyn(FieldName$) <> Null Then

        ' Format the current field's value
        Result$ = dyn.Fields(FieldName$)
        ' Find the field's value in the current combo box
        For N% = 0 To (WndName.Controls(Cntl%).ListCount - 1)
          i% = WndName.Controls(Cntl%).ListIndex + 1
          WndName.Controls(Cntl%).ListIndex = i%
          If Len(WndName.Controls(Cntl%).Text) <> 0 Then
            Exit For
          End If
        Next N%
     End If

     ' If the control is a text box
  ElseIf TypeOf WndName.Controls(Cntl%) Is TextBox Then

     ' If the current field's value is blank then skip
     If dyn(FieldName$) <> Null Then

        ' Store the formatted value in the text box
        WndName.Controls(Cntl%).Text = dyn.Fields(FieldName$)
```

(continues)

V

Optimization

Listing 34.1 Continued

```
        End If
    End If
Next Cntl%

Screen.MousePointer = vbDEFAULT

End Sub
```

Listing 34.1 contains the subroutine LoadFormData. You could reference this subroutine in the load event of any form. Simply provide the name of the dynaset containing the data, position the table at the appropriate record, place the names of the fields that you want in the appropriate control's tag property, and run this routine. In instances where you cannot use Bound controls, this routine works amazingly well. Notice that the use of vbHourGlass and vbDefault makes it clear what the program is doing to the mouse pointer.

From Here...

An application's appearance is as important as what the application does. A poorly thought-out application interface detracts from the application's usefulness because users focus on the bad interface rather than what it does. Be careful how you use 3-D graphics and how you position controls on your screens. Also be careful to ensure that the user knows what is going on and doesn't see a mouse pointer during processing. All of these are elements of a user-friendly interface.

To find information on related topics, see the following chapters:

- For more information on the toolbar and status bar, see Chapter 30, "Advanced Control Techniques."

- To find out more about MDI and SDI applications, see Chapter 31, "Advanced Form Techniques."

- For a treasure trove of styles for different kinds of screens and designs, see *Look for the Windows Interface* (Microsoft Press, 1992). Use this book in conjunction with the *Visual Design Guide*.

Appendix A

Preparing for Visual Basic 4.0

Visual Basic has arguably had a part in the success of the Windows operating system. Windows is not a static type of graphical interface, but rather a constantly changing operating system. Thus Visual Basic has had to change to adjust to the everchanging Windows. Visual Basic 4.0 incorporates many of the changes to the Windows operating system, enabling programmers to create even better and more powerful applications. Many of these changes make it necessary for programmers to change the ways in which they program.

Is Visual Basic 4.0 worth changing the way that you program? Yes. Everyone is understandably reluctant to adapt to changes that affect familiar and comfortable ways of working. But as this chapter will demonstrate, Visual Basic 4.0's new features provide advantages that make it worthwhile to adjust your old programming habits.

In this appendix, you learn about the following:

- How to prepare your projects written in previous versions of Visual Basic for conversion to Visual Basic 4.0

- How the Visual Basic 4.0 language and code have changed from previous versions

- How familiar controls have changed, and what new controls Visual Basic 4.0 introduces

- How forms have changed from previous versions

- What new controls Windows 95 introduces

Discussing Preconversion Concerns

Visual Basic 4.0 is a major revision of the Visual Basic programming language. Microsoft wrote all previous versions of Visual Basic in assembler. Visual Basic 4.0 makes the jump from assembler to C++, and thus had to rewrite the entire language from scratch. Considering this momentous change, you must proceed carefully with any mission-critical applications written in previous versions of Visual Basic.

Saving Previous Versions

Visual Basic 4.0 has a built-in conversion utility. When you try to access a project written in another version, Visual Basic 4.0 prompts you to indicate whether you want to convert the project to the current version of Visual Basic. Unfortunately, Microsoft has provided no conversion utility for changing a Visual Basic 4.0 project back to Visual Basic 3.0.

Microsoft expended great effort to make Visual Basic 4.0 as downwardly compatible as possible. Nevertheless, you can expect some problems when converting a mission-critical project from version 3.0 to 4.0. For this reason, you must keep backups of Visual Basic 3.0 as well as your project source code in Visual Basic 3.0. If you then encounter problems that take a long time to fix, you can at least return to the previous version to fix minor bugs.

Saving Forms as Text

Before converting a project, you first must ensure that you have all the forms saved in text rather than binary format. For programmers moving from version 1.0 to 2.0 and from 2.0 to 3.0, Visual Basic forms and modules saved in binary format caused several random problems. You can easily avoid such problems by ensuring that all files are in the correct format.

Checking the format of every form and code module in your projects is well worth the time and effort. To do so, simply choose the appropriate file on the Project screen and type Ctrl+A. The Save File As dialog box (see fig. A.1) appears. The check box Save as Text should already be selected; if not, left-click on it. Then click OK. Since you can no longer save files in binary format in Visual Basic 4.0, this will not be a problem in the port to the next version of Visual Basic.

Before continuing, choose Options, Environment Options. Note that the dialog box's Setting list includes the option Default Save As Format (see fig. A.2). Simply changing the setting in this dialog box does *not* affect the format of any previous project's files. You still must use the File Save As dialog box to change the format of any binary files.

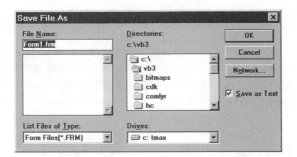

Fig. A.1
Visual Basic 3.0's
Save File As dialog
box.

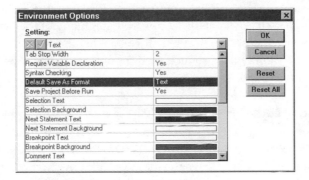

Fig. A.2
The Visual Basic
3.0 Default Save As
Format option.

Using Third-Party Controls

When converting your projects to Visual Basic 4.0, your greatest challenge
is to maintain compatibility with third-party VBX controls. In version 4.0,
Visual Basic moves from the 16-bit-format VBX controls to the new 32-bit-
capable OCX controls. Most of your existing third-party controls should work
under Visual Basic 4.0, but there are always exceptions.

The first time that you open a Visual Basic 3.0 project, Visual Basic 4.0's Custom Control Upgrade dialog box (see fig. A.3) asks whether you want to upgrade the current VBXs. You cannot selectively upgrade only some of the
Visual Basic controls. If you choose No, Visual Basic 4.0 ignores all your
project's third-party controls. Therefore, choose Yes in this dialog box to
upgrade all the controls that you can.

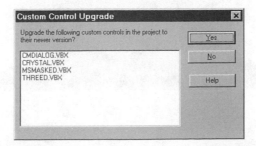

Fig. A.3
The Visual Basic
4.0 Custom
Control Upgrade
dialog box.

> **Caution**
>
> Make sure that you keep on your system all the VBXs that belong to your projects. Visual Basic 4.0 often needs these controls during the conversion process. If you remove them before conversion, you get errors during the conversion process.

Exploring Interface Changes

In Visual Basic 4.0, Microsoft has improved the Visual Basic interface as well as the language itself. Visual Basic 4.0 incorporates many of the new features found in newer Windows applications. If you are familiar with the "look and feel" of the Microsoft Office products, you should feel right at home with the Visual Basic 4.0 interface.

The Toolbar and Floating Help Text

Visual Basic now has an attractive, colorful toolbar. A major addition to the Visual Basic toolbar is floating Help text. You no longer need to guess what a toolbar button does. Simply leave the mouse pointer over a toolbar button for a few moments and Visual Basic displays Help text that indicates the purpose of the toolbar button. Figure A.4 shows what this toolbar Help looks like in Visual Basic 4.0.

Fig. A.4

The Visual Basic 4.0 floating Help text for toolbar buttons.

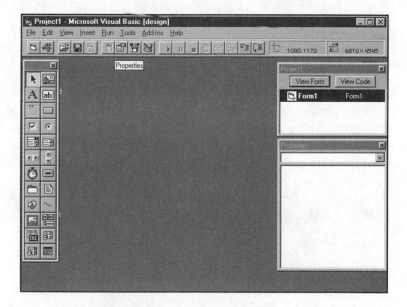

This floating Help text feature is even more useful with the Toolbox. You need no longer be confused by a Toolbox full of unfamiliar controls. Now you can simply leave the mouse pointer over an unfamiliar control and wait a few seconds for Visual Basic to display Help for the control. This new feature is a godsend if you have a hard time memorizing the purpose of each control. Figure A.5 shows what Toolbox Help text looks like.

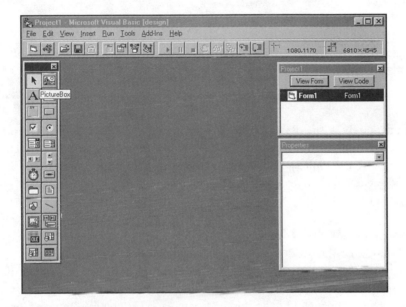

Fig. A.5
The Visual Basic 4.0 floating Help text for Toolbox controls.

Shortcut Keys

One of the most glaring omissions of Visual Basic 3.0 was the lack of shortcut keys for many of the important features. If you wanted to display the Toolbox by pressing a shortcut key, for example, you were out of luck unless you had a third-party add-in. Fortunately, many of Visual Basic's different windows have shortcut keys. Unfortunately, Microsoft has changed some of these shortcut keys to be more consistent with other Microsoft Office products. Table A.1 lists some of the most useful shortcut key combinations.

Table A.1   Visual Basic Shortcut Keys

Shortcut Key	Feature
Ctl+S	Save project
Ctl+F	Find

(continues)

Table A.1 Continued

Shortcut Key	Feature
Ctl+H	Replace
F7	Show Code
Shift+F7	Show Form
Ctl+G	Show Debug window
Ctl+R	Show Project window
F4	Show Properties

Unfortunately, Visual Basic 4.0 still does not enable you to change the shortcut keys. Perhaps a third-party vendor will come up with a product that enables you to customize Visual Basic 4.0 further. For example, most users would greatly appreciate a feature that enables them to change as well as assign shortcut keys.

Visual Basic Add-Ins

In Visual Basic 3.0, third-party add-ins like Sheridan Software's VB Assist added value to many programmers' Visual Basic environments, particularly in cases where Microsoft failed to provide a utility to make certain processes easier. The vendors will have to upgrade such add-ins before they can work properly with Visual Basic 4.0. This upgrading is necessary because Microsoft now provides a method for incorporating add-ins into Visual Basic 4.0. With Visual Basic's addition of an Add-In facility, however, you can look forward to some new Visual Basic enhancement utilities that help make your work easier. These add-ins should start appearing soon after Visual Basic 4.0's release.

Understanding Language Changes

More than any previous version of Visual Basic, version 4.0 incorporates some of the biggest code changes. Microsoft has worked hard to minimize the impact of these changes on your existing projects. The built-in conversion utility handles many of the changes for you automatically. However, Microsoft wisely chose not to convert many things. In such cases, Visual Basic 4.0 is downwardly compatible so that both the new and old methods work.

Old versus New Techniques

Visual Basic 4.0 works fine whether you use older ways of writing code or the newer ones. But should you change the code that you are writing to match the new ways of writing code? The answer is probably yes. You need to start getting used to the new ways of writing code. You need not adapt immediately, but you should gradually as you start to take advantage of Visual Basic 4.0's newer features. By switching to the new techniques, however, you enable newer programmers reading your code to better understand what you have done. The longer you cling to the older techniques, the more difficult you make it for newer programmers to understand your older, less familiar code constructions.

The Line-Continuation Character

Often you want to view all of a long line of code on-screen at the same time. If you are familiar with C and C++, you are aware of how useful it is to view all the code that belongs on the same line. Visual Basic 4.0 now includes support for the much-awaited continuation character, which provides exactly this new capability. If you have a long line, you can now break it by ending the first half of the line with a blank space followed by an underscore character (_). Although the screen now displays the code line as two individual lines, Visual Basic still processes the two code lines as a single line of code because of the line-continuation character.

Code Changes

Visual Basic 4.0 introduces many basic changes to the appearance of code. These changes were necessary to make Visual Basic 4.0 code more consistent with other Microsoft strategies. None of these basic changes are difficult to handle. However, several take some getting used to if you are familiar with older versions of Visual Basic.

The Code View

Notice that the new code view system displays in the Code window only those subroutines that include code. To add a new event, simply choose it from the Object and Proc combo boxes (see fig. A.6). The event then displays in the Code window.

Fig. A.6
The Visual Basic code view for the Calculator project showing the positioning of the Object and Proc combo boxes.

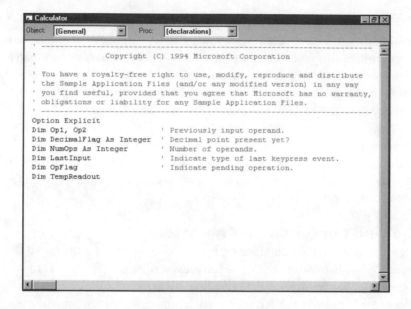

Private Subroutines

The following examples demonstrate the differences between Visual Basic 3.0 and 4.0. Here's a Load event for a Visual Basic 3.0 form:

```
Sub Form_Load()
End Sub
```

Now here's a Load event for a Visual Basic 4.0 form:

```
Private Sub Form_Load()
End Sub
```

Visual Basic 4.0 adds the word Private before the code identifying a form's event. Therefore, only code within the same form can access the code. At a glance, you can tell whether the code works on a form level or application-wide level.

Public Subroutines and Variables

To identify variables that were available throughout a project, Visual Basic 3.0 applications used the keyword global. In Visual Basic 4.0, projects use the keyword Public. The previous practice of using global still works in Visual Basic 4.0 and remains unchanged by the conversion process. For this reason, all code that uses the older global construction still functions properly under Visual Basic 4.0. To remain consistent with this new language upgrade, you should change your global constructions to Public constructions as time permits.

Constants

Visual Basic 4.0 changes the language's constants. Constants in Visual Basic 3.0 were all uppercase with underlines between the words. Although Visual Basic had few built-in constants, you could add the CONSTANT.TXT file to a project to use the ones that Microsoft recommended. In Visual Basic 4.0, the constants are available without the addition of CONSTANT.TXT and they appear in a different format. Constants now appear as upper- and lowercase characters with no underlines between words.

Table A.2 shows the differences between the format of constants in Visual Basic 3.0 and 4.0. These differences do not cause any applications that use the Visual Basic 3.0 constants and constant format to fail to work properly. Simply be aware that Visual Basic 4.0 changes the means by which you access constants, and act accordingly.

Table A.2   Comparing Visual Basic 3.0 and 4.0 Constants for `MsgBox`

Visual Basic 3.0 Constant	Visual Basic 4.0 Constant
MB_OK	vbOKOnly
MB_OKCANCEL	vbOkCancel
MB_ABORTRETRYIGNORE	vbAbortRetryIgnore
MB_YESNO	vbYesNo
MB_RETRYCANCEL	vbRetryCancel
MB_ICONSTOP	vbCritical
MB_ICONQUESTION	vbQuestion
MB_ICONEXCLAMATION	vbExclamation
MB_ICONINFORMATION	vbInformation

Compilation

Visual Basic 3.0 seldom handled large projects quickly. Improvements in Visual Basic 4.0 provide relief to some of the most troubling compilation problems. Now projects compile in the background while you work with the first loaded form. Loading large projects is no longer a tedious process.

Background Compile

Running projects within the development environment no longer takes as long as it used to. Visual Basic 4.0 doesn't compile your project all at once anymore. Now when you start an application, Visual Basic compiles only enough to load the first form. Afterward, compilation continues only during idle times. This greatly speeds up the compilation process.

Background Project Load

In Visual Basic 3.0, you had to wait (often impatiently) for every single form, module, VBX, and DLL to load into the project window. If you had to do so a couple of times an hour with the same project, you could lose a lot of valuable time. Visual Basic 4.0 now includes several new features designed specifically to make large projects load faster.

Exploring Form Changes

Visual Basic 4.0 makes some major changes to forms. These changes enhance your capabilities as a programmer and enable you to create Visual Basic applications with a "look and feel" matching that of other current Windows applications.

The *Appearance* Property

Applications with a three-dimensional (3-D) appearance are becoming increasingly common. The current versions of Microsoft Word, Excel, Access, Project, and PowerPoint all have a consistent 3-D appearance that users are beginning to expect in their applications. In fact, new applications that lack this familiar appearance are the exception to the rule. Before the release of Visual Basic 4.0, providing a 3-D appearance in Visual Basic was fairly difficult. However, Visual Basic 4.0 provides an Appearance property that makes the task much simpler.

Figure A.7 shows the appearance of the Form1 form of a new project after you set its Appearance property to 3D (which is the property's default). The form's backColor property does not affect the color of the form's 3-D appearance. The 3-D appearance is quite similar to that which you find in many dialog boxes in Microsoft Office applications. Figure A.8, for example, shows the Open dialog box for Word for Windows. Notice the similarities between this dialog box and the form shown in figure A.7.

Fig. A.7
Form1 from a new project, showing the 3-D appearance that the Appearance property provides.

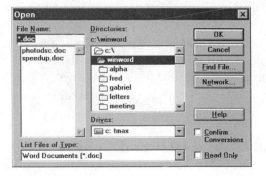

Fig. A.8
Microsoft Word's Open dialog box.

The *NegotiateMenus* Property

Visual Basic 4.0 includes full support of OLE 2.0 technology. Therefore, you now can place an object on a Visual Basic form and have the object change appearance when the user works with it. A form's NegotiateMenus property determines whether a form's menu choices change when the user works with an OLE object. For example, when you set the NegotiateMenus property to True, a user working with a Word for Windows 6.0 document sees the Microsoft Word menu choices on the Visual Basic form.

Note

You need to add the File menu choices manually to a form as they will not appear automatically from a Word OLE object.

The *AutoShowChildren* Property

Sometimes you want to reduce the number of children viewable on the multiple-document interface (MDI) parent, but do not want to remove them from memory yet. Visual Basic 3.0 did not enable you to make MDI children invisible at run time. Fortunately, Visual Basic 4.0 fixes this problem by adding the AutoShowChildren property to the MDI parent form. By using this useful property, you can use the load method to put an MDI child in memory but invisible.

Using the New Controls

Visual Basic 4.0 does more than simply give its interface a facelift and add a bunch of new features. Before the release of Visual Basic 4.0, programmers had to look for third-party vendors to provide common windows features. The newest version of Visual Basic includes new data-bound grids, lists, and combo controls. For Windows 95 and Windows NT 3.51 applications, Visual Basic includes the new tabstrip, status bar, slider, treeview, RichText, Sheridan Tab, and toolbar controls.

Data-Bound Grids, Lists, and Combo Controls

Data-bound grids, lists, and combo controls were among the most glaring omissions from Visual Basic 3.0's feature set. Such features are now integral parts of Windows applications. Without such data-bound features, you practically had to obtain third-party controls to write database applications. Fortunately, Visual Basic 4.0 includes these types of data-bound controls.

Toolbars

Toolbars are an integral part of every popular Windows application on the market. Visual Basic 3.0 provided no straightforward method for adding toolbars to your applications. For this reason, programmers wrote Visual Basic applications with a variety of behaviors and capabilities. Such now-common features as tooltips required code. Visual Basic 4.0 resolves this problem by adding a toolbar control. Figure A.9 shows an example of this type of toolbar control.

Toolbar

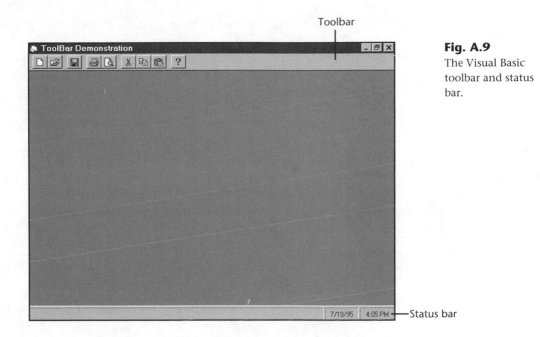

Fig. A.9
The Visual Basic
toolbar and status
bar.

Status bar

Status Bars

Status bars are becoming another integral part of every popular Windows application on the market. Users demand constant indications of what an application is doing. If an application is processing a new report, users want to see some kind of message indicating what is taking place, or better still, a percentage indicator that shows how much more time they must wait for processing. One of the most common places to find such information is on a status bar at the bottom of an application's window. Visual Basic 4.0 includes a status bar that you can add to your applications. Figure A.9 shows a standard status bar.

Tabstrips

Sometimes a screen doesn't have enough space to place all the information that a user wants. No established standard addresses this problem.

One possibility is to place the information on a grid, with any extra columns forcing the user to scroll to the right. However, most users don't like screens that force them to scroll horizontally. Another possibility is to place the information on several different screens. Of course, users find this method confusing and unintuitive.

The best solution is to create a form with tabstrips (see fig. A.10). You divide your information into categories that you associate with a series of tabs; when the user clicks on one of the tabs, the application then displays the appropriate category of information. Before the release of Visual Basic 4.0, you had to create such tabs by writing code or using third-party controls. Visual Basic 4.0 now provides a tab control.

Fig. A.10
A Visual Basic tabstrip.

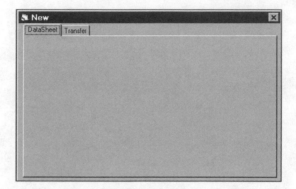

Sliders

To provide a graphical method to enable users to enter a value within a range, Visual Basic 4.0 provides a new slider control. With such a control, the user can enter a value into an interface by dragging the control within a scale that presents the range of values. Many new features of Windows 95 include a slider control. This control provides a welcome alternative for Visual Basic programmers.

Fig. A.11
A Visual Basic slider.

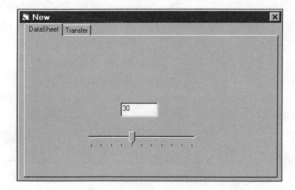

Introducing the Object Browser

Visual Basic 4.0 provides a feature in which you can look up all the controls
and attributes in your project's forms: the Object Browser (see fig. A.12). This
utility is an excellent resource for keeping track of your forms and their
contents.

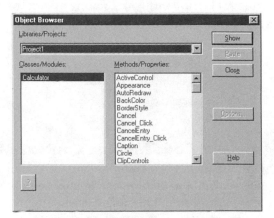

Fig. A.12
The Object
Browser displaying
objects that belong
to the Calculator
form in the Calc
project.

Introducing Uninstall Support

Removing an unwanted program from your computer is no longer as easy as
deleting that application's directory and files. Windows applications place
files in the system and Windows directory, so the user cannot easily identify
and remove them. In addition, another application might be using a file that
you want to remove. Removing a shared file can cause other applications to
cease functioning properly. Visual Basic 4.0 enables you to program applications that users can easily uninstall without encountering such problems.

Examining IDE Enhancements

Visual Basic 4.0 includes many enhancements to the integrated development
environment (IDE). Formerly, one of Visual Basic's greatest deficiencies was
how difficult it was to place controls on a form in exactly the right spots and
then keep them there. Visual Basic 4.0 enhances your capability to place
controls precisely and permanently.

Control Lock

Visual Basic 3.0 offered no method to prevent users from inadvertently moving controls on a form. After you have painstakingly placed a control on a form, accidentally moving it with a double-click can be truly aggravating. The Control Lock feature enables you to lock controls in place on a form. You can easily turn this feature on and off by clicking the toolbar's Lock Control button, shown in figure A.13. The control lock setting for one form does not affect the setting for another form.

a.   b.

Fig. A.13

The Lock Control toolbar button indicating that your controls (a) are unlocked or (b) remain locked.

Form, Control, and Code Module Context Menus

A standard Windows mouse has two buttons. For most Windows 3.x applications, you use only the left mouse button and ignore the right. Applications that did use the right button used it for different purposes. Windows 95 creates a new standard in which you click the right mouse button to access a context menu of common functions. Visual Basic 4.0 provides specialized context menus for each of the types of windows, including code modules, controls, and forms. Figure A.14 shows a form's context menu.

Fig. A.14

The context menu for the Calculator form in the Calc project.

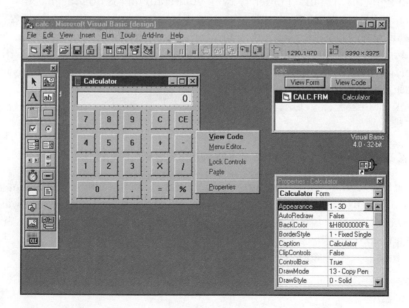

Control Nudge

Previously in Visual Basic, placing a control on a form at run time was a tedious process of playing with the control's left and top properties until you placed it just right. In Visual Basic 4.0, you can use the Shift key with the arrow keys to move a control one pixel at a time. You can also use the Ctrl+arrow keys to adjust sizes. This "control nudge" feature is a great time-saver that makes working with controls much easier.

From Here...

To learn more about topics related to porting to Visual Basic 4.0, see the following:

- Part II, "Using OLE," provides more information about OLE technology.

- Chapter 30, "Advanced Control Techniques," explains more about the status bar.

- Chapter 31, "Advanced Form Techniques," provides more information about multiple-document interface (MDI) and single-document interface (SDI) applications and explains how to make complex changes to forms.

- Chapter 34, "Designing Windows Applications," describes the Windows programming standards that Microsoft has set.

Index

Symbols

G

H

I

S

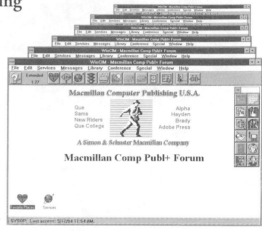

EXPERT ADVICE FOR EFFECTIVE APPLICATIONS FROM QUE

Special Edition Using Windows 95
ISBN: 1-56529-921-3
Price: $34.99 USA
Pub Date: 8/95

Special Edition Using Delphi
ISBN: 1-56529-823-3
Price: $29.99 USA
Pub Date: 3/95

The *Special Edition Using* series remains the most-often recommended product line for computer users who want detailed reference information. With thorough explanations, troubleshooting advice, and special 'Techniques from the Pros' sections, these books are the perfect all-in-one resource.

Special Edition Using Visual C++, New Edition
ISBN: 0-7897-0401-3
Price: $49.99 USA
Pub Date: 12/95

For more information on these and other Que products, visit your local book retailer or call 1-800-772-0477

Special Edition Using Access for Windows 95
ISBN: 0-7897-0184-7
Price: $34.99 USA
Pub Date: 11/95

Source Code ISBN: 1-56529-998-1

Complete and Return this Card
for a *FREE* Computer Book Catalog

Thank you for purchasing this book! You have purchased a superior computer book written expressly for your needs. To continue to provide the kind of up-to-date, pertinent coverage you've come to expect from us, we need to hear from you. Please take a minute to complete and return this self-addressed, postage-paid form. In return, we'll send you a free catalog of all our computer books on topics ranging from word processing to programming and the internet.

Mr. ☐   Mrs. ☐   Ms. ☐   Dr. ☐

Name (first) ☐☐☐☐☐☐☐☐☐☐☐☐   (M.I.) ☐   (last) ☐☐☐☐☐☐☐☐☐☐☐☐☐☐☐☐

Address ☐☐☐☐☐☐☐☐☐☐☐☐☐☐☐☐☐☐☐☐☐☐☐☐☐☐☐☐☐☐

☐☐☐☐☐☐☐☐☐☐☐☐☐☐☐☐☐☐☐☐☐☐☐☐☐☐☐☐☐☐

City ☐☐☐☐☐☐☐☐☐☐☐☐   State ☐☐   Zip ☐☐☐☐☐ ☐☐☐☐

Phone ☐☐☐ ☐☐☐ ☐☐☐☐   Fax ☐☐☐ ☐☐☐ ☐☐☐☐

Company Name ☐☐☐☐☐☐☐☐☐☐☐☐☐☐☐☐☐☐☐☐☐☐☐☐☐☐☐

E-mail address ☐☐☐☐☐☐☐☐☐☐☐☐☐☐☐☐☐☐☐☐☐☐☐☐☐☐☐

1. Please check at least (3) influencing factors for purchasing this book.

Front or back cover information on book .... ☐
Special approach to the content .... ☐
Completeness of content .... ☐
Author's reputation .... ☐
Publisher's reputation .... ☐
Book cover design or layout .... ☐
Index or table of contents of book .... ☐
Price of book .... ☐
Special effects, graphics, illustrations .... ☐
Other (Please specify): _____ ☐

2. How did you first learn about this book?

Saw in Macmillan Computer Publishing catalog .... ☐
Recommended by store personnel .... ☐
Saw the book on bookshelf at store .... ☐
Recommended by a friend .... ☐
Received advertisement in the mail .... ☐
Saw an advertisement in: _____ ☐
Read book review in: _____ ☐
Other (Please specify): _____ ☐

3. How many computer books have you purchased in the last six months?

This book only .... ☐   3 to 5 books .... ☐
2 books .... ☐   More than 5 .... ☐

4. Where did you purchase this book?

Bookstore .... ☐
Computer Store .... ☐
Consumer Electronics Store .... ☐
Department Store .... ☐
Office Club .... ☐
Warehouse Club .... ☐
Mail Order .... ☐
Direct from Publisher .... ☐
Internet site .... ☐
Other (Please specify): _____ ☐

5. How long have you been using a computer?

☐ Less than 6 months   ☐ 6 months to a year
☐ 1 to 3 years   ☐ More than 3 years

6. What is your level of experience with personal computers and with the subject of this book?

	With PCs	With subject of book
New	☐	☐
Casual	☐	☐
Accomplished	☐	☐
Expert	☐	☐

Source Code ISBN: 1-56529-998-1

7. Which of the following best describes your job title?

Administrative Assistant .... ☐
Coordinator .... ☐
Manager/Supervisor .... ☐
Director .... ☐
Vice President .... ☐
President/CEO/COO .... ☐
Lawyer/Doctor/Medical Professional .... ☐
Teacher/Educator/Trainer .... ☐
Engineer/Technician .... ☐
Consultant .... ☐
Not employed/Student/Retired .... ☐
Other (Please specify): _____ ☐

8. Which of the following best describes the area of the company your job title falls under?

Accounting .... ☐
Engineering .... ☐
Manufacturing .... ☐
Operations .... ☐
Marketing .... ☐
Sales .... ☐
Other (Please specify): _____ ☐

9. What is your age?

Under 20 .... ☐
21-29 .... ☐
30-39 .... ☐
40-49 .... ☐
50-59 .... ☐
60-over .... ☐

10. Are you:

Male .... ☐
Female .... ☐

11. Which computer publications do you read regularly? (Please list)

_____
_____
_____
_____
_____
_____
_____
_____
_____

Comments: _____
_____
_____

Fold here and scotch-tape to mail.